ABLAZE

DAVID G. ATWOOD II

Cadmus Publishing
www.cadmuspublishing.com

Copyright © 2021 David G. Atwood II

Published by Cadmus Publishing

www.cadmuspublishing.com
ISBN: 978-1-63751-030-8

All rights reserved. Copyright under Berne Copyright Convention, Universal Copyright Convention, and Pan-American Copyright Convention. No part of this book may be reproduced, stored in a retrieval system, or transmitted in any form, or by any means, electronic, mechanical, photocopying, recording or otherwise, without prior permission of the author.

CONTENTS

INTRODUCTION	1
PROLOGUE	4
CHAPTER ONE	20
CHAPTER TWO	28
CHAPTER THREE	36
CHAPTER FOUR	45
CHAPTER FIVE	56
CHAPTER SIX	66
CHAPTER SEVEN	77
CHAPTER EIGHT	88
CHAPTER NINE	100
CHAPTER TEN	113
CHAPTER ELEVEN	127
CHAPTER TWELVE	143
CHAPTER THIRTEEN	163
CHAPTER FOURTEEN	172
CHAPTER FIFTEEN	182
CHAPTER SIXTEEN	192
CHAPTER SEVENTEEN	203
CHAPTER EIGHTEEN	214
CHAPTER NINETEEN	226
CHAPTER TWENTY	237
CHAPTER TWENTY-ONE	250
CHAPTER TWENTY-TWO	262
CHAPTER TWENTY-THREE	274
CHAPTER TWENTY-FOUR	287
CHAPTER TWENTY-FIVE	308
CHAPTER TWENTY-SIX	332
CHAPTER TWENTY-SEVEN	347
CHAPTER TWENTY-EIGHT	360
CHAPTER TWENTY-NINE	376
CHAPTER THIRTY	388
CHAPTER THIRTY-ONE	400
CHAPTER THIRTY-TWO	411
CHAPTER THIRTY-THREE	424
CHAPTER THIRTY-FOUR	430
CHAPTER THIRTY-FIVE	443
CHAPTER THIRTY-SIX	455
CHAPTER THIRTY-SEVEN	469
CHAPTER THIRTY-EIGHT	481
CHAPTER THIRTY-NINE	499
CHAPTER FORTY	513
CHAPTER FORTY-ONE	526
CHAPTER FORTY-TWO	538
CHAPTER FORTY-THREE	553
CHAPTER FORTY-FOUR	567
CHAPTER FORTY-FIVE	581
CHAPTER FORTY-SIX	598
CHAPTER FORTY-SEVEN	615
CHAPTER FORTY-EIGHT	627
EPILOGUE	639

INTRODUCTION

Being inside a federal courtroom can be a daunting and frightening experience. It is infinitely more so when one is a defendant or a plaintiff. A federal courtroom is no place for amateurs, yet I found myself there in some quite interesting circumstances.

I'd been waiting for hours and I passed the time by adjusting and straightening my tie for the hundredth time and indifferently picking the lint from my suit, but I was terrified inside.

As I and the others with me waited, I slowly looked around the courtroom and saw the assistant attorney general who was representing the state of Mississippi. He sat in a chair chugging lukewarm water from a plastic pitcher that had been discretely filled by a deputy U.S. Marshal earlier that morning.

A door finally screeched open and the judge appeared, quickly followed by her polite and efficient staff. We all immediately rose and came to attention.

The judge took her seat and announced that *my* jury had reached a verdict. And let there be no misunderstanding, this was *my* jury; I helped pick them. They were deciding my future, and everyone was in federal court because of me. It literally was my jury and my future.

What made the occasion all the more terrifying was that I was representing myself without an attorney, something the courts refer to as acting *pro se*. And throughout the recent trial, I often thought back to that age-old adage from Abraham Lincoln that the person who represents himself has a fool for a client.

Everyone told me that a *pro se* litigant could never, and would never, win a jury trial in federal court. After all, I didn't have any formal legal training. I'd never represented myself before and had never argued a case to a jury. Judges hated *pro se* litigants. Every legal expert I consulted said it was a waste of time to even try. Yet, I remained convinced that justice and righteousness would win me the day, and I was determined to prove them wrong.

The next few moments hung in the balance as the jury entered and took their places in the jury box. Time passed in a blur until I heard the words that I'd been waiting to hear for almost eight years, and it was all happening too fast. It began, "We the jury . . ."

I closed my eyes as time stopped and thought back to how I had gotten there. I'd been charged with arson and had faced a life sentence of imprisonment for a horrible fire that destroyed a beloved ancestral mansion.

The fire garnered the attention of the federal government, the governor, and dozens of law enforcement agencies throughout the state. It fostered the commission of a half dozen more crimes and, at the conclusion, utterly destroyed the reputations, credibility, and lives of the corrupt law enforcement officers that committed them and who then tried to cover it all up.

This book is a history of that case. It is a story of how politics and lust for power almost overcame the rule of law.

If ever there was a time when a group of evil and corrupt law enforcement officers attempted to subvert the Constitution and destroy our system of justice—to cover-up and hide their crimes against humanity—this was it. And they almost got away with it.

At times in this story I take the sanctimonious moral high ground in condemning the atrocities committed by these corrupt law enforcement officers. But as it stands today I am a convicted felon. I am far from perfect. I've made mistakes in my life which will follow me to the end of my days. I've seen the underbelly of society and the constant struggle between good and evil.

When reading this book it must not be assumed that the line between good and evil is clearly demarcated between those who wear a badge and those who don't. In this story the lines are often blurred.

I am not the hero in this story, though. Although I am the central character there's more to this book than just *my* side of it. It is a story of good versus evil, told by a flawed person. I tell it, though, through the eyes of one whom has seen and experienced both the good and bad, and in this story is the seemingly uncommon contradictions of good doing bad and bad doing good.

No one emerges from this story with a clean moral character. However, if there is one hero in this book, one constant, moral unequivocation on whose shoulders rested the fate of the Battle of Good versus Evil, it could be no person other than the federal judge who ultimately organized the eccentric chess pieces of this gargantuan battle and brought order from chaos and justice to those who deserved it.

If my jury was my judicial sword, the federal judge was my shield; for the trial that occurred in the summer of 2017 was a marshaling of forces brought together by a spark of flame which ignited the worst in what otherwise should have been decent and honest people.

Unlike *my* jury, this is not *my* story. I tell it, but in doing so I draw on the exact words of those who lived it. Their words are drawn from thousands of pages and hundreds of hours of depositions, trial transcripts, affidavits, interviews, and letters. At other times I've had to rely on reasonable inferences of dialogue based on official records and my not-so-perfect memory.

Some have cooperated in helping tell this story, others have not. Some have threatened more evil and more violence. There are those desperate to keep their secrets hidden and their evil deeds from the light of day. But several have atoned for their sins. No one, though, including myself, feel better about themselves.

This fire killed no one, but it claimed all of our lives. This book should bring closure to those who lived it, justice to those who deserve it, and remembrance to those who need it.

PROLOGUE

It began with a spark, but from what origin whom can say. It was later determined to have started in the kitchen, near the electrical box. But that important fact was later conveniently ignored by investigators.

The fire quickly spread throughout the house, gaining in momentum and intensity. Nothing stood in its destructive path. Within minutes the entire house was engulfed in flames, burning out of control.

Nearly one hundred years of history was being destroyed. Family heirlooms, pictures, and memorabilia were lost forever. While these priceless articles burned, ammunition being stored in the house began exploding, followed by the house's propane tank. The noise from the inferno had to of been deafening, and as it burned it destroyed more than just the tangible property of the family. Being burned away forever were the memories and, in some ways, the ghosts of the Atwood family.

The Atwood Lakehouse and the lake it sat near had been part of the family since the early 1800s. The land itself had been given to an Atwood ancestor in the 1820s as part of a land grant. Throughout the years it served as a cotton and sugarcane plantation until the destruction wrought by the American Civil War. From thence till more recent times it served as the cradle for a new generation of Atwood offspring.

The Atwood Lakehouse itself was built as a family retreat, hunting lodge, and as a place for weddings, birthdays, and other festive occasions. In its more hedonistic days it served as a hideaway for extramarital affairs and as a meeting place for the Kosciusko Klavern of the Ku Klux Klan, of which several members of the Atwood family have claimed membership. It was even claimed to have been haunted.

Approximately one hundred yards from the ongoing fiery holocaust lived Kade Atwood. Kade's father, Herman Bush Atwood, always known affectionately in the family as Uncle Bush, had built a small wooden cabin directly across the lake from the Atwood Lakehouse. Bush had been born on the property and had spent his entire life there, but had sadly died in early 2001.

As the lake house burned, Kade, who moved into his father's house after his death, apparently slept quite soundly through the noisy and bright destruction taking place literally in his front yard. By the time he allegedly woke up on the morning of November 11, 2009, the Atwood Lakehouse, and everything in it, was utterly and totally destroyed.

Surprisingly, Kade never called the fire department. Instead of immediately reporting the burning house to the local fire department and law enforcement, Kade called his uncle, the owner of the Atwood Lakehouse, Emmett Atwood.

Emmett lived in Vicksburg, Mississippi, which is approximately two hours from the lake house in Kosciusko, Mississippi. Kosciusko is the county seat of Attala County, literally in the center of the state. Attala County is the ancestral home of the Atwood family.

Emmett immediately left Vicksburg and drove the two hours to the lake house. When he arrived he was met by Kade and other members of the Atwood family who had assembled to inspect the aftermath of the fire.

Once Emmett arrived on the scene the decision was finally made to officially inform the local authorities. No explanation was later given for the extended delay. A call was placed to the Attala County Sheriff's Department and Chief Deputy Tim Nail responded to the lake house property. Enroute, Deputy Nail placed a call to the Mississippi State Fire Marshal's Office and requested that a state fire marshal be dispatched to the scene to meet with him and start the investigation into the origins of the fire.

The Fire Marshal's Office assigned the case to one of their senior investigators, but when informed of the fire, Deputy Fire Marshal James O'Neal Jackson continued to celebrate his Veteran's Day holiday and told Deputy Nail that he would respond to the scene in several days to conduct his perfunctory investigation. Apparently, Jackson was too busy to be bothered with conducting an investigation that conflicted with his preplanned holiday celebration.

Instead, Deputy Nail begins his own investigation upon arriving on the scene of what remained of the Atwood Lakehouse.

His first task was to meet with Emmett and Kade, whom he knew previously. Everyone knew of the Atwood family in Kosciusko, and Deputy Nail was especially familiar with Kade because of Kade's work with the local ambulance company and fire department.

Immediately upon meeting with Emmett, Deputy Nail was told by him that the fire was an arson, that it had been started by Emmett's grandson (me), and that Deputy Nail should solely concentrate his investigation on me. Emmett wanted Deputy Nail to believe that I was responsible for the fire because of a long-running feud that we'd had.

Because Deputy Nail had very little training in arson investigations, he decided to wait until Jackson completed his holiday vacation and would be available to meet to officially start the inquiry.

This delay was not acceptable to Emmett. He wanted immediate action taken to have his oldest grandson arrested and he was not willing to wait to achieve that long-desired goal.

When Emmett was told that Jackson would not be able to respond to the fire scene for at least several days, Emmett decided to use his political connections to effect a faster result.

Mike Chaney was the elected commissioner of the Mississippi Insurance Commission. This also made him the de-facto Chief Fire Marshal for the state of Mississippi, and James Jackson's boss. He was from Vicksburg, and was best friends with Emmett. In fact, whenever Chaney ran for political office, Emmett contributed heavily to his campaign. If anyone could help Emmett achieve his personal goals of framing me for a crime, Chaney was his man.

When Chaney was told that Jackson was dragging his feet in beginning the investigation, a quick phone call and "get-your-ass-moving" message accomplished its intended goal.

On November 13, 2009, two days after the fire, Jackson finally appeared on the scene of the Atwood Lakehouse fire. Meeting him were Emmett, Kade, and Deputy Nail. The first topic of conversation was Emmett's belief that I was responsible for the fire. Jackson acknowledged that he had spoken to Commissioner Chaney and that I was their primary suspect. They were convinced that the evidence would soon be in their hands to prove it.

The first step in Jackson's investigation was to attempt to obtain forensic evidence supporting their already preconceived belief that I was responsible for the fire. This required Jackson employing a forensic instrument called a hydrocarbon detector.

Hydrocarbon detectors are used to measure whether an accelerant was used to start the fire. Unfortunately for the conspirators, Jackson's hydrocarbon detector could not detect any trace of an accelerant used to start the fire. Having failed at attempting to prove that the fire was started with gasoline, diesel fuel, or another accelerant, Jackson then tried determining where the fire began. In this endeavor he was a bit more successful.

Through measuring and marking burn patterns, Jackson determined with a very high probability that the fire began in the kitchen in the exact area of the electrical box. But because Jackson, a state fire marshal, had no formal training in the origins and aftermath of electrical fires, he was unable to determine or rule out whether the fire began because of an electrical malfunction.

The group of investigators then began rummaging through the remains of the fire. They were specifically looking for a cache of firearms that Emmett had left in the lake house in order to rule out a possible burglary.

Found in the remains of the fire were four or five rifles and shotguns and spent cartridge casings. One of the rifles even showed an exploded breech. If anyone ever questioned Kade as to how he was able to allegedly sleep through this raging, noisy inferno of destruction, no one later admitted it.

Quickly wrapping up the cursory investigation, Jackson and Deputy Nail were then shown some "suspicious" footprints that had allegedly been found near the remains of the lake house. What made these footprints suspicious to Jackson could never be determined because he was aware at that time that dozens of people had walked in and around the burnt lake house in the days after the fire. The scene had been unsecured for almost three days, and neither Deputy Nail, Emmett, or Kade had taken any steps to prevent friends and family from walking around in the area in the days after the fire. But for good measure, plaster of Paris molds and photos were taken of the suspicious footprints for later comparison.

Although it is common practice for arson investigators to inquire into the financial and insurance arrangements of the owner of a house that has burned, Jackson never questioned Emmett about the structure of his insurance coverage on the lake house. Had he done so, Jackson would have learned that Emmett had recently drastically increased the insurance coverage on the Atwood Lakehouse.

Had Jackson performed anything more than a simple, cursory investigation, he would have also learned that Emmett had recently had insulation installed in the attic for the first time in the Atwood Lakehouse's history shortly before the fire, and that a day or two previous to the fire, several people had been staying there. But this line of thought would require Jackson to set aside the already agreed upon "fact" that I was solely responsible for the fire.

Even though not one single scrap of evidence had been obtained indicating that the fire was arson, or that I was responsible, Jackson, Deputy Nail, Emmett, and Kade ended their meeting that day, all understanding that the fire was, in fact, an arson, and that I was responsible. And nothing could sway them from this accepted assertion.

Jackson was so convinced that the Atwood Lakehouse fire was an arson—despite no evidence indicating it—and that I was responsible, that he never attempted or even considered questioning me about the fire. As far as he was concerned the case was solved.

Deputy Nail felt somewhat different about the case, though. Nail had spent his entire career with the Attala County Sheriff's Department. He didn't have any connections with Mike Chaney or the other politicians in Jackson, the state capitol. Deputy Nail was an old-school detective, less dependent on fancy forensics, but instead big on actual gumshoe police work. Despite what he was hearing from Jackson and Emmett, Deputy Nail decided to continue his investigation.

After participating in the perfunctory investigation with Jackson, Deputy Nail decides on his own to contact me. And he does so with a phone call.

Talking to Deputy Nail on the afternoon of November 13, 2009, was the first time I had learned of the destruction of the Atwood Lakehouse. Although I knew immediately that I was a suspect because of my long-running feud with Emmett and that side of my family, I was also devastated at the loss of the place.

The Atwood Lakehouse was more than just an old building to me. The lake house was a place that I loved. Many years of my youth were spent there and on the land that surrounds it. I've fished in the lake, hunted in the woods, rode horses, and camped out in tents. The place ran through my blood and it destroyed part of me when I learned that it had burned.

As Deputy Nail asked me to come speak to him about the fire, I couldn't help but think of all the other crimes that I might have committed rather than burn the lake house.

It was no secret that Emmett and I hated each other. I despised everything that my paternal grandfather stood for and believed in. But the Atwood Lakehouse was not Emmett's house, no matter what a title in the courthouse may have said. The lake house was the family's lake house, it belonged to all of us, and its loss was an irreparable loss that can never be replaced. Of all tangible things to lose, the Atwood Lakehouse was the worst, but I wanted to help Deputy Nail clear my name and help determine who was responsible, if indeed, an arson had occurred.

The next day I went to meet Deputy Nail at the Attala County Sheriff's Department with my boyfriend at the time, Joshua Langston Chamblee, and my maternal grandfather, Aaron Tolleson.

My maternal grandfather was also from Kosciusko and knew Deputy Nail and the sheriff of Attala County, William Lee, very well. Known as "Papaw" to the grandkids in the family, Aaron Tolleson was the closest thing to an earthly saint as ever walked in the mortal world. He believed in my innocence and he knew as well that burning the lake house would have been the last thing I'd ever do.

Upon arriving at the sheriff's department, Deputy Nail separated Josh and I and put us in different interview rooms. Until my face-to-face meeting with Nail I'd not been told when the fire occurred and I had no idea the extent of the damage. But because Josh and I were together everyday, I knew he would be needed as an alibi witness.

In our respective interview rooms we were told the date and approximate time of the fire and asked to write out statements attesting to where we were and what we were doing the night of the fire.

Apparently, the deputy sheriff that was interviewing me got the actual date of the fire wrong. I was asked where I was on the night of November 9, 2009. In response, my statement said that Josh and I were together at his family's house in Carthage, Mississippi, on that specific night—which was true.

During Josh's interview, he was asked where we were and what we were doing on the night of November 10, 2009. In response to that question Josh's statement said that we were at his apartment in Starkville, Mississippi, on that specific night—which, again, was true.

I cannot explain the failure of Deputy Nail and his other investigators in mixing up the dates of the fire, but Josh's and I's statements were honest, true, and completely accurate. And no one is claiming that the investigators were always competent. Neither one of us had anything to do with the fire, and we both protested this very forcefully to Deputy Nail.

Before allowing us to leave we were also asked if we were willing to supply Deputy Nail with the sizes of our feet and the tread patterns of our shoes. In this we readily complied. We later learned that Deputy Nail then compared the sizes and tread patterns of our feet and shoes to the imprints taken from the scene of the fire. None matched.

The last significant part of Deputy Nail's investigation consisted of obtaining our cell phone numbers and then comparing our cell phone records, GPS, and cell tower location data to try and determine whether our cell phones had been used in or near Attala County during the time the fire occurred.

Our cell phone records clearly showed that we were using our phones in the exact same areas, at the exact same times, that our written statements said we were in Carthage and Starkville. Deputy Nail was especially interested in the time of approximately midnight to four, November 10 into the morning of November 11. And the cell records clearly proved that both Josh and I were texting and using data on our phones during this time period while our cell phones were connected to a specific cell tower in Starkville more than 70 miles from the Atwood Lakehouse.

At this point, Deputy Nail closed his investigation. By conducting a substantially more in-depth investigation, Deputy Nail was conclusively able to determine that there was not any direct evidence of arson and that no evidence existed linking me to the fire. According to him, it was simply undeterminable.

After my November 13, 2009, meeting with Deputy Nail, I had no further contact with him or with Jackson, who never attempted to contact me. Despite the lack of evidence proving arson, or that I was responsible, Jackson had, at the insistence of Mike Chaney and Emmett, concluded that I was guilty. But without any evidence his investigation closed as well.

Jackson made one final attempt to collect evidence in the case when he decided to interview Josh Chamblee in March 2010.

The previous month Josh and I ended our relationship on very bad terms. By February 2010 our friendship had lasted five months. We had always gotten along very well, but Josh was a compulsive and pathological liar. At first, it was small things, but by the early part of 2010 things had begun to spin out of control. The final straw that ended our relationship was when I discovered that Josh was HIV-positive and had hidden that important fact throughout the time we dated.

The fact that Josh was HIV-positive didn't concern me so much as he had continually lied to me and fabricated a fake HIV test which he claimed proved he was not infected with the virus. It became too much and I ended any further communication between us.

When Jackson found out that Josh and I were no longer together, he tracked Josh down in Carthage, Mississippi, where Josh lived, and requested that Josh provide him another statement detailing where we were on the night of the fire.

Despite having recently separated from me on bad terms, Josh stuck by the truth and provided Jackson with a written statement in which he maintained that we were together on the night of the fire at his apartment in Starkville.

By this time, Emmett had offered a reward of $20,000 for information leading to the arrest of the person responsible for the Atwood Lakehouse fire—if, in fact, someone *was* responsible. The State Fire Marshal's Office also offered a reward of $5,000.

At this March 2010 meeting between Jackson and Josh, Jackson promised Josh the reward if he would write a statement that implicated me in the fire. But again, Josh decided to tell the truth and stuck by his story.

Without any evidence to secure an arrest warrant, Jackson finally closed his investigation into the lake house fire in March 2010. Officially, it was ruled an undeterminable fire.

From November 2009 until Jackson and Nail both closed their investigations, I lived in a constant state of fear. I knew the power that Emmett Atwood wielded in the world of local and state politics, and I knew that Emmett was doing everything possible to have me arrested and imprisoned for the lake house fire.

Being falsely accused of a crime, especially a crime which carries a potential life sentence, is a terrifying experience. So for several months my life came to a standstill. But once the investigations were over, I felt as though a thousand pounds of weight had been removed from my shoulders.

Although the constant memory of the loss of the Atwood Lakehouse would plague me forever, my life moved on. During the summer and fall of 2010 I turned my attention to finishing an autobiographical book of my life that I eventually titled *Into Hell I Rode*.

This autobiography was going to be the story of my life, but included within the twisted entanglements of telling my story was the definitive account of law enforcement and political corruption in my hometown of Vicksburg, Mississippi.

Into Hell I Rode exposed more than thirty years of rape, murder, corruption, and misconduct involving the Warren County Sheriff's Department and the politicians in Vicksburg. It was specifically timed to be published in July 2011, several months before the reelection of the corrupt sheriff, Martin Pace.

On July 2, 2011, the Miss Mississippi Pageant was being held at the City Convention Center in Vicksburg. It is the biggest event held in the city and it was a perfect opportunity to advertise my recently published book. Many people, including Sheriff Pace and his deputies, knew that I was writing a book that contained some negative information about them, but no one knew that *Into Hell I Rode* would expose some of the darkest and most evil secrets and crimes ever committed by law enforcement.

Prior to the Miss Mississippi Pageant I created brochures to distribute at the event that contained information about my book, including previews of some of the bombshells contained therein. The brochures also encouraged people not to vote for Sheriff Pace in the upcoming November election.

During years that elections are held, the pageant is an excellent opportunity for campaign workers to distribute election literature. Many people owning businesses in the area also advertise and promote their wares during the pageant. In fact, it is so common, many politicians announce their candidacies immediately prior to the pageant.

Although I knew my book would attract attention because of the revelations it contained, I needed the pageant and the crowd it brought in order to maximize the effect.

But on the night of July 2, 2011, I was quickly intercepted by officers and deputies from the Vicksburg Police and Warren County Sheriff's Departments who told me that they would not allow me, or the people I'd hired, to distribute my brochures.

One especially sniveling officer named Daniel Thomas was so enraged with self-righteous indignation that he proceeded to defend with vehement ardor a former deputy named London Williams who had raped and molested his own daughter and then admitted to doing it before being sent to prison for the crime. London's case composed a short chapter in the book. Apparently, Thomas was upset that I had written about a fellow law enforcement officer whom raped and molested his own child.

Daniel Thomas's defense of a fellow officer of the caliber of the child rapist, London Williams, is indicative of the problem with law enforcement corruption in Vicksburg.

I'd known Daniel Thomas previously when we were teenagers and young adults. Even though Daniel Thomas was a police officer, it'd not been many years before that I remember him smoking weed, drinking and driving, and acting a punk bully to those who appeared weaker than him.

Like most bullies, however, when someone with courage stands up to them they cower in fear. Thomas was this type. He was also in 2011 trying to get hired as a deputy under Sheriff Pace. And when Daniel Thomas told me to leave the City Convention Center and not to pass out my brochures, I complied. Instead, I went to the police department and filed a complaint.

While I was at the police department filing a complaint, Thomas was consulting with Sheriff Pace, whom he had made aware of the brochures. According to Sheriff Pace, he told Thomas to handle the situation.

During this conversation, Thomas learned that I was at the police department filing a complaint against him. In order to curry favor with Sheriff Pace in hopes of securing employment, and to exact retaliation,

Thomas decided to arrest me as I left the police department.

Being arrested was nothing new for me. I've been arrested several times, but I have only been convicted of one felony in my life. Thomas, though, was determined to get me for trespassing.

I sat in jail only for about an hour before I was released, but this type of retaliation was the exact example that gave my book, *Into Hell I Rode*, so much credence and accuracy in detailing the local police's corruption.

A few days after my arrest for trespassing, Jackson received a phone call from his boss, Mike Chaney. Chaney wasn't happy, along with a lot of Chaney's friends.

Mike Chaney lives in Vicksburg. He has his place of business there. More importantly, Chaney is best friends with Sheriff Martin Pace, Emmett Atwood, and numerous other people that I wrote about in my book. The only people happy about my book are those who follow the law and don't take advantage of the position they hold. This certainly doesn't include Chaney and Pace.

Jackson didn't know about my book at the time he was called in to meet with Mike Chaney. He hadn't even thought about the Atwood Lakehouse fire in well over a year. To Jackson, it was a closed case. But Chaney never meets personally with deputy fire marshals about their investigations. So Jackson suspects that the purpose of his meeting Chaney is to discuss the lake house fire.

Since people first learned about the book on July 2, 2011, Chaney had been receiving phone calls from Sheriff Pace, Emmett, and others demanding that his office take action to have me incarcerated. The State Fire Marshal's Office was the only law enforcement agency with any miniscule pretext on which to possibly investigate me for a crime.

Sheriff Pace was especially frantic because he was facing a tough re-election campaign against a popular, former deputy of his. *Into Hell I Rode* had been timed to be released in July 2011, specifically for the purpose of influencing the sheriff's election in Warren County in the hopes of having Martin Pace beat. Desperate for help, Sheriff Pace reached out to Chaney.

Emmett was likewise frantic when my book was released. *Into Hell I Rode* revealed the Atwood family's past membership in the Ku Klux Klan and Emmett's extramarital affair that he had with a poverty-stricken African-American woman that he fathered a child with and then later utterly abandoned.

According to sources within the family, Emmett didn't care so much that the Atwood's past connections to the Ku Klux Klan were revealed. Instead, Emmett was incensed that I exposed his long-running affair with the black lady whom he had fathered a child with. This was one of the Atwood family's biggest secrets. Apparently, Emmett finds it acceptable to advocate white supremacy while propagating offspring with black women.

Even though Mike Chaney found Emmett's extramarital affairs with black women hilarious, he was more concerned with the damage that the publicity from the book was causing Sheriff Pace.

Chaney, Sheriff Pace, and Emmett immediately concluded that something must be done to staunch the bleeding that the book was causing. Thus enters James Jackson, and the inception of the Axis of Corruption.

Chaney ordered that Jackson immediately procure a warrant for my arrest and have me incarcerated. Jackson attempted to protest by arguing to Chaney that there was not any evidence whatsoever to support the justification for obtaining a warrant for arson. This didn't sway Chaney.

Jackson continued to protest, but this only infuriated Chaney more. It finally came down to either Jackson arresting me or losing his job.

According to Jackson, Chaney told him to get off his ass, get a warrant, and arrest me or Jackson would be fired immediately and lose his job. When faced with choosing the path of good or evil, Jackson chose evil.

Not willing to lose his job, even though it meant breaking the law, Jackson was nonetheless disturbed by Chaney's obsession with this case. The immediate problem facing Jackson was obtaining some pretext in which to base an arrest warrant.

In all criminal cases, the United States Constitution mandates that law enforcement officers have probable cause before making an arrest. In obtaining arrest warrants, the Constitution requires probable cause before a judge can issue a warrant.

In my case, Jackson had no proof that the fire was arson. This was problem number one. Without proof that the fire was arson, Jackson had no indication that a crime even took place. Without proof of a crime, Jackson could never convince a judge to issue a warrant.

Then Jackson thought of Joshua Langston Chamblee. According to Jackson's thoughts, Josh was the key to unlocking the door of evil that

Chaney had orchestrated. But finding Josh proved to be a problem.

After we ended our relationship, Josh moved to Indianapolis and enrolled in a technical college to learn how to fix engines. But only a few people knew where to find him.

Jackson began with Josh's parents, Teresa and Paul Lyle. They lived in Carthage and were practically the only people that knew Josh's location. But they were not cooperative with Jackson. Despite Jackson's numerous requests, they refused to tell him where Josh was or put him in contact with Josh.

Jackson then turned to the Internet in an attempt to discover Josh's location. Using a commercial website that collects information on American citizens, Jackson obtained a comprehensive consumer history on Josh. However, not all of these records were accurate.

The commercial report that Jackson obtained on Josh sent him on a wild goose chase from North Carolina to Washington state. The only relevant information that Jackson obtained was an arrest report from when Josh had previously been arrested by law enforcement for filing a false police report and lying to police officers.

Despite being unable to find Josh, Jackson's most important discovery was Josh's arrest record. Knowing that Josh had previously been arrested for filing false police reports and lying to law enforcement officers should have given any competent investigator pause in deciding to use such a source to base an arrest warrant. But not Jackson.

Finally, Jackson decided that the only way to get Josh to cooperate with him would be to threaten Josh with arrest. To further that goal, Jackson drove to Kosciusko, Mississippi, and appeared before Judge Ronald Stewart of the Attala County Justice Court.

Jackson filled out an affidavit swearing under oath that he had evidence that the fire was an arson, that I maliciously started it, and that Josh helped cover-up the crime.

Believing that Jackson was telling the truth, Judge Stewart issued an arrest warrant for Josh for accessory after the fact to arson. Jackson, and a team of investigators from the Fire Marshal's Office, immediately took the warrant to Carthage where they found Josh's family at the Neshoba County Fairgrounds.

For a few moments Jackson thought that one of Josh's cousins, who remarkably resembled Josh, was in fact Josh. This poor human was roughed up and made to believe that he was under arrest until Jackson quickly learned of the misidentification.

Fortunately for Josh, he was not at the fair at the time Jackson and the other investigators arrived.

Jackson showed Josh's mother the arrest warrant and told her that unless Josh came to meet with him and provided him a statement, which implicated me in the fire, then he'd be arrested. Josh's mother promised to convey the information to Josh and arrange a time for Josh to come meet with Jackson.

On July 29, 2011, Jackson finally obtained his long sought after justification he needed to obtain a warrant for my arrest.

Josh agreed to appear with his parents at the Leake County Sheriff's Department and give Jackson a statement which implicated me in the fire. In return, Josh would not be arrested and upon my conviction he could obtain the $25,000 being offered as a reward.

The statement that Josh ultimately provided to Jackson on July 29, 2011, was not artful, detailed, or informative. And, of course, it was neither truthful or under oath.

A significant portion of the written statement had been crossed out and rewritten after, apparently, Josh's original didn't contain enough information to base a warrant on. At no time did Josh's statement ever directly say that he saw me start the fire. At the very least, Josh's statement alleged that I told him verbally that I started the fire that destroyed the Atwood Lakehouse.

Despite Jackson needing more information, Josh was unable to state with specificity the date of the fire. He couldn't recall specifics about the location of the lake house, what time I allegedly burned it down, whether the house was actually situated on a lake or not, or even where I allegedly started the fire in the house. His statement solely consisted of a vague and general allegation that I told him I burned down the house.

During the recorded part of the interview, after Josh provided this vague statement to Jackson, he asked the assembled law enforcement officers if they needed him to put anything else into his statement that might help them. Even without specifics, Jackson thought he had enough.

With Josh's most recent statement in hand, Jackson went back to Judge Stewart at the Attala County courthouse.

Jackson told Judge Stewart that he had direct evidence that the fire was arson, that he had an eyewitness, and that I committed the crime.

Jackson never told Judge Stewart that Josh's "confession" was obtained under the threat of arrest and a promise of a $25,000 reward. He never told the judge that Josh had previously been arrested for lying to law enforcement and filing false police reports, he never told Judge Stewart that the cell phone records and footprints exonerated me from having started the fire, and he certainly never told the judge that the fire was never proven to be an arson. The only evidence presented to Judge Stewart was Josh's coerced third statement.

Based on this flimsy evidence, Judge Stewart issued a felony arrest warrant and prematurely set me a $200,000 bond.

Late in the afternoon of July 29, 2011, Jackson and members of a Warren County Sheriff's Department SWAT team surrounded my house.

Despite having recently published a book which severely criticized several members of the Warren County Sheriff's Department for a wide-range of crimes and corruption, Sheriff Pace decided to assign the warrant execution to a deputy named Mike Traxler.

I spent considerable ink and paper in my book writing about Traxler and the long list of atrocities and acts of corruption committed by him. Traxler was hated by colleagues and members of the public. But as I wrote in *Into Hell I Rode*, Traxler had the "goods" on Sheriff Pace and was blackmailing Sheriff Pace into keeping him on the job despite many public calls for his termination.

A deputy on the Warren County Sheriff's Department had been a source for a lot of the information on the corruption that I wrote about in my book. Known as "Deep Six" in *Into Hell I Rode*, he kept me abreast of a lot of the internal machinations of the sheriff's department.

Deep Six later told me that Sheriff Pace specifically appointed Traxler to serve my arrest warrant in the hopes that Traxler would find some cause or pretext to use his firearm and kill me while serving the warrant.

I fully and completely believe Deep Six. These are evil people who were still furious over *Into Hell I Rode* being published earlier that month, none more so than Mike Traxler. And it was with a specific intent that Sheriff Pace gave Traxler my arrest warrant and instructions to kill me.

Sheriff Pace had over sixty different deputies that he could have assigned to executing and serving the arrest warrant. Instead, Sheriff Pace specifically selects the exact same deputies that I wrote negatively about in my book. It was clear that violent retaliation was his and their motive.

The deputies wasted little time in surrounding and then kicking in the door of my house. Screaming, and with firearms at the ready, desperately searching for their target, the deputies rushed into my home.

CHAPTER ONE

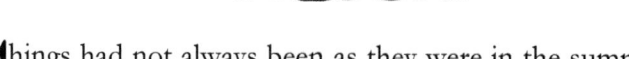

Things had not always been as they were in the summer of 2011. For many years I was the great hope of the Atwood family. Emmett and I shared a regular grandfather/grandson relationship. The Atwoods, by all appearances, reflected a typical upper-class family.

The Atwoods began their ancestral journey to America from Europe in the mid-1700s. My great-great-great-grandfather, Turpin Green Atwood, plied his trade as a watchmaker in Rhode Island prior to being given substantial land grants in Mississippi for his service in the United States Army.

Turpin settled on a 5,000 acre tract of land in Attala County, Mississippi. This land eventually passed into the hands of my paternal grandfather, Emmett Atwood. It was also where the Atwood Lakehouse was built in the early 1900s.

Although cotton and sugarcane were the main crops grown on the Atwood land, Turpin's primary source of income derived from improvements he made on the Eli Whitney cotton gin.

By the mid-1800s, Turpin had transformed his skills as a watchmaker and applied them to making the harvesting of cotton more efficient and productive. The Atwood gins quickly became the most sought-after cotton gins in the country.

Prior to the American Civil War, the three biggest cotton gin manufacturers were the Atwood gins, the Pratt gins, and the Whitney gins. According to the book *Inventing the Cotton Gin*, Turpin Atwood's cotton gins were the best constructed and most productive gins in the world.

Of all the cotton gin producers, Turpin was by far the largest and was ranked third wealthiest manufacturer in the 1860 census. With this wealth came the curse of slave ownership, but little is known about how Turpin utilized the people he owned or how he treated them. If the behaviors towards blacks of some of Turpin's descendants were to be an indicator, though, I would assume he treated his slaves rather poorly.

At the outbreak of the Civil War, Turpin's eldest son, David Chase Atwood, enlisted in the Confederate Army and served under General Robert E. Lee in the Army of Northern Virginia. But by the time he returned to Mississippi at the end of the war, the Atwood family and their gin business were in ruins.

Because the other gin manufacturers based a significant portion of their industrial gin-making capacity in the northern and border states, they were spared the ravages of war. The Pratt and Whitney companies eventually merged to form the largest manufacturing company of aircraft engines in the world.

Since the Civil War ended, and the older generations of the Atwoods have passed away, the family has recovered their financial security.

In the early 1950s, using capital obtained from my paternal grandmother's parents, Emmett opened a Chevrolet dealership in Vicksburg. Since then it has exponentially increased the power and influence that the Atwoods have. And Emmett is at its center.

When I was born in August of 1983 my father had not yet joined the family car dealership in Vicksburg. But that doesn't mean he wasn't employed in the family business. Emmett has for the past several decades engaged in land speculation consisting of buying and enhancing unimproved farmland.

At the time of my birth, my father, David Garland Atwood, was farming a large tract of land in Camden, Mississippi. He had married my mother, Joan Tolleson, the year prior to my birth. My mother, whose family hailed from Kosciusko as well, was the youngest daughter of Aaron and June Tolleson.

When I was two years old we moved from Camden to Vicksburg and moved in with my paternal grandmother, Vivian Atwood.

Vivian was from North Carolina and had married Emmett in the early 1950s. Their marriage produced four children: Emmett Ray, Vivian June, my father, and Alan Quinn. But in 1979 Emmett and my grandmother divorced. The cause of their divorce was the extramarital affair that Emmett had been having with an African-American woman named Georgia Hicks. Her son with Emmett was named Emile Hicks.

Georgia Hicks filed a paternity lawsuit against Emmett asking for child support for their child. Emmett vehemently denied that the child was his and for the next ten years Emmett and Georgia litigated the paternity of the child in the courts of Mississippi.

Eventually, Emmett was forced to submit to a court-ordered DNA paternity test. When the results came back several weeks later, it not only proved beyond all doubt that Emmett was the father of a biracial child, but it forced Emmett to immediately settle out-of-court with Mrs. Hicks for a very large and substantial sum of money. And ever since Emmett's paternity of the biracial child was proven through DNA, he's done everything he could to conceal the extramarital affair that he had with Mrs. Hicks.

The fact that Emmett had extramarital affairs during the time that he was married to my grandmother doesn't surprise me. I've grown up in the Atwood family surrounded by serial abusers and womanizers. What was shocking to me, and the others whom knew Emmett best, was the fact that Georgia Hicks was African-American.

Speaking solely from personal experience, I can say unequivocally that most members of the Atwood family are latent racists and white supremacists, Emmett especially.

I grew up surrounded by racism and bigotry. At times in my life I have struggled with shedding the skeletons and ghosts of my childhood. I was not taught any better than to verbally espouse racism, but deep in my heart and mind I knew that it was wrong. But when one is a child and surrounded by family members such as Emmett and my father, one doesn't know better.

I escaped the strictures of that part of the Atwood family. Emmett and his children never did. And the irony of him fathering children with black women, while at the same time preaching racial hate and white superiority, has never escaped the hypocrisy that those actions imply.

When we moved to Vicksburg we initially moved into my grandmother's house where we lived for the next several years. By the time I started school we'd moved into our own place.

Every summer I visited Kosciusko. My mother's father lived there and

I spent as much time as I could with him. Aaron Tolleson, or "Papaw" as he was known to me, was the surrogate father that I never had.

My father was an abusive, hateful alcoholic who treated me bad and my mother worse. When I went to spend weekends and summers with my Papaw and Mamaw in Kosciusko, it was literally an escape from a horrible household.

One of the first casualties of my father's abusive behavior was his marriage to my mother. They finally divorced when I was seven, and for the next several years I was passed back and forth between family members.

When I turned twelve, Vivian bought a small farm south of Vicksburg in Warren County. On this farm my dad built a house and Vivian and her daughter, June, built a house and barn.

Because I loved the outdoors, and the peace and quiet that having a farm brought, I stayed on the farm with my father for several years. This was the first time in years that my father actually attempted to be a parent to me. He'd quit drinking and the times were almost idyllic. But that all changed when my father married my evil stepmother.

Elizabeth "Buffy" Greenlee had entered our lives a few months prior to their sham marriage. She was never meant to be anything other than a sex toy to my father. But then she got pregnant with what many in our family doubted was my father's real child. Nevertheless, to avoid scandal, they were married in early 1995. Their marriage signaled the beginning of their new lives, but the end of mine.

Buffy was about twenty years younger than my father. That made her only a few years older than me. We both sought attention from my father, and when neither one of us seemed to get enough, we blamed the other.

Within months of their marriage my father was consuming whiskey as though prohibition had recently been lifted. Buffy and I fought and screamed at each other everyday, and I became so depressed that I seriously considered suicide. But then Buffy began to suspect that I was gay and told my father.

If there is one thing in the Atwood family that they hate more than blacks it is gay men and lesbian women.

On the day that my father began believing that I liked men instead of women, our relationship effectively ended and I moved into the house with my grandmother.

Vivian had known for several months that the relationship between my father, Buffy, and me was deteriorating. Buffy had taken proactive steps to separate my father from his mother, brothers, and other family members. But because he had a child with Buffy, he was trapped. I believe that my father was living in an alcohol-induced haze at this point in his life and was not able to make coherent decisions. He wouldn't physically abuse Buffy, but he made my life miserable.

Moving in with my grandmother was the best thing that ever happened in my life. Vivian, of course, was nothing like the Atwoods. This also became a very fortuitous decision.

Soon after moving in with Vivian, my father divorced Buffy, sold his house to his sister, and moved to another part of the county. I look back on that time period in my life and I realize that I don't have memories, I only have scars.

My Aunt June had previously lived with Vivian before I moved in to escape the physical and emotional abuse from my father and Buffy.

June Atwood had always been a pariah in the family. Always suspected of being lesbian, June had briefly married a man before that relationship ended in divorce and ruin. Since then alcoholism and prescription drug use has plagued June's life.

It would be remiss not to mention the intense sibling rivalry and jealousy that permeated throughout the Atwood family. Emmett's favorite child was always his youngest, Alan. His least favorite was June.

Alan, though, would eventually disappoint Emmett's expectations when he became entangled with the law himself. But when Alan was arrested and eventually convicted of poaching-type wildlife charges, Emmett did everything he could to conceal and hide Alan's criminal convictions.

While Emmett could certainly bend the rules and beg for political favors to have his least-favorite grandson incarcerated in prison, by no means would Emmett ever allow anyone to think for a moment that his favorite child could ever be responsible for any misconduct, no matter how guilty Alan might actually be. That is the hypocrisy that one must live with in the Atwood family.

To be fair, the only member of the family with any business competency was my father. My father was a man to be depended upon when it came to the basics of business. But as a father, he was an utter failure.

Emmett's oldest, my Uncle Ray, owned his own car dealership but had been rescued from bankruptcy and alcoholism himself by Emmett several times. Ray's son, Chase, and I were close in age and spent part of our childhood together.

It was always suspected in the family that Chase was gay because he was slightly effete as a child and teenager. I, on the other hand, was the masculine grandson in our family. Chase, however, turned out to be straight and, surprisingly, I gay.

To my knowledge, I have no direct evidence that anyone else in the Atwood family is gay. This was something that I struggled with for a very long time because I knew the ostracism that I faced from the family. But as I grew from a young, naive teenager and into adulthood I quickly realized that no amount of reward or money from the Atwoods could make up for my happiness. So at a fairly young age I developed an independent streak unlike anyone else our family has ever seen. But this would end tragically for me.

Two seminal events occurred in late 2003 that drove a wedge of disunity and acrimony between me and the Atwood family unlike any ever experienced before.

It began over a Christmas party. Every year Emmett hosted a party at his house for the family several weeks before Christmas. There was never much love and celebration at these events, only greedy expectations of extra money. I am just as guilty, though. I eagerly sought the petty cash that Emmett doled out at Christmas and on birthdays to compensate for the lack of love and affection. But I was not invited to the Christmas party in 2003.

As petty as it was, my father had become so consumed with my sexuality—and his hatred of it—that he essentially told Emmett that if I came to the Christmas party, he wouldn't. Emmett, of course, sided with my father. And in an extremely cold exchange I was told that since I'd chosen to live a "lifestyle" that wasn't conducive to the expectations of the Atwood family, I was no longer considered to be part of that family. Needless to say, unlike the other grandchildren in the family, I didn't get a Christmas present from Emmett that year.

As bad as this seemingly was, what came next was the real catalyst that took the internal squabble within the family and multiplied it to an exponential level unheard of in family feuds.

Immediately after Christmas, my grandmother discovered that her daughter June had conned and fooled her into signing over a portion of the house and land that Vivian owned. This was a scam orchestrated by my Aunt June to illegally obtain control over Vivian's house and land upon her death.

It had always been Vivian's intention to leave me her house and a small portion of the land which surrounded it, and then the rest of the land to her granddaughter, Julie.

June wanted the house and land for herself and tricked my grandmother into signing over a deed giving her ownership. Had it not been for a routine audit of the property taxes on the land, Vivian and I never would have learned of June's treachery.

I have in times past refused to accept responsibility for my actions. When I was young, I often acted young. This included being irresponsible and allowing my emotions to override my sense of right and wrong. But I have never acted in a manner which put another human being in danger. Nor have I ever plotted to commit a crime.

What should have remained a relatively minor matter for the local courts to decide, soon blew into a destructive force which forever altered the lives of everyone in my family.

June's abuse of her mother's trust was capable of being rectified in a matter of weeks. But Emmett sided with June because the Atwood family had decided that they did not want their mother giving me, or anyone else but them, her property and house.

In Mississippi all of the judges are elected. They depend on wealthy business owners like Emmett to help them obtain office. In situations such as this, it allows unethical people like Emmett to illegally influence judges' decisions in relatively minor matters such as the land dispute between me, Vivian, and June. For years, I had heard the popular refrain within the family that Emmett could never be beaten in court. And as the land dispute gained in intensity I became a believer.

The dispute over June illegally gaining ownership over her mother's house and land changed for the worst in March 2004 when a tractor belonging to June was damaged. Someone had apparently used a rifle or pistol to shoot out the tires.

Without any evidence whatsoever that I was responsible, June went to a local judge whom she and Emmett had supported for political office and convinced him to issue a warrant for my arrest.

Officially charged with felony malicious mischief, I was arrested by Detective Todd Dykes from the Warren County Sheriff's Department. I bonded out of jail and was released the same day.

This false arrest, without evidence, truly began the feud that devastated the Atwood family and brought disgrace and embarrassment to everyone involved.

CHAPTER TWO

Being arrested by the Warren County Sheriff's Department was not the first time that I'd had negative interactions with them, and Detective Todd Dykes's involvement with the Atwoods was certainly nothing new.

Like many deputies on the sheriff's department, Dykes used his privileges as a deputy to obtain financial favors and other gratuities from businesses in Vicksburg, and my grandfather was more than happy to extend his greedy hand to groveling deputies and politicians there.

Dykes can only be described as the law enforcement version of the nutty professor. Large, obese, born in the early 1960s, one expects to see Dykes with a candy bar in his hands at all times.

Most would describe him as not very bright, more hulking and intimidating than smart, but as an investigator investigating petty crimes in the trailer parks of Warren County, he would have no equal.

Sooner or later everyone living in the South has to purchase a vehicle; the deputies on the sheriff's department were no different.

In return for favorable treatment, Emmett has always provided vehicles at extremely discounted rates to law enforcement officers and the politicians in Vicksburg. And as far as I can tell, of the five or six major car dealerships in our city, only Emmett strives to assure that anyone holding a position of trust or authority is able to obtain a vehicle at his drastically discounted prices, but not without stipulations.

Not only are law enforcement officers assured of special discounts at Emmett's dealership, but Emmett has gone the extra step of employing the brother of Sheriff Pace to help ease and facilitate these, essentially, bribes in return for special favors.

Emmett and Atwood Chevrolet have been sued by numerous people for a wide-range of reasons, usually involving shady business practices. At one point Emmett and the dealership were criminally indicted by a grand jury for a fraud that they were perpetrating against customers. But by greasing the right palms, Emmett was able to avoid being convicted.

When Emmett or anyone in the Atwood family needed help with law enforcement, their go-to person was Detective Todd Dykes. Dykes had personally been assigned to handle the special needs of Emmett and the Atwood family by Sheriff Pace. If there was a problem, big or small, Dykes was eager to assist. Anything for a donut.

It was with these corrupt obligations in mind that Detective Dykes jumped at the chance to help Emmett have me arrested. It didn't matter if there wasn't any evidence, Dykes had never been concerned with evidence, he was solely concerned with returning the favors that had been extended to him by Emmett on numerous occasions. And no one seemed to care that the brand new Chevrolet truck in his driveway, which came from Atwood Chevrolet, raised any sort of conflict-of-interest concerns.

This was not an isolated incident of police and political corruption. The Warren County Sheriff's Department had a long history of it, and Todd Dykes and his ilk were only the latest incarnation.

The real history of corruption and malfeasance began in the late 1960s when Paul Barrett was elected the sheriff of Warren County.

The patronage that propelled Sheriff Barrett into political office was given from Maggie Bryant, an extremely wealthy landowner and businesswoman from Virginia who owned a 20,000 acre wildlife preserve in north Warren County, approximately thirty minutes from Vicksburg. To people in the area this preserve is known as Tara Wildlife.

Maggie Bryant's son, J.C. Herbert Bryant, owned a private paramilitary organization that was known as the Armed Response Group of the United States (ARGUS).

The genesis of the modern corruption of the sheriff's department began in the early 1980s when President Reagan and his administration began looking for alternative financial means in which to support the Nicaraguan contra rebels who were advocating the overthrow of the legitimately-elected leftist government of President Daniel Ortega.

The United States Congress had previously outlawed financial and military support for the Nicaraguan contras due to significant evidence that the contras had been importing large amounts of cocaine and marijuana into the United States to fund their war.

When Congress outlawed support for the contras, members of Reagan's administration, controlled by Lt. Colonel Oliver North, began looking for alternative means in which to provide the continuing support which the contras needed.

Into this void stepped Herbert Bryant and the private arsenal of weapons, airplanes, and other military goods that the contra rebels were desperately in need of.

In order to continue providing the contras with support, an alternative means of raising money was needed to pay for the weapons and supplies that were being funneled to them. Bryant turned to his friend, Sheriff Barrett in Vicksburg, in an attempt to open a new source of revenue.

Using airplanes owned by Bryant and his ARGUS organization, the conspirators, headed by Colonel North, began transporting contra cocaine and marijuana into the United States. Corrupt law enforcement officers like Sheriff Barrett were then used to offload the drugs and then funnel money and weapons back to the contras.

To further this plan, Sheriff Barrett and Bryant built a small grass airstrip on the wildlife preserve owned by the Bryant family. Tara Wildlife, for a brief time, went from a private hunting camp to a major epicenter of international conspiracy.

It has always been known that Sheriff Barrett was connected to what used to be known as the Dixie Mafia. These connections served Sheriff Barrett a very fruitful purpose. Barrett used his connections with the Dixie Mafia in Mississippi to distribute and sell the drugs being offloaded from Central America and, in return, the money and weapons obtained from those transactions would be funneled to the contras to assist them in their ongoing war with the Sandinistas.

Their plan worked brilliantly for a short period of time until one of their pilots, Barry Seals, was caught by the Drug Enforcement Administration.

The DEA immediately turned Seals and recruited him to work as an informant for the Agency. They even wired his airplane, owned by ARGUS, with audio and video recording devices. This portion of the conspiracy was made famous in the Tom Cruise movie, *American Made*.

For several months the DEA used Seals to gather evidence on Sheriff Barrett and other deputies in the Warren County Sheriff's Department whom were assisting him in the drug and weapons conspiracy. Barrett's main conspirator and right-hand man was Martin Pace, the deputy who replaced Barrett and is currently the sheriff of Warren County.

Although Sheriff Barrett played a small part of the larger conspiracy, his actions had drawn intense federal scrutiny. But, fortunately for him, Colonel North discovered that Seals was working as an informant for the DEA and illegally disclosed that fact to the newspapers.

Outed as an informant for the DEA, Seals's life was in immediate danger. In order to protect their asset, the DEA placed Seals in a halfway house in Baton Rouge, Louisiana, in an effort to hide him until his testimony could be presented to a grand jury in an attempt to obtain indictments against the targets of the DEA's investigation.

Seals didn't remain hidden for long. Shortly after being placed in the halfway house, two drug cartel assassins, whom had tracked him there, gunned him down in a hail of bullets.

With the death of their only witness, the part of the DEA's investigation into Sheriff Barrett and his deputies fell apart, and, having been tipped off that they were under investigation, Sheriff Barrett curtailed his involvement in what became famously known as the Iran-Contra Affair.

Even though Barrett and the other conspirators barely missed a federal indictment in the Iran-Contra Affair, federal investigators kept them under close scrutiny.

In September 1992, Herbert Bryant was arrested in Washington, D.C., for impersonating a federal officer. Bryant had previously been a Special Deputy U.S. Marshal by virtue of his ownership of the ARGUS organization.

After the *Washington Post* published a series of articles critical of Bryant and ARGUS, the U. S. Marshal's Service stripped Bryant of his status as a deputy marshal.

To continue to obtain favorable treatment in the guise of law enforcement authority, Bryant convinced Sheriff Barrett to deputize him as a deputy with the Warren County Sheriff's Department. But even after being stripped of his U.S. Marshal status, Bryant continued to flaunt his marshal's badge and identification credentials.

He was eventually indicted and convicted of impersonating a U.S. Marshal in 1994. Called to testify in Bryant's criminal trial was Sheriff Barrett.

During the proceedings leading up to Bryant's criminal trial, Barrett provided several false statements to investigators and then ultimately lied under oath.

Barrett was also eventually charged and convicted of several federal felonies and served fifteen months in prison. When Barrett went to prison, Martin Pace became the new sheriff and continues to serve in that position as this book goes to print.

One would think that Pace would use this fresh opportunity to cleanse the sheriff's department of the taint of Barrett's corruption. But rather than sweep the building clean, Sheriff Pace consolidated his power.

A physical description of Sheriff Pace is not hard to write. Skinny, red-headed, and always impeccably dressed in a suit and tie, Sheriff Pace maintains a public image of one whom is intelligent, college educated, and a capable administrator. Born in the late 1950s, he has aged better than most.

Those that know him best can also argue that he is cunning, sly, and very adroit at playing the two roles of maintaining a positive public persona and being a ruthless manipulator.

Yet, despite Sheriff Pace's intelligence and extensive education, his most salient failing is his inability to control, manage, and discipline his deputies when needed. The employees of the Warren County Sheriff's Department, in my opinion, do not respect Sheriff Pace, do not respect the office he holds, and believe that they are immune from his oversight and direction.

As a person, one-on-one, Sheriff Pace is an extremely likeable guy. He has to be to garner votes. And throughout our many, many interactions we have never resorted to anything less than a cordial and respectful conversation. But his failure as sheriff is his inability to effectively administer the personnel employed by him.

I also feel that he is all too willing to allow himself and the office he holds to be used and abused by some of his deputies to advance their own personal political retaliation agendas. Detective Mike Traxler is the perfect example of this.

At one point in my life I had determined to effect change myself by running for political office in Vicksburg. In the fall of 2002 I entered my name in the race for a constable's position in Warren County.

Constables in Mississippi are mostly an anachronistic throwback to an earlier time of community-based law enforcement. Their intended purpose is to serve papers and misdemeanor warrants issued by the justice courts. But in most cases the constable positions are a stepping stone to higher office, most often the sheriff's position itself.

When I announced my candidacy for the constable's office in Warren County, I left no doubt that I was on an anti-corruption crusade and my target was the Warren County Sheriff's Department. Ironically, the constable's position that I was running for was being vacated by an incumbent who'd recently been convicted of extortion and removed from office.

In the fall of 2002, the Warren County Sheriff's Department had faced a recent wave of allegations of misbehavior in what was an overall bad year for many politicians in our town.

Deputy Lionel Johnson, a bully and braggart, had in the months prior to my election, killed an unarmed black student whom had been protesting the illegal and violent arrest of his aged grandmother. Although a grand jury refused to indict him, even Sheriff Pace had to admit the killing justified refusing to continue employing Deputy Johnson.

One of the judges in Warren County, Gerald Hoseman, had beat his mistress so badly in a fit of domestic violence that she barely survived. Thankfully, in a rare demonstration of independent thought, the voters in Warren County had sense enough not to reelect Hoseman. Eventually, he was convicted of assault charges and fled Vicksburg in disgrace.

In another example of the deeply ingrained stench of political corruption, the son of a popular city councilman, Michael Mayfield, allegedly raped an underage girl, but using his political influence, Mayfield was able to convince the authorities to not press charges.

This had been followed by a botched investigation by the sheriff's department—which many insisted was not botched at all, but was instead an effort to help protect the officer from prosecution— into a Vicksburg Police officer named Bart Henriques.

Henriques had been accused by several underage girls of inappropriate and illegal sexual behavior. Henriques was eventually convicted in federal court of possession of child pornography, but the Fifth Circuit

Court of Appeals overturned his convictions on appeal.

Had the sheriff's department conducted a competent and thorough investigation, Henriques could have been prosecuted in the state courts for a wide array of sexual crimes against his victims, but, as law officers, they protected him from further prosecution.

Another perfect example would be the investigation and prosecution of a city police officer named Bo McCleod who was arrested for raping and sexually assaulting his own cousin. Despite overwhelming evidence that this officer incapacitated and then raped his cousin, the sheriff's department under Martin Pace botched the investigation so badly, especially the forensic DNA collection part, that the prosecutors were eventually left with no evidence other than he-said, she-said.

In fact, the investigation was so shoddy and unprofessional that I am utterly convinced that it was done on purpose to protect—who everyone admits was a very likeable and popular officer—Bo McCleod from a life sentence of imprisonment. But while admittedly screwing up the investigation and forensic evidence so badly that even the prosecutors had difficulty bringing the case to trial, Bo McCleod's reputation and career as a law enforcement officer was effectively over, because, even he had to admit that he did, in fact, have sex with his cousin—just not forcefully. It was a tragic situation for all involved, but the corruption begged for a strong leader to counter it.

My campaign for constable centered on the the naive, but serious belief that as constable I could help clean up the corruption that Sheriff Pace refused to do himself. I tailored my campaign literature and speeches accordingly.

At the time it was naive of me to think that this anti-corruption crusade wouldn't engender push-back and retaliation from the sheriff's deputies, but this was what happened. However, enough citizens in my community agreed with my stances that out of five candidates running for the same office, me and another earned enough votes to qualify for a run-off election.

Although I didn't win the run-off election that followed, I had acquired a large enough following to generate serious support for a later campaign. People constantly told me that my ideas were correct, I was just too young.

The enemies that I made amongst the corrupt deputies on the sheriff's department wouldn't forget my campaign for constable for a long time. Years later I would often be told by former and current deputies that my race for constable and the ensuing anti-corruption message had reverberated within Sheriff Pace's office unlike anything had before. And Sheriff Pace and his deputies never let me forget it.

Things became so difficult for me after the November 2002 election that I decided to move to Orlando, Florida, to get away from the stress and chaos that surrounded my life after the election.

When one is nineteen-years-old and is being threatened with violence from law enforcement in one's own town, it is a scary experience. Added to the mix was a repressive community for any gay man. These combined into motivation to leave.

I left Vicksburg and moved to Orlando shortly after the election. I chose Orlando because several of my gay friends had moved there and were living very happy, open lives. But my stay in Orlando did not last long.

Upon arriving in Florida I enrolled in a flight school to learn how to fly. I never wanted to make a career of being a pilot, but I've always been fascinated by airplanes and wanted to make that dream a reality. But two other factors contributed to me deciding to return to Vicksburg approximately a year after I'd left.

My grandmother had been getting feeble and unable to care for herself alone as she once had. But the main reason that I returned to Vicksburg was that I was homesick. I'd never been away from home for that long of a period and I missed my family. So I moved back to Vicksburg shortly before Thanksgiving in 2003. In hindsight, this decision and the resulting feud with the Atwoods changed my life for the worst.

CHAPTER THREE

It wasn't long after moving back to Vicksburg that the feud with Emmett and my Aunt June began. And coming down from a tightly and emotionally contested election campaign that turned many corrupt law enforcement officers against me didn't help my cause. Sheriff Pace and his deputies were looking for any pretext to exact revenge. Emmett Atwood provided it to them, but the majority I brought down upon myself.

During this time in my life I was what people in the gay community call a "closet case." Closet cases are gay men whom are overly obsessed with hiding their sexuality. I'd been raised in my father's household to hate and judge anyone that was not white, Anglo-Saxon, heterosexual, and Protestant, and that included hating myself and what I was.

As people around me, which certainly included my family, began discovering that I was gay, I often heard the refrain from them that I didn't "look" or "act" gay. But what they refused to understand was that their preconceived notions of gay men were based solely on the gay men who were open and flamboyant about their sexuality. Because people "like" me often hid their sexuality, mainstream America failed to take notice that we existed.

In Mississippi, those around me already had their perception that all gay men were feminine and flamboyant and that "straight-acting" gay men like me didn't exist. This was mostly because closet cases like myself didn't go to gay bars or hang out with other gay men. I certainly didn't at that time in my life. Instead, I turned to Internet chatrooms to meet men.

Having become more comfortable with my sexuality, I set aside my self-imposed prohibition against meeting any gay men who lived close to me.

For a short time I had been in a long-distance relationship with a Marine who was stationed in Washington, D.C.

The Marine that I was dating had an extremely high-profile position in the Marine Corps. Amongst other duties, he saluted President Bush and Vice President Cheney as they arrived and departed from Marine One and Two. But in late 2003, I met Zach Booth in an Internet chat room for gay men in Mississippi.

At the time, I was nineteen-years-old, but shortly after beginning our on-again, off-again-relationship I turned twenty. Zach was fifteen-years-old when we first met on the computer, but turned sixteen before the first time that we ever met in person.

I was vaguely aware of the age of consent laws in Mississippi, and it was with this in mind that I purposefully did not meet Zach until after he turned sixteen. According to Mississippi law, sixteen is the age of consent.

For several months we continued our friendship until the pivotal event of my life changed on July 2, 2004. On that date I was arrested by the Federal Bureau of Investigation for allegedly sending a threatening email to a homosexual pedophile in Virginia.

Immediately upon my arrest I knew who the FBI was referring to as my alleged victim, but I also knew that I had never threatened the person.

Allen Cousby Jacques had been someone that I met in an Internet chatroom while I lived in Orlando. Jacques had represented himself to me as a young adult, stationed with the Air Force in Washington, D.C., and had sent pictures to me of an attractive guy. At the time I believed the stories he told me and the fake pictures that he sent, but before long I began to suspect that he was not who he said he was.

I was finally able to unveil Jacques's fraud and he admitted to me that, in fact, he was a much older man who enjoyed talking to and trading pictures with younger gay men.

Upon learning about Jacques's pedophilia, I immediately decided to cease contact with him, but this was not what Jacques wanted. So for several months Jacques harassed and stalked me on the Internet and I was helpless to stop it because I could not turn to law enforcement for help.

In frustration I cursed Jacques, I called him names, but I never threatened him. But as I was soon to discover, even the FBI doesn't rely on evidence when making arrests.

I, of course, was not given bond, but was instead locked up in the Madison County Jail in Canton, Mississippi, while the FBI searched for the alleged threat. However, after extensive reviews of the five computers taken from me in their search, the FBI was never able to find anything even remotely threat-like on my computers against Jacques or anyone else. Without evidence, the FBI had to drop this charge. But during their fruitless search for the nonexistent Jacques threat, the FBI found the emails between Zach Booth and I.

In the interest of full disclosure, I have always readily admitted that Zach and I engaged in sexual chat on the Internet. This would be the equivalent of "sexting," what many people do today.

In order to bring federal charges for having these conversations with Zach, the FBI had to prove that (1) we used a computer to communicate and that those communications traveled across state lines; (2) that I persuaded or coerced Zach into having sex; (3) that the sex would violate the law; and (4) that Zach was under eighteen years old.

The FBI could easily prove numbers one, three, and four, but there was never any persuasion or coercion involved which would fit the definition of number two.

Zach was a willing participant and, in most every conversation, the aggressor. Without any proof that I did anything to persuade or coerce Zach into having sex, the FBI's case hinged on proving that I actively sought to pursue the relationship.

I strenuously deny, and refuse to admit, that I did anything to persuade or coerce Zach. It was a completely consensual relationship on both our parts. There will be many who disagree with my interpretation of the evidence, but none can disagree that at the conclusion of the FBI's case I was ultimately convicted and sent to federal prison for sixty-three months. The federal judge also sentenced me to five years of probation.

The only immediate positive outcome of my being convicted was that I was able to be transferred away from the Madison County Jail.

I wrote considerably about the Madison County Jail in my book, *Into Hell I Rode*, but until one actually spends a night or more there one will never be able to understand the horrors which take place there.

The jail was administered by Major Charles "Chuck" McNeil, a grossly overweight and disgustingly sorry excuse for a human. His guards were even less impressive and their interactions and abuse of the inmates reflected their low stature. It was only with the grace of God that I survived the terror that was the Madison County Jail.

When one is convicted and sentenced to federal prison the U.S. Marshals transport inmates from their pretrial holding facilities and into the Federal Bureau of Prisons. The FBOP operates several hundred federal prisons throughout the United States, but my federal judge recommended that I be sent to the federal prison in Yazoo City, Mississippi.

The FBOP has several layers of security in which they construct their prisons. Most people are familiar with the "Camp Cupcake" prisons which the FBOP are famous for.

FBOP camps are classified as the lowest security institutions in the FBOP arsenal. They do not have fences, barbed-wire, or locking doors. Inmates are solely expected to stay there based on the honor system. Surprisingly, it works.

The next security level are low-security prisons. These are classified more closely with inmates that have little violence but require closer scrutiny. Low-security prisons have barbed-wire fences, locking doors, but no cells. Inmates are confined in large, open dorms.

Since I had little criminal history I expected to be sent to a camp or low-security prison. Instead, I was informed that I would be going to the medium-security facility at Yazoo City.

Mediums in the FBOP are known for violence. Not only do they have impressive barbed-wire fences, but inmates are housed in two-man, lockable cells, and there is a higher staff-to-inmate ratio.

Mediums house inmates with histories of violence, gang affiliations, severe sexual misconduct, and other crimes which pose management issues for staff. I was not pleased at being assigned to one.

Above mediums are the United States Penitentiaries, or USPs. These prisons are maximum-security facilities with gun towers, electrified fences, and more controlled movements. I was told that I never wanted to go to a USP.

I arrived at Yazoo City in August 2005. It had taken nearly a year to litigate my criminal case in the federal court in Jackson. Compared to Madison County the federal prison was heaven.

I was assigned to a two-man cell where I had my own sink and toilet, a metal locker, and a bunk bed. But we were only locked in the cell from ten at night to six in the morning. With the exception of official counts we were able to remain outside of our cells for the rest of the day.

Every week I could go to commissary, similar to a small convenience store, and buy snack foods, hygiene, stamps and writing paper, clothes, and tennis shoes.

In each unit there were six or seven televisions and we could control which stations we watched. There was even a large recreation yard where inmates were able to exercise, play handball, football, softball, and basketball, and walk a track. Some prisons even had weights for inmates to bodybuild with, but Yazoo City was not one of them.

One of the more peculiar particularities of medium-security prisons was that the entire inmate population of the prison was segregated by race. Whites only lived in cells with other whites, blacks only lived with blacks, and the same for Mexicans. Sometimes, though, whites and Mexicans could live together, but never white and black or Mexican and black.

The same was true for the chow hall. Each race had their own tables to sit and eat at and, like a religious ritual, everyone followed this unwritten code. Even the televisions in the housing units were unofficially assigned to certain races.

As a freshly new twenty-two year old inmate, I had a significant learning curve to obtain. But I quickly developed a routine which included working in the law library during the day and exercising on the rec yard in the evenings. My family even came to visit me every weekend, and it was especially these visits which I looked forward to the most.

The following year I was transferred to the medium-security prison in Memphis because a distant cousin of mine on the Atwood side of the family was hired at the prison in Yazoo City. According to the FBOP, it was policy not to allow an inmate and relative to both be at the same facility at the same time. Despite the trouble that this transfer caused me, Memphis turned out to be a better place to serve time than had Yazoo City.

The prison at Memphis had been built in the 1970s and the mentality there was different than at Yazoo City. There was also a different class of inmates assigned there.

While Yazoo City mostly contained inmates from the Texas, Mississippi, and Louisiana areas, Memphis had inmates from Tennessee, North Carolina, and Kentucky.

Inmates from Texas, especially white inmates, are the worst to do prison time with. Most white Texas inmates are involved in one of the Aryan white supremacist gangs and they are constantly causing strife and discontent on any yard in which their numbers are high.

Yazoo City had a lot of gang violence between the Aryan Brotherhood, Aryan Circle, and Aryan Nation white supremacist gangs. Their counterparts among the Mexicans were the Barrio Aztecas, the Mexican Mafia, and Texas Syndicate. These two racial gangs were counterbalanced by the Vice Lords, Bloods, Crips, and Gangster Disciples of the black gangs.

Memphis, though, had very little racial strife or gang activity. The different races lived together, ate together in the chow hall, and there was no partitioning of the televisions. I was approximately three hours from home, but Memphis was a decent place to serve time.

Memphis, though, became a headache for me during the holidays of 2006 when I ran afoul of a black Vice Lord from Los Angeles.

Prison rape and sexual misconduct is a serious misnomer and stereotype of prisons. I can't speak for some state prisons, but sexual abuse is taken seriously and punished severely in the FBOP. Because of such, instances of sexual abuse are not common. But on occasions it happens. But rape is less likely than is a pressure-game used by bullies to try and force other inmates into engaging in sex.

I ran afoul of such a bully during the holidays of 2006. Darwyn Horey was the leader of the Vice Lords at Memphis and he was a sexual bully. I was placed in a position by him of being made fearful for my safety, and rather than turn to the officers and staff for assistance, I chose to fight.

Knowing that I couldn't win without the element of surprise, me and a friend waited until Horey was distracted and then attacked. Using a homemade prison shank, or knife, and a padlock attached to a belt, we made quick work of the bully. But in doing so I knew that I could never be allowed back to the prison. Instead, the FBOP transferred me to a small, medium-security prison in Upstate New York called Ray Brook.

My first impression of Ray Brook was awe. I'd never seen so much snow in all my life. When I arrived in February 2007, Ray Brook was in the midst of a blizzard. It reminded me of the spring storms in Mississippi, but instead of the side blowing rain, it was torrential snow.

The prison itself had been constructed in 1979 to initially serve as the dormitories for the 1980 Winter Olympic athletes. After the games were over the buildings were converted into a prison. But by the time I arrived in 2007 one could not have discerned the prison's prior famous history.

Besides the cold, Ray Brook was not a bad place to serve time in prison. The food was better than Yazoo City and Memphis had served, there were not any Texas or Vice Lord inmates, and with my unique Southern accent I became popular with the Boston and New York crowd.

I remember Ray Brook best for the hockey games that I used to play every weekend. It was always the Boston inmates against the Canadian ones, but I played with both. I also obtained my first black eye in one of the hockey games which I always jokingly attributed to having come from my cellmate.

I had initially hidden my sexuality when I first came to prison. I'd heard that gay men were not treated well in prison and I did not want to add to the burdens which I was already carrying. So while I was at Yazoo City I carried myself in a very confident and masculine manner and never allowed my desire for companionship to overcome my need for safety. But that changed at Memphis.

Memphis was much less tense and violent than Yazoo City. It also had numerous transgender and openly gay inmates there. I could clearly see upon my arrival that there was no point in hiding who I was. I expected to have other guys, most of whom were undesirable, make passes at me if I was openly gay, but I saw so little trouble that the other gay inmates there dealt with and I made the decision not to hide.

I spent a year at Ray Brook and, as far as prisons are concerned, enjoyed my time there better than I had at Yazoo City and Memphis, but being so far from home made it difficult for my family to come visit.

Each inmate in federal prison is assigned a case manager to help assist inmates in their transition to the free-world. My case manager at Ray Brook was one of the best I'd ever had and she was very helpful in obtaining a transfer for me back to the South so that I could be closer to home.

In February 2008, I was transferred to the medium-security prison at Forrest City, Arkansas. What Ray Brook and Memphis were, Forrest City was not, but it was the closest facility to my family that I could be sent to.

Like Yazoo City, Forrest City had a lot of gang activity and inmates from Texas, but with less than a year left on my sentence I was determined to make the best of it.

I spent the summer of 2008 doing the best that I could in preparing myself for release. I exercised constantly, playing handball, softball, and working out. But my favorite afternoon activity was sunbathing. By the start of fall, not only did I have a very dark tan, but I was in the best shape of my life. I not only passed my last year of incarceration in a blur, but my body benefitted as well. I'd never felt more ready for release than I did then.

On Friday, January 23, 2009, I was released from federal prison. My family rented an oversized, stretched Hummer limousine and picked me up at the prison. We spent the weekend in Memphis and the following Monday morning I reported to my probation officer, William Jay Simpson, at his office in Jackson.

Jay appeared to me to be old enough to have been born in the early 1970s, but not so old that he hadn't been a recent graduate of a college university.

He appeared to me to be utterly competent as a person and probation officer. However, a probation officer is probably the plateau of his professional career and intellectual abilities.

He has red hair that was beginning to go gray by the time that we had our first introduction. His medium build easily reflected a past history in sports, but like many men, he'd given up any hope of staying in shape past college and the marriage that the wedding band on his ring finger indicated.

I believe that Jay is indifferent to my sensitive political situation and could care less whether the cops in Vicksburg loved or hated me. But it was clear that when facing any moral, ethical crossroad, Jay would always fall back and side with his fellow law enforcement officers and superiors regardless of whether or not their position was legally acceptable.

As I came to know Jay better, I soon learned that I could count on him to be fair towards me—as I am sure he was to other probationers—but there was no doubt in my mind that if faced with a choice of being fair towards me or siding with the corrupt cops that I went to war with, he could always be counted on to tow their line, hide wrongdoing, and cover his boss's ass.

At our first meeting, though, I was determined to try and do the best I could to always be honest, straightforward, and professional with him.

Going from imprisonment to probation was like going from one type of incarceration to another, but I was determined to make the best of a bad situation and let nothing, or anyone, stand in my way of making a successful transition.

CHAPTER FOUR

Upon my release I moved back home with Vivian. For the four and a half years that I'd been in prison Vivian had deteriorated in health, both physically and mentally.

Back in 2004, Vivian and I had filed a lawsuit against her daughter June in an attempt to regain the legitimate title to the land that June had stolen from her mother. The land dispute case had been slowly winding its way through the Mississippi court system for longer than I'd been incarcerated. But several weeks before my release, June decided to compromise in an effort to settle the case.

One must keep in mind that in the early 1990s, using solely her money, Vivian bought a large tract of land in south Warren County. At that time, she intentionally gave a piece of that land to both June and my father.

My father built his house on the land that Vivian gave him, but June, instead, used the land that she was given to build a horse barn. If she had wanted, June would have still had plenty of available land to build her own house, but June was very greedy and wanted everything for nothing. This is what led June to defraud Vivian out of her own land and home.

Any loving and caring daughter would never have done what June did in the first place, but once caught, June attempted to double down and fought Vivian tooth-and-nail in order to keep what she had fraudulently stolen.

In December 2008, however, a compromise was reached. To settle the lawsuit, June agreed to return ownership of Vivian's house to her. In turn, Vivian would sign over additional land that she owned to June.

Although June wouldn't get the house, she increased her landholdings by forty very valuable acres. This left Vivian with her house and approximately eighteen acres of land.

During my incarceration, Vivian and I often discussed selling the house and land upon my release if we were able to wrestle control of them back from June. Having accomplished that, our discussions turned more serious once I was out of prison.

In March of 2009, we placed the house and eighteen acres up for sale. We did not have any idea where we would go if the place did sell, but our desire to get away from June was so intense that our potential future home seemed pale in comparison to the immediate problem that June posed for us living on the same property. But while our housing and family issues occupied my thoughts, more pressing business garnered immediate action.

I thought that I had adjusted well to my release from prison, but one of the most embarrassing and awkward duties that I had to perform was registering as a sex offender at the Warren County Sheriff's Department and the driver's license station. It galled me to the core to have to appear at the sheriff's department and undergo the indignity that registering required. But I knew that several of the deputies were no better than me. Their only consolation was that they had not been caught for their crimes.

The legal case involving the malicious mischief arrest that Emmett and June had instigated in early 2004 had been pending for all the years that I'd been incarcerated, but sooner or later it would have to be brought to trial, and even though I was attempting to maintain a low-profile, some of the deputies wouldn't let me forget that they were going to try and have me returned to prison when my case was called for trial later in 2009.

By then I knew that there was not any evidence linking me to the malicious mischief crime. Their entire case was based on circumstantial evidence and innuendo. Emmett and June were depending on their connections with the cops to secure a conviction.

There was one wrinkle in the case, though, that cannot be left out of the story and which provides some needed context into my character and the depths that law enforcement will go to in order to obtain illegal convictions.

One of my closest friends was Richard Dane Davenport. Dane was a state trooper on the Mississippi Highway Patrol and had been a friend of my family for many years.

In the early 1990s, Dane married Tammy English and they began a family. Unfortunately for Dane, Tammy previously had three sons with another husband prior to her and Dane's marriage. Shortly after their marriage, Dane and Tammy jointly began a physical therapy business and over the next decade became millionaires from the successful operation of their company.

Marital troubles began in 2006, and by the next year their marriage was headed for divorce. Because Dane's family had provided the capital for them to start their business, he was slated to receive a substantial part of the money from the company. Tammy apparently couldn't abide this notion and shortly before their divorce two of her sons accused Dane of molesting them.

Dane was ultimately charged in two different jurisdictions, but by the time I had been released from prison he had gone to trial and obtained hung juries in both instances.

Needing to toughen their cases in order to obtain a conviction, the Mississippi Attorney General's Office began looking for additional evidence in which to convict Dane with. Because the Attorney General's Office was also prosecuting my malicious mischief case, their interests immediately settled on me shortly after I was released from prison.

The prosecutors that were prosecuting Dane gave me a choice. Because they knew that Dane and I had been friends when I was underage, they offered to dismiss my malicious mischief case if I agreed to testify against Dane and say that he had molested me. This was something I refused to do. Whatever Dane's shortcomings may be, I do not believe that he molested his stepsons. And ultimately the juries agreed and found him not guilty of all charges. But once Dane's case had concluded, the prosecutors began preparing for mine.

In the meantime, shortly after placing our house for sale, we found a buyer who wanted to take immediate possession. Once the sale concluded, Vivian and I had less than thirty days to find a new house to live in.

We discussed moving closer to Jackson, or even to the Mississippi Gulf Coast to get as far away from the Atwoods and the sheriff's department as possible, but we ultimately bought a new house in north Warren County.

Our decision to stay near Vicksburg turned more on housing availability than it did on the need to get away from the source of my troubles. In hindsight, it was a horrible decision with far-reaching consequences.

From the very beginning, Vivian had always wanted for me and my cousin Julie to inherit her estate. Since the late 1980s Vivian had structured her wills to reflect her desire that Julie and me be given her property and money. In furtherance of this desire, Vivian put our new house solely in my name. At the same time, to compensate Julie, she put the majority of her money in Julie's name.

Vivian knew that all four of her children had been financially secured through Emmett's generosity. The only other grandchildren that Vivian had were Ray's and Alan's children, and they were financially secure.

The two grandchildren in the family that did not have fathers to depend upon were Julie and me. Julie's father was Ray, but like my father, Ray disowned Julie when he divorced her mother and remarried Vivian's other grandchildrens' mother. This essentially left Julie and me without fathers and Vivian had always saw a need to fulfill. So putting the house in my name and leaving Julie the majority of the money was not a surprise to anyone who knew. Vivian voiced these desires to numerous people, including, obviously, the attorneys who did the official work.

When we moved into our new house in north Warren County, Vivian didn't expect to live much longer. She'd been hospitalized for heart failure, she needed knee replacements, and dementia had begun its slow deterioration of her mind.

By June of 2009 Vivian was almost bedridden and we needed help taking care of her. Finding someone to help was difficult, but I ultimately decided on permanently hiring a friend, Scott Andrew Zimmerman.

Scott was a friend of mine that was in his late forties when he came to work for us in 2009. He was overweight, with several certain nerdy qualities to him, and his severe acne scars on his face made him look more like a surviving victim of the worst smallpox epidemic to ever hit this country. But I didn't hire him for his looks; he was there to help me at a desperate time.

At the time, Scott was recovering from alcohol and prescription opioid abuse. I believed him when he said he needed a job and a second chance. Having just been released from prison, I sympathized.

At first Scott was a helpful, resourceful asset to have when I needed assistance in taking care of Vivian. Scott had a history in the medical field and he and Vivian hit it off immediately. But as the months passed I began noticing some red flags of concern.

Taking care of Vivian became a twenty-four hour a day job, and when she had her first knee replacement surgery in early July it became more intensive. I worked part-time at night and during those times Scott would stay with Vivian. Some days we were all three at the house, but Vivian was quickly going downhill and it concerned me when she began forgetting who I was or where she was. The more I depended on Scott, though, the more he disappointed me. It was quickly becoming apparent that I would need more professional help in taking care of my grandmother.

Before I could resolve the problems with my grandmother's welfare, I was forced to stand trial in September for the malicious mischief case.

Shortly before we began picking a jury the assistant attorney general prosecuting my case offered to drop the charges to misdemeanors if I would plead guilty and pay Emmett and June the costs of repairing the tractor. I told them to go to hell in the nicest way possible.

The first witness that the assistant attorney general called to the stand was a firearms ballistic expert who testified that the bullets pulled from the tractor didn't match any of the guns that were taken from my house for comparison. His testimony was quick and pointless. It helped me more than Emmett and June's case.

Detective Todd Dykes was called to testify next, and after Dykes squeezed his obese frame into the witness chair, he proceeded to destroy whatever credibility as a competent investigator he may have had.

What little evidence the sheriff's department had implicating me in the shooting was quickly discredited when it became known that Emmett and June had actually provided Detective Dykes with the evidence that they collected themselves.

Any competent and capable investigator is supposed to collect forensic evidence themselves. However, Detective Dykes, instead of looking for evidence himself, asked Emmett and June to collect it for him. This "evidence," which the Attorney General's prosecutors were hoping would convict me, completely destroyed whatever hope they had of securing a conviction.

My malicious mischief arrest was instigated specifically by Emmett and June; they provided law enforcement with the evidence they allegedly found implicating me in the crime, and they depended on Sheriff Pace and his cronies' hatred of me to secure a conviction.

When June testified after Detective Dykes, she vehemently denied finding and providing the circumstantial evidence to Dykes. It was at this point that several jurors openly laughed and rolled their eyes at June's absurd testimony.

The prosecutors, heads hung low, rested their case once June's testimony concluded. As June left the witness stand everyone in the courtroom noticed the stumbling walk and disjointed movements that June made. And no one could ignore the slurred speech during her testimony.

I leaned over and told both of my attorneys that June was either drunk, high on pills, or both. After all, June had been abusing alcohol and drugs for years.

One of my attorneys, Tom Setser, quickly requested permission to ask June one more question before she left the witness stand. As June took her seat one more time, Tom asked her if she was drunk or under the influence of prescription pills. As clear as it was that there was something mentally wrong with June at that moment, the prosecutors from the Attorney General's Office jumped to their feet and made an objection and asked that the court not allow Tom's question to be answered. The judge agreed with the prosecutors and let June leave without having to answer, but the jury knew exactly what was happening, and I knew, just like I had all my life, that June was an alcoholic and pill-popper.

Once the prosecutors' case concluded it was my turn to rebut and refute their allegations. I did this solely by testifying myself and destroying their case.

The prosecutors tried to discredit my testimony by informing the jury that I had been sent to prison five years earlier, but I had truth on my side and most of the jurors knew it.

When it was finally time for the jury to leave the courtroom and debate my fate, I was confident that I would be exonerated. Those supporters of mine that had watched the trial agreed. But as the jury's deliberations carried over into their fifth hour many of us began to get nervous.

When the jury had deliberated for almost six hours the judge had us assemble in the courtroom so that he could inquire of the jury and question them on how close they were to a verdict. By this time it was dark outside and everyone wanted to go home.

After being recalled to the jury box, the judge asked the jury how close they were to a verdict. Without hesitation, every juror stated unequivocally that they would never reach a verdict and were deadlocked ten for not guilty and two for guilty.

Faced with no choice but to declare a mistrial, the judge did so and dismissed us for the night.

Before leaving the courtroom several jurors approached me and my attorneys and told us how impressed they were with my testimony and our defense. They told us that they clearly saw this prosecution as a witch hunt.

Our obvious question at that point was how we were unable to convince the two conviction-minded jurors to vote not guilty. None of the other jurors knew why the two maintained their desire to convict, but thought it might of had something to do with me being gay.

I thought that my being gay may have given pause to some jurors, but I didn't think it would overcome their conscience when debating whether to send a man to prison in light of the clear exonerating evidence that we put on. I decided to dig deeper.

I began research on the two jurors that voted to convict me. During jury *voir dire* all of the jurors were asked if they knew the Atwoods, ever bought cars from the dealership, or had any connection whatsoever to Emmett, June, the sheriff's department, the attorneys and prosecutors, or myself. Every juror that was eventually selected answered in the negative.

But once I began my research at the county courthouse's tax and motor vehicle registration office, I quickly discovered that one of the jurors that voted to convict me had been a long-term customer of Atwood Chevrolet and had bought several vehicles from there. This directly contravened what the juror had stated prior to being accepted, and it made me extremely suspicious.

A little more digging revealed that this juror was friends on Facebook with three Atwoods in my family, including Emmett's wife, Camille.

These discoveries infuriated me because the only conclusion that any reasonable person could draw was that Emmett had deliberately intervened with this juror in an underhanded scam to have me wrongly convicted. But no one cared when I attempted to bring these facts to the court's attention.

Facebook searches also proved fortuitous when it came to trying to discern the motive for the other juror wanting to convict me. Although all the jurors swore under oath that they had no connections with current or former Vicksburg and Warren County law enforcement officers, the second juror was friends on Facebook with Georgia Lynn.

Not only was Georgia Lynn an investigator with the district attorney's office, she was also the aunt of Zach Booth and best friends with my Aunt June. I had written extensively about Georgia Lynn in my book, *Into Hell I Rode*, because she had, while an investigator with the district attorney, been arrested for and convicted of DUI. She then exponentially made the situation worse when she attempted to illegally cover-up her arrest and dangerous intoxication by using her law enforcement status and political position with the district attorney to attempt to intimidate the arresting officer into not taking her to jail.

It only crossed my mind to check and see if any of the jurors were friends with her on Facebook when Georgia Lynn appeared at my trial with my Aunt June to watch the final day's testimony and closing arguments. But as it was with the other juror, no one seemed to care that this presented a huge conflict-of-interest. Because there had neither been a conviction or not guilty verdict, no one seemed to care what had happened during the trial.

Everyone knew that the Attorney General's Office wouldn't waste their time with another prosecution because they could never hope to win, and this is what eventually occurred. My malicious mischief charge was dismissed and no one cared whether any of the jurors had been illegally influenced; the case was over. But the fact that the wrongful collusion occurred still rankled me. However, shortly after the trial concluded, Scott Zimmerman destroyed my world.

Two weeks after my malicious mischief trial ended, I discovered that Scott had met a thirteen-year-old gay boy off the Internet and had taken him back to my house for a night during one of Vivian's many stays in the local hospital.

It was then that I decided that Scott had to leave, and once I began inventorying Vivian's medications, I found out that Scott had been stealing her narcotics and using them himself.

I fired Scott around the first of October 2009 in a meeting where he profusely apologized for his misbehavior and begged to be allowed to stay at my house. I wouldn't listen and I gave him less than an hour to pack his belongings and leave.

With Scott out of the picture, taking care of Vivian's day-to-day needs fell to me, but I soon found much better assistance from a private healthcare agency.

Scott, having been denied access to my grandmother's narcotics and kicked out of my house, decided to retaliate.

Upon being forced out of my house for having sex with a thirteen-year-old boy and for stealing my grandmother's narcotics, Scott immediately called Emmett and told him that I was physically abusing Vivian and that she wasn't being taken care of.

Emmett, having been recently dealt a bloody nose by me in the malicious mischief trial, decided that he could use Scott to exact vengeance.

Shortly before I had to fire Scott, I began dating a guy that I'd known years before named Joshua Langston Chamblee.

Josh was my age and very athletic with many physical attributes reminiscent of his days as a baseball and football player in high school. He certainly wasn't intellectually gifted, nor could he be counted on to solve complex problems, but he was good at working on broken cars and trucks, building things, and playing sports.

Josh grew up in Carthage, Mississippi, but had joined the Coast Guard after high school and spent several years in different stations, including New Orleans, Louisiana. Upon being discharged from the Coast Guard, Josh enrolled in the East Mississippi Community College near Starkville, Mississippi. Some time after leaving the Coast Guard, but before meeting me, Josh contracted HIV, however I was unaware of this when we began dating.

Josh was present for a lot of the drama that occurred between Scott and me in the immediate aftermath of me firing him, but Josh was also there quite often when I spent the majority of my time taking care of Vivian and making sure that she was provided for.

On Tuesday, October 13, 2009, however, I was contacted by Detective Dykes and told that a warrant had been issued for my arrest and to come turn myself in.

When I arrived at the sheriff's department, Dykes provided me with a misdemeanor warrant signed by Scott Zimmerman for simple assault.

Upon being fired, Scott went immediately to Emmett. Emmett then took Scott to Detective Dykes, and somewhere in between, Scott cooked up a lie that I had threatened to assault him several weeks before on the day when I'd fire him.

Before I could bond out of jail on the misdemeanor charge, Detective Dykes handed me a restraining order forbidding me from returning to my house or going near Vivian.

With Scott and his lies, Emmett had gone straight to one of the judges that he was friends with and convinced him that Vivian was in danger and needed a protective order to keep me from her. No hearing was held, no one sought to confirm Scott's story, and no one attempted to speak to Vivian's doctors and the nurses from the home healthcare agency that I employed to help take care of her.

Vivian, unfortunately, had declined rapidly, both physically and mentally, and was in no condition to dispute the proceedings. According to Emmett and the other Atwoods, Vivian's dementia was so severe that she was incapable of determining her own best interests. Even though Vivian had had nothing to do with anyone on that side of her family, or even spoken to them for over twelve years, the judge felt it best that these people would keep Vivian's best interests at heart, and not those whom had taken the best care of her over the years.

I had to hire an attorney, but I was effectively frozen out of my own house. Emmett and the other Atwoods, using Scott's lies, were finally able, after twelve years of me living with Vivian, to separate us. And neither Vivian or I were able to stop it.

Until a judge could sort out the problem, Vivian's day-to-day care was in the hands of the Atwoods and I was forced to move into my mom's house.

I immediately provided Detective Dykes the name of the thirteen-year-old boy that Scott had had sex with, along with the date and time it occurred. All Detective Dykes had to do would be to talk to the boy's parents, search either the boy's or Scott's computers, or make a simple effort to investigate, but Dykes, the sheriff's department, and the Atwoods needed Scott, and it didn't matter that Scott was a pedophile or a narcotics addict. So Dykes never attempted to investigate the crimes.

Unfortunately, the courts in Mississippi allow one, or a group of relatives, to challenge another relative's care and control over an infirm family member. This is essentially what the Atwoods did with Vivian.

ABLAZE

Scott provided the Atwoods with enough lies that they could, at least temporarily, gain control over Vivian's care, and I was helpless to stop it. Events in my life were quickly about to spin out of control.

CHAPTER FIVE

Shortly after gaining control over my grandmother's care, as if she were a toy to be shared between siblings, my Atwood family members moved to sever any and all contact between Vivian and I.

The judge that the Atwoods used to accomplish this nefarious purpose was Edwin "Eddie" Woods, a justice court judge in Vicksburg. This was another Atwood lackey at the beck and call of Emmett.

After they wrestled control of Vivian's care from me, the Atwoods then moved to have my federal probation violated, and the only way they could do that was through Judge Woods.

Shortly after Scott pressed simple assault charges on me, the Atwoods, under Emmett's control, pressed for the sheriff's department to charge me with elderly abuse based solely on the lies told to them by Scott.

Eventually, both charges ended up in front of Judge Woods in the justice court. Because of Judge Woods's close contact with Emmett, we moved for him to recuse himself from the case and let another judge handle the trial, but because Judge Woods was working for Emmett, he refused to do so, and when I went to trial on the misdemeanor charges in December 2009, Judge Woods found me guilty, basing his verdict, again, solely on Scott Zimmerman's lies.

Thankful for a unique clause in Mississippi's law, any person convicted of a crime in the justice courts is entitled to an automatic *de novo* appeal to the county or circuit courts.

A *de novo* appeal of a criminal conviction means that a defendant gets to have a second, brand new trial as if the first trial and conviction had never occurred. This procedure essentially negates any corrupt judge's rulings which are decided wrongly towards a defendant. I, of course, availed myself of this right, and in a new trial, in front of a six-person jury, I was found not guilty of both assaulting Scott and abusing my grandmother.

This was the second jury trial that I had faced in less than four months, but in the second case, my jury deliberated less than fifteen minutes before returning their verdict of not guilty. It was a stunning reversal of Emmett and the Atwood's desire to incarcerate me again, and an astounding win for justice and fairness. Had I been convicted by the jury, my federal probation officer, Jay Simpson, would have moved to have my probation revoked and me sent back to prison for, no doubt, several years. But, thankfully, the six men and women on my jury saw through the sham that was the Atwood's case. And not only that, it was a direct slap in the face to the corrupt idiot, Judge Woods.

Much to my everlasting regret, this was the last time I ever saw my much beloved grandmother. She was conveniently used by her estranged children and ex-husband and then tucked away to spend her final days alone and uncared for.

Vivian's greatest fear was that she would die alone, without family or friends there with her in the final days. And that is what happened when her estranged children tore her from the only family that had selflessly taken care of her for the last fifteen or twenty years.

Vivian spent the last few weeks of her life in a hospital room in Vicksburg. Not once did any of her children come visit her, stay with her at night, or show an interest in her care. She passed away alone without so much as a final goodbye from anyone in the family.

The same final, lonely moments of life occurred to Scott, too, except for different reasons. Having spiraled out of control, Scott's life ended as a result of his own doing in what was clearly a drug-induced suicide.

When the Atwoods took my grandmother from me, and used Scott's lies to do so, I knew that karma would eventually catch up to them. Scott's did so before the others, but Emmett's and the rests' were soon to come.

During the latest legal wrangling with Emmett and the Atwoods, Josh Chamblee and I had continued to pursue our relationship. We spent almost every day and night together since we'd become a couple. Some of those nights were spent in Vicksburg at my mother's house, but some were spent at Josh's parents' house in Carthage or Josh's apartment in Starkville.

Early on the morning of November 13, 2009, Jay called me on my cell phone and told me that a deputy at the Attala County Sheriff's Department in Kosciusko needed to speak with me. My first inquiry began with a question as to the deputy's reason for needing me to call him, but Jay would tell me no more. At this time, I was still unaware that the Atwood Lakehouse had burned down.

I was with Josh that morning at his apartment in Starkville, but I immediately called the deputy back on the number that Jay had given me.

This was the first time that I'd ever spoken to Tim Nail. At that time Nail was the chief deputy on the sheriff's department and William Lee was the elected sheriff.

Deputy Nail appears to me as one might expect a country deputy sheriff from the backwoods of Mississippi to look like. He was clearly in his late fifties, with rosy skin, a paunch belly, cowboy boots and a large cowboy hat.

I imagined that Nail lacked formal criminal justice training, but had nonetheless gained competent experience in investigations from years of down-in-the-dirt police work. Attala County wasn't known for serious crime, but I approached the situation knowing all too well how serious the situation really was.

My maternal grandfather, Aaron Tolleson, was born and raised in the Kosciusko area, was an Attala County elected leader himself, and was friends with Sheriff Lee, and although I'd met Sheriff Lee on numerous occasions, I'd never had the opportunity to meet or speak to Deputy Nail until our first phone conversation.

Deputy Nail was polite and cordial to me during that phone call, and he was honest. He told me that the Atwood Lakehouse had burned down and that he wanted to question me about my whereabouts on the night of the fire.

The initial shock of learning that the lake house had burned was greater than learning that I was suspected of starting it. I loved that lake house and I had too many good memories from there to ever consider committing such an atrocity.

This was a time of immense stress and frustration with what I had to deal with on a daily basis from the Atwoods and Emmett regarding Vivian. Added to the mix were the two recent criminal trials that threatened to return me to prison.

I was horribly on the edge of wanting to lash out and hurt Emmett and the Atwoods as badly as they were hurting me. Because I'd been denied a fair hearing in the courts before Judge Woods, I'd lost almost all respect and confidence I had in attaining fair treatment there. But as bad as I wanted to lash out, I never would have considered burning down the Atwood Lakehouse. It would have been too similar to burning and destroying my own house, and when it finally sunk in that the lake house was indeed gone, it destroyed a part of my soul. And that is what Emmett and the investigators didn't understand and would never understand about me. If I was going to destroy something valued by Emmett, it would not have been the lake house.

I wanted desperately to explain these thoughts to Deputy Nail, but I'd been counseled by my attorneys not to cooperate with him in any way except to provide him my alibi for the night of the fire. And my alibi was Josh Chamblee.

My Papaw went with Josh and me to the Attala County Sheriff's Department and met with Sheriff Lee and Deputy Nail. While Josh and I were separated into different rooms to provide our alibi statements, my Papaw tried to explain to Sheriff Lee about the ongoing feud between my other grandfather, Emmett, and me.

Even though my attorneys had cautioned me about cooperating too much with Nail's investigation, I had no problem providing him with my shoes so that he could make Xerox copies of the patterns and record their sizes. Josh did the same, but Deputy Nail both told us that our shoes—sizes thirteen—did not match the much smaller shoe impressions that they'd found near the fire scene. Even at this early stage, two days after the fire, the evidence was proving my innocence.

Deputy Nail already had my cell phone number, but he asked Josh for his too. I immediately knew that Nail and the other investigators would be obtaining my cell phone records to see what cell towers my phone was using during the time of the fire, but I wasn't worried. Josh and I both had been in Starkville during the fire.

While waiting for Deputy Nail to Xerox my shoe's tread patterns, I noticed another deputy in the parking lot making charcoal-on-paper impressions of my car's tires. I was amused by this, but worried, too, because I had a Chevrolet Impala and its tires were factory generics. But whether or not these tire impressions helped Deputy Nail or not in his investigation, I'll never know. After I left the sheriff's department I never heard anything further about my car's tire treads.

While at the sheriff's department, Deputy Nail told me that a deputy fire marshal named James "Jimmy" Jackson, from the Mississippi State Fire Marshal's Office was officially in charge of the investigation and would definitely want to speak with Josh and me next. We left, assuring Deputy Nail that we would speak with Jackson if he desired, but I never heard from him.

After the interview with Deputy Nail on November 13, 2009, I did not officially hear anything further about the Atwood Lakehouse fire. I heard some rumors from the Atwood family that the cause of the fire was undetermined, but with nothing concrete, I was still worried.

My federal probation officer, Jay Simpson, had questioned me very little about the fire, but I knew that he was constantly keeping tabs on the investigation with Deputy Nail and Jackson.

Prior to my release from prison on January 23, 2009, I'd never been on any form of probation. It was a new experience having to follow a set of unique rules adopted by the probation department for people like me, but fortunately, Jay assisted me quite well and was a competent and fair probation officer.

In January 2010, however, Jay petitioned the court to revoke my probation. I never knew, though, that Jay was considering sending me back to prison. My first inkling of something amiss was when the U.S. Marshals kicked my door in with a SWAT team on the morning of January 12.

I have over the years become more and more critical of law enforcement and their move to a quasi-like military response to any problem. In my case, the marshals had no cause to kick in the door to my mother's house and run in with guns pointed at everyone's head.

Jay Simpson had always been able to reach me by telephone and I'd always promptly appeared at his office when he requested me to do so. Yet, he and the other officers involved resorted to a military-like tactic that was totally uncalled for and terrorized my family, including my underage brother and sister. But this would not be the last time.

As I was being led from the house in handcuffs, I saw Todd Dykes's extremely large, obese frame leaning against a cop car smiling at me. I wasn't wearing my glasses or contacts that morning, but I was almost certain that I saw a glazed donut in his hand.

The marshals took me to the Madison County Jail again and dropped me off. I was told that I'd appear before a judge a few days after my arrest for violating the terms of my probation, in part, because I was believed to have started the fire that destroyed the Atwood Lakehouse.

The Madison County Jail was even worse than it had been when I was there last in 2004 and 2005. Chuck McNeil was still in charge of the jail and had only consolidated his psychotic dictatorial control over everything there.

Until one meets Chuck McNeil and really has an opportunity to observe his behavior and treatment of inmates at the jail, one can never truly understand how the terrors of the Nazi Holocaust, or the Stalinistic murders of the former Soviet Union were allowed to happen.

McNeil is the quintessential textbook case of a cruel and despotic human being. I am the first to recognize, though, that jails are meant to house bad people. When people commit crimes they deserve punishment. But punishment and sadistic abuse are two separate and distinct things.

The other factor to consider is that jails are not meant to punish. There is a difference between jails and prisons. Jails exist solely to house pretrial inmates awaiting trial. This pretrial status makes these inmates innocent people until they are fairly and justly convicted of their crimes.

We have a maxim in this country that everyone is presumed innocent until proven guilty. Yet, inmates in jails, such as the one run by Chuck McNeil and his ilk, serve solely as a facility to inflict pain and punishment.

Most of the guards at the Madison County Jail are from the poor, uneducated classes, and have little or no training and understanding in human-to-human relations. Because of their lack of training, the guards there are quicker to resort to unnecessary violence.

At a higher level, the failed leadership of the administrative staff under McNeil contributes to officer-on-inmate violence going unpunished. While I was at the Madison County Jail in 2010 I was viciously abused by the guards and placed in constant fear of assault. And Chuck McNeil did nothing to stop it. In fact, he encouraged it. Thankfully, my probation revocation hearing was held fairly quickly after my arrest.

Judge David Bramlette, the same judge who sentenced me in 2005, again handled my probation revocation case.

As hard as they tried, the U.S. Attorney's Office was never able to connect me to the fire that destroyed the Atwood Lakehouse because they literally had zero evidence. Instead, they tried to concentrate on innuendo and hearsay that came mostly from Emmett. But taken together with the other evidence about how well I'd done since being released from prison, Judge Bramlette decided to give me a break and released me after five months of imprisonment.

Prior to my release, Josh and I ended our relationship on extremely bad terms. Trying to maintain any type of friendship in the midst of the chaos that was my life after the drama began with the Atwoods was enough to ruin anything positive in anyone's life, but Josh and I's relationship had begun taking a turn for the worst after the holidays.

It took nearly three months, but I learned a hard lesson about sociopathic people. Josh was, in every sense of the word, a compulsive, pathological, lying sociopath.

I consider myself a very understanding and forgiving person, but by New Year's 2010, Josh had pushed my understanding nature to the breaking point. And it all revolved around lies about the most inconsequential stuff. But when I found out that Josh was HIV-positive and had been lying to me about having the disease, including going so far as to fake a negative HIV test, it was more than I was willing to deal with.

This was the primary reason that we ended our relationship. But in the process of breaking up and finally separating ourselves from the other, things became more acrimonious and hateful. Most people have been in at least one of these types of toxic relationships and know too well to what I refer, but I'd never dealt with anything such as what I did with Josh Chamblee in all my life. So when we finally did separate completely it was more with relief than it was with regret.

When James Jackson learned through the grapevine that Josh and I had ended our relationship he decided to pounce. Jackson had been waiting in the shadows like an evil spider, and when Josh and I went our separate ways Jackson thought that he would have the ammunition he needed to start his own war against me—one the Warren County Sheriff's Department and Emmett Atwood had been unable to complete.

Josh had called my mother after learning that Jackson wanted to interview him. My mother knew about Josh's HIV status and their phone conversation did not go well. But one thing that Josh made clear to my mother was that if we attempted to prosecute him for exposing me to HIV, or pursue any other legal remedy, then he would implicate me in the fire.

In our argument-filled break up, I'd often told Josh that I was considering reporting him to the authorities for exposing me to HIV, but he always used the lake house fire as a bargaining tool to try and convince me not to.

While I was in the Madison County Jail awaiting resolution of my federal probation revocation proceedings, my mother kept me informed of Josh's meeting with Jackson.

Immediately upon being threatened by Josh with retaliation, both my mother and I contacted Deputy Nail and Jackson, but only Deputy Nail returned my mother's phone call. James Jackson at the State Fire Marshal's Office had no desire to communicate with my mother, me, or anyone else who didn't fit with his preconceived plans. We passed along to Nail the threats that Josh had made, but what, if any actions Deputy Nail took afterwards are not known.

Deputy Nail told my mother that Jackson had met with Josh in Carthage and that Josh had provided Jackson a more detailed statement, which was substantially the same as Josh had given Nail several months prior. Surprisingly, Josh maintained the truth and stuck with it even though Jackson had promised Josh a $25,000 reward that was being offered by Emmett and the Fire Marshal's Office.

Learning that Josh had decided to tell the truth and stick by the facts actually surprised me. Josh had lied, schemed, and plotted so much during the few months that we were together that I honestly believed that he would lie to Jackson in order to screw me and collect the reward money, but for some unknown reason, Josh again told the truth.

This had been the second time that Josh had been interviewed by law enforcement about the fire, but I'd only been interviewed once. Even with me confined at the Madison county Jail—literally minutes from Jackson's office—Jackson and the other fire investigators never attempted to interview me. I knew that I was their primary suspect and I knew that any competent investigator would at least make some attempt to interview the person suspected of the crime, but as the days passed I detected more sinister plots in the works.

Sitting in the Madison County Jail, being mentally, emotionally, and physically tortured daily, knowing that Jackson, Chaney, Emmett, and the Warren County Sheriff's Department were plotting to hang me for the fire, and that there was nothing I could do about it, disturbed me greatly.

Unbeknownst to me, after Jackson obtained Josh's second alibi statement in March 2010, he closed his investigation. At that point, neither he nor Deputy Nail had any evidence that the Atwood Lakehouse fire was an arson, and they had even less evidence that I was the one responsible.

What they did have was suspicion and possible motive. Emmett had always maintained, ever since the fire, that I deliberately burned the lake house down in retaliation for him bringing the malicious mischief charges against me and for leading the effort in the family to separate my grandmother from me.

No one, least of all me, could ever argue that I wasn't furious with Emmett, my Aunt June, and the rest of my relatives that were involved in the ongoing legal and family disputes. The scheme they devised to tear my invalid grandmother away from me, in the final hours of her life, for no purpose other than their greedy desire for her money, did more to generate hatred and animosity between me and them than anything else that had ever occurred in our family. But it wasn't a strong enough motive for me to burn the Atwood Lakehouse to the ground and destroy it.

When one has been mentally and physically abused for as long as I was by my father and Emmett, one can't help but let one's thoughts drift to violence and mayhem. But it is a far cry from having thoughts about harming Emmett and taking concrete actions to commit arson, which in Mississippi carries a life sentence of imprisonment.

If Emmett's house in Vicksburg had suspiciously burned down, or if Atwood Chevrolet had been demolished in an instant of heat and explosion, then, and only then, might my motives been questioned. But this was the Atwood Lakehouse that we were talking about. Even though Emmett owned it officially, I still felt kinship to the place, and burning it in a plot to seek revenge against Emmett would not have been in my playbook.

Whatever happened, though, to the lake house provided Emmett and my detractors exactly what they needed at the most opportune moment.

I was in an extremely vulnerable position, and they were hoping that they could use the fire to have me sent back to prison, hopefully for longer than five years, but that's not what ultimately happened.

At this time I had no idea about Emmett increasing the insurance on the lake house before it was destroyed; I didn't know that he had the attic filled with insulation immediately prior to the fire; I didn't know that the fire originated in the kitchen near the electrical box; I had no idea that Kade Atwood had allegedly slept through the inferno and never called the fire department; and I had no clue that Jackson never found any evidence that the fire was arson. All of this came in the future.

In the summer of 2010, the only thing that I knew was that the lake house had caught fire and that I was suspected of starting it. Everything else remained hidden from me. But Deputy Nail knew, and Jackson knew, and almost assuredly Emmett knew, that there wasn't any evidence proving that the fire was arson or that I was involved. And it was with deep regret on their parts that both Nail and Jackson closed their investigations in early 2010 without arresting me, having both concluded that the cause of the fire was undeterminable and nothing linked me to it.

When I was released from federal custody in June 2010 I went back to my mother's house under the belief that the fire investigation was over and that nothing further would come from it.

My Papaw had been in regular contact with Deputy Nail. Nail told my grandfather in early 2010 that there wasn't any evidence that the fire was an arson or that I was responsible. I believed that. So upon my release from prison for the second time in my short life, I gave the fire investigation no further thought, but I certainly never forgot the loss of the Atwood Lakehouse.

CHAPTER SIX

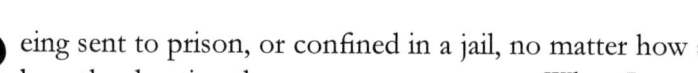

Being sent to prison, or confined in a jail, no matter how short or long the duration, has many consequences. When I was released from custody for the second time in June 2010 it was like beginning my life all over again.

In an effort to begin a new life, with better priorities, I decided to exclude from my surroundings all negative people and energy. I was finally free of Josh Chamblee and what I hoped were the allegations involving the fire that destroyed the Atwood Lakehouse.

I have always shared a close relationship with my mother, her husband, Jerry Campbell, and my half-brother and half-sister, Fisher and Hannah.

Jerry was an attorney in Vicksburg and had helped me tremendously in defending myself against the federal charges from 2004 and the malicious mischief charge in 2009. Had Jerry not represented me, along with Thomas Setser, I truly believe that the Mississippi Attorney General's Office and the Warren County Sheriff's Department may have been able to convict me.

Unfortunately, I had to return to Vicksburg after my second release. I certainly did not want to because I knew that trouble would soon ensue, but I was not financially capable at that time of supporting myself independently.

Other major factors that I had to consider were the restrictions placed upon me by my sex offender status. Not only had I endured imprisonment for whatever it ultimately was that Zach Booth and I had done wrong, but when I was released I had to report every ninety days and register as a sex offender at the Mississippi Highway Patrol Office. It was not a pleasant experience, but I endured it, nonetheless, because I was making a serious attempt to do the right thing and abide by the conditions of my release.

It was not easy maintaining my composure and not being embarrassed about my status. Even though we had a completely consensual relationship, I was still viewed by some as being a predator. It didn't matter either that we were only three years different in ages. What mattered to those wanting to use it as a weapon was the sole fact that I was a convicted sex offender, and it didn't matter what the actual facts were, I was classed the same as rapists and child molesters.

As most reasonably intelligent people know, the gay community is often a vicious and vindictive group. I believe this is more so in Southern states where homophobia is still an ingrained part of society.

Gay men, raised in the South, tend to internalize homophobia and hatred in many ways that true homophobic people do. I've traveled this country and I've met many openly gay men both on the East and West Coasts and the interior. I can say affirmatively that gay men from the South are different, and usually not in a good way.

For example, Cody Womack was a gay guy around my age that was from the Jackson, Mississippi, area. We met in 2009 at the only gay bar in town.

Cody seemed nice at first, but when I found out that he was a drug user I decided not to pursue our friendship any further. But Cody didn't like that I had spurned his feelings towards me.

Without any provocation, Cody used Facebook and social media to post extremely derogatory comments about me and my status as a sex offender. It didn't matter that a week before Cody made these postings he was desperately trying to have sex with me. All that mattered to him was that I'd turned down his sexual proposals and was therefore a suitable victim for his slander and libel.

The gay community in Mississippi is small, and it didn't take long for Cody's Facebook posts to make its rounds through the online community. I, however, never hid the fact that I was a felon, and the majority of people recognized Cody's acts of desperation, but it still aggravated me.

Cody Womack would later interject himself into my life again nine years after I spurned his sexual advances. I use Cody as an example of the type viciousness that I've mostly only seen in the South, especially Mississippi. It seems to be endemic there.

Another observation that I continually make is the rather easily explainable phenomenon of "gay flight."

Almost all of the gay men in Mississippi, who are either educated significantly beyond a high school level and who are reasonably financially secure, seem to flee the restrictive environs of Mississippi. Usually, what is left are the undesirables.

I'm not trying to say that all gay men in Mississippi are bad, but I feel it is a rational judgment to infer that if educational and financial opportunities are available, most gay men prefer to leave Mississippi. I, however, as much as I desired to, could not leave Mississippi due to my probation status. I had to complete my five years of probation in the state.

In the fall of 2010, though, I met Patrick Bryant on a gay dating app for iPhones called Grindr. This was the first relationship that I'd involved myself in since Josh Chamblee and I had broken up. But dating Patrick Bryant posed several problems.

Patrick was the only son of Mississippi's lieutenant governor, Phil Bryant. At that time, Phil Bryant was in the process of running for governor of Mississippi because the current governor, Haley Barbour, was at the end of his term limit. Phil would go on to win the governorship by a very large margin.

Prior to meeting Patrick, I had no idea that Phil Bryant had a son that was gay. Governor Bryant was a hardline Republican, and as far as I knew did not support gay rights.

After Phil was elected governor of Mississippi in November 2011, he quickly moved to restrict gay and transgender rights. Governor Bryant intentionally set out to curtail the marriage equality rights that the United States Supreme Court had recently given to gay and transgender men and women in the famous *Obergefell v. Hodges* case that granted gays and lesbians the right to marry.

Governor Bryant was not alone in this endeavor. Many legislators in Mississippi felt that gays and transgenders should not have the same rights and freedoms as the white, Protestant majority that composes the vast amount of voters in Mississippi.

To counter the steps towards equality that many gays and transgenders have made in the past decade, Mississippi continually passed unconstitutional laws which restricted their rights. Mississippi was the first state, however, to ban gay marriage by executive order.

In the mid-1990s, Mississippi's then governor, Kirk Fordice, an ardent opponent of same-sex marriage, moved to ban gay marriage by executive fiat after the Hawaii Supreme Court first recognized the possibility that gays may have a right to marry. The Mississippi Legislature quickly followed Governor Fordice's executive action with a bill officially outlawing the act.

In 2003, when the United States Supreme Court ruled that state laws criminalizing private, consensual sodomy violated the Constitution, Mississippi amended their constitution to include an amendment forbidding the state from recognizing gay marriage performed in any state which did recognize same-sex marriage.

The issue should have been affirmatively resolved on the day that the United States Supreme Court announced its decision in the *Obergefell* case.

In case the Supreme Court's meaning had been missed, the Fifth Circuit Court of Appeals in New Orleans issued a mandate to all lesser federal courts that the recent *Obergefell* case was the law of the land and must be followed. But Governor Bryant and the Mississippi Legislature failed to take heed.

Any high school student knows that in physics every action has an equal and opposite reaction. It is likewise true that in politics every action has its overreaction. It was this overreaction that Mississippi passed House Bill 1523 in 2016.

Governor Bryant, in spite of the *Obergefell* case becoming the law of the land, felt that the case "usurped [states] rights to self-governance and has mandated that states must comply with federal marriage standards—standards that are out of step with the wishes of many in the United States and that are certainly out of step with the majority of Mississippians."

During the debate over House Bill 1523, Governor Bryant repeatedly compared gay sex to bestiality and other abnormal behaviors. House Bill 1523, as it was eventually overwhelmingly passed by the Legislature, allowed business owners who disagree with gay rights to deny services to gays and lesbians based on their religious beliefs.

The bill also allows a government employee with authority to issue marriage licenses to recuse him or herself from that duty if doing so would violate his or her religious beliefs. Allowing this dereliction of duty would effectively invalidate the Supreme Court's ruling in *Obergefell*.

From the very beginning it was apparent that Governor Bryant would support any and all efforts to curtail and deny equal rights for gays, lesbians, and transgenders in Mississippi. This applied in equal force, if not more, to Governor Bryant's own gay son.

The battles that pitted the state of Mississippi and Governor Bryant against the federal courts and the United States Constitution were in the future as Patrick and I began our relationship in the latter part of 2010, but we knew they were coming, and our discussions about how Patrick's father would handle these human rights issues as governor consumed a lot of our time.

For the first time in many years, the holidays of 2010 were a very happy time for me. Patrick and I's relationship had been much better than that which I'd shared with Josh Chamblee, and we thoroughly enjoyed spending time with one another.

During that time Patrick was living in Hattiesburg and going to interior design school at the University of Southern Mississippi. One might expect that any male attending interior design school was gay, and that proved equally true in Patrick's case. But Patrick was a sincerely gifted interior designer.

Patrick's schooling at the university's interior design school would prove extremely beneficial to the state of Mississippi after Patrick's father became governor and invited Patrick to help redesign and restore portions of the Governor's Mansion in Jackson.

Patrick's family included his mother, Deborah, and his sister, Katie. It was no secret in their family that Patrick was gay, but neither was it a problem. Patrick's sexuality was accepted by his father and mother, and it didn't seem to cause concern, despite the hypocrisy of Governor Bryant's stance on homosexuality.

Patrick and I were together for about two months before I met his father and mother for the first time. Phil was still the lieutenant governor at that time, but everyone knew that he would soon be elected governor at the next election. I have always loved to discuss politics, and despite making Patrick uncomfortable at times, I readily enjoined in political discussions with Governor Bryant about modern issues facing any serious candidate for governor of a Southern state. This certainly included the main social political topics such as abortion, gay rights, and immigration.

I was quickly surprised to discover that Governor Bryant was a hardcore, pro-life candidate whom held sincere beliefs about protecting the lives of unborn children. In this I could sympathize because I believe abortion is a bad thing, but because I am not a woman, I do not think my personal views should be imposed about what others do with their bodies. The governor and I respectfully disagreed on this point, but it was a thrilling intellectual exercise.

When discussing immigration, Governor Bryant and I had surprisingly similar views. I believe that America has a legitimate and needed interest in securing our borders and stemming the tide of illegal immigration. But the millions of immigrants in this country illegally today, who work, raise families, and abide by our laws, deserve to have a path to legal residency.

Governor Bryant's views, as far as I could tell from our conversations, were in accord with mine. Immigration certainly poses a problem, but it is impractical to remove millions of illegal immigrants that have already reached our borders.

Most surprising of all, Governor Bryant had a very indifferent view to the rights of gays, lesbians, and transgenders. This was several years before the contentious debates over the Supreme Court's *Obergefell* decision and House Bill 1523, but I can't imagine Governor Bryant's true feelings have changed.

Governor Bryant knew that Patrick and I were in a sexual relationship. At first, it astonished me that the governor could be so nonchalant and unconcerned with the relationship that I was having with his son. It was even more so because the governor knew that I was a convicted felon and had recently been released from prison. But Governor Bryant genuinely didn't care that Patrick was gay. That is why it was shocking to me when Governor Bryant became so rabidly anti-gay and virulently homophobic in the later battles over same-sex marriage and gay rights in Mississippi during the debates over House Bill 1523. It wasn't the governor I knew.

The closest that Governor Bryant and I ever came to having a detailed discussion about gay rights was in November 2010. Looking back to that day, with the benefit of hindsight, I see that conversation as revealing the true nature of a born politician.

Governor Bryant told me that his job dealing with modern social issues, like gay rights in Mississippi, was akin to what Governor Ross Barnett had to do in the 1960s.

As a student of civil rights history, I was well aware of the battle fought by Mississippi's segregationist governor, Ross Barnett, against school integration at the University of Mississippi in 1962.

The United States Supreme Court had ordered Ole Miss in Oxford, Mississippi, to admit James Meredith, a black student, to the all white college. But Governor Barnett and thousands of Mississippians viciously opposed the end of racial segregation.

The three-day riot that resulted in the eventual integration of Ole Miss claimed several lives and left a permanent stain on Mississippi's history.

During the fight to keep Mississippi's schools white, Governor Barnett maintained a public persona in which he fiercely espoused hatred, racism, and continued segregation. But beneath Governor Barnett's public statements was a man willing to work with the Kennedy administration to achieve what the governor recognized as a losing battle.

Years later, secret recordings made of the conversations between Governor Barnett and the Kennedy brothers during the Ole Miss riots would be released, showing that the governor no more believed in segregation than the Kennedys did. But as Governor Barnett told the Kennedys, he had voters in Mississippi to appease.

Governor Bryant conveyed to me that his stance on gay rights was no different than Barnett's hypocritical positions on racial segregation.

By this point in my life I was thoroughly sickened with hypocrisy. I'd grown up in a family that espoused racial hatred and white superiority, while at the same time freely indulging in their despicable sexual desires with black women. My family was the textbook case of hypocrisy.

Drawing a line from my family's own hypocritical views when it came to race relations to Governor Bryant's on gay rights wasn't a stretch for me to make, but I certainly never pointed this fact out to him. I simply nodded my head as though I thoroughly understood, but it did concern me.

As the son of a politician, one would think Patrick would have strong opinions or emotions on the political beliefs of his father, but Patrick was as attuned to the ambitions of the governor as I was to New York fashion, which isn't saying a lot.

I finally gave up trying to reason with Patrick about the governor's indifference to gay rights, but I warned him that if the governor ever faced a choice between supporting gay discrimination and supporting his son, the governor would no doubt err on the side of discrimination. The extent to which Governor Bryant eventually went in attempting to curtail gay rights astonished me, though.

In the early spring of 2011, Patrick and I temporarily ended our relationship while he finished college and I tried to make sense of my complicated life.

Having my grandmother snatched from me as I did by Emmett and the Atwoods took away from me the center of my universe, and it certainly wasn't helped when incarcerated again. But a plan had to be put in place for me to become more independent.

That spring, I had several irons in the fire, but my long-term goal was to obtain my commercial driver's license and hire on with a trucking company. I'd always loved to drive and travel, and going into the trucking business appealed to me. The pay was outstanding, but most importantly, it removed me from Vicksburg.

I eventually was accepted to a driving school in June 2011, but before I began taking classes I needed to finish my autobiography, *Into Hell I Rode*.

We were under a strict deadline to have my book published before the Independence Day holiday in July, and I literally was working every day to accomplish that goal. Ultimately, due to the deadline, we were forced to leave a large section of the original manuscript from the finished edition.

Sheriff Pace and his deputies knew that I was writing a book, and I even gave them an opportunity to answer questions and comment on what I'd written about them, but no one took me up on the offer.

Earlier that summer, Sheriff Pace had filed his papers to seek reelection to the sheriff's office. But for the first time in several election cycles, Sheriff Pace was facing serious competition from a former deputy of his named Bubba Comans.

Comans had served on the sheriff's department for over twenty years, some of that time under Sheriff Barrett. Comans knew that there were serious problems within the sheriff's office, mostly caused by deputies like Mike Traxler.

In 2011, I seriously believed that Comans had a really good chance to beat Sheriff Pace in the November election. Me and many others believed that this was our one and only chance, and I certainly believed that once my book was published, and the true story of the sheriff's crimes were known, that people would no longer support him.

It was this line of thought that led me to decide to announce the publication of *Into Hell I Rode* at the Miss Mississippi Pageant in Vicksburg.

When I ran for constable in 2002 I'd used the gathering at the pageant to announce my candidacy and promote my message. This was nothing more than a long continuation of an accepted policy of allowing political candidates and their supporters to advertise and distribute their messages during election season. There was nothing odd or unusual about people at the pageant doing this, so I thought I was safe.

On July 2, 2011, me and some friends of mine went to the pageant with several thousand brochures which advertised my book and had information about the illegal activities of Sheriff Pace and his deputies on them.

We had previously purchased tickets to the pageant and we attended the main event that night, but purposely left about thirty minutes before the end of the show. We wanted to have enough time to distribute the leaflets and place them on the cars in the parking lot before too many people left.

Before we could saturate the area and pass out my leaflets, I was accosted by a detective from the Vicksburg Police Department named Daniel Thomas. Thomas was furious that I was passing out the leaflets that were critical of law enforcement.

Thomas's immediate goal was to prevent me from passing out the leaflets to anyone that was leaving the City Convention Center where the pageant was being held. Thomas told me to immediately leave the area, but that I could go to Washington Street— which was about a fourth of a mile away, and very far from any pageant patrons—and pass out my leaflets there. But once I went to the Washington Street area I could tell that no one would be coming to that area and I'd be unable to pass out the leaflets there.

At that point I stopped trying to pass out the leaflets and I went back to Thomas's location and asked him for his badge number. Thomas gave it to me in his best sissy, hissy-fit attitude and I left and went to the police department.

When I arrived at the Vicksburg Police Department, about a half mile from the City Convention Center, I spoke to an entirely retarded and clueless sergeant there named Penny Jones. Officer Jones provided no assistance whatsoever other than to call Thomas and tell him that I was filing a complaint against him.

Once I'd finished complaining about Thomas, I left the police department and went back to Washington Street. I was in the exact area where Thomas told me to go when he again approached me and told me I was under arrest. I asked, "What for?," but the only thing that Thomas told me was that I was being arrested for "Pissing off the police." I'd have to wait until I got to the city jail before I was officially told that I'd been arrested for trespassing.

I bonded out of jail within a couple hours and I returned to my house. There, waiting on me, were my mother and stepfather, neither of whom were happy that I'd been arrested.

For the first time in the many dealings with the corrupt police that I'd had, I decided to take legal action in the federal courts.

Shortly after my arrest for trespassing I filed a federal civil rights lawsuit against Detective Thomas, Sheriff Pace, and their respective departments. I knew that Sheriff Pace had ordered my arrest that night, and I knew Thomas only arrested me in retaliation for the message that my leaflets tried to convey, and I was determined not to let them get away with it. And it all started with a lawsuit that I filed against them for false arrest.

The only consolation I had about my false arrest was that my decision to broadcast the publication of *Into Hell I Rode* at the Miss Mississippi Pageant launched it to the top of everyone's gossip list and it began bringing in a steady income for me.

While these machinations were going on with my book, I was enrolled and taking classes everyday at a truck-driving school in Jackson. This forced me to travel about two hours round-trip to and from school.

I'd recently purchased a motorcycle and I loved to ride, but sometimes it proved impractical or dangerous when I didn't closely follow a weather report and I was caught out in the rain.

Sometimes, due to the course work at the trucking school, I wouldn't finish classes until eight or nine at night. Neither I, or my mother, wanted me driving home at night on the bike. To make it easier and safer, I stayed some nights with a friend of mine who lives in Jackson near the trucking school. My friend, Roger Cole, was gay and someone that I knew from the gay club that I'd been to a few times, but our relationship was purely platonic and only friends.

Roger managed an apartment complex in Jackson and my plan was to eventually get a job driving a truck and move into my own apartment at Roger's complex. When I graduated school and was offered a job with a local trucking company, I gave Roger a $200 check to hold as a deposit so I could move into one of his apartments. But while I was in school I did stay some nights with Roger, but not more than seven, and certainly never more than one night in a row. Before I could start my new job and move into an apartment on my own, other events intervened that changed the course of everything.

It started when Patrick and I got back together in May of 2011. Patrick was not in school and we began spending more and more time together again.

In late July we decided to take a vacation together and get away from the stress of his having finished school and me having released my book and getting arrested.

As we were headed back to Vicksburg on the last day of our vacation, I received a phone call from my mother. We were about thirty minutes from my house when she told me that a SWAT team from the sheriff's office and the Mississippi State Fire Marshal's Office had kicked in her door looking to arrest me for arson.

CHAPTER SEVEN

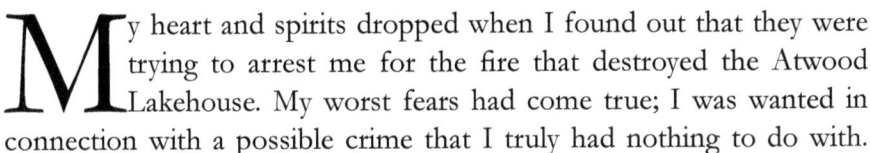

My heart and spirits dropped when I found out that they were trying to arrest me for the fire that destroyed the Atwood Lakehouse. My worst fears had come true; I was wanted in connection with a possible crime that I truly had nothing to do with. What was worse was knowing immediately that I was being retaliated against because of my book.

Had Patrick and I been forty minutes earlier we would have been at my house when the SWAT team busted open the door.

When I learned that I was wanted for arson, I immediately turned the car around and we headed to Patrick's place in Hattiesburg. I also called Deep Six, a deputy on the Warren County Sheriff's Department that had secretly provided me information for my book about the corrupt deputies that he worked with.

Deep Six was more frantic than I was about the SWAT team that had just kicked in my door. He wasted no time in telling me that Sheriff Pace had specifically given the responsibility for arresting me to Mike Traxler. Deep Six was very clear when he told me, "David, you know what will happen if Traxler catches you. If you give him the slightest reason, he will kill you. In fact, I think that's why the sheriff gave your warrant to him. I think Sheriff Pace wants you dead."

It made perfect sense to me and I completely believed Deep Six about Traxler and Sheriff Pace wanting to kill me. Nothing else made sense. I'd written pages and pages in *Into Hell I Rode* on the corruption of Mike Traxler. No other deputy, except Pace himself, had received as much attention in my book as Traxler did. Traxler was literally the redneck bogeyman with a gun and badge.

The irony of my situation didn't escape me even then at that moment. And it wouldn't have escaped the corrupt law enforcements' sense of irony either had they known. What is tremendously scary about the situation, and their plan to kill me, is that they had no way of knowing that I was at that moment with the governor's son.

If Patrick and I had arrived at my house only minutes before the SWAT raid, Patrick would no doubt have been placed in extreme physical danger. Sheriff Pace and his cronies with the Fire Marshal's Office had no way of knowing that their illegal actions were placing the governor's son in serious danger. But they were so intent on exacting retribution against me they were blinded by the laws of unintended consequences.

The second irony to be gleaned from this ironic situation is that, until I could figure things out, I'd have to go into hiding. No doubt that Sheriff Pace and the fire marshals had flagged my name in their crime computers and distributed descriptions of my vehicles. If I was to avoid their dragnet I'd have to have somewhere to go until I developed a plan.

From the moment my mother told me that I was wanted for arson, Patrick knew what was going on and became a willing conspirator in harboring a fugitive.

No one, besides my immediate family and Patrick's mother and father, knew that we had rekindled our relationship. Patrick's place would be the very last location that anyone searching for me would think to look. And I certainly doubt that anyone would have thought to ask the governor whether he had knowledge of the whereabouts of a criminal fugitive.

Even though I had to laugh at my absurd situation—hiding from the police and being assisted by the governor's son—it destroyed whatever sense of coherence I had. I knew that an arson charge was very serious—it carried a life sentence—and that I would have to raise several thousand dollars for bail, but for the moment the only thing I could do was hide out at Patrick's place until I could determine how much my bond was and find a way to turn myself in to someone besides the Warren County Sheriff's Department or the Mississippi State Fire Marshal's Office.

Patrick tried to make me feel better, though, by telling me that even if I was convicted he'd get his daddy to pardon me, but his jokes didn't cheer me up much.

Two days after learning that I was wanted for arson, I finally decided to come out of hiding at Patrick's place and start the process of turning myself over to law enforcement.

Deputy Nail had from time-to-time kept my Papaw up-to-date on the process of the investigation, but once it had been closed in early 2010 they had not spoken about it.

On August 1, 2011, I said my goodbyes to Patrick and drove from Hattiesburg to Jackson. My grandparents were waiting on me at my aunt's house. Until I arrived they did not know that I was wanted for arson.

My Papaw had been very sick for over a year with chronic lung and heart disease and wasn't expected to live much longer. I was cherishing every minute that we spent together, and I knew that telling him about the arson warrant would kill him, but there was no way to avoid it.

At my aunt's house, my mother and I sat everyone down and I broke the bad news about the pending arson arrest. The first word uttered by my grandfather was, "Shit!" I felt the description very apt for the situation.

After informing the rest of my family, and inquiring about the best possible route from then forward, we decided to contact Deputy Nail and tell him that I would turn myself in to him and Sheriff William Lee at the Attala County Sheriff's Department later that afternoon.

Deputy Nail was very courteous to me and made sure that I knew that he was not the one pursuing the arson arrest. "David, this is something that came from the fire marshal. It didn't come from me. I didn't even know about it until the fire marshal called me."

I believed Deputy Nail, but I was also disappointed at what I considered the general failure of justice and fairness within the overall law enforcement community. Deputy Nail did point out to me, though, that James Jackson had originally asked Judge Ronald Stewart to set my bail at over $200,000. According to Nail, Judge Stewart lowered my bail to $50,000 after Nail intervened personally with him to have it lowered.

A $50,000 bail was still ridiculously high. Rapists and child molesters were sometimes released from the jail on less than a $10,000 dollar bail, but the objective of the fire marshal was to have my bail set so high that I would be unable to afford to bond myself out.

Being unable to afford the cost of bond would serve Sheriff Pace and Emmett's goal of having me incarcerated again for something which I didn't do. Emmett would have the satisfaction of having his grandson in jail and Sheriff Pace would achieve the goal of having me removed from the Vicksburg scene so that I could not meddle in his reelection efforts. In one fell swoop their goals would be accomplished. But I had friends, too.

My Papaw called Judge Stewart personally on the ride from Jackson to Kosciusko to turn myself in. My Papaw explained in detail to Judge Stewart the lack of evidence in the case, the ulterior motive of the fire marshal, Sheriff Pace and Emmett Atwood, and the impossibility of me being able to pay the ten percent of the $50,000 dollar bail needed for me to be released on bond. Judge Stewart listened to my Papaw, but ultimately refused to lower my bail. He had been utterly convinced by Jackson's lies that an arson had taken place and that I was responsible for it.

This was an extreme slap in the face to my Papaw. Papaw and Judge Stewart had been friends for over fifty years. My Papaw had always supported Judge Stewart for political office, they'd gone to school together, and my Papaw had sold his house to Stewart. But when it came to the power and political pressure being brought down upon Judge Stewart, even he refused to allow a half-century friendship to stand in the way of the political steamroller headed his way over the arson warrant. His subsequent refusal to listen to my Papaw destroyed whatever alleged friendship they may of had. Truth be told, it sorely disappointed my Papaw that Judge Stewart would take the word of an ambitious, corrupt law enforcement officer, with clear ulterior motives, rather than someone whom he had been friends with for most their lives.

I next turned to my friend, Richard Cain. Rich grew up in Kosciusko, knew the Atwoods, and had become friends with me earlier that year. Fortuitous for me, Rich was also a bail bond agent, and his boss, Sherry Williams, was also a friend of mine.

I called Sherry and explained to her the circumstances and pleaded with her to work with me on the cost of paying the bail so I wouldn't have to stay in jail. Sherry was more than a friend that day, she was an angel of mercy who was more than happy to help me stay out of jail. We quickly agreed that I could pay her half of the $5,000 needed to bond out, and then make monthly payments to her on the remaining $2,500.

Once the details were in place, my mother and I met Sherry at the

Attala County Sheriff's Department and officially turned myself in to Deputy Nail.

Although I'd been to jail before, and it was seemingly becoming a common occurrence in my life, I certainly wasn't in a pleasant mood, especially when the booking process at the small, redneck county jail was stuck in the pre-computer age and everything seemed to take forever. But a little more than an hour after turning myself in to Deputy Nail I was released on my $50,000 bail.

Before I left the sheriff's department, I told Deputy Nail that I believed this arrest was motivated purely by a desire on the part of the fire marshal, Mike Chaney, Sheriff Pace, and Emmett Atwood to retaliate against me for having recently published *Into Hell I Rode*.

Deputy Nail refused to comment on my speculation, but he certainly was aware that there were a lot of people that weren't happy with my book, but were exhilarated about my arrest. It fell to Deputy Nail to inform them, though, that I had bonded out. Of that, they would not be pleased.

Before leaving the sheriff's department, Deputy Nail told me that I'd have to appear in Judge Stewart's court several days later for an initial appearance. I wrote the date down and, when I'd finished, my mother and I left.

From the first moment that we'd learned about the arson warrant, we knew that it was a contrived and false charge, done solely to retaliate against me for having published *Into Hell I Rode* several weeks earlier.

We knew then that even though the corrupt cops had won a small victory that day, they'd never win a conviction on the arson arrest. There was never any doubt in my mind that I'd eventually be found innocent, and there was never any doubt that I would one day make these corrupt sons of bitches pay for their treachery.

I also thought of Josh Chamblee when I learned that I was being arrested, but I never thought that he would have been the sole reason that I'd been arrested. After all, Josh had previously provided two statements to two different law enforcement officers swearing that I did not have anything to do with the fire. At that time I sincerely doubted whether a competent law enforcement officer would give credence to a potential witness who had given the two alibi statements that Josh did. This view changed the day I turned myself in.

My stepdad, Jerry Campbell, who is an attorney in Vicksburg, had talked to one of the deputies on the Warren County Sheriff's Department and had been told that James Jackson and the Fire Marshal's Office had an "eyewitness" who saw me burn down the Atwood Lakehouse.

This insider's information had come from Billy Higgins, one of the senior deputies in the sheriff's department. I had a somewhat indifferent opinion of Billy Higgins, but it was well-known that Billy was being groomed to take over from Sheriff Pace when he retired.

I felt fairly competent that what he was telling my stepdad was true. If that was the case, then the only person who could possibly claim to be an eyewitness involving me and the fire would be Josh Chamblee. But the circumstances involving the why and how of Josh's cooperation with the Fire Marshal's Office still eluded me.

Soon after I was released on bond another serious issue arose which threatened to throw a wrench into the equation.

I was still on federal probation from my 2005 conviction involving Zach Booth, and my probation officer, William Jay Simpson, was not happy that I'd been arrested for arson. My concern was that Jay would attempt to violate my probation again and send me back to prison since I'd twice been arrested in less than a month.

When I left the sheriff's department in Kosciusko, I immediately drove to Jackson to Jay's office at the federal courthouse to discuss with him my future. In spite of getting arrested, I'd recently been offered an excellent employment opportunity driving a truck for a local company, but it required me to travel across state lines and that would require Jay's approval.

Since I'd been on probation, Jay and I had gotten along quite well. I felt that Jay was a fair and competent federal probation officer, but I knew that since my book had been released the pressure on him to violate my probation had increased exponentially.

During our first conversation since I'd been arrested on the arson charge, Jay refused to spare me the details about the manner and amount of calls that he was getting from other law enforcement officers questioning why U.S. Probation had not violated my probation and sent me back to prison. I believe that had it been solely in Jay's discretion, he would have locked me up then, but thankfully, for a brief few weeks I had the law on my side.

Since the fire that destroyed the Atwood Lakehouse had occurred in 2009, before my probation was violated in 2010, the term of probation I was serving in 2011 could not be revoked. My current term of probation could only be revoked for crimes that occurred after I was released from prison in June 2010. This prevented Jay and U.S. Probation from violating my probation for the fire.

In theory, my federal probation could be violated for getting arrested for trespassing, but Jay had already told me that it was his policy not to violate someone's probation until the underlying charges had been resolved first. In August 2011, the pending charge of trespassing was still in the Vicksburg City Municipal Court awaiting trial.

Jay was very clear with me that he was under intense pressure to do anything and everything to have me sent back to prison, but I believe that at that time Jay was attempting to do the ethical and fair thing, but when I asked him to allow me to take the job driving a truck, he refused.

Being denied the opportunity to accept employment was not only unfair, but it was directly contrary to U.S. Probation's stated mission of assisting probationers in obtaining gainful employment.

Jay had previously written me a letter allowing me to take a driving job which required crossing state lines, but once the book was published and I was arrested for arson, Jay rescinded that permission. I'd spent almost $4,000 in the truck-driving school and two months in training, and because of Jay's capriciousness it was all wasted.

Instead of being allowed to obtain gainful employment and move on with my life, which would have been an extremely positive step forward for me, I was forced instead to return to my mother's house and idle my time away while waiting for the charges to be disposed of.

On August 4, 2011, though, I drove back to Kosciusko for the initial appearance before Judge Stewart. At that hearing Judge Stewart formally read me the arson charge, entered a plea of not guilty for me, and appointed me an attorney to represent me in court.

The attorney that was appointed to represent me was Rosalind Jordan, a local Kosciusko attorney, whom upon meeting, I really liked.

Mrs. Jordan appeared to me to have been born in the early 1970s and one could say that she had many beautiful qualities. She was blonde, polite, professional, and certainly looked legally competent. I soon came to find out that not only was she physically attractive, but she was an aggressive, extremely competent attorney and one of the best cross-examiners I'd ever seen.

I explained to Mrs. Jordan that the arson charge was a fraud and that it was only brought in retaliation for my book, but even she was skeptical of my theories. But that would change.

As I left the Attala County Courthouse that day to go back home to Vicksburg, I stopped to visit with my Papaw. My Papaw was an elected official in Attala County and had his office at the courthouse, near Judge Stewart's, but on this day Papaw refused to enter Stewart's courtroom for fear that he would be tempted to express his true feelings in a negative way towards the judge. Instead, Papaw remained downstairs while I was in court.

I dropped by my Papaw's office before leaving the courthouse and I assured him that one day I'd be vindicated on the arrest and that I'd do everything I could to make the corrupt officers who fabricated this outrage pay for their mistake. We hugged, said our goodbyes, and I left Koscisuko. This would be the last time I ever saw my beloved grandfather.

A little more than a month later, on September 29, 2011, he passed away. And as much as he believed in my innocence, and as much as he wanted to be there when I proved it, he couldn't. His death only made me push harder to have my ultimate day in court.

Shortly after the initial appearance, I requested and was granted a preliminary hearing by Judge Stewart. Preliminary hearings are an opportunity for a criminal defendant to listen to what evidence the prosecutors have against him, and then for the judge or magistrate to determine whether there is probable cause to forward the case to the next grand jury.

Mrs. Jordan was representing me at the preliminary hearing, but I had previously prepared a dozen or so important questions that I wanted her to ask the witnesses when they testified.

The first witness that the prosecutor called was James Jackson, the deputy fire marshal. Jackson brought with him to the witness stand a skinny file folder containing the "evidence" against me. I thought to myself that if the only evidence he had against me was in that skinny folder, I was in good shape, indeed.

My first look at Jackson didn't impress me. He neither looked like an able investigator or an effective witness.

He looked like he was born in the mid-1950s, tall, slim, but with a slight paunched belly. He reminded me of an ogre that had some limited success with the Jenny Craig weight loss program. If I saw Jackson's picture in black and white, I'd suspect he would be a poor, dirt farmer from the Great Depression.

He did not make a good first impression then, nor would my subsequent interactions with him change that view.

Under questioning, Jackson affirmatively testified that when he was called to the fire scene he conducted a hydrocarbon test in different areas of the burnt lake house in an attempt to determine whether any accelerants were used to start the fire. He testified clearly that he did not detect any accelerants. Mrs. Jordan and I conscientiously recorded Jackson's answers to all the questions.

When pointedly asked whether he'd been able to determine whether the fire was an arson or not, Jackson clearly testified that he did not find any direct evidence that the fire was arson, just a deep suspicion that it was. We recorded his answer.

Jackson also testified that he relied solely on Emmett Atwood's word in making the ultimate determination that I was the sole suspect. He even admitted that he was getting pressured by his boss, Mike Chaney, to make an arrest.

There were approximately a dozen pictures that Jackson possessed of the lake house that were dated and time-stamped four days before the fire. He testified that Emmett had recently increased the insurance on the Atwood Lakehouse and had, four days before the fire, taken the pictures for "insurance purposes."

One of the pictures showed a large, roaring fire in the fireplace, with significant charring and fire damage above and along the outer walls of the mantel. When Jackson was asked if the fire in the fireplace could have contributed to the fire that destroyed the lake house due to the unsafe fireplace, Jackson conceded that it was possible.

When specifically asked what evidence he had linking me to the fire, Jackson replied that he had a statement from Joshua Langston Chamblee which generally stated that I told Josh that I'd burned the lake house down. Other than this statement, Jackson testified that he had no other evidence.

At the preliminary hearing, Jackson never testified about the details behind how he procured the third statement from Josh. Because Jackson failed to inform us, we didn't know that he had obtained a warrant for Josh's arrest for accessory after the fact to arson, and then threatened to arrest Josh unless he provided Jackson a statement which implicated me in the fire. We were left with the impression that Josh was a willing witness.

When we asked about Josh's credibility, Jackson answered that according to a crime computer search that he did on Josh, Josh had been arrested for lying to law enforcement officers and filing false police reports. Jackson refused to admit, though, that these arrests would give him pause or concern for using Josh's credibility to base an arrest warrant on.

Although Jackson's testimony at the preliminary hearing lasted for about an hour, we clearly and unequivocally established that Jackson could not detect an accelerant, could not determine that the fire was an arson, and besides Josh's third statement, had no evidence linking me to the fire.

The more Jackson testified, the more disbelief was expressed in the courtroom. As Jackson continued with the testimony pertaining to his investigation, I saw Judge Stewart becoming more and more exasperated with Jackson. I could tell that Judge Stewart had realized that he'd been scammed into issuing a false arrest warrant.

We called Deputy Nail to the stand to testify after Jackson. We felt Nail was a bit more sympathetic to my situation. After all, every aspect of his investigation had exonerated me of any wrongdoing.

Deputy Nail's testimony was fairly short, but he was clear in his testimony that my cell phone was in use in another part of the state during the time of the fire and that the sizes of my feet and the treads of my shoes didn't match any castings and measurements that he took of the footprints surrounding the lake house.

After the testimony of the two witnesses concluded, Judge Stewart expressed his doubts about the case. "I have reservations—doubts about the evidence in this case, but I am going to nonetheless bind this case over to the grand jury and allow the district attorney to sort it out."

With that, my preliminary hearing was over and I was more and more convinced that my arrest was nothing more than political retribution. Any doubts I had about the evidence were dissolved after hearing Jackson's pathetic recitation of the evidence, or lack thereof.

Mrs. Jordan was likewise incredulous. "This case is bogus, okay? I don't even think the grand jury will indict you, so don't worry. It's all just bogus."

I made my decision then that if the grand jury didn't indict me I'd sue the hell out of the fire marshal, Sheriff Pace, Mike Chaney, and any other piece of shit corrupt cop that got in my way. If I couldn't receive justice in the state courts, then I'd take it federal.

CHAPTER EIGHT

After my arrests for trespassing and arson, I literally was walking on egg shells everywhere I went. I didn't even feel safe in my own home anymore. There was perpetually a cloud of doom and gloom hanging over my head, but I was determined to give the corrupt law enforcement officers that were after my ass no other reason to arrest me.

The deputy on the Warren County Sheriff's Department that was a friend of mine, and who had provided me secret, inside information about the department, had warned me to stay away from Vicksburg as much as possible.

Deep Six was seriously concerned for my safety and continually passed along to me what he was hearing from inside the department.

I had used Deep Six's information about the corruption in the sheriff's department in much the same way as Bob Woodward used Deep Throat's (i.e., Mark Felt) information in his book, *All the President's Men*, about the Watergate scandal. I was told that Sheriff Pace was furious that one of his deputies was cooperating with me and leaking information about what was going on inside his office.

Shortly after my book came out, my federal probation officer, Jay Simpson, showed up at my house with another federal probation officer named Chris Counts. Counts had previously been a deputy on the Warren County Sheriff's Department, but I'd never had any occasion to have interactions with him.

On the day he and Jay showed up at my house their primary goal was to determine who Deep Six was. They hoped to accomplish this task by confiscating all of my computers and cell phone. Part of the conditions of my probation was that federal probation could search me, my house, my computers, and my cell phones at anytime.

Jay and Chris Counts spent almost two hours searching my room, no doubt frustrated because they couldn't find anything that would disclose Deep Six's identity.

When they couldn't find anything that would tip them off to who Deep Six was, Jay and Counts tried the direct approach. Another condition of my probation is that I report to Jay anytime that I was "questioned by law enforcement." Jay tried to bluff me into believing that I had an obligation to report to him anytime Deep Six and I spoke. Jay knew I wasn't stupid enough to fall for this bluff, and I didn't. I absolutely refused to reveal to them who Deep Six was and they soon abandoned this approach.

Hoping to find out my source's identity, Jay and Counts took my computers and cell phone and had an FBI agent forensically search for Deep Six's identity, along with any other evidence of misconduct I may have been engaged in. But after a two-week search they found nothing, and around August 12, 2011, they gave my computers and cell phone back to me. They made their point, though, and from then forward I was determined to be more careful about how Deep Six and I communicated.

By the middle of August I was literally spinning my wheels trying to determine what to do. I needed to work, but Jay was not letting me. I needed out of Mississippi, but I couldn't move. All I could do was wait until things cooled off.

I was literally scared to stay in my own house, so I spent most of my time with Patrick at his place in Hattiesburg, but there was no way this could be permanent. It was like waiting on one's execution without knowing the date or time. I knew that the corrupt cops were still scheming, but I knew not where their axe would fall next.

I was doing the best I could to remain invisible and not provoke another retaliation. I'd even drastically cut back on the manner in which I promoted my book. I didn't want to do anything else that would draw attention to myself until things cooled off from my most recent arrests.

Any time that I was in Vicksburg I felt constantly watched. The only freedom that I felt was when I was not in Warren County. I knew I couldn't stay away from my home forever, but I wasn't going to make it easy for them to get me. That changed on the night of Monday, August 15, 2011.

I'd been staying with Patrick two or three nights a week, spending the rest of my time at my house in Vicksburg. On the night of August 15, though, Patrick had a small party at his place in Hattiesburg.

At the party that night were two younger guys named Ethan Patrick Robinson and Colton Scott Kendrick. Ethan was from Puckett, Mississippi, in Rankin County, and Colton was from Collins, Mississippi, in Covington County. The two of them had only been dating each other for several weeks and were solely the friends of Patrick's. Until the party that night I'd never met either of them, but I had spoken to Ethan through Grindr, a gay friendship app on iPhones, about a month or so before Patrick and I got back together.

Although Ethan and I had texted each other only long enough to trade pictures and briefly get to know each other, we'd had no other communications.

During our one-time texting communication, Ethan told me that he was nineteen-year-old, lived in Puckett, and was starting college that fall. We traded g-rated face pictures, but I did not find Ethan to be an attractive guy so I respectfully informed him that we could be friends, but nothing more. Sissy, feminine guys just were not attractive to me.

Ethan's response to my denial of his affections was a typical immature reply for someone his age, but he soon took the hint and began talking to someone else. In this case, Colton Kendrick.

Patrick's parties at his place in Hattiesburg had always been fun, but that night Ethan and Colton started arguing over some aspect of their new relationship and ended up screaming and cussing at each other so loudly that we became worried that the police might be notified.

In an eruption of anger and drama, Ethan left the party and, in doing so, denied Colton a ride home. Apparently, Ethan had picked Colton up at his house in Collins earlier that night and, once abandoned, Colton had no ride back home.

The party quickly ended and Patrick and I's attempts to get Ethan to come back to Patrick's place and get Colton to take him home were ignored. But since I had to drive back to Vicksburg that night I offered to give Colton a ride back to his house.

We left Patrick's around eleven that night for the forty-five minute ride to Collins. Just after leaving Hattiesburg, Ethan started calling and texting my phone demanding that I bring Colton back to Hattiesburg so that Ethan could talk to him. But Colton told me to absolutely not turn around. He didn't want anything else to do with Ethan and he repeatedly told me that Ethan was psychotic, crazy, abusive, possessive, and mentally unstable.

I finally answered my phone because Ethan was literally ringing and texting my phone to death, but Ethan only wanted to scream, yell, and threaten me. I've often known gay men to be emotionally unstable, but Ethan Robinson that night put them to shame. So both of us had no choice but to ignore Ethan's calls.

As Colton and I approached his house in Collins, we noticed several police cars parked outside. I immediately knew that the situation had taken a serious turn for the worst and that Ethan caused it, but I had no choice except to face the music.

When we pulled up to Colton's house we were met by members of the Covington County Sheriff's Department who had their guns drawn, but respectfully requested that we step out of the car.

We were separated immediately, but no one made an effort to come speak to me. About ten minutes later Ethan showed up in a hysterical state of agitation, alleging that I'd kidnapped Colton. As I rolled my eyes and made a lunge to choke the life out of Ethan Robinson, the deputies grabbed me, cuffed me, and put me in a patrol car.

I was taken back to the Covington County Sheriff's Department and handcuffed to a restraint chair for over eighteen hours before anyone ever came to speak to me. When a sheriff's detective finally came to talk to me in the late afternoon of August 16, I was told that I was being arrested for felony enticement of a minor, another state charge which carried a life sentence of imprisonment. Apparently, Colton was sixteen years old. He certainly didn't look sixteen, and I never thought to ask when I offered him a ride home, but it was too late by then. But what was most important was that Colton and I had never had sex, never talked about sex, never touched, kissed, held hands, or did anything other than talk about how crazy and psychotic Ethan was. Unfortunately, no one apparently believed that. I was a convicted sex offender and that automatically made me guilty of any other sexual allegations.

Detective Pamela Wade Smith told me that it would help my case if I cooperated in her investigation and provided her a written statement, but I was too smart to fall for this tactic. Covington County was one of the least populated counties in Mississippi, and its uneducated, redneck sheriff's office reflected their country ignorance. There was no way in hell I was going to help these Keystone Cops put me in prison.

Detective Smith did not inspire much faith in her abilities as a law enforcement officer, much less an investigator.

I could tell that at one time she was probably an attractive woman by country South Mississippi standards. She was probably even once the Trailer Park Queen of Covington County, but too many cigarettes, tanning bed sessions, and clumsy sex acts in the back seats of farmers' trucks had faded those nice looks far beyond what Botox and hairdye could hide.

Her frumpy, short frame did nothing to convince me that I would ever receive any fair benefit of the doubt from her in the investigation. In fact, I am convinced as much today as I was then that her position as an investigator was far beyond her abilities as a person and law enforcement officer.

At this point in time, my life, my self-esteem couldn't have been lower. I was on federal probation and facing a maximum of six years in prison if I violated it. I'd been arrested for trespassing the month prior. I faced a mandatory life sentence for arson, and I'd just been arrested again for a crime that also carried a life sentence if I was convicted. I've never been suicidal, but things were looking bleak.

After I was processed and booked for my latest felony charge, the deputies walked me through a small door the size of a submarine bulkhead and locked me in a small, twelve by twelve foot cell and closed the door.

The Covington County Jail was literally a three-celled lock-up facility that had once been a brig inside a World War II military ship. And it was severely overcrowded. Inmates had to sleep on the floor, there was only one toilet for thirty or forty inmates, no hot water, and inmates were not given any hygiene or personal care items. In fact, the jail didn't even have jumpsuits or uniforms for the inmates. One wore exactly what one had been arrested in. I immediately noticed about twenty constitutional violations.

Refusing to provide Detective Smith a written statement certainly didn't endear me to her. I attempted to protest my innocence, but because I was already a convicted sex offender, no one would believe that I'd not committed a second sex offense. What was worse, no one was telling me any details about what occurred after Colton and I were separated by the deputies. I didn't know what he said or what Ethan had lied about. But I knew it wouldn't bode well for me at all.

I was only in the cell with the other inmates for about thirty minutes when they learned that I'd been arrested for a sex offense. My immediate safety was put in danger by the deputies telling the inmates the details of my crime, and if I was going to survive, the next few minutes would be critical. I'd learned to show no fear and this is the posture I took.

I wish I could say, though, that things turned out well for me at the jail, but I ended up getting into a fight with several inmates. But when I recognized that things were quickly going south for me, I didn't wait to be attacked, I immediately struck out at the ring leader of the commotion and am almost certain that I broke his nose. After that, though, I was on the losing end of the scuffle, but I'd made my point.

The next morning I woke up and my face was puffy and my busted lip had swollen to about twice its normal size, but at least some of the other inmates looked just as bad. I made the mistake, though, of requesting medical treatment and this led to a second brawl that morning. The deputies finally separated us and took me back to the restraint chair that I'd been chained to the night before.

After several hours in the time-out chair, the deputies came and got me and drove me to Brandon, Mississippi, and locked me in the Rankin County Jail.

When I arrived at the Rankin County Jail I was told that Ethan Robinson had also pressed charges on me for enticing him to have sex. As with Colton, Ethan was underage, too. But Ethan had told me he was nineteen when in actuality he was seventeen. When the detective there tried to question me about this alleged offense, too, I merely laughed in his face and refused to answer any further questions.

I had been told by Detective Smith, and was now being told by the detective in Rankin County, that the FBI had my cell phone, along with Ethan's and Colton's phones, and that they would soon have the evidence to send me away forever. For once I was even more sure of the eventual outcome than I had been about the lack of evidence in the arson case.

I'd only had one text message communication with Ethan, and it was only to briefly talk, and it ended with me, not him, wanting to end our future communications because I was not attracted to him. But until this evidence was obtained by the FBI, I'd have to sit in jail.

Rather than be placed in the inmate general population, I was placed in a cell and holding area by myself and was relatively comfortable. Like the Federal Bureau of Prisons, I could order food and hygiene from a commissary, I could use the phone, and my mother could send me clean underwear, socks, and t-shirts.

As I sat and waited I couldn't help but take stock in my latest troubles. Let me tell you now, it is the worst feeling in the world to sit in jail, charged with something you haven't done. When one is charged with a false crime, and is incarcerated, the anger and frustration is sometimes more than one can bear. It certainly was true for me. I was in jeopardy of spending the rest of my life in prison for three "crimes" that I'd had nothing to do with. But in my case, the only thing that kept me from despair was my anger. Anger would fortify me, and my quest for justice would sustain me no matter how long it took to clear my name.

I finally obtained a preliminary hearing in the Rankin County courts, but the only evidence presented to the judge was a patently false, and clearly inaccurate written statement made by Ethan which basically said that I had threatened and coerced him into having sex, and then, once he had agreed, I'd used force to rape him three nights prior to me being arrested in Covington County.

I immediately knew that this was an easily disproved allegation. Three days before my arrest in Covington County I'd been down on the beach with my mother. And immediately upon leaving the beach I'd gone to stay with Patrick. I'd been no where near Rankin County in over a month. This was flaw number one.

Ethan's second mistake in his contrived and false story, was that I had repeatedly threatened and extorted him into having sex through text messages, but both he and I had Apple iPhones. I'd learned a long time prior that all iPhones' text messages are saved and become available for retrieval by law enforcement. This was flaw number two in Ethan's lie, both being fatal to any story he could tell.

I walked away from the courtroom that day knowing what Ethan had done and why he had done it. He was a hateful, jealous, vindictive drama queen who was upset that I'd spurned his advances towards me and then had the temerity to ignore his psychotic demands when it came to bringing Colton back to Hattiesburg so that Ethan could abuse him some more. But when it came to the allegations in Covington County in regards to Colton, I was at a loss.

The judge in Rankin County apparently recognized the absurdity in Ethan's lies because he released me from custody on a $1,000 bond. After the preliminary hearing, I sensed a clear reluctance on the part of the prosecutors there to give any credence to Ethan's story. I left the courtroom, as I had the arson case's preliminary hearing, with a firm belief that a conviction never would be obtained on such outlandish lies.

Within hours of being released from Rankin County, though, a deputy from Covington County arrived to take me back to their jail to await a disposition of their charges. Thankfully, though, they had sense enough not to house me with the other inmates. Instead, I was given my own cell, my own toilet and sink, and my own television, while the other thirty to forty inmates had to share only one of each.

Upon my return to Covington County, I immediately requested to be provided a preliminary hearing. Preliminary hearings are not a privilege; they are a right that every criminal defendant is entitled to under the United States' and Mississippi's constitutions. In an ethical and responsible court system, preliminary hearings are never denied to defendants.

When I'd requested preliminary hearings in Attala and Rankin counties I'd been given them, and predictably everyone had learned that those cases were based on lies and false allegations. But when I requested a preliminary hearing in Covington County to exercise my constitutionally-protected right to hear the evidence they had against me, I was ignored and my requests were summarily denied. No reason was given for denying me my right to the hearing, and the judge refused to grant me bond.

I soon learned that the justice court judge in Covington County that had control of my case was not an attorney, did not have a college education, and was nothing more than a popular, backwoods redneck that had convinced some of the poorest and most uneducated populace in Mississippi to elect him.

It didn't matter than the United States' and Mississippi's constitutions required a preliminary hearing. The Covington County judge wasn't going to let me hear what evidence they had, or more likely, what evidence they didn't have.

Learning about the failures and corruption of the Justice Court of Covington County wasn't the only thing I was learning about the area's crookedness. Shortly after being returned to Covington County I learned that the sheriff, Ben Ford, was best friends with Sheriff Martin Pace in Vicksburg. The subconscious lightbulb lit up with that tidbit of information and I knew immediately that Sheriff Pace had struck again.

It had not previously occurred to me that Sheriff Pace in Warren County would be friends with Sheriff Ford in Covington County, but Mississippi's law enforcement world is very small.

Within days of being returned to the Covington County Jail, Sheriff Ford brought me into his office for what was, apparently, a friendly chat.

Because I'd been denied a preliminary hearing, and because the conditions in the jail were unconstitutionally atrocious, I'd been filing motions and lawsuits in the federal and state courts complaining about my treatment. Phone calls had been made and Sheriff Ford was not happy.

"Listen David, I know all about your little war with the police up in Vicksburg. Sheriff Pace has filled me in. But that shit isn't going to work down here. You see, I run Covington County, not you. And while you are in my jail I am the one in charge. So file whatever you want to file in the federal courts. It's not going to do you any good. You're headed to Parchman, and I am going to be the one to take you there."

Sheriff Ford was sincere in his belief that I was going to be convicted and sent to the Mississippi State Penitentiary at Parchman, but I knew his bravado was only a facade. If they had any real evidence against me they'd of provided me a preliminary hearing. But they wouldn't, and that said a lot about their case.

During our conversation that day, Sheriff Ford made it clear to me that since my arrest he'd been receiving phone calls from Sheriff Pace and from Mike Chaney and James Jackson at the Fire Marshal's Office. Everyone saw Covington County as their best chance to get me sent away for life and they were willing to do anything to make that dream a reality. But I had plans too.

The county elections were scheduled to take place that November and Sheriff Ford had a strong contender named Stann Smith who used to be the sheriff of Covington County years before. I felt that the best way to beat the false charges in Covington County was to help Stann Smith beat Sheriff Ben Ford in the election. A strong defense is always a good offense.

I quietly had my family reach out to Smith and explain to him the predicament I was in and offer to help him get elected if he'd promise to take a fair and impartial review of the criminal case against me.

Smith assured my family that one of the reasons that he was running for the sheriff's position again was because Sheriff Ford had abused his authority so much by using the sheriff's department to exact political revenge in their small town.

Smith said that if he was elected that he always had the intention of reviewing every pending case to make sure that politics or corruption hadn't played a part in Sheriff Ford's decision to have that person arrested. I felt this was good enough for me, and in the last few weeks of the campaign we threw money and support behind Stann Smith.

In November 2011 Stann Smith was elected by extremely thin margins and beat Ben Ford in the race for the sheriff's office. But Smith wouldn't take office until January 2012, and until that time Ford was still in power.

The repercussions came immediately. Inmates at the jail were only being fed twice a day. We received a small breakfast in the morning and a meager dinner at night. It was barely possible to subsist on such a scant source of calories, but after Ford went down in defeat, his anger turned on us.

Sometimes our meals in the morning consisted solely of a piece of toast and a boiled egg. Other times we were given two pieces of bacon and a small scoop of scrambled eggs.

At night, they started cutting our calories more by providing us only half the portion of food than what had been normal before the election. We bitched, we moaned, we complained, but Ford would only tell us that because of the election the sheriff's office no longer had the money to provide "full" meals to inmates.

My normal weight is around 180 pounds at a height of 6'2. Within two months my weight dropped to 120 pounds. I honestly felt like a concentration camp survivor. And I wasn't alone.

There were numerous inmates there with serious medical needs, but they were never taken to a doctor. One inmate, a diabetic, went into diabetic shock numerous times but was never taken to the hospital. It was absolutely criminal what Ben Ford was doing to the inmates and I was determined to make sure that someone held him accountable.

When Sheriff Smith finally took office in January 2012 he fired almost every single deputy that worked at the Covington County Sheriff's Department.

According to Sheriff Smith, an internal audit and investigation of the department under Ben Ford revealed thorough and complete corruption and malfeasance justifying the termination of almost every person who worked at the department. I could only agree and applaud his efforts.

True to his word, Sheriff Smith began reviewing every single arrest record of the current inmates to make sure that those arrests under Ford had been lawful and free of political influence.

Shortly after he took office, Sheriff Smith brought me into his office and told me that he had spoken to the district attorney and everyone had agreed to dismiss the felony enticement of a minor charge for lack of evidence.

According to Sheriff Smith, Colton Kendrick's parents were friends with Sheriff Ford and had demanded that I be arrested. Despite not having a single shred of evidence that I had done anything wrong, Sheriff Ford had ordered Detective Pamela Wade Smith to proceed with an arrest anyway, apparently, mostly because Colton's parents wanted me in jail, but most certainly because Ford was getting pressured from Sheriff Pace and the Fire Marshal's Office. This was my belief from the beginning, but Sheriff Smith only confirmed it for me.

Several days later the felony charge was officially dismissed by the Covington County Circuit Court and I was released from the jail and taken into custody by the U.S. Marshals.

Shortly after my arrest the previous August, my U.S. Probation officer, Jay Simpson, had filed a warrant to violate my probation for the Covington County arrest. This legal maneuver is somewhat convoluted.

One would think that the double jeopardy clause of the U.S. Constitution would protect a defendant from having to defend against the same charge in two different courts, but if one is on federal probation the law allows his probation to be violated for, like in my case, enticement of a minor under Mississippi law, even if the state courts dismiss the charges.

So even though the Circuit Court of Covington County said that there was not any evidence to support charging me with enticing Colton, Jay

Simpson could still attempt to have my federal probation violated for the state charge. This essentially required me to leave Covington County and go next to federal court to defend against the exact same charge.

After the U.S. Marshals picked me up in Covington County they took me to the Madison County Jail. To say the least, I was not happy to see Major Chuck McNeil again. Not only had the jail gotten worse, but Chuck McNeil's gut had gotten larger, his ass bigger, and his attitude more horrible.

I was taken to court several days later and met with an attorney from the Federal Public Defender's Office. At that point I was so underweight and sick from been starved and abused by Ben Ford that my attorney immediately requested that I be sent to a federal medical prison that could evaluate my medical situation and hopefully restore me to full health.

The government didn't oppose this request and the magistrate judge, Keith Ball, readily approved. I was taken back to the Madison County Jail but was told by the marshals that they would soon be transporting me to a federal medical center somewhere in the country. By that time I was ready to take the next step in fighting the false charges and sorely needed the opportunity to regain my health and prepare for court.

CHAPTER NINE

Within days of the charges being dismissed in Covington County the U.S. Marshals had me on an airplane headed towards Lexington, Kentucky.

The Federal Bureau of Prisons operates several prisons dedicated solely to providing a higher, more intensive care of inmates with severe medical issues, and Lexington had probably one of the best.

The medical center at Lexington had been built in the 1930s and had a prior history of operating as a narcotics recovery hospital for heroin addicts. Its most famous patient was Ray Charles, the blind singer who had struggled for years with a heroin addiction. Most of the patients at Lexington had orthopedic problems, not addictions. The local University of Kentucky Orthopedic Center had a contract with the prison and, according to most inmates, provided excellent medical care. There were inmates, though, at Lexington who had minimal or less complex medical problems that helped "run" the prison by cooking the food, repairing the different things that broke in an eighty-year-old prison, and helping provide medical care to the sicker inmates.

What the previous prisons like Forrest City and Memphis were, Lexington was not. No one was trying to foment gang violence. There were few, if any, physical fights. Most of the population was over fifty years old, and there were a lot of sex offenders at the facility who rarely, if ever, caused problems. I immediately liked the place. Most importantly for me, though, at that moment, was that the food was really good and they gave us plenty of it.

Until one has been literally starved into a former shell of their prior selves, one can have no idea what it is like to face systemic hunger. Like pregnant women, a starving person develops weird and unexplainable cravings for food. At my hungriest moments at the Covington County Jail I craved peanut butter and jelly sandwiches. I don't know why because I usually despise eating them, but when I was starving I craved them more than I had craved anything before in my life. So when I got to the medical center in Lexington I hoarded all the peanut butter, jelly, and bread that I could find, and I crammed my stomach with as many of them a day as I could, but I was always still hungry.

Lexington had a commissary and I bought cereal, candy bars, honeybuns, Twinkies, and cupcakes. I stuffed my face with high-protein tuna and energy bars, but it was never enough. For my first two months at Lexington all I did was eat, and by March 2012 it was paying off.

The medical department there was fairly good; the best I'd seen in a prison, and they followed my health and weight weekly.

When I arrived in January 2012 my weight was 120 pounds. At the end of March it had risen to 155. By May it was above 160 and I was feeling normal again. My cheekbones were no longer hollow and my hips didn't flare as bad as they had when I'd left Covington County. I could tell I was on the mend and the tortures that Ben Ford had thrown at me were almost long past me.

From the day I'd arrived in the Covington County Jail I'd thought about and then became determined to file a civil rights lawsuit against Ford for the mistreatment that he had subjected me to. But except for the false arrest lawsuit that I'd filed against the Vicksburg Police and Warren County Sheriff's Department for illegally arresting me for trespassing at the Miss Mississippi Pageant, I'd had no extensive experience in filing lawsuits while in prison. But the thought never left my mind.

While at Lexington I was still waiting on Attala County and the fire marshals to take action on my pending arson arrest, but the grand jury in Kosciusko only met twice a year.

After the preliminary hearing, my attorney, Rosalind Jordan, told me that it would be shocking if the grand jury indicted me for arson. There simply was not a single piece of credible evidence for them to do so, and without credible evidence a grand jury cannot indict someone for a crime.

The Attala County Grand Jury finally met in March 2012, and although we were not privy to what occurred during their conference, we were told immediately that the grand jury returned a no-bill, refused to indict me, and cleared me of any wrongdoing.

When I discovered that the grand jury had investigated the arson case and cleared me of any criminal misconduct, it was one of the happiest days of my life. I finally felt completely vindicated against the fraud which Emmett, Sheriff Pace, Mike Chaney, and James Jackson had tried to perpetuate.

In two months I'd been cleared of any illegal activity in both Covington and Attala Counties, and I knew it was only a matter of time before Rankin County did the same. In fact, we had been told that Rankin County had no desire to prosecute the case for the same reason as Covington County—lack of evidence.

What made the Rankin County case more certain was the fact that we had clear evidence that Ethan had lied and tried to fabricate evidence and that I was three hours from Rankin County with a rock solid alibi during the time Ethan said I was raping him. It was all lies and they were slowly falling apart.

The more I thought about filing lawsuits against the corrupt cops that had illegally arrested me, the more I liked the idea of trying to right the many wrongs and acquire justice from the injustice that had been done to me.

Since I'd began recovering my weight, and with it my health, I spent more and more time in the law library at Lexington. The doctors told me that they were going to hold me there for observation until at least the late fall, but I was okay with that. Lexington was not a bad place to do time and I wanted to use that time to fully prepare for the eventual probation revocation trial that would occur as soon as I was transported back to Mississippi.

The Federal Public Defender's Office in Jackson, Mississippi, had officially assigned an attorney to represent me named Omodare Bruce Jupiter.

When told my attorney's name I must admit that I was somewhat hesitant to extend full faith to his abilities as an attorney, and I was more sorry later to learn that my initial hesitancy about Jupiter's competency as an attorney was correct. But in early 2012 I was ready to fight the final battle, even if it was in federal court over a probation violation.

Jupiter and I talked about once a week on the phone, and after he had been provided the evidence by the government, he agreed with my initial assessment that there was not any credible evidence in which to violate my probation for the allegations made by Ethan Robinson and Colton Kendrick.

Because the proceedings had never gone past the preliminary hearing stage in Rankin County, I'd never been provided the actual evidence that they had to support their having arrested me for allegedly enticing Ethan. The same was true for Covington County. None of the authorities had turned over to me any actual evidence. But once I was taken into custody by federal probation, the government had to disclose to Jupiter and me what evidence that was in their possession which they were going to use to try and violate my probation.

When Jupiter finally sent me the discovery packet that had the government's "evidence," I was not surprised to find but very little. The sole evidence was a long, convoluted written statement by Ethan which basically said that I had texted him repeatedly, threatened him through text messages, and ultimately had non-consensual sex with him.

As I'd learned in Rankin County, there were several serious problems with Ethan's story. First, Ethan repeatedly made the assertion in his written statement that I'd threatened and coerced him through text messages using my iPhone. Because Ethan and I did have one short text message conversation, he knew and listed my correct cell phone number linked to my iPhone.

The Rankin County authorities, in conjunction with Covington County and the FBI, subpoenaed the cell phone records of Ethan's phone, Colton's phone, and my phone. And when those records came back in January 2012 they proved that I'd only exchanged about a dozen text messages with Ethan the previous year—much less than the hundreds of texts that Ethan claimed I sent him when I allegedly threatened and coerced him into having non-consensual sex.

The second fatal flaw to Ethan's story was that we had non-consensual sex several days before my arrest in Covington County. He even listed the specific date and time.

Fortunately for me, I was in Biloxi, Mississippi, on the beach with my mother during that last weekend before my arrest. And one of the ways we proved this, when the Rankin County authorities asked, was through surveillance video at the Beau Rivage Casino almost at the exact time that Ethan alleged I was raping him three hours away in Rankin County.

The amateurish plot devised by the psychotic and mentally unstable Ethan Robinson fell apart the moment my alibi was established. That was the main reason why Rankin County and federal probation never tried to pursue a prosecution based off of Ethan's lies. It was all a sham set-up and they knew I was being framed.

The evidence from Covington County was an altogether different matter and it was harder to disprove than the sham case that Ethan had tried to conjure in Rankin County.

When Colton was first interviewed by Detective Pamela Wade Smith at the sheriff's office, he firmly and unequivocally denied that he and I had sex. In fact, the first written statement that he provided to the detective was very clear that nothing improper occurred between us that night. But that wasn't what Detective Smith wanted to hear. So she tightened the screws.

Unfortunately, what occurred between the time that Colton wrote his first statement denying anything improper took place, and his second statement which my arrest was based on, is not fully known. But this is what we do know.

Because Ethan was angry at Colton for not wanting to talk to him anymore, and jealous in his convoluted mind that I was driving Colton home, he decided to call the Covington County Sheriff's Department that night and tell them that I'd kidnapped Colton. The sheriff's deputies immediately went to Colton's house in Collins and roused his parents from sleep to check and see whether Colton was actually there or not. His parents had no idea what had been going on at Patrick Bryant's house or the fight between Ethan and Colton.

As the deputies and Colton's parents were trying to sort out the confusion, Colton and I drive up in the midst of their discussion. But after Ethan had told the deputies that I was a convicted sex offender and had kidnapped Colton, tensions were palpable. And when I made a lunge to choke the last breath of life from Ethan's body, the deputies decided that it'd be a good time to place me in handcuffs.

Everyone was eventually taken to the sheriff's office to sort the mess out. While I was chained to the time-out chair, Colton and his family, along with Ethan and his mother, arrived at the sheriff's office and were interviewed by Detective Smith. However, before their interviews began, both Colton and Ethan continued to use their cell phones to text each other even after they'd been separated at the jail to await their individual interview.

I don't know what type conversation took place between those two after my arrest, but before their phones were confiscated. So I can't speculate. But I doubt it was anything to my benefit.

Nearly twelve hours after my arrest, Detective Smith finally decided that it might be important to confiscate the cell phones of Colton and Ethan. It was at that point that our three phones were bagged as evidence and sent to an FBI expert to have the data extracted.

When that information was returned to Covington and Rankin Counties in January 2012, not only did it absolve me of any wrongdoing, it implicated Ethan in a clear, unequivocal plot to frame me for a crime I didn't commit.

The records also showed that not one single time did I ever text or call Colton on his phone. The cell phone records showed that there had never been any communications between us because, before the night of my arrest, Colton and I had never talked or texted. It clearly proved me innocent. But Colton had been forced into providing Detective Smith a second statement alleging wrongdoing, much like James Jackson at the Fire Marshal's Office had forced, coerced, and extorted Josh Chamblee into writing a statement in the arson case, implicating me in the crime.

Colton's second statement was generically similar to the first statement that he provided Detective Smith, except the second alleged that after I pressured him into having sex he reluctantly agreed and we, in fact, had intercourse before I brought him home.

There were several significant issues with Colton's latest statement because it practically pitted my word against his, and if it had been left as it was there might have been some doubt about my innocence. But Detective Smith needed the proof, so she arranged to take Colton to the local hospital for a DNA and rape kit to be performed on him.

Thankfully, several months later, the DNA and rape kits came back as a negative match to me. It was another clear indication that the allegations were fraudulent.

This was practically the sole evidence that the government was going to try and use to violate my federal probation after I returned from obtaining the medical treatment at Lexington. Both Jupiter and I agreed that the government would have a hard time meeting their burden of proof.

Another aspect of the case gave us great pause and led us to eventually file a motion challenging the constitutionality of my arrests and the pending probation violation. Our challenge was based upon the belief that because both Colton and Ethan were sixteen-years-old or older at the time of the allegations in August 2011, no crime could have occurred because sixteen is the legal age of consent in Mississippi.

The age of consent is the age in which a person sixteen-years-old or older can legally consent to having sexual intercourse with someone over eighteen. The law in Mississippi was very clear about that. Even if Colton and I did have sex, which we did not, no crime could have been violated because Colton was sixteen-years-old.

The authorities in Rankin and Covington Counties were well aware of the age of consent laws in Mississippi. Therefore, they never charged me with having illegal sex with either Colton or Ethan. Instead, they relied on a vague child pornography law that criminalized one's actions when one coerced or enticed a minor under eighteen to engage in sexually illicit behavior.

The definition of "sexually illicit behavior," as meant by the Mississippi Legislature, had solely to do with producing, receiving, or distributing child pornography. That definition certainly didn't apply to me in the least, but the corrupt cops were desperate for anything they could use to keep me in jail. And their ignorant interpretation of a clearly defined statute was the best they could do.

Our argument in our constitutional challenge was that even if I had enticed Colton and Ethan, which I certainly didn't, one can't entice another to do something which is clearly legal. It was a novel argument and Jupiter and I were going to pursue it all the way to the United States Supreme Court if we had to, but our first step would be the upcoming probation revocation hearing that would occur once I'd return to Mississippi from Lexington, Kentucky.

I believe that the U.S. Attorney's Office was well apprised of the fact that they had an extremely weak case. In fact, as soon as the assistant U.S. Attorney prosecuting my case, Carlos Tanner, was made aware of the lack of evidence, he ordered Jay Simpson and the other officers at the U.S. Probation Office to begin looking for something more than Ethan's fantastic fabrications.

In July 2012, Jupiter told me that Simpson had added additional charges to my case and that they were trying to violate my probation based on totally different circumstances that had nothing to do with the Covington County situation.

The first new charge that Simpson put on me alleged that I had violated my probation by getting arrested for trespassing at the Miss Mississippi Pageant the year before. It didn't matter that I'd never been actually convicted of trespassing. It wasn't important that I was clearly exercising my First Amendment rights and was arrested in retaliation for exercising that right. The only thing that mattered to Jay Simpson, U.S. Probation, and their lackeys in the other law enforcement departments was that I be charged with something, anything, that might stick and justify me getting sent back to prison.

Another new charge they added was that I had left the judicial district of Mississippi without permission of my probation officer. Even though Simpson had given me permission numerous times to go to New Orleans on short, overnight trips, the FBI located on my cell phone a picture of me taken on Bourbon Street and had extracted its metadata, which apparently showed that the picture was taken on a date that I'd not had permission to be in New Orleans.

The last and most serious allegation that Simpson added to the new list of charges was that I had violated Mississippi law by failing to register as a sex offender.

Simpson had been told that I'd stayed some nights with my friend, Roger Cole, the previous year when I was taking the truck-driving classes down the road from Roger's house. Even though no one could determine how many nights I'd actually stayed there, Simpson concluded that this was a violation of Mississippi law.

Federal law is very clear about sex offenders having to register. Basically, federal law requires every sex offender to register any address where they live permanently for thirty days or more. There is no obligation under federal law for a sex offender to register any temporary addresses where they might stay sporadically, though.

Under the 2010 version of Mississippi law, however, sex offenders are required to register any place that they stay permanently thirty days or more out of the year and any place they stay temporarily fourteen times or more, non-consecutively, out of a year.

Simpson and the government were alleging that I had violated Mississippi's temporary residence sex offender registration law by staying at Roger Cole's house approximately fourteen or more times in 2011 while I was going to the truck driving school. I knew immediately that I'd never stayed with Roger that many times. I may have stayed with him seven or eight times total over those few months, but I'd never stayed with him more than two nights in a row and certainly not fourteen times. But this was the latest allegation that they stuck me with when their Covington County case fell apart, and although it infuriated me that I was again facing another uphill, adversarial battle, the anger fortified me for the fight. And the angrier that I became the more determined I was to do something about it.

I had a lot of free time on my hands at Lexington and I literally spent as much time as I could in the law library reading up on constitutional rights. The more I looked, the more I thought about filing a lawsuit against the cops that had wronged me. But from the beginning I knew that I could never allow myself to become what so many know as a jailhouse lawyer. I only wanted to file serious lawsuits, alleging true violations of my constitutional rights. To have something of mine called frivolous would impart the same meaning to me as I was assigning to the corrupt cops that I bitched and moaned about so much.

In early 2012, I sat down at an old, manual typewriter and began composing my lawsuit against the officers that had falsely arrested me for arson.

I knew the case would have to be filed in the United States District Court in Aberdeen, Mississippi, and I knew that in addition to James Jackson, Mike Chaney, and Sheriff Pace, I'd also have to add Tim Nail, who had become the sheriff of Attala County in January 2012, to the lawsuit.

I then methodically listed out in chronological order the facts exactly as I knew them. I included everything I'd learned at the preliminary hearing and I prominently displayed the fact that the Attala County Grand Jury had no-billed the charge and cleared me of any wrongdoing.

I alleged that I was suing the defendants for false arrest, false imprisonment, malicious prosecution, and abuse of process. I asked for compensatory damages in the amount of $5,000 to replace the money I'd had to spend to bailout of jail. I also asked for emotional distress and punitive damages. Finally, I requested that I be provided a jury trial.

When I'd completed the lawsuit, or complaint, as it is called, it ran for fifteen pages, but I was proud with what I'd accomplished. I felt like I was actually taking proactive steps in righting what I knew was a horrible injustice.

As part of my complaint I attached a motion to be allowed to proceed *in forma pauperis*. This was a request to the court that I be allowed to proceed with filing the lawsuit without having to pay the high costs and fees of filing a case with the clerk's office.

In forma pauperis status is usually granted to poor persons and prisoners that do not have the ability to pay the court to file their lawsuits. Because I was incarcerated and didn't readily have the $400 needed to pay the filing fee, I requested the court to allow me to file the lawsuit without having to pay that fee.

Part of the application process includes attaching a financial disclosure form itemizing my income, expenditures, and current balance of money and then getting a prison official to endorse the accounting and certify that my answers were true. I dutifully listed the information requested, but when I attempted to get an official at the prison to endorse the application, I couldn't find the right person.

I was soon directed to one of the officers from the accounting office at the prison and he dutifully reviewed my *in forma pauperis* application, signed off that my answers were true, and gave me my form back.

Having completed both my complaint and the *in forma pauperis* application process, I mailed everything to the clerk's office in Aberdeen. Then I waited.

Several weeks later I received my first communication from the court. Their first letter informed me that my lawsuit had been received and filed. They gave me my case number, which was #1:12-cv-168-SA-DAS, and requested that I be sure to utilize it in all future correspondence with the court.

My case number had meaning. It wasn't just a set of randomly assigned numbers. The first number represented the judicial district. The second two numbers represented the year that the case was filed. In this case, 2012. The two letters represented that this was a civil case and the following three numbers were the case numbers assigned specifically to me.

Finally, the last two group of letters designated which judges had been assigned to the case. The "DAS" stood for David Sanders, the magistrate in the case. "SA" stood for Sharion Aycock, the district judge who would have overall supervision of my lawsuit throughout its litigation.

Magistrate judges in the federal court system perform a kind of preliminary review process for civil and criminal matters that occur pretrial. This is to help litigants' cases proceed more quickly and ensure that the district judges have more time available to dedicate to resolving the actual merits of the litigants' claims.

Unlike the lifetime appointments of the district judges who are selected by the President and confirmed by the Senate, magistrate judges are appointed to renewable eight year terms.

In Aberdeen, Judge David Sanders was the magistrate appointed to handle the initial legal steps of my lawsuit, determine whether I qualified for *in forma pauperis* status, and review my claims to determine whether or not my case was frivolous or had merit.

Judge Sanders was appointed to his judicial post in 2008 after having previously served as a law clerk to Judge David Bramlette—my original sentencing judge from 2005—and as an assistant U.S. Attorney in Oxford, Mississippi. He'd also graduated from the University of Mississippi with degrees in English before attending law school where he eventually served as the Editor-in-Chief for the Mississippi Law Journal.

At the time I filed my lawsuit I knew nothing about Judge Sanders or the ultimate role that he would play in helping me litigate my case. But his credentials were impressive and all I asked for was fairness.

The district judge who had overall jurisdiction of my case was Judge Sharion Aycock, a lifetime resident of Tupelo, Mississippi, where Elvis Presley had been born.

Judge Aycock graduated from Mississippi State University in Starkville before graduating from law school at Mississippi College School of Law in 1980. After law school Judge Aycock was in private practice before being elected a circuit court judge in the First Judicial District of Mississippi. Based on her outstanding performance as a state court judge, Mississippi's two United States senators recommended to President Bush that she be appointed to a federal judicial post in 2007. Since that time, Judge Aycock has conducted federal proceedings in the small federal courthouse in Aberdeen.

As with Judge Sanders, at the time I filed my lawsuit I had no idea who Judge Aycock was or whether I would receive a fair opportunity to present my false arrest claims in her court. All I'd ever asked from the court system was fairness, and at that point in my life I did not feel as though I'd been treated fairly, but I was certainly looking to Judge Aycock and Judge Sanders for hope.

In the late fall of 2012, I was still at Lexington and was at the point that I considered myself fully restored in health and spirit from the concentration-like confinement at the Covington County Jail. I was attending mailcall in my unit when I received my second correspondence from the federal court in Aberdeen.

When I went to my cell and opened the letter I was crestfallen and sick to my stomach when I read that Judge Sanders had dismissed my lawsuit because, according to him and the officials at the Lexington prison, my *in forma pauperis* application was not truthful.

When Judge Sanders received my application to proceed *in forma pauperis*, his staff had called the prison to verify that the financial information that I listed on the application was correct. When Judge Sanders did so, some unknown person at the prison clearly provided, whether deliberate or not, inaccurate information to him.

The law is very strict in this regard. When an *in forma pauperis* applicant supplies false information in the application process, their lawsuit is automatically dismissed and they are not allowed to file another. Because some unknown person provided inaccurate information to Judge Sanders, my lawsuit was over before it ever began, and I thought there was nothing I could do about it, but it made me angry and furious. I immediately set out to fix this egregious mistake.

I went and pulled all of my financial records and reports from the entire time that I'd been at Lexington, which included every dollar that I'd been sent, every dollar that I'd spent at commissary, and even the itemized receipts showing what I'd bought from the commissary. I attached these records to a motion asking Judge Sanders to reconsider his order dismissing my case. I then mailed it as quick as I could back to the clerk in Aberdeen. And again I waited.

And while I was waiting for Judge Sanders to review the additional information that I'd sent him, which should have proven that I'd provided a completely correct accounting of my finances, I was finally transported back to Mississippi two weeks after Thanksgiving.

It had taken the competent, but slow medical staff at Lexington nearly ten months to restore me back to health, but I felt Jupiter and I were ready for the probation revocation trial that was scheduled for February 7, 2013. And I was certainly ready to finish the thing once and for all. I didn't know whether I'd be violated and sent back to prison, or if I would be freed, but I was more than willing to fight to find out.

CHAPTER TEN

By Christmas of 2012 I'd been returned to Mississippi for my upcoming revocation trial, but upon my arrival, Jupiter and I requested that I be housed at the Grenada County Jail rather than Madison County.

I'd written quite a bit of negative information about Chuck McNeil and the Madison County Jail in my book, *Into Hell I Rode,* and I'd been told by one of the U.S. Marshals that because of my book there had been some positive changes made there.

When I wrote *Into Hell I Rode* and published it in July 2011, the sheriff of Madison County, Toby Trowbridge, was running what could be called nothing more than a complete financial scam.

Sheriff Trowbridge submitted certified financial claims to the federal government asserting that it cost Madison County and the sheriff's office more than forty dollars a day to house the federal pretrial inmates at their jail.

While claiming to the federal government that it cost him forty dollars a day to feed, house, and care for a federal inmate, Sheriff Trowbridge was simultaneously submitting certified claims to the state of Mississippi and local municipalities, claiming that it costs less than six dollars a day to house their inmates at his jail.

Sheriff Trowbridge and Major Chuck McNeil were submitting clearly fraudulent financial claims to the federal government, overstating the actual amount of money necessary to house a federal inmate, and they scammed the federal government out of this money because they knew that there was no other facility in the area that had the capacity to house the federal pretrial inmates.

My book exposed this clear fraud and I was told that subsequent to this public revelation Madison County had to audit and adjust their accountability procedures as it pertained to housing federal inmates.

Sheriff Trowbridge also left the Madison County Sheriff's Department under a cloud of suspicion of misconduct and he was replaced by Randall Tucker, one of the deputies whom had worked under Trowbridge before his retirement.

To say the least, no one could argue that it was a good idea to house me at the Madison County Jail after what I had written and published about the people that worked there. Instead, upon our request, the marshals kept me at the Grenada County Jail approximately an hour north of Madison County.

Before my probation revocation trial began on February 7, 2013, Jupiter drove to the jail and met with me to discuss a strategy for the upcoming trial.

I tried to sum up my first look at Jupiter in a positive light, but couldn't. My first impression wasn't impressive. Jupiter definitely looked like a nerd with glasses, more fittingly placed in a chemistry lab than a federal courtroom.

He was born in the early 1960s in the U.S. Virgin Islands and his light skin tone revealed his island heritage.

Unfortunately, Jupiter looked overworked, underpaid, and with a wardrobe from the 1980s. By this time I was trying to direct every aspect of my defense with some success and some not—so I chose to overlook his shortcomings. I had an idea of how my defense should be conducted, and as long as Jupiter could put that into effect, I didn't care how he looked.

Since the government added three new charges to the original petition to revoke my probation, they also had to turn over to us whatever evidence they had which was going to be used to prosecute me. The only thing that the government gave us in reference to the trespassing arrest at the Miss Mississippi Pageant was the police report filed by Officer Daniel Thomas the night I was arrested. Thomas's written report was a conglomeration of grammar and punctuation errors which completely demonstrated the uneducated and ignorant background from which he came. More importantly, it was clearly not an accurate reflection of what occurred that night.

Thomas's arrest report concentrated almost solely on the fact that he and the other officers that night arrested me because they did not agree with the message that my leaflets conveyed against Sheriff Pace.

Rather than concentrate on anything to do with criminal activity, Thomas's report said that he believed my leaflets to be slander against Sheriff Pace and that I was being arrested because my book and leaflets posed a "threat to law enforcement" throughout Warren County and the state of Mississippi.

I later compared Thomas's report to the Nazi and Soviet Stalinist justifications for book burnings and suppression of free speech in those countries before their collapse and could not distinguish one from the other.

Daniel Thomas and his uneducated, pro-fascist propaganda espousing ilk are leading the frontline war against any free speech that runs counter to the accepted belief they've been brainwashed into propagating. Thomas's report couldn't have been more clear that I was arrested only because they did not like that I was distributing a message that was negative towards Sheriff Pace and police corruption. And they abused the power and authority they'd been given to effectuate a Gestapo-like arrest. Their actions that night should send a chill of fright through the hearts and spines of any true American patriot who believes in justice, freedom, and equality. I was sure that once Thomas's report became public at trial, and people knew the truth, that I'd be freed of this charge.

Jupiter and I next moved to the allegation that I'd left the judicial district without permission. The government's sole "proof" on this charge was a picture of me on Bourbon Street and some metadata printout alleging that the picture was taken in September 2010 during a time that I did not have Jay Simpson's permission to be in New Orleans. We'd have to wait until the testimony at trial before we'd know anything more.

The last allegation that we discussed was the most serious—that I'd failed to register as a sex offender while staying at Roger Cole's house from "May 2011 through August 2011."

To prove this allegation the government was going to offer the testimony of Roger Cole. To counter whatever testimony the government was going to offer, I had Jupiter gather three friends of mine, plus my mother; all of whom could testify that I never moved into Cole's house, never lived with him, and never stayed the fourteen or more times with him to be in violation of the law.

Even though I had doubts about Jupiter's legal and trial abilities as a lawyer, I had no choice but to proceed to the trial with what I had. But the more I worked with Jupiter to prepare the case, the more I felt like I was the one with the legal training and not him.

In addition to having doubts about Jupiter's capabilities, I immediately had doubts about the fairness of the new judge that had been assigned to conduct my revocation trial.

Judge Bramlette had originally been assigned jurisdiction over my case, but he took retirement and the case was reassigned to Judge Henry Travillion Wingate.

Without reservation, with more than nine years of hindsight dealing with Wingate, I can say that he is one of the worst, most despicable judges to ever have worn the black robe. And this view is held by plaintiffs, defendants, attorneys, other judges, and the public at large. But the horrible thing about Judge Wingate is not just that he is evil, it's not just that he's a moron, it's not just that he's a blathering idiot, it's that the prosecutors, attorneys, and the other judges have all gotten used to the way he is.

Wingate was born and raised in Jackson, Mississippi, but left the state to obtain his undergraduate education at Grinnell College in Iowa.

After being given preferential treatment under the affirmative action system, which was being implemented in the early 1970s, Wingate obtained admission to Yale University Law School where he graduated without honors in 1972.

While at Yale, Wingate befriended Clarence Thomas, a future Supreme Court Justice and fellow sex abuser, who was two years behind him. Their relationship would continue, and over the years Wingate patently attempted to emulate his judicial twin in the Supreme Court.

The allegations of sex abuse committed by Justice Thomas are well-known; Judge Wingate, not so much. But former Yale classmates remember Wingate and Thomas as a predatory team, acting together, preying upon innocent, virtuous, WASPish women throughout the distinguished halls of the Yale Campus. Forty years removed from these events, Wingate's abuses of these women are still vividly remembered by his victims.

Before being appointed a federal judge by President Ronald Reagan in 1985, Wingate briefly held a number of different legal positions, never being able to remain in one job for very long, or able to perform with any outstanding ability.

For less than a year Wingate worked as a legal clerk, then for several months in private practice, then other short stints as an adjunct lecturer at three different colleges, which was then quickly followed with a four-year assignment as an assistant attorney general with the state of Mississippi.

According to former coworkers of Wingate's, while he was at the Attorney General's Office, his work there was continuously plagued with errors and he was constantly criticized for spending more time playing racquetball than he did in the courtroom. Allegations that Wingate persistently sexually harassed his female coworkers would also plague his reputation. Predictably, his employment didn't last long anywhere he worked.

After being released from his employment with the Attorney General, Wingate moved down the employment ladder to a job with the district attorney's office as an assistant prosecutor. When his work didn't pan out there either, he finally sought and obtained employment with the U.S. Attorney's Office in Jackson.

For thirteen years Wingate held eight different jobs without distinguishing himself in any of them. The sexual harassment he inflicted on his coworkers and his difficulty performing well in jobs, and ultimately keeping them for any significant length of time, did not bode well with those that would eventually find themselves in his courtroom.

During the Reagan administration of the 1980s, critics had condemned the President and his advisors for appointing mostly white, male, Anglo-Saxon, conservative judges to the federal courts.

To counter this trend the administration began looking for African-American candidates to appoint to judicial posts to reflect their false beliefs in racial equality.

At the same time, Wingate knew that if he was ever to compete with his white, Ivy League-educated colleagues, he would have to reinvent himself as a hardcore, conservative black Republican. With this he had a willing conspirator in his quickly rising judicial twin, Clarence Thomas—another black Republican judge constantly plagued by allegations of sexual abuse against women.

Despite Wingate's lackluster performance in every job that he had held prior to his appointment, the Reagan administration was quick to recognize that Wingate would be an easy and willing participant in their campaign to make it appear that they were strong on racial diversity in the judicial system. Wingate's appointment, though, would, in many future cases, set the black civil rights movement back many years—this despite Wingate being African-American himself.

A repeated refrain throughout Wingate's thirty-plus years on the bench is that he continuously is harsher on racial minorities, and rules more favorably to individuals and groups allied with the Republican Party, than those that reflect his actual background and social stature.

Many people find this perplexing since Wingate is a minority himself and benefited from affirmative action programs that earned him a coveted spot at Yale Law School and eventually a federal judgeship, despite his lack of abilities and competence.

Wingate's harsh sentencing history and favoritism towards conservative parties is rooted in his narcissistic desire for higher authority and power. Ignorance in conjunction with power, are the worst enemies justice can have.

Judge Wingate's mental pathology and psychological neurosis is a thousand times more dangerous than the worst serial rapist and murderer. Its genesis is tied directly to the self-loathing, internal malevolence generated by Wingate's awareness that no matter how much he wishes to be like his white, conservative colleagues, he will forever be casted as an "Uncle Tom" on the periphery of polite Anglo-Saxon society.

Deep within the neurotic recesses of Wingate's subpar brain is the realization that without the assistance of the liberals' affirmative action system—of which he was, no doubt, a beneficiary of—his acceptance to Yale, and ultimately his graduation, would have been no more than a mythical fantasy of a poor minority lacking in intellectual capability.

But acknowledging that liberal Democrats and their affirmative action programs gave Wingate the undeserved chance at an Ivy League education, which his ability alone could not secure him, is a truth which Wingate would rather suppress more so than his desire to keep secret the names of the many women—and assuredly a few men—who have been the victims of his insatiable sexual appetite.

Just as a closeted homosexual will overcompensate for his lack of masculinity, so has Wingate overcompensated in his desire to be like the white, conservative, Ivy League masters who gave him an almost unlimited tool of power by appointing him a federal judge—a decision many have lived to deeply regret.

While Clarence Thomas was meteorically riding the coattails of the Republican Party's anti-liberal, anti-minority crusade throughout the 1980s, Wingate was languishing in his relatively minor, backwater judicial appointment in Mississippi. But Wingate had higher power aspirations, too. However, when the Republican wave of the 1980s subsided to the Clinton-led era of the '90s, any hope Wingate had of attaining an appointment to the Fifth Circuit Court of Appeals in New Orleans vanished.

It was no secret to the legal community then, or to them now; Wingate desperately wanted a coveted appointment to the Fifth Circuit. In fact, he rabidly craved the prestige and honor that a circuit judgeship bestowed, and Wingate truly believed that to accomplish his promotion he would have to double down on his faux conservative values and reflect in his judicial rulings the core Republican judicial principles of harsh sentencing, stricter limits on constitutional rights, and curtailment of social freedoms.

For all intents and purposes, the African-American Wingate wanted desperately to be the white, Anglo-Saxon, male, Protestant, legitimate Ivy Leaguer of his conservative Republican masters, and if Wingate had to severely punish his own people to achieve his dreams, then the black community would be damned. It became clear that if Wingate ever had an unselfish thought in his self-absorbed, narcissistic life, it no doubt died a lonely, miserable death.

Wingate's best opportunity for an appointment to the Fifth Circuit was during President George W. Bush's reign of power from 2001 to 2009.

For the eight years of the Clinton presidency, Wingate had followed a carefully scripted judicial manifesto designed by him to make himself more appealing as a potential appointee to the Fifth Circuit. But after having spent almost twenty years on the bench, and an almost equal amount of time shuffling from one failed job to another, even the Bush administration was keen enough not to promote Wingate further than his abilities and competence warranted. The allegations of serial sex abuse didn't help his chances either.

One has to realize that Wingate was not appointed by President Reagan in 1985 for his judicial capabilities. Wingate was appointed to help make the Reagan administration appear more palatable to racial minorities. Simply put, the Republicans needed an Uncle Tom. But the blacks in Mississippi saw right through Reagan's racial window dressing, and for that, the unfortunate African-Americans who have to appear in Wingate's court are left feeling betrayed, abused, and mistreated. But the hypocrisy doesn't end there.

Despite Judge Wingate routinely handing down harsh, vindictive sentences of imprisonment to impoverished minorities and liberal whites for relatively minor crimes, all in the name of "law and order," Wingate had no hesitation in rabidly attempting to excuse his own criminal conduct when he was allegedly accused of violently physically abusing his terminally ill wife, Turner Arnita Wingate, in early 2008 while she was in her final months of life.

In fact, during research for this book, this author spoke to numerous family members of Wingate's—all of whom had totally disowned him after his wife's death—that confirmed the allegations that Wingate had repeatedly abused his wife since their marriage in 1974. This is the man who expected—no, deserved—an appointment to the court of appeals.

One of the repeated refrains from Wingate's estranged family and his former law clerks is their almost irrational fear of Wingate and how he can and does use his federal judgeship to bully, intimidate, and silence his critics and sexual abuse victims.

"David, you have no idea the lengths Henry will go to punish anyone that criticizes him," said one of Wingate's estranged relatives. "He has the FBI, U.S. Marshals, and the U.S. Attorney's Office in his back pocket, and he will use them in a heartbeat to retaliate against anyone that crosses him. You could not believe the depth of this man's vanity and madness. It's why we [his family] no longer have anything to do with him. We cut him off as soon as we found out that he was physically abusing Arnita [Wingate's deceased wife]."

Wingate's willingness to abuse his judicial post and intimidate his sexual abuse victims was underscored in his response to allegations by a former law clerk that he raped her in his chambers at the federal courthouse in Jackson.

The former law clerk, who wishes that her name remain confidential for fear of further reprisals, had only been clerking for Judge Wingate a short time before he forced himself on her in his chambers, made her perform oral sex on him, and then used his fingers to penetrate her vagina. "The only reason he didn't rape me was because he couldn't get an erection. His impotence was the only thing that saved me that day," she said.

Shortly after this first sexual assault, and after repeatedly rebuffing Wingate's further attempts to sexually assault her, the law clerk quit her job. "I just couldn't take it anymore. The way he looked at me. What he did to me. I wasn't that kind of girl. I was young enough to be his granddaughter for God's sake. It just made me sick. I had to get out of there," she said.

Judge Wingate, though, would ensure that her punishment continued. And this included blackballing his former law clerk and doing everything possible to prevent her from obtaining employment elsewhere. Wingate went so far as to threaten a partner at a prestigious law firm with ruling against them in a pending litigation if they hired his former law clerk. [It's no wonder Judge Wingate was never considered for an appointment to the Fifth Circuit Court of Appeals.]

In the many conversations with his former employees and sexual abuse victims, I couldn't help but press them on what other sexually aberrant behaviors they witnessed from Wingate. "I don't know if this would qualify," one said, "but Judge Wingate was infatuated with Nancy Reagan. Like, literal idol worship. For the first ten years that he was on the bench, Judge Wingate kept dozens of pictures of Nancy around his office, his house, and even above his toilet in his bathroom. It definitely raised some eyebrows."

The most amusing revelation to come from Wingate's former staff was his penchant for not wearing pants and boxers under his black robe with conducting court. "Judge Wingate had no hesitation in walking around his chambers without any pants on. But he repeatedly went into court wearing nothing but his robe. We just laughed at it at the time. Now we all recognize it as just another of his many sexual aberrations."

Rumors of Wingate's psychopathic sexual deviancy swirled around the federal courthouse in Jackson for decades. But it never registered to Wingate that he was his own worst enemy when it came to obtaining his long-desired, coveted appointment to the Fifth Circuit. There were plenty of people, though, working to ensure this never happened. And, based on his blatant sexual misbehavior, not to mention the total lack of intellectual competency, it was no wonder that Wingate was never considered for an appointment.

Upon President Obama assuming office in 2009, the aging Wingate realized that his chance for an appointment to the Fifth Circuit had evaporated into thin air, and the quality of which he conducted his affairs thereafter reflected his sour attitude at being denied what he essentially felt he was entitled to. And subsequently, Wingate became more and more unmoored from reality.

Since losing his chance for a circuit court appointment, Wingate has apparently lost interest in conducting the judicial functions of his job. Relatively simple legal cases assigned to Wingate linger for years without action. Parties involved in lawsuits who reflect liberal beliefs must wait months or years for Wingate to enter simple judgments allowing those parties to collect those judgments entitled to them. Many criminal defendants are deliberately more harshly punished by Wingate without justification even when the Fifth Circuit continuously remands those cases for egregious trial errors.

In other criminal trials, Wingate deliberately denies defendants the ability to introduce evidence proving their innocence. He assumes a judicial posture hostile to the defendants' lawyers and in several specific cases Wingate has ordered defendants held without bond solely for the purpose of encouraging them to plead guilty and not take their cases to trial.

Despite being repeatedly reprimanded by the Fifth Circuit for dereliction of duty, Wingate continues to act in a patently clear manner that is hostile to defendants, sympathetic to the prosecution, and continually confusing to all others.

Judge Wingate was never known for being intellectually gifted, but I've personally seen Post-it notes with more intellectual depth than the judicial opinions and orders that he issues from the bench. The man was clearly promoted beyond his abilities and station in life. But he is pro-prosecution, so despite his idiocy, the U.S. Attorney's Office provided him an audience of adoring idiots.

When asked by reporters from the Clarion-Ledger newspaper in Jackson why he is repeatedly reprimanded by the Fifth Circuit, rather than demonstrate responsibility, Wingate blamed his shortcomings on his law clerks rather than take the blame himself. This demonstrates clearly the lack of character in the man and his unfitness for the office he holds.

Wingate's favoritism towards government prosecutors and his antipathy towards liberal or Democratic defendants in his courtroom was underscored in the case of *United States v. Whitfield, et. al.* a criminal case filed against a lawyer and three Mississippi state court judges—all Democrats—in the federal criminal court in Jackson.

In that case, Paul Minor, an extremely successful trial attorney and fundraiser for the Democratic Party was charged in a sixteen-count indictment by the U.S. Attorney's Office with bribing John Whitfield, a circuit court judge in Biloxi, Wes Teel, a Chancery Court judge also in Biloxi, and Oliver Diaz, a Mississippi Supreme Court Justice.

At the heart of the government's case was their belief that Minor had guaranteed financial loans for these three judges to help finance their judicial election campaigns in return for favorable rulings in big litigation cases that Minor would file in their respective courts.

Even though Minor made the loans for the judges, it was clear that he never received any special favors or favorable treatment in the cases which he was involved with in their courts. And in order for the government to prove that a crime had been committed, it had to prove that Minor received distinct *quid pro quo* favoritism. In this I believe the government failed.

During the first bribery trial in the summer of 2005, Judge Diaz was acquitted of all charges, Minor was acquitted on six counts, and Whitfield on one. The jury hung on the remaining counts, including the ones against Judge Teel. Judge Wingate, who had assumed jurisdiction of the case, declared a mistrial and rescheduled the retrial for spring of 2007.

Prior to the retrial, Judge Wingate, who clearly despised the remaining three defendants for their liberal beliefs and work on behalf of the Democratic Party, refused to allow evidence to be presented to the second jury, which had been allowed to be submitted to the first jury, that would help establish all of the defendants' innocence.

During the first trial, Judge Wingate allowed evidence of Minor's history of contributing heavily to other judicial candidates in Mississippi, his history of guaranteeing loans to friends and other attorneys, his history of filing big litigation cases in other judges' courts whom he had never contributed money to, and Wingate allowed the defendants' attorneys to present evidence of government misconduct and prosecutorial vindictiveness.

After the first trial, Wingate, and everyone else involved, knew that the first jury had failed to convict the defendants because of the overwhelming exculpatory evidence proving Minor's, Whitfield's, and Teel's innocence.

To ensure that an acquittal or a hung jury didn't occur in the second trial, Wingate specifically excluded and disallowed the defendants' previous exculpatory evidence which he had allowed to be introduced during the first trial. Only Judge Wingate could argue two self-contradictory positions and, apparently, not have the intelligence to realize it. It's no wonder prosecutors adore him.

All of the defendants attempted to have Wingate recused for this clear favoritism towards the government, but Wingate was determined to see the popular Democrats in prison. Predictably, Minor, Whitfield, and Teel were convicted on all counts at the second trial and Wingate sentenced them to an extremely harsh amount of prison time.

At sentencing, Wingate sentenced Minor to a total of over eleven years in prison and over four million dollars in fines.

Whitfield was sentenced to one hundred and ten months imprisonment and fined $125,000.00. Teel got off the easiest with a sentence of seventy months imprisonment. Predictably, all of the defendants appealed their cases to the Republican-controlled Fifth Circuit Court of Appeals.

In December 2009, the Fifth Circuit issued an opinion which overturned some of the defendants' convictions while leaving others intact. However, on remand, Judge Wingate was forced to reduce all of the defendants' sentences, based, in part, off the egregious errors that he made at trial.

I had become intimately familiar with the *United States v. Whitfield, et. al.* case because John Whitfield and I were incarcerated together at the Federal Medical Center in Lexington, Kentucky.

During our time together, Whitfield brought me up to speed on the atrocious behavior of Wingate, Wingate's judicial schizophrenia, and neurotic behavior, and the impossibility of me ever receiving a fair trial in his court. Whitfield reminded me that when I went in front of Wingate for my revocation trial there would be two prosecutors there trying to put me in prison, but the one to beat was the one wearing the black robe.

Whitfield couldn't overstate it enough to me the impossibility of being able to beat the government in a bench trial before Wingate. But I was naive. I believed my innocence would carry the day. I trusted Jupiter to ensure that I was treated fairly. And I'd never seen Wingate in action, so I had no real reason to doubt his ability to perform his judicial duties in a fair and impartial manner. But my date with the executioner was coming and I could only hope that Jupiter had the sense to steer my case in a competent manner.

Several days before my revocation began, Jupiter came to visit me one last time and we discussed Wingate and my chances at a fair trial. Jupiter wouldn't say one way or the other, but he told me that he thought my case was better than most. He did remind me, though, that Wingate's former law clerk, Carlos Tanner, was prosecuting my case and that Wingate would have a hard time divorcing himself from his protégé's arguments in the court.

The last thing that Jupiter and I discussed was a recent piece of evidence that the FBI and government had only disclosed to Jupiter several days before the start of the revocation trial.

After reviewing my cell phone the FBI did not and could not find any evidence of wrongful or improper activity. However, when they reviewed the phone of Colton Kendrick, the FBI discovered thousands of nude pictures of other men, some men of whom were very old, and thousands of pages of texts and chat conversations where Colton had been using gay dating sites to meet older men for sex.

Although evidence of Colton's promiscuous past didn't prove my innocence, it indicated instead his propensity to meet other men. Most disturbing, Colton's phone contained hundreds of pages of evidence, and hundreds of pictures of older gay men that Colton was meeting for sex, going back to when he was fourteen-years-old.

In one particular disturbing case, evidence from Colton's phone showed that he was chatting, meeting, and having sex with an older man in his early fifties named John Gillespie.

What was so disturbing about Colton and Gillespie's communications was that Gillespie was a dentist in Jackson and a reserve officer in the United States Air Force. However, the government made clear that they were not interested in pursuing any type of prosecution against Gillespie or the multiple other older men that Colton was meeting for sex when he was under the legal age of consent.

I felt that this was just another clear indication of the government's willfulness in pursuing selective and vindictive prosecutions against me, but Jupiter refused to make that argument in court. Instead, we would have to rely on the other evidence, such as it was.

CHAPTER ELEVEN

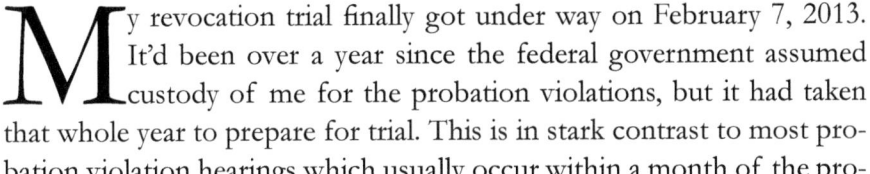

My revocation trial finally got under way on February 7, 2013. It'd been over a year since the federal government assumed custody of me for the probation violations, but it had taken that whole year to prepare for trial. This is in stark contrast to most probation violation hearings which usually occur within a month of the probationer being arrested for the violation. But as I was quickly learning, my case was always special.

Before the revocation trial began, Judge Wingate ordered that all potential witnesses who might be called to testify in the trial leave the courtroom so that they could not hear the testimony of the other witnesses. Upon Wingate's command, both Ethan Robinson and Colton Kendrick left the courtroom along with the other witnesses.

Surprisingly, though, both Ethan's and Colton's mothers were attending the trial and watching the proceedings. It was not a surprise to find that Colton's mother, Susan Coulter, was attending the trial. I'd expected as much. But learning that Ethan's mother, Cassandra Welker, was attending the trial was truly puzzling, not because she was pursuing justice, but simply because since the case began Mrs. Welker pursued nothing but money.

After my arrest in Rankin County, Mrs. Welker communicated her desire to drop the charges if I would make a monetary settlement with her and Ethan for several hundred thousand dollars to compensate them for their "inconvenience."

Any doubt I had about the motives of Ethan and his mother were erased when I was told that they were willing to drop the charges if I would pay them some money.

When my investigators were collecting information to help me defend my case, one of the first things they noticed was the abject poverty that Ethan and his family came from. They lived in a small, dilapidated trailer in Puckett, Mississippi, and it never surprised me that their first motivation was money. But even if I had several hundred thousand dollars to give them, I'd rather rot in jail than be the victim of their extortionate scams to escape their destitution. And I was very clear to my attorneys about this.

I had sincerely but wrongly thought that Welker would avoid the trial to escape being called to testify about her extortionate attempts to scam me out of money, but despite this danger she was there nonetheless.

The government decided to begin the trial by first attempting to prove the violation that I'd broken the law by trespassing at the Miss Mississippi Pageant the night I'd been exercising my First Amendment rights.

To prove this violation, the government first called Detective Daniel Thomas to the stand to testify, and after being sworn in, Thomas was first asked to state his name, employment, and work history.

After the brief preliminaries, Thomas explained that he was on patrol, on a Segway, in the parking lot of the City Convention Center when he first encountered me placing the leaflets on the cars in the parking lot. Thomas explained that once he saw the leaflets, and realized that they were critical of Sheriff Pace, he ordered me to stop distributing the leaflets in that specific area, but granted me permission to go pass them out on Washington Street, one of the main thoroughfares in downtown Vicksburg.

Thomas then said that I left the area, but came back a few minutes later and requested his badge number. After that he didn't see me for approximately forty-five minutes. When I did reappear, however, Thomas said that I was on my motorcycle on Washington Street, leaving the area. Because this was the third time Thomas saw me in less than an hour he decided to execute an arrest.

This concluded the questions that the government, through Carlos Tanner, asked Thomas.

When I first saw Tanner in court, my first impression was that if Carlos Tanner were white, he would look exactly like the TV journalist,

Tucker Carlson.

Tanner wore bowties and frat boy-type suits. Wingate was his mentor and I could tell that Tanner's eyes glistened with adoration every moment that he could strut and prance in front of Wingate.

He was a young guy, though, and the longer I observed him in court, the more I realized that despite having the handicap of being Wingate's protégé, Tanner was a fairly competent prosecutor and cross-examiner, despite, obviously, getting the entirety of my case wrong.

My attorney, Jupiter, was then given an opportunity to cross-examine Thomas.

Jupiter began his questioning by getting Thomas to admit that on the night of my arrest he was in the process of attempting to obtain employment as a deputy with Sheriff Pace. I'd been told this important fact by Deep Six, the deputy who had been working secretly with me to write *Into Hell I Rode*, and the fact that we knew this genuinely surprised Thomas.

Thomas next admitted that there were other people at the pageant distributing campaign literature, but that he never asked them to stop their distribution. Asked why they were allowed to pass out their campaign literature and I wasn't, Thomas explained that my leaflets were "slander" against Sheriff Pace.

Jupiter next played an audio recording of the walkie-talkie radio traffic that night between the officers. In that recording, an unidentified officer made some clearly disparaging remarks about me to Thomas that led me and Jupiter to believe that Thomas was being encouraged to arrest me in retaliation for me exercising my First Amendment rights.

The next recording that Jupiter played was Sheriff Pace calling Thomas on the walkie-talkie radio to tell Thomas to "Answer your phone!" However, during the trial, Thomas conveniently could not remember what Sheriff Pace told him during their phone call immediately before my arrest.

This was followed with the revelation from Thomas that immediately prior to my arrest he had also been told that I was at the police station, two blocks away, filing an official complaint against him for denying me the ability to exercise my First Amendment rights.

After this, we felt we had made our most important points and Jupiter concluded his cross-examination, and since the government had no more questions for Thomas he was allowed to be excused.

The government then called Deputy U.S. Marshal Johnny Davis to the stand to provide testimony to prove their allegation that I'd violated Mississippi law by failing to register as a sex offender at Roger Cole's address in Pearl, Mississippi.

After describing his career with the Marshal's Service, Deputy Davis testified that he'd been assigned to investigate me for possible "violations of SORNA, the Sex Offender Registration and Notification Act."

As part of his investigation, Deputy Davis testified that he went and talked to Cole and was told that I'd stayed "some" nights with him from May 2011 through August 2011, but that Cole was unsure how many nights total it was. This was the sum of Deputy Davis's answers to Tanner's questions.

Jupiter then had an opportunity to question Deputy Davis and scored a little better than Tanner did. In doing so, Jupiter was able to get Deputy Davis to admit that the sole determination of whether I'd violated the sex offender registration laws was totally dependent on how many days I'd actually stayed there.

The first indication that Judge Wingate was going to also assume the role of a prosecutor in my case was when he began asking the witness questions upon Jupiter and Tanner concluding theirs. This is normally not correct procedure. But one of the main things that John Whitfield had told me when we were at Lexington together was that when I went into the courtroom with Wingate, there would always be two government prosecutors in the room, but that the one to actually beat was the one wearing the black robe. On my first day in court I saw that this omen was true.

Wingate proceeded to ask Deputy Davis numerous questions, all designed to provide Wingate a better underlying basis in which to revoke my probation on this violation. But despite the intense questioning, Deputy Davis could provide no other information. Simply put, he just had not conducted much of an investigation.

The government's next witness was Roger Cole himself, and whether I'd be found guilty of this failing to register violation rested in the hands of a person that I thought at one time was a true friend.

Tanner's first inquiries were in regards to how Cole and I met. Roger patiently explained that we'd met at the local gay bar in Jackson called

"Dick and Jane's."

When asked why I eventually came to stay at Cole's house, he told the court that I needed a place to stay sometimes when it was bad weather and "a place to come chill out and get away kind of."

Tanner next asked the most pivotal question of the entire proceedings.

> **TANNER:** First off, how long of a time frame did Mr. Atwood have this living arrangement with you?
> **COLE:** Oh, I would say the whole total, maybe two weeks.
> **TANNER:** Two weeks? About 14 days total?
> **COLE:** Yeah, just here and there.

There it was. This was the answer we'd been waiting for. It neither helped nor hurt. And no one was sure what to make of Cole's testimony. His doubt about the exact number of times I stayed there should have helped me more than it hurt, but it also made it look like Cole was trying to help me.

Tanner quickly wrapped up his questions in the hope that Cole would do no more damage and Jupiter began his cross.

> **JUPITER:** You estimated that David actually spent the night at your house maybe on 14 occasions?
> **COLE:** Yeah, in that area. I actually only saw him maybe two weeks total out of that time. He came and went a lot.
> **JUPITER:** Did David ever say that he was coming to live with you permanently?
> **COLE:** No, sir.
> **JUPITER:** Did David ever spend more than two nights in a row at your house?
> **COLE:** No sir. He was only just in and out.
> **JUPITER:** Ok, so when the investigators came to interview you, you didn't get an opportunity to explain to them that David, in fact, was just someone who stayed there a number of times, maybe 14 times total, over that time period. Correct?
> **COLE:** True.

This was it. I thought that Jupiter had destroyed the government's case. No matter how hard anyone tried, neither Jupiter or Tanner could get Cole to say with any certainty how many nights I'd actually stayed with him. This was the most important fact in the entire case, because if the government couldn't prove that I stayed exactly fourteen or more times at Cole's house, then I'd have to be found not guilty.

Mississippi law was very clear when it came to the temporary residence sex offender registration law. In order for one to be in violation of that law, one would have to stay at an unregistered address for exactly fourteen or more times, non-consecutively, in a single year.

In a fair and impartial court system, doubts, uncertainty, and equivocal speculation is not enough to convict someone beyond a reasonable doubt. And without Cole being able to say with exact certainty that I stayed at his house fourteen or more times should have entitled me to an acquittal. But there was more to come.

On what lawyers and judges call "redirect," Tanner had the opportunity to question Cole again, and in doing so, Tanner went right to the heart of the matter, because, more than anyone, Tanner knew that whether he was going to win his case or not depended on tying Cole's testimony down even further.

> **TANNER:** Is your best recollection about fourteen days of how many days Mr. Atwood stayed with you?
> **COLE:** It's hard to say, you know. He was in and out so much. He would stay a night, be gone two days, stay a night, you know. I would probably say two weeks total.
> **TANNER:** Okay, and that's about 14 days?
> **COLE:** Yeah.

This apparently wasn't enough for Wingate, because as soon as Tanner wrapped up his last question, Wingate poured in with unusual and unnatural gay-related inquiries that quickly led me to believe that Judge Henry T. Wingate was a latent, closet homosexual himself and had a weird, unexplainable curiosity about all things homosexual. I began to wonder whether Wingate was also a sexual abuser of men, too.

> **JUDGE WINGATE:** Did you share the same toothbrush?
> **COLE:** No, sir.
> **JUDGE WINGATE:** The soap?

COLE: I think we shared the same soap.

JUDGE WINGATE: Did you sleep in the same bed?

COLE: No, sir.

JUDGE WINGATE: What about the food? What kind of food did you eat?

COLE: We eat whatever we want. He bought groceries one time because he eats a little more richer than I do.

JUDGE WINGATE: What do you mean by that?

COLE: I don't know quite how to say it. People that's rich eat different than people that are poor.

JUDGE WINGATE: Did you two hang out together?

COLE: We went jet-skiing. We went to the gay bar together.

JUDGE WINGATE: Tell me about that.

COLE: We just went and hanged out.

JUDGE WINGATE: Were there males and females there?

COLE: Yes sir, both gay men and lesbians (Cole said the word "lesbian" as one might say ISIS, Taliban, or Nazi).

JUDGE WINGATE: Where is this bar located?

COLE: Right here in downtown Jackson.

JUDGE WINGATE: Where about in downtown?

COLE: It's right here by the federal building.

JUDGE WINGATE: So, what is your relationship like with the defendant right now? Is he still a friend?

COLE: Yes, sir.

The purpose for which Wingate questioned Cole about these seemingly mundane and unimportant matters was never clear. Jupiter said that Wingate just does this sort of thing in intriguing cases, but I was convinced that there was something more meaningful and, in fact, I later heard rumors from the gay community that an unknown, older African-American cross-dresser that resembled Judge Wingate in many respects was seen at the gay club next to the federal courthouse shortly after my trial concluded.

It honestly would not surprise me if Wingate was a latent homosexual and cross-dresser. Wingate, in my opinion, certainly fits the stereotype of a self-hating, internalized homophobic homosexual, and his unusual inquiries into the relationships that I shared with other gay men did nothing to assuage my concerns. And as the trial continued Wingate would repeat his unusual homosexual interests.

I later learned that Wingate had an unnatural predilection for masculine, tomboyish women. This made total sense to me. His deceased wife, Turner Arnita Wingate, was not only known as the "handyman" of the marriage, but was a star athlete in many men-dominated sports. So while it may have been nearly impossible for Wingate to secretly satiate his homosexual desires, he could no doubt quench his thirst for men by targeting manly women.

Once Wingate fulfilled his gay curiosity surrounding Cole and I's friendship, Cole was excused from the witness stand and left the courtroom. It was the last time I ever saw him.

The government next called my probation officer, William Jay Simpson. Simpson can only be described as a Mississippi redneck with a mediocre education. But let me be the first to say that there is nothing more dangerous in the South than a redneck with some "book learning." This was Jay Simpson. However, in all fairness to him, I've always felt that Simpson made more efforts than most to be fair, and that respect holds true to this day, at least in comparison to most of his coworkers.

Tanner first had Simpson describe how it came to be that he filed the petition to revoke my probation based off my arrest in Covington County.

Simpson was unable to provide any firsthand knowledge about my arrest other than the police report and written statement provided to him by Detective Pamela Wade Smith at the Covington County Sheriff's Department. And Simpson's recitation of these reports and statements was nothing new to us. Tanner was going to wait until Ethan and Colton testified to further prove that allegation.

Tanner next moved to the photograph that was found on my iPhone which showed me on Bourbon Street in New Orleans, Louisiana. Simpson testified that this photo was found on my iPhone and that they took the phone and "used a program off the Internet" which provided them a date and time stamp for when the picture was taken and the latitude and longitude coordinates for where the picture was taken. However, Simpson could not remember what the name of the Internet program was that allegedly provided him this information.

At this point, Jupiter objected to Simpson providing what was essentially expert testimony that he was not qualified in providing and the government conceded that they did not have the proof to support a violation on this allegation. Score one for me.

Jupiter next had an opportunity to cross-examine Simpson and he began with questions that established the fact that Sheriff Pace and other members of the Warren County Sheriff's Department contacted Simpson and the Chief U.S. Probation Officer after my book was published in an effort to harass me. It was after these phone calls were made that Simpson and Chris Counts came to my house to conduct a search in an effort to determine the identity of Deep Six.

Jupiter then moved to establishing the fact that pursuant to the search neither Simpson, Counts, or the FBI were able to locate any information on my computers or cell phone that indicated I'd been harassing or threatening anyone, much less Ethan.

> **JUPITER:** So you found no text messages where Mr. Atwood was harassing young boys?
> **SIMPSON:** Correct.
> **JUPITER:** And they got Ethan's phone from Rankin County. And Colton's phone from Covington County. The phones of the complainants?
> **SIMPSON:** Yes.
> **JUPITER:** And the FBI did a thorough search of everyone's phones?
> **SIMPSON:** Yes.
> **JUPITER:** And were any threatening or harassing text messages or communications ever found?
> **SIMPSON:** Not to my knowledge.

Jupiter then directed Simpson's attention to the dozen short text messages that did occur between Ethan and me when I told him that I wasn't interested in pursuing any type of relationship with him.

> **JUPITER:** And these are the text messages that go on between Ethan and Mr. Atwood?
> **SIMPSON:** They are.
> **JUPITER:** And, once again, you don't have anything—there's nothing in there that indicates that Mr. Atwood had any threatening communications with Ethan?

SIMPSON: There does not appear to be anything threatening.

JUPITER: In fact, doesn't Ethan refer to Mr. Atwood as his "babe" or "baby?"

SIMPSON: Yes.

JUPITER: And going back to the first statement that Colton Kendrick gave to the Covington County Sheriff, doesn't he state that he and Mr. Atwood never had sex?

SIMPSON: It indicates that they did not engage in sex.

JUPITER: Thank you.

After Simpson finished his testimony about the Covington County case he was allowed to be excused but was able to remain in the courtroom for the rest of the testimony. Tanner eventually called Ethan to the stand as a witness to help float their floundering case.

Tanner quickly moved through a list of questions that established, according to Ethan, that he and I met on a gay app for iPhones called Grindr. This was followed by an extremely complicated, and clearly fabricated narrative in which Ethan tried to back off his original story that I'd threatened him, extorted him into having sex, and then raped him. But no matter how hard he tried, he was never able to make sense or sound believable.

Throughout Ethan's initial testimony there was no doubt that he had been coached and was attempting to position himself so as to appear mentally ill and unstable, caused, of course, by my alleged actions.

We knew that he and his mother's sole concern was to somehow extort me in order to obtain money. When that didn't work they began attempting to lay the groundwork for a lawsuit. And Ethan's own testimony in court portrayed him as mentally unhinged.

TANNER: Have you had any psychological treatment?

ETHAN ROBINSON: Yes, sir. I had to go to Pine Grove, a place where a bunch of kids that have a lot of problems go. And since I wasn't eating and I was crying all the time, they felt it was best that I go there.

TANNER: And how long did you undergo psychological treatment there?

ETHAN ROBINSON: About one week.

At this point in the trial I realized what a joke and circus this part of the testimony had become. The government was completely avoiding the actual physical and forensic evidence which unequivocally proved that everything Ethan was saying was a complete lie.

Cell phone records do not lie. FBI forensic searches do not lie. Surveillance video does not lie. But Ethan Robinson does. And his entire motivation was money, and although I was having to sit in my chair and maintain a polite composure, the wrath of anger I felt at his charade was reaching its boiling point. However, I knew that my chance to prove Ethan a psychotic liar was soon to come.

Tanner only spent a few more questions trying to tie up loose strings, but he knew that the more Ethan talked, the worse the case looked. It was clear that by the end of Tanner's direct examination he'd regretted ever putting Ethan on the stand.

By the time Tanner ended his convoluted questioning of Ethan, Jupiter was chomping at the bit to tear Ethan and his credibility apart.

> **JUPITER:** Ethan, my name is Omodare Jupiter. Do you remember me or my investigator coming and trying to speak to you about this incident?
>
> **ETHAN ROBINSON:** Yes, sir.
>
> **JUPITER:** And you refused to speak to me or my investigator? Right?
>
> **ETHAN ROBINSON:** You talked to my mom.
>
> **JUPITER:** Okay. But your mother refused to let you speak to us?
>
> **ETHAN ROBINSON:** I don't know.

These lines of questioning were asked to clearly show that Ethan and his mother, Cassandra Welker, were attempting to hide their real reasons for pursuing these charges. Jupiter and his investigator wanted to talk to them about their attempts to extort money from me, but they couldn't deal with having their plan exposed. So they refused to cooperate.

Jupiter next moved to prove that Ethan was portraying himself on the gay dating apps and websites as being nineteen-years-old.

> **JUPITER:** As you mentioned before, this gay dating app, Grindr, you have to be over 18 to legally use it. Correct?

>**ETHAN ROBINSON:** Yes.
>
>**JUPITER:** And you were portraying yourself as being over 18. Correct?
>
>**ETHAN ROBINSON:** Yes.
>
>**JUPITER:** And the guys that you were meeting on Grindr and having sex with, you actually told them that you were 19. Right?
>
>**ETHAN ROBINSON:** I think I told them 18, but I could have been telling them 19.

This line of questioning was necessary in order to satisfy one of the requirements of the Mississippi enticement of a minor law. Under that law, one of the elements that needed to be met was showing that I'd "knowingly" enticed someone under the age of eighteen. One of the defenses to that specific crime was a complainant, such as Ethan and Colton, who was portraying himself as being over eighteen. And Ethan was clearly doing that. Score another for me.

Jupiter's next questions to Ethan were meant to establish the sexual promiscuity with which Ethan was conducting himself on Grindr.

>**JUPITER:** You wanted people to believe you were over 18. And actually, you wanted to meet people over 18 for sex?
>
>**ETHAN ROBINSON:** Yeah, I guess so.
>
>**JUPITER:** So you were meeting multiple people.
>
>**ETHAN ROBINSON:** I was dating girls and I was dating guys.
>
>**JUPITER:** How many people have you sent your nude pictures to?
>
>**ETHAN ROBINSON:** I don't know.
>
>**JUPITER:** Ten?
>
>**ETHAN ROBINSON:** Yeah, probably.
>
>**JUPITER:** More than ten?
>
>**ETHAN ROBINSON:** I honestly don't know. I don't keep up with how many people I sent my nude pictures to.

After Jupiter finished establishing that Ethan was dating multiple people, some at the same time, he moved on to Ethan's relationship with Colton.

JUPITER: You met Colton Kendrick in June of 2011 and started dating then?

ETHAN ROBINSON: Yeah, we did.

JUPITER: But you weren't the only person that Colton was dating at the time? Correct?

ETHAN ROBINSON: Yeah.

JUPITER: And Colton was interested in older men. Wasn't he?

ETHAN ROBINSON: Yeah.

JUPITER: And this made you jealous?

ETHAN ROBINSON: Probably.

JUPITER: And if Colton wanted to have sex with someone else you were determined to stop that. Correct?

ETHAN ROBINSON: No.

JUPITER: But isn't that the real reason you went to Colton's house that night?

ETHAN ROBINSON: No. I just didn't want him going with David.

JUPITER: But it made you mad that Colton was with someone else.

ETHAN ROBINSON: Yeah. It would make anybody mad, definitely, if you're dating someone.

This concluded Jupiter's cross-examination of Ethan and when the government had no more questions either, Ethan was allowed to leave the witness stand.

This should have concluded the government's case. Ethan had destroyed himself, his credibility, and the monetary-inspired machinations of his mother, but Carlos Tanner decided to double down and put Colton on the stand next.

We'd expected Colton to testify, and both Jupiter and I had prepared numerous questions designed not so much to embarrass him, but only to establish that we'd never had sex, never communicated, and never knew each other prior to that night.

The government began Colton's testimony by having him recite the version of events with which he wanted everyone to believe had really occurred. Tanner then moved to establish early on that Colton was talking to, trading pictures with, and meeting multiple other gay men all at the same time that he was talking to Ethan.

One of the most salient points that Tanner made early on was the fact that Colton's gay lifestyle was very deeply hidden from his parents. It was the first time that I truly felt sorry for him and the problems that the jealous Ethan Robinson had caused not just me, but him, too.

The last unintended point that Tanner was able to elicit from his witness was Colton's statement that since the incident with Ethan he was not as "promiscuous" as he was before. Tanner shrugged his shoulders and passed the witness to Jupiter.

Because I felt so much empathy for Colton and what he had been through because of Ethan's actions that night, I'd specifically asked Jupiter not to press Colton during the testimony, but simply try to elicit his answers in the most respectful way possible. Jupiter agreed with this decision and moved forward in asking his questions in a very respectful manner.

Jupiter was quickly able to get Colton to admit that when first asked by Detective Pamela Wade Smith whether we'd had sex, that he'd vehemently denied us doing so. Colton also admitted that Detective Smith was not happy with his answer, didn't believe him, and became more aggressive in her interrogation.

Detective Smith had apparently then gotten Colton's parents involved in the interrogation and, under pressure, he changed his story and told everyone what they apparently wanted to hear.

Jupiter then had to establish that Colton was trading pictures of himself with numerous other gay men, including John Gillespie, the dentist and Air Force Reserve officer in Jackson whom was apparently having sex with Colton when he was as young as fourteen years old.

> **JUPITER:** And you had tons of nude pictures on your phone, didn't you?
> **COLTON:** Yes.
> **JUPITER:** Nude photographs of older adult men. Correct?
> **COLTON:** Yes.
> **JUPITER:** And John Gillespie, the doctor in Jackson, he sent you shirtless and nude pictures of himself?
> **COLTON:** Yeah, probably.

My attorney then moved to questioning Colton more in-depth about why he changed his story when Detective Smith tightened the screws on him during their interview.

> **JUPITER:** You wanted to keep all this from your parents, didn't you?
> **COLTON:** Yes.
> **JUPITER:** And when David was arrested that night there was no way that you could keep this secret from them any further. Correct?
> **COLTON:** Yes.
> **JUPITER:** But you knew that this secret world that you'd been hiding from your parents was all going to get brought out. Right?
> **COLTON:** Right.
> **JUPITER:** In public and at least to your parents. Correct?
> **COLTON:** Yeah.
> **JUPITER:** And you knew they were going to find hundreds of pictures of older gay men on your phone. And they were going to find where you were talking and having sex with other older men. Correct?
> **COLTON:** Yes.
> **JUPITER:** So you decided it would be easier to explain your secret world—your secret life—to your parents if you made it look like David pressured you to have sex. Isn't that the real reason why you changed your statement? Correct?
> **COLTON:** I don't think so.

After establishing the underlying real reason for why Colton had changed his story—which in a way Jupiter and I understood—Jupiter moved on to establishing the reason why Ethan and Colton were fighting on the night of my arrest.

> **JUPITER:** The two of you were upset at each other. And Ethan thought that you were cheating on him with other guys? Correct?
> **COLTON:** Yes. Ethan did think I was cheating on him.
> **JUPITER:** Okay. And were you cheating on Ethan?
> **COLTON:** I had before. Yes.

At this point both Jupiter and I felt that we'd solidified the major points that we needed to make and he ceased his cross-examination of Colton. However, both Colton and his mother, along with Ethan and his mother, remained in the courtroom for the rest of the proceedings.

The government had no other witnesses and they rested their case. Because we'd gone nearly all day, Judge Wingate, who'd been suspiciously silent throughout Ethan's and Colton's testimony, released everyone and decided to reconvene the hearing the following day.

Before the U.S. Marshals removed me from the court, Jupiter told me not to worry that our turn was next and we had a good chance of demolishing the government's case.

CHAPTER TWELVE

By the time my revocation hearing reconvened the following morning on February 8, 2013, I felt confident that Jupiter and I could refute the government's points on all the issues.

We began by calling to the witness stand a friend of mine that lives in a house next door to my mother's. I'll call this friend Demarcus Donaldson. Demarcus had lived in the same neighborhood as my mother and stepfather for several years and he and I had become good friends since my release from prison in 2010. We didn't see each other everyday, but it was close.

Jupiter called Demarcus to the stand for the sole purpose of showing that I never moved out of my mother's house and into Roger's, and that I was seen at my house during the May 2011 to August 2011 time frame.

Demarcus began his testimony by informing Judge Wingate that he regularly saw me "walking my dog and mowing the grass," and passed by my house every day. He was very clear with Wingate, and everyone else in the courtroom, that throughout the summer there were hardly more than two or three days that he wouldn't see me at my house.

When the government had their opportunity to cross-examine Demarcus, Tanner concentrated mostly on trying to establish that Demarcus didn't know me very well.

TANNER: How well do you know Mr. Atwood?
DEMARCUS: I know him. I know his family. I don't know his birthday, though, or his social security number.

TANNER: Do you know his phone number?

DEMARCUS: I have it. But I don't know it.

TANNER: When you two first met, did you become fast friends or just know each other casually?

DEMARCUS: Casually.

TANNER: Did you and Mr. Atwood ever hang out?

DEMARCUS: I think we have once or twice.

At this point Wingate broke in with another gay-themed, inquisitive question of his.

WINGATE: What did you two do when you were together?

DEMARCUS: I think we were going to a restaurant together with some other friends.

WINGATE: Okay. Go ahead.

Tanner, following Wingate's sexually-themed interests, then attempted to determine whether Demarcus and I had ever had sex or any other relations that might be used to discredit his testimony.

TANNER: Have you ever been inside Mr. Atwood's house? His bedroom?

DEMARCUS: No sir.

Without being able to get Demarcus to commit to anything scandalous, or able to provide Wingate any further fodder for his later fantasies, Tanner closed his questioning.

We next called my friend Seth Lusk to the stand to testify. Seth and I had dated briefly before Patrick Bryant and I rekindled our relationship, but even though we'd broken up, we remained close friends.

After establishing the background of our friendship, Jupiter launched right to the heart of the matter.

JUPITER: I want to direct your attention to the time period between May and August 2011. Were you in communication with David during that time?

SETH: Yes.

JUPITER: And you were dating and seeing each other regularly?

SETH: Yes.

JUPITER: And where did David live during this time period?

SETH: At his mother's house in Vicksburg.

JUPITER: And how would you know that?

SETH: Because I went there to pick him up almost every day.

The next part of our strategy was getting Seth to provide some background on the friendship with Roger Cole and the group of people that we hung out with.

JUPITER: Do you know Roger Cole, and if so, how do you know him?

SETH: Well, through the gay bar. And through friends. We all kind of hang out together. A group of us.

JUPITER: In May through August 2011, did you ever go to Roger's with David?

SETH: Yes. Once or twice.

JUPITER: Is your relationship with David such that if he moved from Vicksburg to Roger's house, or moved in with Roger, that you'd know about it?

SETH: Definitely. I would have known, yeah.

JUPITER: Did David ever tell you he was moving in with Roger Cole?

SETH: No. Never.

At this point Jupiter and I felt that we'd clearly established a baseline for the testimony and that our point had been gotten across to Wingate clearly. So Jupiter ceased his direct-examination and Tanner was given an opportunity to cross Seth.

Tanner spent his first ten minutes on cross questioning Seth about his employment and educational history before ever getting to a substantial question concerning the purpose for which we were in court that day.

TANNER: On a weekly basis, how often did you see Mr. Atwood?

SETH: Almost every day. Certainly on the weekends.

Without getting what he was looking for in this line of questioning, Tanner then moved to trying to get Seth to admit that there were times when he had no idea where I was.

>**TANNER:** On those times that you didn't see him, you didn't know where he was unless he told you somewhere. Right?
>**SETH:** When I talked to him on the phone he would tell me. And I am pretty good at telling when people are lying to me about things. So there were usually things that he would say that would tell me that he was at his mother's house.

This pretty much concluded Tanner's questioning of Seth, but before he could finish I could see the salivating look on Wingate's face as he prepared to launch question after question at Seth about all aspects of our private, sexual lives.

>**WINGATE:** What kind of personal belongings would the defendant have when you saw him?
>**SETH:** I mean, I don't know really what all he had along the lines of personal belongings.
>**WINGATE:** And with regard to where he slept at night, and you said you would talk at night. What did you talk about?
>**SETH:** Uh. Just about life. How he was doing. What I was doing. Uh. That's all I can think of.
>**WINGATE:** So you wouldn't have any idea if he was sleeping with someone else?
>**SETH:** Uh. I think I would know that.

During these weird and unnerving questions, the only thing I could do was look back and forth between Wingate, Jupiter, and Seth and marvel at the obvious unnatural homosexual curiosity that Wingate was fixated on.

It was at this point that I realized that when the witnesses were talking about the pertinent testimony, Wingate would slip back in his chair and stare at the ceiling. But when something particularly gay was being discussed, Wingate leaned forward toward the witness, wrote on paper everything being said, and continually licked his lips as a lion would after a particularly satisfying kill.

My mother, Joan, was the next witness that we called to testify, and, we hoped her testimony would be the final clincher.

After establishing the family dynamics of our home in Vicksburg, and describing the layout of the house itself, Jupiter had my mother testify about my numerous attempts to obtain employment, my attending the truck-driving school and Jay Simpson's eventual obstruction tactics when it came to me getting permission to accept a job.

One of the first things that my mother tried to convey to Judge Wingate was the utter failure of Simpson and U.S. Probation to provide me any assistance whatsoever in helping me reintegrate into society upon my release from prison.

The conversation then turned to Roger Cole. My mother patiently explained to Wingate, while he contentedly stared off into space, that because I was driving primarily my motorcycle—keep in mind gasoline was upwards of four dollars a gallon during this time period—back and forth to the truck-driving school everyday, that it was sometimes necessary for me to stay with Cole due to inclement weather.

The questioning then moved to whether or not I'd ever actually moved in with Roger, or stayed with him a significantly longer time than fourteen days, non-consecutively, over four months.

> **JUPITER:** Did you ever understand David to believe that he was going to move in with Roger?
>
> **JOAN:** No. Never.
>
> **JUPITER:** Did David ever transport anything to Roger's house?
>
> **JOAN:** No. Not that I am aware of. No.
>
> **JUPITER:** When David spent the night at Roger's house, would he always return to your house the next day?
>
> **JOAN:** Yes.

We felt these lines of questions buttressed our argument in defense of the allegation that I'd moved into Roger's residence. After a few more perfunctory questions, Jupiter ended his direct-examination and Tanner was allowed to ask his questions.

Tanner began his questioning by attempting to establish that my mother was not at home during most of the day because of her job. However, my mother works a lot from home and Tanner was unable to advance any points in that regard. He next tried to commit my mother to a specific number for how many times I'd actually stayed at Roger's house in that four month period.

>**TANNER:** How many times was your son at Roger Cole's house during this whole period?
>**JOAN:** Maybe seven times during that whole time.
>**TANNER:** And what was your intention for him staying at Cole's house during that period?
>**JOAN:** Well, my intention was for him to have a safe place to stay if it was bad weather so he wouldn't have to drive back home on the motorcycle the hour or so from the school back to our house in Vicksburg.

Wingate could clearly see at this point that Tanner was stuttering and his questioning was foundering in relevance. So, in order to allow Tanner—who had previously been Wingate's law clerk and likely secret, homosexual lover—an opportunity to collect his thoughts and reformulate his strategy, Wingate called a recess and reconvened court later that afternoon.

After the recess Tanner again began questioning my mother about the exact same topics he'd been covering before we took the break. Jupiter objected to this redundant questioning, but Wingate continued to give his prosecuting protégé paramour much more leeway than he ever gave Jupiter and me.

Tanner's continued line of questioning, of which we'd previously spent half the morning covering, soon wrapped up, but not before he attempted to get my mother to provide the government and Wingate more evidence in which to convict me.

>**TANNER:** Between May 2011 and August 2011, did you ever allow your son to bring any 16-year-old boys to your home?
>**JOAN:** No. Never.
>**TANNER:** Did he ever ask you?
>**JOAN:** Absolutely not.

This concluded Tanner's frivolous questioning and Jupiter was given an opportunity to reexamine my mother and highlight the major pertinent parts of her testimony.

>**JUPITER:** When you left in the morning to go to work,

would you see David in bed before you left?

JOAN: Yes. Always.

JUPITER: And before you went to bed at night would you always know that David was in the house? In his room?

JOAN: Yes.

Jupiter's redirect was short, but as he wrapped up his questioning I could see Wingate chomping at his prosthetic dentures, waiting for his opportunity to portray the prosecutor that he always has been.

WINGATE: How much do you know about your son's social (read: gay) life?

JOAN: I know some.

WINGATE: Do you know his friends?

JOAN: Most of them.

WINGATE: His gay friends?

JOAN: I knew Josh (Chamblee) and Seth.

WINGATE: Did you ever travel with them and your son?

JOAN: We'd go out to eat. But no, we never traveled anywhere together.

WINGATE: Did your son ever invite you to the gay club?

JOAN: He did.

WINGATE: Did you go?

JOAN: No.

WINGATE: Why didn't you go to the gay bar?

JOAN: Because I have two other children and they are very involved and active in school and the community, and I was usually either with them or needing to sleep. I couldn't stay out at a club until late at night.

WINGATE: Hmmm.

JOAN: I did go to the gay club with David one time during the day.

WINGATE: And what did you do when you went in there?

JOAN: Well, it was during the day. It wasn't open. I think we just went by there for David to talk to a friend of his.

WINGATE: Did you ever go out to eat with any of these friends of your son's from the club?

JOAN: I think we may have.

WINGATE: Where did you go?

JOAN: Shapley's. (A very nice steak restaurant in Jackson; probably more than Wingate could afford).

WINGATE: Who paid?

JOAN: I did.

WINGATE: Let me turn to something else. Your son has been convicted of a felony. I guess you know that?

JOAN: Yes.

WINGATE: What do you think of that? Do you think he was guilty?

JOAN: Well, on the crime he was convicted of, I mean, it happens all the time. That particular thing happens everyday. But no one else is getting prosecuted for it or put in jail for years.

WINGATE: So you think it was unfair?

JOAN: In a way I do. David was 19 and Zach was 16. And I see it happening all the time and the government never prosecutes those people.

WINGATE: So you think that we are unfairly picking on your son?

JOAN: In a way, yes I do. Absolutely.

WINGATE: And do you have any particular reason why you think he was picked on?

JOAN: Well, obviously you know he has a feud with the sheriff's department, the Warren County people.

WINGATE: But why would they target him?

JOAN: Because of some of the negative things that he has exposed about their corruption.

WINGATE: So you don't think your son has been treated fairly by the criminal justice system?

JOAN: No. My honest opinion is probably no.

WINGATE: Let me switch back to the gay club. How long has your son been going there?

JOAN: Uh. I don't know. (Quizzical looks of disbelief appear on my mother's face).

WINGATE: You said earlier that you never had the opportunity to experience the atmosphere of the club at peak hours? (I believe Wingate was at this point already planning his rendezvous at the gay club as a cross-dresser so he could experience the "atmosphere" of the club himself).

JOAN: No, I didn't.

WINGATE: So you don't know if it is a bawdy club where danger is always lurking around?

JOAN: Uh. No. David never mentioned anything like that.

WINGATE: So do you think he keeps secrets from you?

JOAN: Well, yeah. But I had my own private secrets, too.

WINGATE: And that's what I wanted to know. (I was left shaking my head at the sick, disgusting, demented fuck that is Judge Henry T. Wingate).

Wingate's questioning of my mother took longer than it had both Jupiter and Tanner's questioning combined. Very few of the judge's questions revolved around actual, pertinent issues pertaining to why we were in court. Instead, I believe Wingate was only satisfying his sick fantasies that revolve around anything gay.

As my mother left the witness stand, I remember Wingate dabbing his mouth with a small handkerchief, no doubt, again, relishing a fresh kill.

The next witness we called was my best friend, Charlie Smith, a guy that I'd been friends with for several years and who lived next door to Roger. Charlie is one of the most optimistic, positive people that I've ever known, despite him being flamboyantly gay in the best way possible. I knew Wingate would fall in love when he met Charlie.

Jupiter began his questions by establishing that Charlie was a nurse, lived next to Roger, and was friends with both he and I.

JUPITER: During the May to August 2011 time period, how often would you talk to David?

CHARLIE: Oh, goodness. Nearly every day. (Said with a distinct gay lisp).

JUPITER: To your knowledge, did David ever move in with Roger?

CHARLIE: Oh lord no. Never.

JUPITER: But he did stay there a few nights?

CHARLIE: Yes. A few times. But he also has spent the night with me a few times, too.

JUPITER: So he never stayed more than a few times with

Roger?
CHARLIE: No. He did not.

Tanner's first questions towards Charlie inevitably led back to the fucking gay club next door to Wingate's courtroom.

TANNER: Did you meet David at the gay club here in downtown?
CHARLIE: Yes, sir.

I doubt that a gay club had ever had such a prominent role in a court proceeding the further the revocation hearing continued. But what Tanner lacked in details, Wingate was determined to make up for.

From the moment Charlie walked into the room and took his seat in the witness chair next to Wingate's dais (throne), I saw love-at-first-sight in Wingate's eyes. And throughout Tanner's cross, Wingate couldn't take his beastly eyes off my best friend.

Tanner only had a few questions, and when he had asked his last, Jupiter and I braced ourselves for the gay questions to begin from Wingate, and he didn't disappoint with the first question he asked.

WINGATE: Did you ever date the defendant?
CHARLIE: Sir?
WINGATE: Did you and the defendant ever date?
CHARLIE: Ha ha. Oh, goodness me. Heaven's no.
WINGATE: So what is your relationship with the defendant right now? (Read: Are you single? I'm interested.)
CHARLIE: Just friends.
WINGATE: You said the defendant spent the night at your house. What were the reasons he stayed with you?
CHARLIE: Oh. We'd just be getting up early in the morning to go fishing. (Despite being flamboyantly gay, Charlie is from South Louisiana and one of the best fisherman I've ever seen.)
WINGATE: Every time he spent the night at your house was to go fishing?
CHARLIE: Well, one time we went tubing.
WINGATE: Tubing? What is that?
CHARLIE: Yes, sir. Down the Bogue Chitto River on an

inner tube.

WINGATE: That's kind of dangerous isn't it?

CHARLIE: Yes, sir. But I'm from down in Louisiana and we used to do it all the time. I lived five minutes from the tubing hole and that's what I like doing.

(Everyone in the courtroom is laughing and shaking their heads)

WINGATE: Can you swim?

CHARLIE: Yes, your majesty. (I swear on a stack of Bibles that Charlie called Judge Wingate "Your Majesty." He meant to say, "Yes, Your Honor," but it came out majesty. This only solidified Wingate's love for Charlie even more.)

WINGATE: Can the defendant swim? (He was wishing he could throw me in the river and drown me.)

CHARLIE: Oh yes. He's a good swimmer.

WINGATE: Was that the only time you have been tubing?

CHARLIE: Well, we've actually gone on a boat trip together, and that was fun. When I say "boat trip" I really mean that we got the boat and took it down the Pearl River, which, actually, it wasn't that fun because we had to carry the boat most of that trip because the water was so dadgum shallow. (More laughs.)

WINGATE: Let me turn your attention to the gay bar. Did you go there with the defendant?

CHARLIE: Uhh Hmmm. (Indicating yes.) But I don't hang out at the club very much.

WINGATE: Why not?

CHARLIE: Well, I'm getting too old for all that mess.

WINGATE: Okay, well last question for your testimony. Have you ever been convicted of a felony? (Read: I need to know that I'm not going to try and fuck a criminal.)

CHARLIE: Oh heavens no.

Neither Jupiter or Tanner had any follow-up questions and Charlie was allowed to leave the witness stand. But before he could do so, I was almost positive I saw Wingate wink at him and pass him his phone number on a piece of paper. As Charlie walked by me sitting at the defense table I told him thank you, but we then turned our attention to the last witness for the day, Sheriff Martin Pace.

We'd called Sheriff Pace to testify about my illegal arrest for trespassing at the Miss Mississippi Pageant on July 2, 2011. My false arrest lawsuit against the sheriff and the police department was slowly working its way through the court system and the City of Vicksburg had made no efforts to actually prosecute me on the charge itself, but this didn't stop U.S. Probation and the government from trying to have my probation violated for what was clearly First Amendment-protected free speech conduct.

Jupiter quickly established that Sheriff Pace was running for reelection in July 2011 and that he was immediately notified by his deputies and the police officers when they became aware of me and my people distributing my political leaflets.

> **JUPITER:** And at this time you were made aware of Mr. Atwood's book?
>
> **SHERIFF PACE:** I don't remember if I knew about the book before I saw the fliers or whether the fliers made me aware of the book.
>
> **JUPITER:** Did you order Mr. Atwood's arrest for trespassing?
>
> **SHERIFF PACE:** No, I did not. The only comments that I made to my deputies was for them not to be involved and to only let the Vicksburg Police handle the situation. (This testimony was done solely to try and limit Sheriff Pace's personal liability in the false arrest lawsuit.)
>
> **JUPITER:** But your deputies actually participated in the arrest of Mr. Atwood.
>
> **SHERIFF PACE:** I found out about that after the fact, and I scolded them for that. (Apparently, Sheriff Pace thinks his deputies are inhuman animals worthy of no more than a firm "scolding." I'd have to agree with this assessment.)

Watching Sheriff Pace and Jupiter do a little judicial sparring back and forth was entertaining. Sheriff Pace knew that his deputies and the Vicksburg Police had royally screwed up and that anything he said could later be used against him in the false arrest lawsuit, but I seriously did not ever consider that Sheriff Pace would attempt to lay the blame entirely on the shoulders of the Vicksburg Police. But by admitting that he warned his deputies not to be involved in my illegal arrest, and despite being warned by their superior, they did so anyway, he gave me all the ammunition I needed to prove that the deputies that arrested me were acting without authority. It was the best information I'd heard all day.

This is entirely indicative of the problem with Sheriff Martin Pace and the Warren County Sheriff's Department. His deputies have no respect for him, the office that he holds, or the authority granted to him under that office.

I've often told people—and certainly have told Sheriff Pace several times to his face—that he is a very likeable guy. He's a great politician. He seems to be a sincere person to one's face. He would have to be to keep getting elected term after term despite the clear corruption in the department.

The problem, however, with the Warren County Sheriff's Department is that Sheriff Pace has no control over his deputies. They literally run wild, and when they screw up—sometimes deliberately and sometimes not—they know that they will not face punishment. I don't know if this is because Sheriff Pace is a weak and ineffective leader, or if he is just by nature incapable of being an able administrator.

During his testimony he made it clear that despite warning his deputies not to become involved in my arrest, they ignored him and did so anyway. What further proof does one need that his deputies do not respect him or the office he holds?

The last thing that Jupiter needed to do was tie Sheriff Pace to Sheriff Ben Ford in Covington County. We'd known through documents that we'd obtained from Covington County that Sheriff Pace had continually been in contact with Sheriff Ford about my case up until Ford was ignominiously kicked from office. And, of course, I'd known about their conversations because Sheriff Ford had told me that he had arrested me because Sheriff Pace had wanted him to.

> **JUPITER:** Were you in communication with Sheriff Ford with regard to charges being brought against Mr. Atwood?
> **SHERIFF PACE:** No, sir.

At this point Jupiter picked up the records proving Sheriff Pace a liar and requested to be granted permission to approach the witness with the documents. Sheriff Pace then quickly changed his story.

> **SHERIFF PACE:** Well, I may have talked to him. I don't recall.
>
> **JUPITER:** Okay. Well did you communicate with anyone to encourage having charges brought against Mr. Atwood?
>
> **SHERIFF PACE:** I don't remember.
>
> **JUPITER:** So when you say you don't remember, you're saying that maybe you did?
>
> **SHERIFF PACE:** I mean, maybe. If I was asked to provide background on the defendant I'm sure I would have.
>
> **JUPITER:** Your Honor, I'm done with this witness.

Besides Charlie, Sheriff Pace had been the best witness of the day. Not only had we proven that his deputies acted without authority when they arrested me for trespassing, but we'd also proven that Sheriff Pace had encouraged Sheriff Ford to arrest me on the false charges in Covington County and then tried to lie about it. It was confirmation of a fact I'd known the whole time.

To finish our rebuttal case the last witness we called to testify was my probation officer, Jay Simpson. Even though he had testified earlier, we needed him to clarify a few matters that had been left to speculation during the government's case.

Covington County had taken my iPhone when they arrested me in August 2011 and turned it over to the FBI and Simpson for a forensic analysis. We wanted to make absolutely sure that Judge Wingate knew that there was not any evidence whatsoever on my phone that was inappropriate, illegal, or even questionable.

> **JUPITER:** The pictures that you found on Mr. Atwood's phone, they were all clothed pictures. Correct?
>
> **SIMPSON:** Correct.
>
> **JUPITER:** But on the phone of Colton Kendrick the examiner found a lot of nude photographs of older men. Correct?
>
> **SIMPSON:** Correct.
>
> **JUPITER:** And even though Ethan Robinson continually said that Mr. Atwood threatened him, harassed him, and coerced him into having sex through text messages on his iPhone, you never found any harassing texts on Mr. Atwood's phone. Correct?

SIMPSON: That is correct.

JUPITER: So again. You got all three cell phones. Two from Colton and Ethan, and then Mr. Atwood's. Yes?

SIMPSON: Yes.

JUPITER: And you found nothing on any of the phones that indicated Mr. Atwood was threatening or harassing either minors. Correct?

SIMPSON: Nothing like that was found.

JUPITER: Thank you. I have no further questions Your Honor.

Tanner was then again given an opportunity to question Simpson, but rather than concentrate on anything to do with the Covington County case—which the government knew they'd already lost—Tanner decided his main line of questioning would be about the failure to register as a sex offender violation, and herein lies the most important crux of the case.

TANNER: Officer Simpson, are you aware of the reporting requirements of the Mississippi sex offender registration laws?

SIMPSON: Yes.

TANNER: In terms of residency requirements, in what circumstances must a sex offender update his residency information?

SIMPSON: They must register either temporary or permanent residences.

TANNER: And under Mississippi law, how many days does a defendant have to stay at a residence for it to be considered a temporary residence?

SIMPSON: According to Mississippi statute 45-33-23(h) an offender has to register any address where he stays fourteen or more days in the aggregate during any calendar year and which is not his permanent residence.

TANNER: And the testimony from Roger Cole was that Mr. Atwood stayed with him fourteen times in the relevant time period?

SIMPSON: Yes.

JUPITER: Objection Your Honor! Cole could not state with specificity exactly how many times. He only guessed.

TANNER: I'll withdraw the question.

This was the last witness and the last question of the guilt or innocence phase of the revocation hearing. Wingate had apparently heard enough testimony for the day—no doubt he was anxious about his cross-dressing performance later that night at the gay club—and he continued the trial until the following week. Wingate's impatience to end the day conveyed to me his desperate need to go suck a dick somewhere.

When we returned on February 14, 2013, Valentine's Day, I noticed a sour mood emanating from Wingate's throne. I thought to myself that either Wingate didn't get to suck a dick on Valentine's Day or his weekend activities at the gay club didn't go so well. It did not bode well for my trial.

Both Tanner and Jupiter were given an opportunity to make closing arguments, with Tanner going first. He chose to concentrate his ten minutes of closing almost entirely on the failure to register violation.

TANNER: Your Honor, for proof on this violation the government offered the testimony of Johnny Davis, a U.S. Marshal, and Roger Cole, the owner of the house where Mr. Atwood stayed. The critical part of the testimony was that the defendant stayed at this home for two weeks. That's critical under the 45-33-23(h) statute which states that a person has to register as a temporary address any place he stays fourteen or more times non-consecutively in any given year. And, so Your Honor, the testimony was clear that the defendant did not do so.

Jupiter was then given an opportunity to make his closing arguments, and while I thought he'd done a fairly good job throughout the trial, I felt he could have done much better presenting a closing argument.

JUPITER: The government hasn't proved with precise specificity that Mr. Atwood stayed with Cole fourteen or more times. But I don't think we can really get to that issue because one of the elements of the crime says that the government has to prove that Mr. Atwood was actually going and changing his residence some type of way. And the testimony was clear that he never did that.

At this point Wingate broke into Jupiter's closing argument and interrupted him. Wingate had respectfully remained silent during Tanner's closing, but before Jupiter could get warmed up, Wingate was hurling aggressive questions at him.

WINGATE: What's the evidence that the defendant didn't change his address to Pearl?

JUPITER: Well, the testimony of his mother and his . . .

WINGATE: That testimony can't be reliable. The mother clearly testified she felt her son hadn't been treated fairly by the justice system. So besides her testimony what else do you have that the defendant was actually living with his mother?

JUPITER: Well, his mother testified that he was living there.

WINGATE: No. That's not reliable. Besides that.

JUPITER: None, Your Honor.

WINGATE: So that hurts your case.

JUPITER: Well, first of all, I mean, I can't change the fact that this would be the person who would be in the best position to testify in this area. But the overall testimony, the overall theme that fell in line with the other witnesses' testimony, it was all consistent that David didn't stay at Cole's house fourteen or more times during that time period.

WINGATE: Move on. Do you have any other arguments on other particular violations?

JUPITER: Well, with regard to the trespassing, we filed a motion with this court directing Your Honor to numerous U.S. Supreme Court decisions which have held that it is a First Amendment free speech right to pass out political leaflets on public property.

WINGATE: But what the defendant was doing was slander against Sheriff Pace. Slander is an exception to free speech. Move on to your next argument.

JUPITER: Okay then. Your Honor we have the very serious allegations from Covington County. But the theme of the government's case, of Ethan's and Colton's testimony was that Mr. Atwood harassed them through text messages. U.S. Probation, the FBI have the phones, the records. There were no records found showing these texts. We saw thousands of pictures, of nude pictures on Colton's phone. They got that. There's no credibility to their testimony. It's not reliable. Second, the statute that they charged Mr. Atwood under, it is inapplicable to this case. It only applies to minors under sixteen and child pornography. And we briefed this issue extensively with Your Honor in our motion to dismiss. We submit that the conduct as alleged was not a violation of any valid law and that the government has not proved this violation. Your Honor, for these reasons and the reasons that were enunciated in our motions that we filed some time ago, we'd ask that the court dismiss all of the counts in the petition.

At this point Wingate removed his prosecutor's hat and resumed his role as judge and executioner in my case. His verdict finding me not guilty of the Covington County charges, but guilty on the others is worth quoting in full.

WINGATE: The defendant is before the court on a petition for the revocation of his probation on several allegations of criminal conduct. The first allegation was that the defendant sexually enticed two youths in Covington County. The government attempted to prove this allegation through the testimony of the two youths. If their testimony was true it would be a most serious incident. But the court has too many questions about the minors' conduct at the time of the alleged threats. The court has questions about their subsequent conduct and the court has questions about the numerous graphic photographs on Colton Kendrick's phone which shows that he was not hesitant to maintain a record of new persons or a record of persons with whom he might have had sex. And from what I have been provided I cannot adjudicate the credibility of these two witnesses. Accordingly, since the court cannot determine whether they are believable witnesses, I must find that the defendant is not guilty. The next point is that the defendant trespassed in Vicksburg. Officer Thomas's testimony proves that the defendant violated the perimeter set up by the Vicksburg Police and that he did it willfully. However, if the defendant would have had a ticket to the event he then would have lawfully been on the premises. But Officer Thomas testified that he did not. Therefore, on this particular charge, the court finds the defendant guilty as charged. Finally, as to the third allegation in the petition that the defendant failed to register as a sex offender under Mississippi's temporary residence sex offender registration law, 45-33- 23(h), some preliminaries are quite clear. First, the defendant is required to register as a sex offender. Second, pursuant to the pertinent Mississippi law he was required to register any address where he stayed fourteen or more times, though not consecutively, but in the aggregate in any year. A failure to do so would be a violation of this law. So then, that is the touchstone that guides our inquiry. Roger Cole's testimony here is critical. And the court accepts Cole's testimony as true. Therefore, the court finds the defendant guilty under the appropriate standard of guilt. This is the ruling of the court.

Wingate wanted then to immediately move into the sentencing phase, and in hindsight we should have acquiesced, but Jupiter had not prepared beforehand, so Wingate granted us a month-long continuance.

Attending a trial is a strenuous experience. And it is more so when one is a defendant. When Wingate told me that I was guilty of failing to register as a sex offender at Roger's house, it made me furious because I knew that I'd never moved there and had never stayed there fourteen or more times. It was also extremely maddening that Wingate had found me guilty of what was clearly an exercise of my First Amendment rights at the Miss Mississippi Pageant.

Jupiter's comforting assurances that I'd have another chance on appeal did nothing at that moment to assuage my anger.

For one, Jupiter had the pageant ticket that I'd purchased and used to gain admittance to the pageant that night. Wingate was clear that if I'd had a ticket I'd then be legally on the premises. But Jupiter made no move or effort to correct this egregious mistake.

Second, Jupiter had Detective Thomas's arrest report and it clearly conflicted with the testimony that he had provided in court. But Jupiter completely forgot about Thomas's report and never questioned Thomas about the clear conflicts between his report and his later false, perjured testimony.

Jupiter had no excuses for why he dropped the ball and failed to introduce this vital evidence. But I knew it was clearly just plain incompetence. It crossed my mind to ask Wingate for a new attorney to conduct my sentencing, but I'd have to think about it. In the meantime I was being returned to the county jail to await my sentencing in late March. I'd also given Wingate a new name. From thence forth Wingate would always be known to me as Judge Losegate. And to me, Judge Losegate was clearly a closet homosexual in addition to a serial sex abuser.

CHAPTER THIRTEEN

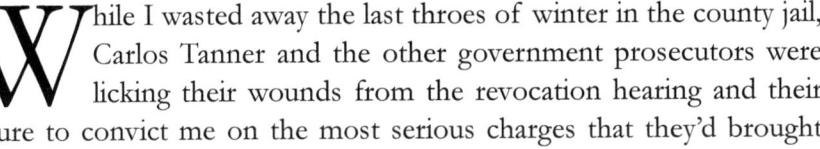

While I wasted away the last throes of winter in the county jail, Carlos Tanner and the other government prosecutors were licking their wounds from the revocation hearing and their failure to convict me on the most serious charges that they'd brought against me. But I was nursing my wounds, too. After all, Wingate had found me guilty of failing to register as a sex offender under Mississippi law. However, when we returned for the sentencing portion of my revocation hearing on March 29, 2013, the government tried a new tactic.

For the entirety of the trial both Ethan's and Colton's mothers had attended the proceedings and heard all of the testimony. And prior to the trial the government never informed us that the mothers might be called to testify. Nonetheless, what began as a sentencing hearing soon turned into another attempt by the government to relitigate a crime that I'd been found not guilty of committing. Tanner wanted to place both mothers under oath to testify about how "victimized" they felt about the whole situation. But the Fifth Amendment and the Double Jeopardy Clause of the United States Constitution prohibits this. Wingate, right or wrong, had already found me not guilty of the exact allegations that the mothers wanted to testify about.

I'd won fair and square and had proven my innocence. I thought to myself, My God, every piece of evidence the government found exonerated me of any wrongdoing. Surely this matter should have been laid to rest upon a finding by the court—no matter how much an idiot he was—that I was not guilty. But the government, once beaten, doesn't give up.

When it came to Ethan's mother, Cassandra Welker, we knew that the only victimization she felt was being unable to cash in on a large chunk of change, much like the extortionist in Michael Jackson's case had done. But with Colton's mother, we genuinely felt empathy. However, it would have to be pointed out to her that not only was no illegal evidence found indicating that I'd done anything wrong, but her son was engaged in some fairly heady sexually promiscuous conduct with a large portion of the central Mississippi gay population over forty years old.

Before we could get to that issue, however, Judge Losegate was forced to deal with an issue concerning the quality of the representation that Jupiter provided to me during the trial.

As mentioned previously, Jupiter totally failed in his obligation to introduce evidence, such as the pageant ticket and Detective Thomas's arrest report, that exonerated me of any illegal conduct.

Jupiter also had made the decision not to introduce my cell phone records, which had location data attached, which, upon review, showed that my cell phone was not in the area of Roger Cole's house anywhere near the fourteen times that they'd alleged during the May 2011 to August 2011 time period.

My cell phone records, which, using the GPS and cell tower information, proved that I'd only stayed overnight at Roger's house approximately seven times total. These records were extremely relevant to answering the question about how many times I stayed at Cole's house. And we had the answer analyzed down to the second. But through Jupiter's incompetence they weren't entered into evidence.

During the month between the time I was found guilty and the start of my sentencing hearing, I'd written Wingate a long letter explaining to him the errors that had been committed during my trial, the evidence that Jupiter had failed to introduce, and the overall lack of confidence I had in Jupiter's future ability to represent me in a competent manner.

When one meets Jupiter face-to-face one is never impressed. Jupiter's overall demeanor and body mannerisms screams night school law graduate. I'd definitely had my doubts about him from the beginning, but by the close of the trial I knew he was just utterly incompetent.

Jupiter was the type of attorney who poses a severe danger to the criminal justice system. He is the stereotypical public defender that gives the rest of the public defender system a bad reputation. But public defending is the highest career competency post obtainable for a person like Jupiter. And the negative impact that has on innocent criminal defendants is frightening. But all I could do was ask Wingate to appoint me a new attorney for the sentencing hearing.

The request for a new attorney was summarily denied by Wingate, though. He also denied any attempt I tried to make to have the evidence proving my innocence introduced. Wingate essentially told me that because Jupiter didn't introduce it when he had the opportunity to during the trial, it wouldn't be introduced now. Too late, so sorry.

This precedent didn't stop Wingate from allowing the government, however, to place both Ethan's and Colton's mother on the stand to testify.

While denying my request to introduce mitigating evidence proving my innocence, Wingate was more than happy to allow the government prosecutors another opportunity to provide more evidence in which to make me look guilty, this notwithstanding the fact that Wingate had already found me not guilty of the Covington County allegations. This, again, was Wingate pushing two self-contradictory positions without the intelligence to realize what an idiot it confirmed him to be.

I'd been told that Judge Wingate was schizophrenic, and I knew how he had screwed over the defendants in the Paul Minor trials, but I never thought that a judge could be so vindictive, hateful, and ignorant so as to allow the government a second opportunity to convict someone of a crime that that person had so recently been found not guilty of committing. But that is exactly what fucking Judge Losegate allowed the government to do—the Constitution be damned.

The first mother that the government called to the stand was Susan Coulter, Colton's mother. Tanner began by trying to establish how Coulter knew me.

> **TANNER:** Do you know Mr. Atwood?
> **COULTER:** No, sir. I only know him since the incident with my son.
> **TANNER:** So what is your knowledge about this incident?
> **COULTER:** I'm only telling you what I've heard since this has happened.

At this point Jupiter did stand up and raise several objections to

Coulter testifying. His first objection was to this being a Double Jeopardy violation. Second, he objected to Coulter testifying because she didn't have any firsthand knowledge about the facts. Finally, Jupiter objected because everything Coulter was testifying to was hearsay. Hearsay is not supposed to be allowed in court trials. But Wingate couldn't be bothered with procedural rules to protect the constitutional rights of an accused.

I still, to this day, don't know what Tanner's intention was with putting Coulter on the witness stand. She testified to absolutely nothing of which she had any personal knowledge. And after a few questions he sat down. As there was nothing that Jupiter could think to question Coulter on, she was allowed to leave the witness stand.

Tanner then placed Cassandra Welker on the stand. Welker was the rabid, money-hungry mother of Ethan Robinson. After I'd been found not guilty of the allegations, she apparently had instituted a public media campaign to put pressure on Wingate to sentence me to a term of imprisonment for which I didn't deserve. Part of this campaign was getting random people to write letters to Wingate asking him to punish me severely for the conduct for which I'd been found not guilty of committing.

> **WINGATE:** Now ma'am. You understand that I found the defendant not guilty of these charges?
> **WELKER:** Yes, sir.
> **WINGATE:** Nevertheless, you submitted multiple letters asking me to take into account that conduct when sentencing the defendant.
> **WELKER:** Yes, sir.
> **WINGATE:** But you've never had any direct conduct with the defendant either?
> **WELKER:** No. I have never had direct conduct with David. I only saw him for the first time in Rankin County at his court hearing. And the only information I have about him came from my son, Ethan.

Jupiter again made some objections about Welker testifying since she had no firsthand knowledge and because everything she was telling the court was something she allegedly heard from her psychotic son or someone else. Welker wasn't a believable witness to begin with, and the fact she was only testifying about information she heard thirdhand solidified that. Nevertheless, Wingate allowed it to be heard.

Welker eventually went into a convoluted tale—told to her by Ethan—that on the night of my arrest Ethan called her after leaving Patrick Bryant's house in Hattiesburg to tell her that I'd kidnapped Colton.

Of course, Ethan hadn't told his mother that he was abusing Colton that night and Colton left the party of his own accord because Ethan had stranded him there without a ride home.

Welker's story continued, though, and she became involved when Ethan told her that I was a sex offender and had kidnapped Colton. She made the choice then to drive to Covington County to meet Ethan and contact the police.

Critical to her testimony was a claim she made on the witness stand that she printed out my picture and information from the sex offender website before driving to Covington County on the night of August 15, 2011.

> **WELKER:** And before I left to go to meet Ethan in Covington County I went on the website and printed off David Atwood's sex offender profile and I took it with me to Covington County. I've had that picture in my purse since that night.
> **WINGATE:** Do you still have it with you?
> **WELKER:** Yes, sir.
> **WINGATE:** Could you get it, please?

Welker then got this print out of my sex offender profile and provides it to Wingate. But after he gets done looking at it (it was actually a pretty good picture of me) he passed it around to both Tanner, Jupiter, and me.

I immediately noticed that the date on the printout was August 17, 2011, two days after Welker says she printed it off the computer. Clearly, Welker was making up lies as she was going along, and this was one crack in the ice. Of course, when asked about this discrepancy, Welker couldn't explain her mistake.

The last thing Jupiter did when questioning Welker, after Tanner and Wingate were finished, was to ask her about her many attempts to extort money from me and my family in lieu of her and Ethan pursuing charges against me. However, Wingate apparently felt that this line of questioning was not relevant and refused to allow Jupiter to obtain an answer.

Basically, what had happened in less than thirty minutes, was that

Wingate had allowed the government, through his former law clerk, Carlos Tanner, to present evidence highly prejudicial to me without an opportunity for either me or Jupiter to refute it, notwithstanding the fact I'd already been found not guilty of these allegations. So much for fairness, or even the *appearance* of fairness.

When in a criminal trial, such as I was in, one of the most important things that the attorneys must do is preserve their objections in the record and make sure that whatever issues are in dispute are clearly introduced and made a part of that record. This is vitally important because once a case is on appeal to the appellate courts, the record is the only evidence that the appellate courts use to resolve the disputes raised in the appeal.

Wingate had been a federal judge for almost thirty years by the time of my trial in 2013, and he knows how vitally important it is to establish a clear record to preserve the issues for appeal, but Wingate is not a fair, competent judge. He's a government prosecutor hiding inside a black robe. He's literally a wolf in sheep's clothing.

Cassandra Welker and her son's attempt to extort my family and me for money, in return for not pursuing a criminal prosecution against me, was critically vital in ascertaining their motives for committing perjury through false testimony and in discrediting their reliability as witnesses. And Wingate knew that. However, he refused to allow us to present any evidence of Welker and Ethan's extortion crimes, and he did it to prevent that issue from being preserved on appeal to the Fifth Circuit.

While denying us an opportunity to present evidence proving my innocence, and utterly destroying whatever credibility Welker and Ethan may of had, Wingate was more than willing to let his (lover?) friend, protégé, and former law clerk, Carlos Tanner, continually present "evidence" throughout the sentencing hearing which was never disclosed to us, never proven to be reliable, and not in the least way relevant to the actual violations that I'd actually been found guilty of committing. The entire sentencing hearing was solely about Cassandra Welker and Ethan Robinson being pissed off because they were unable to use their scams and impoverished background to extort money from my family and me. And despite our best attempts to counter that, Wingate continually denied us the same opportunity that he more than willingly provided to the government.

As I sat through and watched the revocation trial and sentencing, while observing Wingate's behavior, I remembered back to a short passage in this country's Declaration of Independence that our founding father's attributed to the character of King George III. After making a few stylistic changes in my mind I realized that it applied just as equally to Judge Wingate. "*A judge whose character is thus marked by every act which may define a tyrant is unfit to be the arbitrator of a free people.*"

There is no doubt that Wingate poses a threat to every freedom-loving American patriot who believes in the Constitution and its Bill of Rights. Our system of justice, and the fairness inherent therein, is crumbling under the weight of tyrants like Wingate who hate themselves, hate the world, and hate those who are perceived to be better than them.

The genesis of Wingate's neurosis apparently lies primarily in his inability to be the white, Anglo-Saxon, conservative Republican that he's so desperately tried to emulate. The resulting psychosis was exacerbated when Wingate could not obtain his desperately coveted appointment to the Fifth Circuit Court of Appeals. And the by-product of his judicial schizophrenia is a courtroom reign of terror for every unfortunate black defendant who Wingate hates as he hates himself, and for every privileged white that Wingate wishes to become, but knows he can never be. Simply put, Wingate is the tyrant whose character makes him unfit to hold the judicial post that he does.

One is unable to lash out, though, at the injustice and unfairness inherent in a courtroom run by a despot like Wingate, so I had to sit quietly while Tanner strutted for his mentor and Jupiter ineffectually sat idle.

I did, though, remember again a famous quote from another ruthless tyrant. Before being defeated in his bid to recapture Texas from the Texans, Antonio Lopez de Santa Anna once said that if he were God, he would wish to be more. This, too, thoroughly applied to Judge Wingate. One day, somehow, I was determined to expose Wingate for the despot criminal and serial sex abuser that he truly was. But for the time being I sat respectfully quiet, not because I respected Wingate—just the opposite was true—but because I respected the office and sanctity of the court.

The next step of the process, after Wingate had allowed the government to relitigate a crime which I'd been fairly found innocent of committing, was to proceed to sentencing.

In the federal criminal justice system there is a group of attorneys and prosecutors appointed by the president which comprise the United

States Sentencing Commission. The Commission's goal is to formulate recommendations to federal judges for how much prison time any one individual defendant should receive for a specific crime. They also propose recommendations for how much imprisonment a judge should impose for violations of probation.

The more criminal history that a defendant has, the more time in prison the Commission recommends he receive. The Commission also recommends lesser time for certain mitigating factors and increases in time for aggravating circumstances.

In my case, the U.S. Sentencing Commission recommended that my sentence for violating my probation for getting arrested for trespassing and for the failing to register violation be no more than twelve months in prison. Since I'd already served more than twelve months after coming into federal custody from Covington County, I should have been released for time served. However, Wingate had other plans.

According to the government, the maximum amount of imprisonment that Wingate could give me would be seventy-two months total. They came to this figure through a complicated means of equating. From the defense's perspective, however, the most that Wingate could impose would be thirty-six months total. But Jupiter, whom had practically given up at this point, made such a weak and ineffectual argument regarding this issue that Wingate didn't even take a moment to address and respond to our argument. Instead, Wingate completely swallowed the government's erroneous assumption that the maximum was seventy-two months imprisonment.

Before going above the sentence recommendation made by the U.S. Sentencing Commission, Wingate first had to find certain "aggravating circumstances" that would justify him giving me an above-guideline sentence, especially one that reached the statutory maximum. Wingate's findings are worth quoting in full.

> **WINGATE:** Now, with regard to aggravating circumstances, there are quite a few. The defendant trespassed over in Vicksburg, and if the court only had that violation by itself in the abstract the court would not be as disturbed about the evidence presented on the violations themselves. However, the defendant did not comply with the strictures imposed on him by his sex offender status. The court has found that he violated the law and

that he violated it intentionally. So then the court finds that this is a serious aggravating circumstance. And since the defendant, inasmuch as he is a convicted offender who has refused to follow the law with regard to his status as a sex offender, is a danger to the community, the court imposes the following sentence of seventy-two months imprisonment and life probation.

This was patently not a finding that I committed the failing to register violation using "aggravating" conduct. For example, according to the Commission, simply failing to register as a sex offender is not an "aggravating circumstance" justifying a drastic departure above what they recommend as the sentence.

If one were to fail to register, move out of state, and then while absconding commit another sex offense, then that would be an aggravating circumstance as contemplated by the Commission. That didn't apply to me because, even if one were to believe the government's versions of events, I did not commit the failing to register violation in any type of aggravating manner. But Wingate's megalomania and God-complex refused to allow himself to be constrained by anything other than his whims and fantasies—the Sentencing Commission's recommendations be damned.

As the U.S. Marshals whisked me from the courtroom, I knew that a serious mistake had been made in my case. I knew that I had not received a fair trial. And I knew that Wingate was one of the most corrupt, incompetent, and least qualified judges I'd ever seen. Everything that I'd heard from John Whitfield and the other people with firsthand knowledge of Wingate's judicial neurosis was true. But what can one do when one is crucified in a court that lacks integrity, fairness, and competency? The answer is simply nothing.

I was quickly returned to the county jail to await my transfer back into the Federal Bureau of Prisons. I had no idea where they might send me to, but if I was going to have to do the seventy-two months then I wanted to be somewhere decent. Doing prison time in a county jail is one of the worst experiences one may ever have to endure, and I was ready for it to be over.

CHAPTER FOURTEEN

It didn't take long for the U.S. Marshals to move me from the county jail in Mississippi. I was taken by van to the airport in Memphis and put on the marshal's large Boeing 737 airplane that they use to transport their inmates. We then flew to Oklahoma City where the FBOP keeps their Federal Transfer Center—a prison literally built on the edge of the airport's runway. From there, the FBOP bused me thirty miles west to the Federal Correctional Institution in El Reno, Oklahoma. I arrived on Thursday, May 30, 2013.

While being processed in the receiving area of the prison I was asked if I identified as gay or transgender. Since I'd never been asked this question before when processing into a prison, I was somewhat surprised and expressed an interest in knowing why the prison staff was interested in this information. I was told it was going to be used as an informational tool to better place me with compatible cellmates.

Apparently, the FBOP had been sued several times after placing vulnerable transgender and gay inmates in cells with sexually violent predators and other inmates whom refused to live in the same cell with those type inmates. This reassured me.

When I arrived in my unit I was assigned cell number 102. My cellmate was then at work, but I struck up a conversation with my new next-door neighbor whom was an Aryan Brotherhood skinhead. He informed me that El Reno was a really decent place to do time and that I didn't have anything to worry about.

"Let me tell you about your cellie, though," he said. "Do you remember the army guy who used a baseball bat to kill the gay soldier back in the 1990s? Well, that's your cellie. His name is Calvin Glover."

I have to admit. My heart stopped cold when the Aryan Nazi told me this. I thought to myself, *These cock-sucking bitch police have done put me in a cell with a bat-wielding, homophobic maniac.* I was very familiar with the story, publicity, and movie called *Soldier's Girl*, that they made about the murder.

Calvin Glover was a soldier at Fort Campbell, Kentucky, and on the night of July 3, 1999, he and another soldier, Barry Winchell, whom many thought to be gay, got into an altercation. Winchell easily won the fight and Glover was made fun of by the other soldiers for letting a gay guy beat him up.

According to the official story, Glover went and got a baseball bat and murdered Winchell with it. Because it was assumed that Winchell was gay and that Glover had murdered him due to this fact, the case received nationwide publicity, including public recognition by President Clinton.

Glover was branded as an anti-homosexual murderer and was given a life sentence. After spending approximately ten years at the military's Disciplinary Barracks at Fort Leavenworth, Kansas, he was transferred into FBOP custody to relieve overcrowding at the barracks.

One cannot describe the hate that I then felt for the officers at El Reno who had placed me in danger by assigning me to a cell with a known gay-killing, homosexual-hating murderer. Without wasting any time I ran and secured two brand new pencils and sharpened them to a razor point. I was determined not to be another Barry Winchell, even if I had to protect myself with sharpened pencils, which actually work surprisingly well as weapons.

At the afternoon inmate recall I was sitting on my new bunk bed waiting on the worst, when in popped a small, effeminate inmate who immediately held out his limp hand and introduced himself as Calvin Glover. As I took his hand and noticed the soft feel, I quickly realized that Calvin Glover was no homosexual-hating murderer. If anything, I quickly realized that there was probably more to the Barry Winchell story than met the eye. My first suspicions, later to be confirmed, was that Winchell died in a lovers' triangle, not in a homosexual-hating induced fit of rage.

Glover and I quickly became friends and I realized that nothing in which the way Glover was portrayed in the news or the movie about the murder was correct. He was a quiet, polite, very shy person. And as I came to know him better, I certainly did not believe that he was capable of cold-blooded murder.

On Friday, May 31, 2013, the day after I arrived at El Reno, I was walking back from afternoon chow when it began to rain. Before I could get to my unit it began to hail. As I walked through the door the sirens in the nearby town began to wail. Minutes later the officers were frantically shouting for us to lockdown in our cells because a monster tornado was heading our way.

Glover and my cell faced to the east. However, several other inmates' cells faced to the west and to the south. Those inmates that could see out their windows to the west and south began shouting that a huge tornado was forming on the horizon. As soon as the inmates began yelling about the tornado, Glover and I heard on his radio that a massive killer tornado had formed and was heading towards us.

Everything happened so fast that it only seemed like a blur. But within seconds the wind around the prison was tearing through so fast you could hear it screaming. Then the hail increased in size to that of softballs.

All of the inmate housing units had clear skylights in the roof and several large pieces of hail punched through and crashed on the floor of our day room. Terrified themselves, the officers retreated to the inside closets of the unit for protection. Everyone knew that one hell of a tornado was wrecking havoc, but no one knew if we were in line for a direct hit.

But then, as soon as it began, it was over. However, the El Reno tornado would never be forgotten. In all, over twenty people would be killed, including Paul and Tim Samaras, the father and son storm chasing team that had their own show, *Storm Chasers*, on the Discovery Channel.

Tim and Paul Samaras had been following the tornado when it abruptly turned and sucked them into its vortex. At this point, the tornado was more than two miles wide with sustained wind speeds of over three hundred miles an hour. The El Reno tornado still holds to this day the record for the biggest and most powerful tornado ever recorded. And it missed the prison by only a mile.

As much as I've desired to see a real tornado in my short life, I've never been able to. As my cell window faced east, I missed everything but the wind, rain, and hail. But I've certainly seen the aftermath of plenty, and it gave me pause to consider the fact that I was in the literal middle of tornado alley.

One of the next persons I met after arriving at El Reno was Kwame M. Kilpatrick, the disgraced former mayor of Detroit, Michigan. Kilpatrick was serving what was essentially a life sentence for multiple counts of extortion, bribery, mail and wire fraud, filing false tax returns, tax evasion, and RICO conspiracies.

Kilpatrick had also been involved in the cover-up of a murder of an exotic dancer that many believed that his wife committed as retaliation for Kilpatrick having an affair with.

But Kilpatrick was not what one would expect of someone who had been the mayor of a major American city. When I first saw him I certainly thought to myself that this was a joke. Kilpatrick looks like a thug from an urban rap video. Not in the slightest way does he resemble someone that would be capable of getting elected to a major political office.

But getting elected was what he did. However, in prison, Kilpatrick went from running the government of Detroit to working in the chow hall cooking and serving other inmates their daily meals. On the side, Kilpatrick ran a sports betting ticket for college and professional football and basketball teams. Betting on sports games wasn't exactly condoned by the officers, but they allowed it to proceed unmolested.

When I first arrived at El Reno it was not a thoroughly safe prison. Texas inmates mostly controlled the hustles, and Texas inmates are some of the worst to do time around.

In the summer of 2013, El Reno had its fair share of inmate-on-inmate violence. That eventually changed, however. But when I was there during my brief stay in the summer of 2013, it was not uncommon for fights to break out daily and, in some not-so-rare cases, inmates to get stabbed.

Shortly after arriving at El Reno I met with the staff psychologist for my initial intake. During our conversation I mentioned to him that the violence level at the prison concerned me and that I didn't feel it was safe for someone like me that had a sex offense.

Without missing a beat the psychologist told me that I should sign-up for a transfer to a sex offender management facility where the majority of the inmate population were sex offenders. Since I'd never heard of one of these facilities—they didn't exist while I was incarcerated between 2005 and 2009—I was intrigued and thought that any prison with majority sex offenders would be way better than a violent prison run by Texas gang members. So I expressed an interest.

I was told by the El Reno psychologist that it was as simple as signing a piece of paper and acknowledging interest. Nothing about sex offender "treatment" was ever mentioned. In fact, besides being told that the majority of the inmate population would be sex offenders, nothing else was told to me about the sex offender management prisons.

I officially signed a consent to be transferred to a sex offender prison in June 2013. Shortly thereafter my case manager told me that I was approved and that I'd be leaving El Reno within thirty days.

In early August, I was told to pack my property and that I'd be leaving the next day to begin the transfer process to a sex offender prison. When I asked where they were sending me to I was told that I'd be going to the Federal Medical Center in Fort Devens, Massachusetts. For the second time in less than three months my heart stopped. Massachusetts was not where I wanted to go.

I was again placed on the U.S. Marshals' airplane and flown to the airport near the West Point Military Academy in Newburg, New York. Waiting for me was a FBOP bus that transferred me to Fort Devens.

Upon arrival at Devens, along with the other half-dozen inmates that were with me, I was told that I would be going to a special unit known as the Residential Sex Offender Treatment Program, also known shorthand as SOTP-R. Unbeknownst to me, I'd been conned into signing up for an intensive eighteen-month to two-year sex offender therapy program designed for sex offenders of the worst caliber. I was like, *What the fuck?*

I literally walked into something that I was neither prepared for, nor had expected. The FBOP's sex offender treatment unit was designed for the worst of the worst of the sex offenders currently serving time in the FBOP. Inmates who'd molested children under twelve, inmates who'd committed rape while armed with a weapon, and inmates who'd horribly and viciously abused vulnerable children were what it was designed for. What the Devens SOTP-R was not designed for were inmates like me with minor sex crimes.

However, at the time the El Reno psychologist signed me up for the program, the SOTP-R was close to being shutdown for lack of volunteers to take the program. In fact, when I arrived in August 2013, only about one-third of the one hundred and twenty beds were filled. To say that the program was desperate for inmates would be putting it mildly. Therefore, they began qualifying inmates to take the program who were never intended to benefit from its intensive eighteen-month to two year process.

The director of the SOTP-R was an older psychologist by the name of Dr. Cheryl A. Renaud. And in my first meeting with Dr. Renaud I expressed shock at having been misled by the El Reno psychologist about where I was going and what I was getting into. He had never told me anything about treatment or attending a sex offender therapy program.

After reviewing my file and the details of my "crime," Dr. Renaud agreed that I did not meet their criteria for placement there. The SOTP-R was designed to treat individuals with multiple, serious sex offenses involving the abuse of children under twelve or involving the use of force. Neither applied anywhere close to what I was in prison for.

On the other hand, however, Dr. Renaud did believe that I had other areas of my psyche that may need working on, including her belief that I had an "authority" problem. And since the SOTP-R was desperate for fresh bodies in order for them to continue justifying their existence, she did everything she could to convince me to stay while also reminding me that anyone who resigned the SOTP-R was placed in solitary confinement for several months until the transfer request back to their parent institution was approved. I think this was when I really began to despise Dr. Renaud.

Shortly after arriving at Devens I was quickly made aware that the Boston Marathon Bomber, Dzhokhar "Jakar" Tsarnaev, was being confined at the facility while he awaited trial.

On occasion, the guards would secure the walkways between units and escort Jakar from solitary confinement to the attorney/client visitation rooms to meet with his attorneys. It was during one of these occasions that I first laid eyes on the infamous terrorist. However, despite his notoriety, I wasn't repelled by looking at him. I actually found him to be a very attractive guy, his murderous inclinations notwithstanding.

I will be the first to admit, though, that I had very little, if any, sympathy for the bombers, their belief system, or motives for committing their crimes. Targeting innocent civilians to advance a terroristic cause is abhorrent, evil, and impossible to condone. But my opinion of Jakar soon changed when I had the opportunity to interact with him on a personal basis.

I was able to obtain an inmate job, cleaning the floors and taking out the trash in the secure area of the prison where Jakar was being celled in solitary confinement. This required me to pass by his door daily, and even though I had been warned not to speak to Jakar through his door, there were many times when I was alone on the cell range with no officers around. My curiosity got the better of me and I couldn't resist talking to him, passing him magazines and books under his door, and providing him toothpaste and other hygiene that some of the guards refused to give him. The friendship that I established with Jakar soon proved beneficial because it wasn't long before Jakar began to break under the pressure of which he was subjected to. And when Jakar began to act out in violent ways—usually because of being taunted by a prison guard—I was always able to talk to him and calm him down.

Devens was the seventh federal institution that I'd been to. This didn't count the innumerable county jails and transfer facilities that I'd passed through on my way to and from the different prisons. But besides Madison County, I had never seen or experienced such hateful, unprofessional conduct from prison guards as I did at Devens. The guards there treated the inmates atrociously and Dzhokhar Tsarnaev worse.

For example, Muslim inmates are supposed to be provided a special pork-free meal. The guards at Devens deliberately put pork products in Jakar's food in their many sick attempts to taunt and harass him. Some guards even brought magazine cut-outs of bacon and pigs and glued them to Jakar's cell window.

In other cases, when Jakar expressed frustration at his situation and became suicidal, some guards would slide razor blades from the shaving kits under his door and encourage him to kill himself, and, in at least one incident, he almost succeeded.

Our mutual dislike of the guards gave Jakar and I something to talk about and relate to, but our conversations always ultimately turned to the marathon bombings and Jakar's belief that the jury would eventually acquit him of any wrongdoing. Jakar no doubt loved his brother, and further, without doubt, supported his brother's more extremist beliefs. But Jakar never led me to believe that he was a full participant in the bombings. I didn't necessarily agree or believe him, but we eventually decided to avoid any discussion of his crimes or upcoming trials. Instead, we mostly talked about the guards and how hateful they were.

The prison guards at Devens were almost, without exception, some of the cruelest, evil human beings that I'd ever seen, and their constant mental torture and harassment eventually drove me to escape Devens in any way that I could.

Dr. Renaud literally ran the SOTP-R in a manner similar to how Dr. Josef Mengele might have run it had he been in charge of "treating" sex offenders. By that I mean that everything that went on there seemed to be more of an experiment of the unknown rather than a program of precedents proven to treat sex offenders and reduce their risk of recidivism.

Sex offender treatment in the Federal Bureau of Prisons was literally a new science, and being new there were not any statistics which tended to prove or disprove an assumption that the treatment protocol Dr. Renaud and her other clinicians developed was effective at reducing the recidivism rate of sexual offenders. It was all experimentation.

However, as one might imagine, there are a certain class of sexual offenders who will never cease committing future sex crimes. Thankfully, these type of offenders are in a very distinct minority. But at Devens, Dr. Renaud quickly identified these participants, and, in most cases, removed them from the program for the slightest of reasons, or, in some cases, actually invented cause to terminate them from the program.

I found this practice disturbing because these are the type offenders most in need of sex offender therapy. They were also offenders that would be releasing to their communities soon and could benefit from whatever therapy that they could obtain. However, they were quickly removed from the program by Dr. Renaud for the slightest pretext. I believe this was done deliberately by Dr. Renaud in an effort to manipulate her SOTP-R graduates' recidivism statistics.

Simply put, Dr. Renaud only allowed the most likely low-risk offender to graduate from her program so that she could say that her personally designed sex offender treatment program was the most effective at "curing" and reducing the recidivism rate of the offenders who completed it. Anyone who posed the slightest risk of reoffending was quickly gotten rid of, yet it was these inmates most in need of treatment.

Another factor which affected my desire to get as far away from Devens as possible—not including the atrocious treatment at the hands of the guards—were the inmates themselves that were participating in the program. While I made several good friends there, some of the other inmates were the most conniving, petty, jealous, hateful, and manipulative individuals I'd ever been around in my life.

For example, after the lights in the unit were turned out for the night the bathroom of the unit quickly became a beehive of salacious sexual activity—the SOTP-R unit was an open dorm and inmates lived in cubicles rather than cells. Yet, the following day if I stole a muffin from the chow hall and sneaked it back to the unit, there would be an inmate who had been having sex the night before challenging me in group therapy for my "criminal thinking" mentality. The hypocrisy was killing me.

In the spring of 2014 I requested a meeting with Dr. Renaud and expressed to her my earnest desire to withdraw from the program. This request definitely disappointed her because I'd been tagged as a participant that was most likely to complete the program and not reoffend. Plus, the SOTP-R was undergoing a FBOP audit because so many inmates had been withdrawing from the program. It did not look good for Dr. Renaud when more than half of the inmates who signed up for the SOTP-R either voluntarily withdrew or were terminated for misbehavior or "treatment failure." Treatment failure was a catch-all euphemism used by Dr. Renaud and the other clinicians for any inmates who didn't swallow her treatment propaganda hook, line, and sinker. I had become one of her treatment failures.

I'd honestly given the SOTP-R my best shot. I'd tried to gain some tidbit of useful information, and besides learning techniques to better express myself, I viewed my ten months there as a wasted endeavor.

What I did get out of the experience was ten months of mental torture and harassment from some of the worst prison guards on earth and a steady stream of sob stories and excuses for why some of the most disturbed inmates currently incarcerated committed their heinous crimes.

Before I officially signed out and withdrew from the program—Dr. Renaud had begged me to reconsider and think about the issue some more—my best friend in the program, Harold Space, was rushed from the prison suffering from what we thought was a stroke.

When he didn't return later that night I called his brother, whom I'd met in a visit earlier that month when my family came to visit at the same time Harold's did. I never told his brother what hospital Harold went to (I didn't know). I didn't tell him any specifics about when Harold left or when he might come back from the hospital (because, again, I didn't know), and I didn't provide any other information other than to tell his brother that we thought Harold had a stroke and had been taken to the outside hospital.

Less than thirty minutes after making this phone call I was called to the lieutenants' office and accused of "facilitating the escape of another inmate." I was quickly handcuffed and led away to solitary confinement. I did, however, have Jakar Tsarnaev as a neighbor, for whatever consolation that provided at the time.

The staff wrote me an incident report for telephone abuse, sanctioned me my phone, commissary, and visits for three months, and placed me in disciplinary segregation for two weeks without access to a radio, books, or any form of mind-stimulating materials.

Several days after getting locked in solitary confinement, Dr. Renaud came to visit and told me that Harold didn't have a stroke, only a pinched nerve in his neck, and that he wasn't even at the outside hospital when I called his brother, but was instead in the prison's infirmary.

I was relieved that Harold did not have a stroke, but this had been the final straw. I made it clear to Dr. Renaud that I would not be returning to the SOTP-R. She could list me as a treatment failure and her program be damned. I wanted out of there as soon as possible and I didn't ever want to hear the names of Devens, Renaud, or SOTP-R again.

My wish was granted and in late July 2014 I was transferred from Devens back to El Reno, Oklahoma. As the bus pulled away from the front gate of Devens, I'd never been so happy in my life. For almost a year I'd sung the lyrics to "Dixie," always wishing I was back in the South, and finally I was headed back there.

CHAPTER FIFTEEN

It would be an understatement to say that I hated my time at Fort Devens in Massachusetts. Not only were the prison guards hateful and abusive, but the cold weather and snow were atrocious. Even though Oklahoma is known to have cold winters as well, nothing could compare to New England.

During the early winter of 2014, while I was still at Devens, there wasn't much to do. Thankfully, I had the time to occupy myself with preparing for an appeal to the Fifth Circuit Court of Appeals in New Orleans.

The last two official acts that my trial attorney, Omodare Jupiter, took was to file my notice of appeal and a motion to withdraw as my attorney. The appeal was a constitutional right, but I'd asked Jupiter to withdraw from further involvement in the case after the appalling and lackluster performance he'd mustered at trial. I specifically requested the court to appoint me a new attorney to represent me on appeal. But I'd made these requests to Judge Wingate in April 2013.

Like he usually does, Wingate refused to take any action on these motions even though criminal appeals are required to be handled in the most expeditious manner possible. Again, as most tyrants and megalomaniacs usually do, Wingate felt the laws and constitutional rights of this country didn't apply to him.

Because Wingate refused to rule on my motion for a new attorney, or in any way take action that would allow me to appeal the convictions and sentence, my appeal stagnated for almost a year.

When a district court, such as what Judge Wingate is, refuses to take action on routine court matters, either through deliberate indifference or incompetence, a litigant has the right to file a petition in the court of appeals asking them to issue a writ of mandamus, compelling and forcing the district court to carry out its duty.

Because Judge Wingate has deliberately shunned his duties as a district court judge, and, in some instances, through utter incompetence, refused to issue rulings, which deny a litigant certain constitutional rights, he is one of the judges most likely to have petitions for writs of mandamus filed against him in the Fifth Circuit.

After waiting many months for him to issue a simple, one-page order appointing me a new attorney, I decided to file a petition for a writ of mandamus against him, and I did so in the early part of 2014. It had the desired effect.

Shortly after filing the petition, but before the Fifth Circuit could make a ruling, Judge Wingate appointed a woman named Eileen Mary Maher from Natchez, Mississippi. Mrs. Maher, as I quickly learned, was not experienced in federal appellate matters. When we researched her litigation history we only found one single federal appeal that she had ever done—and she lost that one big time. Her lack of qualifications in federal appeals concerned me, but I was willing to give her the benefit of the doubt. However, I was positively convinced that Judge Wingate had deliberately appointed me the most inexperienced attorney that he could find to represent me on appeal.

Soon after Mrs. Maher was appointed to represent me, I began trying to contact her through the telephone and through letters, but I didn't have any luck reaching this new attorney. My mom and stepfather tried next, but neither of them could reach Mrs. Maher either and she did not return their phone calls.

After more than a month had passed without being able to reach this attorney, who was supposed to be competently representing me on appeal, I finally got fed up and wrote her a letter requesting that she either respond or withdraw from the case. I also sent a letter to Wingate informing him that the person he appointed to represent me was not communicating with me.

Shortly thereafter, my mother received a call from Mrs. Maher, but it wasn't pleasant. My mother, who is normally an extremely cultured, polite, and respectful person, was utterly shocked at the way Mrs. Maher spoke to her.

In a hateful and aggressive voice, Mrs. Maher told my mother that she would not discuss my case with her or my stepfather, who is an attorney, that communicating with them was a waste of time, that she was not getting paid enough money to devote lots of time to the appeal, and that she would not accept my phone calls from the prison, even though they were prepaid and not collect.

When my mother told me later that day the details of the contents of the conversations she had with Mrs. Maher, I was utterly shocked. I knew then that no matter what, there was no way I was going to let this Eileen Mary Maher woman handle anything remotely connected to my case. I didn't know what kind of attorney she was, but I knew she was a horrible person, and I definitely didn't want to find out anything more.

Not only was Mrs. Maher not experienced in federal appeals, but her refusal to communicate with my family and me about my appeals, or in anyway consider me assisting her in preparing the appeal, made me determined not to proceed any further with her. Subsequently, I filed another motion with the court asking that she be forced to withdraw from the case due to irreconcilable conflicts and that another attorney be appointed to represent me on appeal.

As he did with the first motion, Wingate refused to take any action. This, again deprived me of a right to an expedited appeal of my conviction and sentence. However, because Wingate had been so dilatory in handling the case, the Fifth Circuit soon took over jurisdiction and made their own rulings that would speed things along.

Because Wingate refused to carry out his duties as a district court judge, the Fifth Circuit was forced to handle the attorney issue. Unfortunately, the Fifth Circuit refused to appoint me a new attorney. I was left with the decision to either use Eileen Maher or proceed with the appeal *pro se*, acting as my own attorney. Since I clearly could not entrust my future to someone as horrible as Eileen Maher, I decided to represent myself on appeal. No one knew the issues better than me, and I felt that no one could do a better job than myself. The only consideration that gave me pause was the fact that appellate courts—honestly, any court—were less likely to rule favorably to *pro se* litigants.

Courts want to deal with attorneys. Even though a litigant has the right to represent him or herself in court, judges, prosecutors, and other attorneys hate when they do so. The reasons are varied.

The most salient reason is that *pro se* litigants are not legally trained. They don't understand the intricacies, decorum, and procedure of the courtroom. But a large part of the antipathy coming from courts regarding *pro se* litigants is the alleged sanctity of law that judges, prosecutors, and other attorneys believe they have, solely because they are law school graduates.

Simply put, no one wants an untrained, *pro se* litigant winning in the courtroom, because, if they do, it negates the sole reasons for attorneys in the first place. So I wasn't keen on representing myself on appeal, but I didn't have a choice.

The first step in appealing a district court's judgment is filing a notice of appeal stating your intent to appeal the ruling to the appellate courts. That had already been done in my case.

The next step is for the parties to file their appellate briefs, or their legal arguments, setting out what issues they are appealing. Because I was the defendant and the one who filed the appeal, I would have the first opportunity to file my first brief. After that the government could file a response arguing why my brief was not meritorious. Finally, I would have a chance to file a reply brief to the government's arguments. Then the case would go to a panel of three judges on the Fifth Circuit Court of Appeals for a decision.

Before I could prepare an appellate brief, though, I had to obtain the transcripts from the revocation hearing. Without knowing what was said and what evidence was presented one cannot file an appeal without the transcripts.

Ordinarily, one would obtain a transcript of a criminal trial by petitioning the district court and asking that the court order the court reporter to prepare the transcript and then file it on the official docket. But with Judge Wingate nothing was ever easy.

Even though I was constitutionally entitled to a copy of the trial transcripts for my appeal, Judge Wingate decided to continue his judicial games of guerrilla warfare and deny me copies. Judge Wingate's reasoning for denying me copies of the transcripts and records was that I "did not need access to the record for the purposes of an appeal."

This was clearly another tyrannical, neurotic act on Wingate's part to further deny me the right to appeal my case. Not only that, he knew it would further delay any appellate review of the actions that he took in my case because once he denied the transcripts I would then be forced to appeal that order to the Fifth Circuit and request that they overrule him.

Fortunately, by this time, even the Fifth Circuit was exasperated by Judge Wingate's childish, immature behavior. No sooner had Wingate denied me the right to the transcripts than the Fifth Circuit overruled him and ordered that copies be provided to me "forthwith."

With transcript copies in hand, I was finally able to begin preparing the appellate briefs and arguments that I would be making to the Fifth Circuit.

The first major issue in my appeal regarded my arrest for trespassing. I felt, and even to this day I know, that I had a First Amendment right to distribute my political leaflets which were critical of Sheriff Martin Pace. And the United States Supreme Court has been clear on this point numerous times.

In *Jamison v. Texas* in 1943, the Supreme Court held that a "state may punish conduct on the streets which is in violation of a valid law, but one who is rightfully on a street . . . carries with him there, as elsewhere, the constitutional right to express his views in an orderly fashion . . . [including] the communication of ideas by handbills and literature."

This case was followed by a long line of others which consistently held that police officers cannot restrict an individual's right to distribute leaflets in a public area short of that individual posing a danger to himself or others.

There was no doubt that my actions on the night of July 2, 2011, were constitutionally-protected First Amendment actions and that I was only arrested by the corrupt, dishonest Daniel Thomas in retaliation for filing a complaint on him and because of the message my leaflets conveyed. I hoped that the Fifth Circuit would see it my way.

My second main issue was that there was not sufficient evidence for Wingate to find me guilty of failing to register as a sex offender.

William Jay Simpson and U.S. Probation accused me of violating Mississippi's temporary residence sex offender registration law under Section 45-33-23(h) of the Mississippi Code of 1972.

Under Section 45-33-23(h) a sex offender has to register as a temporary residence any place he or she stays in a non-consecutive fashion fourteen or more days in any calendar year. However, Roger Cole had been clear in his testimony that he could not remember how many times I stayed with him, but could only guess that it was "maybe" or "about" fourteen times total from May 2011 through August 2011.

Any days less than fourteen would not be in violation of the law. So Cole's testimony was critical. But the government could never tie Cole to anything more than a guess about how many times I stayed with him.

In criminal trials, a defendant cannot be held liable for a crime unless it is proven "beyond a reasonable doubt" that he or she committed that crime.

In my case, the only evidence that the government had that I stayed with Cole was his testimony. And his testimony was very clear; he could not state with any specificity how many nights I stayed with him. He could only guess. Guesses are not a sufficient basis to deny one's liberty.

The last major issue that I raised in my appeal was a double jeopardy argument. Judge Wingate had found me not guilty of all the allegations from Covington County involving Colton Kendrick and Ethan Robinson. And his verdict was clear. Not guilty is not guilty. In the criminal justice system a not guilty verdict is the same as a proclamation of innocence. But Wingate being the schizophrenic judge that he is couldn't let the issue die.

It was only after Ethan and his mother were thwarted in their attempt to extort money from me and my family that their tactics changed. And once I'd been found not guilty of any crimes related to them, legally they were unable to file any type of lawsuit against me.

Their next step involved instituting a letter-writing campaign involving their relatives and friends in the community in an effort to place pressure on Wingate to sentence me harshly. For this, Wingate fell hook, line, and sinker.

The Fifth Amendment to the United States Constitution, and a long list of Supreme Court cases, is also very clear that the government, with all its resources and power, should not be allowed to make repeated attempts to convict and harass an individual for an alleged offense.

According to the Supreme Court case of *Yeager v. United States*, the double jeopardy clause of the Fifth Amendment prevents the government from relitigating any issue that was decided by an acquittal in a prior hearing or trial.

At the liability phase of the revocation hearing, Judge Wingate listened to the evidence, heard testimony, and ultimately concluded that it was not reliable, that Colton and Ethan were not credible witnesses, and that there was not enough evidence to convict me. And in finding me not guilty he stated with specific particularity the facts he used to base his not guilty verdict on.

However, these exact same "facts" that Wingate considered and relied on in finding me not guilty were the exact same "facts" that the government was allowed to reintroduce at sentencing, and these were also the exact same "facts" that Wingate used to base my seventy-two month statutory maximum sentence on. And not once did Wingate ever attempt to explain or justify himself in violating the Fifth Amendment and the Double Jeopardy Clause.

Like normal, Wingate conducts himself in a manner that reflects his apparent omnipotent belief in unlimited, unreserved power. And this was the posture that I took in my appeal. No one familiar with my case felt that I received a fair hearing, least of all me. I hoped that the Fifth Circuit would see it my way and conclude that Wingate had overstepped the limits of his power.

On April 4, 2014, I filed my first appellate brief with the Fifth Circuit Clerk's Office. From that point, the government had sixty days to file their response to my brief. However, the government only took twenty-six days to file their arguments.

In response to my first issue, the government never attempted to argue that my conduct on the night of July 2, 2011, was not First Amendment constitutionally-protected free speech. Nor could they. The U.S. Supreme Court was very clear that distributing political leaflets on public property was protected speech.

Instead, the government argued that I repeatedly breached a "secured" perimeter established by the Vicksburg Police despite being warned by Officer Daniel Thomas not to. However, this was not part of the evidence and it certainly wasn't the reason I was arrested according to Thomas's written arrest report. The government also specifically argued that I was on the property illegally because I did not possess a ticket to the event. This, again, goes directly back to Omodare Jupiter's legal incompetence and his utter failure to introduce the arrest report and pageant ticket into evidence.

Thomas's written arrest report, made on the night of my arrest, was clear and its meaning obvious. Thomas told me that I could go to Washington Street to pass out my leaflets, but after filing a complaint against him, and after he had talked to Sheriff Pace, he arrested me in the exact area he told me to go.

I even found out later that between the time he told me to go to Washington Street and my arrest, Thomas had spoken to Sheriff Pace and no doubt was told to arrest me in retaliation. But the government didn't add this salient point to their appellate brief.

The government's response to my next issue, the sex offender registration violation, was even more erroneous, factually incorrect, and not an accurate representation of the issue.

The testimony from Roger Cole had been crystal clear. He could never, despite multiple attempts by the government, say with any specificity how many nights I stayed at his house. Instead, he only guessed that it was "about" or "maybe" fourteen times total. Not one single time did Cole ever testify that I stayed with him "for at least 14 days." Yet, that exact phrase, attributed to Cole, found its way into the government's brief.

Essentially, what the government did was credit a testimonial statement to one of their witnesses that was never made. This comes alarmingly close to perjury. Yet, again, the government made a false argument to the Fifth Circuit and claimed that Cole testified specifically that I'd spent "at least 14 days" at his house.

The phrase "at least 14 days" means that I definitively stayed with Cole no fewer than fourteen times. But that was not Cole's testimony and it wasn't even close to what he said. The most that Cole was willing to say was that he guessed I stayed with him "maybe" or "about" fourteen times total. That's a big difference than saying he was sure that I stayed with him "at least 14 days" total. But that didn't stop the government from making false statements to the appellate court.

On this issue, however, the government needed the testimony to reflect their desire that I stayed with Cole at least fourteen times total, and if they had to alter the testimony then so be it.

In response to my double jeopardy arguments, the government essentially argued that because my attorney and I hadn't made a sufficient objection at trial to the double jeopardy violation, I was now precluded from raising it on appeal.

Their last argument was one which was seemingly cast to convince the appellate court that the evidence introduced at sentencing wasn't prohibited by the Double Jeopardy Clause, but was instead evidence solely about my character, which was relevant for sentencing purposes. So, again, the government completely side-stepped the main issue.

Lastly, even if the testimony and evidence was allowed at sentencing, the last people in the world that would be qualified to give evidence about my "character" would be the mothers of Ethan and Colton.

Character evidence, as defined in the law books, is evidence given about a person's traits, reputation, and honesty. However, people such as Ethan's and Colton's mothers, who have never met me and never heard anything about me prior to the incident, are not qualified to give evidence of my character that they know nothing about. That's not character evidence. But that was the government's argument.

In my reply response that I filed to the government's brief, I used the testimony from Officer Thomas to discredit the government's own witness. And it couldn't have been clearer. Not only did I have a First Amendment right to distribute my leaflets, but it was clear that I was arrested in the exact area where Thomas told me to go and that the arrest was done in retaliation.

In regards to the sex offender violation my main response was that the "government deliberately misrepresented the facts in their brief by characterizing [my] stay at [Cole's house as being] for 'at least 14 days.' " No where in the trial transcripts is there any mention, by any witness, that I stayed "at least" fourteen times or more at Cole's residence. The government simply invented testimony.

Finally, in response to the government's argument that my double jeopardy rights weren't violated, I quoted a Fifth Circuit case that was almost identical to mine.

In *Bullard v. Estelle*, the Fifth Circuit ruled that if the same facts are presented at the liability phase of a trial, and the defendant is found not guilty, then those same facts cannot be the basis of a second fact-finding proceeding at sentencing. But that's exactly what happened to me.

I filed my reply brief on May 23, 2014, and began the long wait. I wasn't sure how long it would take the appellate court to issue a ruling, but I expected a four to six month wait. In the meantime, my miserable existence continued at the prison in Fort Devens, Massachusetts, until my return to El Reno, Oklahoma.

CHAPTER SIXTEEN

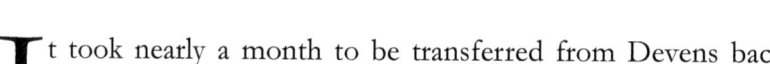

It took nearly a month to be transferred from Devens back to El Reno, but when I returned it wasn't the same prison that I'd left the year before.

During the past year El Reno had been taken over by a new warden and a new captain. Prior to me leaving, El Reno was a violent, gang-controlled prison yard. But upon my return none of that nonsense was apparent anymore. The new warden and captain had made it their goal to clean up the prison and make it safe for every inmate.

Any inmate—whether a gang member or not—who wanted to cause problems was quickly locked in solitary confinement and shipped to a different prison.

El Reno itself had been turned into a programing facility designed to provide maximum rehabilitation educational programs for the inmates, and any inmate who might try to interfere with that mission was quickly gotten rid of. On top of that, the recreational outlets were superb and so was the food. Simply put, none of the inmates wanted to screw off their time there and get shipped. As a result, the violence level dropped and all the inmate bullshit stopped. El Reno turned into one of the best prisons I'd ever been to and I was easily able to turn my attention back to my legal work.

Since dismissing my false arrest lawsuit case, the federal court in Aberdeen, Mississippi, hadn't taken any action. I'd sent numerous letters to the clerk's office, but I'd always receive a polite response that my motion for reconsideration of the dismissal was still pending. Until the judge or magistrate reconsidered that motion nothing could be done.

While I was waiting on the federal court in Aberdeen to take some action on the false arrest lawsuit, I also decided to file a separate lawsuit against Covington County for the atrocious treatment they subjected me to while I was incarcerated there.

In this lawsuit I claimed that Sheriff Ben Ford, Detective Pamela Wade Smith, and several other defendants subjected me to a false arrest, falsely imprisoned me, and then denied me needed medical care and caused me to be harmed by other inmates in the jail. This lawsuit was filed in the federal court in Hattiesburg, Mississippi, and district court judge, Keith Starrett, and magistrate, Michael T. Parker, were assigned to the case.

From prior experience dealing with Judge Wingate and researching his background, I quickly learned that Judge Starrett was best friends and close colleagues with Wingate. In fact, they were almost judicial twins in their beliefs of strict, harsh sentencing and partisan politics against Democrats in Mississippi.

Judge Starrett also had an extremely conservative background and was not known to be sympathetic to criminal defendants or litigants raising the claims that I was attempting to raise against Covington County. But there was no doubt that Covington County was wrong in how they treated me. I was abused, starved, and left to wither away.

Added to the atrocious treatment was the fact that Covington County arrested me without any evidence that I'd harmed Colton or Ethan, and, in fact, they arrested me for something that was not even in violation of any law. They simply invented a crime. And as I had promised to myself back in 2011 when I was incarcerated there, I was not going to let them get away with it.

Lest not forget either that the false arrest lawsuit that I had filed against Officer Daniel Thomas, the Vicksburg Police Department, Sheriff Pace, and the Warren County Sheriff's Department was also still pending and had not moved forward at this time as well.

It can truly be said that my arrests in the fall of 2011 began with my false and illegal arrest for trespassing at the Miss Mississippi Pageant.

Since then, it had been patently clear that I'd not committed arson, nor was there ever any evidence of arson, and that I'd not committed any type of crime against Ethan and Colton. The last tenuous toehold that the government had against me was my probation revocation con-

victims. But even in that, when it came to the allegations that had been made against me by Ethan and Colton, I'd proven beyond a reasonable doubt that they lied, fabricated evidence and testimony, were motivated by extorting me for money, and that I was completely innocent of those actions.

Pursuing lawsuits against Covington County and the Vicksburg defendants was important to me, but the one lawsuit that I wanted to win the most was the false arrest arson lawsuit in Aberdeen. It had been my arrest for arson that I believed had finally sent my beloved Papaw into his final spiral of health that took him from us, and I was determined to avenge him.

My Papaw had believed in my innocence. He knew the evil, immoral wickedness that was Emmett Atwood and that side of the family. And even though he was gone I knew that he would want me to pursue justice against those whom had been so quick to deny it to me.

Finally, on September 10, 2014, Judge Aycock reopened my lawsuit, and after reviewing the correct *in forma pauperis* affidavit, granted my motion to proceed without having to pay the costs and fees of the case.

Once the case had been reopened, Magistrate David Sanders set a hearing for me to appear in court and answer questions and provide testimony regarding exactly what my claims were against the defendants and to clarify any questions that the court may of had. A hearing of this type is called a "*Spears*" hearing.

Spears hearings are to dig beneath the conclusional allegations of a *pro se* complainant and ascertain exactly what the prisoner alleges occurred and the legal basis of the claims. This affords the person an opportunity to verbalize his complaints in a manner of communication more comfortable to him.

Judge Sanders set the *Spears* hearing for February 18, 2015. But while I waited on the *Spears* hearing and the slow process that accompanies a lawsuit, I also had to wait on my criminal appeal to be ruled on by the Fifth Circuit. That decision came on September 9, 2014, and it wasn't good.

Unfortunately, the Fifth Circuit did not rule in my favor, and their opinion upholding my convictions was shocking. More unbelievable was the fact that in many instances the Fifth Circuit utterly failed to address many of the main arguments that I made. It almost appeared that the

Fifth Circuit copied and pasted the government's argument out of their brief and incorporated it into their opinion upholding my convictions and sentence.

In response to my First Amendment arguments, the Fifth Circuit completely failed to consider whether my conduct was constitutionally-protected speech. Instead, they sided with the government's argument that I had "breached the established perimeter" that law enforcement set up that night and that doing so justified an arrest for trespassing. But the court would not and did not address Officer Daniel Thomas's conflicting testimony and police report, or the pageant ticket that I possessed the night of my arrest. It was clear the panel judges didn't even read my briefs.

This was reinforced further when the Fifth Circuit concluded that I had specifically violated Mississippi's temporary residence sex offender registration law under Section 45-33-23(h) of the Mississippi Code of 1972 "by staying at the home of Roger Cole in Pearl, Mississippi, for at least 14 days between May 2011 and August 2011."

There was that phrase that didn't exist in the record: "at least 14 days." The government had pulled a fast one. They completely fabricated false testimony and attributed it to a witness who never made that statement. And despite the clear refutation in the record, the Fifth Circuit fell for the government's lies.

Finally, when it came to my arguments about the double jeopardy violation, the Fifth Circuit stated that "double jeopardy does not apply to a [probation] revocation proceeding." However, the Fifth Circuit was quick to add that the case they relied on in coming to this determination was decided in a totally different context than mine was.

Essentially, the Fifth Circuit made a ground-breaking determination that completely reinterpreted a major amendment in our Constitution without any precedential history or explanation on which to base the decision on. So much for fairness, justice, and integrity in our judicial system.

Of course, upon learning that I would not be getting out of prison anytime soon, I became depressed. I knew deep down in my heart that I'd not had a fair hearing. I knew that Judge Wingate was wrong and that the Fifth Circuit had issued a clearly erroneous opinion that wasn't based in law or based in accurate facts. But what can one do?

I was back at El Reno and the only consolation that I had was Kwame Kilpatrick's repeated assurances that President Obama would be implementing drastic changes to the federal criminal justice system which would result in prisoners earning more good-time credits and being released from prison earlier.

It was well known that Kilpatrick was at one time friends with President Obama. Whether their friendship extended to the present day I cannot know. But Kilpatrick firmly and fully believed that Obama was going to commute his sentence before leaving office. We now know that that was not to be the case, but in 2015 Kilpatrick believed it with all his heart. Without that commutation Kilpatrick still faces decades in prison.

I, on the other hand, faced about two more years in prison after the denial of my appeal. My release date was in April 2017, but with six months halfway house I was actually slated to be released in October 2016. That was not too much time to have to wait, but I was extremely disappointed nonetheless.

On February 18, I appeared via video conference before Magistrate Sanders for my scheduled *Spears* hearing. Because it was impractical to transfer me from El Reno back to Mississippi, the prison and court arranged for me to be connected via a Skype-type video conferencing system set up inside the prison. This would be the first time meeting Magistrate Sanders.

For the several days prior to the hearing I'd studied the evidence, memorized the previously filed complaint and legal documents, and I felt I was ready to answer any and every question that the magistrate may of had.

When we started the hearing I was placed under oath and told to answer every question truthfully. Magistrate Sanders was very professional, polite, and seemed to exercise every caution to make me feel relaxed and comfortable.

To begin, Magistrate Sanders asked me to explain in detail the who, what, when, where, how, and why of my arrest for arson and the basis for the lawsuit that I filed.

I felt that to get any full understanding of the genesis of the case, that I'd have to begin with my book, *Into Hell I Rode*. After explaining that, I briefly mentioned the trespassing arrest, then the arrest for arson, my preliminary hearing and the testimony James Jackson and Tim Nail provided, the ultimate exoneration by the Attala County grand jury, and the constitutional violations that I felt were committed against me by the defendants.

My entire recitation took about thirty minutes, but I felt that when I concluded Magistrate Sanders and any other person that may have been listening would have the best understanding of the case as possible under the circumstances.

Magistrate Sanders may have asked me a question or two, but if he did I don't remember what they were. However, the most salient point that I remember from the hearing was at the conclusion when Magistrate Sanders complimented me on being so well-prepared, organized, and articulate. He also told me that the hearing had been one of the easiest he ever had to preside over.

Magistrate Sanders concluded the hearing by informing me that he would review my original complaint, consider the evidence and testimony, and then issue a report and recommendation about whether or not he believed the case had merit and should be allowed to proceed.

This report and recommendation was issued less than a month later on March 13, 2015. In his report, Magistrate Sanders concluded that there had not been a sufficient basis to include Sheriff Martin Pace as a defendant in the lawsuit, but that I had "allege[d] facts that support the elements of the cause of action in order to make out a valid claim" of false arrest and that the lawsuit could proceed against Mike Chaney, James Jackson, and Tim Nail. Score another point for me.

At this point, the next step in the process is for the court to actually send a copy of my lawsuit to the defendants and require them to file an answer within a certain fixed time, usually twenty-one days. In the legal world, this is called "serving" the complaint, and my lawsuit was served on all the defendants by the first of May 2015.

Sheriff Tim Nail's lawyer, Daniel J. Griffith, was the first to file his appearance in the case, officially informing all of the parties involved that he was representing the sheriff. Unfortunately, not until the end of the case would Mr. Griffith and I have anything close to what could be called a "working relationship."

Mr. Griffith's practice was based out of Cleveland, Mississippi, deep in the heart of the Mississippi Delta. Apparently, his practice mostly consisted of representing local county and city defendants when they are sued by litigants such as myself.

Wilson Douglas Minor was the next attorney to enter an appearance in the case. As an assistant attorney general for the state of Mississippi, Mr. Minor would be representing the state defendants, James Jackson and Mike Chaney.

Mr. Minor's uncle was Paul Minor, the Democrat lawyer that Judge Wingate had so unfairly convicted, punished, and sent to prison. Mr. Minor's career had been spent in the Mississippi Attorney General's Office in their civil litigation division. From what I knew, Mr. Minor represented state defendants, too, like Jackson and Chaney, when they were sued by litigants like me.

Unlike Mr. Griffith, Mr. Minor and I would establish an early, friendly working relationship and would maintain it throughout the entirety of the case.

I never did get to meet Mr. Griffith face-to-face, however, when I did finally meet Mr. Minor, he struck me as a competent, professional, business-type individual. He wore conservative suits and looked every inch the government lawyer I expected him to be. The one quality lacking in his personality was a sense of humor.

Throughout the whole case I never heard or saw Mr. Minor laugh or express humor in any type of way. I guessed that he was in his mid-thirties, but his flat, monotone way of speaking, and his no-nonsense way of handling business, struck me as odd. But upon reflection, it was probably because he and I had not met on the best of terms and because he was always trying to undermine my abilities as a *pro se* litigant.

More than once Mr. Minor expressed to me his devout belief that I would never win the case and that I was just wasting his, the court's, and everyone else's time. I politely demurred and didn't express a view one way or the other—I knew the odds—but I was determined to do my best regardless.

Although it is extremely common for *pro se* litigants such as myself—especially *pro se* prisoners—to file lawsuits in federal court, it is not common for that same litigant to file such a meritorious lawsuit that it actually proceeds all the way to a jury trial.

Almost all lawsuits filed by *pro se* prisoners are dismissed as frivolous, malicious, or for failing to state a claim upon which relief can be granted. Simply put, a lot of people in my circumstances who are frustrated with the criminal justice system, file a lot of nonsense that are neither worth the court's time or is anything close to being a constitutional violation.

I hoped my false arrest lawsuit would be different. For starters, it was not even apparent that a crime had occurred. James Jackson was clear when he testified at the preliminary hearing in Attala County that there was no proof the fire was arson.

Second, there was no doubt that the only reason Jackson reopened the closed fire investigation was because of the book I published and the content of the message that it conveyed about the corrupt cops in Vicksburg and Warren County.

Finally, even if the fire was an arson, there was absolutely zero evidence linking me to it. And what evidence did exist exonerated me of being involved. That left, however, the one problem that was central to the whole case: Josh Chamblee's third statement which implicated me in the fire.

Chamblee's third statement could never be, without more, grounds for an arrest for arson when one takes into consideration the fact that the third statement was given under threat of arrest, a promise of collecting a $25,000.00 reward, and Josh's lack of credibility as a witness.

One mustn't forget that Josh had previously been arrested in Louisiana for lying to law enforcement officers and filing false police reports, and Jackson knew this posed a severe problem with Josh's honesty and credibility as a witness. But Jackson needed something, anything, in which to base an arrest warrant for me on, and if he had to conceal exonerating evidence from the judge in Attala County in order to effect that arrest, then he was determined to do so.

With these facts in mind I felt that my false arrest lawsuit was more meritorious than most and that if I could just get a fair hearing before a fair and impartial judge I might have a chance of obtaining justice for my family and I. But in order to get to a trial there were many more steps on the judicial ladder that we had to climb.

Once Mr. Griffith and Mr. Minor obtained a copy of my lawsuit and had opportunities to review it, the next step was for them to file the defendants' specific answers, or responses, to the lawsuit.

Mr. Griffith filed Sheriff Nail's answers and responses by May 2015, which then was quickly followed by Mr. Minor for Jackson and Chaney.

The answers and responses that a defendant files after being served with a lawsuit is their opportunity to plead their agreement or disagreement with each fact that is alleged in a complaint.

In Sheriff Nail's case, his attorney mostly filed answers claiming that Sheriff Nail either didn't know whether the facts, as alleged in my complaint, were true or not, or that he disagreed completely with my version of events. This is truly when the obstructionist tactics began from Sheriff Nail's attorney.

Mr. Minor's answers and responses to my lawsuit were more thorough and complete. Unlike Sheriff Nail, Jackson had more knowledge of the facts of my case and was able to either accept or deny my version of events as I alleged them in my complaint. The same was true for Chaney.

After the answers had been filed by the defendants, the next logical step was for us to proceed with discovery, or the exchange of evidence and information related to the litigation.

At this point in the case I did not have any discovery to turn over to the defendants. However, the defendants had plenty of discovery to turn over to me. And by the end of June 2015, both Mr. Griffith and Mr. Minor had disclosed to me everything related to the case that was in the possession of Sheriff Nail, Jackson, and Chaney.

Sheriff Nail's discovery packet contained a hundred-page file that he had accumulated during his part of the investigation into the fire. This packet contained pictures of the Atwood Lakehouse after the fire, a detailed, hand-sketched drawing of the lake house, its electrical box, layout, and utility pole, Sheriff Nail's notes, the written statements that Josh and I made on the day we were interviewed, our cell phone records proving our phones were in Starkville on the night of the fire, and the jail records from my arrest and brief stay there.

Seeing the pictures of the destroyed Atwood Lakehouse was the first time I had seen the destruction caused by the fire. It was total devastation. Nothing remained at all but bare brick columns. It was absolutely heartwrenching.

The pictures of the lake house had been the first thing in the discovery packet that I took time to study. Because Kade Atwood had not called the fire department when he saw the house on fire, everything was totally destroyed.

In one set of pictures, though, were what appeared to be numerous remains of rifles and shotguns that had been destroyed in the fire also.

In one picture a person could clearly see that a shell had been chambered in one of the weapons and had exploded during the fire, bursting the breach.

There also was, no doubt, hundreds of rounds of ammunition that had exploded in the fire. How Kade could ever legitimately claim to have slept through this raging inferno was beyond my ability to comprehend.

After studying the pictures, I moved to the next piece of evidence I felt was the linchpin of any probable cause determination—my cell phone records.

Included in Sheriff Nail's discovery packet was a court subpoena that Sheriff Nail had filed with the local Attala County Circuit Court wherein he makes a claim in October 2009 that "the fire was determined to have been arson" and that my cell phone records, including the location data information, were needed to determine if my cell phone was in use near Attala County on the night of the fire.

Because Sheriff Nail had been in touch with my Papaw prior to my arrest, we already knew that my cell phone records didn't place me at the scene of the fire. But after I filed the false arrest lawsuit, apparently, some of these vital cell records came up missing. The others were almost unreadable.

The cell records were the key to the entire case. If the cell records definitively showed that my cell phone was in use, connected to a Starkville tower, and that I was actually using it to text, make calls, and using apps during the time of the fire, that significantly made it harder for anyone to claim that I was almost two hours away burning down the Atwood Lakehouse at that time.

The only problem with the cell records that Sheriff Nail disclosed to me was that they were almost unreadable and were clearly incomplete. Most importantly, the cell records were missing the data and text records from the time period in question.

Sheriff Nail had clearly subpoenaed the entire records for mine and Josh's phones, but when his attorney disclosed the records to me after the lawsuit was filed, the only records I received were the call history and the tower location data for when those calls were made. This was problematic because I made far fewer calls than texts, and because during the time period in question I hadn't made any phone calls at all even though I knew that I had made at least a few dozen texts while in Starkville during the exact time that the Atwood Lakehouse was supposed to be burning.

I immediately filed a motion with the court asking one of the judges to compel Sheriff Nail and his attorney to disclose the entire cell records and to provide legible copies that were actually readable. Unfortunately, Sheriff Nail and Mr. Griffith were never able to provide anything more than what they'd already given.

Discovery is a long process, and without complete cooperation from all parties on both sides it can be an arduous and frustrating procedure. I realized early on that Mr. Minor was much more capable of getting along with me and hashing out the discovery details than Mr. Griffith was. Although I had never conducted discovery before in a lawsuit, I tried to become as knowledgeable about the process, and professional and helpful as possible. To that end it benefited both Mr. Minor and myself, but not Mr. Griffith so much.

CHAPTER SEVENTEEN

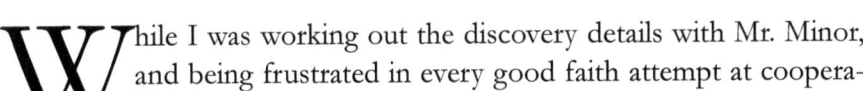

While I was working out the discovery details with Mr. Minor, and being frustrated in every good faith attempt at cooperation with Mr. Griffith, I was still doing time at El Reno, but it was not going well.

Over the holidays in late 2014 I developed a severe sinus infection that refused to respond to treatment. The nurse practioners and one doctor that El Reno had kept telling me that it was sinus drainage from a minor cold. When that lasted more than a month their diagnosis changed to a bacterial infection, but nothing they prescribed seemed to work.

From my viewpoint at the time, I cannot describe the amount of sinus pressure and pain that this infection caused me. My face was puffy, my throat hurt, and I was developing horrible migraine headaches. When I hit the three-month mark and hadn't gotten any better I knew that something was seriously wrong.

In early February 2015, I woke up in my cell one morning and could barely breathe. I felt my neck and discovered that it was swollen to about three times its original size. I immediately went to medical, and upon being seen by the nurse, I was whisked away in an ambulance to the local El Reno hospital.

Unfortunately, the doctors at the El Reno hospital misdiagnosed me as well. For two days they pumped me full of powerful antibiotics and corticosteroids, waited until the swelling went down, and then sent me back to the prison. As soon as I finished the course of antibiotics they prescribed—which only minimally helped—the infection and symptoms came roaring back and I was sicker than before.

Two weeks after returning from the El Reno hospital I woke up again with a swollen throat. However, I also felt like my brain had swollen so much that it would explode at any moment and that liquid fire flowed through my veins.

When I went to medical and had my vitals taken, my temperature registered 104.3 degrees and I began losing my vision. They immediately called me another ambulance.

Instead of going to the small first aid station that was the local El Reno hospital, I was whisked away lights and siren to Saint Anthony's Medical Center in Oklahoma City. Accompanied by a prison guard in the ambulance, and another behind us in a prison police car, I barely remembered the trip because I was so sick.

Saint Anthony's Hospital sits at a sharp angle to the site of the federal building that Timothy McVeigh destroyed in 1995. After his arrest he was even housed in solitary confinement at El Reno, but at the time I arrived in the emergency room at Saint Anthony's I wasn't aware of my closeness to history.

From the moment I arrived at the hospital the doctors there knew that I was suffering from something very serious. My blood work showed a serious infection and none of the antibiotics proved effective at killing whatever it was that was killing me.

The doctors immediately took cultures and samples of my sinuses, but those take days to grow to a point where the lab would be able to determine what it was that I had. In the meantime the doctors kept me on tons of antibiotics and lots of morphine.

About a week after I was hospitalized we finally found out what it was that was causing so many problems. I had somehow caught a deadly, flesh-eating fungal infection, known as Rhizopus, that had started in my sinus cavity and then spread throughout the bones in my face and into the tissues surrounding my brain. I was told by their experts that if we'd waited any longer, and the infection would have passed into the brain, I would not have survived.

Their ultimate treatment protocol was both complex, painful, intense, and was not something that I was looking forward to undergoing.

The first step was for the surgeons to put me to sleep and then cut out all of the fungus and infected tissue and bone. However, there was no guarantee that they would get all of the infection on the first round, and this is ultimately what occurred.

Over the course of thirty-three days I underwent four different surgeries in an attempt to remove all of the fungus and infected tissue and bone from my face.

Because of the rarity of the fungal strain itself, there was only one anti-fungal medication that had been proven to treat it. Unfortunately, this medication was not easily obtainable and it was not cheap.

Once it was determined that I needed this specific medication, the doctors at Saint Anthony's needed to obtain approval from the Federal Bureau of Prisons to pay the $1,500.00 a day price tag of this medication, and because I would need to be on it for at least three months, the FBOP didn't give their approval quickly.

Once I had undergone the four surgeries and began taking the anti-fungal medication I improved extremely quickly. Literally, the day after beginning the regimen I felt better than I had in years. I could breathe through my sinuses again, I wasn't in pain, and I was hungry, ravenously hungry.

Saint Anthony's had a food menu that I could order from three times a day and the food was outstanding. My favorite meal that I ordered most often was pancakes, fried eggs, bacon, sausage, oatmeal, orange juice, coffee, and milk. The nurses were superb and I gained about ten pounds. The best thing was that anytime I wanted I could go lay in a big bathtub and soak in the hot water. I'd not had a bath since getting arrested and I reveled in this short-lived luxury.

Unfortunately, all good things must come to an end, and after being a patient in the hospital for thirty-three days I was returned to the El Reno facility as a prisoner.

Prisons by their nature are not clean places. Some inmates, by their nature, are not clean people. We were provided cleaning supplies and disinfectant, but it is not always effective. And even with cleaner and disinfectant, some inmates either don't use it properly or use it at all.

An FBOP infectious disease intervention team scoured the prison looking for the source of the fungal outbreak, but I was never told whether their searches were fruitful. But when I returned to my cell I spent the good part of a day cleaning and disinfecting everything from the floor to ceiling, bunks to the toilet.

No explanation was ever given, though, for how I caught the infection. However, there was no doubt that the medical staff at the prison dropped the ball and continually misdiagnosed me for almost three months. Their misdiagnoses could have cost me my life, but it didn't, and for that I was thankful.

Soon after returning to El Reno, rumors began circulating through the prison that President Obama was going to visit and tour the facility on his upcoming trip to Oklahoma City. If this proved true, which it ultimately did, it would be the first time in history that a sitting president had ever visited a prison.

I have not always been a Democrat. At one time in my life—the time period I call the dark years—I had thought that I was a Republican. Even today some of my personal beliefs reflect a conservative viewpoint. But in the summer of 2015 I had firmly and undoubtedly established myself as a liberal Democrat. And I loved President Obama.

Since taking office in January 2009, President Obama and the Democrats in Congress had been slowly attempting to make changes to the criminal justice system. Most of these efforts centered on reforming laws that unfairly targeted black defendants at higher rates than whites. The crack-to-cocaine sentencing disparities being the most well-known.

President Obama had also been working with his attorney general to reduce the use of solitary confinement in the FBOP.

Unfortunately, officers in the FBOP are sometimes very quick to use solitary confinement as a temporary cure, or fix, for inmate issues that could have been resolved in a less intense manner.

It is now scientifically proven that solitary confinement leads to permanent mental illness, personality disorders, schizophrenia, and a host of other negative behavioral traits. Yet, the FBOP turns to solitary confinement quicker as a form of control and punishment than any other method of discipline. And it is leading to severe mental illness for thousands of inmates who will one day be returned to our communities.

The President and Congress had also been trying to work together to pass prison rehabilitation legislation that would improve an offender's chance of not reoffending upon release from imprisonment. This legislation would help offenders like me obtain the maximum amount of halfway house possible as we neared the end of our sentences.

The specific purpose of President Obama's visit to El Reno was to publicize his recent push to reform sentencing laws that resulted in life sentences for relatively minor drug offenses.

There were several inmates at El Reno who, besides their current drug crime, had no criminal history, yet were serving life sentences without the possibility of parole for drug offenses that state courts were barely punishing. Some inmates had not even been caught with drugs in their possession , but were convicted of conspiracy to possess instead.

On the day of President Obama's visit we were locked in our cells early that morning shortly after breakfast. We were told only that the President was visiting and would possibly be touring one of the housing units. We were strictly warned that if the President or anyone else entered our unit we could not bang on the doors, yell, make noise, obscene gestures, or anything else that may have been considered offensive.

It was obvious that the majority white officers and staff at the prison did not like President Obama and were not pleased at being the center of a media storm related to his visit.

The inmates, with few exceptions, couldn't have been more pleased. The only inmates who weren't happy that the President of the United States was coming to visit were the Aryan Skinheads who maintained their hatred of everything related to Obama.

Because I had changed cells over the holidays, my new cell window faced to the south, towards the interstate and El Reno Airport.

I'd expected that President Obama would fly into the local airport on Marine One since it was about a forty-five minute drive from downtown Oklahoma City, where he was staying, out to the prison. But shortly before his appointed time to arrive, the local news said on the radio that the President would be motorcading from the city out to the prison. I could only imagine the traffic nightmare along the interstate.

Both my cellie and I stayed with our faces fixed in our cell window until we saw the lead elements of the motorcade approach. We couldn't see much detail because of the distance, but I was impressed with the number of police cars and other vehicles with their flashing lights. Within a few moments I saw two limousines turn into the prison that resembled the President's, but then nothing more.

Approximately twenty minutes after the limousines arrived, the front doors of our unit opened and the dayroom was flooded with Secret Service and a few prison guards. By this time my cellie and I had moved from the outside window to the small window in our cell door.

The Secret Service and other guards established themselves in select areas of our dayroom and then they were followed by several individuals carrying large video cameras. The unit was quiet as a church mouse, but I knew what was coming next.

Much still to my astonished eyes President Obama walked through the doors of my prison unit followed by a small retinue of staff members, our warden, our SIS lieutenant, and other people I'd never seen before. He was quickly guided over to the first cell and he began a slow walk up the range viewing each cell and the occupants inside. I was so nervous I didn't know what to do. Both my cellie and I were fighting for space to look through our small cell window, but when President Obama passed in front of my door, less than three feet away, the only thing that I thought to do was give him a "peace sign" with my right hand. Surprisingly, the President returned my gesture with his own peace sign and continued the tour.

As I watched my president leave the housing unit I knew that I'd never loved him more. Certainly, no Republican president would have ever visited a federal prison. And certainly if one had, no Republican president would have been cool enough to return my peace sign with one of his own. I truly felt special that day. I honestly believed that some of the broken parts of our criminal justice system were on the track to being fixed. And it started with President Obama's visit to the El Reno federal prison in the summer of 2015.

One might think that getting a visit by the President of the United States would be a joyous occasion, but that was not the case with most of the guards at the prison.

I later discovered that the majority of the guards who were not needed for the presidential visit were locked in the inmate library for over three hours and were never given the opportunity to meet or even see the President. Many, who were not Democrats to begin with, found the entire spectacle pointless and fake. But we, as inmates, felt differently.

I had long realized that there were problems with the criminal justice system that began on the street-level when law enforcement conducted arrests. These problems flowed through the judicial pipeline into the courts and ultimately into the prisons. And when these inmates were discharged out the other end, after having served in some cases years more than what is necessary to properly punish and rehabilitate, the resulting effluent is neither prepared for reentry or rehabilitated.

We cannot continue to feed lawbreakers into a violent, hard system and expect them to be released and conduct themselves in accordance with the standards set by our society. But these problems begin at the local, street-level.

Too many times law enforcement carry out policies that lead to too many arrests when less serious, less far-reaching consequences can be imposed instead. The result is that many people get fed into the next step of the criminal justice system that is even less prepared to meet their individual needs, along with society's needs in deterring crime, than local law enforcements' are.

The court system today is geared more towards punishment than determining guilt or innocence. This is completely backwards. Courts should, first and foremost, be concerned with obtaining the truth. And the truth is that not every person arrested by law enforcement is guilty of the charged crime.

As in my case, law enforcement officers—who assume an "us versus them" mentality—are too often willing to cut corners, abuse their authority, fabricate evidence, and lie to the courts in order to clear cases from their files. Without court oversight of these illegal actions it will continue.

Unfortunately, because most courts adopt the same rationale as law enforcement, they are just as unwilling to make initial guilt or innocence determinations as the arresting officers are. This leads judges to deny bond to a disproportionate amount of defendants, resulting in months or years of incarceration before a defendant is formally found guilty or not guilty of their crimes.

Just as it was in my case, had my family not been able to secure the $5,000.00 needed to bond me out of jail, unlike most families of criminal defendants, I would of had to sit in the disgustingly atrocious Attala County Jail for months until the grand jury exonerated me. Incarcerating an innocent person, no matter how short a time, is abhorrent and is a direct threat to our concept of freedom and liberty in this country.

This is why, in theory, our Founding Fathers created in our system of justice a checks and balances procedure to ensure that a police state without oversight didn't occur in this country like it had under the reign of King George III and past monarchs.

Once police make an arrest it falls to the prosecutors and courts to "check" that arrest and ensure it was legal, proper, and supported by the evidence. And if those criteria were not met, or were only partially met, then the court was supposed to "balance" the interests of society and the rights of the defendant in determining guilt and, if necessary, crafting a punishment. But this system is failing, and it's failing just as seriously in the correctional arm of the criminal justice system as it is in the courts and on the streets.

Once a defendant has been convicted—and by my use of the word "convicted" I by no means wish to convey "fairly convicted"—an individual is then transferred into the custody of the prison system.

In an ideal environment our prison systems would be safe, violence-free facilities where inmates would be required to obtain educational and job skills, work with psychologists on any mental and emotional issues, and prepare for their eventual release back into society. The reality is quite different.

Of the more than twelve federal prisons that I have been to, every single one was filled with illegal drugs, violence, corruption on the part of the guards, and only token efforts were made at meeting the stated rehabilitation goals of the FBOP. In many cases, the inmates controlled almost every aspect of prison life.

From the perspective of someone whom has experienced all three levels of our criminal justice system, I am more qualified than most to unequivocally state that the system is broken at the local street-level, in the courts, and in the prisons. And until society determines to fix some or all of these problems then crime will continue to rise, drugs will remain part of the daily life of millions of Americans, and countless thousands will become victims to the unfortunate life choices of those who could have been helped, but weren't.

As President Obama highlighted numerous times towards the end of his administration, the broken criminal justice system affects blacks and other minorities much more so than it does whites. But as any demographic study of prisons will show, whites have their own problems that are nonetheless as serious as other ethnic groups.

What cannot be discounted, however, is the clear fact that blacks are targeted with violence from law enforcement at higher rates than any other demographic. It's a frustrating, disturbing problem that has existed for centuries and whose genesis began in the American antebellum South with officially sanctioned slave patrols.

As long as blacks and other minorities are targeted at higher rates than whites, there will always be the perception of animus, racism, and injustice at the hands of police. The by-product of these horrible attributes is a higher ratio of blacks in prison than whites and the undeniable fact that blacks receive longer and more harsher sentences than whites for comparable crimes.

This is what President Obama's visit to El Reno, and the media coverage that it brought, were all about. It's that time in America when we must start taking hard looks at some of our entrenched belief systems about crime, justice, and punishment. We were headed in the right direction. And many were hopeful that a Clinton Presidency would continue some of the reforms, or at least the discussion, that Obama began. But that wasn't to be the case.

Any objective look at our system, though, must begin at the street-level where local law enforcement interact with the community on a personal basis and make the ultimate first-tier decision about whether or not to conduct an arrest. And in carrying out those arrests law enforcement must conduct themselves according to an established acceptance on use of force.

Too much force results in the violation of citizens' rights and leads to an unacceptable escalation of police authority. Too little force puts officers' and citizens' lives at risk.

Unfortunately, violence is a part of policing our communities. We theoretically live in a society where the government allows its citizens to possess weapons and maintain a strong sense of individualism. In instances of confrontation, police must be able to meet threats on an equal basis.

However, it is the police that represent the most direct means by which the government imposes its will on the people. And when the government's will is imposed in an abusive manner, it is the police and their willingness to use violence that effects their policies.

Law enforcement respond with varying degrees of violence in differing situations. For the lucky, the police may use an unjustified, illegal arrest to impose their will and authority. For the unlucky, police use the most extreme form of violence—death.

Whether a victim of police violence is arrested, beat, or murdered, or all three, there must be some level of accountability both at the local, state, and federal levels.

Law enforcement culture also plays a large part in whether or not police corruption and abuses are allowed to flourish or wither. But one must ultimately ask, *who* polices the police? Who sets the standards? And who tells the police what is right and wrong? In theory, the individual communities—the citizens—should set the standards as to what is acceptable policing authority. But in many instances that is not to be the case.

We, in turn, are supposed to trust our police and law enforcement administrators and supervisors. And if they cannot be held accountable then we, as voting citizens, have the power to turn their bosses—the politicians—out of office. But too many times that doesn't and won't happen. Let's use my case as an example.

As you, the reader, will come to see, both through the evidence and testimony produced in this case, it is undeniable that James Jackson reopened the closed fire investigation case, coerced and extorted Joshua Chamblee into providing a false confession, and then obtained an arrest warrant for me without any evidence of arson. This was done solely because I had published a book which was critical of law enforcement.

Upon learning of the book's existence, Sheriff Martin Pace, and some of the other politicians and law enforcement in Vicksburg, contacted my U.S. Probation officer in an attempt to secure more harassment of me and my family, and they used their friendship and connections with the State Insurance Commissioner/Fire Marshal, Mike Chaney, to have me arrested and incarcerated for a fire that was never determined to have been an arson.

Lest not forget either that once the arrest warrant had been obtained, Sheriff Pace gave the warrant to the one deputy who had the most reason to murder me—Mike Traxler—who, then, ultimately led a violent, destructive, and totally unnecessary raid on my home that not only put my family in imminent danger, but had I been home, would have also put not only myself, but the son of the Mississippi governor in grave danger, too.

At every level of the criminal justice system my case failed to live up to our Constitution's guarantees of protection from tyrannical abuses of authority from government actors like Sheriff Pace, Mike Chaney, James Jackson, and U.S. Probation.

It was only when the Attala County grand jury—a body of independent citizens—met and considered the evidence and actions of law enforcement that I was exonerated of any wrongdoing and my name was cleared. Had this case remained in the hands of the corrupt arresting officers there's no doubt I'd be serving a life sentence for a fire that I had nothing to do with.

The system very nearly failed me. It certainly failed at the lowest and most important level. And it failed because corruption, like cancer, lives and breathes in the heart of people like Sheriff Pace, Chaney, and Jackson.

It failed, in that, not only was Jackson—the lowest level of the justice tier—allowed to conduct an illegal, politically motivated arrest, but his actions were ordered, approved, and condoned by the highest authorities in the justice tier even though they knew their actions to be illegal, morally and ethically wrong, and criminal.

These law enforcement officers and politicians constituted an axis of political corruption that I only hoped I could defeat in federal court. And as the case progressed I felt surer not only of my eventual exoneration, but vindication.

CHAPTER EIGHTEEN

Shortly after President Obama's visit to El Reno in the summer of 2015, I was told that I would soon be transferred to another prison. This shocked me because normally, when one doesn't get in trouble or have their custody points drop, the FBOP doesn't transfer inmates without just cause.

In my case, I was never told why I was being transferred. But I eventually assumed it was because I had spent so much time at the hospital, which required the already short-staffed prison to provide guards, that they didn't want to fool with me anymore. It may also have been that the medical department dropped the ball and exposed themselves to a malpractice lawsuit.

Whatever the reason, I found myself headed to the medium-security prison in Beaumont, Texas, immediately after Labor Day. The medium-security prison in Beaumont is known colloquially as "Bloody Beaumont" to the inmates who are sent there, and it lives up to its reputation.

Bloody Beaumont is one of the most dangerous, violent federal prisons in the system. It is literally run by the gangs, and the guards neither attempt to exert authority or necessarily care to. The food is horrible, the conditions worse, and there are very few recreational outlets to pass one's time.

What I did to deserve to go to Bloody Beaumont I still do not know. But I knew that I was in a place where I didn't want to be after I saw bullet holes in the walls surrounding the recreation yard. These had been put there by a trigger-happy guard during a recent inmate-on-inmate riot.

As much as I hated being at Bloody Beaumont I didn't let it distract me from the task of litigating the false arrest lawsuit in Aberdeen.

I had recently been granted limited authority by Magistrate Sanders to begin the discovery process outside of what Mr. Minor and Mr. Griffith had provided to me from their clients. I began my discovery attempts by submitting a list of interrogatories to the defendants and a list of questions that I wanted submitted to other witnesses in depositions.

Interrogatories are written questions, usually limited to twenty-five total, that are submitted by one party to the other before trial. The person who receives the interrogatories must give his answers in writing and under oath.

Depositions, on the other hand, are a written record of oral testimony in the form of questions and answers, made under oath, that can later be used in a trial. Since I was representing myself, I would have to convey the questions to the witnesses and they would have to respond with their answers under oath, which would all be recorded by a court reporter.

Since I was incarcerated I would be unable to depose, or ask the questions of the witnesses myself. Instead, the federal courts allow a procedure called "deposition by written questions." This procedure is very similar to interrogatories, but instead of being submitted to the defendants, depositions in the form of written questions would be submitted to the witnesses who were not being sued in the actual lawsuit.

While at El Reno I had composed multiple interrogatories of multiple questions that I wanted submitted to the defendants, Mike Chaney, James Jackson, and Sheriff Tim Nail. I also composed multiple depositions by written questions that I wanted submitted to Judge Ronald Stewart, Josh Chamblee's mother, Teresa Lyle, Emmett Atwood, and Kade Atwood.

I also asked the court to allow me to subpoena the insurance records from Mississippi Farm Bureau Casualty Insurance Company pertaining to the increase in insurance that Emmett did shortly before the fire at the lake house.

Any juror considering whether or not there was probable cause to arrest me would, no doubt, be interested in Emmett's recent increase of insurance and the pictures that were taken of the lake house four days before the fire that related to that increase.

The court also allowed me to subpoena the Attala County Justice Court records relating to the warrants issued for Josh's and my arrests.

In October 2015, while I was at Beaumont, Magistrate Sanders issued an order allowing me to submit the interrogatories to Chaney, Jackson, and Sheriff Nail, and also allowing me to conduct the depositions of Emmett, Kade, Mrs. Lyle, and Judge Stewart.

As part of the depositions the court issued me four subpoenas that had to be served on the four deposition witnesses. The interrogatories could be sent through the mail to Chaney, Jackson, and Sheriff Nail, so I didn't have to worry with having them served with subpoenas by a process server.

The purpose of the interrogatories, depositions, and subpoenas was for a singular purpose—to find the truth. There were so many unanswered questions that one was at a loss on where to begin. But I had to try.

The interrogatories that I propounded to Mike Chaney concerned what knowledge he had about my book, the interactions that he subsequently had with Sheriff Pace, and the ultimate thought processes and decisions he made when ordering Jackson to reopen the closed fire investigation case and obtain an arrest warrant for me at any cost.

The interrogatories to James Jackson were mostly concerned with exactly what evidence he had that the fire was arson, his communications with Chaney, the actions he took in obtaining the arrest warrants, and the procedures he followed when investigating the fire.

In Sheriff Nail's case, things were a little different. The interrogatories to him were mostly a reflection of my desire to know the details of the early part of the fire investigation, specifically the conclusion he made when obtaining my cell phone records in November 2009 when he alleged to the court that the "fire was determined to have been an arson."

Besides that one, unsubstantiated claim, there was nothing else in the record prior to Chamblee's third statement that indicated that any of the investigators had any possible clue that the fire was arson.

One might conclude, however, that Sheriff Nail's claim in November 2009 that the "fire was determined to have been an arson," was nothing more than a bald-faced lie to the local judge to justify the issuance of a search warrant. This point of contention would become crucial as the case unfolded.

If Sheriff Nail was filing false statements under oath, claiming that a crime had occurred, when in actuality nothing could be further from the truth, then my lawsuit against him would be justified on numerous grounds, the least of which would be a clear violation of the Fourth Amendment. But that would be a contentious point that could only be hashed out at trial.

Moving past the interrogatories to the defendants led me next to the witnesses that I felt would be crucial to proving my claims at a trial.

My first deponent, Emmett Ray Atwood, was the most crucial. And the information that he provided under oath would, I felt, make or break my case. It was with this in mind that I formulated his deposition questions to allow me to inquire into the insurance policies he maintained on the property, his whereabouts on the night of the fire, how he was notified of the fire, his interactions with Sheriff Pace, Chaney, and Jackson after the fire, and how he ultimately spent the proceeds from the insurance payout after the fire.

I was especially interested in any communications he may of had with Chaney after the fire. I knew that Emmett and Chaney were good friends and that Emmett contributed lots of money to every political campaign that Chaney was involved in. And I knew that Emmett had been putting Chaney under a lot of pressure to have me arrested for the fire, but I needed the details, and my deposition questions were designed with those goals in mind.

Kade Atwood, on the other hand, posed a different challenge. If the fire was indeed an arson, then Kade, from my perspective, was the most likely suspect for having started it.

To begin, I knew that Kade had allegedly slept through the raging fire even though guns and ammunition were exploding and the resulting inferno was by no means quiet. I found his excuses implausible because Kade lived across the open expanse of the lake, less than one hundred yards from the lake house.

Furthermore, Kade's bedroom windows were floor-to-ceiling, with beige-colored blinds. The lake house was so huge that any fire had to of filled his entire bedroom with bright light. Unexplainably, though, Kade not only didn't hear the fire, he didn't see it either.

More tellingly, when Kade finally "discovered" the fire, he never called the fire department. He didn't even immediately call law enforcement. By all accounts, Kade called Emmett first, waited on Emmett to drive two hours from Vicksburg, and then, together, they contacted law enforcement.

One has to wonder what occurred in the "lost time" between Kade discovering the fire, Emmett arriving, and them finally calling Sheriff Nail. I certainly wondered, and as the case progressed so did everyone else.

My deposition questions to Kade concentrated almost solely on these unexplainable failures. I felt that if the truth to discovering the true cause of the fire was ever to be found, then Kade Atwood would hold the key to that information.

I had also propounded deposition questions to Josh Chamblee's mother, Teresa Lyle, in a vain effort to determine Josh's location. Since providing his coerced third statement, Josh had disappeared and no one could find him. However, it was obvious to the court and everyone else that if the case eventually went to trial then Josh's testimony would be needed. But no one could find him.

My deposition questions to Mrs. Lyle were short and to the point. We wanted to know where Josh was and we wanted to know how to get in touch with him. To that end I had hoped that Mrs. Lyle would be cooperative, but that wasn't to be the case either.

The last deposition that I was granted leave to take was for Judge Ronald Stewart. Judge Stewart had been the one that Jackson had gone to to obtain the arrest warrant for Josh and me, and whom had conducted the preliminary hearing shortly after my arrest.

The deposition questions to Judge Stewart were designed to discover what, if any, information he remembered receiving or being told by Jackson when he issued the arrest warrants. Critical to any determination in the federal false arrest lawsuit was whether or not Jackson withheld any probative or exculpatory information from Judge Stewart when he obtained the arrest warrant. I was hoping Judge Stewart would be cooperative.

Judge Stewart and my other grandfather, Aaron Tolleson, had been very good friends over the course of about fifty years. My grandfather had even sold one of his houses to Judge Stewart and supported him in his election campaigns. However, this friendship was broken on the day of my arrest when Judge Stewart chose to believe Jackson over my Papaw when he was asked to lower my bail.

Since my arrest and the preliminary hearing before Judge Stewart in

October 2011, Judge Stewart had been beaten in his reelection efforts by a first-time candidate.

Even though Attala County is a conservative, Republican county, many people believed that Stewart was beat because he refused to perform any further marriage ceremonies after the U.S. Supreme Court's *Obergefell* decision legalizing gay marriage. Rather than be forced to marry gay couples, Stewart decided to cease performing any marriages at all, and many believed this cost him his election.

I wasn't concerned with Stewart's political beliefs, or whether he gave a shit about performing gay marriages. As far as I was concerned I wasn't even sure that openly gay people existed in Attala County, but I did care whether or not Stewart could help or hurt my false arrest case. And that was what my deposition questions were meant to answer.

While I was busy working out the details of the interrogatories and depositions, Sheriff Nail's attorney, Mr. Griffith, filed a motion in October 2015 to dismiss my claims against his client, also known sometimes as a motion for summary judgment on the pleadings. This essentially asked the court to dismiss my lawsuit against Sheriff Nail before any discovery could be completed.

My claims against Sheriff Nail were based on the fact that he had conducted the majority of the investigative footwork and that he was the one to personally arrest me.

Under my theory of liability, based upon numerous federal case law, if a law enforcement officer conducts the majority of the investigation into a crime, and is therefore familiar with the evidence, and conducts the actual arrest, he can be held liable for that false arrest even if he was not the one to procure the warrant. This is what occurred in my case.

Sheriff Nail knew, through his own investigative efforts, that there was not any credible evidence to support the issuance of an arrest warrant for arson. Yet, despite knowing the arrest warrant was not supported by evidence, he nonetheless executed it against me and incarcerated me in the county jail. I felt federal false arrest case law was clear on this point even though Sheriff Nail didn't himself procure the warrant from Stewart.

When he arrested me, Sheriff Nail knew the warrant wasn't supported by the evidence, yet, he chose to use it to arrest me anyway. By conducting that arrest, knowing it wasn't supported by the evidence, it opened

Sheriff Nail to liability, or at least that was my theory.

Mr. Griffith argued the opposite on behalf of his client in the motion to dismiss that he filed in October 2015. However, before the court in Aberdeen would rule on Sheriff Nail's motion to dismiss, they wanted for the parties to conduct, at least, some limited discovery on the issues raised in my lawsuit. This was a small win for me.

I felt that after the interrogatories and depositions had been answered and responded to, I'd have a much better understanding of the situation and the evidence to support my claims. Most importantly, though, I'd have the evidence I needed to defeat Sheriff Nail's motion to dismiss and the ultimate motions to dismiss that I knew Jackson and Chaney would ultimately be filing.

Meanwhile, while the discovery process was playing itself out, I decided I no longer wanted to be at Bloody Beaumont and was able to obtain a transfer to the medium-security prison in Talladega, Alabama. And what Bloody Beaumont was, Talladega was not.

When I arrived at Talladega the week before Christmas 2015, I was impressed with its small size, laid back environment, lack of violence, and improvement in food and conditions. Simply put, Talladega was a really decent place to have to do time.

Unfortunately for me, once I met with the doctor at the facility and he saw where I'd recently had the sinus surgeries for the fungal infection, it was decided that Talladega was not medically equipped to continue treating me. So less than three weeks after arriving at Talladega I was once again whisked away to a new facility.

This time, the FBOP moved me to one of the medium-security prisons in Butner, North Carolina. Butner maintains five prisons in the same general area. One is a medical center, two are mediums, one is a low, and the last is a camp. I went to the first medium and, like Talladega, it was also a pretty good spot to do time.

Butner was a unique prison in that it was designated by the FBOP as a facility solely for sex offenders and former gang members who no longer wanted to participate in the gang lifestyle in prison.

One of the first inmates that I met upon arriving at Butner was Bernie Madoff, the Ponzi schemer who bilked billions of dollars from innocent investors. Madoff was serving one hundred and fifty years for multiple federal crimes relating to the Ponzi scheme that he conducted for decades.

At the time, Madoff was probably the best known federal prisoner currently incarcerated in the United States. However, his presence at Butner was low-key, unobtrusive, and surprisingly never generated more than a brief passing notice by the inmates.

There were not many intelligent, "normal" inmates at Butner that I felt were capable of meeting me on an intellectual level, and that is how Madoff and I first became friends; there simply weren't many decent people to talk to there.

During the nine months that I was at Butner, Madoff and I developed a close friendship, built not only on shared likes and interests, but also on mutually beneficial assistance. I knew my way around the federal legal system and Madoff knew his way around money, although I am the first to admit that neither of our knowledge about those two topics served us very well in the past.

Even though Madoff didn't have any hope of ever receiving any type of helpful assistance from the federal courts, he truly believed that he had a chance of obtaining freedom through the compassionate release program run by the FBOP.

Madoff was quickly approaching old age and had rapidly declining health. Furthermore, Madoff did have quite a few influential friends whom were advocating on his behalf for a compassionate release. I thought that what was more important was that Madoff, who is Jewish, had the backing of the Israeli government for a presidential commutation of his sentence.

With President Obama going out of office in January 2017, Madoff sought my help in quickly preparing the legal documents and letters of support which argued that he should be given compassionate release or a commutation of his sentence.

While I didn't believe that Madoff had a harebrained chance in hell of ever getting released, either through compassionate release or a commutation, I was more than willing to help him prepare the documents to make the requests. Hope is both a blessing and a curse in prison, and in Madoff's case, hope is what kept him alive and I was more than happy to help him.

Another inmate that I met soon after my arrival at Butner was Nicodemo "Nicky" Scarfo, the former "boss" of the Philadelphia Mafia.

Scarfo was in his mid-eighties and was serving a life sentence that he'd been given in the late 1980s for multiple crimes, including extortion, murder, and all the other federal offenses that go with being the boss of a major Mafia family.

Scarfo, by all accounts, was one of the most vicious, violent, bloodthirsty gangsters of all time. According to those familiar with his case, Scarfo was responsible for over forty murders, including a state court judge. He apparently ruled Philadelphia and Atlantic City with an iron fist and was known by other Mafia bosses as the most ruthless boss of the families.

But the Nicky Scarfo that I met at Butner in February 2016 was a small, unassuming man, no more than five feet, four inches tall, weighing less than one hundred and ten pounds. At first glance, Scarfo could have been anyone's beloved grandfather. He didn't look like a Mafia boss. He didn't look violent or ruthless. In fact, upon first meeting Scarfo, I fell in love with him as a mentor, friend, and an upstanding person.

I found it impossible to believe what other inmates told me about his past and what I later read about his life. During my nine months at Butner, Scarfo became almost a surrogate grandfather to me. Never, not a single time, did I ever see the "boss" that Scarfo once was crack the facade of gentleness that he constantly maintained.

If Scarfo was the most vicious and ruthless gangster to ever rule the New England coast, I certainly never saw it at Butner. Scarfo was the epitome of sophistication, politeness, and gentlemanly behavior. One would think that a Mafia boss from Philadelphia would be reluctant to maintain a friendship with a gay white boy from Mississippi, but Scarfo and I never found a dull moment in our conversations about history, prison, and politics.

He even regaled me with numerous stories of how he used to provide prostitutes to Donald Trump and accept cash bribery payments from him. During the 1970s and 1980s, one couldn't operate a hotdog stand in Atlantic City without Scarfo's approval—much less a casino. And Trump, no doubt, used and was used by the Italian Mafia to build and operate his casinos and hotels there. Allegations that were later proven true by the Steele dossier and the Mueller Report.

Scarfo reminded me most of the Mafia character, Sonny LoSpecchio, from the movie *A Bronx Tale*, who is played by the actor, Chazz Palminteri.

In the movie, Sonny befriends a young Italian kid in the neighborhood and takes him under his wing, but doesn't allow the kid to become involved in the Mafia lifestyle. Sonny is all about respect; all about honesty.

Scarfo was like Sonny in many ways. His biggest lessons to me were the sanctity of one's word and the need to always give respect to those who deserve it and demand respect from those who need to give it.

Unfortunately, several months after I was released from prison Scarfo passed away in January 2017. I didn't learn about it, though, until I was reading Scarfo's Wikipedia page several months later. Regardless of what Scarfo might have been, and what he might have done, to me he was a great friend and was almost like a grandfather.

Unlike Scarfo, I didn't share a positive opinion of Carmine "Junior" Persico, the former boss of the New York Colombo family. He, also, was serving a life sentence at Butner for a wide-ranging accumulation of federal crimes.

Persico, who was also in his eighties, spent most of his time by himself, ate alone, lived alone, and except for the person that pushed his wheelchair, didn't speak to many people. The comparison between Scarfo and Persico was like night and day. But although I didn't like Persico personally, I respected him because of the position that he once held and his decision never to cooperate with the government and snitch on his fellow La Cosa Nostra Mafia compatriots.

The last interesting point to be made about Butner and its idiosyncrasies as a prison was its maintenance of a separate unit known in the FBOP as "Maryland Unit."

In 2006 the United States Congress passed the Adam Walsh Act to deal with the problem of interstate control of sexual offenders in the country. Part of the Act allows the government to indefinitely confine in prison any individual that a judge deems to be a "sexually dangerous person." Unfortunately, the definition of a "sexually dangerous person" has been interpreted fairly broadly and liberally.

Under the Adam Walsh Act, at the completion of a sex offender's prison sentence, if the government believes that he may qualify as a "sexually dangerous person" it can petition the local federal court to continue to incarcerate that sex offender for the rest of his life under the assumption that if that sex offender is released back into the community he would be incapable of not committing another sex offense.

I vehemently disagree with this approach. To begin, I believe that our criminal laws are more than sufficient to take into account a sex offender's past criminal history and the current charge for which he is incarcerated and provide for a punishment commensurate with his crime.

Second, compared to every other felon, it is scientifically proven that sex offenders have the lowest rate of criminal recidivism. Releasing them back into the community poses, statistically, a far lesser chance of them committing new sex crimes than does murderers, thieves, and drug dealers.

Finally, by essentially incarcerating an American citizen because of what that citizen *might* do in the future goes against every tenet of a free society. It is never acceptable, no matter how unpopular the defendant, to imprison someone without them having committed a crime. But that is what the government is doing. And when one is civilly committed as a "sexually dangerous person" they are placed in the Maryland Unit at Butner to essentially serve out a prison sentence for the rest of their lives for something that they've never been convicted of in a court of law. It's not fair. It's not justice. But it's happening everyday at Butner.

While at Butner several other interesting things happened to me that would be remiss without mentioning. The first was, obviously, I was preparing for my release back into the community. Even though my actual release date wasn't until April 2017, I was eligible to receive up to six months in a halfway house in Mississippi prior to the April 2017 release date.

Before release, however, there were several legal developments that proved beneficial for me. The first was that the attorney that Covington County hired to defend them in the lawsuit that I'd filed against Sheriff Ford and the other deputies was interested in settling the case with me.

Will Allen, an attorney in Brookhaven, Mississippi, had been hired by the Covington County defendants shortly after they'd been served with my lawsuit. I believe that once Mr. Allen saw the evidence in the case, he recognized that his clients were on the losing end of what would have been a long, drawn out process.

From the first, Mr. Allen and I developed a great, friendly, professional relationship. Mr. Allen was one of those rare opposing attorneys that everyone involved in the litigation should have no problem getting along with. At all times through the litigation he treated me with respect and dealt on an intellectual level with me that was neither condescending or belittling. This, again, was unlike Mr. Griffith, who was representing Sheriff Nail in the false arrest lawsuit trial.

Interestingly enough, Mr. Allen and Mr. Griffith were hunting buddies and close friends. But I never understood why I could deal so well with Mr. Allen but not Mr. Griffith. However, as Mr. Minor had, Mr. Allen continually informed me that I could never win a false arrest lawsuit against a law enforcement officer in Mississippi. According to him, jurors simply wouldn't condemn a cop. His and his clients' interests in settling the lawsuit with me was done solely to save resources and money.

This desire to save the costs of extensive litigation led Mr. Allen and the Covington County defendants to settle the lawsuit for a confidential, but substantial sum of money in the spring of 2016. With that lawsuit over, I moved on to the two remaining ones.

My lawsuit against the Vicksburg Police and Warren County Sheriff's Departments had been pending before Judge Wingate since it was filed in July 2011. For what was completely typical of the lack of competency on Judge Wingate's part, the lawsuit had been pending without any action for five years.

In the summer of 2016 I reached out to the attorneys that were representing the separate departments and, surprisingly, both sides were willing to settle out-of-court for confidential sums of money. Any part, though, of any deal, would also entail the Vicksburg Prosecutor's Office dismissing the actual criminal trespassing charge too, and by August we had reached a deal. I was given a certain sum of money, I dismissed the lawsuit, and the criminal charge went away.

Even though I knew that I was in the right, and that I was exercising my First Amendment rights, I felt that the City of Vicksburg finally did the right thing after five years by settling the lawsuit and dismissing the criminal charge. I was currently two and zero on winning federal lawsuits in court. I was hoping that the false arrest arson lawsuit would be number three.

CHAPTER NINETEEN

When the Fifth Circuit Court of Appeals denied my criminal appeal in September 2014 one of the last avenues of legal review that I could obtain on my revocation convictions and sentence was through a petition for a writ of certiorari to the United States Supreme Court, but the chances of that petition being accepted were less than one percent.

Getting the Supreme Court to review one's criminal convictions is not a matter of right, solely judicial discretion. No one has a constitutional right to have their appeals heard by the highest court, and those petitions that are granted are only for compelling reasons.

Normally, the only time that the Supreme Court agrees to hear a federal criminal case is if a United States circuit court enters a decision that is in conflict with the decision of another federal court or if a circuit court has decided an important question of constitutional law that has not been, but should be, settled by the highest court.

I knew that the chances of getting my petition accepted by the Supreme Court were slim to none, but usually the highest court is particularly sensitive to criminal cases dealing with First Amendment rights. I fully believed that my arrest for trespassing, and Judge Wingate's erroneous assumption that my conduct was not constitutionally-protected speech, violated the First Amendment. There might be a chance that the highest court would accept my case on this ground.

I filed my petition for a writ of certiorari to the U. S. Supreme Court shortly before Christmas 2014. Unfortunately, nothing ever happens quickly, and it was June 2015 before the highest court denied my petition, which wasn't a surprise.

According to the procedural rules of federal law, I then had one year from the date that the highest court denied my petition to file what is known as a habeas corpus petition, or as it is officially known, a motion to vacate a federal conviction or sentence pursuant to 28 U.S.C. Section 2255.

Habeas corpus is Latin for literally, "You have the body." These type of petitions are usually employed to bring a person before a court, most frequently to ensure that the person's imprisonment is not illegal.

Since my appeal had been denied by the Fifth Circuit there had been quite a bit of discovery about my revocation case before Judge Wingate. And all of it was a direct reflection on how innocent I was and how ignorant and oblivious Wingate and the government was in my case.

Let it be remembered that I was sent back to prison because Wingate found me guilty of trespassing and failing to register as a sex offender under Section 45-33-23(h) of the Mississippi Code of 1972 by allegedly staying at Roger Cole's house approximately fourteen times, non-consecutively, between May 2011 and August 2011. Based on that alleged criminal activity, Wingate sentenced me to seventy-two months in prison.

When Wingate found me guilty of trespassing he stated that if I would have possessed a ticket to the Miss Mississippi Pageant I would have lawfully been on the premises and not subject to arrest.

As stated before, my attorney, Omodare Jupiter, had in his possession the ticket that I bought and used to gain admittance to the City Convention Center property the night of my arrest. Yet, he failed to introduce it into evidence. This incompetent failure caused me to be found guilty of this probation violation.

Likewise, Jupiter possessed Officer Daniel Thomas's arrest report that he wrote on the night of my arrest. However, when Thomas later testified in court, his testimony conflicted significantly with his report. But again, Jupiter failed in questioning Thomas about these lies and inconsistencies.

More important than the problems with the trespassing conviction, since my appeal was rejected by the Fifth Circuit, I had learned that the Mississippi Legislature repealed Section 45-33-23(h) in April 2011 and replaced it with a law that only required sex offenders to register addresses where they stayed seven or more *consecutive* days.

Cole's testimony at the trial was clear, and the government admitted in their arguments on direct appeal, that I never stayed more than two nights in a row at Cole's house. There was no way that I could have violated the new law by staying at Cole's house seven or more times in a consecutive fashion.

What is absolutely horrendously shocking about this revelation is that the United States government and Judge Wingate prosecuted and imprisoned me under a law that had been repealed and was no longer in effect at the time I allegedly stayed at Cole's house without registering as a sex offender.

During the time frame from May 2011 to August 2011 there was not a single, valid law in effect that criminalized me staying at Cole's house fourteen times or more, non-consecutively, without registering it. Even if the government's allegations were true, I was sent to prison for six years for something that was not a crime.

I suspect that the government and Wingate knew that they were sending me to prison for conduct that no law criminalized. I am positive that they knew that Section 45-33-23(h) had been repealed by the Mississippi Legislature and was no longer in effect. And if they did they had an ethical and legal obligation to inform us.

There can be nothing more morally, ethically wrong and evil than imprisoning an innocent person. But that's exactly what the government did. They sent me to prison for something that wasn't illegal.

What shocked me more was that Jupiter was so incompetent that he couldn't even do a simple Google search to determine whether the law that the government was accusing me of violating was still valid or not. Any simple search would have uncovered the fact that the Section 45-33-23(h) law had been repealed in April 2011—one month before I was alleged to have begun staying with Cole—and was no longer in effect.

If one thinks that I didn't punch the cinderblock walls of my cell and scream bloody murder into the stuffing of my prison pillow when I learned of this judicial atrocity, then they'd be highly mistaken.

When the Mississippi Legislature repealed Section 45-33-23(h) and replaced it with a law that only required sex offenders to register addresses where they stayed seven or more consecutive days in a year, that eliminated any requirement that I may of had to register Cole's residence even if I did stay there fourteen or more times between May 2011 and August 2011. And if Jupiter would of been anything more competent than a first-year law student then I'd of had to of been found not guilty of this violation and I wouldn't currently be in prison. The injustice was infuriating.

At that point, the only avenue of judicial relief available to me to challenge this injustice was filing the habeas corpus petition pursuant to 28 U.S.C. Section 2255. And as the one-year deadline neared for me filing the habeas corpus petition I was convinced that I would eventually be cleared of this accusation.

Ultimately, the habeas petition that I filed raised numerous grounds, or issues, for relief. The two most important grounds argued that I'd been incarcerated for conduct that was not criminal and that my attorney provided ineffective assistance of counsel by not properly researching the Section 45-33-23(h) statute and raising a proper defense to me being prosecuted under that repealed law.

I also argued that Jupiter was an incompetent and ineffective attorney for not introducing the pageant ticket and questioning Officer Thomas on his lies and false testimony at trial that conflicted so significantly with the arrest report that he filed on the night of my arrest.

In addition to several other procedural mistakes that I argued rendered my conviction illegal, I also argued that Judge Wingate sentenced me to thirty-six more months in prison than what the statute allowed.

I felt that the law regarding the amount of imprisonment that a district court could impose upon the revocation of one's probation was no more than thirty-six months. Jupiter never made this argument in court during my trial so it couldn't be raised during the direct appeal. And, ultimately, Wingate sentenced me to double what I thought the statute allowed.

I based my belief that I was sentenced beyond the statutory maximum on the law that specifically governs imprisonment upon revocation of probation. That law, 18 U.S.C. Section 3583(e)(3) reads that "a defendant whose term [of probation] is revoked under this paragraph may not be required to serve on any such revocation more than 3 years in prison if the offense that resulted in the term of [probation] is a Class B felony."

It was never contested that at the time of my 2005 conviction that the crime they said I committed was a Class B felony. Therefore, the most that Wingate could give me should have been three years in prison.

This was just another atrocity on the long list of judicial incompetency examples committed by Wingate. As I stated earlier, Wingate rules his inner sanctum according to his own rules and sense of what is right and wrong. And because Wingate is so jaded due to his inability to obtain his long desired, coveted appointment to the Fifth Circuit, he sincerely believes that he retains the power and intellectual capacity to make decisions that are clearly contrary to established appellate and Supreme Court case law. My only hope was that with the habeas corpus petition I'd finally get a fair hearing.

As with many habeas corpus petitions, the district courts aren't quick to act on them. I filed my habeas petition in May 2016, shortly before I was scheduled to be released from prison and go to the halfway house in Hattiesburg, Mississippi. And, as expected, Judge Wingate took no action even though anyone who read the habeas petition could clearly see that Wingate and the government had seriously screwed up and that I was incarcerated for something that was not illegal.

I knew that I'd eventually be successful if I ever received a fair hearing on the habeas petition—which would never happen in front of Wingate—but while I waited the false arrest lawsuit in Aberdeen was still slowly working its way through the system.

After obtaining permission by the court in August 2015 to submit the deposition questions to Emmett, Kade, Teresa Lyle, and Judge Stewart, the next step in the process was setting up the actual depositions with a court reporter in Jackson, Mississippi, and then having the witnesses served with federal subpoenas which legally required them to attend the depositions.

After contacting a court reporter and scheduling the depositions for February 22, 2016, I had all four of the federal subpoenas delivered to each witness personally. By being personally served with the federal subpoena, this obligated each witness by law to attend the deposition or face being held in contempt of court. I'm by far naive, but I didn't expect Emmett and Kade to just completely ignore the subpoenas.

When a federal subpoena is served on someone, whether he or she is a party to the litigation or is a witness, there are several avenues available for that person to contest the issuance of that subpoena. The most common way is to file a motion with the court to quash the subpoena.

Usually, there are only several reasons why a court will grant a witness's request to quash a subpoena. The most common reasons are that the witness will be unduly burdened by complying with the subpoena, that the subpoena requires the witness to travel beyond the allowed geographical limits, which is about one hundred miles from the witness's place of residence, or that by complying with the subpoena a trade secret or other confidential research, development, or commercial information would be unnecessarily disclosed. Obviously, none of these would apply to the witnesses in my case.

All of the witnesses lived within one hundred miles of Jackson. The subpoena gave each witness more than three months notice that they had to appear and answer questions on February 22, 2016, and each witness would be providing answers that had nothing to do with commercial trade secrets. It should have been open and shut that each witness had to attend as ordered.

When February 22, 2016, came, only Mrs. Lyle and Stewart showed up and answered the questions that were submitted to them—sort of.

Mrs. Lyle absolutely refused to answer the questions regarding where Josh was living or working. Her reasons were that Josh felt threatened by me and didn't want to answer any questions regarding his and my arrest or his past criminal history. However, a witness in a deposition doesn't have the right to refuse to answer relevant questions. And since Magistrate Sanders had already approved the questions that Mrs. Lyle was supposed to answer, refusing to answer them was tantamount to violating a court order.

Stewart on the other hand took a more subtle approach. Every question that was submitted to him regarded his actions in issuing the arrest warrants for Josh and me, his conversations with James Jackson, and his memory about the evidence and testimony submitted to him at the October 2011 preliminary hearing in the Attala County Justice Court.

Unfortunately, Stewart answered every single question with the response, "I don't know" or "I don't remember." His deposition was an absolute waste of time because no matter how the question was asked, or how many times it was asked, Stewart was always going to claim that he couldn't remember any details. It seriously made me consider that he may have legitimately been suffering from dementia or Alzheimer's disease.

Emmett and Kade, however, refused to attend the deposition. They didn't even acknowledge the subpoenas and deposition or attempt to contest them by filing a motion to quash. They simply ignored a federal subpoena.

Their actions, at first, confused me, but later it was kind of shocking. I knew Emmett was used to being provided special treatment by the local courts in Vicksburg. After all, he had financially supported in one form or another almost every judge there. But this was a subpoena issued by a United States district court. It wasn't something to be trifled with. But that's exactly what he and Kade did.

When a witness refuses to attend a deposition, after being duly subpoenaed, there is only one step to take to compel their attendance. In March 2016, I filed several motions with the court to hold Emmett and Kade in contempt of federal court for ignoring the subpoenas and not showing up for the scheduled depositions.

On August 19, 2016, Magistrate Sanders issued an order directly to Emmett and Kade that compelled them to attend a future deposition. Magistrate Sanders specifically put in his order that "[f]ailing to attend these depositions is tantamount to violating a court order, and as such, whoever does not attend could be held in contempt of court and sanctioned."

I scheduled a new deposition for December 6, 2016, in the hopes that Emmett and Kade would attend this one. New subpoenas were issued and I had my process server again personally serve Emmett and Kade with the subpoenas, plus a copy of Magistrat Sanders's order compelling them under threat of contempt to attend. I was told by the process server that Emmett tore his new subpoena and Magistrate Sanders's order to pieces and threw them on the ground.

Once I was successful in getting a new court order requiring Emmett and Kade to attend a second deposition under penalty of contempt, I moved on to Mrs. Lyle's refusal to answer the deposition questions that were submitted to her in regards to where Josh was.

After Mrs. Lyle refused to disclose Josh's location, I had to file a compliance motion against her and ask that Magistrate Sanders issue an order compelling her to answer the questions.

On August 19, 2016, the magistrate issued an order that required, under threat of contempt, Mrs. Lyle to disclose to me and the court where Josh was living and what his contact information was. With this order in hand, I had Mrs. Lyle served with a new subpoena which required her to attend the deposition on December 6, 2016, that Emmett and Kade were supposed to also attend.

As part of the discovery process I'd felt it absolutely essential to obtain the insurance records on the Atwood Lakehouse because I knew that Emmett had recently increased the insurance shortly before the fire. In furtherance of this goal the court issued a subpoena to Mississippi Farm Bureau Casualty Insurance Company.

The Farm Bureau insurance agent in Vicksburg who provided Emmett his coverage on the lake house was Jan Hyland Daigre. Daigre was not only Emmett's insurance agent, but she was also a relative by marriage and the Circuit Clerk of Warren County. Of course, she and I despised one another.

The genesis of our mutual dislike originated during my battle with the City of Vicksburg over their illegal trespassing arrest of me.

As the Circuit Clerk of Warren County, Daigre was responsible for filing all of the legal documents that originated regarding the case. Circuit clerks are supposed to be neutral, unbiased government bureaucrats who are supposed to administer the paperwork and details of legal cases in the courts. Daigre, however, on numerous occasions took exception to the legal work I was filing in the trespassing case in an effort to assist the City of Vicksburg in covering up the illegal arrest. In the end, though, it was I who won and the City and Daigre who lost.

When Daigre was served a copy of the federal subpoena, which required her to disclose the details of Emmett's insurance coverage on the lake house, the first thing that she and Farm Bureau did was try to have the subpoena quashed. Apparently, both Daigre and Emmett knew that something shady and possibly illegal had occurred regarding the increase in insurance shortly before the fire and they were going to do everything possible to cover it up.

On February 12, 2016, Farm Bureau and Daigre, through their attorneys, filed a motion to quash the subpoena on the grounds that complying with it would pose an undue burden on their office and that the information contained in the records was privileged, protected information and not subject to disclosure.

On March 11, 2016, the magistrate issued an order that Daigre and Farm Bureau had to comply with the commandments of the subpoena and disclose to me the contents of the insurance records related to the lake house in the year prior to the fire in 2009.

The whole purpose of obtaining the insurance records was to prove that Emmett drastically increased the insurance coverage on the lake house shortly before the fire, and that purpose was stated clearly in Magistrate Sanders's order requiring them to comply with the subpoena.

Desperate to try and continue the coverup, Daigre and Farm Bureau provided me copies of the insurance records that they maintained, but tellingly, they redacted and deleted the exact information that the subpoena called for. Without knowing the numerical figures for what the insurance coverage was before the increase, and not knowing by how much money Emmett increased the coverage, the whole disclosure was pointless. This proved my assertion that Daigre, Emmett, and Farm Bureau were attempting to cover up something that had been done illegally or unethically.

To obtain the unredacted copies of the insurance records I had to file a compliance motion with the court on August 22, 2016, asking the magistrate, again, to compel Daigre and Farm Bureau to comply with the subpoena.

Finally, after going through a process that was more difficult than pulling the teeth of an African crocodile without a sedative, Daigre was finally forced to comply with the subpoena. And as I had believed all along, the records proved that Emmett had drastically increased the insurance coverage of the lake house shortly before the fire to something to the effect of a little over $500,000.00.

For a house that was almost a hundred years old, and which was more similar to a hunting cabin than a true lake house, the $500,000.00 sum was staggering. But the main question of why Emmett had so drastically increased the coverage shortly before the fire still eluded me. But at least I was getting closer to the truth.

The last subpoenas that I had issued were to the Attala County courts asking them to provide me with the records from Josh and I's arrests in 2011.

Mrs. Wanda Fancher was the Circuit Clerk of Attala County, and what Jan Hyland Daigre was, Mrs. Fancher was not. From the beginning, Mrs. Fancher cooperated fully with the discovery process, was more than helpful, and maintained a polite and courteous manner at all times.

I'd met Mrs. Fancher before and she was good friends with my Papaw in Kosciusko, whom was also an elected official in Attala County. When my first book was published my Papaw took me around the Attala County courthouse and introduced me to people as his grandson who was a published author. Unfortunately, it wasn't long after those introductions that James Jackson abused the court's trust in Attala County to have me falsely arrested.

What Mrs. Fancher disclosed to me in response to the subpoenas were the affidavits that Jackson signed swearing under oath that he had evidence of arson and that Josh and I were guilty, the actual arrest warrants that Judge Stewart signed, and then the grand jury verdict exonerating me of any wrongdoing.

The affidavit that Jackson signed under oath, swearing that a crime had been committed, was the one single piece of evidence that would later come back and bite him in the ass. With no evidence of arson, and even less evidence that Josh and I were responsible, Jackson committed a serious felony when he lied under oath.

With all of the subpoenas that had been issued I'd been able to collect a small bit of information that proved helpful in piecing together the ultimate story. But without being able to question Emmett and Kade, or receiving the answers from the interrogatories that I'd sent to Chaney, Jackson, and Sheriff Nail, a good portion of the story, and the majority of the major questions, remained unanswered.

The next step in the process was to get those interrogatories and file a response to the motion to dismiss on summary judgment grounds that Sheriff Nail's attorney had filed in October 2015 asking Judge Aycock to dismiss the case.

By this point in the process Mr. Griffith and I had no possible way of ever being able to communicate or cooperate together on any portion of the discovery process. It was frustrating and I felt it totally uncalled for because not I only had I been able to get along extremely well with Mr. Minor, but I'd also been able to effectively communicate and work with the attorneys that represented the other defendants that I'd sued in Covington County and Vicksburg, Mr. Allen being the best example.

One of the first contentious issues that we faced was obtaining clear, legible copies of the cell phone records that proved Josh and I were using our phones in Starkville during the time of the fire.

The records that Mr. Griffith provided to me, which came from Sheriff Nail, were blurry, small, and almost completely unreadable. But this was a vital piece of evidence and I requested multiple times that I be provided readable copies. I never got them.

This lack of cooperation by Mr. Griffith was only the beginning, but as the case progressed it would get worse before, ultimately, it surprisingly got better.

CHAPTER TWENTY

The first defendant to file answers to my interrogatory questions was Sheriff Nail. On December 9, 2015, Mr. Griffith sent me the copies of his client's sworn answers to my questions and also filed them with the court. To say that I wasn't pleased would be an understatement.

Sheriff Nail's answers to my interrogatories were vague, blame-shifting, and in some cases simply outright avoidance of the question asked.

For example, Sheriff Nail, not surprisingly, did everything he could to minimize his role in the investigation and shift the blame entirely onto Jackson's shoulders.

Specifically, though, when I asked the question about his November 2009 request to the local court for a subpoena for my cell phone records, wherein he states under oath that "the fire was determined to have been an arson," Sheriff Nail absolutely refused to answer the question about what evidence he relied on in making that assertion.

It was clear that Sheriff Nail did not have one scrap of evidence that would lead an investigator to conclude that the fire was determined to have been an arson, and from his interrogatory answer it was also clear that he could not provide a justification for that assertion. But I wasn't going to let him get away with it.

I immediately filed a motion asking the court to compel Sheriff Nail to provide an answer, but before the court could rule on that motion Mr. Griffith provided another interrogatory answer from Sheriff Nail that contained the statement that Sheriff Nail concluded that the fire was arson based on the third statement that Josh Chamblee provided to law enforcement in July 2011.

When I read that answer I was even more dumbfounded. My interrogatory question specifically asked what evidence Sheriff Nail had in *November 2009* to conclude that the fire was determined to have been an arson. Josh's third statement two years *after* Sheriff Nail submitted that false assertion to the local court had nothing to do with what evidence he had in November 2009. The legal smoke screen was clever on Mr. Griffith's part, but I wasn't fooled. It was also perjury, as all interrogatory answers are under oath.

On February 22, 2016, I filed another motion to compel full and complete interrogatory answers from Sheriff Nail regarding what specific evidence he had, specifically in November 2009, that led him to conclude that the fire was an arson.

By this time, both Judge Aycock and Magistrate Sanders were tired of the intricate legal ballet dance that Mr. Griffith and Sheriff Nail were doing, and in a March 30, 2016, order they required that Sheriff Nail provide a complete and *truthful* answer to my question regarding what evidence he had in November 2009 to conclude that the fire was an arson.

Finally outmaneuvered, both Sheriff Nail and Mr. Griffith conceded in a March 31, 2016, response that there wasn't any evidence to conclude that the fire was arson. Sheriff Nail had lied under oath to the Attala County courts. Another small win for me.

In late February 2016, Jackson finally provided the responses to the interrogatory questions that I submitted to him. This is when the major pieces of the puzzle finally began fitting together.

According to Jackson's answers, he was never able to rule the fire an arson because when he arrived at the fire scene on November 13, 2009, the ground was too hot and was still smoking, which prevented him from getting accurate readings on his hydrocarbon detector.

This answer was a shock to me because at the preliminary hearing before Judge Stewart in October 2011, Jackson had clearly testified that when he used his hydrocarbon detector at the fire scene he got all negative results. Not a single time did he mention that the ground was still smoking or was too hot to get an accurate reading.

If one were to believe Jackson's interrogatory answer, though, one would still be left to wonder why Jackson didn't wait until the ground cooled off and quit smoking to go back and try his hydrocarbon detector tests again.

I knew the answer to this inquiry, though. Jackson didn't need to go back out to conduct accurate tests because the first time he tried it he got all negative readings and, because, from the first moment he was instructed to investigate the case by Mike Chaney, he already was convinced that the fire was an arson and that I was responsible.

His interrogatory answer that said he couldn't get an accurate reading because the ground was too hot, and was still smoking, was just an excuse so that he could claim that it was possible that accelerants were used to start the fire. But using that logic still left the question hanging about why he didn't go back out to test the ground again once things cooled off and quit smoking.

The next interrogatory question that I was most interested in was about what exactly Chaney told Jackson prior to my arrest. According to Jackson, Chaney's only involvement in the investigation was a simple directive to "work the case and arrest the person responsible."

I knew this was a crock of shit and that Chaney was much more involved than issuing a simple directive to work the case and arrest the person responsible, but interrogatory answers are prepared by an attorney and I knew Jackson's answer to this question was specifically designed by Mr. Minor to shield Chaney from liability at all costs. I would have to find other ways to prove that Chaney specifically ordered my arrest.

Mike Chaney provided his answers to my interrogatory questions last. Unfortunately, his answers weren't very helpful either. They consisted almost entirely of denials regarding every aspect of the investigation.

I knew without a doubt that Chaney, Sheriff Pace, and Emmett were the driving forces behind Jackson reopening the closed fire investigation in July 2011 and procuring the arrest warrants. And I thought that the interrogatory questions to Chaney would ultimately give me the information I needed to prove the conspiracy. I was highly mistaken, though.

While not denying communicating with Sheriff Pace about the fire investigation, Chaney claimed to have no specific memory of any specific conversation that he may of had with Sheriff Pace. He, likewise, denied specifically ordering Jackson to arrest me in retaliation for my book. Chaney only claimed that he told Jackson to investigate the fire and arrest the person responsible.

Once the interrogatories had all been answered by the individual defendants, and after I'd received all of the information from the multiple subpoenas that had been issued, the next step in the process was for the defendants to file their motions to dismiss my lawsuit on summary judgment grounds.

Before a civil lawsuit can go to trial, defendants often file motions to dismiss on summary judgment grounds in an effort to get the lawsuit dismissed. This procedural rule allows the speedy disposition of a controversy without the need of a trial.

Summary judgment is basically a decision by the court concerning the merits of a lawsuit when the pleadings, depositions, interrogatories, and other evidence show that there is no genuine issue as to any material fact alleged in the lawsuit.

At the heart of my lawsuit were several legal claims that Judge Aycock would ultimately have to determine whether they were meritorious or not. The most important claim was that Chaney, Jackson, and Sheriff Nail violated my Fourth Amendment rights under the U.S. Constitution to be free from a false arrest when there was no probable cause to support the arrest warrant.

As part of that argument, I had to show that not only was there no evidence to support the issuance of an arrest warrant, but also that Jackson withheld vital and important evidence from Judge Stewart that should have been considered before the judge issued the warrant.

The U.S. Supreme Court has defined probable cause as only a probability or substantial chance of criminal activity, not an actual showing of criminal activity. Probable cause exists when the entire facts and circumstances of the case are sufficient for a reasonable person to conclude that a suspect had committed an offense.

In my case, the legal consideration was whether any reasonable, well-trained officer in Jackson's position could legitimately conclude that an arson had taken place and that I was responsible. My argument was that no one could reasonably conclude that the fire was arson and that I was responsible.

The last element that had to be proven to hold the defendants responsible for my false arrest was whether or not they were entitled to qualified immunity. Qualified immunity protects public officials from civil liability in lawsuits when their conduct does not violate clearly established constitutional rights, even if their actions were wrong.

To overcome this protection, I had to show that the defendants specifically knew they were violating my constitutional rights by arresting me when they knew that there wasn't any evidence to support the arrest warrant.

Taking the entire facts and circumstances into consideration I believed that anyone could reasonably conclude that Jackson was the most liable for my false arrest because he was the one to actually procure the arrest warrant. I knew, however, that he was only acting under orders from Chaney.

Sheriff Nail was liable, too, even though he didn't take any part in procuring the arrest warrant. However, he knew that there wasn't any evidence to support the arrest and he shouldn't have taken part in executing it.

Back in October 2015, Mr. Griffith filed on behalf of Sheriff Nail his motion to dismiss the lawsuit on summary judgment grounds. His argument was that Sheriff Nail only participated in a small part of the initial investigation, wasn't aware of the evidence in the case, and that he relied on what was, to him, a facially valid arrest warrant when he took me into custody at the Attala County Sheriff's Department on August 1, 2011.

I knew that Sheriff Nail's argument wasn't exactly accurate. He, in fact, was the officer that conducted the majority of the investigation and at all times he was familiar with every piece of evidence that had been gathered in the case.

On December 14, 2015, I filed my response to Sheriff Nail's motion to dismiss arguing that because he was the officer to conduct the majority of the footwork in the investigation he was familiar enough with the evidence to realize that the arrest warrant that Jackson procured on July 29, 2011, wasn't facially valid because there was no probable cause to base it on.

The case law in the Fifth Circuit was somewhat confusing and not clearly defined with regard to this issue. Even though I felt that the U.S. Supreme Court's case law was more on point, there simply wasn't a case similar enough to mine to be able to gauge how Judge Aycock might rule in regards to Sheriff Nail's liability in executing my arrest.

On December 18, 2015, Mr. Griffith filed a reply to my response to Sheriff Nail's motion to dismiss on summary judgment grounds. His reply contained an argument in a recent Fifth Circuit case that stated that the appellate court was, in most cases, unwilling to extend liability for a false arrest beyond the person who actually procured the warrant. There was a glaring exception, though.

The exception was if the officer who executed the arrest should have known that the facts supporting the arrest warrant were baseless, false, and didn't state sufficient grounds to support the arrest. This interpretation required us to examine the affidavit that Jackson filed under oath on July 29, 2011 which he presented to Judge Stewart to obtain the arrest warrant.

When a law enforcement officer approaches a judge to procure an arrest warrant for a suspect, that officer is mandated under law to provide that judge with specific facts and details which support the judge's ultimate decision that there is probable cause to issue the warrant. Without those facts and details in the affidavit, the judge cannot make a fair determination whether or not probable cause exists.

The affidavit that Jackson provided to Stewart was nothing more than a simple generic recitation of the elements of the crime of arson. It stated: "*David Garland Atwood, on or about the 11th day of November 2009 in the said County did unlawfully, willfully, maliciously, and feloniously set fire to and burn a dwelling house, the property of Emmett Atwood located on Youth Center Road.*"

This affidavit clearly did not contain any facts or details that would lead Stewart, or any other person for that matter, to conclude that there was probable cause for my arrest.

Sheriff Nail knew that arrest warrants must be supported by probable cause. This is police training 101. And when he executed the baseless arrest warrant on me at the sheriff's office, he knew that Jackson's affidavit did not state sufficient facts and details to support the warrant. Hence, he was liable for my false arrest.

On April 8, 2016, Mr. Minor filed motions to dismiss on summary judgment grounds for both James Jackson and Mike Chaney.

Chaney's motion to dismiss asked that Judge Aycock dismiss the lawsuit against him because he was entitled to the protection of the *respondent superior* doctrine.

The *respondent superior* doctrine shields government supervisors from civil liability when the actions of their subordinates violate the constitutional rights of a citizen.

I knew that Chaney ordered my arrest as retaliation for publishing my book. However, at that point in time I didn't have any direct evidence that Chaney specifically ordered Jackson to arrest me. Without proof that Jackson was acting directly under Chaney's orders—according to the motion to dismiss filed by Mr. Minor—Chaney couldn't be held liable for my false arrest.

In making a response to Chaney's defense, I argued that he made himself liable in the case when he ordered Jackson to work the case and arrest the person responsible. I thought I had clearly shown that had Chaney not given this directive to Jackson in July 2011, I'd never of been arrested. That was my argument anyway and Judge Aycock would have to work that out herself.

From the beginning, everyone involved in the case knew that Jackson was going to have the most difficulty in obtaining a dismissal of the lawsuit against him. After all, he was the one that actually procured the warrant and attempted to have me prosecuted for the fire.

Mr. Minor attempted to explain Jackson's liability away by arguing that because Stewart issued the arrest warrant that this somehow shielded Jackson from being sued. There was validity to this argument, though.

According to Fifth Circuit and U.S. Supreme Court case law, when an arrest is made pursuant to a warrant issued by a judge, if all of the facts and circumstances regarding the case are presented to that judge, with no exculpatory evidence being hidden, then the arresting officer is shielded from liability even if the suspect is ultimately exonerated of the crime.

But there are several very important exceptions to this rule. The most pertinent exception states that if the law enforcement officer somehow taints or interferes with the independent deliberations of the judge during the judge's decision process in determining whether to issue the warrant, then that officer can later be held responsible for the false arrest.

Likewise, if the officer withholds any exculpatory or relevant evidence from the judge, which tends to demonstrate a suspect's innocence, that officer can be held liable for the false arrest.

Mr. Minor, in Jackson's motion to dismiss, argued that Jackson did not withhold any relevant evidence and that he provided Stewart with Chamblee's third statement which allegedly implicated me in the fire. According to Mr. Minor, this was sufficient for Stewart to make an independent decision regarding whether there was sufficient probable cause to issue the warrant for my arrest.

There were multiple problems with this argument, the least of which was the fact that Jackson utterly failed to provide Stewart with any of the evidence that proved my innocence.

On April 25, 2016, I filed my response to Jackson's and Chaney's motions to dismiss on summary judgment grounds. I argued that not only had Jackson failed to provide the judge with my cell phone records proving my phone was in use in Starkville during the time of the fire, along with my shoe impressions proving that my shoe tread and size didn't match the footprints found at the scene, but that Jackson had also failed to inform Stewart about the credibility problems with Josh Chamblee's third statement.

Jackson knew not only that he had obtained Josh's third statement under the threat of arrest and the promise of a $25,000.00 reward, but that Josh also had past criminal arrests for filing false police reports and lying to law enforcement officers. Jackson also failed to inform Stewart that Josh had previously provided me two alibi statements swearing that we were together in Starkville on the night of the fire and that I was in no way responsible.

It is undisputed that the only information that Jackson gave to the judge was the generic affidavit and Chamblee's third statement, which, when one reviews, contained only a single hearsay statement which implicated me in the fire. This clearly did not comport with the due process requirement under the Fourth Amendment of the Constitution.

The last major argument that I made in my lawsuit was that the defendants had violated my First Amendment rights under the Constitution when they arrested me in retaliation for me publishing my book, *Into Hell I Rode*.

There was no doubt in my mind that Jackson was ordered by Chaney to reopen the closed fire investigation shortly after my book was published. And there was no doubt that Chaney issued this order on the recommendation of Sheriff Pace and Emmett Atwood.

Sheriff Pace was in a desperate run for reelection against a popular, former deputy of his and the last thing he needed was my book dredging up the old ghosts of his involvement in Sheriff Barrett's drug dealing and the other law enforcement and political corruption that had plagued him, the sheriff's department, and Vicksburg in general.

Likewise, Emmett was furious that my book exposed the Atwood family's past membership in the Ku Klux Klan and the extramarital affair that he had with the African-American woman that he fathered a child with and then utterly abandoned.

It was clear that had it not been but for the book, the fire investigation would have remained closed, tucked away forever in the inner confines of Jackson's file drawers.

In First Amendment retaliation claims the U.S. Supreme Court has been very clear that the First Amendment prohibits not only direct limits on individual speech, but also adverse governmental action against an individual in retaliation for the exercise of that protected speech.

Under the legal test established by the highest court, I had to prove that I was engaged in constitutionally-protected activity, that the defendants' actions caused me to suffer an injury, such as a false arrest, and that the defendants' actions were motivated by the constitutionally-protected speech. I felt that my lawsuit and the defendants' actions clearly met this standard.

After I filed the responses to all of the defendants' motions to dismiss on summary judgment grounds, I had a short time to sit back and reflect on all that had happened, all that was happening, and what was about to happen.

The FBOP had approved me to release from prison on November 9, 2016, and go to the Dismas Charities Halfway House in Hattiesburg, Mississippi. To finally receive my actual release date was extremely satisfying and exciting.

I'd been given a six year sentence by Judge Wingate for doing absolutely nothing wrong or illegal. When I was released on November 9, I'd of done almost five years total on that sentence. Although I was still hopeful that my 2255 habeas corpus petition would eventually get granted, and I'd have the probation aspect of my sentence removed, going to the halfway house was essentially the end of my prison sentence.

Halfway houses, in theory, are designed to help offenders reintegrate into society by placing newly released inmates in a structured environment that provides them access to jobs, education, and social support services while that inmate transitions back into society.

A lot of inmates hate going to a halfway house because of the strict rules involved in living there. In addition to being forced to obtain employment, an inmate at the halfway house is obligated to provide the halfway house twenty-five percent of their gross earnings. As far as I was concerned, I didn't care if I had to pay them one hundred percent, halfway house was bound to be better than prison and I was ready to go home.

During the summer of 2016, I spent most of my time exercising and playing softball at Butner. Bernie Madoff and I spent a considerable amount of time together and he was genuinely happy that I was releasing back to the community. My mother and sister even flew into the Raleigh-Durham airport and visited me one weekend.

I also religiously watched the unfolding drama in the 2016 presidential election, and not only supported Clinton and the majority of the issues in the Democrat platform, but I was also thoroughly convinced that in November there would be a Clinton landslide against the abomination of what is Donald J. Trump.

Every few weeks I kept tabs on the status of the defendants' motions to dismiss, but while their motions were pending every other action in the case had been put on hold. Not only did I believe that Clinton would win in November, but I also suspected and believed that by November Judge Aycock would rule in my favor and deny the defendants' summary judgment motions.

Thankfully, Judge Aycock's order and opinion regarding the motions to dismiss came down a lot quicker than I suspected. I was at mailcall one afternoon and received a large, rather thick manila envelope bearing the return address of the clerk's office in Aberdeen. I immediately knew what it was.

I ran to my cell and tore open the envelope. Without waiting to read the contents of her opinion I skipped straight to the last page. Clearly written in black and white was her decision, handed down and issued on July 14, 2016.

The motions to dismiss on summary judgment grounds filed by Sheriff Nail and Mike Chaney were granted. This meant that my lawsuit against these two defendants was dismissed. James Jackson, on the other hand, was a different matter. Judge Aycock denied his motion to dismiss and allowed the lawsuit to proceed against him. It wasn't a complete victory, but it was victory enough.

In dismissing the lawsuit against Sheriff Nail, Judge Aycock stated that it was undisputed that Sheriff Nail's only role in my arrest was taking me into custody at the sheriff's department. He wasn't involved in procuring the arrest warrant or in obtaining Josh Chamblee's third statement. Finally, the judge concluded that because the record indicated that the sheriff had no knowledge of the circumstances leading to the issuance of the warrant, his motion to dismiss should be granted.

It wasn't what I wanted to hear, but it was a fair, competent assessment of the available evidence and the law.

Judge Aycock dismissed the lawsuit against Mike Chaney on the grounds that I expected she would. She concluded that at that time there wasn't any factual basis in the record to conclude that Chaney directly ordered my arrest or that Jackson conducted the arrest specifically on Chaney's orders.

However, I knew that if competent evidence came out during the subsequent trial, that Chaney was more involved than what the evidence was able to prove at the time of Judge Aycock's opinion in July 2016, then I could go back and pursue those claims against Chaney. Again, I didn't agree with the opinion, but I felt like Judge Aycock based the dismissal on a fair assessment of the evidence as it existed at that time. Her assessment of Jackson's involvement, though, was a totally different matter.

The judge wrote in her opinion that, unlike Sheriff Nail and Chaney, Jackson was the driving force behind the investigation and procurement of the arrest warrant, and that it was undisputed that the only evidence that Jackson presented to Judge Stewart was Chamblee's third statement.

Judge Aycock recognized Chamblee's third statement for what it was—a convoluted fraud of deceit and dishonesty that was apparent to anyone who read it. This led her to conclude that although an accomplice's statement, without more, is enough to sometimes establish probable cause, the circumstances in which it was obtained, the reliability of the witness, and the corroboration of the facts contained in the statement are all relevant to the probable cause determination.

Judge Aycock wrote that multiple factors called into question the reliability of the information that Chamblee provided in his third statement.

First, the third statement was obtained under the threat of arrest and the promise of a $25,000.00 reward. Second, even with no evidence that the fire was arson, Jackson relentlessly pursued Chamblee, harassed his family, and threatened his mother with her son's arrest if she didn't help him convince Chamblee to implicate me in the fire.

Lastly, Judge Aycock concluded that the third statement was severely lacking in detail because Chamblee didn't know the date of the fire, he couldn't mention specifics about the location, how far away it was, what time it was, whether the house was on a lake, or even how and specifically where the fire was started.

According to her view of the case, there were strong indications that Chamblee was not a credible witness and that the information in his third statement was both vague and unreliable.

After considering the fact that Jackson also ignored the exculpatory evidence proving my innocence, such as the cell phone records showing where I was using my phone in another part of the state, Judge Aycock concluded that any reasonably well-trained officer in Jackson's position should have known that his affidavit failed to establish probable cause and would not have applied for a warrant.

By Jackson failing to provide Judge Stewart with these important details, the exculpatory evidence, and by failing to inform him of the problems with Chamblee's credibility, Jackson deprived Stewart of the opportunity to conduct an independent evaluation of whether or not to issue a warrant based on probable cause.

When I finished reading Judge Aycock's patent indictment of Jackson's actions, I was shocked. Her opinion left no doubt that she clearly did not approve of Jackson's actions and that his conduct would not be allowed to go unpunished. It was a damning condemnation. And it was a gigantic victory for me.

This was the first time that I had ever had a judge, much less a federal judge, rule in my favor. Overnight, Judge Aycock became my new hero. She left me totally convinced that there was still justice in the system. For once I felt that I'd finally found a judge who still honored that age-old concept of fairness, integrity, and justice.

The next step was for Mr. Minor and Jackson to get together and try to settle the case with me, or for Judge Aycock to set the case for trial before a jury.

Soon after her opinion was issued, I spoke to Mr. Minor about a possible settlement. He let it be known, however, that they would never settle. He also reminded me that I'd never win at a trial.

When they didn't offer to settle, Judge Aycock set the case for a jury trial at 9:40 A.M., on March 6, 2017, in the U.S. Courthouse in Oxford, Mississippi. By then, I knew I would be ready and I hoped that I would eventually win.

CHAPTER TWENTY-ONE

Once the case was set for trial there were numerous things that both Mr. Minor and myself had to do before we ever set foot inside Judge Aycock's courtroom.

For starters, I was still in prison. Emmett's and Kade's depositions still had not taken place and there was no guarantee that they would show up for the one scheduled on December 6, 2016.

I also wanted to take a deposition with Josh Chamblee, but without his mother's cooperation, there was no easy way to find out where he lived. The last address that he was known to have resided at was in Indianapolis, but due to Josh's itinerant nature, he no longer lived there.

While I was incarcerated I'd signed up for a prison pen-pal service and had met several people that turned out to be good friends. But one person that I met that turned out to be the best friend of all was a retired physician named David Ferguson from Indianapolis, Indiana.

Through the years, during my incarceration, David and I stayed in constant touch through prison email and letters and he knew all about my ongoing struggle against the defendants in all of my legal cases.

When I began taking a hard look at seriously locating Josh, I turned to David for help, and like a true friend he was more than happy to help me.

I was released from federal prison on November 9, 2016, after being given a little over five months in the halfway house in Hattiesburg. The night before my release, though, was a devastating, jaw-dropping shock as I listened to the radio and learned that Donald Trump would be our next president rather than my beloved Hillary.

One would imagine that one's thoughts would be on one's imminent release from prison if one was in my shoes, but the only thing that went through my mind on the night of Trump's election was the horrible nightmare of scandal, dishonor, corruption, and degeneracy that Trump and his administration would bring to our country. The only consolation that I took from the situation was that I was being released from prison the next day.

At ten in the morning, my mother and aunt were waiting to pick me up, and once we all had our hugs, kisses, and a good cry, we piled in the car and started our fourteen hour drive back to Mississippi. I had a little over twenty-four hours to report in at the halfway house and I didn't want to get off to a bad start by being late, so our plans were to drive straight through.

My first meal upon release from prison was an Egg McMuffin from McDonalds and a large orange juice. By the time we reached Georgia, though, we stopped at one of the chain restaurants and ate a more substantial meal. I didn't know what the halfway house would serve, but I wasn't taking any chances. I needed some good food after doing five years in prison.

When I arrived at the halfway house I was immediately met by a team of friendly, helpful staff members called "resident monitors." The terms "guard" and "inmate" were not used. Overnight I went from being a prisoner to being a "resident." And I also quickly realized that I had a lot more freedom and was treated more like a human being than I had been in prison.

My mother and I had done some shopping before dropping me off, so I had everything that I needed to make an easy transition from prison khaki to civilian clothes at the halfway house. I was assigned a bunk in a six-bunk room. I had to share a shower and sink with the other five guys, and our meals were served to us in a small cafeteria, but overall I realized that I shouldn't have any problems making the adjustment.

The director of the halfway house, Christopher E. Kelly-Patton, was another matter altogether. I could definitely tell that the staff members at the halfway house were wonderful people and were there to genuinely help us transition successfully back into society, but I didn't get the same feeling about Kelly.

From the start, my opinion of Kelly was not good. I felt that he was a braggart and show-off, and I was even less impressed with how he treated his employees. Numerous times I observed him, in front of the residents, berate, belittle, and demean the people that worked for him, which ultimately would delegitimize any authority that the resident monitors may of had over the residents.

I felt that Chris Kelly also had a tendency to feel threatened by any resident that appeared or was smarter, better dressed, and more intelligent than him. Kelly's ostentatious behavior manifested itself in a number of ways, including him bragging about the BMW car that he drove, the Rolex watch on his wrist, and his allegedly extensive educational background. By the end of my stay in the halfway house I was utterly convinced that Chris Kelly was a megalomaniac, and that opinion was shared by many others besides me.

One of the requirements of halfway house placement was that a resident obtain employment as soon as possible. Unfortunately, employment opportunities are limited for residents in a halfway house because many businesses are already reluctant to hire felons, and they become even less likely to hire someone that's in a halfway house because the resident monitors have to verify the resident's employment, call the employer every day to verify that the resident is at his job, and the employer is required to sign mountains of paperwork and waiver of liability forms that ensure the halfway house isn't sued. A lot of employers don't have time for all that or the inclination.

However, the one employer in Hattiesburg that hired halfway house residents without hesitation was the local chicken processing plant. They ran three shifts a day and, with their high turnover rate were willing to hire anyone for any job then available. I was told that this was my best option for immediate employment.

When a resident obtains employment they are given special privileges not normally given to others in the halfway house. I wanted the special privileges of being able to obtain social passes to go out to eat, go to the gym, the movies, the mall, or anywhere else that I wanted to go as long as it was for a legitimate purpose and I could verify my attendance, usually through purchase receipts.

One week after arriving at Dismas Charities I went to work on the night shift at the local chicken plant on their sanitation crew. I knew I was in trouble, though, on my first night.

My belief system is complicated when it comes to animal rights. I used to be a hunter, and I still believe in hunters' rights for people who want to own guns and hunt animals. But as for me, I no longer believe in killing animals myself, although this poses problems for me because I still enjoy eating meat. However, I was not prepared for the chicken apocalypse which greeted me upon my arrival at my new job.

Everywhere I looked there was a mass scattering of every conceivable chicken part imaginable. Blood was strewn around like some sick movie set from a *Saw* production. Equipment designed for the mass extinction of the chicken population jutted overhead and around corners. I had honestly never imagined what I was seeing, but a job was a job and I wanted those social passes.

I was given a rubber smock, rubber boots, gloves, face masks, a bucket of soap, green scrub pads, and a high-pressured water hose and told to get to work. I had approximately six hours to make my section of the plant inspection ready by 6:00 A.M. I was not enthused, but I learned to do my job and I did it well to the best of my ability from thence forth.

One of the most effective means in which a former prisoner can reintegrate into society successfully is by having a reliable means of transportation. Thankfully for me, due to the recent monetary settlements made by most of the law enforcement defendants that I'd sued, I was able to buy a new vehicle shortly after arriving at the halfway house.

Having a vehicle allowed me not only to drive back and forth to work everyday, but it also allowed me to take my social passes around Hattiesburg without having to depend on friends or family. The first altercation that I had with Chris Kelly involved the December 6, 2016, depositions of Emmett, Kade, and Teresa Lyle. I'd set them up with Magistrate Sanders's approval more than three months before and I couldn't miss them. However, Kelly wouldn't allow me to attend them because they were going to be conducted in Jackson, which was nearly ninety minutes away.

I failed to comprehend Kelly's logic, though, because there were numerous residents who worked in Jackson that were allowed to drive back and forth between there and Hattiesburg everyday. With no other option, I placed a call to Magistrate Sanders's office and explained my dilemma to his law clerk, Rylee Zalanka.

This was the first time that I had spoken to Rylee, but he was extremely helpful, polite, and professional. Not once did he ever treat me any differently than he might an attorney that was approaching him with similar issues. Most importantly, he was more than willing to assist me in obtaining my attendance at the depositions.

Shortly thereafter, Kelly informed me that I'd been approved to go to Jackson on December 6 for the depositions, but that I'd have to call him upon arriving at the court reporter's office and upon leaving when the depositions concluded. I didn't have a problem with these conditions and I called Rylee to thank him.

When I showed up for the depositions, Emmett and Kade were noticeably absent, however, Teresa and her husband, Paul Lyle, were present. I introduced myself and was surprised that they didn't recognize me from the several times that I'd met them when Josh and I were together. They were, likewise, surprised to see me because they thought that I was still in prison. But all-in-all they were polite and I made an extra effort to remain so as well.

Once the deposition began though, Mrs. Lyle again refused to answer the question about where Josh was. In response to the questions Mrs. Lyle pled the Fifth Amendment and refused to answer.

I'd anticipated that that would be her response and I placed a call on the speakerphone to Magistrate Sanders in an attempt to resolve the issue.

After explaining to Rylee what our issue was, Magistrate Sanders came on the line and questioned Mrs. Lyle about her reasons for refusing to answer the deposition questions about Josh's location and contact information.

According to her, Josh felt threatened and did not want to be involved in any of the trial, nor did he want to provide testimony in a deposition. Essentially, Josh wanted to avoid being a man and was hiding behind his mother and throwing her under the bus to escape the web of lies which he had so stupidly weaved.

Instead of holding Mrs. Lyle in contempt for what was a direct violation of the court's earlier order, Magistrate Sanders allowed Mrs. Lyle to refuse to answer the questions on that day, but required her to help arrange a deposition with Josh directly through the court so that Josh wouldn't be required to disclose his location.

I thought that this was a fair and practical approach, but knowing Josh Chamblee I knew he would never live up to his end of the bargain. Instead, he would leave his mother holding the bag while he again skipped out on his obligations to finish what he had started. And this is what ultimately occurred. Josh lied again.

When Mrs. Lyle was finished and they were allowed to leave, with promises of enlisting Josh's full cooperation, I waited another hour for Emmett and Kade to appear, but more than two hours after their scheduled appointment it was clear that they were not going to honor the second subpoenas or the court's order for them to attend or risk contempt.

As soon as I made it back to the halfway house I typed up and filed another motion asking the court to hold Emmett and Kade in contempt and sanction them the costs that I had incurred for having them served new subpoenas and for having the court reporter set up their depositions. The expenses were building against them for their idiocy.

Apparently, Judge Aycock and Magistrate Sanders were furious with Emmett's and Kade's clear violation of the court's order and their patent disrespect for the legal process.

Soon after failing to attend their second scheduled depositions, Judge Aycock set a contempt hearing for March 7, 2017, during the false arrest trial, which required Emmett and Kade to appear before her and explain why they had blatantly ignored the subpoenas and the court order. To be honest, I was looking more forward to their contempt trial than I was the false arrest trial against Jackson.

Once Judge Aycock set the date for the contempt hearing, it apparently finally sunk in to Emmett and Kade that they were in serious trouble. Mr. Minor called me a few days later and informed me that he had arranged a deposition with both of them for February 3, 2017, at his office in the Mississippi Attorney General's Office in Jackson.

Allowing Mr. Minor, through the Attorney General's Office, to arrange the depositions proved beneficial to me in several respects. Most importantly of which was the financial consideration.

If Emmett and Kade appeared for one of my depositions then I would be responsible for the payment of the court reporter and the transcripts. However, since Mr. Minor arranged their depositions, his office would be responsible for paying the costs.

In addition to taking the depositions of Emmett and Kade, Mr. Minor also wanted to take my deposition. At first, I thought it may not be a good idea to willingly consent to a deposition. After all, Mr. Minor had recently refused my request to conduct a deposition with Jackson and Chaney, but my goal from the beginning was to find the truth about the fire, not obstruct any process that might further that endeavor. Jackson and Chaney had done enough already to suppress the truth and I was not going to play the same game.

After more than a decade since last seeing Emmett, I was looking extremely forward to having him under oath with a legal obligation to answer my questions, but I was under no illusion that Emmett would be totally truthful. I expected him to commit perjury and I began formulating my deposition questions for him in an effort to deny him the ability to lie.

While I was preparing for the February 3 depositions I was involved in an accident at the chicken plant that required me to get my ass away from the nightly chicken apocalypse, social privileges be damned.

My sanitation routine at the chicken plant normally consisted of me spending six hours of the night scrubbing metal parts, washing away the suds, and making sure everything was inspection ready for the following morning. One night, however, I was given the task of sanitizing, with highly concentrated chlorine bleach, large vats used to store chicken waste.

These vats were so large that I could walk into them and not have to bend down. That night I had to wash out all the chicken parts and blood, scrub them inside and out with soap, spray them down with the bleach, then wash out the bleach with the high-pressured water hose. No one gave me or even told me about the need for protective respiratory masks.

After cleaning all the vats, which took up my entire six hours of work time, I went back to the halfway house, showered, and then went to bed around the time that the sun was peeking over the horizon.

Shortly after 9:00 A.M. I awoke with a severe burning sensation in my eyes, throat, and nose. And it was quickly spreading into my lungs and making it difficult to breathe. I, and those around me, immediately knew that I'd burned my sinus cavities, esophagus, and the linings of my lungs with the atomized spray of the chlorine bleach.

I immediately requested permission to leave and go to the emergency room at the local hospital, but without Chris Kelly's approval, I could not leave the halfway house without exposing myself to an escape charge. Unfortunately, Kelly was not at the halfway house and when the resident monitors contacted him on his cell about me needing to go to the hospital, they were told not to approve the move request until he returned.

I waited more than three hours before Kelly made it back from whatever errand he was apparently running that was so much more important than my obtaining medical treatment. This was when I first really began to despise Chris Kelly.

Fortunately, once I arrived at the hospital and sought treatment, I was assured that the chemical burns were not as severe as I felt they were. I was doubtful of this prognosis because at the time I could barely breathe and I was having uncontrollable fits of coughing, but I wasn't the only resident at Dismas Charities that had had chemical burns from the bleach at the chicken plant, and I knew, too, that I wouldn't be the last.

After having the linings of my esophagus burned to a crispy red, I was no longer willing to work at the slaughter house. I'd had enough of the blood, guts, heads, and feet that I had to clean every night. And I didn't care about losing my social passes for a while, but I also was convinced that I'd soon find new employment.

For the first time in my life I seriously had to hit the ground and look for a job. This ended up being much harder than I expected. And until I found new employment, Kelly was not going to approve any passes for me to go to the mall, the movies, or out to eat at restaurants.

Many residents at the halfway house obtain legitimate passes to leave the facility and go apply for jobs or to interview. As proof of their job search, residents were required to have the potential employers sign a form stating that the resident had applied or interviewed for that specific job at that specific date and time. These job search verification forms were to be returned to the resident monitors each time the resident returned to the facility from an approved movement.

Unfortunately, many residents used these job search passes to go shack up with their girlfriends in a local hotel, cruise around town, or go off and do their own thing. They'd then forge a name and signature on the forms.

The resident monitors rarely called the potential employers listed on the job search verification forms so this scam would usually work if it wasn't used too often. I, however, didn't want to risk being kicked out of the halfway house and returned to prison, so I never abused this privilege. But some did, and when they were caught they went back to finish out the rest of their halfway house time in the local jail.

Shortly after the new year I became aware of an ongoing project to remodel one of Hattiesburg's downtown buildings and turn the bottom floor into a restaurant and the upper floor into a gay club.

I immediately contacted the two owners and asked if they had a need for someone with handyman or construction experience.

The building had been bought by a local physician named L.B. Bell and the remodeling effort was being overseen by Dr. Bell's friend, Gary May. Upon meeting both of them I was impressed with their desire to provide an entertainment venue for the small gay population in the local area and their idea to create a unique restaurant that serves mostly organic, homemade food.

I was completely honest and upfront with them about my situation at the halfway house and my recent release from prison, but I think them giving me a chance had a lot to do with the overall theme of the restaurant and club, which was to be called Black Sheep's Cafe.

Gary agreed to hire me to help them finish the remodeling effort and, in addition to me, there were two other people, both gay, that worked to help get the place ready for a June 2017 opening.

At first, Kelly did not want me working for Gary. He tried using the excuse that residents were not allowed to work at any establishment which served alcohol. The point was lost on Kelly that the restaurant was an empty shell and was nowhere even close to being ready to open for business. So I eventually succeeded in getting Kelly to approve my employment.

With Gary willing to sign all of the paperwork that was required for me to work for him, I was able to get to work in the middle of January. And from that day forward I never had a bad day at Black Sheep's Cafe. Gary was a great boss, my coworkers and I got along great, and I thoroughly enjoyed doing the remodeling work.

Things were going too well for me, though. By the time I went to work for Gary I'd been noticing some slight pain in my hips when performing certain types of twisting movements. At first, I thought it might be related to lifting weights in the gym, but lightening up on my routine didn't make the pain go away. Then I thought it might be a pulled muscle. But the pain only got worse.

Shortly after going to work for Gary, the pain had increased enough to require me to seek medical attention, but the first x-ray I obtained showed nothing out of the ordinary. It was only after obtaining an MRI that I was informed that I was suffering from a rare bone disease known as avascular necrosis in both my hips.

Some physicians refer to avascular necrosis as osteonecrosis, and there are not many treatment options for it. Essentially, avascular necrosis is the lack of blood supply to a bone. It usually, most often, affects people's hip joints first. The lack of blood supply causes the bone to die and collapse.

The vast majority of new avascular necrosis diagnoses—upwards of ninety-four percent—are from known causes, such as long-term corticosteroid use, long-term alcoholism, and past injuries to the joint. None of those causes pertain to me.

Avascular necrosis is listed as a rare disease because there are usually only about twenty thousand new diagnoses per year in the United States. Of those, about ninety-four percent are from the known causes category.

That leaves around eight hundred idiopathic, or unknown causes diagnoses. I fell into this last category.

The first orthopedic doctor that I saw in Hattiesburg explained to me the numerous complexities involved in treating someone with idiopathic avascular necrosis. To begin, the left hip was more damaged than the right and the only option available was a total hip replacement.

The right hip, however, had not collapsed and might be savable. This would require bone decompression surgery to stimulate blood flow and possible bone and vascular grafts to replace the damaged or dead bone and vessels.

Unfortunately, the doctor in Hattiesburg didn't know of any surgeons capable of doing the surgeries required to save the right hip. Instead, he referred me to a team of orthopedic specialists at the University of Mississippi Medical Center (UMMC) in Jackson. It was the only public hospital in the state, but it was an excellent research and teaching facility for the medical community. My first appointment was for March 14, 2017.

The only advice that the doctor in Hattiesburg could offer was to stay off my feet as much as possible so as to prevent further collapse of the left hip and to prevent the collapse altogether of the right. This didn't bode well for my obligations at the halfway house.

Gary and Dr. Bell were both understanding about my new diagnosis and were more than willing to work with me in a flexible manner at Black

Sheep's Cafe so that I could still work for them and contribute something positive to their endeavor. But it was clear that it wouldn't be long before chronic pain became a constant problem.

While working, serving time in the halfway house, preparing for the false arrest trial, and dealing with my new medical issues, I still found time to try and track Josh Chamblee. But it was proving harder than I thought.

Thankfully, my friend David, in Indianapolis, was proving to be a one-man hunting machine when it came to finding Josh. We knew that his last location was in Indianapolis, but we lost track of him there.

Fortunately for us, though, Josh's employer there placed his name and picture on their website when he was recently hired to come work for them. Once this showed up in the Google search, finding him no longer became a problem. We knew where he worked and we knew where to find him to serve him with a subpoena. My problem then was getting a deposition set up and a subpoena in his hands without tipping him off.

I knew that if Josh found out that we knew where he worked, and that we were about to serve him with a subpoena, that he would run. He had conducted himself from day one as a coward would, and I was fully convinced that any service on him with a subpoena would have to be done quickly and stealthily.

Josh knew that he had utterly ruined whatever reputation and credibility he may of had as a witness. He'd lied multiple times, he'd helped Jackson fabricate evidence, and he'd thrown his mother to the judicial wolves and placed her in an untenable legal position.

The simple thing for Josh to have done would of been to submit to a deposition along the lines that were outlined by Magistrate Sanders at the December 6, 2016, deposition of his mother. But as usual, even though there was an agreement for Josh to do a deposition from an undisclosed location, he refused to follow through on those false promises.

This required me to resort to cloak-and-dagger tactics to find him and get him served with a subpoena. And I didn't care if I had to involve his employer and those around him to get it accomplished. With David in Indianapolis helping me, I knew it was only a matter of time before we caught him.

Setting up a deposition with Josh was easier said than done. But with Mr. Minor's assistance we were able to locate a court reporter in Indianapolis who had a flexible enough schedule to accommodate us in the short timespan.

With Judge Aycock's approval, we set Josh's deposition for February 27, 2017, at 1:00 P.M. Now all we had to do was get him served with the subpoena.

Knowing where Josh worked, and what shift he worked, made our jobs easier. I overnighted my friend, David, a copy of the subpoena and the next morning he arrived at Josh's employer's office, subpoena in hand.

Needless to say, Josh was absolutely furious that we had been able to track him down and serve him at his place of business. When he realized what the piece of paper was that he was holding in his hand, he crumpled it up and threw it back at David, but Josh had been officially served, and if he didn't show up for the deposition he'd have to explain the reasons why to Judge Aycock, much like Emmett and Kade would eventually be required to.

The last step that needed to be completed for the depositions was obtaining Chris Kelly's permission to travel to Jackson on February 3 so that I could be present at Emmett's and Kade's depositions. Without my presence the whole endeavor would be pointless. Like the first deposition, however, Kelly wouldn't cooperate, nor would he give me a reason for why he was denying me permission again to go to Jackson for legitimate court-related business.

Kelly's obstinacy was quickly rectified by another call to Rylee in Magistrate Sanders's office. By this time, I think even the magistrate and Judge Aycock were getting tired of dealing with Kelly's megalomania. But the problem was solved and I prepared for the upcoming confrontation with my grandfather and cousin.

Not only would the February 3 depositions prove highly entertaining and ultimately fortuitous for me, they also gave me my long-desired opportunity to confront Emmett about his past sordid history. It also put me in the position of being one step closer to discovering the truth about the fire that destroyed the Atwood Lakehouse.

CHAPTER TWENTY-TWO

February 3, 2017, dawned bright and early for me. I showered, dressed in my best suit and tie, ate a hearty breakfast, then rolled out of the halfway house around 6:30 A.M. Emmett's deposition was set to begin at nine and I didn't want to be late.

As I drove to Jackson I began going over the list of questions that I'd prepared in anticipation of the depositions. However, because Mr. Minor arranged the depositions, he would be given the first opportunity to ask the questions. So even though I had numerous questions of my own, there were some inquiries that I could only make after Mr. Minor made his and Emmett answered.

The butterflies in my stomach were also churning because the deposition would be the first time I'd seen Emmett face-to-face in almost a decade.

If the fire was indeed accidental, then there was a good chance that Emmett would legitimately believe that I started it. However, if Emmett or Kade started it themselves, their false indignation would also be palpable. Either way, I expected the tension to be extremely high.

After arriving at the Attorney General's Office and being cleared through security, I was escorted to Mr. Minor's office. My first impressions of him were certainly different than my impressions that I'd developed over the years of talking to him on the phone and reading the legal documents he filed.

Mr. Minor appeared to be in his mid- to late thirties, medium build, black hair, with a working man's demeanor that conveyed a high level of competence. His suits were neither Savile Row or bargain-basement. Even though he'd told me numerous times that I'd never beat him in court and win a judgment against his client, he never treated me any different than one might treat the opposing counsel, and I sincerely appreciated this.

Soon after arriving at his office, Emmett, Kade and Kade's wife entered the room and my nerves immediately frazzled. But I remained stoic and completely professional. Emmett on the other hand couldn't help mouthing off a few choice words and displaying his middle finger to me. I was astonished that Emmett hadn't seemed to age at all since the last time I'd seen him years before.

Kade, on the other hand, looked like death. It'd been even longer since I'd laid eyes on him, but from his looks it appeared that Kade had been living quite a rough life.

While Kade and his wife were escorted from the office, Mr. Minor and I began Emmett's deposition by having him placed under oath. Mr. Minor's first questions concerned Emmett's full name, his age, and his occupation.

When Mr. Minor asked Emmett how he and I were related, Emmett said that he didn't consider himself to be my grandfather and doubted that my paternity was actually biologically connected to the Atwoods.

One of the most contentious issues regarding Emmett's hatred of me concerned my exposing his extramarital affair with the African-American woman that he fathered at least one child with.

Mr. Minor immediately opened the door to this issue by asking Emmett how many children he had. Without hesitation he replied that the answer was four—which wasn't true when one counts his black bastard child. I made some notes on my notepad and Mr. Minor moved on.

He next had Emmett establish who owned the Atwood Lakehouse, when it was built, and how the house was situated on the surrounding lake and property.

From there, Emmett testified that the weekend prior to the fire several people and their family members had been staying in the lake house, but even Emmett couldn't remember the exact dates.

Mr. Minor then moved into questions about Emmett's actions upon learning about the fire.

MR. MINOR: Do you know who discovered the house

burned to the ground?

EMMETT: Yes, my nephew Kade did that morning and when he discovered it he called me in Vicksburg.

MR. MINOR: What did you do?

EMMETT: Well, as soon as I got dressed I went up there to the site of the fire.

The topic then changed and turned to the amount of insurance that Emmett had on the lake house, which I knew to be in excess of $500,000.00. However, Emmett testified that it was only around $160,000.00. And most importantly, he vehemently denied that he had increased the insurance shortly before the fire.

This was lie number three. Not only had Emmett lied about how many children he had (which I believe is many more than just five), but he also lied about how much insurance he had on the house, and he lied about increasing it shortly before the fire. And I had the insurance records to prove it.

When asked whether he immediately had a suspicion about who may have started the fire—if it was indeed an arson—Emmett didn't hesitate to accuse me.

In one long, convoluted tale, Emmett accused me of everything from the burning of Atlanta during the Civil War to the crucifixion of Christ. Without any proof that the fire was started intentionally, Emmett spilled forth tons of verbal abuse that any sane man never would. But it was expected and I took it in stride without comment. If I was going to look like an attorney that day, then I was determined to act like one.

Around this time in the deposition, though, I noticed Kade at the door to Mr. Minor's office attempting to listen to everything that was being said.

There was a reason that Kade and his wife were removed before Emmett's deposition started. We didn't want the witnesses to hear each others' testimony and tailor their answers accordingly. But Kade decided to ignore this directive. However, Mr. Minor solved the problem by having Kade removed to the waiting area.

We then moved on to Emmett's interactions with Jackson when they met for the first time. Before Emmett could answer the questions, though, I knew what his answer would be.

> **MR. MINOR:** Did you ever have occasion to talk to a man named James Jackson with the Fire Marshal's Office?
>
> **EMMETT:** Yes, and I told him the same thing, that I knew who burned the house.
>
> **MR. MINOR:** And who was that?
>
> **EMMETT:** That fella sitting right there. Dave Atwood.

After identifying me as the culprit for starting everything short of World War Three, Emmett was then asked about the footprints around the lake house that he and Kade felt were indicative of foul play.

> **MR. MINOR:** Where were the tracks that Kade found?
>
> **EMMETT:** There is a levee that has two levels. And he walked down the lower level where Kade couldn't see him because if he would have walked on top of the levee Kade would have saw him. So his footprints were on the lower level.

When I heard this reasoning from Emmett I couldn't help but laugh. According to this logic, Kade would have seen the person walking across the top levee that night, but somehow missed the blazing, fiery, noisy inferno that engulfed the lake house a few minutes later. *Yeah right*, I thought sarcastically.

Shortly after this exchange Emmett went on and accused me, again, of damaging his tractor. As with the fire, despite the lack of evidence, Emmett spent considerable time trying to explain to Mr. Minor how he came to the unsupported conclusion that I was responsible for the tractor. Mr. Minor, however, quickly moved on. It was his office that had tried to prosecute me for the tractor damage and he didn't want to reopen that door.

To my surprise, though, Mr. Minor did repeatedly ask Emmett what proof he had that I committed these atrocities. Despite his internal unwillingness to do so, Emmett had to concede that there was no proof, no proof at all.

The next part of the deposition concerned Emmett offering a $20,000.00 reward, which he admitted to advertising in the local newspapers. However, no one ever contacted him with any relevant information about the fire.

Surprisingly, Mr. Minor quickly wrapped up his questions at this point and turned the deposition over to me. By this time, I was chomping at the bit to get my figurative hands around Emmett's neck.

My first questions were designed to establish some of the family history involving my mother, alleged father (Emmett's words), and myself. Emmett's whole demeanor changed and one cannot truly understand what an evil, hateful, vindictive person Emmett Atwood really is until they see and witness that part of his personality.

It was apparent from the beginning that Emmett was not going to be cooperative, helpful, or polite. I was determined, though, to do my best to remain above the fray, avoid the deep-seated emotions, and try to stick with my goal of finding the truth.

Emmett's first tactic was to complain to Mr. Minor that my questions about our family had "nothing to do with this lawsuit." But Mr. Minor realized that a foundation had to be laid and that I was building up to a point. He made Emmett answer my questions.

I wanted to establish through his testimony that the genesis of his hatred of me began because he found out I was gay; not because I committed any crime or did something horrible and terrible to him. I was estranged from that family because of something that I had no control over in my life. And I was determined to get that into the record, but it was becoming clearer by the minute that all Emmett was interested in was making unfounded allegations without being willing to support his accusations with evidence.

After trying to establish some of the details of the family feud I moved to my first home run question of the day.

> **ME:** Okay. Earlier in your deposition you were asked how many children you had, and you stated that you had four.
> **EMMETT:** That's correct.
> **ME:** But that's not entirely true, is it?
> **EMMETT:** That is totally true. And you're building up to lie, which go ahead and tell your lie.
> **ME:** Was there a paternity suit filed against you?
> **EMMETT:** Yes.
> **ME:** And did you settle that lawsuit out-of-court with the African-American woman?
> **EMMETT:** No, I did not. We went to court, and the court ruled in my favor. And some of the lies that you've told on that,

you so-called showed where a paternity test was done that showed that I was guilty. That was lies. Total lies. I never took a paternity test. That's a lie.

ME: So you're saying that you never fathered a child with the African-American woman?

EMMETT: It's never been proven that I fathered a child with her or anybody else except my four children.

ME: Did you have sex with the African-American woman?

EMMETT: None of your business.

My point at this juncture had been proven. Not only did I have the actual court records from the Chancery Court proving that a DNA test had been done and that the child was Emmett's, but I also had the actual settlement agreement that Emmett signed wherein he agreed to provide the African-American woman a very large sum of money in return for her dropping the paternity suit.

Emmett had no idea at this time that I'd found the court file and DNA tests in the basement of the courthouse and had made copies of the entire case. I didn't tell him about the file either. I planned to spring it on him at trial in front of the jury. And he had cooperated fully in setting himself up for perjury.

My next questions concerned whether or not Emmett had dementia or Alzheimer's disease. After all, he was ninety-two-years-old. I knew from listening to him that his memory was superb, but he had just committed a serious felony by lying under oath in a federal deposition. I needed to establish, through his own testimony, that his memory was impeccable so that he couldn't later claim that he had dementia and had forgotten about fathering a child with the African-American woman and settling out-of-court with her after the DNA test proved the child was his.

My next questions concerned the allegations that Emmett had repeatedly made that I'd damaged the tractor in 2004. What didn't make sense to me was the fact that the tractor was allegedly damaged in 2004 on the same property where Vivian and I were living, and Emmett clearly believed that I was responsible, yet when I got out of prison in 2009 Emmett continued to store the same tractor on the same piece of property where it had allegedly been damaged by me in 2004.

If the tractor had truly been damaged in 2004 on the property that I lived on, why would Emmett continue to store the tractor there knowing that I was getting out of prison and was going to be literally yards away from where the tractor was? It didn't make sense.

If Emmett truly believed that I damaged the tractor in 2004, why in God's name would he leave the tractor in the same spot if he thought that I'd committed all these crimes? If I was as bad as Emmett accused me of being, then he should have immediately moved the tractor and all his other farm equipment away from there as soon as he knew that I was getting out of prison. But he didn't, and that is indicative of Emmett's paranoid schizophrenic mind when it came to accusations about me committing crimes.

Prior to the deposition, Emmett provided Mr. Minor with a five or six page list of different alleged crimes that had been committed against Emmett and the Atwood family. Mr. Minor, though, only briefly had Emmett read off the list and then moved on. I, however, took each allegation of wrongdoing in detail.

What quickly became apparent, though, was that for every criminal allegation on the list that Emmett accused me of committing, not one single time did Emmett or the Atwoods have law enforcement officers investigate or file police reports involving these allegations. The deposition was quickly becoming a mudslinging affair with nothing but false and, in some cases, patently hilarious allegations of wrongdoing.

During one especially contentious question, I asked Emmett to explain how one person could commit what would essentially be one of the worst, unsolved crime sprees in the history of the United States. All Emmett could say was that I was "slick as a lizard."

The lists of unproven, never-reported-to-the-police criminal allegations that Emmett accused me of committing were also nothing more than hearsay, told to Emmett by third-parties. And even Emmett admitted that he had no proof whatsoever.

At this point in the deposition Mr. Minor requested that we go off the record and he and I stepped out for a private conversation.

Mr. Minor essentially asked me to move on from questioning Emmett about the unfounded allegations because Mr. Minor had no plans or intentions of trying to get the allegations introduced at trial, therefore making any further inquiry or argument on the subject pointless. I agreed to move on and we went back into the office.

When we went back in, Emmett was standing up on the floor and made the statement that he was not going "to sit here and listen to this B.S. from this criminal sitting over there. I'm done answering questions."

I shrugged my shoulders and told Mr. Minor and Emmett that I was going to place a call to Magistrate Sanders and seek an order from him requiring Emmett to finish the deposition.

At the mention of the magistrate's name, Emmett's demeanor quickly changed. He sat back down, accused me of being a "jackass" and "playing lawyer," but told me to continue asking my questions. Score another victory for me.

During the follow-up questions I was able to get Emmett to admit that prior to my birth in 1983 there had been several suspicious fires on the Atwood Lakehouse property that destroyed other buildings and houses and a good portion of the timber on the south side of the property. Obviously, since these occurred before my birth, I couldn't be accused of being responsible.

I then changed topics to Scott Zimmerman and how he became involved in the legal fight with my grandmother and the rest of the Atwood family. To my utter shock, though, Emmett informed me that Scott Zimmerman was dead.

This caused a short pause in the proceedings while I digested this information. I'd not known that Scott had died, but I wasn't displeased. I later found out that Scott had overdosed on illegal drugs and was quietly buried in 2013. It was a fitting death for a person so evil.

I next moved to the financial situation of Atwood Chevrolet at the time of the November 2009 fire. If the fire was indeed an arson, and that Emmett purposely had it destroyed, I suspected that some of the insurance payoff might of been used to prop up the dealership's financial problems that were bound to have been occurring during the recession of 2009.

Every car dealership in late 2009 was suffering terribly under the recession. I seriously doubt that Atwood Chevrolet was any different. But Emmett was prepared for this line of inquiry and I suspect he was because of a guilty conscience.

ME: Would you agree that in 2009 that most car dealerships, including Atwood Chevrolet, were having a tough time due to the economy?

EMMETT: That did not include Atwood Chevrolet, that's

a lie.

ME: Are you familiar with the dealership's finances or profit loss?

EMMETT: Reasonably so. Yes.

ME: Would you agree that Atwood Chevrolet was in a better financial situation in 2007 than it was in late 2009?

EMMETT: I don't remember.

ME: But you just testified that you're reasonably well acquainted with the finances of Atwood Chevrolet?

EMMETT: Of course.

ME: But you cannot tell me whether you were making more of a profit in 2007 than in 2009?

EMMETT: There's no way I can remember that.

ME: Okay. Can you answer this: Do any properties that you own, and that includes land, houses, buildings, businesses, in 2009, of those properties that you owned, did you have financing and mortgages on any of those properties?

EMMETT: I don't recall. I doubt seriously we owed anything.

It was clear to me, in my opinion, that Emmett was trying to hide something. It was impossible for me to believe that Emmett would have a crystal clear memory about some alleged minor crime from thirteen years before, but couldn't remember anything about the finances of Atwood Chevrolet or whether or not he had any mortgages on any property. I was beginning to believe the worst about the Atwood Lakehouse fire and why it was started.

This then led me to question Emmett about the insurance on the lake house. Mr. Minor had touched on the issue, but not gone into any depth. I planned to mine the information from Emmett like a 49er would a nugget of gold.

ME: Prior to the fire, had you recently increased the insurance?

EMMETT: I don't recall. It's possible, though. For many years the insurance company wouldn't increase it because the house was so far from a fire station. So it's possible we got them to increase it, I think way before the fire, but I'm not sure.

I next handed Emmett a set of photos taken of the lake house four days before the fire. During the preliminary hearing in the Attala County Justice Court, and in Jackson's interrogatories, Jackson testified that these photos were provided to him by Emmett, and at the time they were given to him Emmett told him that the photos were taken at the insistence of the insurance company for purposes related to the recent increase in insurance. Emmet, though, had a different story.

> **ME:** I'm going to hand you a set of photographs of the Atwood Lakehouse. Can you look at the date and tell me why those photos were taken?
>
> **EMMETT:** They were taken—that was a weekend that a employee of mine, and his family, stayed there. And he took those pictures. But I also took pictures just in case we had storms and tornados come through. And that was the primary reason the photos were taken.
>
> **ME:** Did you give these photos to the State Fire Marshal?
>
> **EMMETT:** I think I did.
>
> **ME:** Did Mississippi Farm Bureau pay out on that insurance policy?
>
> **EMMETT:** Yes. Paid out with no problem.
>
> **ME:** Do you remember what you used the money for? How did you spend it?
>
> **EMMETT:** I rebuilt the house and used it as part payment.
>
> **ME:** So did you use all of that money to rebuild the house?
>
> **EMMETT:** Why do I have to answer that? That has nothing to do with anything except to satisfy your two-bit ego.
>
> **ME:** But did you take any of that money and apply it to any of your businesses or personal funds?
>
> **EMMETT:** Didn't need to. No business that I had, that I was involved with, needed any money.
>
> **ME:** Okay. Let me ask you this: If the fire marshal testified that you told him that you took these pictures for insurance purposes, would that be incorrect?
>
> **EMMETT:** It's very possible that the pictures got mixed up, from two different sets. I can't recall.

It was clear that I was never going to get honest answers from Emmett, nor was he going to give me anything that would lead one to believe that he was responsible for the fire and had taken the insurance money to save his other businesses from collapse during the 2009 recession. So, after squeezing all the blood that I could from the turnip, I moved on.

> **ME:** Did you have any guns in the house at the time that it burned?
> **EMMETT:** Yes, for people like you. I kept it loaded and ready.
> **ME:** So ammunition, too?
> **EMMETT:** We might have.
> **ME:** The fire marshal's report stated that the fire began in the north rear of the house. What did the north rear of the lake house contain? Inside.
> **EMMETT:** Well, the kitchen. I think that's where you set the fire.
> **ME:** And isn't that also where the electrical box is?
> **EMMETT:** Yes.
> **ME:** Do you remember having insulation installed in the lake house shortly before the fire?
> **EMMETT:** Yes. They put it in the attic.
> **ME:** Did the fire marshal ever tell you that he determined that the fire was, in fact, an arson?
> **EMMETT:** No, I don't recall him telling me that.
> **ME:** Do you have any evidence that the fire was arson?
> **EMMETT:** I don't have any evidence one way or the other.

I was beginning to get weary of Emmett's aggressive attitude and constant attempts to avoid answering the questions that were being asked. But before I could end the deposition I had to know about his connections with Mike Chaney.

> **ME:** Do you know a person named Mike Chaney?
> **EMMETT:** Yes. He is the Insurance Commissioner and State Fire Marshal.
> **ME:** Would you consider Chaney to be a friend of yours?
> **EMMETT:** Yes. He's from Vicksburg and he is a friend.
> **ME:** And have you donated money to his election campaigns?

> **EMMETT:** Yes.
>
> **ME:** I'm almost done with my questions. But let me ask this: How do you account for Kade sleeping through the fire and not hearing it?
>
> **EMMETT:** You'd have to ask him or a psychiatrist.

This was the one thing that I wanted to know more than anything else. No one, least of all me, could understand how Kade was able to allegedly sleep through the lake house burning down when he was so close to it. If it indeed was an accident, Kade's inability to hear the fire is totally unexplainable.

There was only one other topic, though, that I wanted to ask Emmett about, and I had purposely saved it for last because I knew it would be the one thing to make Emmett come unglued more than anything else.

> **ME:** Are you familiar with my book, *Into Hell I Rode*?
>
> **EMMETT:** Yes, I am. And it is misnamed. It should be *Dave's Lies*. A book full of Dave's lies.
>
> **ME:** Have you read it?
>
> **EMMETT:** No, but I've been told all about it. I was not happy about it at all. It's all lies. That's what everyone tells me that reads it. Just lies.
>
> **ME:** Did you ever file a libel or defamation of character lawsuit over what I wrote?
>
> **EMMETT:** No. But I thought about it. And I am not going to answer anymore questions about your book and stroke your ridiculous ego.

This essentially concluded Emmett's deposition. Mr. Minor didn't have anymore questions and frustratingly told Emmett that he could leave and go wait in the waiting room.

It had been a long two hours of constant mental struggle between Emmett and I, but at the end I felt that I'd won the intellectual exercise.

Emmett had violated federal law numerous times by lying under oath. I'd caught him trying to hide information about the insurance, he'd not been truthful about the photographs, and it was clear that any jury reading or listening to his testimony would come away despising Emmett Atwood and everything he stood for. It was clearly a win for me and I was ready to take Kade Atwood on next.

CHAPTER TWENTY-THREE

I was intellectually drained after sparring with Emmett for over two hours. No doubt that Mr. Minor was, too. But the one thing that I had proven to myself and to him was that no matter how morally low Emmett went in his personal attacks, I would not follow.

It had been years since I'd seen Kade, probably closer to two decades, but he and I had never had a negative interaction. In fact, his father and me, my Uncle Bush, got along really well before he passed away in early 2001.

Uncle Bush had always been sympathetic to my situation with my own father, and in many ways had been more than just a distant relative. He was not only an authority on family history, but a close friend. Unfortunately, his son didn't share his sentiments.

Kade's attitude upon entering Mr. Minor's office was just as cold and angry as Emmett's had been. I couldn't tell if this was a false bravado or genuine hatred. It all depended on whether or not Emmett and Kade were actually responsible for the fire or if they believed I was.

Mr. Minor began the questioning the same as he had with Emmett. After establishing that Kade had lived on the Atwood Lakehouse property for his entire life, Mr. Minor had him estimate the distance that his house was from the lake house. Although Emmett estimated that it was more than five hundred yards, Kade gave a more accurate figure when he stated that it was about one hundred.

It was soon clear, though, that Mr. Minor was not going to get any relevant information from Kade. It seemed to me that Kade was doing everything he could to avoid answering the questions. At almost every turn Kade claimed to not recall any memory regarding the details asked in the questions.

Kade told us that he dozed off around midnight on the night of the fire and when he woke up the following morning the lake house was gone. Other than that, he had no other memory of that night. He also couldn't remember anything about the weather on the night of the fire, but he did inform us that Emmett had recently told him that it was windy that night.

This tidbit of information intrigued me and immediately raised alarm bells in my mind. Emmett had testified that he was in Vicksburg—more than two hours away—when the lake house burned down. Yet, Kade just made a statement that would lead one to believe that Emmett was in Kosciusko, at the lake house, the night it burned. How else would he know that it was windy at the lake house the night it burned? I made a notation in my notebook.

When asked if he called the fire department or the sheriff's office when he discovered the fire, Kade couldn't remember. Tellingly, though, Kade did say that on the morning he discovered the fire, numerous family members came out to the scene and walked around looking at everything.

This ran counter to the argument that two days after the fire "suspicious" footprints were found that led investigators to conclude that there might be foul play. If there were several family members at the scene on the morning it was discovered, this could surely account for why they later found footprints.

After several more questions, and I-don't-know answers, Kade informed Mr. Minor and myself that he had recently survived being infected with Rocky Mountain Spotted Fever after having almost died. I looked at Mr. Minor, and he casted a sideways glance at me, but we kept trying to move forward on gaining something useful.

The first useful piece of information that we pulled from Kade concerned the footprints that Jackson and Sheriff Nail had claimed, in response to my lawsuit, were indicative of foul play.

MR. MINOR: Do you recall seeing or finding any footprints on the property?

KADE: Yeah. I remember seeing a bunch of them. They was right there where everybody was walking around. I mean, it's people walking about everywhere.

There went another piece of evidence that Jackson was trying to hang his hat on to justify his belief that the fire was arson. Apparently, he never took the time to try and determine where the footprints came from when he was shown them two days after the fire. Mr. Minor quickly moved on, though.

> **MR. MINOR:** Do you believe that the fire was an arson?
> **KADE:** Yeah.
> **MR. MINOR:** And why do you believe that?
> **KADE:** I just don't believe that it stood for 77 years and didn't burn, and all of a sudden it burns.

I could tell then that Mr. Minor was running out of questions for Kade and was about to turn the questioning over to me. But before he did so he had to obtain Kade's opinion on my real paternity.

> **MR. MINOR:** How are you related to the Plaintiff, David Atwood, II?
> **KADE:** He's my first cousin's son.
> **MR. MINOR:** So y'all are second cousins?
> **KADE:** I wouldn't say that.

This, in a way, kind of tickled me. After seeing how bad Kade looked, physically, I was hoping that we didn't share the same DNA. But in my mind I've always known that the Atwood blood flowed through my veins. There are too many similarities. Mr. Minor was almost done, though, with Kade.

> **MR. MINOR:** Do you believe that David burned the house down?
> **KADE:** Yeah.
> **MR. MINOR:** And why do you believe that?
> **KADE:** He's just the type person to do something. He's just an evil little man.
> **MR. MINOR:** Has he ever done anything to you personally?
> **KADE:** No.

Mr. Minor sat back in his chair and took a drink of water. Despite Kade having very little memory about anything to do with the fire, he possessed quite sharp mental faculties when it came to his belief that I was responsible for the fire. But now it was my turn to question him and, like Emmett, I wouldn't let him get away with unsupported allegations.

My first questions revolved around what Kade did the morning he woke up and discovered the house gone. I asked him what family he had, knowing that he was married and had a son, but surprisingly, Kade answered that he did not have any children. This shocked me and I didn't understand because I knew for a fact that Kade had a son. I'd spent part of my childhood playing on the lake house property with him. So I didn't understand Kade's answer, but it was irrelevant and I moved on.

It wasn't until I left the deposition and called my mother that I learned that several years prior, while I was in prison, Kade's son had become involved in dealing illegal drugs and had been killed in a drug deal gone bad. Had I known this, though, I would have never asked Kade anything about his son. It'd been a line I wouldn't have crossed.

I asked Kade why he did not call the fire department, but all he said was that there wasn't a need to call them. But every other question, regarding who he called and when, Kade claimed to have no memory or recall from that time period. But I kept trying.

> **ME:** Before you lived in the house that you live in now, your father, Bush Atwood, lived there, my Uncle Bush?
>
> **KADE:** I wouldn't say he was your uncle, but yeah, he lived there.
>
> **ME:** And to your knowledge he and I had a friendly relationship?
>
> **KADE:** Yeah.
>
> **ME:** And you'd agree I've been in your house?
>
> **KADE:** Yeah.
>
> **ME:** And your house, your bedroom, has large, floor-to-ceiling windows that face the lake?
>
> **KADE:** Yes.
>
> **ME:** And what kind of coverings do you have over the windows?
>
> **KADE:** White plastic blinds.

The purpose of this line of questioning was to establish the improbability of Kade being able to sleep through the fire. His bedroom windows were huge, taking up more than half the total wall area that faced the lake house. The blinds were plastic and they were white. White plastic window blinds would let in a ton of light from a fire that was as big as the Atwood Lakehouse fire was. But somehow, neither the noise or the light woke Kade up. I wasn't buying it.

I tried next to get Kade to remember details about some of the other fires that had occurred over the years on the property, ones that I certainly could not be accused of committing. And Kade threw me another unexpected gold nugget.

> **ME:** Besides the lake house burning down, do you remember any other fires out there?
>
> **KADE:** It's possible there were. I think Emmett burned off this year, or last year some of the fields and underbrush. It seems like Emmett's done some burning out there.

This was useful information to me and I saw Mr. Minor emit a short sigh. We had just listened to Emmett expound for more than two hours about me being a pyromaniac, yet here was Kade admitting that Emmett was doing a lot of burning himself out on the lake house property.

I wanted to go back and tie Kade's story down regarding the footprints. This would prove, I hoped, to be another unravelling of one of the fire marshal's strands that he claims gave him probable cause to get an arrest warrant.

> **ME:** Both the fire marshal and Sheriff Nail have stated that two days after the fire you showed them some suspicious footprints. Do you remember this?
>
> **KADE:** I don't remember this. I've heard people talk about the footprints, but I don't remember who might have found them. I don't remember finding any.
>
> **ME:** So, if footprints were found two days after the fire, it's a possibility that one of the Atwood family members could have left them?
>
> **KADE:** Well, everybody out there left footprints.

I wanted to then go back and get Kade to expound on his opinion that I was an evil person. Since I'd not had any contact with Kade since before I was a teenager, I needed to know what he based this belief on. I, of course, knew that it was based on what he heard from other people, but I needed it on the record.

>**ME:** You testified that I was an evil person. What do you base that on?
>**KADE:** Well, you've been to the pen (prison).
>**ME:** Would you agree that everyone that's been to prison is evil? (I was hoping that Kade would not answer in the affirmative because I knew that Mr. Minor's uncle, Paul Minor, had recently been released from prison and, no doubt, Mr. Minor was thinking of him when I asked Kade this question.)
>**KADE:** I would not agree with that.
>**ME:** Can you tell me then why I went to prison?
>**KADE:** Nope.
>**ME:** So it would be fair to say that your opinion of me is based on things you've heard from other people?
>**KADE:** Well, everybody's got an opinion, Dave.
>**ME:** Okay. Thank you.

These were essentially my last pertinent questions. I felt that every question that I'd wanted information about had been asked, although Kade certainly hadn't been cooperative in providing any information.

As Kade was walking out of Mr. Minor's door, I made the comment to Mr. Minor, in a sarcastic fashion, that I thought the two depositions had gone well. Apparently, Kade heard me, turned on his heels, and moved in an aggressive manner towards me. I could tell Kade was trying to intimidate me. But I'd just been released from some of the most violent prisons in the federal system. Kade Atwood and his depleted, weakened body was not going to bully me.

Mr. Minor froze as he watched what was about to happen. I stood up from behind the desk and met Kade face-to-face. I didn't realize how short Kade was until I looked down on him. His eyes refused to meet mine, but I was clear when I told him, "You need to sit your stupid ass down before I hurt you old man."

Kade apparently remembered the young, skinny kid I'd been the last time we met face-to-face decades before. Who he met on February 3, 2017, was a grown man willing to do violence without fear of repercussions. And upon this realization Kade blinked, turned around, and left Mr. Minor's office, just like the coward he'd always been.

I had thought that Mr. Minor would make a move to call security, but once Kade left the office everything went back to normal and we proceeded to prepare for my deposition next. I doubt, though, that the Emmett and Kade Atwood depositions would be shortly forgotten. Mr. Minor had certainly not dealt with as much hostility as we did that day. But as with Emmett, I felt that I conducted myself as professional as possible.

After being sworn and placed under oath, Mr. Minor began questioning me. I quickly realized, though, that Mr. Minor's questions were going to have nothing to do with the fire, but instead, concentrated almost entirely of criminal allegations from years before and the lawsuit that the Atwoods brought against me to steal Vivian's property.

Mr. Minor first, though, wanted to know about Emmett's claim that I wasn't his biological grandson.

> **MR. MINOR:** There was some discussion during Emmett's deposition that you are not his offspring. Do you have a comment about that?
>
> **ME:** I am his grandson biologically. Emmett and the Atwoods are very racist, very anti-gay. I can't imagine that they would want to admit that they have a blood relative that's gay.

I was then questioned about my relationship with Vivian, how I came to live with her, the details of us selling our house and farm in south Warren County, and then moving to the new house shortly after my release from prison. We then moved to the reasons why I went to prison in July 2004.

Mr. Minor then asked me to explain the lawsuit that Vivian filed against her daughter, June, in 2004 after we learned that June had frauded her out of the title to her house and land.

This led into a discussion about the tractor that was allegedly damaged on the property that I got blamed for. This obviously wasn't relevant to the fire that destroyed the lake house, but I was trying to be cooperative. I made sure, though, that Mr. Minor was reminded that his office failed to secure a conviction against me for the crime.

I was then asked about Scott Zimmerman. Despite the fact that I didn't know that Scott had killed himself, I explained to Mr. Minor that Scott and I were only friends, nothing sexual, that he was hired by me to do cleaning and cooking chores around our house, and eventually took over trying to help me care for my grandmother.

We kept coming back to the time, though, that Vivian put the house and property in my name and put the money in my cousin Julie's name. Mr. Minor just couldn't seem to understand why Vivian would do this. I explained to him, however, that Vivian had always intended that Julie and I inherit her estate, and that she was scared to death that her children would try to contest her will when she died. Vivian was more correct in this supposition than we could ever have thought.

Mr. Minor then wanted to know about the elderly abuse charge that Emmett had gotten the sheriff's department to file against me based on Scott Zimmerman's wild accusations that I'd harmed my grandmother.

Judge Woods—one of Emmett's good friends—in the Justice Court of Warren County, had found me guilty of this charge based on Scott's testimony. However, when I appealed the conviction to the County Court and was given a new trial, the jury spent less than fifteen minutes returning a not guilty verdict. And I made sure Mr. Minor knew this.

We then moved to a discussion of the five or six page list of alleged crimes that Emmett had composed and provided to Mr. Minor that he accused me of committing. Fortunately, Mr. Minor realized that it was almost all bunk.

For my part, I patiently explained my belief that it was all a creation of Emmett's tortured mind. How else can one explain being the alleged victim of dozens of crimes, yet never reporting a single incident to law enforcement? I believed these allegations were solely created by Emmett the moment he realized that he would have to testify in my false arrest trial. But I had plans to deal with that.

We finally moved on to a more relevant topic: Joshua Langston Chamblee. In this, I felt Mr. Minor was finally addressing an issue worth talking about. Obviously, he wanted to know everything about how Josh and I first met, where we met, how often we stayed with each other in Starkville and in Vicksburg, and what Josh and I were doing on the night of November 10, 2009.

Josh and I had been friends for awhile, but we didn't actually begin a romantic, dating relationship until September 2009. And from the beginning, we were almost inseparable. I was either at his apartment in Starkville, his parent's place in Carthage, or my house in Vicksburg.

I explained to Mr. Minor that on the night of the fire I was in Starkville. Josh had to work that night at Applebee's, where he was a waiter, and that when he got off work he came back to the apartment. We went to sleep and didn't wake up until the next morning. Not once did we leave that night.

Mr. Minor then asked how I learned about the fire that destroyed the lake house. I explained to him that on November 13, I received a call from my probation officer, Jay Simpson, who told me to contact Sheriff Nail at the Attala County Sheriff's Department. When I did so I was informed about the fire. I went on to explain that I cooperated fully with Sheriff Nail and both Josh and I went there later that afternoon and provided him alibi statements for where we were. Curiously, though, Mr. Minor had the same confusion over my statement as I did.

When I was interviewed at the sheriff's office I was asked where I was on the night of November 9. Josh was asked where we were on the night of November 10. We both answered truthfully, not knowing that we each were being asked different questions about two different dates.

Mr. Minor wanted to know why there was this discrepancy in our statements, but it was not something that I could answer. Only Sheriff Nail and the other deputy who took our statements could explain why they asked us about two different dates when only the November 10 date mattered. I chalked it up to law enforcement investigatory inefficiency and incompetence.

I could quickly see that Mr. Minor was having as much difficulty wrapping his mind around this confusion as I was. But it wasn't my statement, necessarily, that mattered. I was the suspect. The only person's statement that really mattered was my alibi's. And Josh was very clear; the night of the fire we were together all night at his apartment in Starkville. I explained this numerous times, in numerous ways to Mr. Minor, too.

We then moved to my cell phone records that Sheriff Nail obtained shortly after I got arrested. Even though there was confusion regarding the dates on Josh's and I's statements, the cell phone records were clear. Our phones were being used, connected to a Starkville cell tower, before, during, and after the time the fire occurred. I, likewise, explained this to Mr. Minor.

I did agree with him, however, that if I were to of left my cell phone at Josh's apartment, and drove to Kosciusko to burn the lake house, then no cell towers in Attala County would be on the cell records.

I had to explain to Mr. Minor, though, that this was improbable because there were few gaps in the communications. The cell phone records showed that I was receiving calls and texts, making calls and texts, and using data almost continuously through the afternoon, evening, and night that the fire destroyed the lake house. That means that I, or at least someone—in all fairness—was using my phone while it was connected to a Starkville cell tower to make and receive calls, texts, and data during the time the house burned. This was beyond doubt, notwithstanding the incompleteness of the records.

I was then asked if I was ever worried whether Josh would implicate me in the fire after our relationship ended. The answer was complicated. Josh had exposed me to HIV, lied to me about having the virus, and fabricated fake HIV tests, which he used to convince me he was negative. Thankfully, I didn't contract the disease, but I could have. And his evil thought processes and lies were what led me to end our relationship.

For almost a year, I lived in fear that Josh had transmitted the virus to me. I had to go get tests every three months. I was placed on PrEP, a pre-exposure prophylactic medication that helps prevent one from being infected with HIV, and I attended multiple counseling sessions with doctors and social workers. Thinking about having Josh charged by the authorities did cross my mind numerous times.

Josh knew that I had spoken to a social worker and informed her that he had exposed me. He also knew that I'd spoken to a law enforcement officer about possible charges. This led him to call my mother and threaten her that if I pursued charges against him for exposing me to HIV, then he would go to the fire marshal and implicate me in the fire. He essentially told me the same thing through text messages.

When Josh threatened us, we immediately contacted Sheriff Nail and told him about the threats. We also tried contacting Jackson, but he never returned either of our phone calls. Interestingly, though, Sheriff Nail told me that Josh's threats didn't matter because the fire investigation was never proven to be an arson and that the case was closed. I believed him.

Explaining all of this to Mr. Minor wasn't easy, though. I didn't get the feeling from him that he was especially familiar with the dangers posed by the gay community and the complexity of gay relationships. But I knew if I couldn't explain it clearly and succinctly to him, I'd never be able to explain it to a jury. So I made the extra effort.

I could tell we were getting close to the end of the deposition because Mr. Minor was having to turn to his notes more and more to form his questions.

The money that I'd spent regarding the arrest was the next line of inquiry from him. I'd had to spend $5,000.00 on the day of my arrest to bond out of jail. Since then, I'd had to pay the costs of the lawsuit, the failed depositions of Emmett and Kade, and numerous other expenses related to litigating the case. Some were documented, others weren't. And I explained this to Mr. Minor.

I was then asked if I knew anyone in the Hell's Angels gang. This question surprised me. When I was incarcerated at Ray Brook, New York, one of my best friends was a major commander in the Hell's Angels on the East Coast. For some reason he took a liking to me—in a non-sexual nature—and made sure that I didn't have any problems there. Unfortunately, he was killed in a shootout with police shortly after he was released from prison in 2014.

In my book, *Into Hell I Rode*, I'd written about my Hell's Angel friend and how he helped me while I was at Ray Brook.

In one of Emmett's many accusations against me he claimed that he was threatened by someone from the Hell's Angels that was acting on my behalf. I found this accusation hilarious because not only did Emmett make this allegation after my book was published—which is no doubt where he got the idea from—but just the thought that I had such a powerful influence with the Hell's Angels was laughable. I could only roll my eyes. This was better than fiction.

The last thing that Mr. Minor wanted to know revolved back to the lawsuit that the Atwoods filed against me to reclaim Vivian's house and money.

They filed that lawsuit on November 2, 2009. But I wasn't served with the lawsuit by a process server until November 18, 2009. When it was filed I did not know about it. I had no clue—like a lot of people—that the lawsuit had been filed until I was actually served with it. And this had easily been proven.

Since I had no clue about the lawsuit's existence until November 18, the lawsuit itself could never have been a motivation for wanting to burn the Atwood Lakehouse on November 10. I understood that Mr. Minor needed something, anything, to use to support Jackson's claim that I had motive to burn the lake house, but using the lawsuit that Vivian's children brought could not form that basis.

Not only was I not made aware of that lawsuit until after the fire, but Emmett's name was nowhere on the document. He had nothing to do with it. If the lawsuit was going to serve as a basis for an arson, then the arson would have been against one of Vivian's children that was suing me. Not Emmett. But I don't think Mr. Minor understood this. However, the deposition was concluded and it was time to move on.

I thought the day had gone well. My confrontations with Emmett and Kade hadn't really answered any lingering questions that I'd had, but I was able to obtain some useful information.

Unfortunately, there was never a Perry Mason moment. Somewhere deep inside of my mind I'd hoped I'd be able to wring a confession from either Emmett or Kade that they were the ones responsible for the fire. There was enough suspicious activities on their part for one to think that, but it was apparent they were well-prepared for any questions in that regard.

The strong sense of something foul in the air permeated the room, though, when they finished their testimony.

Kade sleeping the night away while the fire raged didn't make sense. Nor did him refusing to call the fire department or sheriff's office when he woke up.

Emmett's refusal to answer truthfully the questions about the increase in insurance and where the payoff money went to from Mississippi Farm Bureau, didn't make sense either.

I had the insurance records, and they clearly showed something different than what Emmett testified to, but it was becoming clear that I would need to subpoena Jan Hyland Daigre to court to explain them.

As the day's events and testimony began percolating in my mind, I was already forming a trial strategy as I made the ninety-minute drive back to Hattiesburg. My ultimate goal at trial was finding the truth. I didn't care about fancy lawyering techniques or concocting complicated stories to explain to the jury what happened. I felt like I would be able to connect with a jury much easier than Mr. Minor and Jackson would.

They were approaching the trial with the attitude that no juror would dare question a thirty-year veteran police officer who made a decision to execute an arrest on an unpopular defendant with a criminal past. But that was the point they missed. I was not a criminal. I was a victim of an unjust, corrupt criminal justice system, and that, I decided, would be my message.

By the time I made it back to Hattiesburg I'd partially developed my strategy and laid out its components. The last major thing left to do was to take Josh's deposition on February 27, 2017. This, I was not looking forward to.

CHAPTER TWENTY-FOUR

As we began preparing for Josh's deposition, Mr. Minor told me that Josh had hired a lawyer to represent him and attend the deposition. The guy's name was Randall Juergensen and he kept his office in Indianapolis.

I did a quick search in all the federal courts for Juergensen's name, but I couldn't find a single federal case that he was involved in. This indicated to me that he wouldn't be familiar with the federal rules and procedure. Even though I wasn't an attorney, I was more familiar with federal procedure than most attorneys who don't practice in the federal courts are.

It also surprised me that Josh would hire an attorney to represent him in the deposition. But as I thought more about it the closer I came to the realization that Josh would do anything, use anyone, and abuse whomever he could in order to avoid his responsibility as an adult.

Herein lies Josh's real mental pathology. In my opinion, at his core, Joshua Langston Chamblee is a psychotic sociopath. He did nothing but compulsively lie, manipulate, and abuse my friendship with him.

When it came time for him to stand up and atone for his sins he chose to hide behind his mother, risk having her held in contempt of court, and avoided every responsibility he had. He wouldn't even follow through on a simple agreement that his parents made with Magistrate Sanders to schedule a private deposition by phone so that he wouldn't have to disclose his location.

Josh is, and was, incapable of accepting any responsibility for his actions, the least of all which was exposing me to HIV. And his hiring an attorney to be his mouthpiece at the deposition was just another incarnation of Josh's avoidance of responsibility.

Because Josh's deposition would be through the phone, there was no reason for me to leave the halfway house in Hattiesburg and travel to Mr. Minor's office in Jackson. However, I did explain to Mr. Minor before the deposition that it would probably go worse than Emmett's and Kade's. We just weren't prepared for how bad it would actually be because of the attitude, stall tactics, and frivolous interruptions and objections made by Josh's attorney in their attempt to hide the truth.

At 1:00 P.M. on February 27, 2017, I placed a call to Mr. Minor's office and was connected via three-way to the court reporter's office in Indianapolis where Josh and Juergensen had assembled. Josh was placed under oath and Mr. Minor introduced himself as a special assistant attorney general who was representing James O'Neal Jackson. After the preliminaries, which required Josh to state his name, Mr. Minor asked Josh if he had ever testified in court before or in a deposition. Josh firmly replied that he had not. Mr. Minor was very specific.

> **MR. MINOR:** Mr. Chamblee, have you ever given a deposition before or testified in court before?
> **JOSH:** No.

Josh was then asked what city and state he lived in, to which he replied "Indianapolis, Indiana." He also stated that he had lived in Indianapolis since 2011 and was currently working for Celadon Trucking as a technical coordinator.

Before moving to Indianapolis, Josh testified that he had lived in Starkville, Jackson, and New Orleans, and that his parents lived in Edinburgh, Mississippi, which is a small community near Carthage in Leake County.

After establishing the basics, Mr. Minor then moved to establishing the relationship that we shared.

In response to Mr. Minor's questions, Josh testified that he and I met at the gay bar in Jackson in 2009 and that we dated for a few months. However, Josh couldn't remember how many months we dated.

Josh was then asked if he remembered James Jackson with the Fire Marshal's Office, which he did. But Josh couldn't remember when he met Jackson. However, Josh did remember meeting Jackson in July 2011 and providing him with the third statement which implicated me in the fire. Mr. Minor concentrated on that meeting first.

> **MR. MINOR:** What, if anything, did you tell him when you gave that statement?
> **JOSH:** What do you mean by that question?
> **MR. MINOR:** What did you tell him about the fire in Attala County?
> **JOSH:** I told them what happened.
> **MR. MINOR:** And what happened?
> **JOSH:** I told him that David picked me up after work at my apartment. We drove to Attala County. We parked the car in a field and walked across a cattle grate to the house and burned it. (There is no cattle grate on the Atwood Lakehouse property.)
> **MR. MINOR:** Was that the truth?
> **JOSH:** Yes.

Josh was then asked whether or not Jackson had threatened him or promised anything to him for changing his story. Josh emphatically stated that he was not threatened or promised anything.

We immediately knew that this was a lie because Jackson himself admitted that he had threatened Josh and Josh's mother with his arrest if he didn't provide a statement implicating me in the fire, and he also admitted that he promised Josh that he could collect the $25,000.00 reward for changing his story. But Josh didn't know that I already had the information.

It was becoming apparent to me at this point that Josh had made the decision to do everything possible to blame me for the fire in retaliation for me ending the relationship with him.

One has to keep in mind that Josh was in deep, deep love with me at the time I ended the relationship. There's certainly no doubt in my mind that Josh claimed to love me much more than I felt I loved him. But is it really love when one is HIV-positive, knowingly exposes his partner, lies about his status, and then is surprised when that partner finds out and chooses to end the relationship?

Josh's response to my ending our relationship was simple hatred, vindictiveness, and scorn for a relationship gone wrong. And like symbiotic twins mutually dependent on the other, Josh and Jackson each provided the other with a means to an evil end. Josh could punish me for ending our relationship and Jackson could use Josh to effect his, Chaney's, and Sheriff Pace's retaliation intentions. It was a perfect storm of maleficence.

Mr. Minor made the mistake, though, of trying to probe deeper into Josh's thought processes than just letting the topic of threats and promises die.

> **MR. MINOR:** So nobody threatened you in order to make you give that statement?
> **JOSH:** No, not at first.

My ears perked at this comment because I knew then that the truth was close to slipping to the surface.

Josh went on to explain that he got arrested in Indianapolis because he wouldn't come back down to talk to Jackson after he gave him the third statement, and that he felt threatened after Jackson and other members of the Fire Marshal's Office began harassing his family. Mr. Minor quickly moved to another topic, though.

Josh was then asked about the night of the fire. Despite testifying a few minutes prior that I picked him up at his apartment and then went and burned the lake house, Josh now stated that he left Applebee's around one or one-thirty that night and went back to his apartment where I was waiting on him.

According to Josh, I told him that I wanted to go for a ride and we headed towards Kosciusko. After driving for an estimated time of thirty to forty-five minutes (it takes almost ninety minutes to drive from Josh's apartment in Starkville to the Atwood Lakehouse property on Youth Center Road in western Attala County), Josh said we parked the car in a field, got out, and walked towards the house.

> **MR. MINOR:** And at that time did you know why you were there?
> **JOSH:** I kind of figured it when he had a can, a green can of something in his hand. I'm guessing it was kerosene, but I don't know to be honest.
> **MR. MINOR:** Did David say anything to you at that point?
> **JOSH:** He just said that his grandfather's house was up there

and that he was going to burn it down.

MR. MINOR: And after that, did you observe anything?

JOSH: We started walking back and I saw the house was in flames.

When Mr. Minor tried to get Josh to state whether or not he actually saw me start the fire, Josh was unable to do so except to say that he only saw me walk behind the house and that after coming back he saw flames coming out of the house.

MR. MINOR: Did David say anything to you after that?

JOSH: I don't really remember much of that night anymore.

MR. MINOR: Did he tell you not to tell anybody what happened?

JOSH: He told me not to say anything or he'll do something to my family, burn my house down.

I found this statement from Josh ludicrous for several reasons. First, if what Josh said is true, then he continued dating me for another three months after I allegedly threatened to harm him and his family if he told anyone.

Second, not only did we keep dating months after the fire, when I got locked up on my first probation violation from January 2010 to June 2010, Josh came to see me in the county jail, accepted my collect phone calls, and wrote me dozens of love letters. This isn't the actions of a person who was an accessory to a serious crime and was then threatened to keep silent.

Furthermore, in the third statement that Josh provided to Jackson, Josh told him that days after I allegedly burned the house down that we ended our relationship, quit speaking, and that Josh told me that if I contacted him again he would pursue criminal charges against me.

If Jackson would of had any ounce of competency as an investigator he could have determined that this was an absurd lie.

Not only did Josh and I continue our relationship for over three months after the fire, Josh tried to continue our relationship even after I went back to prison, despite allegedly, me threatening him and his family. It didn't make sense and it never would. But we moved on.

Mr. Minor then questioned Josh about the two prior alibi statements that he'd given Sheriff Nail on November 13, 2009, and then Jackson in March 2010. Josh explained, however, that the only reason he gave these two alibi statements was because I'd threatened him.

Again, in March 2010 I was locked in jail. There was no reason for Josh to lie for me. I posed no threat to him and he knew that he could have implicated me in the fire then and had me locked away in prison forever. But the truth was, in March 2010, Josh told the truth to Jackson because Josh still expected he and I to continue our relationship whenever I got out of prison. It was only when I ended things with him that he turned against me.

The last question that Mr. Minor had for Josh concerned whether or not he'd received any threats from me since I'd been released from prison.

> **MR. MINOR:** Since you gave the third statement, have you been threatened by David Atwood since then?
> **JOSH:** Besides him calling my parents and trying to find out my information, no.
> **MR. MINOR:** Okay, thank you Mr. Chamblee.

Up until this time, Juergensen had been quiet and had not interrupted Mr. Minor a single time in the deposition. That would change, though, as soon as I began my questions.

Mr. Minor had briefly touched on how Josh and I began our relationship, but I felt that if the jury was going to truly understand Josh's mental pathology they would have to hear as many details as possible.

> **ME:** Did you and I develop a friendship first when we met, or did we immediately develop a relationship upon meeting?
> **JOSH:** How is this relevant?
> **JUERGENSEN:** Let him just ask for now.
> **JOSH:** We were friends first.
> **ME:** To the best of your recollection, can you state the date that we actually began our relationship?
> **JUERGENSEN:** I'm going to object to this series of questions. I don't see how it's relevant or designed to lead to any relevant or discoverable evidence in this case. You know, I've let you go ahead and ask some preliminary questions, but I don't see

where you're going with this or how this has any relevancy to the issues that's pending in your case.

ME: So are you recommending that your client not answer any further questions of mine in this regard?

JUERGENSEN: I don't know what you mean in reference to "with regards to this." If you have some point you're trying make we'll entertain that. Or if you want to go on to other areas that may be relevant to the issues in your pending litigation, that's fine. But if the questions are designed to embarrass or harass my client, then we'll have to see what the questions are. But your questions about your relationship has no relevancy to the issues pending in your case.

I could immediately tell that Juergensen was not going to make it easy for me to get any information from Josh that would be helpful in my case. Not only that, I felt that Juergensen was a complete Yankee asshole. Not only did I feel like the man was a dick-eating bitch, but I also began to feel that Josh and Juergensen were probably sexually involved.

I knew Josh's history and how he sought out older, wealthy men to support a lavish lifestyle that he likes to live. The hostility in Juergensen's voice convinced me that this was not merely a client/attorney relationship, but was probably, in my opinion, a boy-toy/sugar-daddy relationship. I kept my opinions to myself, though, and tried to remain professional. But I wasn't going to let Juergensen bully me.

ME: Well, again, Mr. Juergensen, I'm not an attorney, but I do have a point and I am entitled to try and establish the evidence in this case.

JUERGENSEN: Then get to the point.

ME: Listen, I will ask the questions, and if your client refuses to answer, then we can get the judge on the phone. He's standing by. So I will just keep going.

I wanted to establish early in the deposition the real reason for why I ended my relationship with Josh. The catalyst for that end was Josh not telling me that he was HIV-positive.

ME: Ay some point did we begin a sexual relationship?

JOSH: Yes.

ME: And at that time did you disclose to me that you were HIV-positive?

JOSH: How is this relevant?

JUERGENSEN: I am going to object on the grounds of relevancy. It's invasive of my client's privacy rights and it is designed to harass and intimidate him, and it's beyond the scope of relevant discovery in this case. But you can answer if you want.

JOSH: The first time we had sex, no, I did not disclose. And as a federal employee I do not have to disclose that information.

What being a federal employee had to do with disclosing to a sexual partner one's HIV status was lost on me. First, at the time Josh and I were together he was not a federal employee. He was a waiter at Applebee's. Second, state law is very clear. One who is HIV-positive must disclose that fact to their sexual partners. And Josh admitted that he did not disclose that to me.

ME: So you're saying that after you disclosed to me that you were HIV-positive we continued having sex?

JOSH: Not until after the fact that you told me that you was fine with my status.

This was news to me. Except for the abject horror and misery I went through after finding out that Josh was HIV-positive, had not told me, and that I might be infected myself, I felt the situation almost surreal. Who in their right minds would continue having sex with a person that was HIV-positive and had lied about that fact throughout the relationship? Certainly not I. But that was Josh's story and I moved on.

ME: Can you give me an estimate on the date when the fire occurred?

JOSH: No, I cannot. I forgot about that night.

ME: Did we end our relationship immediately after the fire?

JOSH: No, not until you went to jail. (Again, this was not what he told Jackson when he gave the third statement.)

ME: But you remember visiting me in the jail? Accepting my collect phone calls?

JOSH: Yes. I wanted to see how you were doing.
ME: Were those calls pleasant?

I wanted to demonstrate the implausibility of Josh's statement that I had threatened him and his family after the fire. If he was coming to visit me in the jail and accepting my collect calls, and those visits were cordial and pleasant, then it would be hard for someone to believe that I'd previously threatened Josh and his family if he revealed anything about the fire. But Juergensen intervened.

JUERGENSEN: Again, I really fail to—we've been extremely patient, and I've sat here and allowed you to go on. So if you have a point you need to make it. I'm going to object. This is just to harass and argue with my client.
ME: Mr. Juergensen, I know you're in Indianapolis and aren't real familiar with this case, but these phone calls and visits to the jail have become important. I know you're not familiar with that, but there is a point. I'd appreciate your continued cooperation.
JUERGENSEN: Well, I'm sure you believe that. But why don't you move on to a different area.

Juergensen was really getting on my nerves and I could tell that he was getting on Mr. Minor's nerves, too, from the sighs and heavy breathing coming from his phone, but I wasn't to the point yet for a head-on collision.

My next area of questioning concerned the personal property of mine that Josh refused to return after we ended our relationship. He had kept several electronic items of mine, including a large screen television, DVD player, computer, printer, and an iPhone. When I tried to get them back from him, he refused. This led to more fights between us, but I eventually conceded that it wasn't worth fighting over and I let him keep the items.

However, when I tried to question Josh about this, he denied he had illegally kept anything of mine when we broke up. So I didn't get far in this line of questioning.

I kept wanting to go back to Josh's statement that I threatened him and his family the night the fire occurred. I just couldn't leave it alone because nothing he said made sense.

ME: Do you remember attending a court trial in Vicksburg involving me? (This was the jury trial where Scott Zimmerman and the Atwoods had me charged with elderly abuse, which I was found not guilty of.)

JOSH: Yes.

ME: And it was after the fire in Kosciusko?

JOSH: I do believe it was.

ME: So even after the fire in Kosciusko, you continued staying at my house in Vicksburg?

JOSH: Yes, I did.

ME: And after the fire you continued having sex with me?

JOSH: Not as sexual as you wanted it to be.

Again, I would have found this assertion hilarious had the seriousness of Josh exposing me to HIV not been in the forefront.

It didn't make sense why I would want to continue having sex with someone knowing they were HIV-positive and had lied to me about it. But again, too, this was Josh's story and the jury would ultimately have to hash out the validity to it.

ME: But we did continue a sexual relationship after I allegedly threatened you and your parents?

JOSH: I guess you could say so. I'm sorry. I am getting annoyed.

JUERGENSEN: Okay. Again, I am going to object here. We've given you a great deal of latitude. And so if you have a point to make, please do so.

ME: Thank you for the objection.

I then went back to Josh's first answer in the deposition regarding whether or not he had ever testified in a trial or deposition before.

ME: You testified earlier in this deposition that you had never testified in a court hearing or deposition before; is that true?

JOSH: That is true.

ME: But did you not appear in court after being sued by a former roommate of yours for not paying the rent?

JOSH: That was when I was 21 years old.

ME: So it would be correct then to say, though, that you have testified in a trial before?

JOSH: But that's not the question that was asked of me. The question was, have you done a deposition or trial for *your* case.

ME: No, the question was, and the attorney general's question was, have you ever testified in any type of trial or deposition and you answered no. So it's true that you've had to testify in a trial before?

JOSH: Yes.

I was slowly dismantling Josh's credibility. And I knew if I gave him enough rope he would hang himself with his compulsive, pathological lying. But I had to turn to a portion of Jackson's investigation next.

As part of the investigation to try and find Josh in the summer of 2011, Jackson obtained a comprehensive consumer report on him that stated that Josh had lived in Oregon and worked for a company named Markee Dragon. But when asked, Josh denied living in Oregon or working for the company.

When Jackson had first approached Josh's mother in his effort to find Josh, Mrs. Lyle had lied and told Jackson that Josh was living in North Carolina and was in the Navy Reserve. These were both lies. And Josh denied in the deposition ever living in North Carolina or being in the Navy Reserves.

This led into questions about Josh's arrest history. According to the comprehensive consumer report that Jackson obtained, Josh had been arrested in Saint Tammany Parish, Louisiana, for injuring public records. When I called the police department there they told me that Josh had been arrested for lying to a police officer and filing a false police report.

This was another gold nugget in the case. Even though Louisiana called the charges "injuring public records," the genesis of the charges began because Josh lied to an officer that was investigating a DUI car crash that Josh was involved in and where he filed an official police report that was not truthful.

Jackson had proof in his hands before he took Josh's third statement that there were serious problems with his credibility. Jackson ignored this vital and extremely important piece of evidence when he obtained Josh's third, coerced statement and used it to convince the judge to give him a warrant for my arrest.

This topic was probably the most important part of Josh's deposition, and this arrest in Louisiana was something that Judge Aycock had specifically had concerns about when she issued her opinion in July 2016 denying Jackson's motion to dismiss on summary judgment grounds. But Juergensen was prepared and he was intent on doing everything possible to hide and conceal Josh's criminal history.

> **ME:** Before your arrest in Indianapolis in 2011 for accessory after the fact to arson, had you ever been arrested before that?
> **JUERGENSEN:** I am going to object to that. This is irrelevant to your issues in your suit. This is invasion of his privacy. It's not discoverable information. And it's, again, designed solely to annoy, harass, and otherwise burden my client.
> **ME:** Objection noted. But I think the rules allow for a witness's credibility to be questioned. Will your client answer?
> **JUERGENSEN:** Well, as you'd know if you had attended law school there are strict limits on what a witness has to answer in a deposition. Whether or not my client has ever been arrested is irrelevant. So, no. My client will not answer.
> **ME:** Okay. We've reached an impasse here, so I am going to call the court and get guidance from the judge.

Both Magistrate Sanders and myself had expected that there would be issues in the different depositions that would need to be resolved with court intervention. Obviously, Juergensen was doing everything possible to hide Josh's criminal history. Yet, it was that criminal history which was the main key to the case. So I called the judge.

> **ME:** Judge Sanders, this is David Atwood. We've reached a point in the deposition where I am asking Josh Chamblee about his criminal history. His attorney has objected and they have refused to answer the question.
> **JUERGENSEN:** Your Honor, this is Randall Juergensen. I asked about the relevancy of these questions and Mr. Atwood indicated that they were designed to question my client's credibility and veracity as a witness. Mr. Atwood insisted on going over questions of my client's arrest history and I made an objection to that. We've been here since 1:00 and I believe these questions

are just fishing expeditions designed solely to harass and annoy and embarrass my client rather than lead to any arguably relevant information.

MAGISTRATE SANDERS: Hold on a minute. I don't think that would be something that would be a problem at all for him to answer. I am going to allow Mr. Atwood to ask because it does sound like something that would be relevant, that it could be relevant at trial based on the allegations in this particular case. So, yes. You can ask a few questions with respect to that. And that's going to be the order of the court.

ME: Thank you, Your Honor.

This was another win for me. Juergensen surely felt like he could bully and intimidate me in the deposition and that the court would back him up because he attended law school and I didn't.

Fortunately for me, Magistrate Sanders was going to ensure I received fair opportunities to develop the record relating to Josh's past history of dishonesty because, after all, it was Josh's "honesty" that Jackson relied on in asking for a warrant for my arrest.

In response to my questions, Josh had to admit that he was arrested in Saint Tammany Parish by the Lake Ponchartrain Police Department for lying to law enforcement officers and filing a false police report. I then had to move to what he and Jackson discussed about his criminal history.

ME: In your multiple interviews with James Jackson, were you ever asked about your criminal history or this arrest?

JOSH: No, not that I recall.

I next moved my questioning to the first alibi statement that he gave to Sheriff Nail when we went to the Attala County Sheriff's Department on November 13, 2009.

ME: This alibi statement that you gave to Sheriff Nail says that we were at your apartment in Starkville the night of the fire. Was that an accurate statement?

JOSH: I made that statement to him.

ME: And did you give a second alibi statement in March 2010 to James Jackson stating that we were together at your apartment

on the night of the fire?
JOSH: Yes.

At this point, Juergensen and I got involved in a shouting match at his inane, frivolous, and pointless objections that were designed for no other purpose than to conceal the truth, harass me, and stall the deposition.

JUERGENSEN: Again, I am going to object. This has already been asked and answered. You can ask one more question and then we can move on.
ME: Listen, Mr. Juergensen, I'm conducting this deposition of your client, and I'll move on when I'm ready to move on. These statements that Chamblee gave are the very crux of this case and I am going to ask him about them. So when I finish my questions about these statements we will move on.
JUERGENSEN: Well, let's just go into them in detail, now, if you have a specific question.
ME: We've not yet identified the third statement that Josh gave. Once we do, then I'll move on.

At this point Juergensen managed to close his mouth for a long enough period of time that I was finally able to ask Josh about the third, coerced statement that he was forced to give Jackson. However, Josh claimed that he couldn't remember giving a third statement that implicated me in the fire, only a verbal recording.

No question that I could ask was even able to get close to getting Josh to admit he wrote a third statement. And this confused me because in the first two alibi statements that Josh gave in November 2009 and March 2010 a distinctly different handwriting was used than the one used to write out the third, coerced statement in July 2011. But when I asked Josh about his different styles of writing, Juergensen made another frivolous objection.

JUERGENSEN: Okay. Again, I am going to object here. Are you asking my client to identify something that's not in front of him? So I don't understand your point in this.
ME: Okay. Josh, can you state to me in what instances would you write in cursive and in what instances you would write in

print?

JUERGENSEN: No. No. No. No. No. We're not going there. We're not going into that. Either move on or get the judge on the phone. (Juergensen sounded just like a petulant child.)

I remember thinking that this deposition had devolved into an immature bitch fight more suited to the backrooms of the gay bars than the federal courts. Juergensen kept trying to dominant the process to protect what I believed was his sociopathic lover. It was clear that Juergensen was doing nothing but trying to wear me down, but I kept chugging forward. I did move on to another lie in Josh's story, though.

ME: Josh, earlier in the deposition you testified that when we allegedly went to the Atwood Lakehouse that I had a green bottle in my hand; is that correct?

JOSH: I think so.

ME: Did you ever tell the fire marshal that I had a bag in my hand and that you did not know what was in the bag? (In Josh's third, coerced statement, he never mentioned anything about a bottle; Josh told Jackson that I only had a clear bag in my hand.)

JOSH: Uh-huh. Yes, I did.

ME: So which is it? Did I have a clear bag in my hand or did I have a green bottle?

JUERGENSEN: Again, I object. He's testified today that he didn't know what the bottle contained, so I think you're splitting hairs whether it was a bag or bottle. He says he doesn't know. So again, I don't know what the relevancy is. He didn't testify what you had, only that it was a bag or bottle.

ME: No, Mr. Juergensen. You're trying to change your client's testimony. He testified very clearly earlier that it was a green bottle that contained kerosene.

JUERGENSEN: Okay.

ME: So I am going to question him on that. Josh, do you remember whether I had a bag or bottle?

JOSH: I don't remember now. It was either a bag or bottle.

ME: Let me move on. You also testified earlier that on the night of the fire I allegedly told you that I would burn your parents' house down. If that was true, why would you continue dating me, coming to my court hearings, answering my collect calls from the jail, and visiting me there?

JOSH: Because it was the right thing to do. I was trying to be nice. (I almost vomited at this point.)

ME: After I allegedly threatened you, did you continue allowing me to come and stay in your apartment?

JUERGENSEN: Again, he's testified that there continued to be a relationship. You can argue about whether that does or doesn't help your case, but those facts are established. Move on.

ME: Listen, Mr. Juergensen. Again, I am conducting this deposition. Not you. And you can't have it both ways where I ask a general question and then you require that I ask a very narrow question and then object to the narrow question. So I will continue the way I want. Josh, did you ever file a police report when I allegedly threatened you and your parents?

JOSH: No.

ME: Let me ask about something else. You testified earlier and told the fire marshal in your statement that when we allegedly burned the lake house, you turned around and saw flames coming out of the house.

JOSH: I never said I saw flames coming out of the house. I only saw flames in the air.

ME: So you never saw the house on fire?

JOSH: I only saw flames in the air.

ME: Did you ever see me strike a match or use a lighter?

JOSH: No.

Despite Juergensen continuing to make his inane and frivolous objections that were designed to hide the truth and obstruct the deposition, I still had quite a bit of information to get through.

One thing that I couldn't understand about Josh's testimony was my allegedly telling him that we were on the way to burn my grandfather's house down and him doing nothing about it.

ME: According to your testimony, I allegedly told you that we were going to burn my grandfather's house down. Did you ever try to convince me not to? Did you ever try to do anything to stop it or call 911?

JOSH: I was in a vehicle with you. What was I supposed to do? Jump out?

ME: What about when we allegedly stopped on the Atwood property? According to your testimony and statement to the fire marshal, we walked a long way together from the car up to the house?

JOSH: Well, let me see. It's dark. It's in the middle of nowhere. Would you stay by yourself?

ME: Why not just insist on waiting in the car?

JOSH: I don't think that's relevant.

ME: So if what you're testifying to is true, that I allegedly burned the house, you were a willing and knowing participant?

JUERGENSEN: I am going to object to that and instruct my client not to answer.

My point had been well-established, and instead of continuing to entertain Juergensen's narcissistic need to hear himself speak, I moved on to Emmett's reward money. Jackson had testified that he had told Josh about the reward and that he could collect it if he gave a statement implicating me in the fire. Josh, though, chose to try and lie about this.

ME: At any point in time were you aware of any type of reward that had been offered for information leading to the arrest of the person who allegedly burned the Atwood Lakehouse?

JOSH: No.

ME: So the fire marshal, James Jackson, never mentioned to you that there was a $25,000 reward?

JOSH: No.

ME: But at some point in time, in July 2011, you were made aware that Jackson and the fire marshals were wanting to question you again about the fire?

JOSH: Yes, because they came to the fair and actually tried to harass my family.

ME: When you finally met with Jackson did you willingly want to talk to the fire marshals?

JOSH: I didn't willingly want to, but they made me.

This led me into another line of questions about what exactly Jackson had told Josh, or promised him, in regards to not being arrested if he would give a third statement implicating me in the fire.

ME: When you met with Jackson, did he ever tell you that if you gave a statement implicating me in the fire that you wouldn't be arrested?

JOSH: He told me that if I told him what really happened that night I wouldn't be arrested. And after he told me that, I wasn't afraid of being arrested.

ME: But you were eventually arrested in Indianapolis and extradited back to Mississippi after refusing to cooperate with the fire marshals anymore?

JOSH: Yes.

ME: Did anyone at anytime ever tell you that if you testified against me that it would help your case?

JOSH: Yes. It was my belief that if I testified against you it would help get my charges dismissed.

ME: Where did you get that idea from?

JUERGENSEN: Objection. That's not what he's testified to. So if you've got another question, ask it. Otherwise, move on. We're coming up on 3:00, and almost 20 minutes ago I told you we needed to draw this matter to a conclusion. So let's get done in the next five minutes.

ME: I wished it were that easy Mr. Juergensen, but, you know, again, this case completely revolves around your client. So, I mean, the more time you spend making pointless objections, the longer we're going to be here.

JUERGENSEN: No. No. No. No. No. Let's get the judge on the phone. You've wasted our time all afternoon. I don't think any of the points you've made are really that important. So get the judge on the phone. I've got other obligations. This has been an exhaustive and ridiculous exercise. So get the judge on the phone.

ME: Okay, then. Stand by. I still have about 15 or 20 minutes of questions.

JUERGENSEN: Well, why don't you get the judge on the phone. I'm getting really sick of your questions. I want to talk to the judge.

At this point there was no more trying to reason with Juergensen or be polite and patient with him. It was apparent that his personal feelings towards what I assume was his psychopathic lover were overriding his sense of professionalism. Or, it may have just been his northern, Yankee attitude. But I knew Magistrate Sanders would be on my side, so I made the call.

ME: Your Honor, I'm probably just going to refer to Mr. Juergensen on this one and let him explain what is going on.

JUERGENSEN: Your Honor, Randall Juergensen here. We've been at this for two hours now. Mr. Minor took a short factual deposition. I fully appreciate that Mr. Atwood is *pro se* and representing himself. We've been patient and accommodating. About 20 minutes ago I advised him that I didn't have all day. I have other obligations. He says now that he needs more time. I want you to limit this deposition. We could sit here all day and not accomplish much.

MAGISTRATE SANDERS: Mr. Atwood. Your response?

ME: Your Honor, I have been limiting for the last hour my questions about what's in the fire marshal's written reports, what's in Chamblee's statements. I've been sticking straight to the evidence and what promises may have been made to him by law enforcement. We've gotten to the point where Josh has stated that if he testified at the grand jury it would have helped him get his charges dropped. I specifically asked what made him think that. Mr. Juergensen has objected to him answering that question and that's where we are now. He insisted that we get you on the phone. This is the crux of the case; why Josh provided two alibi statements and then changed his statements. So I am really trying to get into his state of mind. We've spent all day hearing objections over and over again from Mr. Juergensen that has taken up the majority of what he considers valuable time. I told him I had about 20 more minutes of questions. Mr. Juergensen does not want to continue. But that's where we are.

MAGISTRATE SANDERS: Okay. Here's what I am going to do. Mr. Atwood, you can ask Mr. Chamblee why he believed his testimony would help get his charges dismissed. You can definitely ask him that. Then, once you get his answer, I am going to give you your 20 minutes to finish asking your questions. We are always lenient with *pro se* litigants, and you've done a fine job so far, Mr. Atwood. So 20 more minutes, then y'all will be done. Okay?

ME: Thank you, Your Honor.

This had been another small win for me and another slap in the face to Juergensen and the trash that he was representing.

Magistrate Sanders's words cannot be adequately expressed on paper, but at the deposition it could not be hidden that he was displeased with Juergensen's attitude and constant need to interrupt the process with his pointless objections.

When the magistrate granted my additional twenty minutes he conveyed in his voice his displeasure at Juergensen. So I felt that Juergensen would calm his bitch ass down a little and let me finish.

ME: Josh, at that point in time, what made you feel like if you testified against me it would help your case?

JOSH: Just the fact that if I testified that it would have helped.

It was apparent I wasn't going to get anywhere else with him. Josh was making up lies and answers as we went along and there wasn't anything that I could do about it. Thankfully, though, I was almost done.

The only thing that I had left to question Josh about was whether he'd had any conversations with James Jackson since he was arrested, and whether or not he had talked to Mr. Minor, or anyone else to prepare for the deposition.

ME: Since your arrest, have you had any other conversations or contact with Jackson or the other fire marshals?

JOSH: No.

ME: And have you had any conversations with Mr. Minor or anyone else in preparation for your testimony here today?

JOSH: I discussed with him the time, and also to find out if I could get a list of questions that was going to be asked between you, him, and me.

ME: Did Mr. Minor give you or tell you what those questions might be?

JOSH: No. He just said pretty much the same statements that I was given back in the day, but no specific questions.
ME: Okay. I'm done. Thank you gentlemen so much.

Without saying their goodbyes, Josh and his attorney hung up and disconnected the connection. I stayed on the phone long enough to express my opinion of Randall Juergensen to Mr. Minor, and I believe he felt the same way. But the deposition was over, I'd been able to attack Josh's credibility, I'd been able to get at least some of the information I needed, and I proved that Joshua Langston Chamblee was a pathological liar when it came to this case.

All in all, I felt that the deposition was more beneficial to me than it was to Mr. Minor. Even though Josh still tried to implicate me in the fire, it was apparent that he was lying, that he had motive to lie, and that he had no credibility as a witness at all. I knew then that a jury would hate him.

This was the last step in the discovery process. The only thing left for me and Mr. Minor to do next was prepare for trial on March 6, 2017. I was determined to be ready.

CHAPTER TWENTY-FIVE

Once Josh's deposition was completed I began gathering and organizing the documents, evidence, exhibits, and deposition testimony that I would need for trial. But before I could start that process, Chris Kelly interjected himself into the false arrest lawsuit trial once more while trying to assert his perceived authority and stroke his megalomania.

Since arriving at the halfway house I'd kept Kelly and my case manager informed of my need to attend the federal trial in March 2017. For three months, though, Kelly had ignored me and not given me permission to go.

The day after Josh's deposition Kelly finally gave me an answer, which, of course, was no. I tried to explain to him that I had to attend, but Kelly told me that he was in charge of my custody, not Judge Aycock. I thought to myself, *Well, I'll fix that.*

Again, I had to call Rylee, Magistrate Sanders's law clerk, and explain to him the problem. This was something that posed a more serious problem because I would actually have to be away from the halfway house for about a week. So Rylee kicked it up to Judge Aycock.

While I waited to figure out how the logistics would work for the March trial, Judge Aycock set a hearing, called a pretrial conference, that both Mr. Minor and myself had to attend in Aberdeen.

Since we were moving into a phase of the case where Judge Aycock was having to take over more and more of the logistics, Rylee passed me off to one of the judge's law clerks, Parker Kline.

My first phone call to Mrs. Kline established a great working relationship with her and the judge's other law clerk, Daniel McHugh. Despite me being a *pro se* litigant, they treated me with respect and professionalism. I believe that these two clerks' attitudes reflect the high standards of ethics that I believe Judge Aycock showed throughout the proceedings. Parker and Daniel were extremely helpful and made everything so much easier.

After explaining to them my need to receive Chris Kelly's approval before being able to attend the pretrial conference and the March trial in Oxford, Parker informed me that she would get me approved to go to Aberdeen for the conference but that Judge Aycock would deal with my need to attend the trial at a later date. Since I was in no position to argue otherwise, I left it in their capable hands.

Early on the morning of the pretrial conference, I left Hattiesburg, and with a friend, drove the four hours to Aberdeen.

Prior to that morning, Mr. Minor and I had communicated multiple times and worked out an agreement on what should be included in the final pretrial order which would be approved by the judge that day.

In a civil trial, a pretrial order sets out the claims and defenses of the litigants that will be the subject of the trial, the agreements and disagreements of the litigants, the evidence expected to be introduced, and the witnesses that are expected to testify.

It took Mr. Minor and I about two weeks to work out the final details of what all should be included in the order, but at the end we came to a mutually agreeable understanding that foreclosed the need for Judge Aycock to intervene. Therefore, the pretrial conference before the judge was expected to go smoothly.

When I appeared before Judge Aycock for the first time that morning, I was immediately impressed with her stately demeanor, professionalism, and quiet dignity. She was not ostentatious, arrogant, or haughty. In fact, by all outward appearances, I thought she was rather pretty.

My mind quickly began making comparisons between Judge Aycock and Judge Wingate, but I quickly realized that what Wingate was, Judge Aycock was not. And I was very thankful for that because I've never wanted special treatment from the criminal justice system, only fair treatment. I was hoping I'd continue to receive that in Aberdeen.

After taking her seat, Judge Aycock took the time to speak to both

Mr. Minor and myself, and then asked how we were doing. Wingate had never done that.

Our first item of business was the pretrial order that Mr. Minor and I had only finished the night before. Because we had reached an agreement on all the issues contained therein, Mr. Minor was able to tell Judge Aycock that it was a mutually agreed order and that we did not have any objections to it. This obviously moved things along fairly quickly that morning.

Once we had disposed of the pretrial order, and it had been accepted by the judge, we were asked by Judge Aycock whether we still wanted a jury to try the matter. I could tell in Judge Aycock's voice that she would have preferred to try the matter in a bench trial without a jury. That would have eased things considerably and shortened the duration of the trial.

Knowing that Judge Aycock was clearly hinting her preference on how to conduct the trial put me in a bad situation by insisting on a jury trial. I believed that Judge Aycock had been, so far, very fair to me, but the only times that I had ever received a fair hearing in a criminal court was when I had a jury. Juries seemed to like me for some reason and I felt safest with them.

However, I did not want to risk losing what goodwill I may of had with Judge Aycock by insisting on a jury trial that was going to be more expensive and take more time than a bench trial would, but as much as I hated to, I was intent on being insistent about requiring the case to be tried by a jury—which was my right to do so.

Thankfully, though, Judge Aycock turned and asked Mr. Minor what his preference was for the trial and placed on him the burden of whether or not to request a jury trial.

Much to my relief, Mr. Minor insisted that he wanted the case tried by a jury. I immediately thought back to one of the many times that Mr. Minor had told me that no jury in Mississippi would award money to a plaintiff that was suing a state law enforcement officer for false arrest. Mr. Minor truly believed that Jackson was immune from liability based on Mississippi's past conservative hesitancy in holding corrupt law enforcement officers liable for their illegal actions.

By Mr. Minor insisting that the case be tried by a jury, this removed from me the fear I had of insisting on a jury trial myself and risk pissing off the judge. But like a lot of other weird things in the lead up to the trial, and eventually the trial itself, things were falling perfectly into place.

Having settled the jury issue, we next turned to my request for the court to issue me several subpoenas so that I could get the witnesses I needed to appear in court for the trial.

I'd previously filed a motion for each subpoena that I wanted, explaining to the court exactly why that witness was needed and what they might testify to, however, Judge Aycock had me briefly explain in court, again, why I wanted the witnesses. After doing so, she granted all of my requests and ordered that the clerk's office issue the subpoenas under their seal.

I had requested that the court give me subpoenas for Mrs. Lyle, her husband, Paul Lyle, Sheriff Tim Nail, Sheriff Martin Pace, my attorney, Rosalind Jordan, James Jackson's direct supervisor at the Fire Marshal's Office, Ricky Davis, and, finally, Mike Chaney himself. That was seven subpoenas that I'd have to get served before the March 6, 2017, trial.

After resolving the subpoenas issue, Judge Aycock asked me to explain to her the reason why I couldn't get permission to attend the trial in Oxford. The simple reason was, of course, Chris Kelly's megalomanic desire to control everything and everyone around him. But being as concise and succinct as possible left me no room to explain what my opinion was of Kelly's mental pathology.

Judge Aycock was not going to be cowed, though, from someone like Kelly. She quickly informed me that if need be she would issue a direct court order to Kelly to have me at the federal courthouse in Oxford on March 6 at 9:00 A.M. if need be, even if the U.S. Marshals had to transport me. I assured her, though, that I had my own transportation and that I could stay with my mother in a hotel room in Oxford for the duration of the trial. I just needed someone with more authority than Kelly to make it happen. And I was assured it would.

That concluded the pretrial conference and my friend and I left the courtroom and went and picked up my subpoenas from the clerk's office. Our plan was to get as many of them served as quick as possible on our way back to the halfway house in Hattiesburg.

Our first stop was the Attala County Sheriff's Department in Kosciusko. My friend approached the desk officer and explained to her that we were there to deliver some federal documents to Sheriff Nail and that we needed to see him as soon as possible.

We were then quickly ushered into Sheriff Nail's office, which, apparently, was the center of a large meeting because there were deputies standing around everywhere pouring over maps, bags of evidence, and other law enforcement incidentals.

I introduced myself again to the sheriff, told him my process server needed to serve him with a subpoena—at which time he was handed the document—and I asked him to contact me if he had any questions. He said, "Thank you," and we turned to leave. As we walked away, though, Sheriff Nail said to all of the deputies in the room, "And *that* was David Atwood." I could only smile.

Our next stop was the law office of Rosalind Jordan. I'd not seen her since my preliminary hearing before Judge Ronnie Stewart in October 2011, but she and I had stayed in touch and she knew that she was going to be called as a witness in the lawsuit case.

Our meeting was very cordial and I was happy to see that her office was full of clients and that her practice was thriving.

Even though the subpoena required her to attend court on Monday, March 6, I didn't expect to call her to testify until the following day. So I told her not to plan to come to court until Tuesday. Otherwise I'd just be wasting her time and that of her clients' if she came on Monday.

After the formalities of having the subpoena served were over, we briefly chatted about my recent release from prison, any interesting cases that she had, and what questions I'd be asking during her testimony at trial. I quickly realized that Mrs. Jordan would probably be one of my best witnesses.

My friend and I then left Mrs. Jordan's office and went to the cemetery about a mile from downtown. I'd been incarcerated since my Papaw, Aaron Tolleson, had passed away in September 2011, and I desperately wanted to visit his grave. I had a deadline to make it back to the halfway house, but I was determined to stop and visit with my beloved Papaw for at least a few minutes.

With that somber duty out of the way, we next headed further south to Carthage. Mrs. Lyle lived and worked in the area and we wanted to try and get her served on our way back. Thankfully, she was at work and my friend was able to get her served with the subpoena. I also included a note to her that I wouldn't need her testimony until the Tuesday after the trial started. I also asked her to call me before the trial.

We then burned out of Carthage and headed back to the halfway house. The rest of the subpoenas would have to be served without my assistance. My friend had served several of the subpoenas for the past depositions, so I had faith in his ability to get them done before trial.

After arriving back in Hattiesburg I immediately began work on preparing for trial. It had always been my belief that James Jackson would be the most important witness on whose shoulders the outcome of the trial would be decided, and I intended to call him as my first witness.

I still went to work everyday and my boss, Gary, was more than willing to allow me extra time at work to prepare for trial—without pay, of course. At night, though, I was given three hours, from five to eight, in social passes to go do about whatever I wanted to in the city. In the lead-up to the trial, though, I spent almost every night possible at the local library researching, reading, writing out questions, and forming a strategy.

I knew from the start that I'd have to make a good impression with my jury and that the best way to do that was through my opening statement. I'd been going over several phrases that I planned to use, but even so short of a time before trial I'd not formulated anything near a finished draft. I'd never conducted a trial before, so I was on a large learning curve.

Several themes began to develop in my mind the further things progressed. It was vitally important that the jury understand from early on that there never was any proof that a crime even took place. I had to make this point by underscoring the fact that none of the investigators could determine that this fire was an arson.

I also had to make a decision as to whether to approach the theory of the case from the standpoint that the fire was accidental and that I was wrongly accused, or whether the fire was intentionally set by, or on the orders of, Emmett for insurance purposes, and that I was purposely framed to coverup the crime. There was enough evidence in the case to support both arguments.

Despite my past history with Emmett, and my ultimate hatred of everything he and most of the Atwoods stood for, my personal belief was that the fire was accidental. But I still couldn't explain the coincidences with the recent increase in insurance, the pictures taken of the lake house four days before the fire for insurance purposes, and Kade allegedly sleeping through the fire and never calling the fire department.

If the cause was accidental it would be impossible to show this because Jackson did not do any competent investigation. He simply showed up, poked around in the ashes, took down Emmett's statement, accepted that statement as true, and then worked the case from Emmett's point of view for the next two years. It was perfectly reasonable to assume that we don't know whether the fire was arson or accidental because Jackson was either an utterly incompetent investigator, or simply decided to follow the path of least resistance and accept a theory advanced by a man who had clear motives to lie, a clear incentive to commit arson himself, and a clear intention to frame his least favorite grandson.

I'd always heard from defense attorneys that one needed to decide on a single theory and stick with that theory throughout the course of a trial. But this case was unlike any other I'd ever heard of.

More than anyone involved, it was I who wanted to know the true story about what happened to the Atwood Lakehouse. Like it being said in *The X-Files*, the truth is out there; and I wanted to find that truth.

This was the approach I ultimately decided to take in presenting my case theory to the jury. This trial was going to be a search for the truth; a search for justice. I wanted it to be a fact-finding mission more than I wanted to win a bunch of money. The truth meant more to me than money from Jackson's checkbook.

Ultimately, I realized, it didn't matter whether the fire was accidental or arson, as long as we were able to find the truth about what really happened. And the only way I felt that we could do that would be to present both theories to the jury and let them decide.

This essentially divided my forces and required me to present a case with two parallel narratives that each was as supportable as the other with the evidence at hand. What I was hoping would happen, though, was that something unexpected would happen at trial that would open the floodgates—a Perry Mason moment.

So as I began preparing the actual opening statement and the questions that I'd have to ask the witnesses, my intent was not to catch witnesses in lies, demean or belittle them, or try to prove some grand conspiracy—although I certainly believed and was going to attempt to prove that that is what brought the criminal charges about—my intention, instead, was to try and find the truth about what really happened.

Trying to find the real truth about the fire, and getting the witnesses to help me, obligated me to follow the dictates of Occam's Razor.

Sometimes the simplest explanation is the most correct. But going into the trial left both Mr. Minor and myself wondering exactly what happened on the night of November 10, 2009.

Jackson's theory, of course, was that Josh Chamblee and I drove from Starkville to Kosciusko and burned the lake house down. This wasn't the simplest explanation, though, because not one single piece of available evidence pointed in that direction. Just the opposite was true.

The second theory, which, in my opinion, Mr. Minor believed personally, was that the fire was accidental, caused by some unknown source. Now, to be fair, Mr. Minor never expressed this viewpoint to me, but I nevertheless gathered from our multiple interactions that this is how he felt.

I also believed that Sheriff Nail felt that the fire was accidental due to his multiple conversations that he had with my Papaw before he passed away. But there was little evidence to support this view.

The only possible indication from the evidence at hand that the fire might of been accidental was the fact that the fire started in the kitchen, near the electrical box, and that shortly before the fire Emmett had paid to have new insulation installed in the attic. But this still wasn't the simplest explanation.

The theory of Occam's Razor is that the simplest of two or more theories is preferable over a more complicated one, and that an explanation for an unknown phenomena should first be used to explain the situation from the known facts. Applying Occam's Razor to this case led me to simply conclude that the Atwood Lakehouse was purposely burned with Emmett's involvement.

First, there was no doubt in my mind that Emmett and his businesses—especially Atwood Chevrolet—were in financial trouble during the hard recession of 2009.

Second, there was no other explanation for why Emmett would increase the insurance on the lake house so drastically so soon before the fire.

Third, there was even less of an explanation for why Emmett would have pictures taken of the inside and outside of the lake house four days before the fire "for insurance purposes."

Fourth, Kade sleeping through the fire can be called nothing but an unexplained phenomena, except if one were to conclude that the fire was intentionally set with his knowledge. Then, his allegedly sleeping through the fire is a perfectly reasonable explanation.

Fifth, Kade never calling the fire department when he did allegedly discover the fire is just as unexplainable, except, of course, if his intent was to destroy the lake house.

Finally, Emmett's unwillingness to admit what the insurance payout was fully used for, except being partially used to rebuild a new lake house, led me to conclude that part of the insurance money was needed to prop up what I felt were his failing businesses. Nothing else made sense.

Taken together as a whole, I felt that the entirety of the evidence pointed to an arson, that Emmett was involved in, for the specific purpose of collecting an insurance payout to avoid bankruptcy, for which I'd be framed and blamed for. That was my theory.

I will, however, be the first to admit, though, that this was only my opinion—my personal assessment of the evidence. Others familiar with the case made their own conclusions. But for trial purposes before the jury, I had to solidify my theories and present them in the most concise, succinct manner possible. I didn't want to go into court spouting some harebrained theories that would only confuse or anger the jury.

So the more I thought about the case and the ways to present it, the more I decided to present all of the theories to the jury and allow them to decide. Because, ultimately, whether the jury sided with Jackson and believed that I was responsible, or whether they believed it was an accident or arson, it would be impossible not to allow the jury to make their own conclusions.

I also felt that honesty was the best policy to adopt when communicating with my jurors.

There are only a few times in a trial when the litigants are allowed to directly speak with the jurors. We'd have an opportunity to ask questions during jury *voir dire* when we selected the eventual eight jurors that would compose our jury, and we'd also have chances to speak to them during the opening and closing arguments. Other than those three times, Mr. Minor and myself would have to communicate our messages to the jury through our witnesses and our evidence.

In this personal communication, I felt that I had the better hand, not just because I've always felt that I was a better communicator, but because of Mr. Minor's indirect style of interaction with people.

When I first met Mr. Minor face-to-face at the February depositions, his personality immediately kind of reminded me of Ben Stein, the monotone-speaking-actor that did Visine dry eyes commercials. One could easily call his manner of speech monotonous.

This made me think more about how to address the jury. While I would be the first to agree that Mr. Minor does spectacular legal work and is thoroughly competent in making his arguments through legal briefs filed with the court, his personality precludes him from making those same arguments in an exciting, charismatic, and appealing way that is absolutely necessary when communicating with a jury.

Granted, the only time I've ever seen Mr. Minor in court is when dealing with my case—which no doubt Mr. Minor felt was a joke, a waste of time, and a case that it was impossible for him *not* to win—so I can't make a judgment on how his courtroom charisma is in other cases. But I knew it was seriously dangerous to underestimate me and the connection that I can sometimes make with people.

In both my previous jury trials, when I'd been charged with malicious mischief and elderly abuse, jurors told me after the trials that they were impressed with my honesty and my willingness to face them in the juror box when I was testifying. It was a personal connection they felt. I'd never formally taken speech and elocution classes, but I knew I had to instantly make a connection with my jury as soon as the trial began.

Whether Mr. Minor underestimated me, or whether he could perform under the pressure of trial to connect with a jury to gain sympathy for his client, was yet to be determined. I couldn't control his case, but I knew that I had to be ready for mine.

Getting ready for my trial, though, wasn't easy. Chris Kelly was determined to do everything possible to make my time at the halfway house as difficult as possible.

Initially, upon being told by Judge Aycock that I would be attending the trial despite his desire that I not, Kelly told me that I could stay at the hotel in Oxford with my mother for the duration of the trial. However, another option presented itself and Kelly was able to maintain his maniacal control of my custody in a limited way.

There was a Dismas Charities halfway house in Tupelo, Mississippi, the birthplace of Elvis Presley, which was about an hour east of Oxford. Kelly ordered me to stay there during the duration of the trial rather than in a hotel with my mother.

I was allowed to leave Hattiesburg on Friday, March 3, and make the four and a half hour drive to Tupelo. Leaving a few days early would give me an opportunity to prepare for the final phases of the trial there, and to meet with my mother on Sunday to prepare for her testimony.

When I arrived at the Tupelo halfway house I immediately noticed that it wasn't anything like Kelly's domain in Hattiesburg. While the staff in Hattiesburg also treated me with respect, the staff in Tupelo were much happier, more accommodating, and seemed to actually enjoy having me visit them.

I met with Mrs. Johnson, the director, upon my arrival and she promised whatever cooperation I needed to prepare for trial. At one point, I even commented on how much different the Tupelo halfway house was than Hattiesburg, and several staff members made the comment that things were done a little different there—for the better—than what Kelly did in Hattiesburg.

On Sunday I was allowed to drive to Oxford and meet with my mother at the hotel. She had driven up from Vicksburg that morning and was waiting on me with all of my dress clothes that I would need for the trial. She also brought me a new laptop to use to work on the case.

The biggest enjoyment of my short visit with my mother was taking a bath in the hotel room's bathtub. This was my first bath since my hospitalization and I enjoyed every minute of it. My mother also ordered us pizza and breadsticks from Pizza Hut and we ate and had a good visit while preparing for the trial set to begin the following morning.

Before leaving the hotel to go back to the halfway house I tried on all my suits and dress shirts; they still fit perfectly after the six years I'd been locked up.

Once back at the halfway house I sat down in their conference room and worked until two in the morning on my opening statement. I took in a lot of input from family members and friends. I based part of it on rhetoric and another part on facts.

From the beginning I wanted to convey to the jury that my arrest was a serious constitutional violation. They had to know that Jackson, Chaney, and Sheriff Pace operated as an axis of corruption in effecting this illegal arrest. I knew I had one opportunity at that early stage to set the mood for the rest of the trial.

Despite never writing an opening statement in a trial before, when I finished I felt that it couldn't have gotten any better. By the time I laid down to catch a couple hours sleep, I was convinced that my opening argument would be an early knockout in what I hoped would be a short few rounds.

Judge Sharion Aycock

Magistrate David Sanders

Deputy Fire Marshal James O'Neil Jackson

Sheriff Martin Pace

Sheriff Tim Nail (far left) and Deputies of the Attala County Sheriff's Department

Judge Henry T. Wingate

Mike Chaney

Joshua Langston Chamblee

Me, my grandmother Vivian, and my aunt Geneva

Me and Governor Phil Bryant
2011

Me on the first day of trial
Aberdeen 2017

DAVID G. ATWOOD II

Me waiting on the jury's verdict
Aberdeen 2017

IN THE UNITED STATES DISTRICT COURT
FOR THE NORTHERN DISTRICT OF MISSISSIPPI
ABERDEEN DIVISION

DAVID GARLAND ATWOOD, II   PLAINTIFF

V.   CIVIL ACTION NO. 1:12-CV-168-SA-DAS

JAMES JACKSON   DEFENDANT

VERDICT FORM

We the jury find:

1. That there (was) OR **(was not)** (circle one) probable cause to arrest the Plaintiff David Atwood.

    a. If you find that there **was** probable cause to arrest the Plaintiff then your verdict must be in favor of the Defendant James Jackson. Your work is finished, stop here and record your verdict (*We find for the Defendant James Jackson*) below, and hand it to the Court Security Officer: _____

    b. If you find that there **was not** probable cause to arrest the Plaintiff David Atwood move to number 2.

2. That Defendant James Jackson (is) OR **(is not)** (circle one) entitled to the protection of the independent intermediary doctrine.

    a. If you find that Defendant James Jackson **is** entitled to the protection of the independent intermediary doctrine then your verdict must be in favor of the Defendant James Jackson. Your work is finished, stop here and record your verdict (*We find for the Defendant James Jackson*) below, and hand it to the Court Security Officer: _____

    b. If you find that Defendant James Jackson **is not** entitled to the protection of the independent intermediary doctrine move to number 3.

3. That Defendant James Jackson (is) OR **(is not)** (circle one) entitled to qualified immunity.

    a. If you find that Defendant James Jackson is entitled to qualified immunity then your verdict must be in favor of the Defendant James Jackson. Your work is finished, stop here and record your verdict (*We find for the Defendant James*

Jackson) below, and hand it to the Court Security Officer: _____

b. If you find that Defendant James Jackson **is not** entitled to the protection of the qualified immunity then your verdict must be in favor of the Plaintiff David Atwood. Record your verdict (*We find for the Plaintiff David Atwood*) below, then move on to number 4: We find for the Plaintiff David Atwood.

4. Damages:
    a. Compensatory Damages: We the Jury award the Plaintiff compensatory damages in the amount of $ 5,000.00 . and/or
    b. Emotional Distress Damages: We the Jury award the Plaintiff David Atwood emotional distress damages in the amount of $ 0 .
    c. Nominal Damages: (award only if no compensatory or emotional distress damages) We the Jury award the Plaintiff David Atwood nominal damages in the amount of $ _____.

Foreperson Signature _Patri C. Donovan_ Date 07/20/2017

The Atwood Lakehouse four days before the fire

The remains of the Atwood Lakehouse

CHAPTER TWENTY-SIX

Monday, March 6, 2017, dawned bright and early. Although I was desperate to catch a few more hours sleep, I was up, showered, and on my way to Oxford by 6:0 A.M. I had to go to my mom's hotel, change into my suit and then be at the federal courthouse, ready for trial at 9:00 A.M.

As we were processed through security by the U.S. Marshals, I looked around and noticed that the potential jurors were also arriving and assembling in the courtroom's spectator area. I knew, however, that I could pass the bar and take my seat at the table on the right where the plaintiffs and prosecutors normally sit.

A few minutes later Mr. Minor and Jackson entered the courtroom and took their seats at the table to the far left. This was my first time seeing Jackson since the preliminary hearing in Kosciusko in October 2011. He didn't look the same as I remembered. He looked older, almost haggard. But he certainly wasn't haggard from the stress of my lawsuit. I could tell that both he and Mr. Minor had a certain swagger to their step that conveyed to me supreme confidence.

As they took their seats and we waited on Judge Aycock and her staff to enter, I slowly unpacked my briefcase and laid out all of the documents and exhibits that I would need for that morning. The most important article that I'd brought with me, though, was a picture of my beloved Papaw who had loved and supported me one hundred percent throughout my entire life.

My Papaw believed in my innocence before he died and I wished everyday that he would have been able to attend the trial and witness the beating that I planned to put on Jackson.

It was this false arson arrest that my family and I really believed sent my Papaw over the edge and caused his already deteriorating health to spiral out of control. If he couldn't be there in person, though, I wanted him to be there in spirit. And that's why I put a picture of him on the desk so that he could sit and watch the trial and be there for me as moral support.

At straight up 9:00 A.M. the door to Judge Aycock's chambers opened, a U.S. Marshal stepped out and called for everyone in the courtroom to stand as the judge entered. Once she had taken her seat we were allowed to sit down and the trial officially commenced.

Judge Aycock began by introducing herself to the potential jurors and then introducing Mr. Minor, Jackson, and myself. She then briefly explained to the potential jurors what the case was about and what would be expected of them. With those simple preliminaries over, Judge Aycock invited me to take the podium and begin the jury *voir dire*.

My obvious concern with picking a jury that would be standing in judgment of a law enforcement officer would be whether they had any close friends or family members that were law enforcement officers. So this composed my first set of questions.

Several potential jurors admitted that they had relatives that were police officers, which then prompted me to ask them whether they could, in good conscience, stand in a judgment of a cop that had been accused of doing something illegal. Surprisingly, some said that they could not. Their names and juror numbers were marked down in my notepad.

I next turned to the question of whether any of the potential jurors were related to Jackson, Mike Chaney, or me and any of my family members. But none admitted to being so.

They were also asked if any of them remembered supporting Chaney when he ran for election as the state insurance commissioner. Some of the potential jurors did, but they quickly added that this fact wouldn't effect their judgment in the case.

At this point in time Judge Aycock had not made a ruling on whether or not to allow my past criminal history in as evidence during Mr. Minor's case. So during jury *voir dire* I needed to make sure that I didn't get any people on my jury that would be prejudiced against someone that had a criminal history like I did.

However, the problem of how to ask those type questions eluded me without immediately giving away the fact that I was a convicted felon. I solved the problem by asking generic questions regarding whether any potential jurors had been victims of crimes and, if they had, what type.

One woman admitted that she'd been the victim of sex abuse. I immediately knew she would have to be struck from the list because my criminal history, if it was introduced, would certainly prejudice her against me since I had a sex offense.

Another potential juror stated that although he hadn't been the victim of a crime, *per se*, he felt that he would not be a good member of the jury because in the past he had been harassed unnecessarily by a state fire marshal and that due to that harassment he believed most state fire marshals were too "enthusiastic" in their jobs.

This was a huge gold nugget thrown my way early in the trial. I knew that if Judge Aycock didn't strike this potential juror for cause then Mr. Minor would, but every other potential juror had heard the man's complaints about the heavy-handed tactics of the state fire marshals and a statement like that was hard to erase. I thanked God for small miracles.

The last round of questions that I had for my potential jurors were whether or not any of them had any biases against gays.

I had to explain to them that this case would revolve around the credibility of my ex-partner, Josh Chamblee. I went on to explain that they would have to listen to some testimony about some aspects of our gay lives that they might find offensive. It was better now to raise the issue than wait.

My potential jury pool was pulled from some of the most conservative areas of Mississippi. I expected numerous people to raise their hands and voice their objections about homosexuality, but, surprisingly, only one older woman raised her hand and admitted that she didn't think she could be fair to anyone who was gay.

I thanked her for her sincere honesty and assured her that her honesty and opinion about gays was a right that she was more than entitled to believe in. But I also explained that the reason I had to ask was because if she was in my position she would want a jury that was as fair as possible. And I think I hit a soft spot with several potential jurors.

With no more reasons to ask questions I sat down and turned the *voir dire* over to Mr. Minor. It was only then that I was able to get a good feel for how Mr. Minor would conduct himself for the rest of the case.

He didn't spend much time asking questions, though, and instead concentrated on some of the areas that I'd already touched on, just more in-depth.

However, once Mr. Minor was finished asking his questions, Judge Aycock stated to the potential jurors that she wanted to make sure, again, that no one in the jury pool had any biases or prejudices against gays.

She explained to them that there would no doubt be a lot of testimony about stuff that had to do with homosexuality and she needed to make sure the jury was as fair and unbiased as possible, but no one else raised their hands.

With jury *voir dire* complete, Judge Aycock had Mr. Minor and myself approach her bench and, out of the hearing of everyone else, we asked her to strike for cause several potential jurors that indicated they had pre-existing biases. Judge Aycock granted all of our requests.

We were then given three strikes each to remove from the jury pool anyone that we didn't want on the jury. I used my strikes to remove several potential jurors that simply looked hostile to me.

Mr. Minor used his strikes to remove almost all of the African-American potential jury members from the pool.

There was no doubt that African-Americans would be more sympathetic to someone that had wrongly and illegally been abused by the police. Mr. Minor and Jackson knew this, so their strategy at the beginning was to remove as many potential African-American members from the jury as possible. But once they had done so, it was time to pick the ultimate eight people that would sit on my jury.

The way federal juries are selected is not random. Once all of the strikes had removed the potential jurors that we didn't want, the first eight left in the group were selected to serve. And that's how my jury was picked.

The rest of the potential jurors that weren't picked were allowed to leave and my jury was then seated in the jury box. But by this point it was time for lunch, and Judge Aycock told the jurors that they could leave, but not to discuss the case amongst themselves or with anyone else. They were then excused and told to return to the jury room at 1:15 P.M.

Judge Aycock then turned to the issue of my criminal history and the motion *in limine* that I'd filed asking her to limit what Mr. Minor was able to introduce to the jury about my past criminal history.

Motions *in limine* are filed before a trial begins, asking the judge to prohibit certain introduction of evidence regarding or referencing that specific evidence in the motion. I'd ask that Judge Aycock not allow the defense to introduce any of the allegations made by Emmett, Ethan Robinson, Colton Kendrick, or any other arrests or convictions in my record.

As soon as the jury left for lunch the judge had Mr. Minor and I again make our arguments about my criminal history.

I argued that to allow any reference to my past conviction would do nothing but prejudice the jury and that it should be disallowed because it had nothing to do with the fire investigation and because the crime of conviction was not related to Emmett.

I also argued that all the other criminal allegations should not be introduced because they were baseless, hearsay, without evidentiary support, and didn't result in any actual convictions.

Mr. Minor, however, argued that my federal conviction should be allowed to be introduced to the jury because he believed the Federal Rules of Evidence allowed a witness's criminal history to be given to the jury. He based this on his belief that my criminal conviction, which, again, had nothing to do with Emmett, gave Jackson partial probable cause to believe that I'd committed arson.

I do not believe that Judge Aycock was inclined to allow the conviction to be introduced, though. So in helping clarify matters she asked Mr. Minor what Jackson's understanding was in reference to my federal conviction at the time he investigated the fire.

> **JUDGE AYCOCK:** What would Mr. Jackson's testimony be about what he knew about the Plaintiff's prior conviction prior to submitting the affidavit for an arrest warrant?
>
> **MR. MINOR:** Only that he did a background search and found that Mr. Atwood had a felony conviction. He would testify about what it was for, but that's it. He won't get into the facts. He did not research the facts.
>
> **JUDGE AYCOCK:** Okay. For the purposes of direct evidence, the Defendant's ability to introduce the Plaintiff's criminal history into the record will not be allowed. I will not allow you, Mr. Minor, to introduce the knowledge of his prior criminal his-

tory for purposes of direct evidence. I don't think the charges are related to the charge of arson. I also think it would be highly prejudicial. So the Court will not allow you or Mr. Jackson to introduce that in its case-in-chief.

This was essentially the ruling that I was looking for. It meant that when Mr. Minor presented his case, or when Jackson testified, they could not mention that I had a criminal history. And Judge Aycock was very clear that my criminal history would not, and could not, be introduced. However, she included an exception.

JUDGE AYCOCK: On the other hand, I think the federal rules do speak to when it might be used for impeachment purposes. So it may be appropriate for that. But as direct evidence it will not be admitted.
MR. MINOR: Yes, Your Honor.
JUDGE AYCOCK: Okay. So, Mr. Jackson, to be clear with you, there shall be no mention of Mr. Atwood's criminal history.

Although the judge wouldn't allow them to bring up details about my criminal history during direct evidence, Judge Aycock was going to let Mr. Minor use it for impeachment purposes if I were to testify.

I'd not made a decision at that point whether to testify in the trial or not. I believed that I could get the full story before the jury without having to take the stand and open myself up to issues—like my federal conviction—that had nothing to do with Jackson's investigation. But when Judge Aycock told us that she would allow Mr. Minor to question me about my criminal history if I testified, this sealed my decision to avoid taking the stand. I did not want my jury to know I was a felon.

Once the motion *in limine* was sustained and we'd been instructed on what was going to be allowed as part of my criminal history, the judge dismissed us and we went to lunch. When we returned it would be my chance to stand and address the jury. I was a bundle of knots, but I was ready.

My mother and I left and went to eat lunch at a small sandwich cafe near the courthouse. To settle my nerves I had a margarita on the rocks, double-shotted with tequila. This probably wasn't acceptable for a real attorney to do before trial, but I needed the calming influence that the drink provided. I was about to address a jury for the first time in my life and I was scared to death.

After lunch we went back to the courthouse and waited for the trial to begin. At 1:15 P.M. sharp, Judge Aycock entered, followed by Parker and Daniel. I was impressed that Judge Aycock carried her own legal books and file folders and didn't rely on her staff to do that for her.

After assuming her seat and saying hello to Mr. Minor and me again, the jury was brought in and told that we would begin with opening arguments.

>**JUDGE AYCOCK:** Okay. Mr. Atwood, you may come forward and make your opening statement.

I rose from my desk and looked down at the picture of my Papaw that I had sitting there. I asked him to give me strength and courage as I approached the podium and faced the jury.

>**ME:** May it please the Court?
>**JUDGE AYCOCK:** You may proceed.

It all came down to this. The trial was officially underway and I knew I had to catch this jury's attention from the gate. I'd done my best to memorize my opening statement as much as possible. I'd written it in a way to give me cues rather than something to read word-for-word. I reminded myself to speak clearly, enunciate properly, and not rely too much on ad-libbing. I took a deep breath, looked at each juror, and began speaking.

>**ME:** Ladies and gentlemen of the jury, good afternoon. President Abraham Lincoln once said, *He who represents himself has a fool for a client.* Well, this week you will have the opportunity to determine whether he was correct in that assertion. As you already know my name is David Atwood and I am representing myself in this case, but it's not a complicated case. The facts are rather simple. So I don't need some fancy Memphis lawyer to come down here and explain to you the facts and circumstances of this case.

I then took a pause, caught my breath, and looked around. I had everyone's attention, including, most importantly, the jury.

> **ME:** There are really only three things in life that cannot long be hidden. That's the moon, the stars, and the truth. The truth is powerful and the truth should always prevail. You have the duty, you have an opportunity this week to help me find the truth. So I have to tell you a story, a story about a horrible fire that occurred on the night of November 10, 2009, in Kosciusko, Mississippi. That's seven years, three months, and twenty-five days ago. On that date, my paternal grandfather's lake house burned to the ground. No one knows how, and no one has ever been able to prove that it was an arson. We simply just do not know. But this was a house that I loved. On paper it belonged to my grandfather, but in actuality, it was a house that belonged to all of the Atwoods. It literally was the Atwood Lakehouse. I grew up spending time in that house. I played on the front porch. I fished in the lake and I hunted in the woods. That house was like my house. And it broke my heart when I learned that it had been destroyed. But I'm estranged now from that side of the family. I'm especially estranged from my grandfather. We have a sad, heartbroken history.

I took another pause and shuffled my feet. I remember that all eight jurors maintained eye contact with me and seemed to be sitting on the edge of their seats. My left hip was hurting at this time so I switched my weight to the right and kept going.

> **ME:** During the course of this trial you will hear the words of my grandfather, Emmett Atwood. You'll also hear the words of the law enforcement officers who investigated the fire and you will see their evidence. But you will ultimately have to come to the conclusion that no reasonable, well-trained and fair law enforcement officer could ever legitimately rely on the evidence at hand to obtain a warrant for my arrest. You're probably going to hear some things that might make your blood run cold. You'll probably hear some things that will turn your stomach. There'll be things that astonish you in this case. And there will probably be a few things that'll make you laugh. But you will never hear or see one shred of physical or forensic evidence indicating that that tragic and horrible fire was an arson. There simply is not one iota

of evidence to suggest that a crime ever even occurred. You'll hear speculation. You'll hear lies. You'll hear contradictions, but you will never hear in this case any credible, believable evidence that the fire was, in fact, an arson.

From the beginning I had to plant in my jurors' heads that there was never any evidence to prove this fire was arson. I had to speak to my jury as a collective in the hopes that they would, together, from the start, view my arguments in my perspective. So I thought I had to hit hard that there wasn't any evidence to support Jackson's affidavit when he went and got my warrant. It was essential the jury believe that.

> **ME:** The evidence in this case is extremely simple and straightforward. I intend to show that the defendant at that table, Mr. James Jackson, a former deputy fire marshal, maliciously and criminally conspired with others to violate the United States Constitution, my rights as a citizen of this country, and my dignity as a human being. I intend to show that the defendant, Mr. Jackson, deliberately and intentionally procured a warrant for my arrest for arson without any evidence that a crime had actually occurred and without any evidence that I was involved. In fact, the defendant ignored multiple pieces of evidence proving that I was not even responsible for the fire.

If I was going to get the jury to rule in my favor, I felt that I would have to try and demonize Jackson as much as possible to get the jurors to view him not as a law enforcement officer, but a rogue vigilante working for a group of corrupt cops and politicians. It was a gamble to do so because of the enormous respect that most have for the police, but Jackson wasn't your normal officer.

> **ME:** There is simply not a single piece of credible evidence to support the defendant's assertion that this fire was an arson and that I was responsible. In fact, what evidence that does exist proves that I was not involved. For example, some of the evidence will show that my cell phone was in use in another part of the state at the time of the fire and that the shoe prints found at the scene were not my size. You'll come to know that my grand-

father, Emmett Atwood, suspiciously and drastically increased the insurance on the Atwood Lakehouse shortly before the fire, and more unbelievably, had taken pictures of the lake house four days before the fire in relation to the recent increase in insurance. Just as unexplainably, Emmett's nephew, my cousin, Kade Atwood—you'll be hearing from him—he allegedly slept through the fire the entire night while the lake house burned and never called the fire department when he discovered it. I think you will find this extremely unbelievable because Kade's house sits adjacent to the Atwood Lakehouse and there were guns and ammunition exploding during the fire. Somehow, though, Kade conveniently slept through this raging inferno. You will end up asking yourselves before the close of this trial whether you believe in coincidences, or whether you believe these are deliberate actions.

This was the part of the opening statement where I intended to plant the seed of doubt in the jurors' minds that this was possibly an arson, and that Emmett and Kade were responsible. It was my first attempt to present my multiple theories to them.

In doing so, I realized that I ran the risk of overrunning the jurors' minds with information overload. But Occam's Razor supported equally the theories that this fire was either an accident or deliberately set with Emmett's knowledge and approval. And this trial was a search for the truth as much as it was a search for justice. So I felt I had to present both theories.

ME: During the course of the trial you'll meet many witnesses, but ultimately, this case is going to revolve around three main people: The defendant, Mr. Jackson; my ex-partner, Josh Chamblee; and then myself. Chamblee's credibility will be the key to this case. Two different times Chamblee provided law enforcement officers with alibi statements swearing that he and I were together the night of the fire in another part of the state. Two years later, after he and I ended our relationship on bad terms, he was approached by the defendant and harassed and threatened into giving a false confession. At the time Jackson went to Josh, the defendant had a warrant in his hand for Josh's arrest for accessory after the fact to arson and a promise of a $25,000 reward if Josh would change his two previous alibi statements and say that I was responsible for the fire. Without second thoughts, and to avoid arrest and collect the reward, Josh changed his story and provided the defendant with a vague, ambiguous statement which said I started the fire. And with no other evidence, the defendant relied on this nebulous, unspecific lie from Chamblee and arrested me. The question you will have to answer in this trial is why Josh Chamblee lied when he gave that third, coerced statement. But more importantly, you must decide why the defendant chose to rely on Josh Chamblee's false, third statement. At the time the defendant obtained Josh's false confession, the defendant knew that Josh had provided multiple alibi statements on my behalf. Defendant Jackson knew that Josh had been arrested before by other law enforcement officers for providing false statements and filing false police reports. Defendant Jackson ignored multiple pieces of evidence proving my innocence and deliberately and willfully concealed that evidence from the Attala County Justice Court judge when he went to obtain my warrant.

Obviously, Chamblee's third statement that Jackson obtained only through harassment and coercive tactics made it essential that I deal with Josh's credibility issues immediately and tell the jury what to expect when it came to his testimony. I hoped to discredit him before his deposition was ever even read.

Hitting on this theme of dishonesty applied not only to Josh, but every other fire investigation investigator and witness, too. Since the arrest, every person except myself had changed their stories, and the jury needed to know that.

ME: It is important that you know that every single person involved in the fire investigation has lied and changed their stories, often multiple times. Defendant Jackson has lied and changed his story. Josh Chamblee has lied and changed his story. Kade Atwood lied and changed his story. Emmett Atwood lied and changed his. Even the sheriff of Attala County, Tim Nail, changed his story after this lawsuit was filed. But the one person in this case, though, that has never lied and never changed stories is myself. I have denied repeatedly that I was responsible for the fire. I cooperated in the investigation and I never changed my story. Even when everyone else in this case was lying, changing stories, and pointing fingers, my story was the one that remained unchanged. I was not responsible for the fire. I have not lied about the fire, and my story has not changed for this trial. Everyone else's has, but mine hasn't.

In adding these statements to my argument I wanted the jury to know, first, that I have always denied that I set the fire and that I have never been accused of lying about it. But my most important reasons for including these statements was so that the jury would be attuned to all the lies and changed stories of everyone involved in the case. I needed the jurors to be listening for all of the contradictions. This was important and I hoped my opening statement would make them ready for that.

ME: No one here today really knows what happened on that night in November 2009. But we have an opportunity this week to try and find out. So, in actuality, we are not just here to decide if the defendant had enough probable cause to arrest me, we're here—we have the opportunity to discover the truth about what happened that night. But you're not the first jury to hear evidence in this case. In 2012 an Attala County grand jury investigated this fire and came to the conclusion that there was not enough evidence to support probable cause for my arrest. They no-billed the charge. The grand jury, at the very beginning of the case, decided there was not enough evidence or probable cause to even indict me.

I wanted this jury to know that they weren't the first average body of citizens to look at this case. I felt it would make their jobs easier to know that a prior jury had already determined that there wasn't probable cause. And I hoped they caught my hints as I strongly pushed them their way.

ME: At some point in this trial you're going to have to ask yourselves what motive the defendant and his coconspirators would have in arresting me. I mean, after all, nearly two years after the fire, in July 2011, the defendant reopened the closed fire investigation, and with quick swiftness, obtained a coerced lie through the harassment and extortion of Josh Chamblee and had me arrested for a fire that was never proven to have been an arson. Why would the defendant and his co-conspirators do this? And why the timing of July 2011? I mean, again, after all, nearly two years had passed since the fire. I'm going to tell you why. (At this point I held up a copy of my book, *Into Hell I Rode*, for all of the jurors to see). This is a book that I wrote and published in June of 2011, and I named it *Into Hell I Rode*. And this book is this most detailed account ever written of the long and abusive history of government and law enforcement corruption in Vicksburg and Warren County, Mississippi. Contained within these pages is the true story about how the citizens of Vicksburg were abused, mistreated, and in some instances raped and killed by members of the Vicksburg Police and Warren County Sheriff's Departments. Contained within these pages are the names of family relatives, friends, and colleagues of Defendant Jackson and his boss, the State Insurance Commissioner, Mike Chaney. Within two weeks of this book being published, Defendant Jackson, at Mike Chaney's direct orders, reopened the closed fire investigation, coerced a false confession from Josh Chamblee, and had me arrested. And that is what makes the defendant's and his coconspirators' actions so evil and malicious. They did not arrest me because of a crime that had been committed. They arrested me in political retaliation for my public and outspoken stance against their corruption and crimes.

I had especially taken care to memorize, word-for-word this part of my opening statement. I wanted to be able to look each individual juror in the eye as I held my book up for them all to see as I told them the real reason that I was arrested. This was both effective and it immediately connected with the jury.

Once the jurors connected the dots about how and why Jackson arrested me, I saw several nod their heads and tacitly agree with what I was telling them. I knew then that I had their attention.

> **ME:** This case became not about a fire in Kosciusko, Mississippi. It became a tyrannical tool of a group of corrupt and dishonest law enforcement officers bent on a quest for retaliation.

And that is why you, members of this jury, must listen to the evidence, hear the lies and changed stories of the fire investigation witnesses, and ultimately hold Defendant Jackson—the man who willingly participated and allowed himself to be used as the tool of political retaliation—responsible for my illegal arrest. In this trial, you will hear the good, the bad, and the ugly. You'll hear bad things about me. You'll hear bad things about Josh Chamblee. You'll hear bad things about Emmett Atwood, and you'll hear bad things about the other witnesses, but you will also hear the lies and changed stories of the fire investigation witnesses. You will meet a group of law enforcement officers whose personal motto has become admit nothing, deny everything, and make counter accusations. From the defendant and the fire investigation witnesses, you're going to hear the three D's of dishonesty. You'll hear discrepancy. You'll hear deception. And you will hear distortion. But by the close of this trial, I believe that the truth will come shining through, and you will rule to hold Defendant Jackson personally responsible for an illegal arrest, for a criminal, wrongful arrest that severely damaged me, my family, and put a government-imposed freeze on the First Amendment rights not just for myself but on all others who might have the courage to stand against government corruption and oppression. I believe you're the jury that's going to stand with me in this and stand with my family and say no to this criminal wrongdoing. Thank you.

Throughout my entire opening statement I was able to maintain eye contact with each juror. I realized that they were on the edge of their seats and were listening to my every word. They were truly interested in what I had to say. They no doubt thought that this would be an interesting trial. And I hoped they thought already that they would rule in my favor if I could deliver on the goods that I'd promised.

I took my seat, sipped on some water, and waited for Mr. Minor to take his place at the podium and make his opening statement on behalf of Defendant Jackson.

There was no telling what Mr. Minor would say. I felt that he may have been the type to really shed his bland demeanor once at the podium and addressing the jury. It was his turn next, and like my jurors during my opening argument, I was on the edge of my seat ready to hear what he would say.

CHAPTER TWENTY-SEVEN

I thought my opening statement had gone well. I specifically looked every few minutes to make sure that I was still connected to the jury and that they were paying attention. I don't think I failed in that endeavor.

After I sat down and replenished my cup of water, it was Mr. Minor's turn to stand and address the jury. He had dressed that morning in a well-fitted dark suit and I was impressed with how he looked. Defendant Jackson was also dressed in a suit, but his smug expression had not changed.

Mr. Minor approached the podium that I had just left with nothing more than a notepad in his hand with a few scrawled lines. I assumed from his meager writings that he was going to ab-lib most of his opening statement to the jury.

As I'd mentioned previously, my only interactions with Mr. Minor had been over the phone, through email, the depositions, and the pretrial conference. I'd never really seen him in action in the courtroom. But that was about to change.

> **MR. MINOR:** Good morning, ladies and gentlemen. Again, my name is Wilson Minor with the Mississippi Attorney General's Office, and I represent former deputy fire marshal James Jackson.

I noticed immediately that Mr. Minor wasn't speaking very loudly and didn't have the microphone pulled close enough to him. Some of the jurors in the back row were leaning forward to try and hear him.

> **MR. MINOR:** Listening to Mr. Atwood, you would think this is a criminal case with him talking about we don't—that the State doesn't have any evidence—that we can't prove that he committed arson. This is not a criminal case. This is a civil case, and Mr. Atwood has the burden of proof. He has to prove his case by a preponderance of the evidence.

I immediately realized that Mr. Minor's tactics in the trial were not going to be centered around attempting to prove that I was responsible for the fire. I don't think anyone with an understanding of the evidence could legitimately conclude that I was responsible for the fire.

Instead, Mr. Minor was going to bypass the theory that I was responsible for the fire and concentrate on a purely legal explanation.

> **MR. MINOR:** The issue in this case is not whether Mr. Atwood burned down his grandfather's lake house. That's not what you're going to be deciding today or this week. The issue is whether my client, James Jackson, had probable cause to go get an arrest warrant for Mr. Atwood from a judge in Attala County and whether he misled that judge by not telling him all of the evidence that he had uncovered during his investigation. Mr. Atwood has to prove that my client intentionally misled that judge and withheld evidence from that judge and that he was aware of evidence that showed that Mr. Atwood did not commit this arson.

As one might expect from a legally-trained mind with the benefit of an extensive law school education, Mr. Minor's argument was going to try and convince the jury that Jackson followed the letter of the law and that Judge Stewart's issuance of an arrest warrant was based on probable cause because Jackson provided Stewart with everything pertinent to the issuance of that warrant.

But we weren't dealing with a jury that had the benefit of a legal background. These jurors were regular people who thought as I did. They were going to want to know, first and foremost, whether this fire was even an arson. Second, and only after they'd determined the first issue, would they consider whether I was responsible for the fire.

My case was going to prove that, regardless of whether it was accidental or arson, no well-trained, fair law enforcement officer could ever conclude that I was guilty.

Mr. Minor's opening argument would of been more suited to an oral argument before a panel of appellate court judges if the case was on appeal, but we were dealing with regular citizens from the northeast corner of Mississippi. They, I was almost positive, would want to know what the evidence, or lack thereof, showed in the case.

> **MR. MINOR:** I agree with Mr. Atwood. This is a pretty simple case. This case does boil down to whether the information and statement that Josh Chamblee—Mr. Atwood's boyfriend at the time this fire occurred—whether the information he provided to the State Fire Marshal's Office was credible, reliable, and worthy of being submitted to a judge to secure an arrest warrant.

This statement by Mr. Minor shocked me. It shocked me because he basically told the jury that he was going to hang his case on whether or not Josh was a credible witness. So from that point I'm sure the jury was thinking about whether or not Josh would be a believable person when they heard his testimony. And as Mr. Minor and I both knew, there was a lot of issues that called into question Josh's honesty and reliability as a witness.

> **MR. MINOR:** Now, Judge Aycock is going to instruct you on what probable cause means. I'm not going into that now, but that's the key point in this whole case. This is the case that we are going to prove this week. James Jackson was called to investigate this fire that occurred in Attala County just outside Kosciusko at a lake house owned by Emmett Atwood, David Atwood's grandfather who had disowned him more than 15 years before that. His whole family had disowned him except for his mother's side of the family.

So far, everything that Mr. Minor had said about the details of the fire I agreed with. I even planned, myself, to go into detail about the disownment from the Atwood family. But I was hoping that Mr. Minor would let me do it on my terms, using my version, rather than his. And he did.

> **MR. MINOR:** James Jackson went to investigate this fire outside of Kosciusko at the lake house owned by Emmett Atwood, who owns a car dealership in Vicksburg. Mr. Jackson attempted to do some forensic testing at the scene, but because the house was made completely of wood—pinewood—and because the fire department was never called, the house completely burned down, so it was impossible to do any forensic testing to prove that an accelerant was used to start this fire.

There was that false statement again from Jackson which he was trying to use to excuse his failure to take the proper steps to investigate the fire.

At the preliminary hearing before Judge Stewart in October 2011, Jackson clearly testified that all of his forensic tests were negative and that he couldn't detect an accelerant. Rosalind Jordan questioned him extensively on this point and not once did Jackson testify that it was impossible to do any testing.

Not only did Mrs. Jordan's extensive notes that she took at the preliminary hearing prove this, her memory of Jackson's testimony was superb, too. It was only when the lawsuit was filed that Jackson, again, changed his story and put forth a version that wasn't true.

> **MR. MINOR:** Now, Mr. Jackson examined the scene and he ruled out several accidental causes of the fire, such as electrical fire or fire caused by lightning. And he also determined that nobody was at the house the night of the fire. Nobody was staying there. It was completely empty. Again, this is a lake house that was used on the weekends by the Atwood family. So James Jackson subsequently goes to talk to Emmett Atwood, the owner of the house in Vicksburg, and Emmett tells Mr. Jackson that, you know there is a longstanding feud between me and David, the plaintiff. And he tells Jackson that he thinks David might have done it. So that's how David becomes a suspect.

This argument fit well into my theory that I was going to advance to the jury that when Jackson talked to Emmett, and was told that I was suspected of starting the fire, Jackson accepted this as the gospel truth and never attempted to pursue any other leads or possible causes of the fire. So far, everything that Mr. Minor was telling the jury fit with what I expected him to say.

> **MR. MINOR:** So James Jackson gets in touch with Joshua Langston Chamblee, who is David's ex-partner. They were dating at the time of the fire, which, again, is November 11, 2009. The evidence shows that the fire most likely occurred in the early morning hours of November 11, 2009, and that the house burned completely down by the time Kade Atwood, who is Emmett's nephew, who lived just across the lake in another house, discovered the fire that morning. He did not call the fire department so it was never put out. So James Jackson tracks down Joshua Chamblee and asks to interview him, and he interviews him at a KFC in Leake County, in Carthage. And Mr. Jackson, you know, asked him did he know anything about this fire. And Chamblee says, no, he doesn't know anything about it and that he was with David in Starkville on the night of the fire. But Jackson notices that Chamblee is very nervous and seems as though he's trying to avoid telling the truth. So James Jackson doesn't believe this statement that he gets from Joshua Chamblee is credible at this point. So he leaves the investigation open. He does not close it. A year transpires without any further leads and Joshua Chamblee moves to Indiana.

Mr. Minor dumped another gold nugget in my lap when he made the argument about Jackson not believing this second alibi statement that Josh made at the KFC in March 2010. This essentially proves my belief that I was arrested for this fire in direct retaliation for publishing *Into Hell I Rode* in June 2011.

If Jackson truly didn't believe that Josh was telling him the truth when Josh gave that second alibi statement, then Jackson would have immediately gone and gotten a warrant for Josh's arrest—like he did in July 2011—and gone back to him and given him the choice of either telling the "truth" or going to jail—again, like he did in July 2011.

Jackson doesn't do this, though. Getting an arrest warrant to coerce more information from Josh never crossed Jackson's mind at the time. It didn't cross his mind at the time because he wasn't under the political pressure to arrest me then like he later was in June and July 2011.

So, without any further evidence, Jackson leaves Josh alone, goes about his business, doesn't pursue the case for more than a year, but then starts shaking the tree limbs again when my book is published.

If Jackson truly believed that Josh was lying he would have gone and gotten that arrest warrant then. Mr. Minor set me up perfectly to make this argument at a later time to the jury.

> **MR. MINOR:** At some point in June 2011, Jackson reopens the investigation (By using the word "reopens" I believe Mr. Minor conveyed inadvertently a Freudian slip indicating that the fire investigation was, indeed, closed.) and attempts to track down Joshua Chamblee. He calls his mom, who lives in Carthage, and she says he's going to come home, but then he doesn't come home. Joshua Chamblee gives Mr. Jackson the runaround for about a month. Finally, Mr. Jackson gets fed up with Joshua Chamblee not coming back to Mississippi from Indiana to talk to him again. So he does go get an arrest warrant for Joshua. But Joshua does come home and he comes home to the Neshoba County Fair, and his parents promise Mr. Jackson that he'll come to the Leake County Sheriff's Department and give another statement.

This argument was the most sanitized, vague rendition of the true story about how Jackson harassed and pestered Josh and his family in those two months that I'd yet heard in the entire case. But this was Mr. Minor's argument to make. However, I made sure to make a notation on my notepad to go back in my case-in-chief and demolish this watered-down version of Jackson's extortionate efforts to coerce that third statement from Josh.

> **MR. MINOR:** You will hear testimony from Joshua Chamblee that he did not feel any pressure. He was not threatened to give this statement and that he did it voluntarily. Mr. Jackson will testify that he never told Josh or his family that he had an arrest warrant and he never served the arrest warrant or arrested Chamblee.

I quickly leaned forward in my seat and turned my head to directly at Mr. Minor. This was a totally inaccurate statement.

Not only had Jackson told Josh's mom that if Josh didn't come give him another statement implicating me in the fire that he'd be arrested, Jackson actually took the step of having Josh arrested in Indiana and extradited back to Mississippi when Josh, again, refused to cooperate in Jackson, Chaney and Sheriff Pace's false, malicious persecution of me.

The more Mr. Minor talked about Jackson's actions, the more easier I saw that it would be to discredit their entire case. I'd been told over and over again by attorneys never to promise anything to a jury in an opening statement that you weren't capable of proving at trial. But that's what Mr. Minor seemed to be doing with this jury.

MR. MINOR: So Joshua appears at the Leake County Sheriff's Department to give another statement. And this time, Josh tells the truth. Josh says that he rode with David Atwood from Starkville, where Josh lived in an apartment, to Attala County and he watched—this is during the night, so you couldn't see much other than the woods. But they got out of the car, and they walked through a field, and he watched David go behind the house with a plastic bag, and then when he came back and as they were walking back to the vehicle, he saw flames coming out of the house. And at that point, he told Mr. Jackson that David said, "I just burned down my grandfather's house." Well, of course, Mr. Jackson asked him, "Well, why didn't you tell me the truth when I interviewed you a year ago?" And here's the key to the whole case. Joshua said, "The reason I didn't come clean earlier is because I was afraid of David Atwood." He was afraid of David Atwood because David had threatened to burn down his parents' house if he told what really happened. That's why he hadn't come clean, and that's why Josh's statement, his third statement, has credibility and why my client, reasonably and in good faith, relied on that statement and took that statement to a justice court judge in Attala County and told that judge, "I have a statement from Joshua Chamblee implicating David Atwood in the fire. I would like an arrest warrant for him." And the judge placed Mr. Jackson under oath and asked him to swear that this information was correct to the best of his knowledge. And Mr. Jackson did swear to that, and the judge found that there was probable cause and issued the arrest warrant.

There were several severe problems with this version of events that Mr. Minor was feeding to the jury. First, the testimony from Josh's deposition, and the evidence available to Jackson in July 2011, clearly showed that there were issues with Josh's assertion that he didn't tell the truth because I'd allegedly threatened him.

I was able to show that even though I'd allegedly made this threat, Josh kept dating me, kept allowing me to stay at his apartment, kept coming and staying with me at my mother's house, visited me in jail, and even accepted my collect phone calls from the jail. No person in their right mind would do all that months after an alleged threat had been made against them and their parents.

Second, even with this third statement, Jackson took no actions to independently verify what Josh was saying was true. He knew that the cell phone location data didn't support this version, he knew that the footprints at the scene didn't match either Josh or me, but most significantly, Jackson knew that there wasn't any evidence that the fire was an arson or that it was started intentionally. And when he left out these important facts when communicating with Judge Stewart, he deprived that judge of making a reasonable decision as to whether to issue an arrest warrant.

I understood, though, what Mr. Minor was trying to do. He was trying to shift the blame and responsibility to Judge Stewart instead of his client. But Judge Stewart's actions were only as good as the information Jackson was giving him. And as it's been shown, that information was doubtful at best.

> **MR. MINOR:** Now, there's a part of the story that Mr. Atwood left out in his opening statement. He didn't tell you that there was a hearing before the same judge a few weeks later. And Mr. Jackson testified at that hearing, and Mr. Atwood had an attorney who cross-examined Mr. Jackson, and the judge heard all of the evidence that you're going to hear today, essentially, all of the evidence that Mr. Atwood says undermines my client's case for probable cause. And guess what? The judge again found there was probable cause and bound Mr. Atwood's case over to the grand jury.

This was the first indication that I'd made my first big mistake in the trial. I'd not subpoenaed Judge Stewart to attend and testify. I'd done a deposition with him, but he conveniently couldn't remember anything about my case.

I'd been told by Mrs. Jordan, though, that in all of her many years practicing in Judge Stewart's court—before he was defeated in his reelection bid—that she had never seen him *not* bind a case over to the grand jury, even when a third-party appeared in his court and confessed to committing the crime rather than the defendant that was actually charged with the offense.

Even though those third-parties confessed to committing the crimes rather than the defendants, Judge Stewart bound those defendants' cases over to a grand jury, nevertheless, for the local district attorney to sort out.

It was clear that Judge Stewart's actions in binding over the cases to a grand jury were nothing more than routine rubber-stamps and that the preliminary hearings didn't serve any real purpose.

I'd failed to realize how important this seemingly unimportant fact was. And it caused me concern. Mr. Minor was going to exploit the rubber-stamp of Judge Stewart "finding" probable cause as much as he could. If he could convince the jury that this finding was legitimate, it could very well cause me to lose the case. But there was nothing I could do at that point.

I did begin to notice, however, that several jurors had disconnected from Mr. Minor's words. A couple of them looked rather bored and were staring off into space rather than looking at Mr. Minor and following along with his rendition of the facts. One juror was even scrapping dirt from underneath his fingernails.

> **MR. MINOR:** Now, Mr. Atwood is going to make a lot of the fact that the grand jury didn't indict him, but he's not going to put on any evidence about what that grand jury heard and what the district attorney told that grand jury. You will not hear anything about that. So you have a judge in Attala County making two findings of probable cause. The grand jury doesn't indict. I submit that's irrelevant.

Obviously, the fact that the grand jury didn't indict me was, in fact, extremely relevant. Mr. Minor tried to explain it away by insinuating that Judge Stewart's "findings" of probable cause took precedence over the grand jury's. But, again, Judge Stewart was not a real judge; he wasn't an attorney. And regardless of whether he found probable cause or not, no finding made by him was dispositive of the case. It was only the grand jury's finding of probable cause—which they affirmatively ruled was lacking—that ended my case.

It dawned on me more and more, though, as Mr. Minor continued with his opening argument, that I'd made a major mistake in not subpoenaing Judge Stewart to testify. It was a rookie mistake and I hoped it wouldn't sink my case.

> **MR. MINOR:** So you're also going to hear a lot of evidence about conspiracies and his grandfather burning his own lake house down for insurance money. The key in this case is not that evidence. The key in this case is what evidence did James Jackson have, what evidence he was aware of at the time he went to go get that warrant. Not any evidence of conspiracies about books and politics and insurance fraud. It's all irrelevant. It's all a red herring, a smoke screen, to distract you.

I thought Mr. Minor's analogy to a smoke screen was not a well put pun given the circumstances of the case. Maybe he made it intentionally or maybe he didn't. But if he really believed that the jury was supposed to ignore evidence that Emmett burned the lake house, or that I wasn't prosecuted because of my book being published, Mr. Minor was in for a surprise.

Likewise, no juror in his or her right mind would overlook Jackson's failure to properly investigate this case and uncover the suspicious circumstances that indicated that Emmett and Kade may of had something to do with the fire.

Mr. Minor wanted this jury to only concentrate on what evidence Jackson conveniently had at the time he arrested me. But I needed the jury to see all of the evidence (e.g., the increase in insurance, the pictures taken four days before the fire for insurance purposes, Kade allegedly sleeping through the fire, how Emmett spent the insurance payout, and how Chaney and Sheriff Pace forced Jackson to reopen the closed fire investigation and arrest me in retaliation for what I wrote about them in my book) that Jackson either ignored or didn't take the time to discover.

A law enforcement officer cannot conduct a shoddy and incompetent criminal investigation, fail to collect evidence, or ignore important evidence all together, falsely arrest a person, and then claim that he didn't know about or didn't have in his possession the evidence that proved that suspect innocent. Incompetency does not shield law enforcement officers from punishment for illegal actions. But that was the argument that Mr. Minor was trying to use to excuse his client's deplorable conduct.

> **MR. MINOR:** Mr. Atwood is also going to try to make a case that Joshua Chamblee was motivated to claim a $25,000 reward for any information leading to an arrest in this case. We'll prove that Joshua never even asked about the money, never tried to claim that monetary reward when he gave his third statement implicating David Atwood.

This was partly true and I couldn't fault Mr. Minor for pushing this fact in front of the jury. But one cannot truly know what went on in Josh's mind.

If one remembers, Jackson admitted in his interrogatories, and in the report he filed detailing his investigatory efforts, that he'd promised Josh the $25,000 reward if Josh would give a third statement implicating me in the fire. So we know Josh was promised that reward.

However, when we did Josh's deposition immediately before the trial, he was specifically asked about the reward. Instead of admitting that Jackson promised him the reward, Josh lied and testified that he was never promised anything by Jackson. So we know there was something fishy and dishonest about that situation and that there was something Josh wanted to hide regarding him trying to collect that reward.

It was another issue in Mr. Minor's opening argument that was easily disproven and I planned to take care of it during Jackson's testimony. I made another notation in my notepad and continued listening.

> **MR. MINOR:** Mr. Atwood also tried to prove that his cell phone records proved that he was in Starkville the night of November 10 through the morning of November 11. However, his cell phone records curiously have a gap of about 12 hours where there are no texts, no calls from about midnight on the tenth

through noon on the eleventh, the exact time frame when the fire started and burned the house down.

I shot up to the edge of my seat when I heard Mr. Minor make this statement. I knew immediately that it wasn't true, and it was a huge mistake to say otherwise.

Although there had been a contentious debate with Mr. Griffith and Sheriff Nail regarding these records, I thought that the cell phone records were clear and legible enough for any person to see that my phone was being used on the night of the fire while connected to a Starkville cell tower.

The only thing that I could understand happening is that Mr. Minor was only looking at the call history in the records and not the text or data history.

Of course, I texted way more than I made phone calls. And there was a gap of about twelve hours from the last call that I received on the night of November 10 and the one I made on the morning of November 11.

However, I felt the records were clear enough to also show that there were dozens of texts made and received up until about 3:00 A.M. on the night of November 10 into the morning of November 11—all of which occurred while attached to a Starkville tower—and that I started receiving texts again around 6:00 A.M. that morning. The records were pretty clear about that and it astonished me that Mr. Minor had made this egregious mistake in his opening.

> **MR. MINOR:** He'll also talk about how there wasn't any forensic evidence that an accelerant was used to burn down the house. We will put on evidence to show that it was impossible to gather any forensic evidence at the house, because, again, it burned completely down. There was nothing left. It stood on brick pilings. The wood that would have been lit on fire with kerosene or gas was all burned up. And Mr. Jackson will testify that he tried to use a device to detect accelerant and it kept going off because there was still smoke coming out of the ground and you couldn't isolate any wood to use it on. So, again, that's another smoke screen. It's not relevant to the issues.

There was that changed story again from Jackson that he kept getting invalid results from his hydrocarbon detector. I knew that he had testified differently at the preliminary hearing, that Mrs. Jordan's extensive notes from his testimony said differently, and that her superb memory from the hearing was different than his now changed story. I'd deal with this issue when I called her to the stand to testify.

> **MR. MINOR:** Again, I would ask that you focus on what information, what evidence James Jackson had, was aware of, at the time he went to go get an arrest warrant. That's the key to the case. And at the end of the case, we will ask that you render a verdict in favor of my client. Thank you.

He'd gone full circle back to the argument that Jackson's illegal actions should be excused because he had failed to properly discover relevant evidence, or ignored the relevant evidence at hand, and didn't present it to the judge.

I didn't think the jury would follow that line of reasoning and I saw immediately how the rest of my case would have to play out. I realized that these type of trials were almost like playing chess. Besides having to correct some serious misrepresentations in Mr. Minor's opening argument—especially about the phone records—I felt that my pawns were in the lead.

After Mr. Minor sat down, Judge Aycock excused the jury for a short break and told us to take a fifteen minute recess. I was told that when we returned to be ready to call my first witness.

Everyone knew that my first witness would be James Jackson, but no one knew how things would turn out. I was still looked at as an amateurish questioner. No doubt I was underestimated. But I knew where Jackson's weaknesses laid, and I would be ready.

CHAPTER TWENTY-EIGHT

I'd never questioned a witness under oath before. In fact, this whole trial had been one of many firsts for me. But Judge Aycock and her staff treated me the same as they would a seasoned trial attorney with a law degree from Harvard.

At no point throughout the entire proceedings did Judge Aycock ever attempt to instruct me, caution me, warn me, or lecture me about what would and would not be acceptable in her courtroom. I don't think this was by accident.

From the beginning I'd taken care to only file meritorious motions, to communicate with Mr. Minor and the other attorneys as professionally and as courteously as possible, and to always address Judge Aycock, Magistrate Sanders, and their staffs with as much respect as possible. And I think Judge Aycock knew that.

The real test, however, would come during my interactions with my witnesses, almost all of whom were hostile or adverse witnesses to me.

Although I'd never questioned a witness in court before, I'd had quite a lot of practice at being an inquisitor in the many gay relationships that I'd been in with other men throughout my life.

It seems to be my lot in life to end up dating some of the worst, most dishonest gay men out there, like Josh Chamblee. I've constantly been lied to, cheated on, used, abused, and treated like shit. So, over the years I developed a keen sense of when someone was lying or telling the truth. And if they were lying I knew I was a good enough inquisitor that I'd eventually be able to discover the truth.

James Jackson was, in a lot of ways, like many of the dishonest boyfriends I'd had in the past. He was an opportunistic liar; a liar who would do and say anything to pathologically manipulate any situation to put himself in the best possible light. But Jackson was also not dealing with someone that had attended the best law school in the country, come from a stable background, or whom only dealt with mostly honest, trustworthy people their entire lives.

I had seen the underbelly of society. By my trial in March 2017 I'd spent almost nine years locked up with some of the worst people in the world—those that lied, schemed, used, and exploited others for no purpose other than a fulfillment of their sick fantasies. So if Mr. Minor and Jackson thought that I wouldn't be able to effectively question him, they'd be in for a surprise.

After the break, with all the parties at their respective tables and ready, Judge Aycock walked into the court followed by Daniel and Parker. The U.S. Marshal called us to attention, we rose, and then remained standing while Judge Aycock took her seat and had the jury brought in. It was only after the jury took their seats that we sat back down.

> **JUDGE AYCOCK:** Thank you ladies and gentlemen. Welcome back. It's time for the plaintiff to call witnesses. Mr. Atwood, who would you call first?
>
> **ME:** Your Honor, I'd call the defendant, James Jackson.
>
> **JUDGE AYCOCK:** Mr. Jackson, come forward, please, and be sworn.

Jackson raised his right hand next to Judge Aycock's bench, placed his left on a Bible, and swore under oath to tell the truth, the whole truth, and nothing but the truth, so help him God. I wondered then how much truth we'd actually hear from him.

I began my examination by having Jackson state his name for the jury, his employment dates with the State Fire Marshal's Office, and then his previous work history prior to that.

Jackson testified that he was employed with the State Fire Marshal's Office from 2006 until 2014 when he retired. Before that he worked as a police officer in Canton, Mississippi. He also testified that he worked as a fire investigator with the Yazoo City, Mississippi, fire department from 1991 through 2005.

My next line of questioning concerned what type of training that Jackson had in fire investigation techniques. Surprisingly, Jackson testified that the last training that he had was in 1991. I wanted to know more about that, though, and how he investigated fires in the modern age.

> **ME:** Since that time, would you agree that forensic tests, criminalistics (for fire investigations) has come a long way?
> **JACKSON:** It has.
> **ME:** Okay. Well, let's talk about some of the tools you use. When you go to a fire scene, what are some of the tools that you use to do your forensic tests?
> **JACKSON:** Well, I bring a rake and a shovel and a hydrocarbon detector.
> **ME:** Okay. We all know what a rake and shovel are used for. But can you explain to the jury what a hydrocarbon detector does?
> **JACKSON:** Sure. A hydrocarbon detector is an instrument that is used to detect accelerants like Freon, kerosene, gasoline, diesel. Anything that's got an odor to it. It has a meter on there that has a negative and positive, and if there is accelerant in the ground or on the wood it would make a loud beeping noise. If it beeps a long time, a steady beep, then you know there's something there, an accelerant. If it just goes beep, beep, it's possible nothing is there. Smoke can set it off though.
> **ME:** So you would agree that in order to get an accurate reading on that instrument that you would need to use it at a time when the fire is completely out and has had a chance to cool down?
> **JACKSON:** Yeah.

I wanted to deal early on with the issue of the hydrocarbon detector and Jackson's assertions in his interrogatories that he couldn't get an accurate reading because the ground was too hot and was still smoking. I'd laid the groundwork for me to later come back to that issue after Jackson had used his figurative shovel to dig himself into a deeper hole.

I then moved to questioning him on how he was made aware of the fire.

Jackson testified that on November 11, 2009, he received a call from

Sheriff Nail—who was still a deputy on that date—informing him that the Atwood Lakehouse had burned down the night before, but that he didn't go out to investigate the fire until two days later because Sheriff Nail "had to get the consent to search form signed by Mr. (Emmett) Atwood in order to go on the property to investigate the cause of the fire."

Bingo! Jackson just told the first lie in his testimony and I was easily able to disprove his assertion. One has to remember that the real reason that Jackson didn't go immediately to the fire scene was because he didn't want to be bothered on his Veterans' Day holiday. It was only when his boss, Mike Chaney, got on his ass that he finally went two days after the fire.

Jackson's excuse for why he didn't immediately go to the fire was to blame Sheriff Nail by essentially testifying that his hands were tied until Sheriff Nail got Emmett to sign a consent-to-search form allowing them to conduct an investigation. It wasn't a lie that I was expecting, but I immediately knew how to crush it.

> **ME:** I'm going to show you a document that's been marked Plaintiff's Exhibit 9A. Mr. Jackson, have you seen that document before?
>
> **JACKSON:** Yes. I have.
>
> **ME:** And how would you identify that document?
>
> **JACKSON:** That is the consent-to-search form that we used to go on the property.
>
> **ME:** And is this the document you just referenced in your testimony?
>
> **JACKSON:** Yes, it is.
>
> **ME:** Mr. Jackson. If you will look on the document at the top right-hand corner, can you tell me the date on there that Emmett Atwood signed this document giving you and Sheriff Nail permission to go on the property to conduct your investigation?
>
> **JACKSON:** November 11, 2009.
>
> **ME:** And you agree that that is the date of the fire?
>
> **JACKSON:** Yes.
>
> **ME:** So if Emmett Atwood gave you permission to go on that property and do an investigation, why wait two days?
>
> **JACKSON:** Because Sheriff Nail told me at the time that it was still too hot. We couldn't do it right then. We go at the re-

quest of the sheriff.

Jackson knew he had been caught in his first lie. But like he'd tried to do throughout the discovery process of the lawsuit, his intention was to blame everyone but himself. And if he had to tell lie after lie to the jury, even when caught red-handed, he was determined to do so.

> **ME:** To your knowledge, was anything done to secure the fire scene for those two days that it took you to go investigate it?
> **JACKSON:** I can't remember. You'd have to ask Sheriff Nail.
> **ME:** Was there any crime tape around the area when you arrived?
> **JACKSON:** No, there wasn't. There was not.

This series of questions laid the groundwork to later explain the "suspicious" footprints that were found around the area that led Sheriff Nail and Jackson to supposedly conclude that the fire might have been started intentionally. But one shouldn't forget that Kade testified in his deposition that on the morning of the fire there were a lot of family and friends out there walking around.

I next moved on to the steps Jackson took to actually try and determine whether the fire was arson.

> **ME:** Can you walk me through the normal steps that you take when you approach a fire scene as part of your initial investigation?
> **JACKSON:** When I get on scene, I walk around the exterior of the property. We look around to see where the meter pole was set, where it's located—all of the utilities—and then we go inside the scene and take our rakes and shovels and start digging around inside to see if we can determine the cause of the fire.
> **ME:** At what point in the fire investigation on November 13, did you decide to use the hydrocarbon detector?
> **JACKSON:** Well, at the time, when we pulled our rakes back, the ashes had piled up, and the fire was still burning two days later on the house. So I used my detector—I stuck it in the ground. But it just started beeping. I did that once or twice and couldn't detect any accelerant.

> **ME:** So to be sure, you did not at any point detect any accelerant?
>
> **JACKSON:** I did not.
>
> **ME:** During the course of this litigation do you remember making a statement that your hydrocarbon detector kept going off because of the smoke from the fire scene?
>
> **JACKSON:** Uh-huh. Yes.
>
> **ME:** And that was because the ground was still very hot and smoking?
>
> **JACKSON:** That's correct.
>
> **ME:** Well, at any point after November 13, did you try to go back out there when it cooled down and quit smoking?
>
> **JACKSON:** No, because once you leave the scene you have to go back then and get a search warrant. You've got to go get a search warrant and explain to a judge what probable cause there is and why you need to go back out there. Once you leave the scene, you've got to leave somebody there—you've got to put someone there, because if you don't, the scene gets contaminated.

This was the first time in Jackson's testimony that I realized—just as I'd said in my opening statement—that there was going to be a lot of bullshit testimony from him that was going to astonish the jury.

Jackson's assertion that he needed a search warrant to go back out to the Atwood Lakehouse property to continue his investigation was absolute hogwash. Emmett had already signed a consent-to-search form and was more than willing to let Jackson pitch a tent on the scene and live there if he thought Jackson would be able to find some evidence that might prove I was involved.

The second assertion that someone needed to be placed at the scene was, likewise, utter garbage. The scene had been unsecured for more than two days before Jackson arrived. Yet, it was becoming clear that Jackson was going to lie, stall, obfuscate, and blame everyone else but himself for his incompetent investigation. But I wasn't going to let him get away with it.

> **ME:** But we're in agreement that for more than two days the fire scene was unsecured?

JACKSON: I don't know. You'll have to ask Sheriff Nail.

ME: Well, did you ever try to get a search warrant to go back out there to continue using your hydrocarbon detector?

JACKSON: I did not. I finished my investigation that day. I was through.

ME: But you made a decision not to go back out and try to detect an accelerant when the ground had cooled off and it quit smoking?

JACKSON: Yes. Just like I explained, once you leave you have to go back and get a search warrant, and if you don't have probable cause a judge won't issue it.

ME: Could the owner give you permission to go back on the scene?

JACKSON: He could.

ME: Did you ever ask Emmett Atwood for permission to come back out and continue your forensic tests?

JACKSON: No, I did not.

There were several interesting things that I learned from this colloquy with Jackson. First, according to his logic, he needed a search warrant to go back on the property. However, he never attempted to go and obtain one because if one doesn't have probable cause, a judge won't issue a search warrant.

This proved my case immediately. There was no probable cause to believe a crime occurred. That's why Jackson didn't go try and get a search warrant. There was absolutely no evidence demonstrating that there was probable cause to believe the fire was arson.

It should have been an open and shut case. No probable cause equals no justification for going and getting a warrant to continue searching. Jackson had made my case for me within the first thirty minutes of his testimony. I wished it was that easy, though.

My next line of questioning dealt with what Jackson found during the course of his brief, cursory investigation. But I made a notation to come back to the search warrant and probable cause issue.

ME: During the course of your investigation, did you find the remains of any guns at the fire scene?

JACKSON: I did.

ME: Okay. Mr. Jackson, I have on the projector screen a picture. Are you able to identify what kinds of weapons remains these are?

JACKSON: It appears to be rifles and shotguns.

ME: Okay. And if you will look at this one (indicating) here, does it look like the breech is exploded on this gun?

JACKSON: I can't tell.

ME: Based on your experience as a fire investigator, is it normal for people to also keep ammunition with their guns?

JACKSON: Yes.

I asked these series of questions to try and establish that not only should Kade Atwood have heard the blazing inferno of the fire, but he should have also heard the ammunition exploding that was stored near and inside the breeches of the guns. The Atwood Lakehouse fire was not a quiet fire, and how Kade allegedly slept through it is beyond belief.

This then immediately led back to my Occam's Razor theory and the simple—and certainly supported by the evidence—explanation that the house was burned for insurance purposes.

ME: When you went and spoke with Emmett Atwood, did you ever ask him how the insurance was structured on the lake house property or how much insurance he had?

JACKSON: All I can recollect is that I asked him how much, and it was four-something-thousand dollars, I believe. I can't remember the exact total.

ME: And did Emmett Atwood ever state to you during your investigation that he had recently increased the insurance on the house?

JACKSON: I can't remember him saying anything about it.

ME: Okay then. In your opinion as a fire marshal, do you quite often run across cases where people destroy their house for insurance fraud?

JACKSON: Occasionally, yes.

ME: So is it normal in the course of your investigations to look fully into the insurance situation of a house that's burned down?

JACKSON: Well, you know, we don't get involved in the insurance part. I just get with the company and they tell me how much insurance he had on the property.

ME: And did you do that in this case? Did you attempt to obtain the insurance records on the house?

JACKSON: I can't remember. I don't think so.

ME: So at the time of your investigation you had no idea that Emmett had recently increased the insurance on the lake house?

JACKSON: No, I didn't.

In Judge Aycock's courtroom, the witness sits immediately adjacent to the jury box. The entire time that Jackson was testifying I could not only look at him, but I could also gauge the reactions and facial expressions of the jurors who were attentively listening to his testimony.

Everyone in the courtroom knew that I was building up to a finale. I was carefully laying the groundwork in the different areas in which I planned to hang Jackson up by his ankles. I was also proving the theory of Occam's Razor that I'd set out to do.

At this point, any reasonable person in that courtroom had a picture in their heads of Emmett burning the lake house down for the insurance money. That is what the evidence indicated, and I was determined to push that theory.

ME: Now, Mr. Jackson. I have a set of pictures here (indicating on the projector). Do you recognize these pictures as those that were given to you by Emmett Atwood?

JACKSON: That's correct. Those are the pictures of the exterior and interior of the lake house.

ME: And can you look on the bottom right of each picture? Can you tell me what the date is on those photographs?

JACKSON: 11/07/2009.

ME: And that's four days before the fire?

JACKSON: Yes.

ME: Okay. Thank you. Will you look at this picture? It's of the interior of the lake house, specifically a roaring fire in the fireplace. Would you agree that there's black charring on the bricks from that fire?

JACKSON: I do.

This questioning turned back to the possibility that the fire was accidental. This specific picture that Emmett took showed where the fire in the fireplace had on occasions grew so large that it charred the wood and bricks surrounding the fireplace. And being four days before the fire, it was quite possible that we were looking at the real cause of the Atwood Lakehouse fire. It fit with my second theory.

>**ME:** In your investigation report, you stated that the hottest point of the fire was in the north rear of the house. Is that an indication of where the fire started?
>**JACKSON:** Yes.

If one remembers from Emmett's deposition testimony, the north rear of the house is where the kitchen and electrical box were located. This, also fit with my second Occam's Razor theory that the fire was accidental. But having now laid the groundwork for that, I switched back to another topic.

>**ME:** We've established, Mr. Jackson, that on November 13, 2009, the ground was too hot and was still smoking and you couldn't do any forensic tests. After that point, what other steps did you take in the investigation as far as forensics are concerned?
>**JACKSON:** Nothing.

I saw several jurors shift around in their seats as though what Jackson said—and how he said it—made them uncomfortable. I think I hit a nerve.

>**ME:** Okay. But at some point you were made aware of an individual named Joshua Langston Chamblee?
>**JACKSON:** I was.
>**ME:** And you remember interviewing him at the KFC in Carthage in March of 2010?
>**JACKSON:** That's correct.
>**ME:** What was your purpose in interviewing Chamblee?
>**JACKSON:** To see if he knew anything about the fire.
>**ME:** And what did he tell you?
>**JACKSON:** It's my recollection that he said you and him were in Starkville and that he didn't know anything about the fire. Af-

ter I started talking to him, I told him that Emmett Atwood was offering a $20,000 cash reward for information leading to the person that burned his camp.

ME: So in March 2010 you specifically remember telling Josh Chamblee about the reward?

JACKSON: Yes. And I also told him that the State of Mississippi offers up to $5,000 upon the arrest of the person that might have set fire to it.

ME: Okay. But even after telling Josh Chamblee about the rewards, he still maintained his story that he and I were in Starkville that night and had nothing to do with the fire?

JACKSON: Correct.

This was another chink in Chamblee's integrity that had been struck loose. In his deposition he flat lied when denying that he'd been told or promised the reward if he changed his story. It was another gold nugget thrown my way.

ME: After you took Josh's statement in March 2010, what steps did you take to complete your investigation?

JACKSON: After that, the trail went cold. I didn't have any other leads to follow at that time.

This is now where we got into the crux of why I was eventually arrested in July 2011. From Josh's March 2010 alibi statement, until July 2011, there were not any new leads or information. It literally was a closed case. But I knew Jackson had reopened the case right after my book was published and I knew he did it at the direct orders of Chaney and Sheriff Pace. Somehow, some way, I was going to prove it.

ME: Mr. Jackson, I am going to refer to your report that's on the screen. According to your report, you contacted Josh's mother, Mrs. Lyle in July 2011. Correct?

JACKSON: Correct.

ME: What prompted you to pick up the phone and call Mrs. Lyle in July 2011?

JACKSON: I can't recall.

ME: According to your report, when you called Mrs. Lyle she told you that Josh was living in North Carolina and that Josh was in the Navy Reserve. Correct?

JACKSON: Yes.

ME: But after contacting the Navy, you found out that Josh wasn't in the Navy. Is that correct?

JACKSON: Correct.

ME: Did you ever find any evidence that Josh was ever in North Carolina?

JACKSON: I did not.

I knew that Josh's mother was lying to Jackson, and he knew it as well. But as bad as I hated to do it, I needed to try and discredit her honesty in case, like I expected, Jackson and Mr. Minor tried to use her communications with Jackson as an indication that Josh knew the "truth," but was trying to hide it.

The next point that I wanted to move to concerned Josh's criminal history in Louisiana where he had been arrested for the equivalent of lying to law enforcement officers and filing false police reports.

ME: I am now going to show you a document that's listed as a *Comprehensive Consumer Report on Joshua Langston Chamblee*. Do you recognize that document to be something you procured?

JACKSON: I do.

ME: And where did you get that document from?

JACKSON: It's a government site that law enforcement use to find criminal records.

ME: Oh. Is it a private company or a government agency?

JACKSON: It would be a government agency because only law enforcement can get on there.

ME: Mr. Jackson, if you'll look at the bottom of the page, here. Do you see that website address?

JACKSON: Yes.

ME: And anywhere on there do you see a .gov?

JACKSON: No.

ME: Do you see a .com?

JACKSON: Yes.

ME: Thank you.

I'd caught Jackson in another little lie. It was important for Jackson to try and make the jury believe that this consumer report had legitimacy because it is what he relied on in finding out about Josh's criminal history.

By saying that the website was a government agency, Jackson could try and lend some credibility to it. However, as I quickly showed, the website was nothing more than a private data collection company.

> **ME:** On the second page of your report, do you see on there where it says that Josh was arrested for injuring public records in Louisiana?
>
> **JACKSON:** Yes.
>
> **ME:** And at the time that you procured this report it was your intention to obtain a third statement from Josh?
>
> **JACKSON:** Yes.
>
> **ME:** And once you obtained Josh's third statement, you relied solely on it in obtaining my arrest warrant?
>
> **JACKSON:** Correct.
>
> **ME:** At some point in time as a law enforcement officer procuring warrants, isn't it important to know the credibility and criminal history of the person that's making the statement that you're basing your arrest warrant on?
>
> **JACKSON:** Yes.
>
> **ME:** But you didn't care about Josh's past criminal history?
>
> **JACKSON:** Well, this is what he was charged with. It was a misdemeanor, not a felony.
>
> **ME:** And you know this how?
>
> **JACKSON:** My legal attorney at the insurance department told me. The document said injuring public records.
>
> **ME:** Okay. But read that first sentence, on the first page, at the very top.
>
> **JACKSON:** It says, *Data is entered poorly, processed incorrectly, and generally not free from defect. Any data supplied by this system must be independently verified.*
>
> **ME:** But you never tried to independently verify anything about Josh's criminal history did you?
>
> **JACKSON:** Nope.

I doubt that Jackson had been placed under such an intense examination in court as that which I was subjecting him to.

I knew what the evidence was, I knew every word, sentence, and paragraph in Jackson's reports, and I was not going to let him get away with even a little white lie. Jackson was a corrupt, dishonest law enforcement officer and I was slowly tearing him apart with his lies and sanctimonious attitude.

The tension in the courtroom had been building for over an hour. It had started off a little slow. But the longer Jackson stayed on the witness stand, the deeper was the hole he dug. I knew, however, that the final knockouts were to come.

> **ME:** Did you at one time explain to Mrs. Lyle in reference to her son, Joshua Chamblee, the severity of the crime and that he was an accessory to the fire even though he didn't strike the match? Did you make that statement to her?
> **JACKSON:** I did.
> **ME:** And did you make that statement to her before you talked to Josh at the Leake County Sheriff's Office and obtained the third statement from him?
> **JACKSON:** Yes.
> **ME:** Okay. So on the date you made that statement to Mrs. Lyle, what evidence did you have that the fire was an arson?
> **JACKSON:** Nothing until I talked to Josh.
> **ME:** But you explained to Mrs. Lyle before that that he was an accessory to the fire. What evidence did you have at that time that Josh was an accessory to a fire that was arson?
> **MR. MINOR:** Objection. Asked and answered.
> **JUDGE AYCOCK:** Overruled.
> **JACKSON:** I can't recall.
> **ME:** You can't recall or you don't know?
> **JACKSON:** I don't know.

This is what the case always swung back to. Without Josh and his lies, there was no case. There was no evidence. No proof the fire was arson. No proof I was involved. No probable cause. And even though it was like pulling teeth, Jackson was making my case for me.

> **ME:** Finding Josh wasn't easy was it?

JACKSON: No, it wasn't.

ME: And you got the opinion that he didn't want to talk to you.

JACKSON: Yeah. I figured that.

ME: But you made multiple attempts to contact Josh and he never would return your phone calls, did he?

JACKSON: I talked to Josh maybe twice on the telephone.

ME: Before the interview at the Leake County Sheriff's Office when he gave you the third statement?

JACKSON: Yes.

He had just told another lie and I had his own investigation report to prove him wrong. Jackson was honestly shocking the hell out of me and everyone in the courtroom with his continual lies that followed one after the other.

ME: I'm going to show you you're supplemental report from your investigation file. Let's look at the first paragraph, which starts in March 2010 and go through, paragraph by paragraph, up until July 29, 2011.

(Jackson reads through all the paragraphs)

ME: Do you see anywhere in your report where it says that you talked to Josh at any time prior to the July 29, 2011, meeting at the Leake County Sheriff's Department?

JACKSON: No.

ME: So you would now agree that on July 29, 2011, was the first time you talked to Josh again since your last meeting in March 2010?

JACKSON: Correct.

ME: So when you stated a few minutes ago that you had talked to Josh twice, that would be inaccurate?

JACKSON: I might have been mistaken.

It was clear that Jackson had lost every ounce of credibility and believability that he may have had with the jury. The more he testified the deeper he dug. And it crossed my mind multiple times that there were probably several innocent people, if not more, that were in prison because of the dishonesty and lies of disgraced deputy fire marshal James O'Neal Jackson. But the worst was still yet to come.

CHAPTER TWENTY-NINE

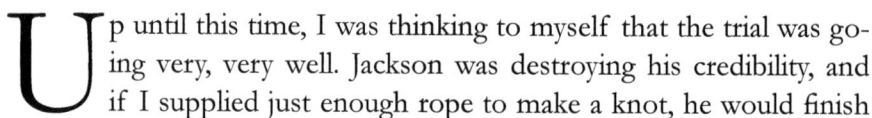

Up until this time, I was thinking to myself that the trial was going very, very well. Jackson was destroying his credibility, and if I supplied just enough rope to make a knot, he would finish hanging himself.

On reflection, it sickens me to have to contemplate the thought that a state law enforcement officer—a sworn protector of the law—would so easily lie, connive, and subvert justice to hide his dishonesty, his corruption, and the misdeeds of his superiors. But that's what Jackson continued to do.

As the trial progressed, I continued to be more and more shocked at Jackson's brazen disregard for the truth, his cocky attitude, and his air of invincibility before both the jury and Judge Aycock. He really believed that the jury would never rule against him. However, that was about to change.

My line of questioning continued regarding Jackson's interactions with Josh Chamblee and the arrest warrant he obtained for Josh's arrest.

> **ME:** At some point in time, Mr. Jackson, prior to your July 29, 2011, interview at the Leake County Sheriff's Department with Joshua Chamblee, before that time, did you go and obtain an arrest warrant for Josh's arrest?
>
> **JACKSON:** I did.
>
> **ME:** And if I showed you the affidavit that you filled out under oath to obtain that warrant, would you be able to recognize

it?

JACKSON: I would.

When Jackson went to get Josh's arrest warrant, he had to fill out an affidavit, under oath, swearing under penalty of perjury, that a crime had been committed and that there was probable cause to believe that Josh Chamblee committed it. I presented it to him on the screen and Judge Aycock allowed it to be shown to the jury without any objections from Mr. Minor.

The affidavit that Jackson filled out stated that he:

> *James Jackson, State Fire Marshal's Office, makes an affidavit that Joshua L. Chamblee, did, or on, or about the 11th day of November, 2009, in Attala County, did willfully, unlawfully, and feloniously aid and assist David Atwood, knowing that he had feloniously assisted in burning a lake house, with intent to enable him to avoid arrest after commission of such felony, in violation of Section 97 1-5, accessory after the fact, contrary to the statute in such cases made and provided and against the peace and dignity of the State of Mississippi. Sworn, under oath, James Jackson.*

ME: You filled that out and swore that that was accurate?
JACKSON: Correct.
ME: Swore under oath that that was the truth?
JACKSON: Correct.
ME: So at the time that you procured this warrant for Josh Chamblee's arrest, what evidence did you have that he was an accessory after the fact to arson?
JACKSON: I can't recall, other than when I talked to Josh later at the Leake County Sheriff's Department.
ME: Well, you procured the arrest warrant for Josh's arrest before you talked to him at the sheriff's office.
JACKSON: That was just to get Josh down here to talk to me.
ME: Oh. Is it normal police procedure to obtain a warrant for somebody's arrest to make them talk to you?
JACKSON: I have done it.
ME: Is it normal to obtain an arrest warrant for someone's arrest without any evidence that they committed a crime?
JACKSON: It all just depends on the case.

ME: But that's what you did in this case. You procured a warrant for Josh Chamblee's arrest without any evidence that he was an accessory to arson.

JACKSON: Correct.

ME: Why?

MR. MINOR: Objection. Argumentative.

JUDGE AYCOCK: Overruled.

ME: Please answer.

JACKSON: Like I said before, to get him to talk to me.

ME: And we know that Josh certainly talked to you. Was Josh ever convicted or indicted by a grand jury for being an accessory after the fact to arson?

JACKSON: No.

This was the first time that I heard members of the jury express a verbal response to some of Jackson's astonishing—and no doubt horrifying to the ears of a freedom-loving American—answers to my questions. No one actually said anything, but numerous jurors took in a few sharp breaths of air, one rolled her eyes as she exhaled, and another nervously popped his knuckles.

By the time Jackson had finished answering, his face was filled with that deer-in-the-headlights look. He saw, too, the reactions of the jurors, and I think everyone in the courtroom knew that this is when the jury incontrovertibly swung in my favor.

Everyone, including Jackson, is aware of the Fourth Amendment to the United States Constitution. But just to reinforce its importance, it is worth repeating:

> *The right of the people to be secure in their persons, houses, papers, and effects, against unreasonable searches and seizures, shall not be violated, and no warrants shall issue, but upon probable cause, supported by oath or affirmation, and particularly describing the place to be searched, and the persons or things to be seized.*

The Fourth Amendment is not an archaic relic of a bygone era when British troops indiscriminately searched, seized, arrested, incarcerated, and impounded the American colonists and their property. Our American forefathers fought and died to protect this unassailable right, yet James Jackson readily admitted that he flagrantly violated not just Josh's and I's constitutional rights, but many others, as well. There was no telling how many innocent people were falsely imprisoned because of Jackson's lies and incompetency.

I'd literally written the book on this type of government abuse. And as I know all too well, this type of conduct is not limited to corrupt, rogue law enforcement officers like Jackson. It's part of a culture; it's part of a culture of continually getting away with destroying the Constitution—chipping away bit by bit—by corrupt, dishonest cops who ultimately desire to inflict upon our way of life a set of controls that fits with their one-world view of a closely monitored police state.

Since at least the year 2000, I'd been shouting from the rooftops that Sheriff Pace and a majority of his deputies on the Warren County Sheriff's Department were corrupt, evil henchmen that were part of a larger contingent of politicians, judges, and other law enforcement agencies in the area that were moving our country closer and closer to a highly controlled, constitutionally-restricted police state.

Jackson was just the latest incarnation of this demon. The unfortunate part for Jackson was that he willingly allowed himself to be used like a puppet by the real crooks that ultimately held and controlled the strings. And if he had to lie, scheme, and connive to cover up and hide these illegal machinations, then Jackson was prepared to do so, even if it meant losing at trial to me.

After all, one has to keep in mind that James O'Neal Jackson meant nothing to Sheriff Pace, Mike Chaney, and Emmett Atwood. Jackson was simply an expedient tool, at a convenient time, that they tried to use to accomplish one of their long sought goals of having me incarcerated for the rest of my life.

If Jackson had been anything more than the blunt tool of a corrupt gang of degenerate politicians, then they would have been at his trial supporting him. But when one looked over to the defense's side of the courtroom, it was completely empty. Chaney and the other supervisors at the State Fire Marshal's Office had hung their incompetent minion out to dry.

And that is the ultimate conclusion that one can draw from the situation. Jackson was the most convenient tool that they needed at the time, but, after botching my investigation, arrest, and prosecution, he was left alone to defend what was essentially indefensible conduct.

I was heading closer and closer to my finale with Jackson. I'd laid the groundwork repeatedly for every screwed up part of his investigation and my subsequent arrest. It was time to start closing the noose a little tighter around Jackson's neck and Mr. Minor's defense.

> **ME:** Mr. Jackson, we were at the point where we had gotten to July 29, 2011, the date that you obtained that third statement from Josh Chamblee where he stated that I was allegedly responsible for the fire.
> **JACKSON:** Yes.
> **ME:** Prior to July 29, 2011, did you ever attempt to interview me?
> **JACKSON:** No.
> **ME:** But wasn't I the main suspect in the case?
> **JACKSON:** You was.
> **ME:** Is it normal police operating procedure not to try and interview the main suspect in the case?
> **JACKSON:** That's correct.
> **ME:** Well, then, why did you not try to interview me?
> **JACKSON:** Because you was in prison at the time.

My mouth fell open and hit the floor. Judge Aycock turned in her chair and stared in astonishment at Jackson. I saw from the corner of my eye that Mr. Minor was dumbfounded.

Jackson had just violated Judge Aycock's direct order she'd made earlier that day not to discuss or reveal anything about my past criminal history or imprisonment in front of the jury. But Jackson did it anyway, and we knew by the expression on his face that he did it on purpose and that he did it to try and prejudice the jury against me.

Everyone knew that I was winning my case the longer I examined Jackson. He was destroying his credibility and indicting himself by his actions in the case. I immediately knew that he purposely disclosed to the jury that I'd been in prison for no purpose other than to try and exact some revenge against me for my tough interrogation and to try and help his case.

Besides directly violating Judge Aycock's order, Jackson's statement that I was in prison during the time of his investigation was completely and totally false.

The fire occurred on the night of November 10, 2009. On January

12, 2010, my probation was violated and I was locked up until June 11, 2010. But for four of those five months I was at the Madison County Jail, less than ten minutes from Jackson's office. There was no excuse for why Jackson didn't try to interview me.

I was available and willing to be interviewed immediately after the fire, and then, anytime after my release from the probation violation in June 2010. But Jackson never chose to try and do so.

I knew, though, that Jackson never made the attempt because he didn't care what I had to say. He didn't care what evidence I may or may not have been able to contribute to his investigation. Jackson's mind about what happened was made up the same day he got his marching orders from Chaney. So my input wasn't necessary.

When Jackson made the erroneous statement that I was in prison and couldn't be interviewed, it left me speechless. The most that I could do while suppressing my rising, boiling anger, was to ask Judge Aycock to strike that statement and instruct the jury not to consider it. But the barn door had already been opened and the horses were loose.

> **JUDGE AYCOCK:** Counselors, would you approach?

I was absolutely furious. If I could have gotten my hands around Jackson's neck I would have squeezed until his head burst. I was so angry I could barely speak, but I could see immediately that Judge Aycock was madder. It took me a moment to gather my thoughts, but once I did I spat venom.

> **ME:** Your Honor, you specifically instructed that defendant not to bring that up, not to state anything about my criminal history or prison. He was in agreement with that. He intentionally and deliberately did it. Second, that statement was completely inaccurate. I was available to be interviewed from the time of the fire until January 2010 when I was locked up for a probation violation. I was available to be interviewed after my release in June 2010. I am going to ask for a mistrial. He was specifically instructed not to and he deliberately did it anyway.
>
> **JUDGE AYCOCK:** Your response, Mr. Minor?
>
> **MR. MINOR:** He was in the Madison County Jail for six months? That's a personal explanation for why he wasn't able to

talk to him. He did not reference the conviction. He explained his whereabouts. I don't think it's an intentional violation of the Court's order.

Judge Aycock then had us return to our respective tables and told the jury to disregard the statement made by Jackson. However, she had the U.S. Marshal remove the jurors from the courtroom so we could finish hashing out this egregious misstep by Jackson.

JUDGE AYCOCK: Mr. Atwood, I am concerned that perhaps everything was not on the record that you were attempting to say at the bench, so I want to make that record, and then I'll give Mr. Minor an opportunity to respond.

ME: Your Honor, before we began you specifically instructed this defendant not to reference any convictions or prison. This defendant knowingly and intentionally and deliberately revealed that fact to the jury. You were very, very clear with him. He did it, though, intentionally and maliciously, which has been the MO with this defendant from the very beginning of this case. This is just the continuing type of method used by this defendant. So it's kinda impossible now to close the barn doors now that the horses are loose. I am going to move for a mistrial. It's impossible now for me to obtain any kind of fair consideration from the jury with a statement like that. The defendant knew that I was available to be interviewed when I wasn't in prison. And now to try to explain his failure to pursue proper police investigation techniques he wants to try and make it like it's my fault. I was available to be interviewed for over a year after my release from prison and before I was arrested on August 1, 2011. The defendant chose not to pursue that route. Instead, to explain his failures as a law enforcement officer, he has revealed the fact that I was in prison to the jury after specifically being warned by the Court not to, and he did it to prejudice the jury. I move for a mistrial.

More than a year removed from when I made this objection, I am still surprised at how lucid and eloquent I sounded. I was so pissed and filled with such hate and anger that I am still surprised I was able to formulate my words as well as I did.

I especially emphasized the phrase "to explain his failures as a law enforcement officer," because there was no doubt that Jackson was a failure as a cop. This whole case had been filled with lies, corruption, dishonesty, and now direct violations of Judge Aycock's orders. It had to end and I was hoping that Judge Aycock would accept my move to declare a mistrial.

JUDGE AYCOCK: Mr. Minor.

MR. MINOR: As I stated earlier, I don't think it was an intentional violation. Mr. Jackson explained that for some of the time when he was investigating the case Mr. Atwood was incarcerated, which is a fact, which is an explanation for why he didn't interview him. I think it's relevant. I don't think it's overtly prejudicial. So he gets to go into whether Chamblee got arrested for some crime in Louisiana and we can't explain that he's in prison. I think he's trying to have it both ways. I don't think the Court should punish Mr. Jackson for referencing a fact that everybody knows for a mistrial.

JUDGE AYCOCK: Mr. Jackson, I instructed you not to speak of this. Can you explain that lapse of judgment?

JACKSON: (Shrugging shoulders) Your Honor, he asked a question, and I just made an answer.

JUDGE AYCOCK: Well, did you understand this pretrial before we started the testimony? What did you understand that discussion to be about no mention of convictions? Did you understand it?

JACKSON: Part of it, yes, ma'am.

JUDGE AYCOCK: Did you ask your attorney for an explanation of what parts you didn't understand?

JACKSON: No, ma'am. No, Your Honor.

JUDGE AYCOCK: Tell me what you didn't understand.

JACKSON: Well, you said we couldn't mention anything about it, but, you know, he asked me a question, and I just answered it without thinking, I guess, thinking it through.

JUDGE AYCOCK: I'll say. I don't see any way to cure the problem. I think it's going to be a mistrial. I'll declare a mistrial. We'll reconvene at a later time. And Mr. Jackson, I will take into consideration about the costs that should be assessed to you for bringing in the jury on this occasion. I'll make a ruling on that at a later date. The Court declares a mistrial. We will follow up with everyone about some dates to retry the case. I wish it hadn't happened the way it happened, but it did, so that's it.

I stood in shock at my table. Not only had Judge Aycock granted my request for a mistrial, she had also stated that it was her intention to sanction Jackson for his having screwed the trial.

Before I could move, Judge Aycock recalled the jury, explained to them that Jackson had divulged information that had previously been excluded from the trial, and that it was now necessary to dismiss them.

I was still so angry over his blatant attempt to prejudice the jury against me that I didn't take the time to notice Jackson's or Mr. Minor's attitudes or expressions when a mistrial was declared. None of us had been outside the courtroom's door since the trial began, so I took the time to step out.

The first person I saw was Sheriff Nail. I explained to him that he could go home because Jackson had just screwed the trial and a mistrial had been declared.

Overhearing me talking to Sheriff Nail was my mother. She, as well, wore a look of shock on her face that the trial was ending so soon. But I took a little longer to explain to her what happened than I did with Sheriff Nail. He could catch the story from Jackson. As far as I was concerned at the moment, I never wanted to see another police officer connected to my case for as long as I lived.

As I was explaining to my mother some of the insane testimony that came from Jackson, all eight members of the jury came out of the courtroom.

Not knowing whether I was allowed to speak with them or not kept me from approaching any of them. However, two quickly approached me and introduced themselves.

Both jurors complimented me on the extraordinary job that I'd done when I delivered my opening statement and when I questioned Jackson. Unfortunately, both jurors—and all the others—still didn't quite understand why a mistrial had been declared.

I took this opportunity to explain to them that I was, indeed, a convicted felon and that Judge Aycock had disallowed evidence of that conviction and imprisonment to be introduced. This, I was told, wouldn't have affected the jurors' decisions on whether to ultimately hold Jackson responsible for what was clearly a false, politically motivated arrest.

As I was talking to one of the jurors and explaining to her the rest of the story that the jury hadn't been able to hear, the other juror was talking to my mom and complimenting me on what a superb job I'd done. My mother couldn't have been prouder at that moment.

As I kept replaying Jackson's testimony through my mind, I quickly realized that having tons of practice at running a gay inquisition had proven quite helpful in questioning Jackson and ultimately responding to his lies and falsehoods in such a way that utterly discredited him.

Dating the numerous gay men that I have—most of whom were pathological, compulsive liars like Josh Chamblee—prepared me tremendously when it came to interrogating Jackson. He was, in a lot of ways, just like these gay men. Jackson would lie, then when caught, lie some more to cover that lie.

The false arrest trial was, to me, an attempt to discover the truth. My goal was to determine the true story about what happened to the Atwood Lakehouse. Everything else, even that about the corrupt cops and what illegal actions they took in other cases, was incidental to that goal.

I sought the truth about the past in order to learn the truth about the present. Jackson was telling lies about the past to try and support his lies about the present. But I was close to the truth.

Anyone leaving that courtroom that day knew that Jackson was a liar, that he was a corrupt cop, and that he had exceeded his authority far beyond what was allowed by law. He was destroying the moral fabric of our free society by his continual destruction of the protections of our Constitution. But this is not uncommon. I literally wrote the book on it.

Police authority, in theory, is supposed to be restricted by both federal and state law. There are good laws with good intentions in place to protect those whom are victimized by corrupt law enforcement officers like James Jackson.

The reality is, though, that police like him commonly exceed that authority and violate those laws everyday. However, they rarely pay the price for doing so.

The rules and laws in place are only as good as their enforcement. But the problem is, they are seldom enforced. The real limits on police power are not often established or limited by our laws and regulations, but by police leadership, the pressure of an informed community, and in cases such as mine with Judge Aycock, the judicial court system.

Lack of effective oversight and punishment for violations of these laws is why the police so often have targeted people or groups who advocate greater oversight and limits to police authority. That's exactly what happened to me the night that I was arrested at the Miss Mississippi Pageant for advocating that the citizenry vote for someone other than Sheriff Martin Pace.

That was not an isolated incident. This political targeting happens all the time. I thanked God everyday that there was a judge who was finally willing to apply the laws as they were meant to be applied when police—like Jackson—exceeded their authority.

Not once did I ever think that Judge Aycock favored me over the defense. She simply did her job and applied those laws as they were meant to be applied. Jackson clearly exceeded his authority and abused it by making an arrest without any evidence of a crime due to political pressure for an outspoken stance I took against government corruption.

Without these limits on abuse of authority, we will, as a country, be transformed from the land of the free to a strictly controlled populist under the armed might of a totalitarian police state.

Whether it is the killing of unarmed African-Americans by white police officers, the violent police responses to peaceful political demonstrations, or in my case, an illegal arrest done in retaliation for my outspoken views against law enforcement corruption in Vicksburg, without firm limits and punishment for this type of conduct it opens the specter of what it might mean if the police were to take over society.

Without restraint, corrupt police might comport themselves and respond in such a way not as the upholders of law and order, but a true criminal force of civil repression that is chaotic, undisciplined, and totally uncontrollable.

Even the United States Supreme Court has repeatedly stated in their opinions that the freedom of individuals verbally to oppose or challenge police action without thereby risking arrest is one of the principal characteristics by which we distinguish a free nation from a police state. This was something I'd been telling people for years.

The trial in March 2017 only proved one thing to me. The law enforcement officers involved in my arrest were going to do anything and everything they could to avoid punishment for their offenses—none more so than Jackson—even if it meant lying under oath and disobeying Judge Aycock's direct orders.

On the day that I drove back to the halfway house in Hattiesburg I stopped in Meridian, Mississippi, to refill my vehicle with gas. While I was doing so, I checked my email. Every time that a document, motion, or court order was filed in the case the clerk's office would send me an email informing me of what had been placed on the docket.

True to her word, Judge Aycock fined Jackson almost $2,000 as punishment for violating her direct orders. Several days later, Jackson presented a personal check to the clerk's office for $1,925.64.

At the same time, Judge Aycock set a new trial date to retry the case. It would now be held on July 17, 2017, at 9:30 A.M. in the federal courthouse in Aberdeen. I wouldn't have the headache of trying to work around the halfway house's restrictions or Chris Kelly's interference by then. And there was no doubt in my mind, come July, I'd be better prepared than I was before.

CHAPTER THIRTY

As soon as I got back to the halfway house I immediately went back to work for Gary at Black Sheep's Cafe. I had some unbelievable stories to tell about the trial and a captive audience to listen. But several days after returning I had to drive to Jackson for a medical appointment with my new doctor regarding my avascular necrosis diagnosis in my hips.

At my appointment, the doctor told my mother and I that due to the extensive damage and femoral head collapse in my left hip, the only option available was a total hip replacement. However, my right hip had not progressed as seriously as the left; the doctors thought that it may be worth trying to save.

If we were going to save the right hip, surgical intervention was immediately necessary and I would need an orthopedic specialist that was trained to perform bone grafts, bone decompressions, and vascular grafting, procedures that would, hopefully, stimulate the blood flow to the femoral head and prevent the starvation of the hip from the blood it needed.

Unfortunately, at the University of Mississippi Medical Center (UMMC), there were not any orthopedic specialists trained to perform those type surgeries, and we were sadly informed of this. However, we were encouraged to begin looking around the country for physicians that could not only treat idiopathic, unknown causes of AVN, but who could also perform the hip preservation surgeries that I needed for my right hip.

It was explained to us that due to my young age, and the relatively short lifespans of artificial hip joints, it was possible that I would face future surgeries to replace the artificial hip joints as they wore out from use. Because the replacement of artificial joints is much more difficult and potentially harmful than the replacements of original joints, I was encouraged to do everything possible to seek a joint preservation surgery for the right hip.

After multiple and exhausting searches for orthopedic specialists trained to treat unknown causes of AVN and perform hip preservation surgeries, we found a team of surgeons in San Diego, California, at Scripps Hospital that was willing to accept me as a patient and treat me for free.

This was excellent news. However, as I was preparing to leave the halfway house I realized that I was only substituting one type of confinement for another. I still would be under the control of U.S. Probation. And they ultimately retained the keys to my movements.

As soon as I knew that I would need to go to California for treatment, I attempted to contact the woman who had been assigned as my probation officer.

Shameka Horton was apparently a new probation officer. Her communications with me on the phone certainly reflected her newness and unpreparedness for the job.

I tried to explain to Horton what my medical condition was and why I needed to go to San Diego. However, without demonstrating the slightest compassion or understanding, Horton informed me that it was her policy not to allow new probationers to leave the state of Mississippi the first two months into the beginning of their terms of probation.

My halfway house confinement ended on April 13, 2017, and my term of probation was set to begin that same day. However, Horton ultimately told me that she didn't care what medical conditions that I had, she would only talk to me on or after April 13. This was not a good sign.

My doctors ultimately wrote numerous referral letters stating that, based on their significantly informed medical opinions, I could not receive adequate medical treatment for my condition in Mississippi and that I needed to be referred to the medical doctors in San Diego for the specialized care that the AVN disease required.

The doctors in San Diego wanted me to come out and meet them as soon as possible. I, unfortunately, had to explain to them that without the approval of my U.S. Probation officer, I would be unable to legally leave Mississippi to come to San Diego for a medical consultation. Even they expressed abject horror at Horton's obstinate refusal to consider my medical condition and need for specialized treatment that the doctors in Mississippi couldn't provide.

Horton, though, had effectively tied my hands. She wouldn't even discuss with me anything about my probation conditions, much less give me permission to go to California, until after my halfway house term ended and my probation began. The doctors at Scripps Hospital did make an appointment for me, however, on Thursday, May 4, 2017.

My official Bureau of Prisons sentence ended on April 13 when I was finally allowed to leave Dismas Charities Halfway House and the maniacal control of Chris Kelly-Patton. I immediately left Hattiesburg and drove to Jackson to meet with my new probation officer at the federal courthouse.

Finally meeting Shameka Horton face-to-face didn't bode well with me. I could work with my last probation officer, Jay Simpson. I could tell, though, that Horton didn't want to work with me. She was cold, rude, certainly not polite, and spoke to me as if I was a child.

My first thought when I saw Shameka Horton was that she looked like the type of female law enforcement officer that took bad boys to jail and bad girls to bed. I later found out that Horton had at one time been a counselor but left that job after having utterly failed to help or keep any clients.

Our first meeting did not go well. My sole concern was getting this emergency surgery that I needed so badly. Horton couldn't have cared less. Her answer was still a firm no. I realized then that I was going to have to go around Horton in everything that I did. It was apparent to me that she had been promoted beyond her abilities, tasked with a job she couldn't perform, and cared nothing about the rehabilitation of a former inmate.

The only option left for me was to file an official petition with Judge Wingate and ask him to give me permission to go to San Diego for medical treatment.

In early April, shortly after my release from the halfway house, I filed an emergency petition for permission from Judge Wingate to travel to San

Diego to meet with my team of medical specialists. My petition included all of the relevant information that he would need to make a ruling, along with, of course, the multiple letters my doctors wrote stating the urgent necessity of me getting this treatment. But as usual, Judge Wingate sat on the petition, neglected his duties as a judge, and ignored me.

As my May 4, 2017, doctor's appointment neared, it was becoming clearer by the moment that Wingate was not going to take my medical needs seriously no matter how urgent.

Thankfully, the federal rules allow for a mandamus petition to be filed with the Fifth Circuit if a lower district court judge refuses to take action on one's case. When it became clear that Wingate was not going to grant me permission in a timely manner to go get the medical treatment I needed in San Diego, I filed a petition for a writ of mandamus with the Fifth Circuit asking them to intervene.

Thankfully, someone in the appellate court recognized the urgency of the situation, and soon after filing the writ, Wingate was forced to grant me permission to travel to San Diego. The probation office, including Horton, were not happy with me going over their heads. I didn't give a shit, though. I was headed to Southern California and I was going to make the most of the trip.

We arrived in San Diego late at night on Wednesday, May 3. By the time we checked into the hotel my mother, sister, and I were exhausted. The next morning, however, we were up early and at the doctor's office right on time.

The doctors that we met with that morning were extremely glad that I'd been able to get permission to come see them, but, unfortunately, after looking at my most recent MRI and x-ray results, they decided that any hip preservation surgery would have too low of a chance at success to risk the complicated and painful surgery.

The only option left at that point was total hip replacements in both hips. This was not good news to me. I wanted desperately to avoid one, not to mention two, total hip replacement surgeries. But that wasn't to be the case. The disease was rapidly progressing and destroying what good bone was left.

Our conversation then turned to what options were available to me surgically. UMMC in Mississippi could only provide me a ceramic-on-polyethylene artificial joint replacement. These type artificial joints only have an average of fifteen to twenty years life expectancy before they wear out and need replacing.

At my young age, I would be facing multiple, future artificial joint replacements when the first artificial joints wore out. And because replacing an artificial joint is much more complicated and painful, with longer recovery times, than replacing the original joints, all of my orthopedic surgeons wanted me to make sure that when I did receive the hip replacement surgeries that I get artificial joints with the longest life expectancy.

At the time, a ceramic-on-ceramic artificial joint provided the longest life expectancy—up to thirty to forty years. Unfortunately, UMMC in Mississippi couldn't offer me this type of joint, but Scripps Hospital in San Diego could. The other major consideration was cost. In San Diego I received free medical treatment and surgery; not so in Mississippi.

Our other major consideration was trying to formulate a treatment plan that not only could try and determine what was causing the AVN to spread to my body's joints, but also develop possible treatments to stop it. Otherwise, without treatment the disease would continue to spread.

Because idiopathic AVN is so rare, finding medical specialists to treat it posed a problem. The only current treatment plans available at that time were through a clinical trial at Stanford University. Without being in the general area, though, I couldn't participate.

The ultimate conclusion that we reached on May 4 with my doctors was that if I was going to receive the best quality treatment in a timely manner—not to mention free of charge—then I would have to at least be able to move to San Diego for a year to eighteen months. I knew then that U.S. Probation would never approve it no matter how dire the emergency. But I was going to try.

For the rest of the weekend while in California we went to the famous San Diego Zoo, the *U.S.S. Midway* aircraft carrier, and several other museums.

The Mexican food was outstanding and some of the Cinco de Mayo parties were even better. But what most impressed me about San Diego was the quality of the gay men that I met. I'd never met more beautiful, more intelligent gays anywhere else that I'd been.

The quality of gay guys in Mississippi always left something to be desired. It's because, in most cases, any gay man with education or financial ability gets the hell out and moves somewhere better.

I had a lot of fun, made several new friends, and finally was exposed to a real gay community and culture. I didn't care at the time what kind of medical issues I had, I knew I wanted to be in San Diego for the rest of my life.

Once back in Mississippi, I made a formal request to Officer Horton and U.S. Probation to be allowed to move to San Diego temporarily for medical treatment.

As part of my request, I included affidavits from my mother, stepfather, and other family members stating that they would financially support me while undergoing the medical treatment in San Diego.

I provided them multiple letters from all my doctors certifying that I needed specialized medical care that I could only receive in San Diego at Scripps. And I provided them with the addresses of several apartment complexes in San Diego near Scripps that wouldn't pose a problem with me living in due to my sex offender status.

I made sure that probation had every piece of information they needed to make a decision in my favor. I needed this transfer for legitimate medical needs, but when I presented this request to Horton she acted as if she actually took pleasure in the pain and difficult medical position that I was in.

I knew things were probably not going to go my way when one of the probation officers that works with Horton reminded me that in my book, *Into Hell I Rode*, I'd written about a sheriff's deputy in Hattiesburg named Paul Amacker that was a good friend of his.

Back in 2001, when I was going to college in Hattiesburg, I started dating Paul Leslie Amacker, Jr., who was a deputy sheriff at the time on the Forrest County Sheriff's Department under Sheriff Billy Magee.

Paul was a degenerate, corrupt cop in the truest sense of the word. Even though I was under the age of eighteen for part of the time we were together, this didn't stop Paul from getting me drunk, having sex with me, or smoking marijuana himself.

Several times, Paul let me ride with him in his sheriff's patrol vehicle and we made traffic stops on people that Paul caught with marijuana and other illegal drugs. Rather than take them to jail I watched Paul confiscate the drugs, release the drug users, and then later use the drugs himself.

When I eventually ended my relationship with Paul he became physically abusive and threatening, but despite me contacting Sheriff Magee and telling him what Paul was doing, the harassment never stopped.

I eventually made contact with an investigator at the Mississippi Attorney General's Office who actually conducted an investigation, made the harassment stop, and would have brought felony charges against Paul had I desired to pursue them. But I just wanted Paul to leave me alone, and the investigator helped that happen.

Astonishingly though, in 2010, Paul Amacker was hired by the Federal Bureau of Investigation as a special agent. When I found out that the FBI was about to hire a criminal that was worse than some felons I'd been locked up with in prison, I immediately contacted them and told them everything I knew about Paul and what he had done to me. This didn't prevent him from keeping his employment with the FBI, though.

My efforts to prevent a blatant criminal drug user and rapist from becoming a special agent with the FBI only proved detrimental to my efforts to receive fair treatment by U.S. Probation because most all of the officers there knew and were friends with Paul. And Officer Horton's colleague made this crystal clear to me.

So I didn't expect that I would ever receive any type of fair consideration or treatment from probation. But I made the effort to be as compliant and polite as possible when dealing with them. I certainly didn't want to give them any reason to set me up and try to get me sent back to prison.

Several weeks after formally submitting my request to transfer my probation from Mississippi to California, I was told that if I could receive approval from the U.S. Probation Office in San Diego then I would be allowed to move out there; probation in Mississippi would not stand in my way, surprisingly.

I immediately made contact with the federal probation officer there into whose hands had fallen my urgent, medically necessary need to transfer out there. Her name was Paula Burke.

Officer Burke at first didn't seem to have a problem with me coming out to San Diego for the twelve to eighteen months that I'd need to get treatment; she certainly didn't seem disinclined to do so in our first conversation. But as weeks went by and I couldn't get an answer from her or Horton, I began to suspect that the eventual decision would not be favorable to me.

While I waited for permission to transfer my probation out to California, I spent the early part of my summer catching up on the life and fun that I'd missed while incarcerated.

Once I'd been told that the doctors could not perform any hip preservation surgeries on me, there was really no need to lay around all day, be inactive, and not put weight on my right hip. I had a lot of catching up to do and I planned on making the best of what little time I had until I became immobile for the year to year-and-a-half that I'd need to recover after my first surgery.

My first big purchase upon release was buying a motorcycle. I'd always loved to ride street bikes, and despite my mother's worrying, I was determined to continue—bad hips be damned.

Not long after I bought my bike I was going too fast on the highway outside of Vicksburg and I got pulled over by a trooper with the Mississippi Highway Patrol. This was the first time that I'd been written a ticket or cited for any type of traffic violation since 1998. I deserved it, though.

After getting the ticket, I immediately called Horton and informed her that I'd been written a traffic citation for speeding and that I was fulfilling my obligation to call her and make her aware that I'd had contact with law enforcement.

My one and only question to Horton was whether or not she would violate my probation and try to send me back to prison for getting a speeding ticket. Horton answered in the negative. She even told me that she'd never violated someone's probation for traffic citations unless they were serious, such as drinking and driving.

Horton did want me, though, to take a picture of the traffic ticket and text it to her. Unfortunately, the cell phone that I was using at the time did not have a good camera, nor was it a smartphone that was designed to text pictures. I told Horton this and explained to her that I'd have to get my mother to use her smartphone to take and send a picture of the ticket.

When I got home I immediately had my mother take a picture of the ticket and text it to Horton. I was then informed by her not to worry about it, but to keep her informed about my court dates and whether I was found guilty or not of speeding. I thought this should have concluded the matter.

When my friend, Dane Davenport, a lieutenant on the highway patrol, found out that I'd been written the ticket, he offered to call the trooper that'd written it and ask him to void it. I, of course, didn't discourage this. I was wrong for speeding, but once cited, I wasn't going to do so again. So Dane fixed the ticket for me.

When I told Horton that Dane had fixed the ticket, and that it was not going to be forwarded for prosecution, I could tell that she was not pleased.

Throughout our entire interactions over the course of nine months, not once did I ever see or hear Horton expressing any type of encouragement or positivity when something good happened for me. I always got the feeling that Horton was jealous of me, didn't like me, and was doing everything she could to hurt me. I'd never gotten that feeling from Jay Simpson, but I did with Shameka Horton, the failed mental health counselor and incompetent probation officer.

Come late June 2017, I finally received a phone call from Horton telling me that Burke had denied my request to come to San Diego for medical treatment. I was told that the reason my request was denied was because Burke had done a "cursory Google search" which revealed numerous orthopedic surgeons in Mississippi that were capable of treating AVN and that the state of California should not bear the expenses of having to pay for my medical treatment.

I was also told that Burke's probationer caseload in California was significantly higher than Horton's in Mississippi, and that she simply didn't want the extra burden of having an additional probationer to supervise.

Despite everything that my doctors had provided, repeatedly stating that I could not get the specialized medical treatment that I needed in Mississippi, Burke and U.S. Probation in San Diego completely ignored them and instead based their decision on a quick cursory search of Google in reaching their decision.

Of course, they were correct that there were doctors in Mississippi that could treat known causes of AVN and provide hip replacement surgeries. Those doctors were capable of isolating the AVN cause and developing treatments for that. However, my AVN was idiopathic, and none of those doctors in Mississippi even knew where to begin.

When eight hundred people or less are diagnosed with idiopathic AVN every year, there aren't a lot of specialists willing to so narrowly specialize in that field. The only ones we could find were in San Diego.

Burke's additional contention that California shouldn't be burdened with my healthcare was also misplaced. Simply put, I was a potentially valuable research asset that could have expanded science's knowledge about this disease. Yet, by denying my request to transfer my probation, Burke and her office were not only denying me the ability to seek specialized medical treatment, they were denying researchers what was an excellent opportunity to discover new treatment methods.

Besides being devastated that I was being denied access to the best—and certainly only—medical care at that point, I was also upset that I wouldn't be able to escape the confines of the oppressive environment of Mississippi. I wanted away from there so bad.

The only thing that I knew to do at that point was to get court intervention. Hopefully, a judge would see the medical necessity of me needing treatment and would order probation in San Diego to accept me. In furtherance of this objective I could file lawsuits and legal petitions in both California and Mississippi.

On June 26, 2017, I filed a lawsuit in the United States District Court for the Southern District of California in San Diego alleging that Officer Burke and her U.S. Probation Office were denying me medically necessary treatment by refusing to allow me to transfer my probation.

I also filed at the same time a mandamus petition asking the same district court to order Burke to accept my probation. Because U.S. Probation is a federal agency, courts have the power to order them to perform a specific function that they are denying to someone entitled to that specific action. So, essentially, I had two avenues of relief in San Diego through the courts.

On the same day, I also filed a motion with Judge Wingate asking him to order that my probation be transferred to California for the medical reasons previously outlined.

The federal courts also have power to order a probationer who is serving his probation sentence in that particular district to serve his time in another federal district. Although I doubted that I would ever receive any favorable action from Wingate, I was at least going to try. If Wingate wouldn't transfer my probation, there was always the chance that the Fifth Circuit would on appeal or that the courts in California would.

As I always did when it came to anything dealing with my probation, I was sure to provide Horton with copies of all of the legal documents that I was filing so that she would be aware of what I was trying to do.

The same morning that my lawsuits were filed in California, and my motion to transfer my probation was filed in Mississippi, I also faxed those same documents to Horton and Burke at their respective offices. As I tend to do, especially since being sent to prison by Wingate for alleged actions that were not criminal, I was going to fight.

The next morning, however, the doorbell at my mother's house rang rather early. When I opened the door I was surprised to see two U.S. Marshals standing there with papers in their hands.

At first, I thought that I was going to jail. I'd associated badges so much with going to jail that I'd come to expect that at first sight. However, when the marshals asked to come inside and talk, I knew that they were there for another purpose—just not the purpose I expected.

The day before, when I'd filed the lawsuits and other petitions against U.S. Probation, both Horton and Burke decided to retaliate and file something against me.

The marshals had in their hands a summons that informed me that Horton was trying to violate my probation for getting a speeding ticket, using an internet-capable phone to text her a picture of the speeding ticket, and for having an active Facebook Page.

Fortunately for me, the summons did not require that the marshals incarcerate me. There would have to be a hearing before Judge Wingate first. The ultimate decision whether to send me back to prison for these "violations" would be decided at a later date. For the time being, though, I was left to stew at the clear retaliatory tactics being used by probation.

Horton is a liar, not to mention an incompetent probation officer and failed therapist. She's no better than James Jackson and the other corrupt cops that I've written about so much. There is no longer any integrity and honesty in federal law enforcement. Decent, honest federal officers have been supplanted by corrupt, dishonest officers like Horton whom, like her, have failed in every other vocation they've ever tried.

Horton had been clear with me, she did not violate probation for minor traffic citations, especially ones that were never prosecuted.

Furthermore, it was at Horton's insistence that I use my mother's smartphone—which was internet-capable—to text her a photo of the speeding ticket. And truth be told, my mother is the one who texted the ticket to Horton, not myself. But I was being blamed for it.

Lastly, my Facebook Page was not a regular account. It was a business page that advertised my book, *Into Hell I Rode*, and had been active since 2011. And there was not a single, solitary post on my Facebook Page that had been made by me since I'd been released from prison.

The terms of my probation didn't allow me to use computers to access the internet, cell phones with internet capability, or any other device that could access the internet. And I abided by those conditions.

Horton's probation violation allegations were a desperate grasp at retaliation which twisted the truth, contorted the facts, and in some ways were just plain, outright lies. But I'd already come to suspect the worst from law enforcement, and Horton's shenanigans didn't really surprise me.

One of the marshals that morning told me that Horton and U.S. Probation was especially pissed that I'd used my friendship with Dane to get the ticket voided. Later that morning, however, when I told Dane what they'd done, he told me that several months prior to that date he was contacted by a U.S. Probation officer in Horton's office and was asked to void a ticket for the son of that probation officer.

The hypocrisy was killing me. A federal probation officer could use a highway patrolman to get a speeding ticket voided for his kid, but if my friend, out of the goodness of his heart, willingly tries to help me, then I get punished and sent back to federal prison. Life isn't fair.

So in addition to having to worry about my medical needs—which weren't being treated, thanks to federal probation—I also had to worry about Horton trying to send me back to prison and also trying to get myself prepared for the second false arrest trial in Aberdeen that was coming up on July 17.

I realized that I could only fight one corrupt officer—one corrupt department—at a time. There would be opportunities later down the road to deal with Horton, but at that moment the only person that I needed to be concentrating on was Jackson and the Fire Marshal's Office. Come July, despite what Horton and U.S. Probation were trying to do, I'd be ready. But I also had a lot to do to get ready.

CHAPTER THIRTY-ONE

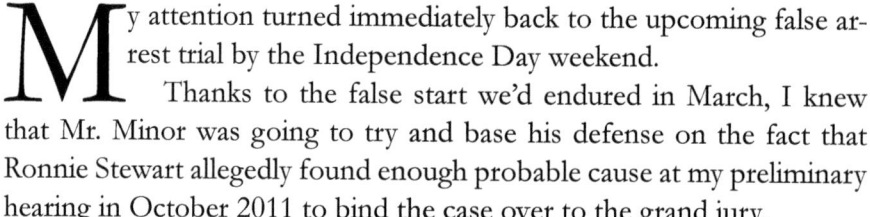

My attention turned immediately back to the upcoming false arrest trial by the Independence Day weekend. Thanks to the false start we'd endured in March, I knew that Mr. Minor was going to try and base his defense on the fact that Ronnie Stewart allegedly found enough probable cause at my preliminary hearing in October 2011 to bind the case over to the grand jury.

I knew, however, that Stewart's finding was nothing more than a routine rubberstamp on a legal document that didn't ultimately mean a single thing. And I was going to prove it using Stewart and Mrs. Jordan.

Since the cell phone records belonging to the iPhones that Josh and I had on the night of the fire were not complete or completely legible, I'd asked Judge Aycock to issue a subpoena for those records. They arrived in late June.

Just as I expected, when one reads the entire cell phone record, which included dates and times for calls, texts, and data usage, it was clear that there was no major gap in my communications the night of the fire contrary to what Mr. Minor had said in his opening statement.

I don't know if Sheriff Nail or Jackson had simply lost them, destroyed them, or just inadvertently failed to turn them over to me during discovery. But the newly subpoenaed records unequivocally showed that my phone was being used to send and receive texts almost throughout the night of the fire while attached to a Starkville cell tower.

When I got these records I immediately sent them to Mr. Minor and made him aware of what they showed. I knew this would foreclose another avenue of argument that he'd be able to make to the jury. And it did.

To this day, I still do not know what Mr. Minor truly believes about what happened the night of the fire, but my cell phone records were pretty damn clear. No one could argue that my phone was not sending and receiving texts and using data that night while attached to a Starkville tower. That's pretty damning evidence that proves my innocence.

In addition to the new cell phone subpoena, I asked and received from Judge Aycock subpoenas to be served on Ronnie Stewart, Teresa Lyle, Rosalind Jordan, Sheriff Martin Pace, Sheriff Tim Nail, Jan Hyland Daigre, Emmett Atwood, and Kade Atwood.

I had the depositions of Emmett and Kade, but I made the decision that their courtroom testimony would be much more entertaining, helpful to me, and damaging to Jackson's defense.

I planned to use Stewart's testimony to discredit himself and render useless the "finding" he made at my preliminary hearing that Mr. Minor said saved his case.

Mrs. Jordan was needed to substantiate her detailed notes that were taken at the preliminary hearing, discredit Jackson's latest claim that his hydrocarbon detector kept getting false readings at the fire scene, and to further establish that Stewart's probable cause finding at the preliminary hearing was nothing more than the routine rubberstamp that we all knew it was.

Nothing had really changed with Sheriff Nail. I still needed him to explain his steps in the investigation, the evidence he uncovered—which was all exculpatory and beneficial to me—and his involvement in my arrest.

By this time, I didn't look at Sheriff Nail as an enemy. After seeing the bigger picture I realized that, like Jackson, Sheriff Nail was being used as a pawn in Chaney and Sheriff Pace's game of political retaliation. I'd even been given permission to interview him at his office shortly before the trial by Mr. Griffith.

Since being released from prison, Mr. Griffith and I had patched up our differences and his attitude towards me had drastically changed. When I called him and asked permission to interview Sheriff Nail to discuss his testimony at the upcoming July trial, Mr. Griffith was more than willing to work with me.

At our interview, Sheriff Nail walked me step-by-step through his investigation—at least those parts that he remembered—and explained to me the evidence that he collected and that which he didn't.

When I specifically asked Sheriff Nail about the subpoena that he obtained in late 2009 for my cell phone records, wherein he claims that "investigators determined that the fire was arson," he was unable to cite any evidence whatsoever that he could have relied on at the time to convince me, much less a judge, that the fire was arson.

When I again pressed Sheriff Nail on this fact, and kept asking him to point me to something in the record that led him to believe that the fire was an arson in late 2009, the only thing that he would say was, "We will have to just wait and see at the trial."

I kind of sympathized with Sheriff Nail's position. Sometimes criminal investigators have to stretch things a little in order to find that one small lead that breaks a case. Unfortunately, Sheriff Nail and Jackson didn't just stretch things too far, the whole process was broken and shattered to pieces.

When the police have to lie, fabricate evidence, and file false legal documents with the courts, then there is a serious problem. And that is exactly what Sheriff Nail had done. Without any evidence that the fire was arson he had made a false statement to a judge in order to illegally obtain what was, he hoped, proof that I was involved in the fire. Thankfully, the records proved otherwise.

It was also becoming clearer to me, after meeting with Sheriff Nail, that he knew nothing about my book which was so critical of the corrupt law enforcement officers in Vicksburg.

Sheriff Nail knew that there was some kind of extreme impetuousness that was driving Chaney's and Jackson's burning zeal to arrest me in the summer of 2011. I believed him, though, when he told me that he knew nothing about my book or the motives of Jackson and Chaney.

Sheriff Martin Pace in Warren County was another matter altogether. Sheriff Pace had a personal history with me of trying to have me arrested and incarcerated for crimes that I had not committed.

Whether it was the malicious mischief case where I was accused of shooting Emmett and June's tractor, the elderly abuse case that Emmett and Scott Zimmerman had brought against me, or the trespassing arrest at the Miss Mississippi Pageant in July 2011, Sheriff Pace had repeatedly shown his willingness to abuse his office and use his deputies to settle political scores. My arrest for arson was just the latest incarnation of his power plays.

Sheriff Pace's testimony was needed to connect him to Chaney and then to Jackson. It was crystal clear that Sheriff Pace and Chaney got together after my book was published and conspired together to get me arrested for the fire. And even if I couldn't get Sheriff Pace to admit it, I could insinuate enough that the jury would catch my drift.

I'll be the first to admit, though, that Sheriff Pace has some charming qualities; he's a politician after all. Without an ability to suppress his undesirable character traits, he'd never get reelected. And those who know Sheriff Pace the best know that he's neither an effective sheriff, a competent administrator, or an honest politician—despite his charming personality.

I have always said that Sheriff Pace is a likeable person. However, he has no control over his department or the deputies that work for him. They are allowed to run crazy without fear of oversight, discipline, or competent direction. They simply don't respect their sheriff or the office he holds.

This has led to some of the most embarrassing moments in Sheriff Pace's administration, including when Deputy Lionel Johnson shot and killed an unarmed black teen that was trying to protect his elderly grandmother from being assaulted by Johnson, and when Detective Mike Traxler got caught by his wife having sex with another woman in his patrol car, which was then wrecked in a fit of anger and road rage. Finally, who could forget when Detective London Williams was convicted and sent to prison for molesting and sexually abusing his own biological daughter.

Sheriff Pace had been warned numerous times about these disgraced deputies that he was employing, but ultimately he refused to take affirmative action to prevent these crimes.

One of the biggest criticisms that Sheriff Pace regularly faces is his compulsive desire to try and attend every single funeral that takes place in Vicksburg. It is jokingly said that Sheriff Pace is the Warren County Funeral Director, not the sheriff.

Attending funerals, directing traffic, hugging widows, and making his presence seen is a high-profile way of keeping in visual contact with the voters. Family members at funerals want to know that their dearly departed loved ones were remembered and cared for by others, especially politicians. And Sheriff Pace exploits these advantages for purposes unrelated to helping the families grieve.

It was unsurprising, then, that when my process server and I went looking to serve the July trial subpoena on Sheriff Pace, that we couldn't find him. And no one at his office would tell us where he was. I immediately thought to check the cemetery.

We left the sheriff's office and drove to the city cemetery where we located, without difficulty, a large funeral taking place. Right in the middle of the crowd was Sheriff Pace hugging the old ladies and shaking the hands of the old men.

As the funeral concluded, we nondescriptly waited by Sheriff Pace's patrol car, and when he came to leave, my process server politely handed him the subpoena. He didn't know what it was at first, but I stepped up, said hello to my old antagonist, and told him it was another subpoena for the false arrest trial. This was the first time we'd seen each other since his testimony at the 2013 revocation hearing.

We stayed and talked for a few minutes and I told him that his testimony would not be needed the first day of trial and that there was no point in him attending until Tuesday, July 18. This was a professional courtesy to him because the subpoena commanded that he attend on Monday, July 17, and stay day-after-day until it was time for him to testify.

I knew that I would spend all day on Monday questioning Jackson and that I wouldn't get to any other witnesses until the following day. There was no point in Sheriff Pace or any of the other witnesses coming any earlier, so, in this, I was trying to be professional and not disrupt their lives anymore than necessary.

Once Sheriff Pace had been served we went to the Warren County courthouse to try and find Jan Hyland Daigre to serve her with her subpoena.

Her testimony was needed to validate the Mississippi Farm Bureau insurance records, to provide information about Emmett increasing the insurance shortly before the fire, and any investigation that Farm Bureau did into the cause of the fire.

I'd never met Daigre, and I didn't want to. She was related to me through marriage, was best friends with Emmett and all the Atwoods, and she'd abused her position as the Circuit Clerk of Warren County by becoming personally involved in some of my pending criminal cases in her office. I wanted no more contact with her than needed.

As we were walking up the stairs of the courthouse, we met Diagre coming down. My process server handed her the subpoena. I introduced myself and explained to her it was a subpoena to attend and testify in the false arrest trial.

I was going to explain to Daigre that she didn't actually need to show up to testify until Tuesday morning—not Monday as the subpoena commanded—but before I could do so Daigre was calling for deputies from the sheriff's office to come make me stop talking to her.

Of course, I complied with Daigre's request, but I did make a snide comment that I'd see her in court. Since she wanted to be a bitch she could just come to Aberdeen and stay all week until I decided to call her to testify. I'd expected nothing less from Daigre, and she proved my thoughts true.

This only left Emmett, Kade, and Teresa Lyle to serve with subpoenas. Thankfully, I'd developed a polite, working relationship with Josh's parents and they assured me that they would attend the trial without the necessity of having to be subpoenaed. I trusted their word and counted on them to be in court for trial on Tuesday.

I definitely did not want any kind of confrontation with Emmett or Kade. Nearly having to whip Kade's ass in the Mississippi Attorney General's Office gave me enough pause to purposely want to avoid another. So I had my process server go to their houses without me and get them served. Of course, neither were happy, but Judge Aycock had put her foot down. They were going to attend and testify and that was that.

This second trial was becoming more a game of chess than the checkers game we'd played in March. At the time, I'd been furious that Jackson violated Judge Aycock's direct orders and forced me to ask for a mistrial. But in hindsight, it allowed me to prepare much, much better the second go around and formulate a better, more complete strategy.

I decided to rewrite a significant part of my opening statement and rely less on rhetoric and more on preempting any of the various arguments that I knew Mr. Minor was going to try and make to excuse his client's deplorable conduct.

There was certainly going to be a time and place for strong rhetoric and fiery speeches during the trial. I had been working on a closing argument that I hoped would blow people away. But I decided to concentrate my opening statement on the evidence and testimony that the jurors could expect to hear.

I wanted to, early on, set the mood for the trial. I knew that Jackson was going to lie and that he was going to try and lie big; it was clear that honesty wasn't a concern of his. So I wanted the jury to expect that.

Mr. Minor's assertion that Judge Stewart's evidentiary findings at the preliminary hearing excused Jackson from making the false arrest also needed to be dealt with at the beginning. I was planning to knock that argument out of the ball park immediately. Stewart was not a real judge, was not an attorney, and did not have any legal training. So whatever findings he may have made were irrelevant.

Everything else was ready. My suits and dress shirts were cleaned and pressed. I bought a new pair of black dress shoes and a belt. And I updated my ties to bold colors like red, blue, and gold. I wanted some individuality in my wardrobe, but I also wanted to appear as a lawyer would trying a serious case in court.

On Saturday, July 15, 2017, I boarded the Amtrak train in Jackson for a three hour ride to Memphis. Sunday morning I was going to pick my friend, David, who had found and served Josh Chamblee with the subpoena, up from the airport.

David and I had met through a pen-pal service for inmates in prison. For more than three years he'd been a great friend, a wonderful communicator, and invaluable as an asset in helping me prepare for trial. He was also a doctor and a Democrat, and we never lacked for intelligent conversation.

Meeting for the first time that Sunday was the culmination of thousands of hours of emails, phone calls, and texts. And I was so glad to finally meet him.

After we rented a car we started the three-hour drive to Aberdeen. Because there weren't any hotels in Aberdeen, we had to either stay in a hotel in Tupelo or in Columbus. Thankfully, though, I found a bed and breakfast house for rent that was less than one block from the federal courthouse. Things were turning out to be perfect.

Aberdeen is a small town in the northeast, upper corner of Mississippi. When one sees the town for the first time it will remind one of a typical, small southern town. There are lots of magnolia trees, flowers and bushes, manicured lawns, and old storefronts in downtown. And sitting slightly off the main street is the United States Courthouse.

In addition to David, one of my other friends, Richard, came to visit and stay with us to watch the trial. However, there would be other friends and family coming and going throughout the week as they tried to juggle their jobs and also watch part of the trial.

There was almost an atmosphere of excitement as we prepared for the start of the trial on the following day. While David cooked barbeque on the grill and fixed drinks for us, I practiced delivering my opening statement.

I didn't know where Mr. Minor and Jackson were, but if I did I'd at least have invited Mr. Minor over to join us. After the way the last trial went I figured that Mr. Minor could have benefitted from a stiff drink, and by the way David was mixing the drinks one could tell that we thought we could benefit from them as well.

All was set, all was ready, and I hoped that this trial would go better than the last. David and Richard told me, though, that there was no way that we could lose. As I went to sleep that night I was hoping that they were right.

By the time we awoke the following morning I was a mass of nerves and anxiousness. As I got up and prepared to shower, David was telling me that we didn't have any hot water in the house. I thought that not having a hot shower was a bad way to start the day. However, upon closer inspection, I discovered that David had simply failed to operate the shower control head properly.

After Richard and I had our refreshingly hot morning showers (separately), I began getting dressed in the same suit that I'd worn on the first day of trial back in March. I wanted to make an instant first impression with my potential jurors and there was no way better than to dress the part.

I was too nervous to eat breakfast, but I seriously considered taking a swig of the previous night's liquor to calm my nerves. I didn't, though, and once everyone was ready we headed to the courthouse.

Compared to the federal courthouse in Oxford, the courthouse in Aberdeen is much smaller, with fewer courtrooms. We immediately noticed that there were a lot of people arriving at the same time we were; no doubt they were my potential jurors.

After being screened through security, David, Richard, and I made our way upstairs to Judge Aycock's courtroom. Already waiting were Mr. Minor, Jackson, and Mrs. Cameron Benton, a new attorney that had recently been assigned as an additional defense attorney for Jackson. After the way the last trial went I wasn't surprised that Jackson had more lawyers.

I took my seat at the table to the right and David sat right behind me. His job for the trial was to be the official paper shuffler and cheerleader. Richard sat with the audience and was ready to shoot texts to my phone if I was missing something, or had overlooked a potentially viable point that needed to be made during a witness's testimony. I wouldn't have traded my trial team for all the best lawyers in the world.

The last thing I did was place my Papaw's picture on the table so that he could watch me and watch over the trial as I did the best I could to make good on the promise that I made to him to vindicate myself.

Before the trial started I walked over to Mr. Minor, shook his hand, and offered to settle the case right then for $5,000—the cost of my bond. Mr. Minor shook my hand back, declined the offer to settle the case, and reminded me again that I would never win the trial. I had a smile on my face that morning, but I was seriously worried, too, that he might be right.

At 9:30 A.M. sharp, Judge Aycock walked in, we rose in respect, and she took her place on the bench. Also present were Parker, Daniel, and a new court employee, Mrs. Melinda. They all greeted Mr. Minor and I warmly and the trial began.

Judge Aycock introduced herself to the potential jurors and then introduced Mr. Minor, Jackson, myself, and then, surprisingly, my friend, Dr. David. The details of the case were then briefly explained to the potential jurors and we began with jury selection.

As in the first trial, I was given the opportunity to conduct jury *voir dire* first. And, as in the first trial, I needed to make sure that none of the jurors had any relationships or kinships to anyone involved in the case; none had.

I then delved into the gay issue. There was no doubt that there would be a lot of talk about gay relationships, gay drama, and Josh and I's relationship. I needed to make sure that it wouldn't be offensive to anyone.

Fortunately, several of the potential jurors raised their hands and explained that they didn't think they could be fair because their religion prohibited them from condoning or accepting anything even remotely related to the word gay.

It's always irked me when people hide behind their religion in order to discriminate against gays, lesbians, and transgenders. And it especially pissed me off when I had to listen to someone say that because of his or her religion they could not be fair and impartial in sitting on my jury. But I was careful not to let my frustration show. I thanked them for being honest, assured them they had a right to feel and believe the way they did, and I moved on to other areas.

Judge Aycock was going to excuse them from the jury no matter what, so I didn't need to spend any further time asking questions of those potential jurors.

I moved on to questioning the potential jurors about any relationships, friendships, or kinships they may of had with law enforcement officers. Almost everyone raised their hands.

It was going to be impossible to find a juror who didn't at least know one police officer or sheriff's deputy. What I needed to know, though, was whether or not their connections with that cop would prevent them from being fair and impartial in the trial.

Surprisingly, several raised their hands and stated that their connections with a cop would prevent them from standing in judgment of an officer like Jackson. From previous experience, I knew that these potential jurors would be excused and dismissed by Judge Aycock, so I moved on.

The last question that I asked was whether or not any of the potential jurors had ever worked for the telephone company or worked as a telephone repair person.

This seemed like an odd question, and I noticed that both Mr. Minor and Judge Aycock raised their heads and looked at me with quizzical expressions when I asked it, but I had a reason which would become clear during the trial.

Thankfully, all of my jurors denied ever working for the telephone company or being any type of utility repair person. I was glad to hear this because if someone had at one time worked for the telephone company, I'd of had to change a few things with my trial strategy.

When I was done with my jury *voir dire*, Mr. Minor had an opportunity to question the potential jurors, too. But his was quick and we moved on to picking the ultimate eight that would sit on my jury.

I knew who the three potential jurors were that I was going to strike. Judge Aycock, though, struck all of the potential jurors that had voiced negative opinions about gays and those whom stated that they could not stand in judgment of a law enforcement officer. That only left about sixteen people in which to choose from.

I already knew that Mr. Minor was going to try and strike all of the African-Americans that he could from my jury. I, on the other hand, was going to try and strike all of the old white men that I could as I felt that those were the type to be the least sympathetic to me.

My three strikes were used to get rid of the first of three old white men sitting on the first row. Richard and David, both, had been texting me during *voir dire* telling me that they were not getting good feelings from the first old white men in the first row, so my strikes were used on them.

Mr. Minor, in turn, struck all the blacks from the first row. With his choice of strikes, that left the first eight people that were going to be selected to serve on my jury. As Judge Aycock called out their names and asked them to come forward and be seated in the jury box I couldn't help but resign myself to the fact that I didn't get the jury demographics that I wanted.

Taking their seats one at a time were two white men, three white women, one black lady, one Hispanic man, and one Indian from India.

The two white men were employed as a salesman and forklift operator, respectively. The black lady was a nurse. The Hispanic man was a healthcare worker. The Indian was a physics professor at Mississippi State University. And of the three white women, one was a teacher, one was a stay-at-home mom, and the last worked as a secretary at her church. Into these hands fell my fate.

All in all, there was no arguing that my jury wasn't an intelligent jury. They all looked eager to hear the evidence and decide Jackson's and I's fate. I could have done worse and I could have done better. But as Donald Rumsfeld said after the disaster of the Iraq War, "It's better to go to war with the army you have than the one you don't."

Once the jury had been picked and seated, Judge Aycock dismissed us for lunch and set 1:00 P.M. as the time to begin opening statements. By this time I was calm again and ready to do battle against Jackson and all that he stood for.

CHAPTER THIRTY-TWO

On our lunch break I nibbled on some leftover barbeque from the night before even though I wasn't hungry. I did decide to have a drink, though, to calm my nerves, which had built back up into a crescendo. But when we returned to the courtroom I was even more nervous than before. It's almost like I felt that the first trial had only been a practice run. This second one was for real, though. And everything depended on my performance.

At one o'clock, Judge Aycock and her staff entered the courtroom and she called for the jury to take their seats in the jury box. I had my opening statement nearly memorized and I hoped it grabbed their attention.

> **JUDGE AYCOCK:** Welcome back everyone. It's now time for opening statements. Mr. Atwood will you come and make your opening statement?

I approached the podium and faced the jury for the first time in an up close and personal sort of way.

> **ME:** May it please the Court?
> **JUDGE AYCOCK:** You may proceed, Sir.

I took another deep breath, glanced back at David and Richard, took a sip of water, and began.

ME: I want to just briefly introduce myself again. As I said in jury *voir dire* my name is David Atwood and I am representing myself in this case. If I thought, though, that this would be a complicated case, or that I would need a slick talking lawyer to present this case to you, I guess I could have gone and found one, but I don't need some fancy Memphis lawyer to come down here to Aberdeen and explain to you one of the simplest and most straightforward legal cases I've ever seen. Let me start here by asking you a question: Have you ever in your life been falsely accused of something you didn't do? If not, let me tell you, it's not a good feeling.

I decided to ask this question to the jury to set the mood for how I was going to proceed with the rest of the case. My thinking was that if I could get the jury to remember a time in their own lives when they might have been accused of something they didn't do, then I could generate sympathy for me.

ME: To get an understanding I have to begin with a story. A story about a horrible and tragic fire that occurred on the night of November 10, 2009, in Kosciusko, Mississippi. That's seven years, eight months, and seven days ago. On that night my paternal grandfather's lake house burned to the ground. No one knows how and no one has ever been able to prove that it was an arson.

At this point, I turned around and pointed directly at Jackson, who was sitting far across the courtroom in between his two attorneys.

ME: The defendant there wishes it was an arson. He wishes that I did it. And he wishes that he had the evidence to prove it. But wishful thinking is one thing and reality is another. There's simply is not one shred of evidence that the fire was arson or that I was involved. This place, this lake house of my grandfather's was a place that I loved. On paper it belongs to my grandfather, Emmett Atwood, but in actuality it belonged to the family. It literally was the Atwood Lakehouse. I grew up there, I hunted in the woods, I fished in the lake, and I loved that house. And it killed me inside when I found out that it had been destroyed. The Atwood family, though, is a broken family. Money, petty jealousies, divorces, and alcoholism has destroyed this family. We are estranged from one another and it is a horrible, horrible situation. But I had nothing to do with the fire that destroyed that lake house.

To understand how the arson charge came about, the jury had to know about how screwed up the Atwood family was. I planned to use Emmett to prove this point, but I needed to lay the groundwork and make the jury aware very early on that they were going to hear some crazy shit involving the Atwoods. But once I'd touched on that topic I then turned my attention to Jackson.

> **ME:** But that defendant over there, James Jackson, a former deputy fire marshal, thinks I did. But the evidence doesn't support that belief and it never did. We are here to decide whether enough incriminating evidence existed to support probable cause for my arrest. If there was not enough evidence to support my involvement in the fire then I will be asking you to find in my favor. You will be deciding that this week.

This is where I left establishing the groundwork for the trial and turned to the rhetoric that was inherent in turning the hearts and minds of any jury that may be on the fence and torn between two competing views.

> **ME:** This case is not for the timid, though. It is not for the meek and mild in manner. This case is for courageous individuals who believe in the Constitution. At heart, this is a constitutional rights case. You are here this week to uphold the United States Constitution—the sole security, the sole protection we have against tyranny and oppression. So while you sit here now, I want you to be thinking about the Constitution and what it means to you. Ask yourselves, is the Constitution just an old piece of paper that we learned about in high school, or is it a living, breathing, guarantee of freedom, justice, and liberty for all? You are here today to protect that document, to protect the Constitution of

the United States of America. So I am telling you now, this is not the case for the shy and timid. It takes courage to defend the Constitution and it takes devotion. This case will require both.

There was an idea in my mind at the time that if I could convince this jury that I was on a crusade, that this case was worth caring about, was worth fighting for, that if I could get them excited about the power and message that they could send to the world with their verdict, then I could empower them to justify sympathizing with my cause very early on.

Mr. Minor was going to concentrate on technicalities and boring legal theories. I wanted to capture their attention and inspire them with their potential. This was a moral cause worth fighting for. And I needed something other than a boring recitation of the evidence and legal theories to convince them.

ME: Now, this trial is about to begin and you will have to sit and listen to the testimony of several witnesses. And I ask you to listen closely because you will never hear or see a single piece of evidence that indicates that this fire was an arson. You will hear speculation. You will hear lies. You will hear contradictions. But you will never hear or see any evidence proving that this horrible fire was an arson. You won't hear it because the defendant didn't do his job.

Over the summer, I'd developed several themes in which I planned to concentrate on throughout the trial. One thing that I kept coming back to was my belief that we could have found out the real cause of the fire if Jackson had simply done his job. But he didn't do his job, and nearly nine years later we are still left to wonder what happened.

This tied into the fact that Jackson didn't do his job because he rushed to judgment. He rushed to conclude that Chaney, Sheriff Pace, and Emmett were all correct in their assertions that I was guilty and he refused to consider any other alternative. He rushed to judgment.

ME: Every individual in the fire investigation has lied and changed their stories, often multiple times. The defendant there, James Jackson, has lied and changed his story. My ex-partner, Joshua Langston Chamblee, has lied and changed his story. My grandfather, Emmett Atwood, has lied and changed his story. Almost everyone in this case has lied and changed their stories. The one person, though, whom has never lied and never changed his story is myself. I have denied that I was responsible for the fire. I fully cooperated in the law enforcement investigation. And I have never changed my story. Even when everyone else was lying, pointing fingers, and changing stories, my story remained the same. I was not responsible for the fire, I have not lied about the fire, and my story has not changed for this trial. Everyone else's has, but not mine.

This was probably over the line about what should be allowed during an opening statement, especially since I was representing myself without an attorney. Essentially, what I was doing was testifying for myself without Mr. Minor having an opportunity to question me. That's normally not allowed in opening statements. But he didn't object and Judge Aycock didn't stop me. I was, however, careful not to try and put testimony from myself anywhere else in the trial.

> **ME:** The only reason we are here today is because the defendant rushed to judgment. He didn't do his job. And because he didn't do his job we don't know what really happened on the night of the fire. Other investigators attempted to do their jobs and the evidence they uncovered demonstrated that I am innocent and not involved in the fire. But this defendant here refused to do his job and instead, relied on the path of least resistance. He relied upon the tainted opinions of others and failed to employ his own ability to think and reason. He rushed to judgment. And because he rushed to judgment I was wrongly and illegally arrested and incarcerated for a fire that was never even proven to be an arson. The defendant knew that there was no proof that the fire was arson. The defendant knew that evidence existed proving my innocence. And the defendant knew that he was being politically pressured by his superiors to make an illegal arrest for political retribution purposes.

I was going to come back to the motives for why I was politically targeted, but first, I needed to inform the jury of exactly what evidence there was so that they could begin forming their opinions about the case based on something more than my rhetoric.

ME: Now, let's talk about some of the evidence in this case. We have physical evidence and we will also have evidence given by witnesses appearing here in court and testifying. The physical evidence will show, first and foremost, that the cause of the fire was simply undeterminable. Nobody knows what happened. Second, the evidence will show that my cell phone was in use in another part of the state at the time of the fire, indicating, of course, that I was nowhere near where the fire occurred. Footprints and tire tracks were found near the scene of the fire, but none of those prints and tracks matched the size or style of my shoe or vehicle. You're also going to see insurance records showing where my grandfather, Emmett Atwood, suspiciously had the insurance increased on the lake house shortly before the fire and had taken pictures of the inside and outside of the house four days before the fire, ostensibly for insurance purposes. Incredibly, Emmett's nephew, Kade Atwood, who lives within several hundred feet of the lake house, allegedly slept through the majority of the fire and never called the fire department when he discovered the fire. This is what we call exculpatory evidence. Exculpatory evidence demonstrates innocence. But let's talk about incriminating evidence. The only evidence, unreliable as it is, was a statement from my ex-partner, Josh Chamblee, telling the defendant that I burned the house down. Now, what the defendant doesn't want you to know is that Josh had previously given me two alibi statements swearing that I was with him in another part of the state on the night of the fire. The defendant doesn't want you to know that he had to force Josh Chamblee into giving that third, incriminating statement by threatening Josh with an arrest warrant if he didn't change his story. He also promised Josh a reward of $25,000.00. Well, what do you think Josh Chamblee did? He faced a choice of either going to jail or changing his story and implicating me in the fire. That day, Josh Chamblee decided to go home rather than go to jail. The defendant relied on this patently false, coerced statement to obtain my arrest warrant even though he knew that Josh Chamblee had previously been arrested and charged with lying and filing false police reports with law enforcement officers in Louisiana.

By this time I hoped I had hooked the jury with the story line and hadn't lost them in the details. It was essential that they understand that Jackson never had any evidence of arson; that almost all the evidence demonstrated my innocence; and that Josh's third statement was false, coerced, and was completely unreliable given Josh's past history. I hope I had made my points.

ME: Throughout this trial you will have to ask yourselves whether a reasonable, well-trained law enforcement officer could legitimately believe that (a) a crime occurred; and (b) that I committed it. I mean, ask yourselves now, and be thinking about this during the trial, does it not mean anything to the defendant that the shoe and tire tracks on the lake house property can't be matched to me? Does it not mean anything that the cell phone records show that I was in a different part of the state at the time of the fire? And Emmett Atwood's insurance records. This defendant rushed to judgment so quick that he didn't even take the time to question Emmett about the suspicious circumstances behind the recent increase in insurance. And the unbelievable fact that Kade Atwood allegedly slept through this fire and never called the fire department when he discovered it. James Jackson wants to have it two ways. He wants you to believe something that is physically impossible, yet he also wants you to believe that he faithfully executed the duties of his office in investigating this fire. Well, he can't have his cake and eat it too. So you're gonna have to ask yourselves at some point whether or not you believe in coincidences. After hearing the testimony in this trial and seeing the evidence can you honestly call the actions of Emmett and Kade coincidences? This case is full of coincidences, though. But not one single coincidence implicates me as being responsible for the fire.

This had been one of the most unexplainable facts about the fire. Occam's Razor led me to conclude that the fire was arson and that it was started with Emmett's and Kade's approval. There was no other way to explain Kade sleeping through the fire, not calling the fire department, and Emmett increasing the insurance by so much so close to the time of the fire.

These coincidences were going to have to be considered by the jury, and the earlier in the trial that they began to consider that suspicious evidence the better. This was in line with my decision to proceed using a two-part theory and allow the jury to hash it out.

> **ME:** Now, the defendant and his team of lawyers are going to try and make a big deal about a little informal court hearing that I had called a preliminary hearing. At that preliminary hearing, an Attala County Justice Court judge rubber-stamped a document declaring there to be sufficient probable cause to bind the case over to a grand jury. In effect, the defense is going to try and convince you that even though James Jackson didn't have enough evidence to prove I was guilty of committing a crime, that he should nonetheless be excused for executing this wrongful and illegal arrest because a justice court judge rubber-stamped a routine legal document handing the case over to a grand jury.

This is where it became clear that having a practice run with the March 2017 trial was going to benefit me the most. It was then that I learned that Mr. Minor was going to base his defense on the fact that Stewart allegedly found probable cause at the preliminary hearing.

Knowing Mr. Minor's strategy helped me form the perfect counterpunch to his belief that Stewart's findings at the October 2011 preliminary hearing excused Jackson from making an illegal arrest two months prior.

The Fifth Circuit case law on false arrest was pretty clear. They've held multiple times that the constitutional violation for false arrest occurs at the moment of arrest and that any probable cause findings by a judge at a later date are not relevant to the analysis for that claim.

There would be plenty of time to argue points of law such as that when we debated the contents of the jury instructions given at the end of the trial. For the time being, though, I wanted to discredit Judge Stewart and the ridiculous notion that his probable cause determination at the preliminary hearing excused Jackson's illegal arrest of me.

ME: You need to know two things. Two very important things. First, that justice court judge, Ronnie Stewart, he isn't a real judge. He's never been to law school, he's never been an attorney, and he doesn't have a legal background. He's spent most of his life as a simple telephone repairman.

I saw several people in the courtroom, including members of the jury, nod their heads in acknowledgment of my earlier questions during jury *voir dire* about whether any of them had ever worked for the telephone company.

My intention was certainly not to demean telephone repairmen. The only point I was trying to make was that telephone repairmen have no business sitting in judgment in criminal cases such as mine. And I believe the jury immediately understood that point.

ME: In Mississippi, however, justice court judges do not have to be attorneys. It's wrong. It's not right. It's a law left on the books from 200 years ago, but the fact remains nevertheless that this justice court judge, Ronnie Stewart—the man the defense is hoping will save their case—was nothing more than a telephone repairman. And they want you to base your independent, fair, reasonable verdict on the rubber-stamp of a man who likes to dress up and play judge.

Having dealt with the now discredited probable cause determination that Stewart made at my preliminary hearing, I turned next to further solidifying my contention that this arrest was illegal and without probable cause.

ME: More importantly, in this probable cause determination, you should keep in mind that you aren't the first jury to decide whether probable cause existed—whether there was enough evidence to suggest that it was more likely than not that I committed a crime. That's what grand juries do in Mississippi. They only decide whether there is enough probable cause to indict a person for a crime. They do basically what you are doing here today. Do you know what the Attala County grand jury did when they heard the defendant and the evidence he had? They threw it out. They kicked it out the backdoor of the Attala County courthouse. The grand jury no-billed the criminal charge. They firmly and clearly stated that there was not probable cause in this case. This lawsuit case, this case were are here on today, is the result of that grand jury decision. They declared that there wasn't any probable cause, and now I am asking you to hold that defendant responsible for pursuing a false criminal case when he knew that there was not any evidence to support his wishful thinking.

I've always thought that the grand jury's decision not to indict me for arson should be one of the main events in the case that the false arrest lawsuit jury should concentrate on when determining whether Jackson should be held liable or not.

If my jurors in Aberdeen knew that a prior jury had already helped decide one of the central decisions of the case in my favor, then it may make it easier for them to decide in my favor, too. That was my thought at least.

ME: Now, I am sure you are asking yourselves, why would the defendant do this? Why would he rush to judgment? Why would he frame this kid knowing there was not any evidence of a crime? And I want to be clear about one thing. This fire occurred on the night of November 10, 2009, and for almost two years the defendant didn't pursue this case. It was pretty much a closed case. He couldn't determine whether the fire was arson, I had a stone solid alibi, and the physical evidence indicated I was not involved. Case closed. Moving on to bigger and better things. But in June 2011, almost two years after the fire, it's like this defendant woke up from a coma and got a shot of adrenaline in the arm. He started shaking the tree limbs hoping that something would fall out. He hounded and harassed Josh Chamblee's family until they finally told him where Josh was. He got the warrant for Josh and forced Josh into a coerced lie. And then he quickly moved to effect an arrest on me. So ask yourselves, Why the urgency? What happened in June of 2011 to spur this defendant into action?

Everyone in the courtroom—except the jury—knew what was coming. In addition to the notes and prompts I'd brought to the podium for my opening arguments, I'd also brought my book, *Into Hell I Rode*, with me. And I'd left it conspicuously sitting on the podium, facing the jury, only feet away.

The last jury in March had instantly made the connection between the book and my illegal arrest. I could tell that I'd pumped and primed this latest jury for this connection, too.

> **ME:** Let me tell you why. This (indicating by holding *Into Hell I Rode* up for the jury to see) is a book I wrote and published in June 2011. It's called *Into Hell I Rode*. This book is the most detailed account ever written of the long and abusive history of political and law enforcement corruption in Vicksburg and Warren County, Mississippi. Contained within these pages is the true story about how the citizens of Vicksburg and Warren County were abused, mistreated, victimized, and in some cases raped and killed by members of the Warren County Sheriff's Department and the politicians and elected leaders that stood by and allowed it to happen. In these pages are the names of friends, family members, and colleagues of the defendant and his boss, the state fire marshal, Mike Chaney. Within two weeks of this book being published, the defendant, at Mike Chaney's direct insistence, reopened the closed fire investigation, coerced a false statement from Josh Chamblee, and had me arrested. And that is what makes this defendant's and his coconspirators' actions so wrong and malicious. They did not arrest me because a crime had been committed. They arrested me in political retaliation for my public and outspoken stance against government corruption and abuse.

As with the first jury, the second jury immediately showed their understanding of what the publishing of my book meant. Several jurors even nodded their heads slightly as though everything in a complicated game of puzzles and riddles had suddenly become crystal clear. I'd succeeded in making the connection again. The only thing left to do was prove it.

> **ME:** This type of political retaliation is exactly why I told you that this case is not for the timid. It's not for the mild and meek in manner. This is a case for the courageous because I am asking you to stop this abuse. To help stop this corruption and uphold

the Constitution and send a message that these type of Gestapo tactics will not be tolerated in America. I am asking you to hold this defendant responsible for destroying the Constitution. And you can do that with your verdict.

I'd finally come full circle with my opening statement and switched back to the rhetoric that I'd need to convince my jury to rule in my favor.

In hard times, in difficult legal cases, people want to be inspired. They want to be entertained. They want to believe in a cause worth fighting for. That was why I laced my opening arguments with hyperbole.

I needed to do more than just convince my jury that Jackson illegally arrested me. I needed to embolden every one of them to go against their base instincts and realize that not every law enforcement officer is the Andy Griffith of Mayberry. They had to understand that Jackson, Chaney, Sheriff Pace, and every other officer involved in my illegal arrest represented a Nazi-like, totalitarian threat to our system of justice and liberty—an Axis of Corruption.

The only way I knew to help the jury understand my zeal, to understand my passion, was to rely on the rhetoric. No jury wanted to be bored with a monotone recitation of facts, figures, evidence, and testimony. And I knew this. So, once again, I turned it up.

ME: In this case you're going to hear the good, the bad, and the ugly. I'm sure there will be name-calling. I'm sure you will hear bad things about me and all the other witnesses. But you will also hear the lies and changed stories of the fire investigation witnesses. You will meet a group of law enforcement officers whose personal motto has become, Admit nothing, deny everything, and make counteraccusations. From the defendant and his team of lawyers you will hear the three D's of dishonesty. You will hear discrepancy. You will hear deception. And you will hear distortion. But I believe that you are an intelligent jury. I hope that you are a courageous jury. Because this is a search for justice. This is an opportunity to take an active role in defending the Constitution of the United States. So don't be fooled by the defendant's game of smoke and mirrors. The defense will now have an opportunity to address you when I finish. I hope you will be able to see through the smokescreen they are about to blow your way. Because what the defendant did to me and my family was wrong. It was malicious, and it was illegal. But you now have the opportunity to right that wrong.

As I finished my opening statement I'd been able to maintain eye contact with all the jurors; they'd been attentive, responded with the appropriate body language, and seemed eager to accept and believe what I was telling them.

In the short fifteen minutes that I had to deliver my opening statement, I'd been able to cover what evidence they would expect—both good and bad—to hear and see, and I'd been able to, in my opinion, undercut any argument that Mr. Minor may have been able to make regarding the preliminary hearing finding that Judge Stewart made.

I recognized Stewart's alleged finding of probable cause as the number one biggest obstacle to me winning my case. I knew, however, that Stewart had always, in every single case, found probable cause and binded the case over to a grand jury. Mr. Minor, to my knowledge, didn't know this fact. So it undercut his assertion that Stewart's findings were legitimate.

I also had Mrs. Jordan. Mr. Minor didn't know that Mrs. Jordan was going to testify that Stewart always found probable cause in criminal cases, even when a third-party appeared before him and confessed to committing the crime rather than the defendant. This, too, undercut the legitimacy of Stewart's findings.

One thing that I could not understand before the trial began was Mr. Minor's failure to question any of the witnesses that I had listed on the pretrial order. He certainly had the right to, but he didn't. And I think that had he interviewed my witnesses he'd of known about Stewart's probable cause findings in the justice courts and their illegitimacy.

It was now, however, Mr. Minor's turn to make his opening arguments to the jury, and I was anxiously awaiting them. I wanted to know what he would change and do differently than he did at the first trial. I don't know if he expected me to change my strategy from the first trial, but I was hoping he hadn't changed his.

CHAPTER THIRTY-THREE

No sooner than I'd set back down in my chair, Mr. Minor came bounding forward to deliver his opening statement. I think at this time that he still believed that Jackson had conducted a competent, fair investigation and had acted appropriately in acquiring both Josh's and I's arrest warrants. I didn't know how his second opening statement in this case would go, but I expected it to be similar to the first.

MR. MINOR: Good morning ladies and gentleman. My name is Wilson Minor and I represent James Jackson, a former deputy fire marshal. This is not a criminal case. The issue in this case is whether my client violated Mr. Atwood's Fourth Amendment rights by going to get an arrest warrant. So the issue is not whether Mr. Atwood burnt down the Atwood Lakehouse or whether the State can prove that. The issue is whether James Jackson lied to a judge and provided false evidence in getting that warrant. That's what we're here to decide.

So far Mr. Minor was proceeding as I thought he would. However, I thoroughly disagreed with him when he tried to argue that the jury shouldn't be concerned with whether I had burnt the lake house down. One of the first things that I had to prove in this case was that Jackson did not have probable cause (i.e., evidence to prove arson and that I committed it) to go get my arrest warrant. So the evidence from the investigation was crucial.

> **MR. MINOR:** There's one thing I agree with, though. This is a simple case. I expect the evidence to show the following: That on 11/11/2009 Emmett Atwood's lake house burned down and on that date Sheriff Tim Nail called Mr. Jackson at the Fire Marshal's Office and told him that he thought an arson had occurred. Two days later Mr. Jackson goes out to investigate at the scene of the fire. And he attempts to collect forensic evidence. He did try to use a piece of equipment called a hydrocarbon detector to try and detect an accelerant. His hydrocarbon detector kept going off because the fire was still going and there's smoke and dust and it keeps setting it off. So he stops doing that.

At this point I knew that Jackson had led his attorney into a bad trap. Jackson was trying, as he did at the first trial, to make it seem like it was possible that an accelerant was used to start the fire, but because of the residual heat, smoke, and dust he was unable to get an accurate reading.

What Mr. Minor hadn't been told, however, was that Jackson had testified at the preliminary hearing before Judge Stewart that he in actuality had used his hydrocarbon detector, that it was working correctly, that it didn't give any false readings, and that he detected no accelerant. The trap had been set.

> **MR. MINOR:** But the investigation does not stop right there. Just because he's unable to collect any forensic evidence does not mean that an arson didn't occur. So Mr. Jackson goes to talk to Emmett Atwood, Mr. David Atwood's paternal grandfather and the owner of the lake house. And he tells Mr. Jackson that he believes his grandson, Mr. David Atwood, burned down the Atwood Lakehouse because of numerous disagreements and feuds they'd been having in the past. So Mr. Jackson then gets in touch with Joshua Langston Chamblee, Mr. Atwood's boyfriend. And he talks to him at Kentucky Fried Chicken in Carthage. And it's true, Mr. Chamblee denied any involvement in the fire and he said that he and David were in Starkville the night the fire occurred. However, my client doesn't believe Josh Chamblee based on his body language and demeanor. He thinks he's lying. And he's trying to cover it up. So he takes Chamblee's statement at the KFC and at that point the trail goes cold. Now it's true that over

a year later Mr. Jackson decides to reopen the investigation and he attempts to get in touch with Josh Chamblee and his family to find out where he is. Chamblee's mother tells my client that Josh is in Indianapolis and that he'll be coming home for the Neshoba County Fair in July 2011. Now, Mr. Jackson made several calls to Chamblee's mother to see where he was to get another statement.

At this point I felt that Mr. Minor was deliberately understating Jackson's attempts at contacting Josh. To imply that Jackson easily contacted Josh through his mother after only one try is a serious attempt to downplay the fact that Jackson's tactics in that regard can be construed as nothing short but pure harassment. But I would take care of that once Jackson began testifying.

> **MR. MINOR:** So finally, Josh comes to the Neshoba County Fair. Now, it is true that my client did obtain a warrant for Josh's arrest. However, he never served the warrant. Josh Chamblee voluntarily came to the Leake County Sheriff's Department and gave a statement. In fact, Mr. Jackson never even told Josh or his family that he had a warrant.

This was another mistake in Mr. Minor's opening that I made note of to disprove when Jackson testified. And it was a glaring mistake. Jackson's investigative report clearly states that he told Josh's mother that he'd be arrested if he didn't come give another statement and implicate me in the fire.

I'd obviously never acted as my own attorney before in a jury trial. But one refrain I'd heard over and over from the legal community was never promise anything to a jury that one wouldn't later be able to deliver. I thought this was a serious mistake to make the argument to the jury that Josh wasn't coerced into making the third statement because he feared for his arrest.

> **MR. MINOR:** So they sit Josh down because his mother had previously indicated to my client that Josh was ready to tell the truth and the only reason that he hadn't told the truth before was because Mr. Atwood had threatened him to do something to him or his family. So my client sits down with Josh and he tells

them that David started the fire, that he drove Mr. Atwood to Kosciusko, and then watched him burn down the Atwood Lakehouse. And Mr. Jackson recorded that statement and you will hear that statement. He also got a written statement and he took it to Attala County to the justice court and then went into the judge's chambers, Ronnie Stewart, who will also testify, and my client gave him an affidavit saying, swearing under oath that he believed that David Atwood had started this fire. He also showed him the written statement from Josh Chamblee. The judge issued a warrant for Mr. Atwood's arrest. A few days later Mr. Atwood turned himself in and bonded out after being booked for about ten minutes. A few weeks later they had a preliminary hearing in front of the same judge. My client testified and told him all the facts and the judge still found probable cause. Now, the Plaintiff wants you to find significance in the fact that the grand jury did not indict him. However, you will hear testimony from my client that he told them about Chamblee's third statement that implicated Mr. Atwood in the fire. And he will also testify that he arrested Josh Chamblee to come testify before the grand jury. But the district attorney never called Chamblee to testify before the grand jury. So the grand jury never heard Chamblee's testimony.

From having read Judge Aycock's order on summary judgment that she issued in July 2016, I knew that whether Judge Stewart or the grand jury later found or did not find probable cause was immaterial to the case. False arrest claims are based on whether probable cause existed at the *time* of the arrest.

In my case, the only issue was whether James Jackson had probable cause on the day I was arrested to believe that I committed arson. Judge Aycock had been very specific about that specific requirement and the Fifth Circuit and United States Supreme Court case law reflected that precedent.

Whether Judge Stewart later found probable cause or not at my preliminary hearing two months after my arrest was irrelevant. Likewise, whether a grand jury later found probable cause to indict me was also immaterial. False arrest cases are judged from the precedent of whether probable cause existed to believe a crime had occurred at the moment of the arrest.

It was a smooth move by Mr. Minor, and I had to give him credit for making that defense. After all, Judge Stewart did find that there was probable cause to bind my case over to the grand jury, even after hearing almost all of the exculpatory evidence proving my innocence.

What Mr. Minor and his client failed to take into account was that Judge Stewart wasn't an attorney, he wasn't a real judge. He had no legal training, and, based on my foresight into interviewing Judge Stewart before the trial, I knew that Judge Stewart, in his twelve years on the bench had never failed to find probable cause in a criminal case.

It was clear that Judge Stewart would find "probable cause" no matter what the evidence showed. And I was easily going to prove that through Stewart's testimony and the testimony of Rosalind Jordan.

This was the point in Mr. Minor's opening statement that I realized that he and his client were going to base their whole defense on the fact that Judge Stewart found "probable cause" at the preliminary hearing two months after my arrest. But this time I was a thousand times more prepared to deal with that defense than I had at the first trial.

In the lead-up to, and throughout the second trial, I realized more and more what a blessing it was for Jackson to throw the case down the tubes in March and require a mistrial. Had I not been granted a mistrial at the first trial, I probably would have lost the entire case because I was so utterly unprepared to deal with Mr. Minor's defense that his client should not be held accountable for my false arrest because Judge Stewart allegedly found "probable cause" at the preliminary hearing.

As I sat and finished listening to Mr. Minor's opening statement I couldn't help but be thankful for the earlier mistrial. That trial had given me such a better opportunity to prepare. And as Mr. Minor hit his two minute mark that signified his time was almost up, I thanked God for small miracles.

> **MR. MINOR:** At the end of the day I think you will find that my client acted reasonably and reasonably relied on Josh Chamblee's third statement. He was not aware of any evidence that Chamblee had a motivation to lie about David Atwood, the plaintiff. He reasonably determined that his statement was credible and that he reasonably relied on that in obtaining an arrest warrant. And at the end of the trial I'll ask that you return a verdict in favor of my client, James O'Neal Jackson.

Some things in Mr. Minor's opening statement had definitely changed from the first trial. But overall I think he'd done a pretty good job. But I knew his client was keeping important facts from him. I also knew that his client was about to massacre himself on the witness stand and, more than likely, commit perjury. I just didn't know that it was going to be as bad as it actually turned out to be.

This time I was thoroughly prepared, my boxing gloves were on, and I was ready for the rounds to begin. As I prepared to call Jackson as my first witness, I had no doubt in my mind that my past capabilities in running a gay inquisition when it came to the scumbag, cheating, lying boyfriends I'd admitted into my life in the past was going to serve me extremely well. As I'd said before, Jackson was a lot like these pathological and compulsive liars I've dated in the past. He would lie about lies and tell more lies to cover past lies. But I would never let him get away with a single one.

CHAPTER THIRTY-FOUR

Judge Aycock had been bright and chipper all morning as we went through jury *voir dire* and opening statements. Just as in the first trial, she had never warned me, admonished me, or cautioned me about my behavior in her courtroom. Too many times I've seen people that weren't attorneys try to represent themselves in court and it usually went horribly wrong. But I knew Judge Aycock expected only the best out of me and wasn't going to cut me any slack. So I made mental notes to myself not to violate that trust.

JUDGE AYCOCK: Mr. Atwood, who would you call as your first witness?

ME: Your Honor, I call the defendant, James O'Neal Jackson to the stand.

JUDGE AYCOCK: Mr. Jackson, will you come take the stand and be sworn?

ME: Your Honor, may I have permission to treat the defendant as an adverse witness?

JUDGE AYCOCK: Yes. Yes, you may treat him as an adverse witness.

Asking the judge to treat a witness as an "adverse" or "hostile" witness allows an attorney—or in this case, me—to ask leading and provoking questions of him. It's almost a superfluous exercise because it's expected that I would automatically be able to ask leading questions to

Jackson, but I'd heard the question asked a thousand times on the television shows and courtroom dramas, so I decided to do it myself.

As we had at the previous trial, I went through Jackson's education, his past employments, and his experience in investigating fires. One of my first questions about his education in fire investigations immediately set the mood for the rest of the day.

> **ME:** What fire investigation manual do you follow when you are investigating possible arsons?
> **JACKSON:** We follow a manual that teaches you the basics of fire investigations, electrical fires, all kinds of fire scenes. It tells you how to do reports and make findings. It helps us determine whether they are accidental or arson.
> **ME:** And you failed that course, right?
> **JACKSON:** I passed it.

I then went through and had Jackson explain what a hydrocarbon detector is and what it does and what type of tools and instruments he brings to fire scenes when he goes to investigate. I wanted the jury to know immediately, though, that Jackson never found any accelerants that may have been used to start the fire, and, when asked whether he'd detected any, Jackson stated that he did not because his hydrocarbon detector kept getting "false positives."

There was a plan that I'd devised before trial to destroy Jackson's credibility little by little. I knew him to be an opportunistic liar who would tell the jury anything in response to a question whether it was the truth or not.

Jackson clearly was only interested in testifying to what he thought, at that moment, was the better answer to provide, regardless of whether it was the truth or not.

My strategy was not to figuratively knock Jackson's credibility out in the first round, but I was definitely going to cause its death by a thousand different paper cuts. So after I'd established Jackson's background, I made my first slash.

> **ME:** How many fires do you think you've investigated?
> **JACKSON:** Probably 300.
> **ME:** Have you ever falsely arrested someone in one of those

cases?

JACKSON: [shrugs shoulders.]

ME: How many counties are you in charge of?

JACKSON: Nine.

ME: Do you remember testifying in the previous trial that you were in charge of eleven counties?

JACKSON: Yes.

ME: Do you remember testifying at the previous trial that you couldn't remember how many fires you've investigated?

JACKSON: Yes.

ME: So now your story is changing?

JACKSON: Yes.

These may seem like insignificant details, and in isolation they would have been. But Jackson was either in the full throes of Alzheimer's or he was just making shit up as we went along. I knew, however, that this was just the tip of the iceberg. I would catch Jackson in many, many more lies as we went along. And I really got the feeling that Jackson was so convinced of his righteousness and eventual vindication that he didn't even try to come across as a competent, honest law enforcement officer; I don't think he cared what happened to him.

We next moved over into his reasons for waiting two days to go investigate the fire. I knew that the real reason he waited was because he didn't want to interrupt his Veterans' Day holiday. But like he'd done in the first trial, Jackson tried to blame his dilatory actions on Sheriff Nail and the ridiculous belief that he had to wait two days for Sheriff Nail to get a "consent to search" form signed by Emmett Atwood.

What Jackson apparently didn't know was that I had Emmett's consent to search form that he signed early on the morning of 11/11/2009, only a few hours after the fire was discovered. But Jackson tried to play it off.

ME: Why couldn't you come back after that first day to investigate more?

JACKSON: I can only investigate for that first day. If I leave, I have to secure the scene. And if you come back the second day you would have to get a search warrant.

ME: If Emmett Atwood said that you could come back on

the second day to investigate, would you still need a search warrant? Or, let me ask the question this way. Can a homeowner give you continuous permission to come back to a fire scene on consecutive days to investigate?

JACKSON: Yes. A homeowner can.

ME: You talked about a scene being unsecured. But this scene was unsecured for two days from November 11th, 2009, until November 13th, 2009. So when you arrived on scene on November 13th, 2009, was the scene secured?

JACKSON: No.

ME: Okay. Let me get something straight. The consent to search form was signed by Emmett Atwood on November 11th, but according to you, Sheriff Nail and you could only investigate on the exact day the consent to search form was signed. So according to your testimony you would have needed a search warrant to go back out there on November 13th?

JACKSON: This search was done under Sheriff Nail's authority. He's the lead investigator, not me. I'm just there to assist.

ME: But did Sheriff Nail obtain my arrest warrant?

JACKSON: No, I did.

ME: Why did you really wait two days before going out there to investigate?

MR. MINOR: Objection. Asked and answered.

JUDGE AYCOCK: Overruled.

JACKSON: Because Sheriff Nail could only meet me on the thirteenth.

ME: But isn't it important to get to a scene and preserve evidence?

JACKSON: It is.

ME: Did you voice any concern to Sheriff Nail about the need to investigate this fire as soon as possible?

JACKSON: No.

ME: Because it wasn't that important at the time was it?

JACKSON: It was important, but I was probably busy working another fire. And as I said, I had to wait on Sheriff Nail.

I moved on at this point because I realized that age old adage that it's impossible to get blood from a turnip. No matter how bad Jackson's testimony became, he would always tell another lie to cover the last lie even if the whole charade looked ridiculous to everyone in the courtroom, even to the ones whose opinions mattered the most—the jury.

One of the most important parts of Jackson's overall testimony that needed destroying the most was his excuse that he couldn't detect any accelerants—which, by this implication, he was trying to imply that there might have been some there because his hydrocarbon detector kept getting false positives from the heat, smoke, and dust.

> **ME:** So at some point in your investigation you used your hydrocarbon detector?
>
> **JACKSON:** Yes.
>
> **ME:** So two days after the fire you finally go out to investigate. You may have taken pictures first, you may have used your rake and shovel. Who knows what you did. You may have even fished in the lake. Who knows. No one knows just what really happened. But at some point you used your hydrocarbon detector. What happened when you used it?
>
> **JACKSON:** It went off.
>
> **ME:** Indicating what?
>
> **JACKSON:** A false positive.
>
> **ME:** Would the ground still being hot give a false positive?
>
> **JACKSON:** Yes.
>
> **ME:** Okay. And as you know the fire department was never called to the scene to extinguish the fire. Correct?
>
> **JACKSON:** Correct.
>
> **ME:** After November 13th, why did you not attempt to go back to the scene when things cooled down and quit smoking to use the hydrocarbon detector again?
>
> **JACKSON:** Because I was done with my investigation. I didn't need to go back. And I'd of needed to ask the homeowner to come back or go get a search warrant from a judge.
>
> **ME:** Did you ever ask Emmett Atwood for another consent to search to come back out and investigate?
>
> **JACKSON:** No.
>
> **ME:** Were you not concerned with determining the cause of the fire? Was it not important enough not to go back out to try and find the real cause of the fire?

JACKSON: Yeah. It was important. I just didn't see a need at the time to go back.

ME: Because you rushed to judgment?

JACKSON: I didn't rush to judgment.

ME: But from day one Emmett and Kade Atwood said that I started this fire.

JACKSON: They implicated you in it.

ME: So case closed? Emmett says his grandson did it. We're feuding. So case closed. You didn't want to go back out to conduct a competent investigation? You didn't want to do anymore tests because you rushed to judgment. Correct?

MR. MINOR: Objection. Asked and answered.

JUDGE AYCOCK: Sustained.

ME: Just to be clear, though, you never, after using your hydrocarbon detector at different areas around the house, found any accelerants?

JACKSON: Correct.

ME: What other steps did you take in the investigation?

JACKSON: At that time, nothing.

ME: Was there ever a desire on your part to do a thorough investigation to try and determine the cause of the fire?

JACKSON: I thought I was thorough. I just didn't see any sense in going back.

ME: But in a fire investigation, isn't determining the cause of the fire the most important part?

JACKSON: It is.

ME: And you were never able to determine the cause of the fire?

JACKSON: No, I didn't.

In order for me to make my argument that I was made a suspect in this fire investigation not because the evidence led them to conclude it was arson and that I committed it, but, instead, was the result of political pressure from Emmett to Chaney and on down to Jackson, I had to prove that Jackson's primary focus was not on collecting evidence but in pursuing me and what Emmett and Chaney wanted.

Jackson is either the most incompetent fire investigator that ever existed, or he simply bought hook, line, and sinker Emmett's and Chaney's beliefs that this fire was arson and that I started it. I believe it was a little of both, and I had to make that point in every way that I could.

> **ME:** Is it possible that if you would have come back at a later date you might have been able to determine the cause of the fire?
> **JACKSON:** It's possible. But then you would have needed to leave someone there to secure the scene until you come back. And we and the sheriff's department don't have the personnel for that—to leave someone there 24/7.

I couldn't let Jackson get away with this one. It was becoming too easy so early in the trial to catch him in his lies, distortions, and discrepancies. It was just as I predicted in my opening statement. Jackson was making my case for me. All I needed to do was ask the right question.

> **ME:** Okay. If that's truly the case, then why even go out there on the thirteenth when the fire scene had been unsecured for over two days? If it's that big of a deal that the scene is unsecured, why did you wait two days to go out there?
> **JACKSON:** Like I said before, I had to go with Sheriff Nail. He's the lead investigator.
> **ME:** Did Sheriff Nail determine for you whether or not you could come back out to the fire scene at a later date to continue the investigation?
> **JACKSON:** I don't think it was discussed.
> **ME:** But you made the decision not to try and go back out to the fire scene?
> **JACKSON:** Yes.
> **ME:** But you don't know what really caused the fire?
> **JACKSON:** I don't.

One might think that before a fire marshal could proceed with obtaining arrest warrants for arson he should have at least determined what caused the fire. But it was clear that Jackson was just as ignorant to the cause as any other person. He didn't need a cause as long as he was willing to accept Emmett's word as the gospel.

The origins of the fire had been accepted as malicious by everyone in the Atwood family. They were absolutely convinced that the fire was arson, though I'm sure they had no idea that Jackson could never prove—and it's fair to say never attempted to prove—that the fire was arson. I felt I had to pound this fact into the jury as much as possible to get them to understand how illegal this arrest really was.

Even though Mr. Minor attempted to convince the jury that we weren't there in court to determine whether I started the fire or not, I knew it was essential to prove that there was never a basis to begin with to make the argument that the fire was arson. And I needed to prove just how incompetent Jackson was to show the jury that not only was he a horrible investigator, but a willing participant in a crime to illegally arrest me even though he knew that he could not prove this fire was an arson. I had to establish that there was a possibility that this fire was something other than maliciously set.

>**ME:** So there's doubt in your mind whether this fire was an arson?
>
>**JACKSON:** Well, there were no storms or lightning.
>
>**ME:** So what other steps did you take to try and determine the cause of the fire?
>
>**JACKSON:** Josh Chamblee's name came up and I met him at the KFC.
>
>**ME:** But that was five months after the fire. We're talking about what caused the fire. So surely there was doubt in your mind and probably doubt today on whether it was an arson?
>
>**JACKSON:** No.
>
>**ME:** Okay. Based on what?
>
>**JACKSON:** Based on there was nothing there to start the fire.
>
>**ME:** Like an accelerant? (Jackson just ignores this question.)
>
>**JACKSON:** We ruled out all known causes.
>
>**ME:** Well, did you find any specific evidence that it was intentionally set?
>
>**JACKSON:** Well, no. But the house was completely destroyed. The only thing left were the pillars.
>
>**ME:** So if it was completely destroyed and nothing was left to indicate that it was an arson, wouldn't the same line of reasoning also indicate that if the house was completely destroyed there wouldn't be anything left to demonstrate that it was accidental?
>
>**JACKSON:** We were able to rule out accidental causes.

ME: So you were able to rule out accidental causes, but not arson?

JACKSON: Right.

ME: Okay. Tell me how you did that. How did you rule out accidental causes?

JACKSON: We look at the weather. It was clear. No rain, no lightning. We look at the receptacles, but they were burned out. The house was made of pine, so if there was a shortage in the house that started the fire we wouldn't know if that caused it.

This was the first crack in Jackson's dam that would eventually release the flood waters on this sham investigation and fallacious assertion that this horrible fire was an arson. It was the moment in the testimony that I'd been waiting for. I'd skillfully maneuvered Jackson into a corner on the origins of the fire that he couldn't back out of. I only had to press home my lead.

ME: So it's possible that this fire could have been accidental?

JACKSON: It's possible.

ME: So you weren't totally able to rule out all accidental causes?

JACKSON: We tried to rule out all accidental causes.

ME: Okay. But we're talking about facts here, Mr. Jackson. What facts did you have to conclusively conclude that it was not accidental?

JACKSON: Nothing other than there were no storms or lightning that night.

ME: Is bad weather the only cause of accidental fires?

JACKSON: No. You've got electrical causes that could start fires. Appliances.

ME: But the house was destroyed. So you weren't able to determine whether one of those may have started this fire?

JACKSON: Well, we looked at the wiring and appliances. But I am not an electrical engineer, so therefore, I cannot say it was an electrical fire or whatever. Because if I say that this appliance started this fire I'll be in court trying to explain if I'm an expert.

ME: But you're a fire marshal! You're charged with the authority to investigate these things. Because this is very important.

Electrical fires happen all the time. You're telling us that you are not trained to determine if a fire was started by electrical shorts, electricity or not?

JACKSON: Nope.

ME: So it's possible that in this case an accidental electrical fire burnt this house down?

JACKSON: I can't say it did and I can't say that it didn't.

This was the first time I heard a collective gasp from the audience and the jury. The crack in Jackson's dam had widened into a large fissure. This was extremely important, though, and I planned to break it wide open.

It was established, and Jackson agreed, that the area where the fire started was in the kitchen area of the lake house, near the electrical box. That was undisputed. Plus, I had Emmett's testimony that shortly before the fire he'd had insulation put in the lake house for the first time in its near one-hundred-year history. If this had been a criminal trial my not guilty verdict would have been secured at this moment. But there was more to come.

ME: Okay. Five minutes ago you said you were convinced that this fire was an arson. Now you're saying it's a possibility that this fire was accidental?

JACKSON: It could have been accidental, but I say it's arson because I had a witness to the fire.

ME: But Josh Chamblee didn't come forward until almost two years later. I'm talking about at the time of the fire.

JACKSON: (very aggravated) I know what you're talking about, Mr. Atwood, but you're pounding on this question about this fire, okay. I've done told you the reason behind it.

ME: A statement from Josh two years later. But you said you were convinced it was arson when you went to investigate. What evidence . . .

JACKSON: I ruled it arson at the time but I didn't have a suspect. Okay? If I don't have a suspect my case stays cold until I get some evidence to help my case.

This didn't make sense to me and I am sure it made even less sense to the jury. Whether Jackson had a suspect or not had no bearing on whether he was able to forensically prove at the time of the fire that it was an arson and had been deliberately set. And my questions to him had been devised to force him into admitting that from day one he did not conduct a competent investigation, that he had no forensic evidence to prove it was arson, and even less evidence to suspect me of committing it. But Jackson had just stumbled into another trap and I was waiting to spring it closed.

> **ME:** But again, Mr. Jackson, you're changing your story because you earlier testified that when you talked to Emmett and Kade Atwood on November 13th they implicated me in the fire. So you had your suspect on day one.
>
> **JACKSON:** But I didn't know you.
>
> **ME:** I'm going to come back to that, but I'm trying to pin this down, however, I'm having a hard time. And I'm being very fair in giving you the benefit of the doubt. So let's say for the two weeks after the fire, all the way up to December 1st, 2009. During that two week time period, what evidence did you have that this fire was an arson?
>
> **JACKSON:** I really didn't have nothing.
>
> **ME:** Now, let's go from December 2009 until June 2011. And I picked June 2011 because that is before you talked to Josh Chamblee again and his family. It's before you got his third statement. During that time period, what evidence did you have that this fire was arson?
>
> **JACKSON:** None.
>
> **ME:** Okay. From June 2011 until today—excluding Josh's third statement—what evidence did you have that this fire was an arson?
>
> **JACKSON:** None.

This was the turning point in the trial. The witness chair that Jackson was sitting in was immediately adjacent to the jury box. And as I questioned Jackson I was able to observe the jury members twist and turn in their chairs and cross and recross their legs. Their body language clearly indicated to me that they were going from neutral, unattached observers of the evidence, to partial believers in my innocence and righteousness.

I had, in the course of a few minutes, established beyond a doubt that there was not a single shred of evidence that could even possibly be interpreted so as to lead one to believe that this fire was an arson. Not only had I disproved Jackson's assertion that he believed it was arson, I'd been able to get him to admit that it was possible this fire was started accidentally.

Now knowing that Jackson couldn't determine whether an electrical short had caused the fire was even more important in consideration with the fact that it was undisputed that the fire started in the area of the kitchen near the electrical box.

In Emmett's prior deposition at Mr. Minor's office, he readily admitted that people had been staying at the Atwood Lakehouse several days prior to the fire. After Jackson's testimony I realized I needed to drop the theory that Emmett may have had the fire started intentionally to collect the insurance money and, instead, focus on the fact that it was more likely than not that whomever had been staying at the lake house prior to the fire had left one of the kitchen appliances on, that after a few days, overheated and shorted out, therefore causing the fire. This is pretty much what I ultimately came to believe.

Now that I'd gotten Jackson to admit the fire may have been accidental, I would then have to move to destroying Josh's credibility as a witness. After all, Jackson had just admitted that besides Josh's third statement, he had no other evidence that the fire was arson or that I started it. So I began laying the groundwork to destroy Josh.

For the next thirty minutes I walked Jackson through the steps he took to investigate the fire. For this I mostly stayed with and followed the dialogue and questions that I'd asked at the March 2017 trial. I knew Jackson hadn't read his testimony from the first trial, and I was hoping that he'd start providing different answers than he had then; I wasn't disappointed.

One of the important facts that I considered relevant to the case were the numerous remains of multiple firearms and ammunition casings that Jackson and Sheriff Nail had found in the burnt debris of the house. Kade had claimed that he slept through the fire, and even until the day of trial I could not understand how he could sleep through the raging inferno that engulfed the Atwood Lakehouse, especially when there were loaded firearms in the house and hundreds of rounds of ammunition.

After I'd picked David up at the Memphis Airport the day before trial we began discussing the details of the case on the drive to Aberdeen. One of the possibilities that David raised as an explanation for why Kade may have slept through the fire was the fact that he may have been drunk. Now, I will be the first to admit that I have no idea what Kade's drinking habits are. However, alcoholism runs rampant in our family and it may have been an explanation for why Kade couldn't hear the fire.

This possibility still didn't make sense to me because I'd been in Kade's house; it used to belong to Kade's father, my Uncle Bush, who loved me and always treated me much better than my own father and grandfather treated me. Kade's bedroom had floor-to-ceiling windows that faced the lake house and Kade had admitted in the deposition that he had white blinds covering the windows. This was important, I thought, because white blinds wouldn't block as much light from the fire as, say, dark or black blinds.

To this day I cannot account for how Kade allegedly slept through this fire. Initially, I believed that the fire may have been arson and been set on Emmett's orders so that he could collect the insurance money to avoid bankruptcy in one of his multiple business ventures that were no doubt facing financial difficulty in the 2009 recession. This would explain why Kade would conveniently "sleep" through the fire.

After Jackson's testimony, though, about not having experience in determining whether certain fires were caused by malfunctioning electrical appliances, in consideration with the fact that people were staying in the lake house right before the fire, and that the fire started in the kitchen near the electrical box, I could not reasonably continue to believe that the fire was started intentionally.

Occam's Razor tilted more to the fact that the fire was accidental. And believing in the theory of Occam's Razor as I do, I felt it best to go with this belief and push that message. There was no doubt at this point by anyone in the courtroom about the origins of the fire. Jackson could say it was arson all day, but as I pounded on him, we were dealing with facts. And the facts can't be ignored. There was simply no proof that the fire was arson. Now, though, I had to move into other areas to make the overall picture in this jigsaw set come together.

CHAPTER THIRTY-FIVE

Even though I no longer fully believed that the fire was arson and had been deliberately set on the orders of Emmett, I still felt that in order for the jury to understand the overall lack of evidence—except exculpatory evidence proving my innocence—in the case, I still needed to move forward on the details that could, one might argue, raise the suspicion that Emmett was responsible for this fire. And that evidence began with the recent increase in insurance that he'd done.

> **ME:** Mr. Jackson, is insurance fraud a motive for arson?
> **JACKSON:** It is.
> **ME:** So, in conducting a competent, thorough investigation, you'd want to know the insurance coverage and details and whether there'd been any recent increase in insurance on the destroyed home?
> **JACKSON:** Well, I just ask for a copy of it. I just ask how much coverage he had on the house. But I don't remember how much.
> **ME:** Did Emmett Atwood tell you that he'd recently had the insurance on the house increased?
> **JACKSON:** No, he didn't. You told me. But Emmett Atwood never told me. So I didn't know.
> **ME:** In an arson investigation do you not think it is important to determine whether the owner of a house that had burned had recently increased the insurance coverage of the house shortly

before the fire?

JACKSON: Sometimes I ask and sometimes they tell me and sometimes they don't. The insurance company sometimes won't tell you that.

ME: Did you ever contact the insurance company and ask for those records?

JACKSON: I can't remember. I just asked Emmett about the insurance.

ME: Do you find it suspicious that someone would increase the insurance on their house shortly before it was destroyed by fire?

JACKSON: It all depends on the situation. He may have had new remodeling or something done that would increase the value.

ME: Did you ask Emmett if he'd done anything to the house to increase the value?

JACKSON: As far as I know I didn't.

ME: But wouldn't it be important to look at whether a house that'd burned down had had any recent remodeling or electrical work done shortly before the fire?

JACKSON: In some cases.

Not only did I and everyone that I discussed the case with find it suspicious that Emmett increased the insurance on the lake house so soon before the fire, but this suspicion was magnified by the fact that Kade slept through the fire and never called the fire department once he discovered it.

What I wanted to demonstrate most of all is that on the day Jackson met Emmett and Kade he'd already been instructed by Mike Chaney to believe anything and everything that Emmett told him. Emmett had already talked to Chaney and convinced him that I was the one responsible for the fire.

Jackson didn't go to Kosciusko to investigate the cause of the fire or try to determine who was responsible. Jackson went to Kosciusko on November 13 with marching orders in hand to do whatever he could to pin me as the culprit. They weren't looking for the truth, they were looking for whatever they could find to have me sent to prison for the rest of my life.

So truly looking for an accelerant wasn't a high priority. Determining whether Emmett may have had reason to destroy his own home to collect insurance money that he'd recently had the coverage increased on wasn't important because it didn't fit with the plan that Chaney, Emmett, Kade, and Jackson had to frame me for this fire. Jackson accepted everything Emmett and Kade said because his boss instructed him to. If he would have found Emmett's fingerprints on a gasoline can and matchbox near the fire scene he would have simply ignored it.

Jackson's ignorance of the facts of this case weren't so much that he was an incompetent investigator. His ignorance resulted from the orders he'd been given by Chaney to do anything and everything possible to blame me for this fire. I knew that, my family knew that, Jackson knew that, Chaney knew that, and Emmett knew that. What I needed next was for the jury to know that.

My next step in my questioning was to introduce the pictures that Emmett had had taken of the lake house four days before the fire for the purposes of the recent increase in insurance. Mr. Minor didn't object to me entering them into evidence and Jackson admitted that Emmett gave them to him.

One of the pictures showed the charring along the wall caused by the roaring fire in the fireplace that was, no doubt, too large for the fireplace. Even though I didn't verbally say it, everyone in the courtroom knew that it was another strong possibility that we were looking at the real cause of the fire.

I also got Jackson to admit that Kade's house had a clear, unobstructed view of the lake house. However, Jackson would not admit that he found it suspicious that Kade would sleep through the fire. Once I'd done that, without objection from Mr. Minor, I then introduced the pictures that Jackson had took of the remains of the lake house after it'd burned down.

Without those pictures it would be impossible for anyone to realize the true, utter devastation that that fire caused. There was literally nothing left. Kade really had let the entire house burn down to where there was absolutely nothing left. Even most of the metal objects in the house had melted. The pictures only caused me pain, though. I absolutely hated that that house was gone.

After a few more questions about the additional steps he took in investigating the fire, I went back to the issue of the origins. David had sent me a text while I was questioning Jackson about the pictures requesting that I try to nail down Jackson's admission that the fire could have been accidental. But then Jackson decided to stop cooperating and return to his habit of lying to cover lies.

>**ME:** Based on the fact that the electrical box and kitchen are in the exact area where the hottest point of the fire was, which you indicated was where the fire started, did it ever cross your mind that this could have been an accidental fire based on faulty wiring or appliances?
>
>**JACKSON:** It crossed my mind. But I ruled out electrical causes.
>
>**ME:** Mr. Jackson. Earlier you testified that you didn't have any experience in investigating electrical fires.
>
>**JACKSON:** Well, I can't determine if it was electrical or not without calling in an engineer.
>
>**ME:** Did you ever call one for this fire?
>
>**JACKSON:** No, the State won't pay for it.
>
>**ME:** So you not calling an expert investigator to try and determine why this fire was started near the kitchen and electrical box isn't your fault but the State of Mississippi?
>
>**JACKSON:** Yes. The insurance company can call their investigators to come look at it, though.
>
>**ME:** So because you don't have any investigatory experience in electrical fires you were not capable of determining whether this fire may have been started by faulty electrical wiring?
>
>**JACKSON:** Yes, that's correct.
>
>**ME:** So there's doubt in your mind that this may not have been an arson?
>
>**JACKSON:** Could be.

This was only the beginning of the extreme equivocation that Jackson resorted to. I had no idea that it would get as bad as it did, but this was the start. Jackson literally could not decide on one specific theory or answer and stick with it. He literally was making up bullshit as we went along.

The reason Jackson still had doubt in his mind that this fire may not have been an arson was because he knew that he'd been caught. He knew he didn't do a thorough, competent investigation. He knew that his steps in the investigation weren't done to find the truth, but were solely done to conform with what Chaney and Emmett wanted him to do. And now that they'd thrown him to the wolves (me) and abandoned him—neither Chaney or any of the other fire marshals had come to court to support Jackson—he knew that the gig was up. So it didn't matter to him if what he said made sense. Furthermore, there wasn't a lot that he could say that made sense. And I exploited that to the fullest.

After establishing once again that this fire may have been started accidentally and that Jackson was an incompetent fire investigator, I wanted to move on to other areas of his investigation.

> **ME:** Isn't it an important step in conducting an investigation to interview the main suspect?
> **JACKSON:** Yes.
> **ME:** Were you aware that Sheriff Nail sought and successfully interviewed Josh Chamblee and me?
> **JACKSON:** I think if he would have talked to y'all he would have told me and what his findings were.

This was another lie that Jackson was pushing. To explain his reliance on Josh's third statement, Jackson wanted to make it seem as though he had no idea about Josh having previously given me an alibi statement at Sheriff Nail's office two days after the fire. But Sheriff Nail had already filed his interrogatory stating unequivocally that he'd turned his entire case file, including Josh's alibi statement, over to Jackson several weeks after the fire.

So when Jackson eventually went to meet Josh for the first time in March 2010 at the KFC in Carthage, he already knew that Josh had previously given me an alibi statement when we met with Sheriff Nail. And even at the meeting with Jackson, Josh still maintained that we were together in Starkville the night of the fire and that I didn't burn the house down. This was, of course, right after Josh and I broke up and ended our relationship. However, even though Jackson promised Josh the $25,000.00 reward if he'd turn on me, Josh told the truth and still maintained that we had nothing to do with the fire. Jackson was forced to admit that at this point his case went cold, and because he couldn't determine the origins of the fire, he closed his case.

The next indication that I had that Jackson was going to change his story from the first trial was when I asked whether he'd gotten any leads from the time he met with Josh in March 2010 until he met Josh again at the Leake County Sheriff's Department on July 29, 2011.

From the first trial Jackson and Mr. Minor knew that I was going to pound on the fact that Jackson admitted he didn't have probable cause to get Josh's arrest warrant on July 27, 2011, for accessory after the fact to arson. He'd admitted as much in the first trial. Jackson clearly testified that he didn't have probable cause and only obtained Josh's arrest warrant solely to make Josh talk to him.

It was at that point in the first trial that Jackson knew he'd made a serious error. One could see the looks of disbelief that came on the jurors' faces when he'd admitted that he done such a thing. And, as we now know, Jackson deliberately threw the trial by revealing the fact that I had been in prison to the jury. He did it because he knew that after what he'd just admitted the jury was not going to look favorably on him. He just didn't count on Judge Aycock granting my request for a mistrial and then fining him nearly $2,000.00 as punishment for his deliberate attempt to prejudice the jury.

During the four months between the first trial and the second one, I know that Mr. Minor and Jackson had to of come up with a new strategy to explain why Jackson felt he had probable cause to believe that Josh had committed the crime of accessory after the fact to arson. I just didn't know stupid it would be. But again, I also didn't realize how much Jackson would lie and cheat to try and win his case.

The jury at the first trial had literally drew in gasps of air when I'd been able to get Jackson to admit that he obtained Josh's arrest warrant without any evidence of a crime. That admission established my case immediately. If Jackson would get Josh's arrest warrant without any evidence of a crime, then he would also do to the same to me.

I did almost feel sorry for Josh and his family. I was certainly empathetic. But I was used to corrupt law enforcement officers bending and breaking the law to enforce a political motive against me. The tactics used by Jackson to harass Josh's family and eventually force Josh to give him the third statement was nothing short of extortion. And he and Mr. Minor had to find a way to justify that.

After talking to Josh's mother and stepfather, Mr. and Mrs. Lyle, at the December 2016 depositions, I finally knew just how bad Jackson had harassed and threatened them. They made it clear to me that they did not want to communicate with Jackson, had not volunteered any information to him, and that at no time did they ever tell Jackson that Josh had admitted to helping me start the fire and then wanted to come clean and admit his involvement. But that's the road Jackson tried to take us down.

    ME: From March 2010 until July 28th, 2011, did you obtain any new leads in your investigation?

    JACKSON: Yes. When I talked to Mrs. Lyle. I called her in June 2011 and told her I need to talk to Josh. She wanted to know what for and I told her it was about the Atwood Lakehouse fire and that I wanted another statement from him. She told me that Josh had come home and told her about the fire and that he wanted to contact me and come clean and tell the truth about it.

    ME: That's brand new news to me. Let's go to page seventy of the March 2017 trial transcript. My question then was: From March 2010 until July 28th, 2011, did you obtain any new leads in the fire investigation. What was your answer then?

    JACKSON: (Reading from the March 2017 trial transcript) *I told Mrs. Lyle that I needed to talk to Josh about the fire. She asked me what for and I told her about the fire . . .* that he was mentioned in the fire and that I needed to talk to him.

    ME: Okay. That was your answer four months ago. Today, you're telling this jury that Mrs. Lyle told you in that phone conversation that Josh had told her about the fire and wanted to come clean. But that wasn't your answer back in March. So now your story is changing again. (Jackson had a deer-in-the-headlights look to him by this time.)

    JACKSON: Well, like I've said before, I've had time to think about it now. It's been so long.

Jackson was a lot like both Josh Chamblee and Emmett Atwood. He was like Josh in that he'd tell one lie to cover three previous lies even though he looked like an idiot doing so. In respects to Emmett, Jackson would maintain a phenomenal memory about anything that was favorable to his case and negative towards me, but would then maintain no memory at all if something was hurtful to him but positive to me. It was just as I'd predicted in my opening statement. Everyone's stories were changing.

> **ME:** What prompted you in June 2011 to pick up the phone and call Mrs. Lyle?
>
> **JACKSON:** I just wanted to talk to Josh again to see if he'd thought about what I told him. And to see if he had anymore information.
>
> **ME:** Okay. Let's stop right there and we'll come back to that. But let me ask you now, who is Mike Chaney?
>
> **JACKSON:** He's the commissioner of insurance and the state fire marshal.
>
> **ME:** Your boss and supervisor at the Fire Marshal's Office?
>
> **JACKSON:** Yes. But he's not my supervisor.
>
> **ME:** So he doesn't have any authority over you?
>
> **JACKSON:** Nope.
>
> **ME:** Hmmmm. So why does he have the title of Chief Fire Marshal, but no authority over you?
>
> **JACKSON:** He's over the office, but he can't tell us deputies what to do.
>
> **ME:** So he's just a figurehead?
>
> **JACKSON:** Well, yeah.
>
> **ME:** I'm having a real hard time understanding that, so we're going to spend a few minutes talking about it. Does Mike Chaney have the authority to hire and fire the deputies?
>
> **JACKSON:** Yes. We are appointed by him.
>
> **ME:** Okay. So he does have some ability to execute control over the Fire Marshal's Office?
>
> **JACKSON:** Some type.
>
> **ME:** Have you ever spoken to Mike Chaney before?
>
> **JACKSON:** Numerous times.
>
> **ME:** And have you spoken to him about this case?
>
> **JACKSON:** He's come to Ricky Davis, my chief, inquiring about the case. And then we met in his office.
>
> **ME:** What did he tell you in regards to this case?
>
> **JACKSON:** To go to Vicksburg and talk to Emmett Atwood.
>
> **ME:** Is that all he's ever told you, ever?
>
> **JACKSON:** Yeah.

ME: Did he tell you to go get a confession from Josh Chamblee?

JACKSON: No, he just told me to go investigate. He was not involved in any part of the investigation.

ME: Of the three hundred or so fires you've investigated, how many has Mike Chaney personally been involved in?

JACKSON: None.

ME: But he was in this one?

JACKSON: Yes.

ME: Did you ever ask yourself why the big, figurehead boss of the Fire Marshal's Office was involved in this investigation?

JACKSON: Yes. He told me he was scared of you.

ME: Okay. And you know that Chaney lives in Vicksburg, is best friends with Emmett Atwood and Sheriff Martin Pace, and that Emmett contributes money to his election campaigns?

JACKSON: Yeah. I found that out.

ME: Okay. So sitting here telling the jury this unsubstantiated allegation that Mike Chaney was scared of me and that's why he got involved in this investigation—you didn't tell the jury that Chaney was best friends with Emmett and the sheriff that I wrote the book about—you didn't tell the jury that he gets money from Emmett and that this might of been motivation for why Chaney was coming down so hard on you to make an arrest, to force a confession, to get some evidence to arrest me?

MR. MINOR: Objection, Your Honor. Is this a question? Is this closing argument?

JUDGE AYCOCK: It's not closing argument, Mr. Minor. I will sustain the objection, though. Ask a question Mr. Atwood.

I knew that I was on to something with Chaney's involvement in the investigation. The fact that he pressed for my arrest—regardless of the lack of evidence—lay just beneath the surface of Jackson's testimony and I knew that if I kept picking at it that it'd eventually come through.

Knowing that I was on the brink of a breakthrough caused me to get a little too animated in my questioning of Jackson. Rather than ask short, pointed, concise questions, I'd allowed myself to start lecturing Jackson about what I knew to be the actual truth. Mr. Minor couldn't let me get away with it, nor would Judge Aycock allow me to. So I had to take a breath, change subjects, and calm down.

There was a deliberate method in the manner in which I questioned Jackson. I'm sure he thought that we were done with the questions about Mike Chaney, Emmett Atwood, and Sheriff Martin Pace, but I had only been laying the foundations for the later kill. I knew it was coming, David knew it was coming, Richard knew it was coming, and I hoped the jury would expect it to come. But for the moment I went back to Josh Chamblee and his mother's involvement in the investigation.

I needed to get the jury to understand exactly what Jackson had put Mrs. Lyle through in order to force her to reveal Josh's location. That's why Jackson's statement that he'd talked to Mrs. Lyle and she'd told him that Josh wanted to come forward and tell the truth didn't make any sense.

Starting in June 2011, Jackson called Mrs. Lyle about five or six different times trying to get her to reveal Josh's location. But Josh had never admitted to his mother that he was involved in the fire and wanted to come clean. That was a total fabrication that Jackson made up. And Mrs. Lyle's and Josh's actions supported that.

For over a month Mrs. Lyle lied time after time when Jackson called her asking to speak to Josh. Mrs. Lyle told Jackson that Josh was in the Navy and lived in North Carolina. When Jackson called the Navy and found out that was a lie, Mrs. Lyle lied again and said he was in Oregon. When that proved false she lied again and said she hadn't talked to Josh and didn't know where he was.

When Jackson reached the end of his rope in dealing with Mrs. Lyle and her lies, he patiently explained to her for the last time that Josh was involved in an arson, that it was a very serious issue, and that if he didn't come forward and give another statement which implicated me in the fire he would be arrested. Jackson even went so far as to have the sheriff of Leake County, who was friends with the Lyles, tell them that if Josh didn't come willingly to give another statement which implicated me in the fire, he'd be arrested. Jackson telling Mrs. Lyle in June and July 2011 that Josh was involved in an arson was a fact that I couldn't go without demolishing.

> **ME:** On the day you explained to Mrs. Lyle the severity of the crime and that Josh was an accessory to the crime, what evidence did you have that this was an arson and that I was responsible?

> **JACKSON:** Nothing other than she told me Josh wanted to talk to me about the fire.
>
> **ME:** Mr. Jackson. We aren't talking about what she said later. You told her that there was an arson and that Josh was an accessory before she allegedly told you that. So again, on that day, what was your evidence that this fire was an arson and that I was involved?
>
> **JACKSON:** I didn't have none.

This prompted me to further establish with the jury the impossibility of Josh having allegedly told his mother that he was part of the crime of me committing arson and that he wanted to come clean. If he'd truly told that to his mother, and if she had truly passed that on to Jackson, then Jackson would not have needed to track Josh down and Josh would never have felt the need of avoiding Jackson.

The entire month of July 2011 was spent by Jackson harassing and threatening Josh's mother into forcing her to reveal Josh's location. That's why Jackson could never be believed when he said that Josh told his mother about the fire and wanted to come clean. Jackson just made that up because he wanted the jury to think he had probable cause to get Josh's arrest warrant. Josh didn't want to come "clean." Josh wanted to avoid Jackson because he knew that they would never leave him alone until they eventually forced him into lying to avoid going to jail. And throughout this whole time Josh was having his poor mother tell lie after lie to Jackson so that Josh could avoid him. And even though Jackson knew Mrs. Lyle was lying to him over and over, he conveniently chose to believe her alleged statement that Josh had told her he was involved in the fire.

> **ME:** Since you knew that Mrs. Lyle was telling you lies, did it ever cross your mind that she might be lying to you about Josh blaming me for the fire? Or that I had allegedly threatened him?
>
> **JACKSON:** No.
>
> **ME:** So you took her at her word on that, but knew she was lying about everything else?
>
> **JACKSON:** I couldn't really say she was lying until I checked it all out for myself.
>
> **ME:** But we have multiple false statements from her that you

knew to be untrue then, but you chose to believe her when she allegedly said that Josh had told her I threatened him. You chose to believe that because it fit with what you wanted this case to be. Isn't that correct?

JACKSON: Yeah. I just wanted to talk to him about the fire.

ME: And you wanted to question Josh again because Mike Chaney was pressing you to make an arrest?

JACKSON: Yeah.

ME: Because I'd published a book . . .

JACKSON: Now, I didn't know nothing about no book.

ME: But this person that you describe as a figurehead with no authority over you was pressing you to arrest me?

JACKSON: He was pressing my chief and my chief was pressing me.

The truth was finally coming out. I'd maintained all along that the only reason Jackson reopened this closed fire investigation was because Mike Chaney ordered him to. It didn't take a rocket scientist to figure out that as soon as *Into Hell I Rode* was published, Emmett and Sheriff Pace, whether collectively or not, began putting pressure on Chaney to have the fire investigation reopened and me arrested no matter what it took.

I'd pursued this theory for almost eight years. I knew it to be true just as I knew that the sun would rise tomorrow. But Jackson and Chaney had both lied in their interrogatories. When they'd answered their interrogatories under oath back in 2015, Jackson answered that Chaney was not involved in the investigation and hadn't pressured him or anyone else to make an arrest. Chaney answered that he, also, wasn't involved in the investigation and only monitored its progress.

Anyone should have been outraged at the outright lies. Chaney and Jackson—sworn law enforcement officers—had committed perjury when they signed under oath on their interrogatories that their answers were truthful. As outraged as I was that they'd outright lied, I was more incensed that my belief all along that this was a politically motivated arrest, done in retaliation for my book, was finally being proven true.

The dishonesty and corruption sickened me. Chaney clearly abused his office and power to accomplish a political motive. That fact was becoming clearer by the minute. The longer I kept Jackson on the stand the more he revealed. So I doubled down and kept pushing.

CHAPTER THIRTY-SIX

One might think that my questioning of Jackson was schizophrenic in nature. I'd spend several minutes on one topic and then jump to the next. But it was a strategy that was working. I knew what was going on in Jackson's mind. I'd judged his psyche and character and found them flawed. He was just like these scumbag, lying, manipulating ex-boyfriends that I'd had the bad luck to date. Just as I could eventually trap every one of them in a lie, I could and did do the same to Jackson.

Just when Jackson thought we'd moved on from a typically sensitive topic, I'd switch on him again and come back to a question and answer from ten minutes before. And, surprisingly, more often than not, Jackson would provide a totally different answer than he had before. He was literally making up lies as we went along, and because everything about him *was* a lie, he often wasn't able to remember the lie he told ten minutes prior. In this I made quick work of.

> **ME:** What did you get Josh Chamblee's arrest warrant for?
> **JACKSON:** Accessory after the fact.
> **ME:** But accessory after the fact to what?
> **JACKSON:** To the fire.
> **ME:** So now it's just a fire and not an arson?
> **JACKSON:** I said fire.
> **ME:** Okay, well, there's a difference between a fire and arson. So now you're saying that you got an arrest warrant for a fire that

you couldn't prove was an arson? Or was it an arson?

JACKSON: Arson after the fact.

ME: So on July 27th, 2011, you went and swore under oath, under penalty of perjury, that *on or about, in Attala County, Mississippi, Joshua Langston Chamblee did assist David Garland Atwood, II, in committing the crime of arson and was an accessory after the fact.* What evidence did you have on that date, at that time, that Josh Chamblee assisted me in allegedly starting this fire?

JACKSON: Well, after I talked to him at the Leake County Sheriff's Department where he implicated you in.

ME: No. Now wait, Mr. Jackson. You got this warrant on July 27th, two days before you met with Josh at the sheriff's department.

JACKSON: Yeah.

ME: But you went before a judge two days prior to that and swore under oath that you had evidence to prove that Josh Chamblee committed the crime of accessory after the fact to arson. Correct?

JACKSON: Yes.

ME: So again, what evidence did you have at that specific time that Josh committed a crime?

MR. MINOR: Objection. Asked and answered.

JUDGE AYCOCK: Overruled.

JACKSON: I don't remember.

ME: Let me refresh your memory. Let's turn to page 89 of the March 2017 trial transcript. I asked you, *At the time you procured Josh's arrest warrant on July 27th, 2011, what evidence did you have that he was an accessory after the fact to arson?* And you answered . . .

JACKSON: I can't recall until we talked at the Leake County Sheriff's Department.

ME: No, Mr. Jackson. I'm talking about before then. Your answer at the March trial was . . .

JACKSON: (Reading from transcript) *To get Josh down here to talk to me.*

ME: So is it fair to say that you procured the arrest warrant for Josh not because a crime was committed, but solely just to get Josh to give you another statement?

JACKSON: True.

ME: Is it normal police procedure to get an arrest warrant for someone solely to get them to talk to you? And you said then . .

JACKSON: (Reading from transcript) *Yes. I have done it.* It all just depends on the case really.

ME: And you've procured warrants for other people's arrest without any evidence, without any probable cause, just to get them to talk to you?

JACKSON: Yes. Sometimes.

ME: And you did it in this case. You did not have probable cause?

JACKSON: No.

ME: You did not have probable cause for my arrest?

JACKSON: No.

ME: So when you went to the Attala County Justice Court and filled out this affidavit, you swore under oath, under penalty of perjury, that you had probable cause that a crime had been committed. But that wasn't true was it?

JACKSON: Well, Josh Chamblee was there.

ME: Mr. Jackson . . .

JACKSON: Yes. Okay. It wasn't true.

ME: Mr. Jackson. You testified that when you went to get Josh's arrest warrant that you didn't have any evidence of a crime. No probable cause. Correct?

JACKSON: Yes.

ME: But you swore under oath, under penalty of perjury before a judge, that you had evidence of a crime. So you've lied under oath?

JACKSON: [Long pause] No . . . well, yes, I guess I have.

ME: So you agree that you did not have probable cause that a crime had been committed?

JACKSON: Yes.

If anyone doubted who was going to win this case, at this point I couldn't tell. I'd glanced over my shoulder and looked at Jackson's two attorneys, Mr. Minor and Mrs. Benton, and they just stared forward in shock with their mouths open. Even Judge Aycock had stopped, turned, and then just stared at Jackson.

In the course of about five minutes I'd succeeded in getting a sworn state law enforcement officer to admit that he'd obtained arrest warrants without any evidence of a crime and that he'd lied under oath and committed perjury. How often does that happen?

It was a shock to everyone else in the courtroom, including Mr. Minor, but although I was astonished that he'd actually admitted it, I wasn't shocked because I knew that this type of corruption and behavior was common, especially amongst law enforcement officers in Vicksburg and Warren County.

Of the eight jurors sitting in the jury box, every single one of them had leaned forward and were sitting on the edges of their seats. It was unbelievable that Jackson had just admitted to committing several felony crimes. Think about that . . . a sworn protector of the law admitting to committing illegal arrests and perjury. I almost sat down at that moment and rested my case. Jackson had proven everything that I'd set out to prove, except one thing—Mike Chaney's involvement.

> **ME:** Let me ask you this, Mr. Jackson. On July 27th and July 29th when you lied under oath to get these false arrest warrants, was it because Mike Chaney was putting pressure on you to do so?
>
> **JACKSON:** No.
>
> **ME:** Then why did you lie under oath?
>
> **JACKSON:** [Extremely agitated now with a look of terror on his face] There was some pressure from him, you know, but the arrest warrant was issued on July 29th.
>
> **ME:** But that was for me, Mr. Jackson. We are talking about Josh Chamblee's arrest warrant on July 27th. On that date and before, were you being pressured to make an arrest in this case?
>
> **JACKSON:** Okay. Yes. I was under a lot of pressure.

When Jackson admitted this I heard Mr. Minor throw down his pen on the table and lean back in his chair with a look of disgust on his face. He didn't have to tell me that Jackson had lied to him about this part in the story. I'd known it all along. But Jackson had lied to his attorneys and not told them this part. I knew it. And the fact Jackson had lied to his attorneys and then admitted to committing multiple felony crimes because Mike Chaney was making him do it was something that I knew pissed Mr.

Minor and Mrs. Benton off more than anything else in the whole case.

Attorneys hate when their clients lie to them. It's a thousand times worse when their clients lie to them and then the attorneys get sandbagged at trial with a massive revelation such as what Jackson had just admitted to.

Since the beginning of this lawsuit I'd maintained exactly what Jackson had just admitted to. But because he'd lied to his attorneys and told them a version of the story—which, unfortunately, they believed—it made them look like idiots and frauds because they'd pushed Jackson's version that he hadn't been pressured into making these arrests and that Chaney wasn't involved in the investigation.

Hopefully, Judge Aycock realized that Mr. Minor hadn't been knowingly pushing a false story throughout the entire course of the litigation. Knowing Mr. Minor now as well as I do, I am firmly convinced he did not have any idea the level of fraud and lies pushed onto him by Jackson and Chaney.

I could see on his face at this moment in the trial the utter shock and disbelief he was in at what Jackson had just admitted. Unfortunately for both him and Jackson, things only got worse.

> **ME:** So it's not your fault that you lied under oath and committed perjury. Mike Chaney was making you do it?
>
> **JACKSON:** Yes.
>
> **ME:** But were you under a lot of pressure in May 2011 to make an arrest?
>
> **JACKSON:** I don't know.
>
> **ME:** But in June 2011, when *Into Hell I Rode* was published, that's when the pressure from Mike Chaney really came down on you? Correct?
>
> **JACKSON:** Yes.
>
> **ME:** So this figurehead, this so-called boss of yours, the State Fire Marshal, Mike Chaney, was telling you, you've got to go get David Atwood, you've got to get him somehow, someway. And you wanted to do what Mike Chaney asked of you. You wanted to be a good deputy fire marshal. You wanted to be a good investigator. You wanted to be liked in the Fire Marshal's Office. So you said, "Sure, Mr. Chaney. I'll do whatever I have to do to be a good deputy fire marshal, even if it means lying under oath

to a judge, even if it means breaking the law to obtain an arrest warrant that you didn't have any evidence to support." Correct?
MR. MINOR: Objection, Your Honor. Argumentative.
JUDGE AYCOCK: It's overruled.
JACKSON: Yes.

I had gotten so excited over proving the most crucial crux of my case that I came from behind the podium and began pacing in front of the jury box when I was asking this long, convoluted question. No doubt my voice was raised several octaves, and as I paced, I resorted to my Southern Baptist preacher-mode.

Before I even finished with asking this long, sarcastic—and what I will admit was certainly a very questionable statement—I knew Mr. Minor would object to it. But Jackson's behavior, along with Mike Chaney's, absolutely sickened me. Their attempts to pervert justice and the Constitution was deplorable. And I felt like I was justified in preaching to the jury, even if Mr. Minor was going to object. But apparently, Judge Aycock was sickened by Jackson's testimony because she did not sustain the objection. She allowed the "question" to be asked and required Jackson to answer it . . . which he did by admitting to it. My disgust was demonstrated by my next questions.

ME: Mr. Jackson. Do you consider yourself to be one who has integrity? Do you even know what that word means?
JACKSON: Yes.
ME: Could at any point when Mike Chaney was pressing you to make this illegal arrest, to commit these illegal acts, could you have said, "I'm not going to be part of this? I'm not going to be part to a crime?"
JACKSON: Yeah. I actually argued that with Mike Chaney.
ME: Oh. So now you argued that with him? You told him that this was wrong? That this was illegal?
JACKSON: Yeah. Briefly.
ME: And what did he tell you? Give me your gun, give me your badge, you're fired?
JACKSON: He told me to get my ass up out of the chair and get out there and get you.
ME: So Mike Chaney told you that if you didn't go get an

illegal arrest warrant for me that you were going to lose your job?

JACKSON: He didn't say exactly that.

ME: Well, did you feel that way?

JACKSON: Yeah. He would have made it very hard on me.

ME: But Mike Chaney was asking you to be part of a crime.

JACKSON: Yeah.

ME: Could you have gone to the attorney general? To the local district attorney? To even the FBI? Could you have gone to them and said that Mike Chaney is asking me to violate the constitutional rights of an individual by arresting him when there is no evidence to support his guilt?

JACKSON: Yeah. I guess I could have if I'd thought about it.

ME: But you didn't. So you willingly took part in this illegal conspiracy?

JACKSON: It wasn't a crime.

ME: Do you not agree that lying to a judge is a crime?

JACKSON: Yeah.

Everyone in the courtroom sat in absolute shock. No one was doing anything other than staring at Jackson as though he'd just been caught in the act of murder. It's not every day that a law enforcement officer admits to committing a serious series of crimes in a clear conspiracy to violate someone's constitutional rights.

This type of behavior would have been expected in a country like North Korea or Nazi Germany; not in America, though. And the fact that the truth had finally come out sickened everyone to the core. We are talking about serious felony offenses that Jackson just admitted committing at the direction of a state-wide elected official.

For a moment I just stood there in shock. I didn't know what more I could ask. Jackson gave me everything that I'd ever wanted from this trial. The jury hated him by now, and for the right reasons. I could have stopped my case then and obtained a verdict in my favor. But I was also looking for other truths that I hoped were out there.

I have to admit, after the phenomenal revelation that Jackson previously testified to, I was left speechless. Where would one go with their questioning after their main antagonist admitted to every allegation made in a false arrest lawsuit?

Jackson admitted he didn't have any evidence, he admitted he didn't have probable cause, he admitted that he committed multiple, serious felony crimes, and he admitted that Mike Chaney forced him to commit these crimes. One could ask what more was needed.

For a moment I stood there in shock. I honestly had expected Judge Aycock to call a short recess to allow everyone an opportunity to cool off, collect their thoughts, regroup, and then proceed on with the trial. But the awkward silence from the bench drew me out of my stupefaction and I moved on into other areas of Jackson's investigation and conduct.

One of the things that I knew I must face was Josh Chamblee's credibility and Jackson's reliance on him to obtain the third statement. Josh had severe credibility issues, and Jackson was at fault for ignoring those issues. But we now knew that anything that posed a problem to Jackson's quest to arrest me was something that he no doubt conveniently ignored because of the pressure he was under from Chaney to effect an arrest on me at any cost.

Josh had previously been arrested by the Saint Tammany Parish authorities in Louisiana for lying to law enforcement officers and filing a false police report. In the comprehensive report that Jackson ran on Josh, his arrest for these crimes was clearly listed in bold type on the second page. So Jackson knew even before he interviewed Josh on July 29, 2011, that Josh had credibility issues and a history of dishonest conduct in police investigations. But this was conveniently ignored.

I asked Jackson whether he had done anything to independently verify Josh's third statement, but as one would expect by now, Jackson answered in the negative. Nothing could stand in his way of obtaining whatever evidence he needed to make this arrest. And furthermore, Jackson was again prepared to lie about his failure to independently verify Josh's statements.

> **ME:** Did you ever question Josh Chamblee about his arrest in Louisiana?
>
> **JACKSON:** Yes, I did.
>
> **ME:** Now, hold on Mr. Jackson. You've previously testified that you recorded the interview with Josh at the Leake County Sheriff's Department, but I've listened to the recording and the jury will hear it later on. You never asked Josh about his arrests on the recording.
>
> **JACKSON:** Let me back up for a minute. I didn't ask him

about the Saint Tammany Parish arrest. I only asked him about the fire.

ME: Did you ever call Saint Tammany Parish and ask them about the details of Josh's arrest there?

JACKSON: I tried to call.

ME: That's news to me. Let's go to page 77 of the March trial transcript. I asked you then, when you were sitting in that witness chair, *Did you call Saint Tammany Parish about Josh Chamblee's arrest?* And you said four months ago . . .

JACKSON: (Reading from transcript) *No, I did not.*

ME: Now you're saying that you tried. Which is it?

JACKSON: I tried.

One would think that after Jackson admitted to committing multiple felony crimes and being forced to commit these illegal acts under the orders of Mike Chaney, that he'd just go ahead, give up, face the music, and tell the truth. I continually asked myself what else could Jackson lie about that was worse than admitting to committing several felony offenses under the direct orders of his boss. But Jackson wanted to continue the dog and pony show.

After shaking my head for a few seconds at the absurdity of what Jackson was doing, I moved on to having Josh's third statement entered into evidence and having Jackson point out to the jury that this statement was severely lacking in detail. Josh didn't know the date of the fire, didn't know whether the lake house was actually on a lake or not, and could not provide a single detail regarding anything about the Atwood Lakehouse property. It was simply a vague statement saying that I told him I burned Emmett's house down.

Even when I brought these lack of details to Jackson's attention and asked him whether it was important to independently confirm what's in a witness's statement, he was unable to do so. The most I could get from him was an equivocal statement that "sometimes" a law enforcement officer should verify the details in a witness's statement.

ME: But you didn't try to verify anything Josh was saying because all you needed was a vague, incriminating statement that fit with the plan that you and Mike Chaney had to have me arrested? Correct?

JACKSON: Yes.

ME: So whatever Josh said that was negative towards me you took him at his word?

JACKSON: Correct.

This is what it came down to. And as I stood there before the judge, jury, and God all I could do was shake my head. But at least Jackson was telling the truth, somewhat.

After collecting my thoughts for a moment, I had Jackson explain to the jury what he did after getting Josh's third statement, where he went to get the warrant, and who he passed it on to after getting Judge Stewart to sign it. Sheriff Nail goes to my Papaw's house in Kosciusko, but I'm not there, Jackson then calls Sheriff Pace at the Warren County Sheriff's Department and faxes the warrant to him which is then turned over to Detective Mike Traxler to have it served.

Traxler gets a SWAT team together, and with assistance from several other deputy fire marshals, goes to my house to serve it. And by "serve it" I mean they busted my mother's door off the hinges and ran in holding her and my other family members at gunpoint until they realized I wasn't there.

Of course, during this time me and the governor's son, Patrick Bryant, are coming home from our vacation and are less than thirty minutes from the house. Had we been any sooner, not only do I believe that Traxler would have attempted to kill me, but they'd of put the governor's son in dire danger—another example of the unintended consequences that this group of corrupt and evil law enforcement officers almost put into action.

Thankfully, my mother called me as soon as Traxler and his coterie of corrupt cops left the house. Upon being informed, Patrick and I swung the car around and headed back to his place to hide out until I could figure out what to do, which, of course, was to turn myself in to a safe, responsible law enforcement officer—Sheriff Nail being the ultimate person.

I planned on introducing into evidence, through the testimony of my mother, the fact that Jackson almost—I fully believed—put the son of the governor into dire danger by his illegal actions. I knew this was almost better than fiction. Multiple times I had to sit and think to myself about the irony of a statewide elected law enforcement officer (Mike

Chaney) putting into action an illegal conspiracy to, at the least, have me arrested, and at the most, murdered by a vindictive, corrupt cop (Mike Traxler), all the while not knowing that their intended target was with, at that moment, the most least likely person in the whole state (the governor's son). If it wasn't so serious it would be comical.

By this point in the questioning I think Jackson was at the point where he would just say anything and admit to any allegation just to get off the witness stand as soon as possible. We'd been going for almost three hours without a break and even I was beginning to tire. However, there were just a few more things I needed.

> **ME:** On the day you procured my arrest warrant, excluding Josh Chamblee's third statement, what evidence did you have that I committed the crime of arson?
> **JACKSON:** That was it.
> **ME:** Just Josh's third statement, given to you under threat of arrest?
> **JACKSON:** Yes.

I also had Jackson explain that Josh refused to come testify in front of the grand jury and had recanted his third statement blaming me for the fire. In response to Josh recanting his statement, which he claimed was forced, Jackson obtained another arrest warrant, had Josh arrested, and then extradited back from where he was in Indianapolis. I could tell at this point that the jury was beginning to hate Jackson.

One of the last things on my list to question Jackson about was his decision not to try and interview me. This had caused the mistrial back in March, and I was honestly terrified what his answer would be to my question. But it had to be asked. And in the lead-up to the second trial everyone involved in the case on my end speculated what Jackson's answer might be to my question. He certainly, though, could not answer that he didn't interview me because I was in prison.

> **ME:** Was I your number one suspect?
> **JACKSON:** Yes.
> **ME:** Sometime between the fire and March 2010 you decided to interview Josh Chamblee?
> **JACKSON:** Correct.

> **ME:** But you never tried to interview me did you?
> **JACKSON:** No.
> **ME:** But I was your primary suspect? Correct?
> **JACKSON:** Yes. Correct.
> **ME:** So from the time of the fire in November 2009 until my arrest in August 2011, did you ever try to interview me?
> **JACKSON:** No.
> **ME:** Is it normal police procedure not to try and interview the main suspect?
> **JACKSON:** It all depends.
> **ME:** Again, that's news to me. Let's go to page 96 of the March trial transcript. I asked you the same question and you agreed that it's normal to try and interview the main suspect. But now your answer is changing.
> **JACKSON:** Look, I can't remember this far back in March.
> **ME:** But you remember me being your number one suspect?
> **JACKSON:** Yes.

Here it came. The question that everyone knew I was going to have to ask, but which everyone dreaded hearing. The jury may not have known the reason why, but as I asked the next question everyone in the courtroom held their breath, no one more so than Judge Aycock.

> **ME:** Why did you not try to interview me, your primary suspect?
> **JACKSON:** Because I didn't know where you was.

I was holding my pen in my hand, but had the end between my teeth. I bit down so hard in frustration that I cracked the plastic casing. Here was Jackson telling another flat lie to cover up another deliberate lie. But what could he have said? Saying that he didn't interview me because I was in prison wouldn't be the truth, and saying that he couldn't find me wasn't the truth either. But what was the truth? Incompetence? Lack of willpower? I never got the answer, but I kept pushing.

> **ME:** Well, you didn't know where Josh was either, but that didn't stop you from trying to find him? Correct?
> **JACKSON:** Correct.

ME: So, it's correct to say that you didn't try to interview me because you weren't interested in what I had to say?

JACKSON: I was, I just couldn't find you.

ME: Okay. But did you *attempt* to find me?

JACKSON: No. (One of the jurors laughed under her breath at this.)

MR. MINOR: Objection, Your Honor. Can we please move along. We've already covered this.

ME: I'm just about done, Your Honor.

JUDGE AYCOCK: I need to know whether you can finish his testimony in about ten minutes or so because I'd like to send the jury home for the day, but if not, we can pick up tomorrow.

ME: No more than ten minutes, Your Honor.

JUDGE AYCOCK: Okay. Proceed.

My last questions for Jackson consisted of getting him to admit that the only thing he showed Judge Stewart when he obtained my arrest warrant was Josh's third statement. Jackson admitted he didn't tell Judge Stewart about my cell phone records, Josh's alibi statements, the recent increase in insurance, the fact that none of the shoe prints could be matched to me, that Josh was my ex-boyfriend, and that Kade slept through the fire—all relevant information that shouldn't have been concealed from Judge Stewart. I couldn't help put prick at Jackson one more time.

ME: So Judge Stewart relied on your word? The word of a law enforcement officer who has admitted lying under oath and committing perjury?

JACKSON: Yes.

ME: That's all, Your Honor.

As I sat down Judge Aycock cautioned the jury not to discuss the case or research anything about it. They were then dismissed and went home for the day. Judge Aycock's law clerk then came and asked me how many witnesses I had for the following day and whether I thought we could get through all of their testimonies in one day. As elated as I was, all I could tell Daniel was that I was going to keep it as short as possible because I needed "to stop while I'm ahead."

The first day couldn't have gone better. Jackson gave me everything I could ever ask for, all wrapped in a nice, big Christmas bow. And although Mr. Minor had the opportunity to cross-examine Jackson after I'd closed my direct examination, he wisely decided to wait and call Jackson back to the witness stand after I'd rested my case and it was his turn to rebut it.

CHAPTER THIRTY-SEVEN

As soon as Judge Aycock had dismissed the jury and was preparing to adjourn the court until the following morning, a pudgy, older man sitting on the front row of the defendant's side of the courtroom rather rudely stood up and began waving his arms and hands at Judge Aycock and started trying to speak to her. With law books and folders in hand, Judge Aycock paused before stepping off her dais and turned to address whom I now knew to be Paul Kelly Loyacono, Emmett's best friend and personal attorney.

Kelly, apparently without any courtroom decorum, began asking Judge Aycock whether Emmett and Kade's contempt hearing would still be held the following morning in regards to them not showing up to the depositions that they'd twice been subpoenaed for.

Because it had taken all day to go through Jackson's testimony, Judge Aycock had told us that she was going to continue their contempt hearing until some time after the trial. Not satisfied, though, with this answer, Kelly starts to criticize me, but is quickly stopped by Judge Aycock. Kelly was attempting to tell her that Emmett and Kade would not be coming to court the following day to testify, but I'd subpoenaed them for court and their testimony was crucial.

When Kelly informed Judge Aycock that they wouldn't be attending because they had not been subpoenaed, she apparently took him at his word. After all, Kelly was an "officer of the court," and it was unheard of for one to lie so blatantly to a federal judge. But Kelly's like Emmett. He doesn't play by the rules. And at first Judge Aycock agreed that since they'd not been subpoenaed they weren't required to appear the following day.

I quickly explained to Judge Aycock that they had, in fact, been subpoenaed to testify the following morning and that I had copies of the subpoenas and the proof of service showing where they had been subpoenaed. Kelly lied again and said that they'd not been subpoenaed. But thankfully, Judge Aycock had copies of the subpoenas and the proof of services that clearly indicated that both Emmett and Kade had been properly subpoenaed to testify in the trial and that they were required to be at the courthouse at eight-thirty the following morning.

As Judge Aycock was reading the subpoenas, Kelly tried to interrupt again and tell her that Emmett and Kade weren't required to be in court and that they wouldn't be. I could immediately tell, though, that Judge Aycock was losing her patience with Kelly, and as he continued to try and speak she cut him off, shut him down, and told him not to interrupt her again.

I knew better than to get involved in this judicial squabble. I was in the right, I knew I was in the right, and I knew that the record would prove me in the right. All I needed to do was sit back and let Judge Aycock confirm it.

> **JUDGE AYCOCK:** So, Mr. Loyacono, Emmett and Kade Atwood need to be here in the morning for purposes of this trial. They will come and stay here until I excuse them. Understood?
>
> **LOYACONO:** Your Honor, your order is only for the contempt hearing on sanctions . . .
>
> **JUDGE AYCOCK:** (Very agitated) And you realize that I'm talking to an attorney who has not made a formal appearance before this Court for the purposes of this case! But I am going to give you the privilege of still speaking. You understand the Court's order today. The Atwoods will be here tomorrow morning, ten till nine. Is that clear?
>
> **LOYACONO:** That is clear, Your Honor.

I laughed and snickered under my breath. Kelly Loyacono had just been made a fool of by Judge Aycock. His antics were entirely inappropriate and disrespectful to me, to Mr. Minor, and to Judge Aycock. We weren't in Vicksburg where all the judges and other attorneys were afraid of Kelly. Thankfully, his and Emmett's influence didn't reach so far as to encompass the federal court in Aberdeen, Mississippi.

By attempting to address the Court without entering a formal appearance and then flatly lying to Judge Aycock had not endeared himself to her, and it was unfortunate because she was the one person whom Emmett's and Kade's fate would hang when it was time for them to explain their failures in not attending the depositions.

As Kelly was leaving the courtroom with his head hung low, David, Richard, and I just shook our heads. The first comment that I made to David, after Kelly retreated from the courtroom was, "And that's Kelly Loyacono, Emmett's attorney." David's first comment was, "Did you see how mad he made Judge Aycock? She was furious." I had to agree. We definitely weren't in Vicksburg before a handpicked judge that was in Emmett's back pocket. And I'd never been prouder to have Judge Aycock as my judge as I was then.

As we drove back to the little house we had rented a block from the courthouse, we could do nothing but talk about how bad the case had gone for Jackson and Mr. Minor. We wondered what the conversation must be like between them. I knew enough that I felt for certain that Mr. Minor and Jackson were having a "come-to-Jesus" moment about his testimony.

What could Mr. Minor do to repair that? We were in elation because we knew that I'd won my entire case in those short three hours. It was even discussed whether or not I should even worry with calling any additional witnesses. After all, everyone felt certain that the jury would rule in my favor no matter what came next. However, I had a story to tell and I also had questions that needed answering. But I will easily admit, I went to bed that night slightly inebriated and totally confident that I'd been vindicated and that I'd win. I just had to have those other questions answered, though.

The following morning—Tuesday—we started court at nine sharp. My first witness for the day was my mother. She and my sister had drove up the previous night and stayed with David and I. This was the first time that my mother had met David, but they became good friends and got along famously.

My mother's testimony was short. I had her explain to the jury the fact that Josh had threatened to go to the cops and tell them that I was responsible for the fire if I tried to pursue charges against him. She then testified that when Josh had done this we immediately called Sheriff Nail and told him, and had tried calling Jackson, but Jackson would never return our phone calls.

My mother also testified how terrified she was when Mike Traxler and the SWAT team from the Warren County Sheriff's Department blew our door off the hinges and ran into the house with machine guns and pistols and held her at gunpoint.

> **ME:** And when this SWAT team led this raid on our house, who did you know that I was with at that exact moment?
> **MY MOTHER:** Patrick Bryant, the governor's son.
> **ME:** And if Patrick and I had been at the house, would the SWAT team have put his life in danger?
> **MR. MINOR:** Objection. Calls for speculation.
> **JUDGE AYCOCK:** Sustained.

I knew that a couple heads had turned behind this testimony. Again, it's stranger than fiction. Jackson had no clue that his illegal shenanigans could have put the governor's son's life in danger.

Finally, my mother testified that we had to pay $5,000.00 for me to bond out of jail and that I still owed her for this money. Without testifying myself, it was the only way that I could prove the compensatory damages part of my claims. I ran the risk of not fully proving that part because I did not want to take the stand and testify. So I rolled the dice and got that evidence in through my mother.

The unfortunate thing about having my mother testify in court when I am the examiner, was her tendency to cry and my tendency to cry when she cried. We had talked before her testimony began and I stressed to her the need to stay strong, not show emotion, and stick to the facts. But she hadn't been on the stand for thirty seconds before crying, and that made my ability to question her all the more difficult.

I wanted her on the stand and then back off as soon as I could. I also had to be very careful not to open any figurative doors about my criminal history that would then allow Mr. Minor to question my mother about my past. Out of all the witnesses that I would question throughout the trial, questioning my mother was by far the hardest one. But we made it through it.

Even though I knew her testimony would come with some tears, I wanted to end it on a positive or funny note. After all, it was my mother.

ME: When I was a child, did I ever play with matches?
MY MOTHER: No, never.

As she answered this question I was watching the jurors out of the corner of my eye. Several of them leaned back in their chairs with a smile on their faces. They knew I was having a hard time questioning my mother and not breaking down in tears. So I think they appreciated the light joke. People in the audience certainly did and it set the mood for the rest of the day.

As I finished my direct examination of my mom, I knew Mr. Minor would have the opportunity to cross-examine her and I was not looking forward to that. I had tried the best I could to prepare my mom for what all he might ask. I, however, respected Mr. Minor, and I knew he wouldn't be like a criminal prosecutor and treat my mother harshly. But, also, I knew he had a job to do. So my mother and I went over every possible question he might ask her. Shockingly, though, Mr. Minor didn't cross-examine my mom. So she was allowed to leave the stand and watch the rest of the trial.

My next witness was going to be Emmett's insurance agent, the Circuit Clerk of Warren County, Jan Hyland Daigre. Now, when I subpoenaed all of the witnesses for the trial, every subpoena commanded them to be at the federal courthouse on Monday, July 17, 2017, and remain there day-after-day until excused.

Rather than have Sheriff Pace, Rosalind Jordan, Ronnie Stewart, and Sheriff Nail come to court on Monday, even though I knew the whole day would be consumed with Jackson's testimony, I'd politely informed everyone that they didn't need to be there on Monday, but definitely on Tuesday. I could have been a dick and made Sheriff Pace and that crew come on Monday and waste a trip. But I was doing everything I could to act like the responsible and mature "attorney" that Judge Aycock expected of me.

When Daigre had been subpoenaed, though, I was at the Warren County courthouse and I tried to tell her that she wouldn't need to actually come to Aberdeen until Tuesday. But before I could do so she called several of the deputies from the Warren County Sheriff's Department and told them that she didn't feel safe talking to me by herself and that she wanted me to leave. So, rather than extend her the courtesy of informing her that she didn't need to drive the five hours to Aberdeen until Tuesday, I simply left her with the impression that she had to be at court on Monday morning, bright and early.

When we took our lunch break Monday afternoon, Daigre was still waiting in the witness room as she had been all morning. I informed her that I couldn't get to her testimony that day and that she'd have to come back the following day. Daigre angrily informed me that she would *not* be staying and would *not* be available the following day.

I couldn't help but explain to her that I would of told her that her presence wasn't needed until Tuesday, but she'd called the deputies to come remove me. So when court reconvened I explained to Judge Aycock's law clerk what the situation was, what had happened with the deputies, and that I needed Judge Aycock to explain to Daigre that her presence would be required the following day. And Judge Aycock did this, even though it pissed Daigre off something fierce. But I wasn't sympathetic; I tried working with her politely. She just wanted to be a dick-eating bitch.

On Tuesday morning, not surprisingly, Daigre was at court and I called her to testify as soon as my mother left. Her testimony was short, though. I had her explain Emmett's insurance policy on the Atwood Lakehouse and the details behind it. When I asked her, though, why Emmett had increased the insurance shortly before the fire, Daigre testified that Emmett didn't increase it; Farm Bureau increased it on their own.

I didn't buy this line because Emmett had testified to something totally different at his deposition, but I couldn't get blood from a turnip, so after about fifteen minutes, and without cross-examination by Mr. Minor, Daigre was allowed to leave. It surprised me, though, that she would lie about the reasons why Emmett increased the insurance. But I thought to myself, Daigre was an elected official in Warren County; that explained her willingness to lie.

After Daigre was allowed to leave, I called Sheriff Tim Nail as my next witness. Prior to trial, his attorney, Mr. Griffith, had allowed me to sit down with the sheriff in Kosciusko and question him about the case and his role in it. By this time I looked at Sheriff Nail, not as an adversary, but a potentially valuable witness to my case.

Jackson had tried blaming his every failure on Sheriff Nail. Had Sheriff Nail known what all Jackson had blamed him for, I doubt very seriously that Sheriff Nail would have ever cooperated in an investigation with Jackson again. But while Sheriff Nail might retain some integrity and honesty as a sworn law enforcement officer, nothing of the such could be expected from the likes of Jackson.

As Sheriff Nail came to the stand to be sworn, Judge Aycock gave the jury a five minute break. While the jury was gone, Judge Aycock explained very carefully to Sheriff Nail—as she would every other witness that testified—not to reveal anything about my criminal history or past incarcerations. I'd already explained this to Sheriff Nail, but Judge Aycock did not want to risk another mistrial, so she was very clear about this portion of any possible testimony.

Sheriff Nail's testimony began with his clear assertion that he was not the lead investigator in the case and that if Jackson had said he was, it would be an inaccurate statement. We then moved over into what steps Sheriff Nail took at the beginning of the investigation.

He testified that he was first made aware of the fire after Kade called him in the late morning of November 11, 2009. Sheriff Nail, though, could not explain why Kade waited so long to call or why he didn't call the fire department as soon as he discovered the fire that morning.

After arriving on the scene, Sheriff Nail met with both Emmett and Kade and they both told him that they suspected me of starting the fire. He then had Emmett sign a consent to search form. After that he called Jackson and informed him about the fire. According to Sheriff Nail, he wrapped crime scene tape around the burnt remains, but admitted that for two days the scene was totally unsecured.

When I asked Sheriff Nail whether he encountered any difficulty in locating Josh Chamblee and I, he testified that he easily found me, easily contacted me, and that I more than willingly cooperated in his part of the investigation. I asked these questions to directly contradict Jackson's fantastic assertion that he couldn't find me to interview me.

When Josh and I met Sheriff Nail at the sheriff's department on November 13, he testified that we provided him our shoes for comparison with the shoeprints that he and Jackson had found earlier that morning, two days after the fire, but the sizes and tread patterns could not be matched to the ones they found around the lake house.

Not surprising to me, Sheriff Nail admitted that Emmett never told him about the recent increase in the insurance coverage, although he did find it somewhat suspicious that not only was the insurance increased, but that Kade had allegedly slept through the fire and never called the fire department.

One of the most important aspects of the investigation that I needed to get across to the jury was the fact that Sheriff Nail subpoenaed our cell phone records and that they clearly showed that our phones were connected to a Starkville cell tower at the time of the fire.

However, when Sheriff Nail procured the subpoena for our cell phone records, he stated to the judge in the request that the Atwood Lakehouse fire was determined by investigators to have been an arson. I'd asked Sheriff Nail, both in his interrogatories and at our meeting prior to trial, what evidence he had at the time he requested our cell records to prove that the fire was arson. Sheriff Nail couldn't answer that question satisfactorily. But now he was under oath and had to answer it.

> **ME:** On November 23rd, 2009, when you filed that motion (for our cell phone records), what evidence did you have on that date that this fire was an arson?
>
> **SHERIFF NAIL:** Well, the footprints for one, by the house. It indicated someone had walked around there. The car tracks. And Kade Atwood said no one should have been around the lake house. So that part of the investigation led us to conclude it was arson. I'm not saying who, but somebody.
>
> **ME:** Okay. So besides some suspicious footprints, what evidence did you have that this fire was an arson?
>
> **SHERIFF NAIL:** I don't remember at the time. I don't remember if the fire marshal ruled it arson at the time or if we just concluded that. I don't know. I can't say.

The footprints had always caused a problem in the investigation. They were allegedly found two days after the fire when Sheriff Nail and Jackson went to the fire scene to allow Jackson to conduct his perfunctory investigation. And at that point in the trial, the footprints did sound suspicious and potentially malicious. Unbeknownst to me, when Emmett later testified that day, he would forever crush the question of where the footprints came from.

After moving on from the cell phone records, Sheriff Nail testified that he kept Jackson informed of everything regarding his aspect of the investigation, that he turned over everything in his file—including Josh's and I's first statements—to Jackson, and that he did not keep anything from Jackson.

I tried to introduce the new cell phone records that contained the text and data entries that I'd subpoenaed the month before trial, but Mr. Minor objected to them being introduced because they had not been the records Sheriff Nail initially obtained in 2009.

These records were vitally important, though. Even though we knew that Sheriff Nail had subpoenaed the call, text, and data records for our cell phones in 2009, only portions of the records were turned over by Sheriff Nail during the discovery phase of the lawsuit. And I have to admit, the call records showed a large gap in between the time Josh said he got off work and the following morning. But when I subpoenaed the text and data records they clearly showed that Josh and I were using our phones during the exact time that the fire occurred while they were attached to a Starkville cell tower. Unfortunately, though, because they weren't the exact records that Sheriff Nail and Jackson had in 2009, they weren't allowed to be introduced. I'd made my point, though.

Prior to the July 2017 trial, I'd sent the newly subpoenaed, complete cell records to Sheriff Nail and asked him to review them so that when I called him to testify he'd be able to say that the cell phone records did, indeed, prove that both Josh's and I's cell phones were being used in Starkville at the time of the fire. However, when Sheriff Nail testified and I asked him if he'd reviewed them, he answered in the negative. It seemed like no one in any position of authority wanted to face the truth about this fire and the investigation that followed.

There were only a few other points that I needed to make before I could finish my direct examination of Sheriff Nail. One of the main things was getting him to admit that he turned Josh's and I's first statements, taken on November 13, 2009, over to Jackson.

Sheriff Nail readily agreed that he did. I then moved on to proving that no reasonable law enforcement officer would ever have relied on the evidence at hand to suspect I was guilty of burning the Atwood Lakehouse.

ME: Outside of James Jackson and the Fire Marshal's Office, did you, or do you have the authority to arrest me for this fire if it was truly an arson?

SHERIFF NAIL: Yes, I do.

ME: Do you agree that you do not have any evidence of an arson?

SHERIFF NAIL: Other than the footprints, no.

ME: Okay. But do you have any evidence that I might have been involved if it was arson?

SHERIFF NAIL: No.

ME: Did you do anything to exclude Emmett and Kade Atwood as suspects?

SHERIFF NAIL: Well, I talked to them. I ruled Kade out because he didn't have anything to gain. As far as Emmett, I had no accusations or reason for him doing that. There's no motive.

ME: But that's based off your conversations with him and the information provided to you by him? Correct?

SHERIFF NAIL: Yes. Correct.

Before I finished my questioning of Sheriff Nail, I attempted to get him to admit that Jackson used his hydrocarbon detector on November 13, 2009, when they went to investigate the scene. I was hoping for more evidence to prove that Jackson was lying when he said his hydrocarbon detector kept malfunctioning and getting false positives. But Sheriff Nail, unfortunately, couldn't even remember if Jackson had used the hydrocarbon detector at all. With this, I finished my direct.

When Mr. Minor came to the podium to cross-examine Sheriff Nail, the first thing that he attempted to do was cast doubt on the cell phone records that Sheriff Nail originally obtained in 2009. As I'd said previously, Sheriff Nail's subpoena requested both the call, text, and data records of Josh's and I's cell phones. However, by the time the lawsuit was filed and we entered into discovery, scant portions were the only thing available. Who knows what happened to the rest.

Mr. Minor was correct in his assertion that the call records showed a gap in use between about midnight and seven o'clock the following morning. This left a huge gap in the record during the exact time the fire occurred. On it's face it could be insinuated that Josh and I left our phones in Starkville and drove to the Atwood Lakehouse and burned it down. That insinuation was the exact reason I'd requested a subpoena and gotten the additional text and data records, which, again, clearly showed that both Josh and I were texting and using data on our cell phones—while connected to a Starkville tower—during the exact time the lake house was burning down.

Unfortunately, though, Judge Aycock had previously excluded these new records from being introduced. And when Mr. Minor questioned Sheriff Nail about the gap in the original call records, Sheriff Nail testified that the cell records didn't rule me in and didn't rule me out as being responsible for the fire. As much as I ground my teeth at this judicial voodoo, without being able to get the complete records in as evidence, there was nothing further I could do.

Mr. Minor also questioned Sheriff Nail about why, during my interview at the Attala County Sheriff's Department, I was asked where I was on November 9, when the fire occurred on the night of November 10. Sheriff Nail admitted he made a mistake. The final question to Sheriff Nail was unexpected.

> **MR. MINOR:** Is it common to rely on witnesses for arrest warrants after they've changed their stories?
> **ME:** Objection, Your Honor. Calls for speculation.
> **JUDGE AYCOCK:** Sustained.

I couldn't let Mr. Minor get away with that one. But after having my objection sustained, Mr. Minor ended his cross-examination and I was allowed a brief redirect, during which I was able to get Sheriff Nail to agree that the cell records he had didn't have the text and data records attached and that people text more than they call.

It was also through Sheriff Nail's testimony that I wanted to establish that I'd suffered the loss of $5,000.00 in paying to bond out of jail. So I had Sheriff Nail testify about booking me into the jail, the steps he went through, and then the process of me paying a bonding agent to bail me out of jail.

Sheriff Nail also was forced to admit that the footprints that Kade showed him two days after the fire could have been made by someone other than an arsonist. Back in the depositions Kade had testified that on the morning of the fire, numerous people came out to the fire scene and walked around and looked at everything and left footprints everywhere.

Since I was beginning to be more and more convinced that this fire was accidental, the fact that numerous people came out to look at the fire scene led me to conclude that one of their footprints was more than likely the cause of Sheriff Nail's suspicion. I would have to explore that further when Emmett testified, but for the moment it was enough to get Sheriff Nail to admit that the "suspicious" footprints could have come from almost anyone. My final question was answered with frank honesty.

>**ME:** What evidence did you uncover implicating me in the fire?
>**SHERIFF NAIL:** There was none.

I thanked Sheriff Nail and he was excused from the witness chair. As I'd thought, Sheriff Nail's testimony actually helped me more than it hurt. Sheriff Nail was a reasonable law enforcement officer and he admitted he had no evidence in which to arrest me. I thought the new day was going very well so far.

CHAPTER THIRTY-EIGHT

The next witness that I called was Ronnie Stewart. My trial strategy had been to use Jackson and Sheriff Nail to establish that there was not any legitimate evidence on which to rely in procuring my arrest warrant. I believed on that Tuesday morning that I'd more than proven that point, and proved it beyond any reasonable doubt.

In addition to proving that Jackson conducted an incompetent investigation that did not uncover any evidence whatsoever that implicated me in the fire, I'd also been able to prove that the investigation was motivated by an illegal conspiracy and that Jackson had committed numerous felony offenses under the direct orders of Mike Chaney. It was another very, very large feather in my hat.

I then needed to turn the jury's attention to Judge Stewart's "finding" at the preliminary hearing in October 2011 that there was "probable cause" for my arrest. After all, Judge Stewart did issue the warrant and he did conduct a hearing during which all of the evidence known to us at the time—both exculpatory and inculpatory—was introduced.

From Mr. Minor's opening statement at the first trial, I knew that they were going to try and base their entire defense on the fact that Judge Stewart made this "finding" at the preliminary hearing. It didn't really matter whether or not a jury is supposed to judge the legitimacy of a false arrest claim from the standpoint of the moment the arrest occurred and not what happened later at a preliminary hearing; all that mattered, according to Mr. Minor, was that the judge made a probable cause finding and bound the case over to a grand jury. But I'd strenuously prepared between the time of the first trial and the second.

This led me back to my assertion that if Jackson's dumb ass hadn't deliberately thrown the first trial down the tubes, I'd been totally unprepared to counter this defense. But Jackson's fuck up was my blessing, and it sunk his case at the second trial.

I knew that Judge Stewart was going to find "probable cause" no matter what evidence was presented to him at the preliminary hearing. I knew that because I'd done my research. I'd talked to Mrs. Jordan, and the morning of the second day of trial I'd finally talked to Judge Stewart. He freely admitted to me that in his twelve years on the bench he'd only declined to find probable cause in a case one time, and that was because it was a civil case, not a criminal case.

So I knew that whatever finding Judge Stewart made was irrelevant. It was irrelevant because any "finding" he made was simply a rubber-stamp on the legal highway down and through the criminal justice system. But I also intended to discredit Judge Stewart's "finding" by casting doubt on his legal abilities as a "judge."

Stewart wasn't a real judge. He didn't have any legal training and he certainly was not an attorney. He spent his entire life as a simple telephone repairman. Not to cast aspersions on telephone repairmen; they obviously perform a very valuable and needed service. But one cannot argue that telephone repairmen are qualified to be criminal judges. Unfortunately, Mississippi allows people that aren't attorneys to run for and be elected justice court judges. Perhaps that's why Mississippi has one of the worst criminal justice systems in the country. People with no legal training are making decisions everyday that seriously affect the lives of unfortunate citizens.

Judge Stewart's testimony was going to prove my point; I knew it. And as Judge Stewart came forward to be sworn and testify, I thanked God that Jackson had caused the mistrial in March. Having Judge Stewart testify was going to smash Mr. Minor's argument that Jackson's deplorable behavior should be excused because Stewart allegedly made this "probable cause" determination at the preliminary hearing.

I first began by having Judge Stewart testify to his educational and employment history and his years as a justice court judge. As expected, he admitted he didn't have any prior legal experience. After a few more perfunctory questions, I questioned him about whether he remembered

James Jackson, remembered issuing both mine and Josh's arrest warrant, or even if he remembered the preliminary hearing. Unfortunately, both for me and Jackson, Judge Stewart claimed he had no memory of these events.

My purpose, though, wasn't to get Stewart to admit he remembered details behind the issuance of our warrants and the preliminary hearing. I simply needed to prove that his "probable cause" determinations were worthless and didn't mean a single noteworthy thing. And after being a bit obstinate at first, Judge Stewart finally accepted the logic of my questions and cooperated fully in my examination.

> **ME:** When a law enforcement officer asks you for an arrest warrant, do you always give it to them?
> **STEWART:** Yes, if the affidavit has the probable cause in it.
> **ME:** Do you normally ask the law enforcement officer what the probable cause is?
> **STEWART:** It's supposed to be in the affidavit.

At this time I placed my arrest warrant affidavit that Jackson filled out and submitted to Judge Stewart on July 29, 2011, on the projector screen for everyone in the courtroom to see. Obviously, it didn't have any probable cause evidence in it.

> **ME:** What in this affidavit is probable cause to demonstrate that a crime has occurred?
> **STEWART:** James Jackson would have had to investigate that and put it in there.
> **ME:** Now wait a minute, Mr. Stewart. You said you always issue these arrest warrants as long as there is probable cause in them. What in this affidavit by James Jackson is probable cause?
> **STEWART:** What James Jackson said.
> **ME:** So again, where is the evidence in this affidavit that a crime occurred?
> **STEWART:** There is no evidence.
> **ME:** So if there is no evidence in the affidavit, there's no probable cause to issue the arrest warrant? Correct?
> **STEWART:** The probable cause comes at the preliminary hearing.

ME: But when a law enforcement officer comes to you asking for an arrest warrant, doesn't he need evidence of a crime to show probable cause for the issuance of the arrest warrant?

STEWART: You have to have an affidavit to get a warrant and you have to have some information in it.

ME: Okay. But do you agree that in this affidavit there is no evidence in it to support probable cause?

STEWART: There is no evidence.

I felt like I was Alice in Wonderland. Maybe it was my naive belief that judges, law enforcement officers, and prosecutors always abided by the Constitution. The Fourth Amendment couldn't be clearer. A law enforcement officer could only obtain an arrest warrant upon providing probable cause to a judge.

This was the perfect example of why people of no higher education than a GED should not be allowed to hold positions as justice court judges in Mississippi. Ronald Stewart didn't know the very basis of the foundation of our Constitution. Any high school student in their government class would be required to know that probable cause must be provided before obtaining a warrant, not later at a preliminary hearing. I silently thanked God that Stewart had been beaten in his reelection efforts and was no longer a judge.

Stewart was making it abundantly clear to those of us in the courtroom that the issuance of arrests warrants without probable cause was a matter of simple routine in his office. James Jackson could have appeared before Judge Stewart and claimed that I committed the "offense" of aggravated cocksucking with intent to swallow and Judge Stewart would have issued a warrant.

As we went through these questions I realized what a favor Jackson did for me and my case when he caused the mistrial back in March. Back then I hadn't even planned on calling Stewart as a witness. But once I saw how much Mr. Minor was going to rely on Stewart's "findings" at the preliminary hearing, that there was probable cause to bind the case over to the grand jury, I was thankful that I'd been given the four additional months to prepare my case.

As we moved on from Stewart's willingness to issue arrest warrants on the flimsiest of grounds, I next had to attack his "finding" at the preliminary hearing that there was "probable cause." This was the crucial crux of the case. And whether Mr. Minor's defense or not would be given any credence hung in the next few moments.

> **ME:** In your twelve years as a justice court judge, have you ever *not* found probable cause and dismissed the case?
> **STEWART:** Yes. One time. It was a civil case; not a criminal one.
> **ME:** Okay. So let me ask you this. If you dismiss a criminal case at the preliminary hearing because there's no probable case, does that stop a prosecution?
> **STEWART:** No.
> **ME:** Can the district attorney continue the prosecution?
> **STEWART:** Yes.
> **ME:** So your probable cause determination has no effect on the prosecution?
> **STEWART:** I don't know what you're getting at.
> **ME:** Okay. I am simply asking, if you were to have found that probable cause did not exist in my case, would it have had any effect on the prosecution if the district attorney would have decided to get an indictment?
> **STEWART:** No.
> **ME:** So really, the real reason we have preliminary hearings in justice court is not to determine whether there is probable cause, but instead to obtain information about the case, the evidence that the law enforcement officers have?
> **STEWART:** That's right.

I took a deep breath and let it slowly escape from my lips. Judge Stewart couldn't have answered better. His "probable cause" determination was nothing more than a superficial rubber-stamp on a document that didn't signify a single noteworthy thing. He was going to make this "finding" no matter what the evidence showed and, ultimately, any finding he made wasn't going to effect the case in any way because the district attorney still retained the ability and right to seek an indictment against me even if Judge Stewart had dismissed the case in the justice court.

This was so important an issue because it completely negated Mr. Minor's defense that his client's culpability should be excused because Judge Stewart allegedly found some type of probable cause at the preliminary hearing that justified the arrest warrant. It was absolutely essential to discredit this "finding." And I believe that I did so pretty well.

After I finished my direct examination of Judge Stewart I sat down and Mr. Minor was allowed the opportunity to cross-examine him. I didn't know what to expect, but it was clear that Judge Stewart's words couldn't be erased from the minds' of the jurors.

Surprisingly, the only thing that Mr. Minor questioned Judge Stewart about was whether or not he remembered what evidence Jackson presented to him on July 29, 2011, when procuring my arrest warrant. I'd asked the same question in the deposition with Judge Stewart back in February 2016, but Stewart alleged that he retained no memory whatsoever regarding Jackson or the obtainment of my arrest warrant.

So when Mr. Minor asked Judge Stewart whether he remembered Jackson presenting Josh Chamblee's third statement to him at the time he obtained the warrant, Stewart was unable to do so. Now, whether I believe Stewart's testimony is a matter of speculation that I'm questioning to this day. Thankfully, though, for the purposes of the trial, Stewart didn't have a memory of Jackson presenting anything at all to him. That fit with my argument that Jackson concealed relevant and important facts from him.

Proving that Jackson deliberately concealed essential facts from Judge Stewart when he obtained the arrest warrant was the second element of my case that I had to prove to the jury. I'd already proved—in my opinion, at least—that there was no probable cause, no evidence, that the fire was arson and that I was involved. I next had to prove that Jackson concealed important information from Stewart when he sought and obtained the arrest warrant.

The independent intermediary doctrine would protect Jackson if he could prove that he did not conceal any exculpatory evidence from the judge. But we knew already he hadn't told Stewart about the cell phone records, Josh's prior alibi statements, his arrests, or the fact that the fire could never be proved to have been an arson. These were all essential facts that Jackson was obligated to provide to Judge Stewart. But he didn't, and because he didn't he was not entitled to the protection of the independent intermediary doctrine.

So when Judge Stewart finished testifying he was excused and I moved on to my next witness—the one I felt was one of the most important witnesses during the entire trial.

Prior to the trial I had met with Rosalind Jordan, the attorney that represented me at the preliminary hearing in front of Judge Stewart in October 2011. Not only had she kept extremely detailed notes of the questions asked and the answers provided by the witnesses at the hearing, she also maintained a phenomenal memory about what Jackson testified to.

Very quickly I realized that Mrs. Jordan was going to be, potentially, my best witness. Through her testimony I needed her to discredit Jackson's newest claim that his hydrocarbon detector kept malfunctioning, preventing him, of course, from obtaining accurate readings on whether an accelerant had been used to start the fire.

Mrs. Jordan could also testify about Judge Stewart's propensity to always issue arrest warrants regardless of what was presented to him and his always "finding" probable cause during the preliminary hearings. This is what Mr. Minor was hanging his defense on, and Mrs. Jordan was my best possible witness to discredit that assertion.

Now, I can't help but think that one of the biggest mistakes that Mr. Minor probably made during the trial was not talking to any of my witnesses before the trial. Had he done so, which was certainly his right to do, I believe he would have discovered the truth behind Stewart's "probable cause" determinations and the extensive details that Mrs. Jordan was going to testify to regarding her memory of what Jackson testified to during the preliminary hearing and then Judge Stewart's "findings" in other criminal cases.

From day one I did everything I could to interview every witness involved in my case. Of course, though, Jan Hyland Daigre wouldn't cooperate and neither would Emmett or Kade. Sheriff Pace briefly spoke to me about his potential testimony when I had him served in the cemetery while he was on funeral detail. But he was as tight-lipped as the bulkheads of submarines. Besides, what I needed from Sheriff Pace wasn't so much his truthful answers to my questions, but the denials that I knew would come from my questioning of him and his involvement in the investigation.

This, however, led back to Mr. Minor's decision not to interview any of the witnesses before trial, except Emmett and Kade, of course. I, however, wanted to be as prepared as possible. And I learned a very, very valuable lesson about the dangers of not interviewing witnesses before calling them to testify. Thankfully, having interviewed most of them prepared me to ask the right questions in anticipation of what their answers might be. I assumed all attorneys did so before major trials.

As soon as Judge Stewart left the witness stand I called Mrs. Jordan to come forward and testify. We began our dialogue by me reminding her that I was waiving all of our attorney and client confidentiality. It was almost a moot point, but the privilege between attorneys and clients is inviolate. So I needed to make sure that Mrs. Jordan could respond openly, fully, and completely to all the questions I asked.

We began by talking about Mrs. Jordan's educational and employment history. Obviously, she was a law school graduate. But she also testified that she'd been practicing law for nineteen years (which I found to be amazing because Mrs. Jordan has a beautiful countenance and doesn't look a day over thirty-five), was a municipal court judge in West, Mississippi, had been a special prosecutor on numerous occasions, was currently a public defender, and had conducted sixty to seventy preliminary hearings a year before Judge Stewart in the Attala County Justice Court. Undeniably, Mrs. Jordan was the best qualified person to critique Judge Stewart's actions.

I wanted to first tackle the issues with Judge Stewart and his "findings" regarding probable cause in both mine and others' criminal cases. I would save the questions about Jackson for last because they, in my mind, were the most important and would utterly destroy Jackson's credibility and Mr. Minor's ultimate defense of Jackson's actions during the investigation.

> **ME:** In your many years of conducting preliminary hearings in front of Judge Stewart, have you ever seen or heard of a case where Judge Stewart has *not* found probable cause?
>
> **MRS. JORDAN:** I have no recollection of any preliminary hearings where Judge Stewart did not find probable cause.
>
> **ME:** Does any specific case come to mind where there was just a total lack of probable cause, yet nonetheless, Judge Stewart still found probable cause and bound the case over to the grand jury?
>
> **MR. MINOR:** Objection, Your Honor. Calls for an improper opinion.

JUDGE AYCOCK: Sustained.

ME: Let me rephrase. Have you ever been involved in a case where an alleged victim appeared in court in front of Judge Stewart and told him that he, the victim, had fabricated the allegation and that the defendant was innocent?

MRS. JORDAN: I know of cases in front of Judge Stewart where victims did not want to pursue charges and I've had cases in front of Judge Stewart where someone else came in and said, "Hey, I'm the person that committed this crime, not the defendant," and Judge Stewart still found probable cause and bound the case over to a grand jury.

ME: In your nineteen years as an attorney and judicial officer, do you find it to be true that preliminary hearings in front of Judge Stewart are more for the purposes of finding out information and the evidence about the case rather than being an actual probable cause determination?

MRS. JORDAN: That has been my experience.

ME: And based on your knowledge, the grand jury in my case did not find enough probable cause to indict me, which was directly contradictory to any alleged finding made by Judge Stewart at the preliminary hearing?

MR. MINOR: Objection, Your Honor. Relevance.

JUDGE AYCOCK: Overruled.

MRS. JORDAN: Correct. The grand jury did not find probable cause in which to indict you.

This testimony, I fully believed, took care of any argument that Mr. Minor could make that Stewart's "finding" of "probable cause" at the October 2011 preliminary hearing had any weight or legitimacy. Judge Stewart always found probable cause no matter what the evidence showed. And, as Mr. Jordan testified to and as he willingly admitted, preliminary hearings in his court were more for the purposes of determining what the evidence was in a case rather than for the actual purposes of finding probable cause.

By the objections of Mr. Minor and the tone of voice he used, I could tell that he was not liking where Mrs. Jordan's testimony was going. Her testimony was blowing his client's defense out of the water. By this time it was clear to everyone in the courtroom—including the jury—that no significance could be attached to Judge Stewart's "finding" at the preliminary hearing. I'd smashed that defense in less than ten minutes.

But to really deliver my knockout blow, I had to get around to Jackson and what he testified to at the preliminary hearing. If Mr. Minor was upset at how Mrs. Jordan's testimony went in regards to Stewart's findings in the Justice Court of Attala County, I knew he would be livid when he heard the next round of questions and answers.

I then had Mrs. Jordan lay the groundwork for later questions about the preliminary hearing. She patiently explained to the jury that after I'd been arrested she was appointed to represent me in the case. She clearly remembered representing me at the preliminary hearing before Judge Stewart, she remembered Jackson coming to testify, the evidence he presented, and she testified that she'd kept extensively detailed notes about what questions she asked Jackson and what answers he provided in response to her questions. I'd been provided a copy of those notes and Mrs. Jordan retained a copy on the witness stand with her. I went straight for Jackson's throat.

> **ME**: At the preliminary hearing, did James Jackson testify about his hydrocarbon detector giving false positives?
>
> **MRS. JORDAN**: No. He said that no accelerant was detected.
>
> **ME**: So at the preliminary hearing, Jackson was very, very clear that when he used his hydrocarbon detector it was working correctly and that he did not detect any accelerants?
>
> **MR. MINOR**: Objection. Asked and answered.
>
> **JUDGE AYCOCK**: Overruled.
>
> **MRS. JORDAN**: Yes. At the preliminary hearing Mr. Jackson testified that he in fact had used the hydrocarbon detector and that no accelerant was detected.
>
> **ME**: Did he ever mention anything about a malfunctioning hydrocarbon detector?
>
> **MRS. JORDAN**: No. He did not.
>
> **ME**: Did he ever mention that he could not get an accurate reading on the hydrocarbon detector because there was still smoke coming from the fire scene?
>
> **MRS. JORDAN**: No. In fact, he came two days after the fire and used the hydrocarbon detector and detected no accelerant.

ME: At the hearing, did Jackson testify that he couldn't use the hydrocarbon detector because the ground was too hot?

MRS. JORDAN: No. He actually testified that he used the hydrocarbon detector and detected no accelerant.

ME: So if Jackson is now testifying that he couldn't use the hydrocarbon detector at the fire scene because there was too much smoke and the ground was too hot, that'd be different that what he testified to at the preliminary hearing?

MRS. JORDAN: Yes, sir. That would be very different.

ME: And whether an accelerant is detected is a very important detail in an arson case, so are you sure you remember his testimony clearly about this?

MRS. JORDAN: Yes. That is correct.

ME: Do you remember Jackson clearly testifying at the hearing that he didn't have any evidence of arson?

MR. MINOR: Objection.

JUDGE AYCOCK: Overruled.

MRS. JORDAN: Correct. I do.

ME: And you know this to be true because as Jackson was testifying you were writing everything down that he said and your notes reflect that?

MRS. JORDAN: Yes. Correct.

ME: One last thing. In your experience as an attorney working before Judge Stewart, are you aware of any time that he has *not* issued an arrest warrant when asked by a law enforcement officer?

MRS. JORDAN: I am unaware of any time he has not issued a warrant.

There it was. Not only had another nail been driven into the coffin of James O'Neal Jackson, but the whole thing had been sealed shut. He'd tried to lie and front the story that an accelerant could possibly had been used to start the fire, but because of a "malfunctioning" hydrocarbon detector, he'd been unable to do the proper tests. Of course, this implied that the fire could have been arson even though he couldn't detect an accelerant. But Jackson had testified very clearly at the preliminary hearing that he'd used his hydrocarbon detector, it was working correctly, and that he'd detected no accelerant.

I knew he'd also lied to Mr. Minor about this. And I could tell by the look on Mr. Minor's face and the tone of his voice that he was pissed that he'd been sandbagged again because of the lies of his client. Everything that Jackson talked about turned out to be a lie. Nothing he ever said was the truth. And with Mrs. Jordan's testimony, the final and last nail had been driven into his judicial coffin.

Mr. Minor tried an ineffectual cross-examination of Mrs. Jordan, but he could only get her to admit that just because a grand jury doesn't indict doesn't mean a defendant is innocent. He discussed with her whether Judge Stewart had been presented all of the exculpatory evidence at the preliminary hearing which demonstrated my innocence—which he had been—but the damage was done. Jackson had been caught in almost every lie that he'd told.

As Mrs. Jordan left the witness stand I quickly realized that she had been, hands down, my best witness. She had credibility, she had experience, and I could tell that the jury liked her. So far she had been the only one to provide testimony about the investigation, arrest, and what happened in court with any resemblance of honesty and respectability.

Not only that, but she gave a behind-the-scenes look at how law enforcement and the courts actually worked in the state of Mississippi. Her testimony certainly proved that things were not done by the book and in-line with the Constitution.

The day was quickly progressing and I was almost done. Sheriff Pace would be my next witness and I was looking forward to finally, after years of desire, getting him in a witness chair, under oath, and with me as the examiner. It was a long-prayed-for wish come true. And I was completely ready.

My purpose in calling the Warren County sheriff, Martin Pace, was for a limited purpose. I needed to establish my belief that my book prompted Sheriff Pace and Emmett to put pressure on Mike Chaney, who then threatened to fire Jackson if he didn't get his ass out of the chair and go arrest me. And again, it wasn't going to so much be what Sheriff Pace admitted to, but what he denied.

Through Jackson's testimony it was clearly established that when *Into Hell I Rode* was published, the pressure for him to make an arrest came down on him the hardest. If Jackson's testimony is to be believed about Chaney pressing him to make an arrest—and I have no doubt about that aspect of his testimony—then it was perfectly also logical for one to assume that Chaney was being pressed by others.

Mike Chaney's name had not been mentioned in my book. Neither had any of the deputy fire marshals or anyone else closely associated with Jackson. In fact, it never even crossed my mind to write anything about the Atwood Lakehouse fire or Jackson's investigation. It didn't cross my mind because at the time I wrote the book I'd been told that the fire was ruled undeterminable and that the investigation was closed. End of story, or so I thought.

So, since neither Chaney nor Jackson had been specifically mentioned in my book, my line of reasoning went that there had to of been some reason why Chaney, in June 2011 when my book was published, began pressing Jackson to violate the law and conduct an illegal arrest. Of course, we know it was because Sheriff Pace and Emmett began pressing him to use the circumstances of the fire to punish me for having written what I did.

Nothing else made sense. There had to of been some reason why Chaney chose June 2011 to have the investigation reopened. And since I'd not mentioned him or Jackson in the book, it stood to reason that his involvement at that time was because of what I'd written about other people (i.e., Sheriff Pace and Emmett). I was determined to get Sheriff Pace to make my point.

Prior to him testifying, though, Judge Aycock sent the jury out on a break and carefully explained to Sheriff Pace the necessity of him not testifying about anything involving my criminal history or past incarcerations. He, of course, knew what had happened at the March trial and I am certain he wasn't about to cross ways with Judge Aycock.

After the jury returned and Sheriff Pace had been sworn I quickly established how Sheriff Pace knew me and my family and how he became sheriff. I would eventually get to the reasons why Sheriff Barrett was forced from office, but I allowed Sheriff Pace to tell the story as he wanted to. Sheriff Pace denied, though, my question about whether he considered Sheriff Barrett his mentor.

In a moment of complete candor, Sheriff Pace did admit that he and Emmett were no longer friends because he wouldn't jump and have me arrested every time Emmett called to tell him that I committed some crime.

When I brought up Mike Chaney, Sheriff Pace admitted that he was close friends with him, had voted for him, and had supported him in all his election campaigns. Sheriff Pace also admitted that when my book came out in June 2011 he was gearing up for a reelection campaign where he faced some potentially strong opposition from one of his former deputies.

He also admitted that he became aware of the book during the Miss Mississippi Pageant, however, he claimed that he had not read it even though most of his deputies had. He also agreed that he knew there was a lot of negative information in my book about him and the sheriff's department.

When I then moved over into his deputy, Lionel Johnson, killing an unarmed black kid while the kid was attempting to protect his aged grandmother from being assaulted by Johnson, Sheriff Pace was quick to admit my version of the events and that Johnson had eventually been fired.

I also succeeded in getting Sheriff Pace to admit that when I'd run for constable back in 2002 that I'd done so on an anticorruption platform that severely criticized his department and his employees.

One of the last areas that I went into concerned Mike Traxler and his involvement in my arrest. Of all the deputies available on the sheriff's department to entrust with serving my felony arson warrant, Sheriff Pace chose the one person who had the most to gain by murdering me.

I'd spent pages upon pages in my book revealing the crimes and unethical conduct of Mike Traxler. Yet, this was the person Sheriff Pace gave my warrant to. It was as Deep Six told me; no doubt Traxler wanted to use the opportunity during the SWAT raid to murder me. There was no other reason why he would be given the warrant. And I forcefully pushed this on Sheriff Pace.

> **ME:** Do you think it is a safe, sound practice to assign that felony arrest warrant to a deputy that is so prominent and has been criticized so much in my book?
>
> **SHERIFF PACE:** I don't have a record that you were ever arrested by us on that warrant.

He was trying to be slick. Obfuscation was Sheriff Pace's talent. He tried answering without actually answering, but he'd never had me as an interrogator before, and I wasn't going to let him get away with it.

ME: Okay. But we are talking about a fire marshal contacting you and then you giving this felony arrest warrant to Mike Traxler, a deputy that I severely criticized in my book as the epitome of a corrupt cop. So I ask again, is that a good idea to give that man a felony arrest warrant to serve on me after I exposed all the corrupt things he's done?

SHERIFF PACE: Mike Traxler, for many years, was the county fire investigator. He would have been the person that the fire marshals knew. So I don't know.

ME: Okay. But that's not my question. So let me ask you again. Is it a good idea to give that man my felony arrest warrant to serve so soon after I'd published a book which revealed numerous crimes and unethical actions that he's committed?

MR. MINOR: Objection. Asked and answered.

JUDGE AYCOCK: It has not been answered. Overruled. You may proceed, Mr. Atwood.

SHERIFF PACE: I don't know. If the book you're referring to was given any validity then that is something that maybe should have been taken into consideration.

ME: But this isn't a small sheriff's department. The buck ultimately stops at you.

SHERIFF PACE: Ultimately, I am responsible. But that doesn't mean I know everything that happens.

ME: Did it ever cross your mind to instruct your deputies that if anything came up with me after I wrote this book to inform you so that things were ensured to be carried out in a safe, fair, and proper manner?

SHERIFF PACE: Not that I'm aware of because I wasn't familiar with what was in the book.

ME: But you knew that I'd recently written a book that had a lot of negative information in it about you, your deputies, and the sheriff's department.

SHERIFF PACE: That's right.

ME: And you're aware that there aren't just one or two chapters about the Warren County Sheriff's Department; the whole book is mostly about the corruption there.

SHERIFF PACE: So you say.

This gave me the opportunity to start citing examples from my book regarding the corruption in Warren County. I was able to get Sheriff Pace to agree that one of his deputies, London Williams, had raped his own biological daughter and was ultimately sent to prison for it. And that some of the allegations against Traxler were valid.

ME: So when I write in my book that London Williams raped his own daughter, that is totally true?

SHERIFF PACE: If it's in the book, yes.

ME: Were you aware that the book contained an allegation that Traxler's wife caught him having extramarital sex in the back seat of his patrol car with another woman and because of that his wife purposefully damaged the government car by repeatedly ramming it with her personal car?

SHERIFF PACE: I don't know.

ME: But to your knowledge that allegation is true. Traxler's wife caught him having extramarital sex in his patrol car, by his wife, with another woman, and that his wife used her car to repeatedly ram the patrol car?

SHERIFF PACE: I don't know the exact details. There was a time either right before I took office or right after that that he had a uh . . . uh . . . uh . . . argument or fight with his wife and I think there was some damage to the car. It's just that I don't remember.

ME: Did you not care?

SHERIFF PACE: It's not that I didn't care; I just can't remember.

ME: But even after becoming aware of this you continued paying Traxler as an investigator?

SHERIFF PACE: Yes.

ME: Okay. So at what point did you talk to Mike Chaney about having his office falsely arrest me for this fire to try and get me out of Vicksburg and in a jail somewhere so I wouldn't be able to interfere with your reelection efforts?

MR. MINOR: Objection. Argumentative.

JUDGE AYCOCK: Overruled.

SHERIFF PACE: I've never asked Mike Chaney that.

ME: But if you did ask Chaney that, you wouldn't admit that today would you?

SHERIFF PACE: I'm under oath; I would.

ME: Okay. But during this June/July 2011 time period, did you have any conversations with Mike Chaney?

SHERIFF PACE: I don't remember, but again that particular period there were a lot of state and federal people that I was talking to.

ME: How many of your deputies have voiced concerns to you about my book?

SHERIFF PACE: A handful of them.

ME: And they weren't happy about it?

SHERIFF PACE: I don't know.

ME: But you know this book came out in June/July 2011 and it accused you of being a drug dealer?

SHERIFF PACE: That's right.

ME: And it accused the sheriff's department of dealing drugs?

SHERIFF PACE: That's right.

ME: And you're aware that within two weeks of this book being released Mike Chaney ordered that the fire investigation be reopened and that I be arrested regardless of whether there was probable cause or evidence to do so?

SHERIFF PACE: At some point someone with the office made mention of the fact that you'd been charged with arson.

With this, I ended my questioning of Sheriff Pace, and since Mr. Minor didn't have any questions for him he was allowed to be excused and left the courtroom.

It's hard to get blood from a turnip. But I thought I established that prior to Chaney having the investigation reopened, Sheriff Pace was made aware of the book, that he and his deputies weren't happy about it, and that the probability of him contacting Chaney to ask what could be done to have me arrested was fairly high.

One of the main points that I tried to make was the utter lack of oversight and short-sightedness in allowing Mike Traxler to serve my arrest warrant. Not only had I published in my book that Traxler physically abused his wife, cheated on her with trailer park whores, had tried offering me a bribe when I'd run for constable, and was the center of the modern day conspiracy to deal drugs out of the sheriff's department, but I also demonstrated that there was a conspiracy to do me harm when he was given the warrant to serve on me.

Why else would he and a large group of SWAT officers, with machine guns and a battering ram, destroy my mother's door, run in with guns at the ready, and attempt to arrest me with such aggression? After all, every single time I'd been arrested in the past, Sheriff Pace or one of his deputies simply called me on my phone and asked that I come turn myself in.

But these past courtesy calls when warrants were issued for my arrest were before I'd written *Into Hell I Rode*. Now the game was personal. And no one had as much to gain by the retaliation and my murder than did Mike Traxler. I could think of no other reason why they'd lead that arrest warrant raid in the manner that they did. And when Sheriff Pace at first tried to avoid answering the question, my suspicions were proven entirely true.

If Sheriff Pace didn't hand the warrant, specifically, off to Traxler to have served on me in the hopes I'd give them a pretext to murder me, what was the point in him trying to lie about it and avoid the question when I asked it of him at trial? His obfuscation revealed wonders to me, as I hoped it would the jury as well.

After I squeezed all I could from Sheriff Pace and he was allowed to be excused, there was only one thing left for me to do; only one witness left for me to call and have testify. I deliberately saved Emmett Ray Atwood's testimony for last. I hoped his examination would be the icing on the already delicious looking cake. But if I was to be successful, I'd have to bring every ounce of wit and intellect as I could. Emmett would not be an easy nut to crack.

CHAPTER THIRTY-NINE

Before I officially called Emmett to the stand to testify, I requested that Judge Aycock allow Mr. Minor and myself to approach her bench for a discussion about Emmett's potential testimony.

I explained to Judge Aycock the difficulty that I'd encountered during Emmett's deposition at Mr. Minor's office the past February, and I was severely concerned that his testimony would revert to the immature and unnecessary name-calling, frivolous accusations of criminal misconduct, and anything else he could think of to portray me as the Gay Bride of Chucky.

I asked that Judge Aycock deliver a stern warning to Emmett about her previous order that my criminal history and past incarcerations were not to be disclosed and testified about to the jury. Judge Aycock immediately understood and sent the jury out on a short break while Emmett took the witness stand.

JUDGE AYCOCK: Mr. [Emmett] Atwood, you are about to take the witness stand to testify and there are some things I'm going to speak to you about prior to your testimony. So listen to me very carefully and if you have any questions ask me.

EMMETT: Okay.

JUDGE AYCOCK: I have made some rulings in this case regarding some things that are not admissible and therefore it is not appropriate for you to testify about Mr. David Atwood's prior criminal history, his prior convictions, the fact he's ever been incarcerated, the fact that he's served time in prison or the fact that there are revocations of probation in his history. Are you clear?

EMMETT: Your Honor, I hate to say it, but I am 90 years old and my memory ain't like it used to be. And that's a lot of items I've gotta remember.

JUDGE AYCOCK: [The judge leaned over her dais and glared down at Emmett.] Mr. Atwood, listen to me very carefully. I *will* hold you in contempt. Do you understand me?

EMMETT: Yes, Ma'am.

JUDGE AYCOCK: So here is how we are going to proceed. I am going to tell you about other things that you may not testify to. Again, you shall not testify to any prior criminal history. Do you understand?

EMMETT: Yes, Ma'am. I understand

JUDGE AYCOCK: And you understand that you are not to testify about any of his prior incarcerations?

EMMETT: Yes, Ma'am.

JUDGE AYCOCK: So here is how we are going to proceed. There may be a question asked of you that you need some direction about whether or not it's appropriate for you to respond. Do not respond. If there is a question in your mind that may involve some of these prohibitive matters, do not respond. I will be watching you. You will look to me. I will get the jury out so they do not hear it. We will then explore what your answer might be, and if it is appropriate for you to respond I will tell you you may. Now, we've already had a mistrial in this case and I am trying to avoid another one. A lot of costs have been involved already, and a lot of time, effort, and resources have been expended. You are the last witness to testify in this case on direct. And I'm trying my best to make sure you understand that you must be very careful about testifying to these prohibited matters.

EMMETT: Ma'am, I understand what you are saying perfectly. And I'll try my absolute best and I hope I don't make an error, but don't fault me if I do.

JUDGE AYCOCK: Well, you're not going to make a mistake because you're going to look to me and I'll give you the go ahead to testify or not. But now, it's on you. And I've warned you. And

I'm telling you. And I'm being as fair as I can be about it. I do not want another mistrial in this case. Alright?

EMMETT: Based on all that that I've got to remember, can I refuse to answer?

JUDGE AYCOCK: I don't know what the question might be that you'll refuse to answer. But Mr. David Atwood knows not to ask you any questions related to these prohibited matters. Mr. Minor knows the same. He's an officer of the court. He understands the court's ruling. He's not going to ask you anything inappropriate. The key is that you don't volunteer anything. Okay?

EMMETT: Okay.

I'd seen firsthand the anger that could arise from within Judge Aycock when her warnings had not been heeded. Jackson experienced that himself at the first trial. I don't know what Emmett was thinking, but when he saw Judge Aycock lean across her dais and glare down at him as she threatened to hold him contempt if he violated her order, Emmett knew then to tow the line. I was doubtful, though, whether we'd make it through his testimony without resorting to the name-calling and the making of frivolous criminal allegations.

Judge Aycock was right, however. We had spent a lot of time, effort, and resources, and Jackson's testimony on Monday had gone so well from my standpoint that I certainly didn't want another mistrial. It couldn't have gone better for me than what it did. So I was extra careful as I began Emmett's questioning to make sure I didn't provoke him too much into losing his temper and venting some aspect of my criminal history to the jury.

ME: Mr. Atwood, do you know who I am?
EMMETT: Yes.
ME: And am I your grandson?
EMMETT: That's what the record shows.
ME: But you don't claim me as your grandson?
EMMETT: I don't. [Then turning to Judge Aycock.] He can't ask me personal questions, can he?
JUDGE AYCOCK: Yes, and you are under oath. Proceed.

I then had Emmett testify about his familiarity of the Atwood Lakehouse, the property it sat on, and what buildings were on the property. He volunteered that the only new building was the one he built to replace the original one I'd burned down.

It was essential for me not to play into Emmett's argumentative attitude. He didn't know what all Jackson had previously testified to about not having any evidence that the fire was arson. And I didn't want to argue with Emmett. I simply wanted to just ask my questions and try to get him to answer truthfully. So I ignored his first comment stating that I burned the lake house.

My next question was asked in reference to an aerial photograph that I'd placed on the projector screen for everyone in the courtroom to see. Google Earth had provided me with some wonderfully detailed aerials of the property and I had Emmett explain to the jury the entire layout of the property, the roads, the lake, and the location where the old lake house sat.

> **ME:** [Indicating on the map.] Do you see where my pen is pointing?
> **EMMETT:** Yes.
> **ME:** And what is that building?
> **EMMETT:** It's where I built the new lake house after you burned the old one.

Again, I didn't play into his game. As much as I wanted to reach forth and slap the shit out of Emmett's face, and forever cure him of that horrible attitude, I knew it was more important to act the attorney that Judge Aycock expected of me. So I silently suffered Emmett's attitude.

> **ME:** When we sat down for your deposition at the attorney general's office, you swore under oath then, as you have now, that your answers would be truthful and accurate. Correct?
> **EMMETT:** Yes. If I swore to that, then I did.
> **ME:** Prior to the fire that destroyed the Atwood Lakehouse, had you recently increased the insurance on the property?
> **EMMETT:** I never increased the insurance on the house. Now, the insurance company itself increased it. But I never increased it.
> **ME:** So you're stating to the jury today that you personally did

not increase the insurance?

EMMETT: I didn't ask them to increase it, if that's your question.

ME: [I placed Emmett's deposition testimony on the projector for everyone to see.] Okay. We've established that you testified in this deposition at the attorney general's office back in February. I asked you then, *Prior to the fire, had you recently increased the insurance?* And your answer was...

[Reading from transcript.]

EMMETT: *I don't recall if I did. It is possible, though, because at first, for many years they wouldn't—the limit on it was very small because of it being out in the country and not close to a fire department. So it is possible that I got them to increase it. We did at some period. I think it was way before the period you're talking about, but I'm not sure.*

ME: So today you've come to trial and testified that the insurance company increased it on their own, but that's not what you testified to at the deposition.

EMMETT: I didn't testify and lie. This is just what my memory has been.

ME: And who was your insurance agent?

EMMETT: At first it was John Hyland. Then his daughter, Jan Hyland Daigre.

ME: Who is related to us through marriage?

EMMETT: Not really.

ME: Your granddaughter is married to her stepson.

EMMETT: Yes, if you want to say that. That's factual.

ME: But today is the first time that you've mentioned that the insurance company—Mrs. Daigre—increased the coverage on their own. Correct?

EMMETT: Well, they've melded together because my thinking on the matter is not good.

ME: So, if you testified in this deposition under oath—that you don't recall who increased it—it's possible, though, because for many years they wouldn't—the limit on it was very small because of being out in the country and not close to a fire department—and you said...

[Reading from transcript.]

> **EMMETT:** *It's possible we got them to increase it.*
> **ME:** But you didn't say anything about them increasing it on their own. But today you've come into court and changed your story.
> **EMMETT:** That could have been the case at one time. They increased it. I couldn't.
> **ME:** You couldn't go and ask the insurance company for an increase?
> **EMMETT:** I couldn't make them increase it. I guess I could have, but I don't recall. Possibly I did increase it.
> **ME:** But you do recall the insurance being increased shortly before the fire?
> **EMMETT:** No, I don't. I think that's totally incorrect. If you have records proving my memory wrong, then my apologies.

At the mention of the insurance records, I placed them on the projector screen and let everyone in the courtroom view them. The records that I'd subpoenaed from Mississippi Farm Bureau clearly showed that very shortly before the fire, Emmett had substantially increased the coverage on the lake house. The records proved it, and it proved that Emmett increased it on his own accord.

Of course, this proved that both him and Jan Hyland Daigre were liars and had come to court and committed perjury in an effort to hide the fact—and by implication the suspicion that goes along with a homeowner increasing the insurance shortly before a fire—that Emmett had obtained a substantial increase in the insurance so soon before the fire.

> **EMMETT:** I told you that if the records showed that that I apologize. My memory is not that good.
> **ME:** Okay. But again, Mr. Atwood. You didn't tell me and Mr. Minor that in February.
> **EMMETT:** I told you what I remembered.
> **ME:** But now you remember differently?
> **EMMETT:** I remember what I just said.

A short comment should be made regarding Emmett's "memory." I found it medically fascinating that when it came to anything negative towards me, Emmett maintained a phenomenal memory. But if there was a fact or event that was positive in my favor, Emmett would always revert to his go-to line that his memory failed him. Of course, we know that even the young have selective memory. And that proved just as true with Emmett as anyone else. I then moved to other areas.

> **ME:** Prior to the fire, had you had any maintenance or anything done to the lake house?
>
> **EMMETT:** Shortly before that, maybe a month before that, I had insulation put in. It'd never been insulated. It was built in 1936 and our whole family loved that old house until you burned it down.
>
> **ME:** Okay. Was the Atwood Lakehouse and property a well-known place in Kosciusko?
>
> **EMMETT:** I would say that's fair to say.
>
> **ME:** So a lot of people other than family would come out there for parties, weddings, and anniversaries?
>
> **EMMETT:** Over the years they did.
>
> **ME:** You just testified about some insulation that was put in the house. And it had never been insulated before? Correct?
>
> **EMMETT:** Yes. And I wouldn't have just put it in there if I'd anticipated you burning it down.
>
> **JUDGE AYCOCK:** Counselors, will you approach please? [Mr. Minor and I both walk to Judge Aycock's dais.] You may state your objections, but I'm about to instruct him to quit making reference to you burning the house down. We've just got to get past this. Okay?
>
> **ME:** Yes, Your Honor. [Mr. Minor just nodded his head.]
>
> **JUDGE AYCOCK:** [Turning to speak to Emmett.] Mr. Atwood, I understand that you believe David Atwood burned this house.
>
> **EMMETT:** That's correct.
>
> **JUDGE AYCOCK:** We are not here about who burned the house. I am instructing you, do not make another reference in your testimony stating he burned the house. Understand me?

[I believe Judge Aycock almost said "the fucking house."]

> **EMMETT:** Yes.

Thankfully, Judge Aycock had gotten tired of Emmett's bullshit too. So I moved on with my questions.

Emmett was quickly wearing out not only my patience, but Judge Aycock's as well. And she was right. We weren't there to prove or disprove whether I'd started the fire or not. We were there to determine whether Jackson violated my Fourth Amendment constitutional rights by having me arrested without probable cause. And it was clear, he did. But I still had other questions that needed answering.

> **ME:** Are you familiar with an individual named Mike Chaney?
> **EMMETT:** Yes.
> **ME:** Who do you know Mike Chaney to be?
> **EMMETT:** Mike Chaney was in the oil business in Vicksburg. He's the Insurance Commissioner. He's also the State Fire Marshal.
> **ME:** Are you friends with him?
> **EMMETT:** Yes I am. I won't argue that.
> **ME:** And have you contributed money to his election campaigns?
> **EMMETT:** Yes. But I've only contributed minor amounts, as I have other candidates. But I don't remember specific numbers or amounts.

Ever since Emmett made this comment I've often wondered what he considers "minor amounts." Amounts of money are subjective. What might seem expensive to one could just as easily be viewed as cheap to another. Because all political candidates have to report any donations they receive, I knew from my research that Emmett had donated thousands of dollars to Chaney. Most, I'm sure, would not consider this to be a minor amount.

> **ME:** Okay. At some point in time in the summer of 2011, were you made aware of a book that I published?
> **EMMETT:** I've heard about it . . . that you've allegedly published.
> **ME:** And has anyone told you that you're mentioned in that

book quite prominently?

EMMETT: Yes, I've had people that have said they've read it and that you mentioned me.

ME: So you weren't happy that this book came out and that you were in it?

EMMETT: I'm unhappy that you told a bunch of lies about me.

ME: Okay. So if there were a bunch of lies in the book about you, did you ever file a libel or slander lawsuit?

EMMETT: No.

I deliberately chose at the beginning of my direct-examination to avoid asking Emmett any specific questions about the Atwood Lakehouse, the fire, and the subsequent investigation. Before I asked him anything about the fire, I wanted to first destroy his credibility by catching him in numerous lies.

Emmett is an opportunistic liar just as James Jackson was. Emmett chose to lie in this case to conceal his embarrassing behavior in the past and to cast doubt about his responsibility in having me illegally arrested. And in order for me to dismantle his believability, I needed to get Emmett to lie about his biggest secret of all.

ME: How many children do you have, Mr. Atwood?

EMMETT: I have, uh . . . uh . . . [long pause] four children.

ME: Just four? [Emmett nods his head.]

ME: Have you fathered any other children?

EMMETT: No. Absolutely not.

ME: Okay. Do you remember at the deposition in February 2017 me asking you about an African-American lady named Georgia Hicks?

EMMETT: Uh-huh.

ME: And who do you know Georgia Hicks to be?

EMMETT: Georgia Hicks was a black woman from Jackson.

ME: Did Mrs. Hicks file a paternity suit against you?

EMMETT: Yes, she did. And in the Chancery Court in Jackson, Mississippi, and the record down there will show it. It was dismissed and that's all that ever happened to it.

ME: But she claimed in this paternity suit that you fathered her child? Correct?

EMMETT: She claimed it, but it was disclaimed.

ME: Did you settle that case out-of-court with her?

EMMETT: Absolutely not.

ME: Did you give her any money?

EMMETT: I gave her some money one time, a very, very small amount, uh . . . uh . . . and I don't even remember the amount it was so small.

ME: Did you give her this money before she filed the paternity suit?

EMMETT: Yes.

ME: Are you sure you didn't give her any money after she filed the paternity suit?

EMMETT: Yes. I'm sure.

ME: And you are aware that that allegation is contained in my book?

EMMETT: Well, it's in your book. It's all a part of your lies. And that's a big lie. A big one. Go to the court records and they will verify what I say. [Turning to Judge Aycock.] Judge, can I ask a question?

JUDGE AYCOCK: Yes.

EMMETT: Judge, how can he ask me that?

JUDGE AYCOCK: You are under oath and you have to answer these questions truthfully unless there's an objection that I will then rule on. Proceed.

ME: So we agree a paternity suit was filed against you by Mrs. Hicks? [I placed the paternity suit from the Chancery Court of Hinds County on the projector screen for everyone in the courtroom to see and read.] Do you agree that this is the paternity suit Mrs. Hicks filed against you?

EMMETT: That's been so long ago I wouldn't recognize it. But I told you what happened to it. It was dismissed.

ME: You never settled out-of-court with her?

EMMETT: No, I did not. Again, I say go get the Chancery Court records. They'll prove it.

Emmett had walked right into my trap. The trap had been set and was about to be so perfectly sprung that I couldn't believe my ears when Emmett said what he did. His self-righteous indignation and dishonesty had led himself right into committing the felony crime of perjury.

He had to of known that I had the proof that not only did Mrs. Hicks file a paternity suit against him and that he settled out-of-court with her, but that the case went all the way to the Mississippi Supreme Court and a DNA test was done proving him the father. But Emmett's racism and apparent self-hatred for getting caught fathering a mixed-race child with an African-American woman overcame any fear he may have had of being charged with perjury in federal court. There was only one thing left to do to close the trap.

>   **ME:** I've put a document on your screen that says: *In the Chancery Court of Hinds County, Mississippi. Emile Hicks, a minor, by Georgia Hicks the guardian, this day this cause having been heard before this court on a petition as filed by Georgia Hicks, as guardian of the said minor child, Emile Hicks, and appearing unto the court the following...*
>
>   **EMMETT:** Yes., I see that.
>
>   **ME:** [I continue reading from the legal document.] *That the said Emile Hicks is a minor of approximately one year of age and along with his mother, Mrs. Georgia Hicks, is a resident of Hinds County, Mississippi, First Judicial District...*
>
>   **EMMETT:** Yes, it says that.
>
>   **ME:** *That Georgia Hicks filed a paternity suit against Emmett Ray Atwood to have the paternity of her minor child, Emile Hicks, determined, and that the said suit is presently pending in the Chancery Court of Warren County, Mississippi. That although Emmett Ray Atwood has denied that he is the father of said child and asserts that he has a good, sufficient and complete defense to the said action as filed against him, nonetheless, Emmett Ray Atwood, as a man of some financial means who contends he has a good reputation in the community in which he resides, and who is a married man with a family that may be adversely affected if a public disposition of said paternity action is made public in Warren County, Mississippi, has, while denying the aforesaid claims has offered to pay to the minor, Emile Hicks, or to some other person for his use and benefit, the sum of $18,000.00.* Correct?
>
>   **EMMETT:** Yes.
>
>   **ME:** That's what this settlement agreement says. Correct?
>
>   **EMMETT:** I don't remember that.

There was that subjective belief again about what "minor amounts" and "small amounts" of money might mean to Emmett compared to another. Just as Emmett thought that thousands of dollars were "minor amounts" to Chaney's election coffers, no doubt $18,000.00 to settle a paternity suit was simply "small amounts." It was laughable.

>**ME:** Mr. Atwood. We have it in black and white. You settled a paternity case with a woman that alleged you had fathered an out-of-wedlock child with her. We have the paternity suit. We have the settlement order. But five minutes ago you told this jury under oath that you never settled this case with her. So you've lied.
>
>**EMMETT:** I don't remember settling and I don't remember that order. My attorney at the time was handling that and I don't recall any of that.

Here, again, was another perfect example of Emmett suffering from selective memory. When it came to things he's perceived I've done wrong, his memory is amazing. But when it comes to his horrible actions and dishonest past, he conveniently suffers from "CRS," can't remember shit. I pressed on, though.

>**ME:** But it's a big deal to be accused of fathering another woman's child.
>
>**EMMETT:** Are you getting pleasure out of accusing me of that in front of the court? You got pleasure out of mailing a false letter to all our family accusing me of fathering that black baby. And I didn't do it. The attorneys proved I didn't do it. I gave my DNA and proved I didn't do it. And this is all just a lie.
>
>**MR. MINOR:** Objection. Can we get off this line of questioning?
>
>**JUDGE AYCOCK:** Overruled. Proceed.

Emmett had made a serious blunder in his anger. Nothing throughout my entire life had I seen get under Emmett's skin more than when proof was given that he'd fathered Mrs. Hick's child and then essentially abandoned them. And in his anger he admitted that he'd given blood for a DNA test. But no sooner did he admit this he remembered that I probably had a copy of the DNA paternity test because it was attached as a legal exhibit to his paternity case. I immediately pounced.

ME: Did you just testify that a DNA paternity test was never done? Or that it was done?

EMMETT: A DNA test was never done.

ME: Okay. On your screen is a document that says, *Introduction to Paternity Testing*. And this, as you see is an exhibit to your paternity suit. On the second page, does the DNA test show a match between the father—you—and the patient—Emile Hicks?

EMMETT: Yes. It's typed on there. But did you do that because this stuff isn't true?

ME: Okay. Let me show you another document. It says, *The University of Mississippi Medical Center, Mrs. Wanda Beck, Attorney-at-Law, 729 High Street, Jackson, Mississippi, Court file #32465. Dear Mrs. Beck. This letter is to confirm the date for paternity testing for Emmett Ray Atwood, Georgia Hicks, and Emile Hicks on the 2nd day of July, 1989, at 9:30 a.m. All persons shall report to room R-213 in the Department of Pathology, University of Mississippi Medical Center, at the scheduled time. The client should be prepared to pay the standard fee of $550.00 to the University of Mississippi Medical Center, Pathology Associates. If you have any questions please feel free to contact me. Dr. Robert Louis, Director of Paternity Testing.*

EMMETT: Are you saying I was part of that?

ME: Well, it says you had a confirmed date for paternity testing.

EMMETT: I don't know whether it was confirmed. But I can tell you for sure, I'm not that baby's father. If all this happened, though, I just don't remember it. If it all happened my lawyer got it set aside.

ME: Well, regardless of whether or not you remember a paternity test being done, do you agree, though, that you did settle out-of-court with her?

EMMETT: Yes. But I don't remember it.

ME: So based on these documents, your earlier testimony that you did not settle this case with Mrs. Hicks is a lie?

EMMETT: Well, if I forget something, I forget something.

ME: Let me show you another document. It says *Emmett Ray Atwood v. Emile Hicks, the Supreme Court of Mississippi*. This case went all the way to the Mississippi Supreme Court. That's a big deal. But you have no memory of this?

EMMETT: I knew it went to the Supreme Court. I think I knew.

ME: But you agreed you settled out-of-court with her?

EMMETT: I already answered that.

It was an immensely stressful tug-of-war with Emmett. On the one hand he had a flawless memory, but on the other his lack of memory was the first excuse he reverted to when things didn't go his way. But the jury saw what kind of person (grandfather) that I was dealing with and they fully understood why Emmett would be the type person to try and send his own grandson to prison for something that was never even proven to be a crime.

Everyone in the courtroom could see that the jury was sickened by Emmett's lies, his past behavior, and the immense hate towards me that he radiated in disgust. I had almost destroyed his credibility, but I needed to establish one more thing before I could move on the Atwood Lakehouse fire.

CHAPTER FORTY

Prior to the July 2017 trial, I'd been doing research on Emmett's background in the Warren County courthouse when I ran across a felony indictment for fraud that Emmett and Atwood Chevrolet had been accused of in the 1960s. From my own experience, it has always been my opinion that Atwood Chevrolet used unethical business practices (what car dealership doesn't, LOL?). But finding a felony indictment accusing Emmett of a crime was a shocker.

Emmett spent almost the entirety of his life after our feud began in 2004 accusing me of crimes, criticizing me for the one I got convicted of, and trying to have me arrested on others. Knowing that he'd been indicted for a felony was just too good to pass up.

> **ME:** Have you ever been accused by law enforcement of a crime?
> **EMMETT:** Not that I recall.
> **ME:** You founded and operated Atwood Chevrolet since at least the 1950s? Correct?
> **EMMETT:** Yes.
> **ME:** Were you responsible for the operations and management of Atwood Chevrolet during the 1960s?
> **EMMETT:** Yes.
> **ME:** And were you indicted for fraud?
> **EMMETT:** Absolutely not.
> **ME:** Let me show you a copy of the indictment and . . .

MR. MINOR: Objection. Relevance.

JUDGE AYCOCK: Let's approach, counselors. [Mr. Minor and I both start talking at once.] Whoa, we can't all talk at the same time. Let's look at the indictment first. [Judge Aycock reads and reviews Emmett's indictment for fraud.] Have you seen this, Mr. Minor?

MR. MINOR: Yes. He's just trying to assassinate Emmett's character. And we can't put on any evidence at all about David's convictions, arrests, and crimes. It's a complete double standard.

JUDGE AYCOCK: You made your record on that, Mr. Minor, and I don't want to hear you speak of it again. Okay? You can take it up on appeal.

MR. MINOR: [Raising his voice.] I'm just saying, he's trying to have it both ways.

JUDGE AYCOCK: And I also don't want you speaking loud enough for this jury to hear you.

MR. MINOR: Sorry.

JUDGE AYCOCK: Okay. Do you want to state your objections to the admission of this?

MR. MINOR: Relevance. And he's trying to present bad prior acts evidence to impeach Emmett Atwood's testimony.

JUDGE AYCOCK: I believe it goes to motive. It's admissible.

MR. MINOR: I don't think it was written in the book.

JUDGE AYCOCK: Let's see. If it's not mentioned in the book, then you're right. It wouldn't be relevant. [Turning to me.] Was it mentioned in the book?

ME: No, Ma'am.

JUDGE AYCOCK: Your whole argument here is retaliation for what was published in that book and that they had you falsely arrested. So if it's not in the book, it's not admissible. Okay?

ME: Yes, Ma'am.

Judge Aycock was right even though I wished she'd let me ask Emmett questions about his indictment for fraud. My whole argument was that I'd been retaliated against because of what I wrote in the book. And Mr. Minor should definitely be given credit for raising that specific objection to the indictment being introduced. It was something that I didn't take into consideration when I decided to try and introduce it into evidence. But the jury at least got to hear part of the question.

After laying the trap for Emmett to commit perjury, which he easily fell into and did, I decided to move on to the important issues surrounding the fire. We'd spent enough time on past bad acts, who-fathered-what, and criminal conduct on the behalf of Emmett. It was now time to get to the meat and potatoes of Emmett's testimony.

> **ME:** You previously stated that you were friends with Mike Chaney. After the Atwood Lakehouse burned down, did you call Chaney numerous times to ask him to make an arrest in this case?
>
> **EMMETT:** That's totally false and untrue. I've never called him numerous times. One time I think I called him about the fire . . . the fact that it'd burned down and I wanted found the person that did it.
>
> **ME:** Did you put pressure on him . . .
>
> **EMMETT:** I didn't put pressure on Mike Chaney. I don't have that kind of power.
>
> **ME:** Okay. How were you made aware that the lake house had burned down?
>
> **EMMETT:** My nephew, Kade, who lived across the lake told me.
>
> **ME:** Did Kade at some point tell you that he had slept through the fire?
>
> **EMMETT:** Yes.
>
> **ME:** Did he ever offer an explanation for why he didn't see it or hear it?
>
> **EMMETT:** No, but I found out the next day why he didn't hear it.
>
> **ME:** Why?
>
> **EMMETT:** The house was set on fire in the northeast corner and that night we had an extremely heavy wind blowing from the northeast to the southwest. And the reason I know that is a bunch of my relatives came out there the next day to see the remains of the burned house and there was an area southwest of there by the lake dam and a lot of debris from the burning house had been blown that way from the house. That's how I know there was a real strong wind. And that took the noise away from

Kade's house. That's why he didn't hear it.

A bolt a lightening shot through my spine when I heard Emmett testify that a "bunch" of relatives came out to the fire scene on the morning of the fire to walk around and look at everything. It immediately explained the "suspicious" footprints that Sheriff Nail and Jackson allegedly found two days after the fire. I didn't waste any time in exploiting that admission.

> **ME:** You just testified that a bunch of relatives came out to the property the day after the fire . . .
> **EMMETT:** I'm sure that makes you happy to know that you stirred them up. But yes, they came out there.
> **ME:** And that morning when they all came out, was their purpose to walk around and look?
> **EMMETT:** Yes. That's why they all came out.
> **ME:** To walk around and look?
> **EMMETT:** Yes.
> **ME:** And y'all got out and walked around?
> **EMMETT:** Yes. We all went around the house and in the woods by the dam (where the "suspicious" footprints were allegedly found two days later).
> **ME:** When you finally got around to talking to James Jackson and Sheriff Nail, did you tell them that all of the family had come out there and walked around the morning of the fire?
> **EMMETT:** I'm not sure if I did.
> **ME:** But before Sheriff Nail and James Jackson came out there to investigate, a bunch of the family came out there first to walk and look around?
> **EMMETT:** Yes. That's correct.
> **ME:** Okay. When you testified that you believed Kade didn't hear the fire because the wind was blowing from the northeast to the southwest, did a law enforcement officer tell you that or did you reach your own conclusion?
> **EMMETT:** My own conclusion.
> **ME:** But you weren't there that night so how could you know it was extremely windy?
> **EMMETT:** Cause I saw all the scattered debris.

ME: And you had guns and ammunition in the house?
EMMETT: Yes, several.

At the time I didn't recognize the significance of Emmett's assertion that Kade couldn't hear the fire—and guns and ammunition exploding—because the wind was blowing from a northeast to southwest direction. One of the seminal questions of my entire case had been answered. Emmett unknowingly erased the last piece of doubt about whether this fire was arson. We now knew where the "suspicious" footprints came from.

Had Sheriff Nail been called back to the stand to testify after learning that the Atwood family came out on the morning of the fire and walked all around the property, and especially down by the dam where he later was shown the "suspicious" footprints, I'm sure he would have had to admit that there was absolutely no indication that the fire was arson. But the jury already knew that, so I didn't waste Sheriff Nail's or our time.

Since I'd gotten Emmett to admit everything that I set out to get him to admit to—and some things I didn't—I finished my direct examination and turned it over to Mr. Minor. As I sat down and he took the podium, I was curious where the case would take us next. As Mr. Minor began to speak, though, Richard passed me a short note written on a small piece of paper. I read it and then kept it my hand until Mr. Minor would finish his cross.

Mr. Minor began his cross-examination by asking Emmett to explain the history of the Atwood property and the lake house. Emmett explained that the property had been in our family since the early 1800s, but that the lake house hadn't been built until 1936.

Emmett also was asked and testified to the fact that he was one hundred percent certain that no one had been staying at the lake house the night of the fire, but he did admit that people had been staying there a couple days before. Mr. Minor's cross was short, but one of the last questions that he asked Emmett was whether, when he met with Jackson, he told him who burned the lake house down. Emmett, of course, answered that he told Jackson that I'd done it.

After this last question, Mr. Minor asked Judge Aycock whether he could make a short "proffer" outside the presence of the jury. I have to admit, I didn't know what this meant. But while Judge Aycock was having the jury sent out on a break, I quickly Googled "proffer" and learned that it was testimony related to a case but given outside the presence of a jury. I didn't know what Mr. Minor was trying to do, but I was going to pretend to be ready for whatever it was.

Once the jury was gone, Mr. Minor began asking Emmett questions regarding my past criminal history and incarcerations that, obviously, Judge Aycock had excluded from being made in front of the jury. His questions mostly centered around the fact that Emmett had accused me of everything from the sack of Rome to the terrorists attacks on 9/11.

On the day in 2009 that Jackson met with Emmett, he'd been provided a "list" of alleged crimes that Emmett accused me of committing that numbered into five or six single-spaced pages. Most of the things on there were clearly the product of Emmett's delusional mind. So after Mr. Minor read through these "allegations" with Emmett, he sat down and Judge Aycock asked me if I wished to "cross-examine" Emmett on these allegations. I tore into Emmett like a Texas tornado.

> **ME:** Mr. Atwood, let's get right to the heart of the matter. There's a lot of allegations in this piece of paper. Has any allegations in this paper ever resulted in any kind of arrests or convictions?
>
> **EMMETT:** Convictions, no. Because you're just like a slick lizard. You're always getting out of it. You have the same luck with the sheriff in Warren County. And you still do. I called him personally to arrest you when you were burning my daughter's pasture and he wouldn't do it. He wouldn't even send a deputy out to arrest you. He was supposed to call me the next day but never did.
>
> **ME:** Do you think that Sheriff Pace didn't call you back because in his experience as an investigator he decided you were delusional about all these things?
>
> **EMMETT:** He knows I'm not delusional. You're the delusional one.
>
> **ME:** But he chose not to investigate these allegations?
>
> **EMMETT:** Yes. Many times we've called him about stuff you did, like the one time you tried to burn down my daughter's barn. He didn't do anything. [This was news to me. I didn't know I'd been accused of that.]
>
> **ME:** So, as the long time owner of Atwood Chevrolet, what training have you had in criminal investigative techniques?

> **EMMETT:** Well, I haven't had any, but I could probably learn from you.
>
> **ME:** So then, without any experience investigating crime, wouldn't it be a better idea if you left it to the judgment of the experts?
>
> **EMMETT:** I tried, but they wouldn't deliver.

Emmett summed up the situation in a nutshell. Because of his position—or his perceived position—in the community as one who wields power and money, he expected to be able to control everyone from Sheriff Pace to the judges whom he helped get elected to office. I was surprised, though, that Sheriff Pace had finally given up and began ignoring Emmett's delusional antics.

> **ME:** Let's go back to this document. Before the lake house burned down, is there any allegations that I committed a crime against you?
>
> **EMMETT:** Well, I don't remember.

This was becoming an exercise in stupidity. Emmett was never going to admit that he could be wrong and he certainly was never going to admit that I could be right. But I still had enough ammunition in my belt to keep taking potshots at him. And without the jury being in the courtroom I could ask and say just about anything without fearing what Emmett's response might be. So I kept digging to get beneath his skin.

One might read this exchange between my grandfather and I and wonder how, what is supposed to be a loving, nurturing relationship between a grandson and his grandfather, could denigrate into a Jerry Springer-like brawl in a federal courtroom. It's honestly a sad, sad situation.

Any person not familiar with the history, though, must keep in mind a few things. First, from my personal experience, I believe that Emmett is an extremely racist, white supremacist who hates blacks, immigrants, gays, liberals, and anyone else who doesn't reflect his white, Anglo-Saxon background.

Second, Emmett is an unhinged control freak. I watched his attempts to control all of his childrens' lives, his grandchildrens' lives, and even his ex-wife's life. My father and his siblings were terrified of Emmett and none of them wanted to risk losing whatever inheritance it was that they expected to receive when Emmett finally died.

I, on the other hand, had been independent in both body, mind, and spirit since I was a child. I don't know why that was either. But if I believed I was in the right, no one could change or control my behavior, although I will admit that this has caused me a lot of trouble.

Finally, Emmett and I's relationship didn't end because I committed a crime against him or anyone else in the family. Our relationship ended because I was gay, I refused to remain in the closet and pretend I was straight, and because I wouldn't live in fear of being cut off from an inheritance that I truly cared nothing about. And when I stood up to Emmett and his bullying—which Emmett had never had someone do to him before, except maybe Georgia Hicks—he went ballistic at not being able to control someone that he believed he had the right to boss around. That's the story of our relationship. And for once, I wasn't going to let him intimidate me or accuse me of something I didn't do, and I certainly wasn't going to let him get away with making frivolous accusations.

> **ME:** So you say you don't remember whether this document contains any allegations of criminal conduct before the lake house burned down. So let's read through it.
>
> **EMMETT:** I remember you threatened us.
>
> **ME:** But your document says that occurred in December 2009, after the fire. I'm talking about before the fire. In this document what allegation states that I committed a crime against you?
>
> **EMMETT:** I don't remember whether it does or not.
>
> **ME:** Okay. But read it. Before the fire . . .
>
> **EMMETT:** Well, I don't see that I did.
>
> **ME:** So when we're talking about motive, there's nothing in this document that occurred before the fire that might demonstrate a motive for me wanting to burn your lake house?
>
> **EMMETT:** I know why you did it. But I didn't put it in this document.
>
> **ME:** Okay. So why?
>
> **EMMETT:** Because I helped try to get Vivian's house back from you.
>
> **ME:** But your report said that occurred on November 17th, 2009, after the lake house burned down.
>
> **EMMETT:** I don't know then.

ME: So when you imply that the motive for me burning the Atwood Lakehouse was because you tried to get Vivian's house from me after the fire occurred, that's a little impossible because that didn't start happening until after the fire.

EMMETT: If this corrects my memory then I stand corrected. This date may not be correct.

ME: Well, if the November 17th, 2009, date may not be correct, is it possible that the other information contained in this document that you put in here may also be incorrect?

EMMETT: Well, a lot of your writings are incorrect. I guess mine could be too.

ME: Inaccurate, as in you fathering a child out-of-wedlock? [Emmett doesn't answer.] The problem is, I'm not making delusional allegations that may or may not be accurate. So I want to ask you again. Prior to the date of the fire, can you tell me what motive I may have had for burning your lake house?

EMMETT: Well, you burned my daughter, June's, pasture. You cut the fences. You damaged the tractors. So yeah, you had motive.

ME: Okay. But Mr. Atwood, June's house didn't burn down. Your house did. So I'm asking you, please tell us what motive I may have had for burning your lake house.

EMMETT: I can't answer that right now, what motive you may have had.

ME: So you can't say what the motive may have been?

EMMETT: Well, I'm sure you had a bunch.

JUDGE AYCOCK: Please give specific answers, Mr. [Emmett] Atwood.

ME: Just one more question about this document. Is there any allegation at all in here that resulted in my arrest?

EMMETT: No. Not that I'm aware of.

ME: Your Honor, I'm finished. Thank you.

JUDGE AYCOCK: Mr. [Emmett] Atwood, I'm about to bring the jury back in. Nothing that's been discussed here may you testify about to this jury. Do not mention any of this. Okay?

EMMETT: Okay.

JUDGE AYCOCK: Do you understand?

> **EMMETT:** Yes, Ma'am. [The jury is then brought back into the courtroom.]
> **JUDGE AYCOCK:** Mr. Minor, did you have anymore cross-examination questions for Mr. [Emmett] Atwood?
> **MR. MINOR:** No, Your Honor.
> **JUDGE AYCOCK:** Any redirect?
> **ME:** Yes, Your Honor. Just briefly. [I then return to the podium and begin my redirect with Emmett.]

The proffer that Mr. Minor had requested was done for the purpose of getting in evidence of other crimes that Emmett believed I committed. This was done solely for the purpose of establishing a record of what Emmett may have testified to had Judge Aycock allowed Mr. Minor to reference my criminal history and incarcerations in our cases-in-chief.

The only thing that was accomplished, though, was Emmett's propensity to blame me for any and everything he could think of. But I also thought that I easily proved that I did not have any motive to burn Emmett's lake house. This line of thinking went back to my earlier thoughts that if—and this is a really big IF—I decided to destroy by fire something of Emmett's, it definitely wouldn't be the Atwood Lakehouse.

I certainly, if I was inclined to commit arson—which I most decidedly wouldn't—I would not have destroyed something that I loved just as much as Emmett did. Now, if Atwood Chevrolet had burned down, or even if Emmett's house in Vicksburg had burned, then maybe, and that's a big maybe, one could say that I might have motive to burn that specific structure. But this was the Atwood Lakehouse we were talking about. I loved that place.

The Atwood Lakehouse was not simply an old house whose title was held by Emmett. It was a house that generations of our family—none more so than me—had grew up on hunting and fishing and enjoying themselves. It was the symbol for the Atwood family, and no one loved it as much as me.

It was a sad fact that Emmett and I's family troubles had culminated in what was essentially a Jerry Springer episode carried out in a small federal courtroom in Aberdeen, Mississippi. I wasn't proud of the fact that I had to embarrass Emmett about his having fathered a bastard child with an African-American woman before abandoning them to fend for themselves.

I didn't like having to insinuate that Emmett may have burned the Atwood Lakehouse for the insurance money to avoid going into bankruptcy in one of his other businesses. I derived no pleasure in trapping Emmett in lies and forcing him to admit that he was wrong on almost everything he said. But Emmett had repeatedly done everything he could to send his oldest grandson to prison year after year for doing absolutely nothing wrong.

Emmett had tried to—and almost succeeded—have me framed for a fire that was never proved to have been arson and which—if convicted—carried a mandatory life sentence in one of the cruelest and harshest correctional systems in the United States. What would one in my position do? Thankfully, I chose to fight. And as I prepared to close out Emmett's testimony, I realized that I'd done one fine job of defending myself.

> **ME:** Mr. Atwood, you testified earlier that the wind was blowing from a northeast to southwest direction the night of the fire and that this is why Kade Atwood did not hear the fire. Correct?
>
> **EMMETT:** Yes. From the northeast to the southwest.
>
> **ME:** Let's look at the aerial photograph of the Atwood Lakehouse property. Do you recognize this?
>
> **EMMETT:** Yes.
>
> **ME:** And you agree that the porch of the Atwood Lakehouse faced south?
>
> **EMMETT:** Yes.
>
> **ME:** So, if the wind was blowing from the northeast to the southwest, wouldn't the wind be blowing almost directly at Kade's house?
>
> **EMMETT:** It blew the debris to the left of Kade's house.

Richard had caught a detail in the testimony that I'd missed, and I was glad he did so. It was just another nail in Emmett's judicial coffin. The fire began in the northeast corner of the house near the kitchen and electrical box. That meant that as the fire progressed southwestward, it was almost blowing directly at Kade's house, which set approximately one hundred yards or so south of the lake house.

Emmett's supposition that Kade couldn't hear the fire because of the wind was ridiculous. The fire was headed south, southwestward almost in a direct line with Kade's house. It was a ridiculous notion. And I let

Emmett and everyone in the courtroom know it.

> **ME:** But it's not blowing away from his house?
> **EMMETT:** That's correct.
> **ME:** So explain to me your earlier statement that because of the wind Kade couldn't hear the fire.
> **EMMETT:** Well, it went to the left.

It didn't make sense. And me and everyone else in the courtroom, no doubt, found it suspicious that Emmett would try to so blatantly pass off a lie as an explanation for why Kade didn't—allegedly—hear the fire. But it also gave me an opportunity to explore one more relevant area of interest, and Emmett played right into the trap.

> **ME:** Were you the only one with a key to the lake house?
> **EMMETT:** No. Almost all my family did. But they weren't going to burn it.
> **ME:** So when you said earlier that no one was at the Atwood Lakehouse the night it burned, you can't be sure of that because many people in the family had access to it and could have gone out there that night.
> **EMMETT:** Well, Kade would have seen them. He lives right across the lake from the house. Anytime anyone goes out there he'll know.
> **ME:** So you expect Kade to see and hear someone drive across the levee to visit the house, but not expect him to see and hear that huge house burn down with exploding ammunition inside?
> **EMMETT:** Yes, because the wind wasn't blowing the way it normally does.
> **ME:** But he should be able to hear someone drive across the levee the same night?
> **EMMETT:** Generally.
> **ME:** But not the house burning down?
> **EMMETT:** Yes, because of the wind.
> **ME:** Your Honor, that's all I have. Thank you.
> **JUDGE AYCOCK:** Mr. [Emmett] Atwood, you may be excused. Thank you. [Turning to the jury.] Ladies and gentlemen, I'm going to send you home for the day. Let's meet back in the

jury room at 9:30 A.M. tomorrow morning. Don't discuss the case. Don't research it. Thank you.

This last and final exchange with Emmett—which I honestly hoped would be the last—provided a little comic relief to the jury and everyone else in the courtroom after all the serious testimony we'd endured all day. And just as it didn't make sense to me, it made even lesser sense to the people that had to listen to Emmett testify.

Not only had I proven that Emmett lied about the increase in the insurance, I'd proven that he'd fathered a child out of wedlock with an African-American woman whom he then abandoned, and that every ridiculous notion he had about the cause and explanation of the fire was not only laughable, but delusional.

If Kade couldn't hear the fire that destroyed the lake house, along with the ammunition and firearms cooking off inside, there would be no way he'd ever hear someone drive across the levee. As Emmett admitted, almost everyone in the family had keys to the Atwood Lakehouse. This included Emmett's children and grandchildren, his brothers' and sisters' children and grandchildren, and numerous other uncles, aunts, nephews, nieces, and cousins.

I also knew that many people in our family, mostly the middle-aged married men, used the lake house for secret rendezvous with their girlfriends and mistresses. There was a good possibility that if the fire was indeed accidental, it might of been caused by someone who went out to the lake house the night of November 10, 2009, and that after it burned they remained quiet and tight-lipped about it.

I was almost ready to rest my case-in-chief when Emmett left the stand, and although I thought we got closer to the truth about what may or may not have caused the Atwood Lakehouse fire, there was still no smoking gun. I began to think that we'd never know the cause. But I was determined to press forward, though, and see it to completion.

CHAPTER FORTY-ONE

As David, Richard, and I drove back to our little rented house off the courthouse square, we couldn't have been more pleased with how the case had progressed. Thankfully, I'd gotten through all of my witnesses in the two days that I'd allotted for myself and without any serious screw-ups.

Emmett's testimony had been, hands down, the most difficult in which to deal with. It had also provided the most comical relief. I had no idea what the jury thought about Emmett fathering the out-of-wedlock child with Mrs. Hicks, or what kind of grandfather he must have been trying to get his own flesh-and-blood sent to prison, but I knew that no one left that courtroom that afternoon liking Emmett or thinking him to be a decent human being.

The last thing I needed to do before turning the case over to Mr. Minor for his rebuttal evidence was to read Mike Chaney's interrogatory responses into the record that he provided back in 2015. Unfortunately, I'd made a deal with Mr. Minor not to subpoena and have Chaney come to Aberdeen and testify in court. It was the biggest mistake that I made in the trial.

After what James Jackson had testified to on Monday, there was no doubt that Chaney should have been subpoenaed to court and forced to either admit to committing the crimes which Jackson accused him of, or deny them and explain why Jackson would commit perjury—again—in accusing him of bringing these false charges against me.

This trial in Aberdeen was the best chance that I ever had—and would ever get—at proving what I had always referred to as an "Axis of Corruption," which permeated Warren County and Vicksburg. From Sheriff Pace, Mike Chaney, Emmett Atwood, and numerous judges and political leaders, the corruption seeped into every crevice which shielded their evil from the light of day.

Mike Chaney, the statewide elected Mississippi Insurance Commissioner and State Fire Marshal, should have been forced to come into federal court and explain his illegal and unethical behavior as it pertained to my illegal arrest for a fire that had now pretty much been proven was nothing more than a horrible accident. It's the biggest regret I have from the trial. Chaney—the coward—deserved to be placed under oath and questioned by me, and no one but me. But like every other fire marshal and corrupt cop involved in this case, he tried to hide his evil deeds, he abandoned the tool (Jackson) of their corruption, and refused to answer for his infamous crimes. Chaney was a coward, a corrupt politician, and an evil human being. And to this day I regretted not asking Judge Aycock to force him to come answer for his malicious deeds.

As we began the third day of trial, there was not a single person who doubted that I was going to win this case. In fact, even though I knew that Mr. Minor was going to call Jackson back to the stand as his first witness in his rebuttal case, I didn't spend a single moment preparing to cross-examine Jackson after Mr. Minor finished his direct. We were that confident in our victory.

Instead of preparing to cross-examine Jackson, we spent all of Tuesday night rewriting, editing, and practicing what my closing argument would consist of. What can one say when one's antagonist has said it all? I didn't need to make arguments to the jury, not when Jackson made my argument for me. What I needed to convey was strong rhetoric, outrage, and a sense of victimization. I determined to make it the best closing argument ever.

Wednesday morning, July 19, 2017, dawned bright and early for us. We had breakfast, got dressed, and headed towards the courthouse. Reading Chaney's interrogatory responses into the record wouldn't take long, and after that Mr. Minor would call Jackson back to the stand to testify. There was a good possibility that we would completely finish our case before the end of the day. That would leave all day Thursday for jury instructions, closing arguments, deliberations, and then, hopefully, a verdict in my favor. So as Judge Aycock walked into court at 9:30 A.M., sharp, I rose from my chair and stood tall knowing that I was on the cusp of victory.

BAILIFF: Court will come to order. All rise. The United States District Court for the Northern District of Mississippi is now in session. Chief Judge Sharion Aycock presiding. God save the United States and this honorable court.

JUDGE AYCOCK: Thank you. You may be seated. Mr. Atwood, are you ready to read Mike Chaney's interrogatory responses?

ME: Yes, Ma'am.

JUDGE AYCOCK: Okay. Bring in the jury please. [The jury is brought into the court and seated in their chairs.] Thank you. Good morning. Let the record reflect that the jury is seated. Next, as part of Mr. Atwood's case he desires for some questions that were asked under oath to Mike Chaney and the responses that Mike Chaney made will be read to you. You will treat this as you would any other testimony. Okay? Mr. Atwood, you may proceed.

ME: Do you consider yourself friends with Sheriff Martin Pace and Emmett Atwood?

CHANEY: [Jackson's second attorney, Mrs. Cameron Benton, read the responses.] Yes.

ME: Has Sheriff Pace or any of the Atwoods ever supported you in your political and election campaigns? And has either every contributed money to any of your election campaigns?

CHANEY: Warren County Sheriff Martin Pace and Emmett Atwood have supported my campaigns in the past. However, only Emmett Atwood has contributed money to my campaigns.

ME: According to deputy fire marshal, James Jackson, you took an active part in the investigation of the Atwood Lakehouse fire, going so far as to even knowing who the witnesses were. As insurance commissioner and state fire marshal, do you normally take such an active and personal role in fire investigations, in addition to your other duties? If not, what specifically about this case drew your involvement?

CHANEY: I was never involved in the arson investigation. I merely monitored the progress of the arson investigation.

ME: Thank you, Mrs. Benton. Your Honor, that's all that I have.

JUDGE AYCOCK: Who would you call next, Mr. Atwood?

ME: Your Honor, the Plaintiff rests his case.

Two full days and a short ten minutes of a third and my case was finished. And as the evidence clearly showed, not only had Jackson conducted an incompetent investigation, but he obtained my arrest warrant without probable cause and he did so as part of an illegal conspiracy initiated at the insistence of his boss, Mike Chaney.

In addition to committing perjury in obtaining my arrest warrant, Jackson had also perjured himself in federal court, which is a serious crime with up to five years in federal prison. Likewise, by ordering Jackson to commit an illegal arrest which violated my Fourth Amendment constitutional rights in retaliation for the book I published, Mike Chaney committed numerous felony federal civil rights violations that could have landed him in federal prison for the rest of his natural life.

If I thought, however, that there would be an FBI agent or U.S. Attorney willing to investigate these clear and undeniable crimes, and ultimately bring charges against these two crooks, I would be dead wrong. Even though Jackson couldn't get away from the reach of my civil lawsuit for false arrest, he nevertheless—along with Mike Chaney—got away with committing the actual crimes themselves, not because they were innocent, but because of the lack of willpower by the FBI and federal prosecutors in Mississippi in bringing any type of prosecution against any person who committed a crime against me.

The simple truth was, that although the federal government would prosecute me and send me to prison for years on end for the slightest transgression—and for alleged actions that were not even illegal—they were unwilling to pursue any person with political influence who was in a position of authority. So while I knew I would win my civil rights lawsuit, I also knew that no matter what crimes were exposed that Jackson and Chaney committed, they would go unpunished. That's what our criminal justice system has come to.

With my case over, it was now time for Mr. Minor to present his. Prior to me resting my case, Mr. Minor had told me that the only two people that he intended to call to testify were Josh Chamblee—through his deposition—and Jackson. I knew beforehand what Josh's testimony would be.

We'd spent a considerable amount of time redacting Josh's deposition from every reference to other criminal activity that I'd been accused of and, of course, all of the frivolous, immature, pointless, and ridiculous objections that Josh's attorney, Randall Juergensen, made during the deposition back in February. So as Judge Aycock took up some "housecleaning" matters after I rested my case, I prepared for what I knew would be another disaster with Jackson's testimony.

JUDGE AYCOCK: Counselors, will you approach, please? [Mr. Minor and I come to her dais.] Are there any motions that I need to take up right now?

ME: Yes, Your Honor.

JUDGE AYCOCK: Okay. I'll get the jury out. [The jury leaves the courtroom to take a break.] What motions are there for the court to hear?

ME: Now that my case has rested and Mr. Minor is to begin his, I'm aware that he plans to introduce a recording from July 29th, 2011, of Josh Chamblee and James Jackson, and I do not object to the overall introduction of the recording, but the reference within this recording to several unsubstantiated criminal allegations that this Court had previously excluded. Mr. Minor edited part of the tape to remove references to me being in prison. But there are sections of the tape where the defendant questions Josh Chamblee about alleged damage at Atwood Chevrolet that allegedly occurred after the fire, which Your Honor has already excluded as inadmissible. Second, the fire marshal—the defendant—does not have authority under State law to investigate non-fire related crimes. So I would ask that Mr. Minor be prohibited from playing that specific portion of the recording.

JUDGE AYCOCK: I'll hear from you, Mr. Minor, regarding that request.

MR. MINOR: We do ask him about the incident at the dealership. That was part of his investigation. They wanted to confirm they both did the arson and vandalism. That was the probable cause and why it was relevant. Josh Chamblee says he knew nothing about the dealership. We've excluded from the deposition and recording anything he's been charged with. It's just mentioned in there.

JUDGE AYCOCK: What do you know about it?

MR. MINOR: On December 30th, 2009, approximately fifty cars and trucks tires were slashed and foam was poured into the tanks.

JUDGE AYCOCK: So it's the same list of allegations typed by Emmett Atwood? It's already been excluded by the Court. It was addressed on the first morning of trial. Take it out. It's excluded.

MR. MINOR: Okay. Now there's the problem of how to take it out.

JUDGE AYCOCK: [Annoyed and agitated.] Well, yeah. That is a problem.

ME: Your Honor, if I may? Prior to court this morning, Mr. Minor and I had an opportunity to listen to this recording. We can identify at what point in the conversation between Chamblee and Jackson regarding the Atwood Chevrolet damages.

This exchange was the result of Jackson and the other deputy fire marshals doing everything they possibly could to find something, anything, in which to blame me for, have me arrested, and sent to prison. Now, I do not doubt that there was damage done to numerous vehicles at Atwood Chevrolet. But I definitely knew I couldn't be blamed for it because on December 30, 2009, I was at my Papaw's house in Kosciusko with over twenty members of my mom's side of the family. And Jackson and the other investigators knew that after they'd begun "investigating" the vandalism.

Why Mr. Minor tried to get that allegation slipped passed me and into the ears of the jury is beyond me. But Judge Aycock excluded it and we identified the point on the recording when to stop it from being played to the jury. And with that being done, we moved on to having parts of Josh's deposition read to the jury.

For Josh's deposition testimony, Mrs. Benton was going to read the responses while Mr. Minor and I read our questions that we'd posed to Josh at the February deposition. Since Mr. Minor asked the questions first in the deposition, and because he was presenting his rebuttal case, he was allowed to ask his questions first in the trial.

JUDGE AYCOCK: Mr. Minor, are we clear on where in the tape you need to stop it?

MR. MINOR: Yes, Your Honor.

JUDGE AYCOCK: Are there any other motions or issues that we need to address before bringing the jury back in?

MR. MINOR: No, Ma'am.

ME: No, Ma'am.

JUDGE AYCOCK: Okay. Let's bring in the jury. [The jury returns.] Thank you for your patience. You may have a seat. Let the record reflect that the jury has returned to the courtroom. Who will the defendant call first?

MR. MINOR: We call Joshua Langston Chamblee.

JUDGE AYCOCK: Ladies and gentlemen of the jury, this is a deposition. You will not hear live testimony. But it is sworn testimony from him. You would treat it the same as you would any other witness. Okay? The Court has ruled that there are portions of this deposition that are inadmissible and they will not be read. So if it seems at times a tad disjointed, you must understand that that's where it is redacted. Mrs. Benton will read Josh Chamblee's answers as if she is Mr. Chamblee. She understands that as an officer of the Court she's to read the response exactly as it was given. Mr. Minor, you may proceed.

At this point in the trial Mrs. Benton took the witness stand much the same as if Joshua Langston Chamblee had appeared in court and testified as the other witnesses. The unfortunate thing about the trial and this part of the testimony was the fact that due to procedural rules regarding witnesses in federal court, it was impossible for me to subpoena Josh to court and actually have him appear and give live testimony.

Because Josh lived in Indianapolis now, it was not allowed by the Federal Rules of Civil Procedure to subpoena him to court from such a long distance away. I could have petitioned Judge Aycock and asked her to order that Josh appear and testify by telephone, but I believed I'd bled the turnip dry at the deposition and I didn't see the need of going through the trouble.

Make no doubts about it, though. I wished that I could have had Josh appear in federal court in Aberdeen and face the music for his actions. At least in Aberdeen he wouldn't be able to hide behind his mother and an asshole attorney like he had been able to do in the past.

Having Josh Chamblee testify in court like all the other witnesses would have ended terribly for him. I've previously stated that when it came to interrogating scumbag, lying ex-boyfriends like Josh, I was a master expert. Josh, under my questioning, would have folded quicker than Jackson ever had and would have crucified himself on the stand.

Just as I'd been able to repeatedly catch Josh in lie after lie during our relationship, I knew that I'd be able to destroy him on the witness stand. To understand Josh Chamblee, one must truly understand the mind of a sociopathic psychopath. Just saying that Josh is an evil person could not begin to describe his true mental pathology.

As much as I'd been willing in the past to describe Josh's behavior in terms such as "evil," "wicked," and "horrible," I soon recognized that his psyche issues are much deeper than that. And this supposition is based not only on my own experience dealing with him, but on the experience and opinions of others whom have known him and dated him. Simply put, Josh is one of the most psychotic people I'd ever met in my life, and as much as I hated to admit it, I'd at one time fallen for his charms, believed his lies, and thought that, surely, I wouldn't be another of his victims.

With that being said, I do recognize the impossible position that Jackson and the other fire marshals placed Josh in on July 29, 2011, when they gave him the choice of either writing out a third statement, which implicated me in the fire, or going to jail. What could one do in a circumstance such as that?

On the one hand, a normal, sane, mentally stable individual would not be so quick as to allow a law enforcement officer to extort him or her into giving a false "confession." But what a normal person might or might not do in the same situation as that that Jackson placed Josh in cannot be judged on the same standard as one would have to judge someone that is as pathologically screwed up as Josh is.

When one lacks the basic human skills of empathy, integrity, and honesty—such as Jackson and Josh—it is easy to see how one could so easily be intimidated into framing someone for a crime, whether it's done in political retaliation—such as what Jackson, Chaney, Emmett, and Sheriff Pace were doing—or done to avoid going to jail, such as what Josh ended up doing.

In the same position as that given Josh, whom can say whether we'd compromise our integrity and make false statements against another person to save oneself from going to jail. I know, though, having faced the worst that the criminal justice system could offer, I could not be cowed into lying to law enforcement and framing another person for a crime. And I knew I wouldn't do it because I'd been placed in that exact same circumstance before.

When my best friend, Dane Davenport, had been arrested for allegedly molesting his two stepsons—which he was later proved innocent beyond all reasonable doubt—his prosecutors offered to drop the malicious mischief felony charges against me for damaging Emmett and June's tractor if I'd lie and testify that Dane had molested me as a kid. I wouldn't do it then and I went to trial knowing that I would be sent to prison if convicted. But I believed in Dane's innocence, and I could not allow another man's conviction to be on my conscience. Josh retained no sense of moral right or wrong when it came to things like that.

So trying to understand why Josh so easily cooperated and lied to Jackson when they gave him the choice of either going to jail or giving them a statement which implicated me in the fire is easy. Josh retained no moral conscience whatsoever. The simple fact that I'd caught him in one lie too many and ended our relationship was enough "cause" for him to so easily lie and assist Jackson and the others for framing me with this fire that was never even proven to be an arson. He simply lacked a moral conscience.

To this day I regret not being able to place Josh on the witness stand and provide live testimony, just as I regret to this day not having Mike Chaney come and testify too. I would have annihilated their credibility and destroyed their reputations—not that Josh's reputation was much to speak about in the first place, though.

I was going to have to be satisfied with having Josh's deposition read into the record and just let the jury hear his words rather than hear his voice. But as Mr. Minor began reading from the deposition, I sat back in my chair and thought about what could of, should of, and would of been done differently if only I'd tried to go through the trouble of having Josh, at least, appear and testify by telephone.

Every reference to other criminal activity that Josh made during the deposition was redacted from the transcript that was read in court. Mr.

Minor read through the part in the transcript about whether Josh had ever testified in a deposition or trial before, which Josh answered in the negative. This was untrue, however, and this first lie of Josh's would be dealt with when I read the transcript part about him being sued by his former roommate and having to testify in court.

The part in the transcript where Mr. Minor asked him if Jackson had promised him anything—such as the $25,000 reward—or threatened him with anything—such as his arrest—was also read. And again, Josh chose to lie when he answered in the negative.

We knew this to be a lie because Jackson had testified, and his own investigative report proved, that he'd told Josh's mother that he'd be arrested if he didn't meet with them and give them the third statement which implicated me in the fire. Jackson's report and testimony also proved that he'd promised Josh the reward for changing his story and implicating me in the fire. So this was another lie in the first three minutes of Josh's "testimony" that destroyed his credibility.

However, when pressed about whether he'd felt threatened by Jackson, Josh eventually admitted that he did feel that way, and this was obviously the case because after Josh gave that third statement he quit cooperating in the investigation, recanted his statement, admitted that he'd lied to avoid going to jail, and then disappeared. It was only after he recanted and quit cooperating that Jackson had him arrested, too. It was hard to tell who was the bigger idiot, Jackson or Josh.

The jury also got to hear Josh's testimony that on the night of the fire, I allegedly used a "green bottle" with kerosene in it to start the fire. However, that's not what he'd told Jackson. He'd told Jackson on July 29, 2011, that I allegedly had a plastic bag and that he didn't know what was in it. This was the third lie Josh was caught in.

We were quickly moving through Josh's testimony and one of the last things Mr. Minor questioned Josh about was his testimony that I'd allegedly threatened to harm him or his family if he told on me about the fire. This presented a problem.

On the one hand, it doesn't make sense for someone who'd assisted in committing an arson, then had his and his family's life threatened if he snitched, continue to be friends with someone as long as Josh did after the fire. Keep in mind, that two months after the fire—all of which Josh and I were still together—I had my probation violated and was sent back to prison for five months.

Even when I was in prison—and Josh and his family were totally safe from anything that I may have wished to do—Josh accepted my collect calls from the jail, came to visit me in jail, and even attended the criminal trial that Emmett had brought against me for allegedly mistreating my grandmother, which I'd been found not guilty of committing.

In light of that evidence, Josh's assertion that he didn't come clean sooner because I'd threatened him was laughable. However, I couldn't present that evidence without revealing to the jury that I'd been in prison. It was a horrible Catch-22.

After Mr. Minor finished his questions I returned to the podium and began asking the questions that I'd asked Josh in the deposition. Mrs. Benton did her best to otherwise be a good "reader," but try as she might, she couldn't fake the prissy voice of Joshua Langston Chamblee.

The first questions we addressed were the ones related to me ending Josh and I's relationship because he'd lied to me about having HIV. This was the exact explanation that the jury needed and wanted to hear that would explain why Josh so easily did what he did to me. Josh was a psychotic sociopath with nothing being so much as a better example as his willingness to expose another person to a deadly disease.

We then moved over into details of the fire, but Josh said that he had "forgotten that night" and didn't remember even the most glaring details of the Atwood property. It was very convenient testimony for him. Almost as convenient as Emmett's selective memory when it came to how many bastard children he's fathered with African-American women.

The other area of the testimony that I think the jury found most unbelievable was Josh's assertion that I told him before we allegedly left Starkville that we were going to go burn Emmett's house down. Josh, according to his testimony, did nothing to stop me, did nothing to try and remove himself from the situation, and furthermore, was a willing and knowing participant. It was laughable.

All in all, even with the redactions, the jury got a brief insight into Josh's character, his honesty—or lack thereof—and his sick mental pathology. But as I finished my last questions, and me and Mrs. Benton went back to our respective tables, I couldn't help but regret not doing everything I could to get Josh to testify live without him being able to hide behind his mother, his "attorney," or anyone else he could use and abuse. But at least I was able to get my version of Josh and I's relationship details across to the jury, even if Josh did continue to maintain that we'd gone and burned the house down.

CHAPTER FORTY-TWO

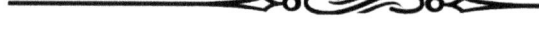

After finishing Josh's deposition testimony, Judge Aycock allowed us ninety minutes to take a lunch break. I knew, however, that as soon as we returned it was going to be Mr. Minor's turn to call Jackson back to the stand to testify. I'd been expecting as much ever since Mr. Minor told me that that was what he was going to do. But all day and the night before David, Richard, and I discussed the inadvisability of Mr. Minor doing that.

Jackson was a horrible witness for himself, for Chaney, for the fire marshal's office, and for the defense. When Jackson was confronted on the stand or got caught in a lie he panicked. And when Jackson panicked he freaked out. And when Jackson freaked out he would lie and say anything and everything that came to mind. As bad as things had gone for him on the previous Monday, we just could not understand how Mr. Minor could realistically put him back on the witness stand and allow him to be subjected to my cross-examination.

But calling Jackson back to testify is what Mr. Minor did. And, unfortunately for him, it did not go well at all. In fact, it went almost as bad as it had on the first day of trial.

JUDGE AYCOCK: Mr. Minor, who do you call as your next witness?

MR. MINOR: Just Mr. Jackson.

JUDGE AYCOCK: Mr. Jackson, will you return to the stand and be sworn? [Jackson returns to the stand and is sworn.]

> **MR. MINOR:** Mr. Jackson, was the testimony you gave on Monday accurate?
>
> **JACKSON:** No, it was not.
>
> **MR. MINOR:** And why was that?
>
> **JACKSON:** Well, due to the fact that I didn't have my report and I was confused.

The main event at the judicial circus had started without even a preshow. Jackson's assertion that his testimony wasn't accurate on Monday because he didn't have his report was insane. I'd spent over an hour on Monday going over his report line by line. But if that's the rabbit hole that Mr. Minor and Jackson wanted to take us down on Wednesday afternoon I was prepared to follow.

> **MR. MINOR:** And have you gone back and reviewed your report?
>
> **JACKSON:** I have.
>
> **MR. MINOR:** And based on your report, did you have evidence to support a request to obtain an arrest warrant?
>
> **JACKSON:** I did.
>
> **MR. MINOR:** What was that evidence?
>
> **JACKSON:** Due to, well, from June 2011 I called Mrs. Lyle and asked her to speak to Josh Chamblee and she asked what for. I told her the situation and she told me that Josh told her that he wanted to talk to me about the fire, but that he'd been threatened by David Atwood. And I told her I still needed to talk to him to get a statement about his involvement in the fire.
>
> **MR. MINOR:** What evidence did you have to obtain a warrant?
>
> **JACKSON:** The probable cause to get a warrant for accessory after the fact due to Josh Chamblee stating to his mother that he wanted to tell me about the fire. I felt like he was withholding information.
>
> **MR. MINOR:** And do you recall whether you actually went and got that warrant?
>
> **JACKSON:** I did. I can't remember the date. I think it was July.
>
> **MR. MINOR:** Why did you obtain that warrant?

> **JACKSON:** To get Josh down here to talk to me.
> **MR. MINOR:** Did you tell his parents about that warrant?
> **JACKSON:** No, I did not.

Again, here was Jackson lying to the jury again and he was too stupid to realize just how easily this assertion was disproved. Jackson's own report that he filled out in June 2011 stated very clearly that he told Mrs. Lyle that if Josh didn't come talk to him and give him another statement—one that implicated me in the fire—that'd he'd go get an arrest warrant and have Josh arrested. I just shook my head as I made a mental note to destroy Jackson again. The next part of Jackson's testimony proved just how caught up in his own lies he really was.

> **MR. MINOR:** So when you testified the other day that when you obtained that warrant without any evidence to support it, was that true?
> **JACKSON:** Correct.
> **MR. MINOR:** No. When you testified the other day that you obtained that warrant without any evidence, was that correct?
> **JACKSON:** No.

It was clear that Jackson was so confused he didn't know whether to scratch his watch or wind his butt. One minute he would testify he had evidence of some obscure crime, but the next he'd admit he never had any evidence whatsoever. Mr. Minor then moved over to Josh's multiple statements that he gave and tried to get Jackson to explain why he didn't believe the alibi statements but did the third one.

> **MR. MINOR:** When Josh gave you this [alibi] statement at the KFC in March 2010, did you believe it was the truth?
> **JACKSON:** No, I did not. I didn't because of his body language. He couldn't sit still in the chair. He was fidgeting with his hands. No eye contact. Every time I asked him a question he'd turn his head.
> **MR. MINOR:** And where did you meet Josh again?
> **JACKSON:** At the Leake County Sheriff's Department on July 29th, 2011.
> **MR. MINOR:** And for what purpose?

> **JACKSON:** To talk to him about the fire. And he gave a third statement in the presence of my chief, Ricky Davis, and Sheriff Greg Waggoner.
> **MR. MINOR:** And did you make a recorded statement?
> **JACKSON:** I did.

At this point in the testimony, Mr. Minor had Jackson introduce the recorded statement Josh made and it was played to the jury, without, of course, the part where Josh was asked about—and denied—our involvement in the vandalism at Atwood Chevrolet. After playing the short recording, though, we ran into another humorous point in Jackson's ridiculous testimony.

> **MR. MINOR:** And after you got this statement, what did you do?
> **JACKSON:** I went to the Attala County Justice Court where I got the warrant for accessory after the fact.
> **MR. MINOR:** You obtained the warrant for who?
> **JACKSON:** Joshua Chamblee.
> **MR. MINOR:** [Agitated.] No, Mr. Jackson. I'm talking about after you got Josh's third statement. Who did you then go get a warrant for?
> **JACKSON:** Oh, David Atwood.

Jackson had been on the stand less than ten minutes and he was already making a fool out of himself. He'd been coached so hard on what his answers should be he couldn't keep even the basic details straight. And it was proven, as I'd said all along, that Jackson was an incompetent investigator and, as we were seeing, an incompetent witness. It didn't stop there, though.

> **MR. MINOR:** What did you do when you got to the Attala County Justice Court?
> **JACKSON:** I met with the clerk and told her why I was there. She got the affidavit book and wrote down the arson statute number. The language out of the book. Then I told her I need to see the judge. So she went and showed him the affidavit. He asked me to come to his office. He had me raise my right hand

and I swore before Judge Stewart that this was true and correct.

MR. MINOR: And when you talked to Judge Stewart, what happened?

JACKSON: He wanted to know what basis I wanted the warrant. I told him that I had a taped interview and a written statement. I then gave him the written statement. He looked at it and then gave me the warrant. I then went to the Attala County Sheriff's Department and turned it over to them.

MR. MINOR: Did you ever have occasion to go before Judge Stewart again?

JACKSON: No.

MR. MINOR: Are you sure about that?

JACKSON: Yes.

MR. MINOR: Did you ever testify in his court?

ME: Objection, Your Honor. He's leading the witness.

JUDGE AYCOCK: Sustained.

MR. MINOR: Do you ever recall going back to his courtroom?

JACKSON: I did. I don't remember when it was. I think it was 2011 on that hearing for David Atwood.

Mr. Minor was, of course, asking Jackson whether he'd gone back in front of Judge Stewart for the preliminary hearing in October 2011. But Jackson was so twisted up in his lies that he couldn't keep the truth from intertwining with the lies. But the circus continued.

MR. MINOR: Did Judge Stewart hear all of the evidence at the preliminary hearing?

JACKSON: Yes.

MR. MINOR: Let me show you a document. Do you recognize this document?

JACKSON: I do. It's from the file from the Attala County Justice Court. It says, *After hearing testimony the court finds probable cause* . . .

ME: Objection, Your Honor. I object to this document being introduced. It isn't a document that was generated by the fire marshal's office or the defendant and the defendant hasn't even testified that he's even seen this document prior to today. It's an internal court document and it shouldn't be admitted through this witness's testimony.

JUDGE AYCOCK: Counselors, will you approach? [Mr. Minor and I approach Judge Aycock's dais.] Let's see the document.

MR. MINOR: Mr. Atwood didn't raise an objection to it in the pretrial order.

JUDGE AYCOCK: What is your objection now since you didn't object to it in the pretrial order?

ME: I don't believe this document should be introduced through James Jackson's testimony. If Mr. Minor wanted to introduce it, he should have brought someone from the Attala County Justice Court to testify that this is a true document from their office.

JUDGE AYCOCK: Let's look at the pretrial order. [We briefly review the pretrial order.] Well, it wasn't objected to. In fact, it states that the authenticity and admissibility are agreed to. Did you have a stipulation on the admissibility of this document?

MR. MINOR: He didn't raise an objection to it. So I thought we had a stipulation.

JUDGE AYCOCK: That's not a stipulation. It's just no objection. So there's no stipulation. Mr. Atwood, are you now questioning the authenticity of it?

ME: Through James Jackson's testimony, yes Ma'am.

JUDGE AYCOCK: Okay. The objection is sustained. It will not be admitted.

This was a small but important victory. Mr. Minor had attempted, through Jackson's testimony, to enter into evidence a form from Judge Stewart's office that he filled out on the day of my preliminary hearing where he literally rubber-stamped on the document that he found "probable cause" and was going to bind the case over to the grand jury.

I didn't object to this document being introduced through the proper channel. However, it could not have been introduced through Jackson's testimony because he'd never seen the document before and didn't know anything about it other than what he read. So preventing the jury from seeing an official court document that had "probable cause" rubber-stamped on it was a small but vital victory. Mr. Minor kept pushing.

MR. MINOR: When you obtained that third statement from Josh Chamblee, did you believe he was telling the truth?

JACKSON: I did.

MR. MINOR: And are you aware of any reason he may be lying?

ME: Objection, Your Honor. Calls for speculation.

JUDGE AYCOCK: Sustained.

MR. MINOR: May we approach Your Honor?

JUDGE AYCOCK: Yes. [Mr. Minor and I approach Judge Aycock's dais again.]

MR. MINOR: Your Honor, I want to make a brief proffer outside the presence of the jury.

JUDGE AYCOCK: Okay. Let me get the jury out. [The jury is led out by the deputy marshal for a short break.] Okay. You may proceed, Mr. Minor.

During the brief proffer that followed, Mr. Minor asked Jackson about the vandalism at Atwood Chevrolet on the night of December 30, 2009, during which time I was at my Papaw's house in Kosciusko with all of my family. When Mr. Minor finished questioning Jackson about his attempts to investigate the Atwood Chevrolet vandalism, I was given a brief opportunity to cross-examine Jackson solely on the issues covered in Mr. Minor's brief proffer. I didn't waste any time on going for Jackson's throat.

ME: Mr. Jackson, what state statute invests you with authority to investigate crime?

JACKSON: I don't know.

ME: Let me read it to you. It says that under State law, *the Fire Marshal's Office has the authority and legal duty to investigate any fire requested by any party in interest, whenever in his judgment there is sufficient evidence indicating that such fire may have been started intentionally.* Mississippi Code 45-11-1. So you didn't have authority to investigate these other criminal allegations that Emmett Atwood was making?

JACKSON: Pertaining to the fire I did.

ME: But these other allegations of misconduct that Emmett Atwood was making didn't pertain to the fire.

It couldn't have been summed up better. Chaney allowed his deputy fire marshals to abuse their power and act as the personal investigators of Emmett Atwood. Chaney and Jackson became Emmett's personal wielders of criminal power to enforce a personal and political motive with me square in the crosshairs. But I wasn't going to let Jackson get away easily with it.

The proffer that Mr. Minor had decided to do only opened up another Pandora's Box which led Jackson straight into another unexplainable explanation of his conduct during the course of his investigation.

> **ME:** Emmett Atwood helped you out a lot with this investigation, didn't he?
>
> **JACKSON:** No, not too much.
>
> **ME:** But almost all of your information came from him? Correct?
>
> **JACKSON:** It did.
>
> **ME:** And you knew that there were problems within the family?
>
> **JACKSON:** I did.
>
> **ME:** So knowing that there was feuding between Emmett and I, did it ever occur to you that the information Emmett was providing you might be biased?
>
> **JACKSON:** It did.
>
> **ME:** But you took him at his word?
>
> **JACKSON:** I guess.
>
> **ME:** And Emmett's checkbook bought that acceptance? Correct?
>
> **MR. MINOR:** Objection.
>
> **JUDGE AYCOCK:** [Turning and giving me the first dirty look of the trial.] Sustained.
>
> **ME:** Let's look at this list of criminal allegations that Emmett gave you. Is there any allegation in there, prior to the fire, that I committed a crime against Emmett Atwood?
>
> **JACKSON:** I don't see anything in there.
>
> **ME:** Do you have authority to investigate any of these alleged crimes?
>
> **JACKSON:** No, but Mike Chaney was making me do it.

I couldn't help at this point but to rock back and forth on the heels of my nice dress shoes and bite down as hard as I could on the end of my pen. My fury knew no bounds at this moment. Every evil, malicious intent that I'd ever expected out of Emmett, Chaney, Sheriff Pace, and Jackson was proving true. I was almost done, though.

ME: Mr. Jackson, you testified earlier that the allegations in this list of crimes gave you probable cause to suspect me of starting the fire. What in this document gave you probable cause to believe I started this fire?

MR. MINOR: Objection.

JUDGE AYCOCK: Overruled.

JACKSON: There is none.

ME: So your basis for believing that this fire was arson was based solely off what Emmett told you?

JACKSON: Yes.

ME: Your Honor, that's all I have. Thank you.

JUDGE AYCOCK: You may bring the jury back in. [The jury returns to the courtroom and Jackson remains on the witness stand to endure my questioning in front of the jury.] Mr. Atwood, you may cross-examine the witness. [Judge Aycock said this as though one might grant a starving child permission to dig into a chocolate cake.]

ME: Mr. Jackson, on Monday we spent several hours on your conduct in the investigation. Do you remember the answers you gave on Monday morning?

JACKSON: I do.

ME: So you agree that you are now changing your story again?

JACKSON: I do.

ME: Since you left the stand on Monday afternoon you've had a chance to sit down with your attorney to talk about your testimony?

JACKSON: Yes.

ME: And did he coach you on what your answers should be today?

JACKSON: No. I just had my report today to better remember.

ME: Okay. Now that you mention it, let me ask you about that report. Do you remember testifying at the mistrial four months ago where you pretty much provided the exact same answers to my questions then as you provided to my same questions on Monday?

JACKSON: Yes. Correct.

ME: But now you're saying you have to change that. That your testimony in March and your testimony on Monday aren't correct after all now?

JACKSON: Correct.

ME: So between Monday and now you've read your report, but you didn't read it from March until Monday?

JACKSON: I just now went back and looked at what all transpired.

ME: But I asked you these same questions back in March. And you gave the same answers on Monday as you did back in March. Correct?

JACKSON: Yes.

ME: After the March mistrial, did you not think it was important to go back and read your report?

JACKSON: I did. I looked over it twice.

ME: Okay. So prior to your testimony on Monday you did go back and read your report?

JACKSON: Yes.

ME: And after reading your report before Monday your answers still remained the same as back in March?

JACKSON: Yes. Correct.

ME: Okay. But now after that horrible day on Monday . . .

MR. MINOR: Objection, Your Honor.

JUDGE AYCOCK: Sustained. Mr. Atwood, don't comment on the testimony.

ME: Sorry, Your Honor. [I turn back to Jackson.] After the testimony on Monday, your attorney didn't tell you, "Hey, Mr. Jackson, we need to clean this up?"

MR. MINOR: Objection. Attorney/client privilege.

JUDGE AYCOCK: It's overruled.

ME: Did you and your attorney have a conversation about repairing some of your testimony from Monday?

JACKSON: We briefly talked.

ME: So you on your own decided to go back and read your report again to see if there's any difference to what you'd previously testified to? Correct?

JACKSON: Correct.

ME: But before you testified to these important matters on Monday we went through your report line by line. So at the mistrial in March and on Monday we read your entire report. And your testimony stayed the same?

JACKSON: Correct.

ME: So when we read through your report on Monday your testimony never changed? Correct? [At this point Jackson took a long pause with a deer-in-the-headlights look and turned his head towards Mr. Minor.] Mr. Jackson, look at me. Don't look at your attorney for the answer.

JACKSON: Yes. Yes, correct.

ME: But now you've had a chance to sit down with your attorney and talk about your testimony and now it has changed?

JACKSON: A little.

ME: On Monday I asked you multiple times if you had committed perjury. And what was your answer?

JACKSON: That I did.

ME: And I asked you multiple times if you had lied under oath. And what did you say?

JACKSON: Yes, I did.

ME: So do you think this jury should consider you an honest witness?

MR. MINOR: Objection.

JUDGE AYCOCK: Sustained.

It is a wonder what could change so much in less than forty-eight hours. Jackson had dug his judicial grave soon after beginning his testimony Monday afternoon. By the end of the day his coffin had been nailed shut and he was six feet under.

What would have been better was if he had come to court on Wednesday, admitted to committing perjury, lying under oath, having me illegally arrested under Mike Chaney's direct orders, blamed everything on Chaney, and then begged for mercy.

If ever there was an opportunity to present the Nuremberg Defense and claim that he was only acting under the orders of his boss, Mike Chaney, Jackson should of availed himself of it. Explaining to the jury that he was pressured, didn't want to lose his job, and that he tried to convince Chaney that what they were doing was wrong and illegal would have been much better than coming back into court on Wednesday and changing his story, telling more lies, and then telling more lies to cover those lies. It was a ridiculous exercise. I kept destroying him, though.

ME: Your testimony was that Mrs. Lyle gave you probable cause to believe a crime had occurred?

JACKSON: Yes. Based on what Josh told her.

ME: After Mrs. Lyle allegedly told you that Josh had information about the fire, did you ever have a conversation, prior to getting Josh's arrest warrant, with him?

JACKSON: Yes. At the KFC.

ME: No, Mr. Jackson. That was before you talked to Mrs. Lyle. Let me be more specific. From the time you talked to Mrs. Lyle in June 2011 and until July 27th, 2011, when you obtained Josh's arrest warrant, did you ever talk to Josh Chamblee during that time period?

JACKSON: I don't believe I did.

ME: Did you try to verify or confirm this alleged statement made by Mrs. Lyle?

JACKSON: No.

ME: Let's talk about Teresa Lyle. From the beginning, Mrs. Lyle wasn't honest with you, was she?

JACKSON: She was not.

ME: And she was trying to hide where Josh was?

JACKSON: Yep. She was trying to protect him.

ME: And throughout you trying to track Josh down in June and July 2011, Mrs. Lyle lied and told you he was in the Navy and lived in North Carolina?

JACKSON: Yes.

ME: So you knew Mrs. Lyle was lying to you about where Josh was and what he was doing?

JACKSON: That's correct.

ME: So if you knew Mrs. Lyle was lying to you, why did you choose to trust her when she allegedly said that Josh allegedly knew something about the fire?

JACKSON: I don't know.

ME: Well, you knew she had credibility issues?

JACKSON: I believed her.

ME: Okay. A few minutes ago you testified that you believed Mrs. Lyle was lying to protect her son. If she truly wanted to protect her son from you, do you think she would tell you that he knew something about the fire?

JACKSON: I can't say.

ME: But you agree she was acting to protect her son?

JACKSON: Right.

ME: So if she was really acting to protect Josh from you, why would she tell you something that would only intensify your search to find and question him?

JACKSON: I don't know.

ME: So your statement to the jury that Mrs. Lyle gave you probable cause to justify getting the warrant for Josh's arrest, that's based on nothing but your word?

JACKSON: Yes.

ME: Your integrity?

JACKSON: Yes.

ME: So you agreed to believe that part of Mrs. Lyle's alleged statement to you because it fit with what you and Mike Chaney were trying to do? Correct?

JACKSON: Yes. Correct.

ME: You chose to believe that part but not anything else?

JACKSON: Correct.

ME: Even though you knew the evidence showed she wasn't a credible person?

JACKSON: Correct.

ME: So when you sit here and say you thought she was protecting Josh, that doesn't really make sense that she would tell you something that would further draw in the involvement of her son? Correct?

JACKSON: That's correct.

ME: And you've admitted multiple times to lying under oath and committing perjury?

JACKSON: Yes. Correct.

ME: And you've clearly testified that you did not have probable cause to get Josh's arrest warrant? Correct?

JACKSON: Correct.

ME: And you've also clearly testified that you did not have probable cause to get my arrest warrant? Correct?

JACKSON: Correct.

ME: But now you've had a chance to sit down with your attorney and you've changed that story again?

MR. MINOR: Objection. Asked and answered. I don't see how this is relevant.

JUDGE AYCOCK: I'll determine if it is relevant. Sustained. Proceed.

ME: When your attorney was questioning you earlier, you said you didn't tell the Lyles about Josh's arrest warrant? Correct?

JACKSON: Correct.

ME: But in your report, which you just said you read again, it clearly says that you did tell them about the warrant? Correct?

JACKSON: I don't know.

ME: Mr. Jackson . . . Let me read you your words . . .

JACKSON: [Reading from his report.] *I explained to Mrs. Lyle the severity of the case and that if Josh Chamblee did not come talk to us a warrant would be issued for his arrest.*

ME: So they were aware that if Josh didn't come speak to you again and give you a statement implicating me in the fire that he'd be arrested? Correct?

JACKSON: Correct.

ME: So when your attorney was asking you whether you had told the Lyles about the arrest warrant and you said no, that wasn't accurate, was it?

MR. MINOR: Objection. Mischaracterizes the testimony.

JUDGE AYCOCK: Overruled.

JACKSON: I didn't remember what was said in my report.

ME: Now wait, Mr. Jackson. Wait a minute. You just testified that between Monday and today you went back and read your report multiple times. But now you're saying you didn't read that part?

JACKSON: Yeah. It's hard to remember everything in the report.

Again, this trial had turned into a judicial circus with the maestro being myself and Jackson the circus clown. Nothing he said made sense; nothing at all. And the longer I kept him on the stand the worse he made it on himself. And let one thing be understood, when we repeatedly referred to Jackson's investigative report, we were not referring to a document that consisted of dozens of pages. Jackson's investigative report regarding his investigation only contained *two* short pages which summed up the steps he took in the investigation.

For Jackson to say that he couldn't remember what all was in his report was a flat lie. There was only two pages and about six short paragraphs. That's it. But after all the lies that Jackson had told, he could neither rely on his memory or the truth, so he doubled down and continued lying, even when he knew it made him look like an idiot.

CHAPTER FORTY-THREE

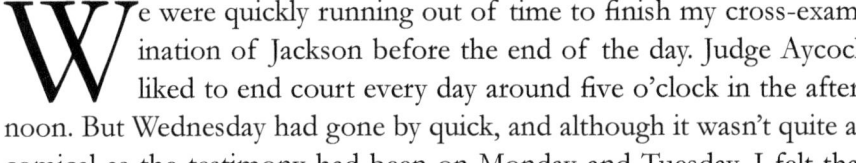

We were quickly running out of time to finish my cross-examination of Jackson before the end of the day. Judge Aycock liked to end court every day around five o'clock in the afternoon. But Wednesday had gone by quick, and although it wasn't quite as comical as the testimony had been on Monday and Tuesday, I felt that if I continued to push hard enough, Jackson would crack again and provide us some more memorable moments. So I kept digging. And Jackson didn't disappoint.

> **ME:** You testified earlier that at the March 2010 interview with Josh at the KFC in Carthage you didn't feel like he was being honest? Correct?
>
> **JACKSON:** Correct.
>
> **ME:** And after that you didn't get any other leads in the investigation? Correct?
>
> **JACKSON:** Yes, correct.
>
> **ME:** But you testified here today that you didn't think Josh was being honest with you?
>
> **JACKSON:** That's correct.
>
> **ME:** Okay. So if you felt that something wasn't right, and that Josh Chamblee wasn't being honest, why wait almost a year and a half to go back to try and get a third statement?
>
> **JACKSON:** The case went cold. I needed some more leads on it.

ME: But you never got anymore leads on it, did you?

JACKSON: No, I did not.

ME: So why did you wait a year and a half to go back to get another statement from Josh?

JACKSON: To see if anymore things had developed with him.

I wanted to make this point because I felt that if Jackson thought Josh was truly lying at the time of the March 2010 interview, he wouldn't have waited over a year to go get an arrest warrant for Josh and force his "confession." The fact is, Josh was telling the truth at the March interview at the KFC and Jackson knew it. That's why he closed his investigation and thought nothing more of it after talking to Josh.

The only reason the investigation was reopened and an arrest warrant was gotten for Josh was because my book was published and Chaney made Jackson take the steps that he eventually did to not only violate my constitutional rights, but Josh's as well.

ME: Okay. But when you made this decision, you testified on Monday that your boss, Mike Chaney, was putting a lot of pressure on you to arrest me? Correct?

JACKSON: A little.

ME: Now, wait a minute, Mr. Jackson. That wasn't your testimony on Monday. You didn't say a little. You testified that Mike Chaney told you to get off your ass and get out there and arrest me? Correct?

JACKSON: Correct.

ME: So he didn't come down just a little bit, he came down real hard?

JACKSON: A little, yeah.

ME: So from March 2010 until June 2011, you didn't care about following up on anything, even though you claim now that you didn't believe Josh Chamblee was being honest at that March 2010 interview? Correct?

JACKSON: That's correct.

ME: So you only reopened this investigation at the time this book was published and Mike Chaney began pressing you to arrest me? Correct?

JACKSON: Now, I didn't know nothing about no book.
ME: But Chaney did?
JACKSON: I don't know if he did or didn't.
ME: But it was in June 2011 when this book was published that Mike Chaney began pressing you real hard to arrest me?
JACKSON: Yes.
ME: And he specifically told you to go arrest me?
JACKSON: Yes.
ME: Did you ever ask Chaney, "Hey boss! Why now?" The case had been closed for over a year after all.
JACKSON: No, I didn't talk to Mike Chaney too much.
ME: Because he'd already given that order to get off your ass and go arrest me?
JACKSON: He told me to get out there and investigate.
ME: No. Now wait, Mr. Jackson. On Monday your testified that you sat in Mike Chaney's office and that he told you to get off your ass and go arrest David Atwood. That was your testimony on Monday? Correct?
JACKSON: Yes. Correct.

It was apparent to me that after Jackson's horrible testimony on Monday, Mr. Minor and he were in a crisis mode. Jackson had been sacrificed upon the altar of the Axis of Corruption. There was no longer any hope in saving him. My case had been won—and his lost—on Monday afternoon.

By Jackson's testimony on Wednesday, however, it was clear that he and Mr. Minor were doing everything they could to further limit and conceal Mike Chaney's role and liability in my illegal arrest. And doing so put Mr. Minor in a terrible predicament.

Essentially, Mr. Minor was representing two clients, Mike Chaney and James Jackson, although only one of those clients appeared in court. Upon testifying that Mike Chaney ordered him to commit multiple felony crimes, Jackson put Mr. Minor in a position of either protecting Jackson's interests or protecting Chaney's interests. He never should have been placed in that position.

Mr. Minor, in my opinion, could not further effectively represent Jackson because by doing so he could only—realistically—argue to the jury that this whole entire case was not Jackson's fault, but his boss's, Mike

Chaney, who had ordered him to commit these crimes or lose his job.

At the same time, Mr. Minor could not effectively represent Chaney's interests because doing so would force him to have Jackson either lie under oath and attempt to conceal Chaney's involvement—like he had been for the entire trial—or admit that Chaney did indeed force him to commit these crimes.

I've always felt that Jackson's best defense should have been the Nuremberg Defense (i.e., admitting to committing the crimes, but blaming it on his superiors because not doing so would be detrimental to his career), but I don't think Mr. Minor seriously was able to consider that theory before trial only because he truly believed in Jackson's innocence and that Chaney had not done what he did.

The testimony from Jackson on Monday changed all that. There was no longer a doubt that Jackson willingly committed multiple crimes in conducting the investigation and that he did so only upon the direct orders of Mike Chaney. This caught Mr. Minor so unprepared that I don't think he ever really considered any other defense. And because Jackson had apparently been lying to Mr. Minor throughout the entire litigation, it did not allow Mr. Minor to prepare for any contingency other than a "totally innocent" defense.

For this, Jackson has no one but himself to blame. His defense fell apart the moment everyone in the courtroom—including his attorney—discovered that everything he'd previously said during the course of the litigation was a lie. By lying to his attorney, Jackson deprived himself of the one means of effective defense for his crimes. But it's his own fault. He was allowed to be used as a tool of the Axis of Corruption, and then, when no longer needed and in trouble himself, abandoned.

I was beginning to almost feel sorry for Jackson by this point in the trial. For the first part of the trial I'd derived much pleasure in seeing Jackson, Emmett, and Sheriff Pace squirm under the intense questioning of my inquisition. But by the third day Jackson was a wounded animal past the stage of fight or flight. He was figuratively lying dead on the witness stand. But I had to continue pressing my case.

> **ME:** In the recorded interview with Josh Chamblee, not one time did you ever ask Josh why he was changing his story? Correct?
>
> **JACKSON:** Correct.

ME: Was it because you didn't care about the reasons he was changing it?

JACKSON: I just didn't think about it at the time.

ME: Was it because this third statement was the long-prayed for gift on y'all's wish list of things you needed to arrest me?

MR. MINOR: Objection, Your Honor. Argumentative.

JUDGE AYCOCK: Sustained. [I got another stern look from her.]

ME: Do you agree that Josh had some very serious credibility issues?

JACKSON: I don't know.

ME: But you are the one who procured the arrest warrant based solely off the word of this witness. So you're telling me that you don't think the credibility of this person who you based your arrest warrant on is important?

JACKSON: I believed what he said because he wanted to come clean.

ME: When you went to get my arrest warrant you testified that you took Josh's third statement to Judge Stewart? Correct?

JACKSON: Correct.

ME: You didn't tell Judge Stewart about the other two alibi statements did you?

JACKSON: I think I just told him about the third one.

ME: So Judge Stewart didn't know about the previous two alibi statements that Josh gave to you and Sheriff Nail?

JACKSON: Correct.

ME: So you hid those from Judge Stewart?

JACKSON: Now, no. I just gave him what I had.

ME: Okay. But you heard Sheriff Nail's testimony yesterday. He turned his investigation over to you and Josh's first statement over to you? Correct?

JACKSON: Correct.

ME: And you agree he did that right after the fire?

JACKSON: Yes.

ME: So for almost two years you had the first alibi statement that Josh gave Sheriff Nail?

JACKSON: I don't know if I had or not.

ME: So is Sheriff Nail lying?

JACKSON: No.

ME: Let's say you didn't have that first statement. You agree, though, that you still had Josh's second alibi statement that he gave you at the KFC in March 2010? Correct?

JACKSON: Correct.

ME: So when you went to Judge Stewart, you didn't tell him about this second statement even though you had it in your possession?

JACKSON: I don't believe I did.

ME: So when making a decision on whether there was probable cause to have issued my arrest warrant, Judge Stewart didn't have all the facts did he?

JACKSON: Just what I gave him.

ME: When you went to Judge Stewart on July 29th, 2011, you testified that you only showed him Josh's third statement? Correct?

JACKSON: Correct.

ME: So when Judge Stewart made this probable cause determination, he didn't have all the facts did he?

JACKSON: No.

ME: Could you have told Judge Stewart about Josh's first and second alibi statements?

JACKSON: I could have if I'd thought about it.

ME: But you didn't think about it, did you?

JACKSON: No.

ME: Was it because you wanted to hide that evidence from him?

JACKSON: No.

ME: But you did.

JACKSON: I just didn't think about it.

ME: Now, Mr. Jackson. You do know the difference between incriminating evidence and exculpatory evidence? Correct?

JACKSON: I do.

ME: And in this case the only incriminating evidence that you had was Josh Chamblee's third statement?

JACKSON: That's correct.

ME: So you agree that there was other evidence in this case of an exculpatory nature?

JACKSON: Like I said, it's been so long ago I didn't think about it.

ME: I didn't ask you if you thought about it. I asked whether at the time you went to Judge Stewart, were you aware of other exculpatory evidence proving my innocence? Correct?

JACKSON: Yes, correct.

ME: And you didn't tell Judge Stewart about that evidence did you?

JACKSON: At the time I talked to him I didn't think to tell him.

It was like pulling the teeth of an angry crocodile. Jackson had decided to shut down again and force me to extract every corruption-coated judicial tooth that I could.

These questions were extremely important because the second element that I had to prove in my false arrest case was that Jackson should not be protected by the independent intermediary doctrine, which simply states that if a law enforcement officer goes to a judge to get an arrest warrant, hides neither exculpatory or incriminating evidence from him, and then reasonably relies on that warrant, then he cannot be later held liable for a false arrest.

Jackson, though, had clearly concealed every piece of exculpatory evidence from Judge Stewart that proved my innocence. He didn't tell Stewart about the cell records, he didn't tell him about Emmett's recent increase in the insurance, he didn't tell him about the footprints, he didn't mention that Kade had suspiciously slept through the fire, and most importantly, he never told Judge Stewart that the fire was never proven to have been an arson.

Because Jackson hid these vital and important facts from Judge Stewart—and I'd certainly proven by now that he did—he was not then entitled to be protected by the independent intermediary doctrine. Getting him to admit that the only thing he showed Judge Stewart—unreliable as it was—was Josh's third statement, essentially assured me victory on this specific element of the false arrest case. But there were still other areas that needed covering.

Unfortunately, we were out of time for the afternoon. And once I'd finished this line of questioning, Judge Aycock sent the jury home while Mr. Minor and myself stayed behind with her law clerk to iron out what the final jury instructions would say prior to being given to the jury. Once that was done we adjourned until the following morning at nine o'clock sharp.

Prior to being dismissed for the day and beginning our work on completing the jury instructions, Judge Aycock had warned Jackson not to discuss his testimony with anyone, including his own attorney. We were supposed to pick up on his testimony the following day at the exact point where we'd left off. I knew I didn't have much more to question him about, but I wanted to make sure that I covered all my bases because this would be my last shot at finishing out my case against James Jackson.

BAILIFF: Court will now come to order. All rise. The United States District Court for the Northern District of Mississippi is now open according to law. Chief Judge Sharion Aycock presiding. God save the United States and the honorable court.

JUDGE AYCOCK: Thank you. You may all be seated. Mr. Jackson, you are still under oath and will continue with your cross-examination. Bring in the jury. [The jury is brought back to the courtroom and seated in their jury box.] Let the record reflect that the jury has returned to the courtroom. We are ready to continue the cross-examination. Mr. Atwood, please proceed.

ME: Good morning. May it please the Court?

JUDGE AYCOCK: Good morning. You may proceed.

ME: Mr. Jackson, yesterday we were talking about Josh's third statement that he gave you. Do you agree that Josh cannot provide you with much detailed information?

JACKSON: About your whereabouts on the night of the fire?

ME: No. I'm talking about dates, times, details of the Atwood property. He can't provide you specific details, can he?

JACKSON: Uh . . . no.

ME: But when he doesn't know a specific detail about the Atwood property, you help him out by providing it to him, don't you?

JACKSON: Just the date of the fire. When I do an interview I tell them a few things.

ME: But when you were asking him about the property you

mention a cattle guard and whether he'd crossed one. You remember that from the recorded interview?

JACKSON: Yeah.

ME: Josh didn't volunteer that information. So in his 2017 deposition, when he talks about a cattle guard, that's a detail that he got from you? Correct?

JACKSON: Possibly.

ME: But you're the one who brought the detail up first.

JACKSON: Yes, I did.

ME: Mr. Jackson, do you agree at the July 29th, 2011, interview, Josh never really provides you any details? Correct?

JACKSON: Yes.

ME: So whatever knowledge Josh has about the Atwood property today probably came from you?

JACKSON: Some.

ME: Do you remember the part in Josh's recorded statement where he says that right after the fire he cut ties with me?

JACKSON: Yes.

ME: And he tells you in that interview that he cut ties and said if I ever contacted him again he would press charges on me?

JACKSON: Yes.

ME: You also knew, though, that Josh testified in his deposition that our relationship continued for several months after the fire?

JACKSON: Yes. I believe so.

ME: But you knew that couldn't be accurate because Josh told you in 2011 that he cut ties with me right after the fire?

MR. MINOR: Objection. Call for speculation.

JUDGE AYCOCK: It's sustained as asked. I will allow Mr. Atwood to lay the predicate and re-ask.

ME: Were you aware on July 29th, 2011, that Josh and I's relationship continued for several months after the fire?

JACKSON: I was not aware.

ME: But you are now?

JACKSON: Yeah.

ME: But you are aware that in Josh's deposition he says our relationship continued for several months after the fire?

MR. MINOR: Objection. He's calling for comment on other evidence.

JUDGE AYCOCK: Overruled. If Mr. Jackson was in the courtroom when that deposition was read, then he has that knowledge. Proceed.

JACKSON: I can't remember.

ME: Mr. Jackson! Five minutes ago you said that you did remember.

JACKSON: I don't know.

ME: So now you don't know?

JACKSON: I can't recall.

ME: Mr. Jackson. Not five minutes ago I asked you if you remembered that part in Josh's deposition where he says that our relationship continued for several months after the fire. And you said . . .

JACKSON: Yes, I believe so.

ME: Now you believe you don't?

JACKSON: I heard it, but I can't remember everything about what's going on.

We had been led down another rabbit hole in this ridiculous exercise in stupidity. But this was important, though. Jackson had interviewed Josh in March 2010—four months after the fire—and at that interview he knew that Josh and I's relationship had continued for months after the fire. So in March 2010 Jackson knew that Josh and I maintained a dating relationship for several months after the fire. He knew that beyond all doubt because Josh told him that at the interview.

However, over a year later when he met Josh again at the Leake County Sheriff's Department, Josh lied in his recorded statement and told Jackson that he ended our relationship immediately after the fire and cut all ties with me. Josh even went so far as to tell Jackson that he'd allegedly told me that if I ever contacted him again he'd press charges against me.

Jackson knew, though, that this statement from Josh wasn't true. Jackson knew this because when he had met Josh at the KFC in Carthage the year prior, Josh had told him that our relationship continued for months after the fire. So on July 29, 2011, Jackson knew—but chose to ignore—that Josh was lying to him about when our relationship really ended. But because that was a detail that only hurt Jackson's case, it was conveniently ignored. I think I made my point, though, to the jury. So I moved on.

>**ME:** Mr. Jackson, on your screen is the affidavit that you used on July 29th, 2011, to get my arrest warrant. You used this phrase: *'maliciously and feloniously set fire to a dwelling house belonging to Emmett Ray Atwood located on Youth Center Road.* My question is, what in this affidavit, or this phrase, shows that an arson was committed?
>
>**JACKSON:** Nothing.
>
>**ME:** So you filled this affidavit out and took it to Judge Stewart and also provided him Josh's written statement. But you heard Judge Stewart; he doesn't remember you showing him Josh's third statement? Correct?
>
>**JACKSON:** Correct.
>
>**ME:** So when you tell this jury that you provided Josh's third statement to Judge Stewart, you have no proof of that other than your word? Correct?
>
>**JACKSON:** Other than I got the warrant.
>
>**ME:** Mr. Jackson, I'm not asking that. I'm asking that when you tell us you took Josh's third statement to Judge Stewart you don't have any proof that you actually did that?
>
>**JACKSON:** I don't know what you're getting at.
>
>**ME:** Okay. Mr. Jackson, I am going to break it down real simple for you. You testified that the only thing you showed Judge Stewart when you went to get my warrant was Josh Chamblee's third statement? Correct?
>
>**JACKSON:** Correct.
>
>**ME:** Okay. And you agree that Judge Stewart testified that he didn't remember you doing that? Correct?
>
>**JACKSON:** That's what he said.
>
>**ME:** Okay. So I am asking you . . . when you state to us that you took Josh's third statement to Judge Stewart, what proof do you have that you actually, did in fact, take Josh's third statement to him?
>
>**JACKSON:** My word.
>
>**ME:** But you've admitted you've lied under oath and committed perjury?
>
>**JACKSON:** No.
>
>**ME:** Wait. Wait. Wait. Mr. Jackson, ever since Monday I've

been asking you the same question and you've admitted multiple times to lying under oath and committing perjury? Correct?

JACKSON: Correct.

ME: So when you ask us to believe that you took Chamblee's third statement to Judge Stewart, you're asking us to accept your word as the gospel truth? Correct?

JACKSON: Correct.

ME: Do you think it's safer to conclude that the truth is you never showed this alleged third statement from Josh?

JACKSON: Nope.

ME: Okay. So in this affidavit that you filled out, do you agree there is no probable cause in there?

JACKSON: Not in there. You go by what the book tells you to write down.

ME: In your experience as a law enforcement officer, do you agree that when applying for warrants you're supposed to provide the probable cause in the affidavit to support its issuance?

JACKSON: Yes.

ME: But in this case you didn't provide any probable cause in the affidavit, did you?

JACKSON: Just the witness statement I showed Judge Stewart.

ME: That's not what I asked, Mr. Jackson. I asked did you provide any probable cause in that warrant application?

JACKSON: I told the judge about the fire. So he said I had probable cause and signed the warrant. [I look at Jackson with a "Are-you-stupid-or-something gaze?"] No. Okay. It's not in the affidavit.

ME: Finally, thank you.

JACKSON: That affidavit is just for the affidavit book. You don't have to put probable cause in there.

ME: Wait. Hold on, Mr. Jackson. Here we go again. A few minutes ago you just testified that you are supposed to put the probable cause in the affidavit to establish the record.

MR. MINOR: Objection.

JUDGE AYCOCK: Overruled. Proceed, Mr. Atwood.

The longer Jackson stayed on the stand the worse he looked. I could have wrapped up the testimony and gone straight into closing arguments. But, as sad as it is to say, I was enjoying seeing Jackson make a fool of himself. That man had willingly allowed himself to be used as a tool of political corruption when he knew there was never any evidence to prove this fire was an arson.

A man of honesty and integrity would have gone to the FBI. Someone who wasn't corrupt and malicious would have refused to do Chaney's evil errand and either resigned or sought protection under the "whistleblower" laws that protect civil servants like Jackson. But Jackson willingly allowed himself to be used. It was as if what I'd said on Monday was literally true. Jackson wanted to be a good investigator. He wanted to be a good deputy fire marshal. He wanted to be liked in the Fire Marshal's Office. So he did anything and everything Chaney asked him to do, even if it meant violating numerous state and federal laws. And because of that, we were now engaging in this ridiculous game of cat and mouse in a small federal courtroom in Aberdeen, Mississippi. I was almost done, though.

ME: Yesterday, when we read through Josh's deposition, do you remember the part where Josh says that on the night of the fire he stepped in some mud and got his feet wet?

JACKSON: Yes.

ME: Let me show you these pictures. It's the pictures that Sheriff Nail and you took as part of your investigation. Were you present when these were taken?

JACKSON: I don't think I was there for these.

ME: Let's set these pictures aside for a moment and go back to your investigative report. Your report reads . . .

JACKSON: *After the investigation we left the scene and went down the road leading out to a highway and were shown some footprints. Photographs were taken of the prints.*

ME: So according to your report, you were there when these photographs were taken?

JACKSON: I just didn't remember if I was there or not.

ME: Okay. And that's understandable. But let's go back to the photos. Do any of these photos of the shoe tracks show a picture of a track in mud?

JACKSON: I can't tell.

ME: Your Honor, may I approach the witness?

JUDGE AYCOCK: You may.

ME: [I hand all of the photographs to Jackson for him to look at.] Do any of these footprints that I'm showing you appear to be tracks in the mud or around water?

JACKSON: No. Just sand.

ME: Looks like firm ground? Correct?

JACKSON: It does.

ME: So it's safe to say that you and Sheriff Nail never found any shoe prints in or around any mud? Correct?

JACKSON: I guess not.

This pretty much concluded my cross-examination of Jackson. And as one can see, it didn't go well for him. If I was Mr. Minor I certainly would not have had Jackson brought back to the witness chair to try and testify and repair the damage he'd done on Monday. His testimony on Wednesday and Thursday only made him look more like the circus clown we now knew him to be.

On redirect, Mr. Minor asked Jackson again whether he'd committed perjury—which Jackson answered in the negative—and whether he still believed that Mrs. Lyle's alleged statements gave him probable cause to get the arrest warrants. Mr. Minor also had Jackson admit that, in his opinion, it was not necessary to put the probable cause evidence in an affidavit for an arrest warrant. But federal case law was most decidedly not in their favor on this opinion.

The last question that Mr. Minor asked was whether Jackson and Sheriff Nail took photographs of every footprint they found. Fortunately for my case, Jackson said "I can't recall." With that, Mr. Minor finished his redirect, Jackson was allowed to leave the witness chair for the final time, and Mr. Minor told Judge Aycock that the defense rested its case. The evidence portion of the trial was finally over.

CHAPTER FORTY-FOUR

When Mr. Minor ended his questioning of his last witness, he rested his case. His role in the evidence portion of the trial was over with. But, according to how civil trials are conducted in federal court, I was then given an opportunity to call rebuttal witnesses. However, everything that could be said, had been said, and it was time to move on.

    JUDGE AYCOCK: Mr. Atwood, do you desire to call any rebuttal witnesses?
    ME: No, Your Honor. The Plaintiff rests.
    JUDGE AYCOCK: [Turning to the jury.] Thank you. Ladies and Gentlemen of the jury, we have now finished all of the evidence portion of the trial. I need to spend about forty or forty-five minutes going over the jury instructions with Mr. Atwood and Mr. Minor. I don't mind if you want to leave the jury room. You may take a walk, but it's hot outside. You may just want to sit and wait on me. We will do this as quickly as possible. At that point I will bring you back in and will read the jury instructions to you. They will then make closing arguments. Because they have argued the case at that point, I'll be sending you to lunch together because I can't let you break up once you've been charged with deciding the case. I can, if you would like, have the lunch brought to you in the jury room, or we can reserve a room downtown at one of the restaurants. But if you want to start your deliberations

during lunch, you can do that in the jury room. Okay. So I'll just ask, yes or no. Would you rather have your lunch brought in? [The majority of jurors nod their heads.] I see more nods than no's. Okay. We will make arrangements to get your food ordered and brought in. Okay. That's the game plan. I'm going to excuse you now. You are not ready to begin deliberations. Don't discuss the case, but you may retire to the jury room. [The jury then leaves.]

After the jury had left, Judge Aycock and all of us remained behind to go over all of the jury instructions. It was at this point that she allowed us an opportunity to either object to the wording of the instructions, or to accept them as is. Without objections from either Mr. Minor or myself, they were accepted.

The jury instructions were both complex, but rather self-explanatory. These instructions would be the guide that the jury would have to use in the maze of testimony, evidence, and arguments that they had to sift through to ultimately reach their verdict and either award me money or not.

Once we'd finished going over the instructions and accepting them as they were, Judge Aycock passed us copies and then we waited on the jury to be brought back in.

> **JUDGE AYCOCK:** Okay. Does everyone have copies of all the jury instructions?
> **ME:** Yes, Your Honor.
> **MR. MINOR:** Yes, Your Honor.
> **JUDGE AYCOCK:** Okay, good. You may bring in the jury. [The jury then returns to the courtroom from their short break.] Thank you. You may be seated. Let the record reflect that the jury has returned to the courtroom. Ladies and gentlemen, I will now read to you your instructions. There are several and I am going to ask you to listen very carefully. You will have a copy of these with you in the jury room so you can read them again if you have questions. Okay?

Judge Aycock then began our jury instructions that would guide the jurors in deciding the issues in the case. They are worth repeating for the reader.

JUDGE AYCOCK: Members of the jury, it is my duty and responsibility to instruct you on the law you are to apply to this case. The law contained in these instructions is the only law you may follow. It is your duty to follow what I instruct you the law is, regardless of any opinion that you might have as to what the law ought to be. If I have given you the impression during the trial that I favor either party, you must disregard that impression. If I have given you the impression during the trial that I have an opinion about the facts of the case, you must disregard that impression. You are the sole judges of the facts of this case. Other than my instructions to you on the law, you should disregard anything I may have said or done during the trial in arriving at your verdict. You should consider all of the instruction about the law as a whole and regard each instruction in light of the others, without isolating a particular statement or paragraph. The testimony of the witnesses and other exhibits introduced by the parties constitutes the evidence. The statements of counsel are not evidence; they are only arguments. It is important for you to distinguish between the arguments of counsel and the evidence on which those arguments rest. What the lawyers say or do is not evidence. You may, however, consider their arguments in light of the evidence that has been admitted and determine whether the evidence admitted in this trial supports the arguments. You must determine the facts from all the testimony that you have heard and the other evidence submitted. You are the judges of the facts, but in finding those facts, you must apply the law as I instruct you. You are required by law to decide the case in a fair, impartial, and unbiased manner, based entirely on the law and on the evidence presented to you in the courtroom. You may not be influenced by passion, prejudice, or sympathy you might have for the plaintiff or the defendant in arriving at your verdict. Plaintiff David Atwood has the burden of proving his case by a preponderance of the evidence. To establish by a preponderance of the evidence means to prove something is more likely so than not so. If you find that Plaintiff David Atwood has failed to prove any element of his claim by a preponderance of the evidence, then he may not recover on that claim. The evidence you are to consider consists of the testimony of the witnesses, the documents and other exhibits admitted into evidence, and any fair inferences and reasonable conclusions you can draw from the facts and circumstances that have been proven. Generally speaking, there are two types of evidence. One is direct evidence, such as the testimony of witnesses. The other is indirect or circumstantial evidence. Circumstantial evidence is evidence that proves a fact which you can logically conclude another fact exists. As a general rule, the law makes no distinction between direct and circumstantial evidence, but simply requires that you find the facts from a preponderance of all the evidence, both direct and circumstantial. You alone are to determine the credibility or truthfulness of the witnesses. In weighing the testimony of the witnesses, you may consider the witness's manner and demeanor on the witness stand, any feelings or interest in the case, or any prejudice or bias about the case, that he or shy may have, and the consistency or inconsistency of his or her testimony considered in light of the circumstances. Has the witness been contradicted by other credible evidence? Has he or she made statements at other times and places contrary to those made here on the witness stand? You must give the testimony of each witness the credibility that you think it deserves. Even though a witness may be a party to the action and therefore interested in its outcome, the testimony may be accepted if it is not contradicted by direct evidence or by any inference that may be drawn from the evidence, if you believe the testimony. You are not to decide this case by counting the number of witnesses who have testified on the opposing sides. Witness testimony is to be weighed; witnesses are not to be counted. The test is not the relative number of witnesses, but the relative convincing force of the evidence. The testimony of a single witness is sufficient to prove any fact, even if a greater number of witnesses testified to the contrary, if after considering all of the other evidence, you believe that witness. The fact that a person brought a lawsuit and is in court seeking damages creates no inference that the person is entitled to a judgment. Anyone may make a claim and file a lawsuit. The act of making a claim in a lawsuit, by itself, does not in any way tend to establish that claim and is not evidence.

This was the first jury instruction that Judge Aycock read to the jurors. It was self-explanatory to all and Mr. Minor and I had not raised objections to this instruction being given to the jurors. As a whole, it was a generic instruction given to almost all juries in civil cases, and it was based on a template provided by the Fifth Circuit Court of Appeals. The real important instructions came next, though.

JUDGE AYCOCK: Plaintiff David Atwood claims that Defendant James Jackson violated the following constitutional right: the constitutional protection from unreasonable arrest or seizure. To recover damages for this alleged constitutional violation, Plaintiff David Atwood must prove by a preponderance of the evidence that: (1) Defendant James Jackson committed an act that violated the constitutional rights Plaintiff David Atwood claims were violated; and (2) Defendant James Jackson's acts were the cause of Plaintiff David Atwood's damages. The Plaintiff David Atwood claims Defendant James Jackson violated his Fourth Amendment right to be protected from unreasonable arrest and seizure. Plaintiff David Atwood claims that the way Defendant James Jackson arrested him violated his constitutional rights. To establish this claim, Plaintiff David Atwood must show that the arrest was unreasonable. An arrest, such as the one involved in this case, is considered unreasonable under the Fourth Amendment when, at the moment of the arrest or warrant application, there is no probable cause for the defendant to reasonably believe that a crime has been or is being committed. Probable cause does not require proof beyond a reasonable doubt, but only a showing of a fair probability of criminal activity. It must be more than bare suspicion, but need not reach the fifty percent mark. Finally, the reasonableness of an arrest must be judged based on what a reasonable officer would do under the circumstances, and does not consider Defendant James Jackson's state of mind. The question is whether a reasonable officer would believe that a crime was committed based on the facts available to that officer at the time he applied for the warrant. To help you determine whether Defendant James Jackson had probable cause to arrest Plaintiff David Atwood, I will now instruct you on the elements of the crime for which he was arrested. Mississippi Code Annotated. Section 97-17-1. First degree arson; dwelling house. Number one. Any person who willfully and maliciously sets fire to or burns or causes to be burned or who aids, counsels, or procures the burning of any dwelling house, whether occupied, unoccupied or vacant, or any kitchen, shop, barn, stable or other outhouse that is parcel thereof, or belonging to or adjoining thereto, or any state-supported school building in this state whether the property of himself or of another, shall be guilty of arson in the first degree, and upon conviction thereof be sentenced to the penitentiary for not less than five (5) years or life and shall pay any restitution for any damages caused. If you find that Plaintiff David Atwood has proved by a preponderance of the evidence that Defendant James Jackson lacked probable cause to make the warrant application and arrest, then Defendant James Jackson violated Plaintiff David Atwood's constitutional right to be free from unreasonable arrest or seizure and you must then consider whether Defendant James Jackson is entitled to protection under the independent intermediary doctrine or is entitled to qualified immunity, which is a bar to liability that I will explain next. If Plaintiff David Atwood failed to make this showing, then the arrest was constitutional, and your verdict will be for Defendant James Jackson on the unreasonable arrest claim.

This first instruction on the elements of a false arrest claim regarded whether or not there was probable cause to arrest me. I fully believed that I'd easily proven that there was no probable cause for my arrest for the reasons previously stated. And Josh Chamblee's third statement aside—unreliable as it was—there was not a single piece of evidence that demonstrated that this fire was a crime. There simply wasn't and I believed the jury would find for me on this element.

JUDGE AYCOCK: The independent intermediary doctrine shields law enforcement officers from liability in some cases where the facts supporting a particular arrest are submitted to an independent magistrate or judge to make the probable cause determination. The independent intermediary doctrine requires that an application submitted to an independent magistrate or judge set forth the particular facts and circumstances underlying the existence of probable cause, so as to allow the magistrate to make an independent evaluation of the matter. This obligation extends to avoiding deliberately or recklessly false statements and to knowingly withholding relevant or exculpatory information. The independent intermediary doctrine does not apply if a reasonable officer in Defendant James Jackson's position should have known that his application failed to establish probable cause and he would not have applied for the warrant. If, after considering the scope of discretion and responsibility generally given to law enforcement officers in performing their duties, and after considering all of the circumstances of this case as they would have reasonably appeared to Defendant James Jackson at the time of the warrant application, you find that Plaintiff David Atwood failed to prove that no reasonable officer could have believed that the warrant application was truthful, reliable, and devoid of deliberately or recklessly false statements, then Defendant James Jackson is entitled to the protection of the independent intermediary doctrine and your verdict must be for Defendant James Jackson on this claim. But if you find that Defendant James Jackson violated Plaintiff David Atwood's constitutional rights and that Defendant James Jackson is not entitled to the protection of the independent intermediary doctrine as to that claim, you must then consider whether Defendant James Jackson is entitled to qualified immunity, which is a bar to liability I will explain later.

The independent intermediary doctrine was the second easiest element of my false arrest claim that I had to prove. Jackson's testimony was clear that he did not tell or provide Judge Stewart with any of the exculpatory evidence from the case that demonstrated my innocence. Likewise, Jackson concealed from Stewart the unreliability of Josh's third statement, Josh's history of lying to law enforcement officers, and the fact that Josh's third statement was obtained under the threat of arrest and a promise of a reward.

When Jackson claimed to Judge Stewart that he had evidence of arson, he "deliberately [and] recklessly" provided a false statement to the judge that deprived him of the ability to make an independent probable cause determination based on all of the evidence. I was totally convinced that the jury would find for me on this element. The qualified immunity element of my false arrest claim was a closer call, though.

> **JUDGE AYCOCK:** As to each claim for which Plaintiff David Atwood has proved each essential element, you must consider whether Defendant James Jackson is entitled to what the law calls "qualified immunity." Qualified immunity bars a defendant's liability even if he violated a plaintiff's constitutional rights. Qualified immunity exists to give government officials breathing room to make reasonable but mistaken judgments about open legal questions. Qualified immunity provides protection from liability for all but the most incompetent government officers, or those who knowingly violate the law. It is Plaintiff David Atwood's burden to prove by a preponderance of the evidence that qualified immunity does not apply in this case. Qualified immunity applies if a reasonable officer could have believed that the warrant application and arrest was lawful in light of clearly established law and the information Defendant James Jackson possessed. But Defendant James Jackson is not entitled to qualified immunity if, at the time of the warrant application and arrest, a reasonable officer with the same information could not have believed that his actions were lawful. Law enforcement officers are presumed to know the clearly established constitutional rights of individuals they encounter. In this case, the clearly established law at the time was the constitutional protection to be free from unreasonable arrest or seizure, and not to be subject to a warrant application that no reasonable officer could have believed was truthful, reliable, and devoid of deliberately or recklessly false information. If, after considering the scope of discretion and responsibility generally given to law enforcement officers in performing their duties, and after considering all of the circumstances of this case as they would have reasonably appeared to Defendant James Jackson at the time of the warrant application and arrest, you find that Plaintiff David Atwood failed to prove that no reasonable officer could have believed that the arrest was lawful, then Defendant James Jackson is entitled to qualified immunity, and

your verdict must be for Defendant James Jackson on this claim. But if you find that Defendant James Jackson violated Plaintiff David Atwood's constitutional rights and that Defendant James Jackson is not entitled to qualified immunity as to that claim, then your verdict must be for Plaintiff David Atwood.

This was the final instruction on the elements needed for me to prove my false arrest claim. Obviously, the first two instructions were clearly in my favor; Jackson didn't have probable cause to support his arson assertion and he concealed relevant information from Judge Stewart at the time he made the warrant application.

I also believed that during the trial I proved that Jackson was an extremely incompetent law enforcement officer and fire investigator. It was a point that I pounded and pounded over and over again. Fortunately for me, everything that Jackson testified to and got caught lying about was further proof of his incompetence. So the first part of the qualified immunity instruction about incompetent officers was clearly in my favor.

At the time of my arrest, it was true, the clearly established law said that an officer could not conduct an arrest when there was no probable cause to support that arrest. This law had been "clearly established" for decades, and all law enforcement officers are taught that they must have probable cause before making an arrest. So there was no dispute that Jackson knew what the clearly established law was in regards to arrests.

Finally, I believe that I had gotten my point across to the jury during Sheriff Nail's testimony that, as a reasonable law enforcement officer, he would not have sought an arrest warrant for me based on the evidence in the case. Sheriff Nail had clearly testified that besides the "suspicious" footprints, he had no evidence of arson and even less evidence that I was involved. Of course, a short while later I proved that the footprints were more than likely left there by family members looking around the scene of the fire rather than some perpetrator.

When Sheriff Nail, as a reasonable law enforcement officer, testified that he didn't have any evidence of arson and no evidence that I was involved in the fire, he sealed Jackson's fate. But Sheriff Nail shouldn't have cared. Jackson had, from day one of the lawsuit, tried to pass off all liability to Sheriff Nail and blame his every shortcoming on Sheriff Nail. Thankfully, though, Sheriff Nail turned out to be a better witness for me than Jackson. We now had to move to the instructions regarding damages. And this part was crucial because I'd not spent as much time during the trial proving actual damages as I had actual liability.

> **JUDGE AYCOCK:** If you find that Defendant James Jackson is liable to Plaintiff David Atwood, then you must determine an amount that is fair compensation for all of Plaintiff David Atwood's damages. These damages are called compensatory damages. The purpose of compensatory damages is to make Plaintiff David Atwood whole—that is, to compensate Plaintiff David Atwood for the damage he has suffered. Compensatory damages are not limited to expenses that Plaintiff David Atwood may have incurred because of his injury. If Plaintiff David Atwood wins, he's entitled to compensatory damages for the physical injury, pain and suffering, and mental anguish that he has suffered because of Defendant James Jackson's wrongful conduct. You may award compensatory damages only for injuries that Plaintiff David Atwood proves were proximately caused by Defendant James Jackson's allegedly wrongful conduct. The damages that you award must be fair compensation for all of Plaintiff David Atwood's damages, no more and no less. Damages are not allowed as a punishment and cannot be imposed or increased to penalize Defendant James Jackson. You should not award compensatory damages for speculative injuries, but only for those injuries that Plaintiff David Atwood has actually suffered or that Plaintiff David Atwood is reasonably likely to suffer in the future. If you decided to award compensatory damages, you should be guided by dispassionate common sense. Computing damages may be difficult, but you must not let that difficulty lead you to engage in arbitrary guesswork. On the other hand, the law does not require that Plaintiff David Atwood prove the amount of his losses with mathematical precision, but only with as much definiteness and accuracy as the circumstances permit. You must use sound discretion in fixing an award of damages and drawing reasonable inferences where you find them appropriate from the facts and circumstances.

This was the instruction on awarding damages to solely compensate me for the damages caused by Jackson's actions. I believe that I proved well beyond any reasonable doubt that I had to pay $5,000.00 to bond out of jail. I knew that if the jury ruled in my favor on all the elements of false arrest, then they'd have to award me at least the $5,000.00.

As stated previously, I decided not to take the stand and testify myself because I did not want to risk having my criminal history introduced into evidence. If I would have taken the witness stand, I would have testified and presented evidence on how much money I'd spent litigating the lawsuit, how much money I lost out on when the trucking company denied me employment based on the arson arrest, and I would have attempted to introduce evidence showing where my book sales declined dramatically after my arson arrest.

The problem with trying to prove that these damages were the result of my arson arrest was very difficult. My arrests in Covington and Rankin Counties for the trumped-up and fake charges came so soon after my arrest for arson that there was only a short, two-week time frame between the two incidents in which to prove that I'd suffered damages. From my arson arrest on August 1, 2011, to my arrest in Covington County on August 16, 2011, gave very little opportunity to prove that during that two-week time frame I'd suffered substantial losses as a result of the August 1 arson arrest.

The first thing that Mr. Minor would have tried to do would be to confuse the jury, argue that my damages were also caused by the arrests in Covington and Rankin Counties—which Jackson could not be held liable for—and that the line between Jackson's illegal arrest of me and my arrests in Covington and Rankin Counties were too blurred to tell what arrest caused what damages. So there was no point in me even trying to testify about what actual damages I'd suffered. But there was more.

> **JUDGE AYCOCK:** To recover compensatory damages for mental and emotional distress, Plaintiff David Atwood must prove that he has suffered a specific discernible injury with credible evidence. Hurt feelings, anger, and frustration are part of life and are not the types of harm that could support a mental anguish award. Evidence of mental anguish need not be corroborated by doctors, psychologists, or other witnesses, but Plaintiff David Atwood must support his claims with competent evidence of the nature, extent, and duration of the harm. Damages for mental or emotional distress must be based on the evidence at

trial. They may not be based on speculation or sympathy.

Where does one whom is representing himself in federal court go to learn about proving emotional distress and mental anguish damages? I honestly had no clue how to go about doing that without taking the stand and testifying for myself. I'd hoped that the jury could see what a distressing situation that Jackson and his co-conspirators put me in; that much was obvious. But I'll be the first to admit I was totally unprepared to prove any of these damages at all. I'd depended entirely on proving Jackson liable for my false arrest and less on proving the damages caused by that arrest.

JUDGE AYCOCK: Nominal damages are an inconsequential or trifling sum awarded to a plaintiff when a technical violation of his rights has occurred but the plaintiff has suffered no actual loss or injury. If you find from a preponderance of the evidence that Plaintiff David Atwood sustained a technical violation of unreasonable arrest but that Plaintiff David Atwood suffered no actual loss as a result of this violation, then you may award Plaintiff David Atwood nominal damages.

Nominal damages are usually one dollar. When this instruction was read to the jury, I prayed that I wouldn't be awarded one dollar. I wanted to win my trial big, and even though a one dollar award would technically mean that I won the trial, having James O'Neal Jackson hand me a dollar bill out of his wallet would be humiliating to me.

The only way that I was going to get anyone's attention was by a large jury award. Five thousand dollars wasn't as large as I wanted it to be, but I knew I would feel as though I'd won a big victory if I could get at least that much. But I certainly was worried about only winning that one dollar.

With the instruction on nominal damages over with, Judge Aycock had only to give one final instruction regarding their deliberations and ultimate verdict. As I sat and listened to the instruction being read, I tapped my teeth with my pen, leaned back in the chair, and hoped beyond hope that I was on the verge of a victory that would forever sear into the minds of the Axis of Corruption that their evil deeds, corruption, and abuse of power would no longer go unpunished.

JUDGE AYCOCK: It is now your duty to deliberate and consult with one another in an effort to reach a verdict. Each of you must decide the case for yourself, but only after an impartial consideration of the evidence with your fellow jurors. During your deliberations, do not hesitate to reexamine your own opinions and change your mind if you are convinced that you were wrong. But do not give up on your honest beliefs because the other jurors think differently, or just to finish the case. Remember, at all times, that you are the judges of the facts. When you go into the jury room to deliberate, you must take with you a copy of this charge and the exhibits that I have admitted into evidence. You must select a jury foreperson to guide you in your deliberations and to speak for you here in the courtroom. Your verdict must be unanimous. After you have reached a unanimous verdict, your jury foreperson must fill out the verdict form, sign and date it. After you have concluded your service and I have discharged the jury, you are not required to talk with anyone about the case. If you need to communicate with me during your deliberations, the jury foreperson should write the inquiry and give it to the court security officer. After consulting with the attorneys, I will respond either in writing or by meeting with you in the courtroom. Keep in mind, however, that you must never disclose to anyone, not even to me, your numerical division on any question.

With that, the jury instructions were over with. It was now time for Mr. Minor and I to come forward and make our closing arguments to the jury. Everything hung in the balance and what was said now would be the last chance we had to speak to the jury directly.

My closing argument had been fine-tuned the night before, it was mostly memorized, and I couldn't have been more prepared than I was then to make what was, no doubt, the most important speech of my life.

JUDGE AYCOCK: I have allowed Mr. Atwood and Mr. Minor an opportunity to make closing arguments. They may actually use these instructions in their closing arguments. I've given each side thirty minutes. They'll be timed. Because the plaintiff carries the burden, Mr. Atwood starts. Then Mr. Minor argues for the defendant. Then Mr. Atwood will have a few minutes to close. Mr. Atwood, do you know how many minutes you may want for rebuttal?

ME: No more than two or three, Your Honor.

JUDGE AYCOCK: Okay. Let's say twenty-five and five. We will keep up with the time.

It was game time; the moment where my skills as a communicator would be proven. I turned and gave one final glance at David and Richard. They both gave me a thumbs up.

CHAPTER FORTY-FIVE

If delivering my opening statement had made me nervous, giving the closing argument terrified me. And what terrified me the most was knowing that I was on the brink of a major victory.

For weeks prior to the trial I'd been formulating the outline of a closing argument based more on the evidence and testimony that I expected to be given rather than any inspiring rhetoric. But James Jackson's testimony and the utter destruction that he inflicted upon himself changed all that.

Any closing argument after a trial such as we had just been through called for high-strung rhetoric.

Despite all odds, I'd proven Jackson, Chaney, and Sheriff Pace guilty of numerous federal and state crimes, I'd gotten Jackson to admit he was a dishonest, dirty cop who lied persistently under oath, and I'd proven beyond a doubt that Chaney and Sheriff Pace were directly responsible for my illegal arrest after they decided to retaliate against me for my book.

The evidence of their crimes was clear. The truth about their illegal, criminal conspiracy had come to the surface and I'd been vindicated beyond all doubt, proving, of course, that I was not responsible for the fire.

The closing argument that I thought I would need was utter garbage. The closing argument that was needed after the testimony we'd heard would have to come from the deepest recesses of my heart and soul. I'd have to bring my A-game and deliver a knockout that would forever settle the question about the atrocity that Jackson, Chaney, Sheriff Pace, and Emmett Atwood almost got away with.

After many rewrites, countless hours of missed sleep, multiple run-throughs with David and Richard, and a miraculous attempt at memorization, I felt ready.

> **JUDGE AYCOCK:** Mr. Atwood, you may come forward and make your closing arguments.

I took a cup of water with me. My hands were shaking and my hip hurt worse than it ever had before. I approached the podium and laid my notes out in the order that I would need them. I also placed my cell phone where I could watch the screen as David and Richard sent me texts to let me know what was going on with Mr. Minor and Jackson, whom were behind me at their table.

Judge Aycock had given us thirty minutes to make our arguments, but my closing had been timed to around twenty-five minutes. I wanted to give myself plenty of time and a significant margin of error.

I took several deep breaths. I looked at my jury and saw that they were all anxiously waiting to see my next stunning performance.

It all came down to this. I realized that I may never again have the opportunity I had that day. I was arguing my own case. I was defending the Constitution. I was standing up against evil, against corruption, against government tyranny. I was on the front lines of the war that I'd always wanted to fight. Now was my opportunity to deliver a death blow to the Axis of Corruption that was James Jackson, Mike Chaney, and Sheriff Martin Pace.

> **ME:** May it please the Court?
> **JUDGE AYCOCK:** You may proceed.
> **ME:** This has been a very difficult trial for some of us. I know it definitely has been for me. But I want to sincerely thank you for your service on this jury. There's been a lot of difficult testimony. We've heard some things that are hard to understand sometimes. But you have been attentive and patient as we've completed this process. In a search for justice there can be no shortcuts, so I apologize for the length of this trial, but I sincerely thank you as well for your service.

I took a sip of water and shuffled my weight from one hip to the other. I braced the edges of the podium with both hands and continued. My nerves and shakes were driving me crazy and I regretted foregoing a swig of liquor earlier that morning.

> **ME:** It is a sad fact in this country that violent crime exists. So when this type of violence occurs it becomes the business of the police. A good, competent investigator will set about the business of carefully investigating crime. He won't be rushed to judgment or motivated by an illegal purpose. But as you know from the testimony, no one knows for sure whether a crime even took place in this case. We don't know because this defendant rushed to judgment. He didn't do his job. And he didn't do his job because he wasn't asked to do his job. He was ordered to carry out a plan of political assassination.

I looked at my watch. I was exactly at the point where I was supposed to be to meet my twenty-five minute goal. I'd calmed down a bit and was slowly feeling myself build into a smooth flow of eloquence.

> **ME:** This defendant has done things in this case that have never been done before. You heard his words, you heard him testify, and the defendant, in his own words, not the words of his lawyer, not the words of Ronnie Stewart, the defendant's own words, you heard him say, "*I did not have probable cause.*" You heard him say, "*I obtained the arrest warrant without any evidence of a crime.*" And you heard him say that the reason he did so—you heard him say that he conducted this illegal arrest—was because his boss was making him do it. And you know now that the reason the defendant's boss, Mike Chaney, was making him commit this crime was because of a book I wrote. And you heard the defendant say himself that he was a willing participant to this crime. So I don't have to go much further with the evidence. You are here to decide whether enough probable cause existed to justify the arrest for arson. And the defendant himself has told you that he didn't have probable cause. He admitted that this was an illegal arrest. He admitted that he was a part—a willing participant—in a crime that was committed against me. It doesn't get any more simple than that. The defendant himself admits that he obtained

the arrest warrant for an illegal reason and that he didn't have probable cause. The defendant said that.

This was about as far as I felt that I needed to go in reciting the evidence and testimony in detail to the jury. They'd heard Jackson testify. They'd heard him make my case for me. They'd seen the defendant himself admit that he didn't have probable cause and that my arrest was illegal. To harp on that testimony any further would be a waste of time.

I knew at that point in the trial that the jury would rule in my favor and conclude that my arrest was illegal. But in order to truly win—to truly send a message—I needed to inspire the jury to award a substantial sum of money. I needed to arouse their passion and send a message that this type of deplorable, illegal behavior by our law enforcement officers would not be tolerated.

> **ME:** Now, there's been a lot of other testimony about cell records, footprints, insurance, and many other things. And I attempted to put that into evidence to give you an understanding—to give you a context—on how this case came to us here this week. And that information was good, but ask yourselves one thing: Did anything you heard or saw this week convince you that (a) this fire was for sure an arson; and (b) that I committed it? The defendant, James Jackson, told you himself that he wasn't convinced, so neither should you be. The defendant's assertion in 2011 that this was an arson we now know was nothing but fantastic speculation. It was a self-serving attempt to justify shoddy police work and to instigate a witch hunt. Now, Emmett Atwood has a God-given right to expect and demand a competent, quick, and accurate investigation. But it was clear in this case that there was another agenda. From the very first moments of this investigation they were more concerned with exacting revenge. They didn't care whether a crime had been committed. They only looked at the potential opportunity these circumstances provided to retaliate against me because I chose to take a stance against political corruption. But that's not how our system operates. We have laws to protect the innocent from this type of government oppression—and there's no doubt here that this is what occurred—there is no doubt because the defendant sat right there

in that [witness] chair and told you that this is what happened. This investigation was infected by a corrupt and dishonest law enforcement officer who sat there and admitted he committed perjury. He admitted that he lied under oath. And he admitted that he did it for an illegal purpose. So you have two crimes that the defendant has committed here. He's lied under oath and he executed an illegal arrest.

At this point it was pretty clear that I had the jury hook, line, and sinker. They were all maintaining eye contact with me, they were leaning forward in their chairs, and a couple had nodded their heads whenever I said something negative about Jackson.

I occasionally looked down at my watch and realized that I was ahead of schedule. I made a mental note to slow down and make sure that I enunciated my words clearly and took the appropriate pauses between my main points.

There were a few instances throughout the trial when I'd gotten overly excited, my voice rose an octave or two, and I'd been admonished to calm down a little bit. But David and Richard were sending me texts telling me what a good job I was doing so far. Richard even invented a new word during my closing argument to describe my performance. He said I was doing "fantabulous."

The best, though, was yet to come. As I had done briefly in my opening statement, I was building into a crescendo. But first, I had to deal with the only hurtful evidence and testimony that was given against me during the trial.

> **ME:** We know that the defendant isn't an honest person because he admitted it, but let's think about Josh Chamblee for a minute. Yes, there is testimony from Josh that is harmful to my case, but Josh is not a credible witness. He's not an honest witness. And he has a clear motive to lie. But you shouldn't be blinded or swayed by what Josh Chamblee said in his deposition in February 2017. What Josh Chamblee said in 2017 had no bearing on what Josh told the defendant in 2011. It doesn't have any bearing because the defendant didn't know about any of the extensive details Josh talked about in this 2017 deposition. The defendant didn't know because in 2011 he did not ask those questions. And

that is what you must look at in this case—the evidence available to the defendant in 2011. In 2011 this defendant knew that Josh was not a credible witness. This defendant knew that Josh had provided multiple conflicting statements. This defendant knew that Josh had been arrested before for lying to law enforcement officers and filing false police reports. So this defendant knew in 2011 that there were problems with Josh's credibility. But the defendant chose to ignore those credibility issues—and you heard him testify—he did not take any steps to independently verify what Josh was telling him. He rushed to judgment. And he did so because his boss was coming down on top of his head to obtain something, anything, to get an arrest warrant. So the defendant chose to ignore Josh Chamblee's credibility issues because doing so fit with the plan he and Mike Chaney had.

At some point during the litigation of this case I realized that Jackson was, in my opinion, an extremely homophobic individual. I felt like he hated gay men and women and probably took pleasure at trying to send me to prison. This gave me an idea that I was sure would get under his skin.

Jackson and Josh Chamblee were alike in a lot of ways. They were both extremely dishonest people. They would lie, scheme, fabricate, and distort in any ways they could to protect themselves and cover their asses. A comparison of the two was totally appropriate.

> **ME:** So when you think about the testimony of Josh Chamblee and Defendant James Jackson, I want you to remember that these are two people that are twins in a lot of ways. They are twins of deception. They are twins of discrepancy. They are twins of dishonesty. Nothing they say can be believed because they've both admitted that they are liars. They've admitted that they are not honest people. The Book of Luke talks about lies. It says if you are dishonest in small things then you will be dishonest in larger things. And that's what we have seen from these two individuals.

A text immediately came across my phone from Richard telling me that Jackson was rolling his eyes, shifting in his seat, and shaking his head behind my back. That was followed with a text from David telling me that Mr. Minor was chugging water from a Styrofoam cup as if he'd recently trekked through the Sahara Desert.

If my closing was having that kind of effect on Jackson and Mr. Minor, I figured the jury was loving it. I kept pushing. It was time for more fiery rhetoric.

> **ME:** The integrity of our justice system is at stake in this trial. You cannot base any verdict finding in favor of Defendant Jackson when the core of the defendant's case is built on lies and deceit. When it's built on fantastic speculation. It is a plague of lies at the heart of their case. Their message—the defense's message—their case—is plagued with lies, distortions, and discrepancies. And we know we can't trust this defendant and we can't trust the message.

Despite having utterly discredited the alleged probable cause determination that Stewart made at the preliminary hearing, Mr. Minor had still tried to build a defense around Stewart's rubber-stamp. I planned to address that defense, slice it to ribbons, and figuratively burn it up.

> **ME:** Now, the defendant and Mr. Minor want you to excuse the defendant's deplorable behavior solely because Ronnie Stewart rubber-stamped a routine legal document binding this case over to a grand jury. Their case swings on the fact that Ronnie Stewart made this determination. Essentially, they are asking you to excuse and turn a blind eye to the fact that the defendant conducted an illegal, criminal arrest without probable cause. They are asking you to excuse the defendant's illegal behavior because some individual who didn't have any legal training rubber-stamped a routine legal document handing this case over to a grand jury that ultimately didn't indict because there wasn't any evidence—there wasn't any probable cause. That's their reasonable, rational theory that you are supposed to buy into, but which I think you will find ridiculous. So you have to think, when the defendant makes a great mountain out of the fact that Ronnie Stewart allegedly found probable cause, you've got to think to yourself what importance did that signify. But you now know the

truth about Ronnie Stewart. And when you know the truth about Ronnie Stewart their mountain becomes nothing but a mole hill. We know that because we know that this determination made by Ronnie Stewart was nothing more than a routine rubber-stamp on a document that didn't signify a hill of beans. Ronnie Stewart was going to rubber-stamp this document handing the case over to the grand jury regardless of what the evidence may or may not have shown. We know that because Ronnie Stewart testified to that. Rosalind Jordan testified to that. You heard her say that Ronnie Stewart had rubber-stamped this document binding other defendants' cases over to the grand jury even when a third-party appeared before Stewart and confessed that they had committed the crime instead of the defendant. You heard her testify to that.

As I'd expected after Stewart and Mrs. Jordan testified, no reasonable person could legitimately believe that Stewart's "finding" of probable cause signified anything important. I think I'd clearly made that point. But David and Richard contributed significantly to the next point, and, once said, sealed Jackson's fate.

> **ME:** So you now know that Ronnie Stewart was going to bind this case over to the grand jury regardless of what evidence was presented to him. So Ronnie Stewart's evidentiary findings in this case don't signify a single, noteworthy thing. Ronnie Stewart didn't provide probable cause in this case. Emmett Atwood's checkbook provided the probable cause in this case.

I amplified and stressed the last two sentences. And when I'd finished saying the word "checkbook," several of the jurors nodded their heads up and down vigorously and a smile or two broke out across the faces of several of them.

This last minute hyperbole had hit a home run with the jury. Not only did it get some of them to smile and nod their heads, but it signified in its entirety how I ended up charged with arson, and it totally discredited the defense's case. But I wasn't done.

> **ME:** The real issue to keep in mind is what the defendant testified to—what the defendant told you—and he was very candid

in his testimony once the truth came out. He kind of gave up. He told you he didn't have any probable cause. He told you he didn't have any evidence. He told you himself that this was an illegal arrest. That is what is most important—not what Ronnie Stewart's rubber-stamp says, but what the defendant himself said.

Here is where I left the testimony and evidence completely, assumed the moral, sanctimonious high ground of a Baptist preacher, and began to preach to the jury as a minister would in church.

I had most of my arguments memorized, and as I began to crucify the evil that was James Jackson, Mike Chaney, Sheriff Martin Pace, and Emmett Atwood, I moved closer to the jury box, I swayed back and forth behind the podium, and I maintained constant eye contact with my jurors.

The trial had all come down to this. Now was the time to win over any doubtful minds and inspire the jury to my cause. They had the evidence, they had the testimony, but now they only needed the inspiration to rule in my favor.

> **ME:** Now, if you chose to do what I do and research and write about political corruption, you come to know that corruption exists. You know that it is out there. You learn very early on that you can't be naive. You love your country but you know it's not perfect. So one must understand that. So it's no surprise to me. But for some of you, you're finding out about the other side of life. That's why this case is so instructive. You're finding out that things are not always what they seem. And it's not just rhetoric. It's the actions of people—these law enforcement officers—it's the lack of courage. It's the lack of integrity in high places. That's what we are talking about here. Credibility and integrity does not attach to a badge; it attaches to the person. So the person that may have a job where he makes two dollars an hour can have more integrity than the person in the highest office. It's something from within. It's from your heart. That's what we are talking about here. And it's not about being anti-police. You heard my mother's testimony—my two best friends are law enforcement officers. So it's not about being anti-police. But anyone who believes that all police are perfect, that they don't lie,

that they don't have the same biases that the rest of society has is living in a dream world. So this case is not for the faint of heart. This is not for the timid. This case is for the courageous. It's for those who understand what the Constitution is all about. And the Constitution is what makes this country so great. The Constitution guarantees us our rights and freedoms. You can be accused in this country of a crime, but that's just an accusation. It doesn't amount to a hill of beans. We are presumed innocent until proven guilty in a court of law. This is a simple, but important concept. Since the beginning of time in this country, this simple, legal concept has been at the heart of our justice system. And that's what trials are all about—an opportunity to come before the people of the community—the consciousness of the community. You set the standards. You tell us what is right and wrong and you use your common sense to do that. Your verdict goes far beyond the walls of this courtroom. Your verdict, finding in my favor, it will send a message that there is still justice in America and that corrupt law enforcement officers are not above the law.

I was having a hard time at this point remembering to breathe. I was wildly gesticulating with my hands and I remember sweat forming on my brow. The Apostle Paul couldn't have been doing a more animated sermon and I could still see that my jurors were on the edges of their seats waiting for more.

I eventually worked my way back over to the podium and I noticed that I was still a few minutes ahead of schedule. I took a few extra seconds to breathe, took a sip of water, and wiped my forehead.

There were several texts on my phone telling me that Mr. Minor was drowning himself with water and that Judge Aycock had stopped all her movement and was concentrated solely on my performance. The courtroom was utterly silent as I continued.

ME: Now, there's something about corruption. There's something about a rotten apple that will ultimately infect the entire barrel, because if others don't have the courage that I've asked you to have in this case, then people will just sit idly by. We live in a society where many people are apathetic. They don't want to get involved. That's why every person in this courtroom thanks you from the bottom of their heart because you know what? You haven't been apathetic. You are the ones who have made a commitment—a commitment to justice. And it can sometimes be a painful commitment, but your courage is much greater than this defendant's. One of the things that have made this country so great is people's willingness to stand up and say, This is wrong! I'm not going to be part of it! I'm not going to be part of the cover-up! And that's what I am asking you to do. Stop this cover-up. Stop this abuse. Because if you don't stop it here today, then who will? You think the defendant's supervisors at the Fire Marshal's Office is going to stop it? You think the Attorney General's Office is going to stop it? Do you think I can stop it by myself? It has to be stopped by you.

I'd gotten entirely too emotional by this point. I was almost yelling. Yet I felt the emotions were entirely appropriate. Jackson's actions were a direct threat to the life, liberty, and the pursuit of happiness of every American in the country. It was good to be passionate because without someone willing to stand up and speak out against this type of government abuse it would only continue unchecked.

I had to take a breath, though, and calm down. I didn't want to lose the flow, but I didn't want to get so animated that the jury couldn't follow my words. And I certainly didn't want Judge Aycock to have to tell me again to calm down a level or two. So after taking a few more breaths and a swig of water—which I wished was strong liquor—I continued in a more level and even tone.

ME: We have not yet reached a point in our country where the deplorable actions of the defendant won't be embraced by those in power. But we are fighting for freedom and equality and justice for all. And when we make this fight we then become guardians of the Constitution. And if you don't speak out, if you don't stand up, if you don't do what is right, then this kind of conduct will continue on forever and we will never have an ideal society—a society that lives out the true meaning of the creed of the Constitution of life, liberty, and justice for all. From the first moments of the fire investigation this defendant concluded that I was guilty. But he can't make that judgment. Mike Chaney can't make that judgment. Ronnie Stewart can't make that judgment. Nobody but you can make that judgment. So when this defendant took the law into his own hands he became worse than the criminals who break the law because this defendant is supposed to be the protector of the law. Who then polices the police? Who polices this defendant? You police this defendant! You police him by your verdict. You are the ones who send the message. Nobody can do that in this society. They don't have the courage. Nobody has the courage! There are a bunch of people running around with no courage to do what is right, except individual citizens like you! You are the ones in this war. You are the ones on the front line. You're the people! You are what makes this country so great. And please don't forget that.

I was almost coming to the top of the mountain with my sermon. I could see the summit, but I wasn't quite done. I was right on schedule according to my watch. I hadn't made a mistake in delivering my closing argument. And everyone in the courtroom had a look of awe on their face when I occasionally turned around to see how my speech was affecting the people in the courtroom.

I was almost at the crescendo and I needed to make sure it was delivered in a picture perfect way. I was about to put James Jackson and his ilk in the history bins as nothing more than a group of evil, corrupt, totalitarian hooligans. My concentration couldn't have been sharper and I couldn't of had a more captive audience.

ME: And so, understand how this happened. Understand how it came about. It's part of a culture. It's part of a culture of getting away with things. It's part of a culture of looking the other way. This defendant thought no one would question him. He thought he could get away with it. But we do not live in Tehran, Iran! This is not North Korea! We are not in Nazi Germany! This is America! We have a right to criticize our government without illegal retribution. We have a right to publish our views and beliefs. We have a right to worship a God of our own choosing. To make a choice to be a liberal or conservative. But that defendant is trying to take away that right. He wants to return us to a police state like Nazi Germany where one can't criticize the government.

This was the second time that I received overt feedback from the jury. At the mention of the police states several jurors nodded their heads again and moved closer to the railing to eagerly catch the rest of the arguments. If they didn't think that Jackson, Chaney, and Pace represented something as bad as the Gestapo of Nazi Germany before the closing argument began, then they did by that point. I'd done my job, I just needed to close out the show.

> **ME:** Do you not think that the actions of the defendant and his co-conspirators didn't scare me to death? You think it didn't terrify my family and make me think twice about ever trying to publish anything about the government again? You're damn right it did. But you can change that. It's not about winning. It's about justice being done. It's about preventing this from ever happening again by your verdict. Your verdict's message. You have the power to stop this.

I'd almost come to the completion of my argument. The summit had been reached, the pinnacle conquered. It was now time to endear the jury to me.

I returned to behind the podium. I caught my breath, drank several sips of water, and placed both hands on the edges of the podium while I looked around the courtroom and reshuffled my notes.

The jury needed a moment to catch their breaths, too. Several readjusted themselves in their seats. I dabbed my forehead and lowered my voice.

> **ME:** Things happen for a reason in our lives. Maybe this is one of the reasons that we are all gathered here today. Maybe there is a reason why you were selected. Maybe there is something in your background or character that helps you to understand that what the defendant did was wrong. Maybe you are the right people, at the right time, at the right place to say, No more! We are not going to have this. Because if the defendant can do it to me he can do it to anybody. He can do it to a teacher. A college professor. He can do it to a salesman. A forklift driver. He could

do it to a nurse or to another healthcare worker. If the defendant is allowed to do this to my family then he can do it to anybody's family.

One of the only parts of the closing arguments that had been a point of contention with the numerous people I consulted was whether or not to specifically list each juror's occupation while simultaneously looking them in the eyes as I said it.

I wanted to make that personal connection and let each juror know that I took the opportunity to learn and remember something about their lives. I wanted them to know that I was emotionally connected to them as they were, hopefully, connected to me. So as I said each juror's occupation I looked them straight in the face and slightly nodded my head.

About half the jurors acknowledged my gesture and nodded back in silent thanks. The other half remained motionless but attentive now that I'd calmed down some and lowered my voice.

> **ME:** If you were in my position you would want someone to fight hard for you. I am fighting hard for myself. Hopefully, in a logical way something I said made some sense to you. Hopefully, as an advocate you can understand my zeal. You know the passion that I feel for this. We all have time invested in this case. But it's not about winning. It's about what is right. It's about my life and it's about the life of my family.

I then turned to trying to make the jury feel empowered again. I needed them to feel like they were invested in the case too. And I did so with the best analogy that I could think of.

> **ME:** It's been a long road to get to this point. This case has been almost like a relay race in many respects—in this search for justice. I had the baton for awhile and I briefly passed it off to Mr. Minor. I've got the baton back for a few minutes, but soon we are going to pass the baton off to you—you will pick up this race and carry the baton. You are now the stars of the show. This is how our system works—this is what makes it so great—we are passing the baton to you. And honestly, I'll be very happy. It's been a long, long road to get here—almost eight years—and now

I am ready to sit back and watch you finish the race.

I was nearing the finale. As I looked at my watch I again realized that I was a few minutes ahead. So I took another sip of water, stared at the floor for a moment, caught my breath, then continued.

ME: So please don't compromise your conscience. Don't compromise your principles. Don't compound the evil that the defendant has already done. Don't rush to judgment like the defendant did. Have a judgment that is well thought out. One you can believe in the morning after you render your verdict. I want you to place yourselves in the day after your verdict when you are back home with your families, when you get up and look in the mirror. But what's important is that you are able to look in that mirror and say to yourselves, Have I been true to my oath? Did I do the right thing? Was I naive or timid? Or was I courageous? Did I believe in the Constitution? Did I believe in justice? Did I do my part for honesty and integrity? Ask yourselves those questions. That's your mission on this search for justice. I want to say one more time; this is a case about an innocent man, wrongly accused. You've seen me now over the last few days. You've heard me ask questions, give answers, interact with the judge and opposing counsel, and argue my case. But soon it will be your turn. You have the keys to my future. You have the evidence and testimony. You not only have the patience and integrity to do the right thing, but I believe you have the courage to do the right thing. Me and my family believe you will do the right thing—that you will give us justice.

The race was nearly over. Mr. Minor would have an opportunity to also make closing arguments, but every juror already knew what his or her decision was going to be. Essentially, I'd already crossed the finish line in first place. The only question left to decide was going to be how much money the jury would award. And that is the last issue that I addressed with them.

ME: And the right thing is to find in my favor and award an amount of money that will not only compensate me for the loss of money, employment, embarrassment, and pain and suffering, but also award an amount that will ultimately send a message that this type of deplorable, reprehensible behavior will not be tolerated. So I ask you to award me a monetary sum of money to compensate me for the money that I have lost. And you heard from the witnesses that I had to pay five thousand dollars to bond out of jail. But I also want you to consider the fact that this illegal arrest caused me to be denied employment. You heard from my mother that because of this arrest a company denied me a job. That's important if you decide to award compensatory damages in addition to the five thousand I had to spend on bail. I believe you will come to a fair monetary figure to compensate me that loss. You may also award damages for emotional distress and mental anguish. You heard from my mother and you know from me that this arrest terrified us. The Gestapo arrest tactics were dangerous and placed our lives at risk. And as you heard this week, I will always be the one accused of starting that fire. I will never be able to escape that accusation. My family will never be able to escape that false accusation. So I am asking you to award substantial emotional distress damages to compensate me for the terror that this defendant and his co-conspirators caused.

I've always hated asking for money. While in prison I made it a firm rule never to ask to borrow from another inmate. I'd never be a good politician because I find it so difficult to ask people to part from their hard-earned money. But asking the jury to award me money was not difficult. I felt they hated Jackson as much as I did and recognized him for the threat to the Constitution and our society that I knew him to be. So I asked them to use their best judgment in coming to a fair figure.

The only thing left for me to do was close out my arguments, thank everyone for their participation, and hope for the best.

ME: Now, Mr. Minor will go on to represent other defendants. Judge Aycock will go on to hear and judge other cases—I at least hope so—but this is my one day in court. This is my one day to try and right a horrible wrong done to my family and I. You are literally carrying my future in your hands. Treat it gently, treat it carefully, treat it fairly, but please, I am asking you, don't be part of this cover-up. Don't be a part of their abuse. Thank you.

I took a deep breath and then exhaled. I'd delivered a stunning, knock-out performance and I did it without making a single mistake. I did it without stuttering, forgetting my words, or getting lost in a sentence that wasn't going anywhere but into oblivion.

The jury sat back in their chairs and took a minute to take in their surroundings. Some even made sideways glances at the other jurors. By the time I made it back to my table my phone was full of texts from David and Richard telling me what a great job I was doing throughout the closing.

I even saw Judge Aycock and one of her law clerks cut eyes at one another as if to silently say that this had been one of the best performances that they'd ever seen. I certainly felt that way and I knew that my closing had been effective with the jury. It was passionate. It was inspiring. And, most importantly, it was persuasive.

It was up to Mr. Minor now to undo some of that damage. But I felt confident. In fact, I felt better than confident. For the first time in the entire case I felt cocky and assured that I would win. And I was ready for whatever Mr. Minor might try to use to alleviate that damage.

CHAPTER FORTY-SIX

I knew Mr. Minor was in his feelings about my closing argument, and I was honestly surprised that he allowed me to go through the entirety of it without objecting to something I'd said. Even I realized that ninety percent of the argument was high-spun rhetoric that had little to do with the actual evidence in the case.

After the testimony, though, and the clear deplorable and illegal conduct that Jackson and Chaney had been caught in, what was needed was something to inspire the jury and tear at their heart strings. As I sat down and Mr. Minor prepared to come make his closing argument, I was curious to hear what he'd say.

JUDGE AYCOCK: Mr. Minor.

MR. MINOR: Good afternoon. I've represented Mr. Jackson throughout this case. He's an honorable man. I am proud to defend the defendant. The Plaintiff tried to make this case about a feud with his grandfather. But this is about whether my client had probable cause for an arrest warrant. Mr. Atwood tried to confuse my client. I showed my client his report, the affidavit, all from different dates and asked what probable cause he had for that. My client got confused. He couldn't remember what court he was talking about and what date he was talking about. He got confused, okay? And Mr. Atwood got my client to say some things that weren't true. He denied that he committed perjury. You heard him. He went back and looked at his report from back in 2011 and after reviewing the report, it confirms that before he obtained that arrest warrant for Joshua Chamblee on July 27th, 2011, he talked to his mother who told him that Josh knew about the fire, but was afraid to tell Mr. Jackson about it because the Plaintiff had threatened him. Now, Mr. Atwood tried to make it about whether my client committed a crime. Then he gets up there and has the gall to tell you that my client admitted to doing something illegal when he arrested the Plaintiff. He didn't admit that. He did not admit it. He denied that the Plaintiff's arrest was illegal. That's a complete distortion.

I think by this time everyone in the courtroom sat with their mouths dropped open. I'd pounded this point over and over again, and each time I did so, whether it was during Jackson's testimony on Monday or his testimony on Wednesday and Thursday, Jackson continually admitted that he didn't have any probable cause, that he had no evidence of arson, that he'd lied under oath, that he'd committed perjury, and that he tried to argue to Mike Chaney that what they were doing was illegal. Jackson even admitted that if he'd thought about it he should have gone to the FBI.

Even though Jackson had gone back on the witness stand Wednesday, and tried to correct some of the testimony that'd he given on Monday, there was no doubt in anyone's mind that Jackson had repeatedly admitted to everything that I'd accused him of. But just as Mr. Minor had sat quietly and endured my closing argument, so I did the same.

MR. MINOR: Now, he gets up here and tells you that he had to pay five thousand dollars for his bond. His mom testified that she paid it. There's no evidence he paid anything. That's not what this case is about. He's trying to make it about all these other issues. This case is about whether Josh Chamblee's recorded statement that you heard gave my client probable cause to go get an arrest warrant from Ronnie Stewart in Attala County. The court's instructions, probable cause does not require proof beyond a reasonable doubt. But only a showing of fair probability of criminal activity. It must be more than a bare suspicion, but need not reach the fifty-percent mark. So to have probable cause you don't need to be one hundred percent for sure that someone committed a crime. You don't even have to be fifty-percent sure.

Just a fair probability. The reasonableness of an arrest must be judged by what a reasonable officer would do under the circumstances. So even though Mr. Jackson may have been under some pressure to make an arrest in this case, his state of mind is irrelevant to the determination of probable cause. The question is whether a reasonable officer would believe that a crime had been committed based on the facts available to that officer at the time he applied for the warrant. Now, what were the facts that Mr. Jackson had available to him at the time he got the warrant? Well, he had just taken Josh Chamblee's statement. You heard that recording where Josh explained that the reason he didn't come clean sooner was because the Plaintiff had threatened him. He threatened that he would burn down his house. And he describes going to the Atwood Lakehouse, driving up the road, getting out, walking to the house, getting water on his feet, which is consistent with my client's testimony. He then described David Atwood going behind the house and setting it afire. Now, Mr. Atwood claims that it was obvious that Josh Chamblee was not a credible witness when my client, James Jackson, interviewed him on July 29th, 2011. It's obvious! [Said with much sarcasm.] He had a clear motive to lie. [More sarcasm.] That was his words. Well, what was Chamblee's motive? That he made a complaint to the authorities that he'd exposed him to HIV? That was allegedly his motive to retaliate? Did you see any evidence that Mr. Jackson was aware of any of that? That was just a little snippet from Josh's deposition. That's the only evidence of that. There's no evidence of any motive that my client was aware of any reason why Josh Chamblee might lie.

Mr. Minor had a point to much of this portion of the closing argument. The entire crux of the case revolved around Josh's credibility and the realistic reliability of the third statement that he gave Jackson on July 29, 2011. However, it had been my assertion all along—a point that I hoped was adequately conveyed to the jury—that Jackson didn't know about the severe problems with Josh's credibility because he didn't take the time to ask those important questions that would have led any other reasonable law enforcement officer to conclude that Josh was a deluded, lying sociopath who would use and abuse anyone in furtherance of his personal needs.

Jackson didn't know anything about Josh's credibility because he didn't *want* to know. My argument was that Jackson could not conduct an incompetent investigation and then claim total ignorance of the relevant evidence when it came time to explain his actions. If one won't ask the important questions, one cannot then legitimately claim plausible deniability. So even though Mr. Minor tried to argue that Jackson didn't know about Josh's credibility issues, it was easily concluded that Jackson didn't know about these issues only because he refused to ask the important questions. And I believed the jury knew that.

> **MR. MINOR:** Now, he says Josh isn't a credible witness because he gave multiple conflicting statements. Yes, it's true. Josh Chamblee did initially deny knowing anything about the fire. But you heard my client's testimony. He said he met him at the KFC to interview him and Josh was fidgety and wouldn't look him in the eye. He was very nervous. So Mr. Jackson didn't believe he was telling the truth. It was like he was scared to tell the truth; like he was hiding something. That was Mr. Jackson's clear testimony. So then they did that interview at the Leake County Sheriff's Department on July 29th, 2011. And Josh explains he wanted to come clean sooner but Mr. Atwood had threatened him. It was reasonable for my client to believe that Josh was telling the truth. Now, he tried to make a lot out of the written and recorded statement that Josh did. They weren't detailed. They weren't real detailed, but they gave some detail and the reason that there was not more details is because my client originally believed that Josh had went to the house in the middle of the night to a piece of land he's never been to before in the middle of the woods. What details could Josh provide?

This was a convenient excuse to explain Josh's inability to provide any details of the lake house property. On the one hand this may seem a viable argument. However, on the other hand, I knew it was an impossibility.

According to Emmett, Kade, Sheriff Nail, and Jackson, they believed that someone parked their vehicle in a cubbyhole section of woods near where the Atwood property meets Youth Center Road. According to their logic, someone then walked a little over a mile from that section of the property all the way to where the Atwood Lakehouse stood.

If this was truly the case, one would have to cross through woods, pine thickets, large pastures, cross a large metal bridge over Atwood Creek, climb a steep hill, walk past Kade's house, cross a levee either on it or below it, before finally coming to the Atwood Lakehouse. This would of had to of been repeated in the reverse after setting the house on fire.

That was their theory to the case. And no matter how hard Jackson, Mr. Minor, and myself tried—at all different times—no one could get Josh to provide any details about the property. This simply doesn't make sense when one takes into account all that Josh and I would of had to go through to get from Youth Center Road back up into the property where the lake house stood.

Josh could not provide a single, solitary detail. It didn't make sense, of course. What did make sense was that Josh didn't know any details about the property or the house because we never went to burn the motherfucker down. It was just more of his pathological lying. And I prayed that the jury was able to see that.

> **MR. MINOR:** Then the Plaintiff says Mr. Jackson didn't do anything to independently verify Josh's statement. There was nothing he could do. Josh Chamblee was the only witness. Mr. Atwood keeps complaining about Mr. Jackson not coming to interview him. But two days after the fire he denies to Sheriff Nail that he had anything to do with the fire. What, then, would be the point of an interview?

This immediately raised a problem with Jackson's storyline. At that first meeting with Sheriff Nail, Josh denied involvement in the fire, too. So, why then, would Jackson continuously seek out Josh for a second and third statement? It was because Josh was the weak link in the armor and Jackson knew that he could eventually make Josh crack with enough pressure. I figured the jury would know this too.

> **MR. MINOR:** Now, the question you must decide is whether Josh's third statement gave my client reason to believe—whether that gave him probable cause to take to a judge to get an arrest warrant. That's the issue in this case. And you heard Chamblee's testimony. He stills maintains to this day that David Atwood

burned his grandfather's house down. Mr. Atwood tried to make it sound like Josh was coerced into making this statement. Well, he was no longer under any pressure and coercion now. And he still says under oath in his deposition that Mr. Atwood burned that house. That speaks volumes. This isn't a case where an eyewitness lied and then later on said he was wrong and made it all up. You heard Josh Chamblee's deposition. He testified that the reason he didn't come clean sooner was because the Plaintiff threatened him. Finally, after Josh's family told him they were fine and could take care of themselves, Josh came forward and did the right thing. He also testified that he wasn't aware that Mr. Jackson had an arrest warrant. So the idea that he was threatened into making this statement is absurd. Josh also testified that he was not aware that Mr. Jackson had threatened his mother to arrest him. And he clearly testified that my client never told him to implicate David Atwood in this arson. He just told him to tell the truth. And that's exactly what my client believes Josh Chamblee did. You heard my client testify that be believed in 2011 that Josh Chamblee was telling the truth, and he still believes that Josh was telling the truth.

There were several problems with Mr. Minor's closing arguments in this regard. First, Jackson knew from the beginning that not only had Josh provided multiple different accounts of what happened on the night of November 10, 2009, but he also knew that Josh had been arrested before and charged with lying to law enforcement officers and filing false police reports. So regardless of whether or not Jackson *wanted* to believe Josh's third statement, Josh's dishonest history should have given him enough pause to stop and go independently verify what Josh was telling him. Jackson didn't do this, of course, because he didn't actually need evidence of a crime. He only needed something—whether true or not—in which to arrest me.

Second, the fact that Josh still maintained in February 2017 that we burned the house down was only the more reason to suspect his ulterior motives. Josh was an opportunistic liar and had been, throughout our brief relationship, jealous of everything that I did.

When my first book was published in September 2009, Josh was jealous of the publicity and name recognition that I received. When I began receiving money from my book's royalties, Josh criticized me for not working a "real" job like he did waiting tables at the Applebee's in Starkville.

Josh hated the fact that I drove new vehicles, had a boat and jet ski, and was able to afford to travel wherever and whenever I wanted. His jealousy of everything that I did and had earned for myself manifested itself in numerous unusual ways both during and after our relationship. Him testifying that I burnt the Atwood Lakehouse—without being able to provide any actual details or proof—and was now litigating, very successfully it might be assumed, a false arrest lawsuit against the people that caused our arrests, was only another manifestation of his jealousy.

Josh could not stand the fact that I was smarter than him—not that it took much to be smarter than him. Josh hated the fact that he couldn't have sent me to prison for the false crime of arson. He wanted me to suffer so bad only because I'd caught him in lie after lie and—when I'd had enough—ended our relationship.

So when Josh testified at the deposition in February 2017, his intention to accuse me of starting the fire was only a continuation of Josh's sadistic goal in punishing me for ending our relationship in 2010. So, of course, he was going to say I burnt the house down. Josh hated me for ending our relationship, he was jealous of the fact that I had more than he did, he couldn't stand the fact that I was too smart to let him get away with lying to me, and he certainly didn't want me winning a false arrest trial in federal court that, ultimately, would cast doubt on his actions, his behavior, and his character.

Even though Josh essentially admitted in his deposition to committing a serious felony crime, his hatred of me overrode any self-preservation mechanism he may have had for denying our involvement in the fire. Josh simply wanted me to suffer and make my life as difficult as possible. That's the only reason why he testified at the deposition that we'd burnt the house down. Unfortunately, as complex of an explanation as this was, I doubted the jury would understand it. I just hoped they were willing to overlook Josh's 2017 deposition.

Third, the fantastic assertion that was put forth claiming that Josh only decided to "come clean" after his parents told him they were fine and weren't scared of me is easily refuted.

Josh lied and said that immediately after the fire he cut ties with me and threatened to press criminal charges on me if I tried to contact him again. Of course, Josh also said that on the night of the fire—November 10, 2009—I'd told him that if he told anyone about us burning the Atwood Lakehouse down I'd harm him and his parents by burning their house down. Again, this doesn't make sense and is easily discredited.

If I had truly threatened Josh and his family on the night of the fire, it cannot explain why Josh would continue our relationship for another four months, why he would accept my collect calls from jail, why he could come visit me in jail, why he would attend court to support me, and why he was waiting on me to continue our relationship when I got out of prison for my 2010 federal probation violation.

Josh and his parents couldn't have been safer—if Josh is to believed when he claims I threatened them—as when I was locked away in prison from January 2010 to June 2010. If he really wanted to "come clean," he could have done so at the March 2010 interview with Jackson at the KFC in Carthage, Mississippi. In March 2010, I was safely locked behind prison walls and Josh knew that if he told Jackson at the KFC interview that I was responsible for starting the fire then there would be a good chance that I'd never leave prison ever again. But thankfully, Josh did the right thing in March 2010 and told the truth. It was only when he was threatened with his own arrest that he changed his story.

Finally, Mr. Minor overlooked an important piece of evidence and testimony regarding Josh's change-of-heart in July 2011. When Mr. Minor claimed in his closing argument that Josh has maintained "to this day" that we burned the house, he was conveniently forgetting an important fact.

Several days after Josh gave the third statement implicating me in the fire, he recanted his statement, claimed that it was a forced false "confession," that he didn't willingly give it, and he refused to come testify against me before the grand jury. And once Josh recanted his third statement and admitted it was false, Jackson retaliated against him—much like Jackson had retaliated against me—and had him arrested and extradited back to Mississippi.

So any argument that Josh's third statement should be given credence even to this day is an assertion that is easily disproven. It is clear Josh had motive to lie, that he still has motivation to lie "to this day," and that nothing he says can ever be believed because he is a psychotic sociopath. And, again, I hoped the jury would see through Mr. Minor's smoke screen and understand what I knew to be true.

> **MR. MINOR:** The Court has instructed you that an arrest such as the one here is unlawful and considered unreasonable under the Fourth Amendment when, at the moment of arrest or warrant application, there's no probable cause for a defendant to believe that a crime has been or is being committed. The moment of arrest or warrant application after Mr. Jackson applied for the warrant. It goes on to say that probable cause only requires a showing of fair probability of criminal activity.

This was an important piece of the puzzle, and it made Mr. Minor's entire arguments throughout the trial to be in conflict with each other. For the entirety of the trial, Mr. Minor had argued that because Ronnie Stewart allegedly found "probable cause" at the October 2011 preliminary hearing, it somehow excused Jackson's illegal actions on July 29, 2011, when he obtained my arrest warrant.

The law was clear. False arrest claims are judged "at the moment of arrest or warrant application," not at a later court hearing. So Mr. Minor's arguments that whatever was done at the preliminary hearing excused Jackson's illegal actions was demonstrably wrong. The jury would only be able to judge the illegality of my arrest at the moment of my arrest or at the time Jackson applied for the warrant.

> **MR. MINOR:** Based on Josh Chamblee's statement, Mr. Jackson had probable cause to go get Mr. Atwood's arrest warrant. He was not aware of any reason Josh would lie and completely make it all up. The fact that Josh had an arrest record for filing false police reports and making false statements has no bearing on Josh's credibility. All my client knew was that Josh had been arrested for it. And the record shows he wasn't even prosecuted for it. So as far as my client was concerned, Josh was a credible person.

Again, this argument failed for several reasons, none so much as the fact that Jackson deliberately did not do a competent investigation, he didn't take the time to investigate Josh's credibility, and he specifically ignored multiple pieces of evidence that disproved Josh's story.

So as I've said before, Jackson cannot conduct a worthless and incompetent investigation, then rely on his ignorance of what he might have discovered had he conducted a true investigation. But he was entitled to rely on whatever defense his attorney could make.

> **MR. MINOR:** The Court instructed that any affidavit or warrant application submitted to a judge must put forth the particular facts and circumstances underlying the facts needed to establish probable cause so as to allow the magistrate to make an independent evaluation of the matter. Mr. Jackson did that. He went to Ronnie Stewart and filled out an affidavit. He swore under oath that David Atwood had committed arson. When you heard his testimony—Mr. Jackson's testimony—he went into Stewart's office and showed the judge Josh's written statement. Judge Stewart made him raise his right hand and swear under oath that the information he was provided was true and correct to the best of his knowledge. Josh Chamblee's statement set forth the particular circumstances underlying the existence of probable cause. That was the basis of it. And my client gave that information to the judge. And he [pointing to me] tries to say that Mr. Jackson shouldn't have relied on this judge because he's not a lawyer and he just rubber-stamps everything. Well, my client didn't know that, so it doesn't really matter because when you give information to a judge, if you don't deliberately or recklessly give false information, or knowingly withhold exculpatory evidence, then that is enough for the judge to issue the warrant. My client gave him the information that he had and the judge issued the warrant. My client was entitled to rely on it as long as he didn't try to mislead him. So my client had probable cause to go get an arrest warrant. You should find that the independent intermediary doctrine shielded my client. If, however, you find that the independent intermediary doctrine does not apply, the next instruction that you will go to is qualified immunity.

The simple argument that Jackson provided all of the information in his possession to Judge Stewart, and didn't hide or conceal anything from him, was laughable. There was no way that any person, including those on the jury, could legitimately argue that Jackson did not conceal relevant information from Ronnie Stewart.

Jackson's own testimony proved that he didn't tell Stewart that he'd never determined that the fire was arson, that Josh's and I's cell phones were in use in another part of the state at the time of the fire, that our footprints didn't match those found around the house, that Emmett Atwood had drastically increased the insurance shortly before the fire, that Kade Atwood had suspiciously slept through the fire, that Josh had provided two previous alibi statements, that Josh had been arrested before for lying to law enforcement officers and filing false police reports, or that Josh's third statement was given under threat of arrest and the promise of a $25,000.00 reward.

All of these details were extremely relevant in Judge Stewart making a probable cause determination when issuing the warrant. And it was clear throughout the trial that the only incriminating evidence that Jackson had was Josh's third statement. So to try and argue that Jackson didn't "deliberately or recklessly give false information or knowingly withhold exculpatory evidence" is ridiculous. Jackson did exactly that and admitted to not providing Stewart with all the relevant information. So I knew that there would be no way that the jury could find in Jackson's favor on this element.

MR. MINOR: The judge has instructed you that qualified immunity bars a defendant's liability even if he violated the Plaintiff's constitutional rights. You can still find in favor of Mr. Jackson even if he violated Mr. Atwood's Fourth Amendment rights. Even if he was wrong. The instruction says, qualified immunity exists to give government officials breathing room to make reasonable but questionable judgments about legal questions. Maybe James Jackson was wrong. Maybe Joshua Chamblee was exaggerating his story to harm Mr. Atwood. Maybe he was wrong. But it was reasonable for my client to believe Josh was telling the truth. Now, based on the evidence, I think you will find that reasonable. It goes on to say qualified immunity provides protection from liability from all but the most plainly incompetent government officer or those who knowingly violate the law. That does not describe Mr. Jackson. He's been in law enforcement for over thirty years. If he was incompetent he'd been fired.

A short comment is needed here about Jackson's incompetency and his thirty years in law enforcement. First off, Jackson never was able, throughout his thirty years in law enforcement, to maintain employment with one department for any length of time. He constantly changed jobs. In all fairness, I cannot say why he changed jobs so much, but I suspect it was because he was incompetent in everything he ever tried to do.

Second, regarding *this* investigation, Jackson clearly conducted an incompetent and incomplete investigation. From day one, Jackson was only concerned with assisting Emmett Atwood, Mike Chaney, and Sheriff Martin Pace with inflicting political retribution against me. He didn't care about whether he could prove this fire to be an arson or not. He, on day one, had his marching orders from Emmett, Chaney, and Sheriff Pace and that's all he cared about.

Finally, the argument that if Jackson had conducted incompetent investigations he'd been fired can also explain itself in the most important and vital way in regards to this case. Jackson's incompetency in this investigation can easily be explained by remembering that every step he took was done under the command of Mike Chaney.

Arguing about Jackson's incompetency is a moot point if Jackson's incompetency is manifested by the orders he received from Mike Chaney. So his incompetency in *this* investigation couldn't, wouldn't, and shouldn't have been judged harshly against him if Mike Chaney was forcing him to conduct an incompetent investigation. After all, he can't be fired for being incompetent if his incompetency was the result of what his boss, Mike Chaney, was making him do.

> **MR. MINOR:** Mr. Jackson did not knowingly not follow the law. He got information from a witness that had no apparent reason to fabricate his story to harm Mr. Atwood. He got a statement. Law enforcement officers rely on statements from witnesses everyday. Even ones that have one arrest, but no convictions. They rely on people with criminal records all the time to get statements to get probable cause. Now, it says qualified immunity applies if a reasonable officer could have believed that the warrant application arrest was lawful in light of clearly established law. That was the information that my client possessed. The information he possessed at the time. He didn't know about the criminal allegations that Mr. Atwood made against Josh

Chamblee. You heard him testify, he didn't know anything about the relationship except that they broke up at some point after the fire. The instruction goes on to say the clearly established law at the time provides for constitutional protection to be free from unreasonable arrests and not be subject to a warrant application that no reasonable officer could ever believe was truthful, reliable, and devoid of deliberate or recklessly false information. But Mr. Atwood has to prove all three. He's got to prove that no reasonable officer in this country and state would believe Josh Chamblee. That none of them would have taken that statement to a judge to get an arrest warrant. No reasonable officer. You heard Josh's recorded statement. If he was lying do you think there'd be a bunch of pauses in his speech? To me, it sounded like he was speaking from memory based on what he observed.

Mr. Minor's psychological interpretation of Josh's voice on the recording fails to take into account that almost all psychopathic sociopaths are able to lie without giving many verbal and physical cues to their dishonesty. Second, trying to claim that Josh was "speaking from memory" was like claiming that the sun wouldn't rise tomorrow.

Every question that was proposed to Josh, both on July 29, 2011, and during his deposition was usually answered with an "I-don't-know" statement. Josh wasn't speaking from memory. He didn't know any details that one whom had done what he said we'd done should know. So there was no way that the jury could infer from Josh's recorded statement that he was telling the truth. He was parroting only what Jackson provided him in way of details.

> **MR. MINOR:** Mr. Atwood did not prove that my client, or all reasonable officials, should or would have known that this statement of Chamblee's was a lie. For that reason you should find in favor of James Jackson. However, if for some reason you find in favor of Mr. Atwood, the instructions say that you may award compensatory damages for injuries that only the Plaintiff, Mr. David Atwood, proved were proximally caused by Defendant Jackson. It says that if Plaintiff David Atwood wins, he's entitled to compensatory damages for pain and suffering and mental anguish that he has sufficiently proved because of the actions

of Defendant James Jackson. So you cannot award damages for speculative injuries; only those injuries that David Atwood has actually suffered or that he is likely to reasonably suffer in the future. This means that damages that David Atwood suffered. He's trying to collect money that his mother spent to bond him out. He wants you to compensate him for that. I didn't hear any testimony establishing a link between his arrest and his grandfather dying. He didn't prove that. You can't compensate him for the loss of his grandfather. He also wants you to award him money for lost wages. He supposedly lost out on a trucking job opportunity. He didn't offer any proof—any documents there was actually a job. His mom just got up there and testified about it. She allegedly overheard some phone calls. Plus, he couldn't even prove that even if he did lose this job that he couldn't go get another one. We don't even know how much wages he lost. You can't award damages for that. He didn't prove it.

Mr. Minor, of course, had a really good point. And this was part of my trial strategy that I gambled on by not testifying. The reason that I didn't testify was that I did not want to risk having my criminal history revealed to the jury.

Judge Aycock had not allowed Mr. Minor to bring up any details about my criminal history during the direct evidence portion of the trial that he, himself, introduced through his witnesses (i.e., Josh Chamblee and James Jackson). She would not allow it. However, Judge Aycock would allow my criminal history to be discussed if I chose to testify because the Federal Rules of Evidence were very clear—any witness with a criminal history could be subject to cross-examination on that history if it tended to prove that that certain witness might not be a credible witness.

So I gambled and made the decision not to testify and, instead, to try and get my proof of damages in through my mother's testimony. And she had clearly testified that although she initially paid the $5,000.00 for me to bond out of jail, it was only a loan and I was required to pay her back. I felt certain that I'd get at least the $5,000.00 back from the jury.

What I hadn't been able to clearly prove was that I suffered any exact damages besides the $5,000.00. I didn't testify. And because I didn't testify the jury was unable to determine what damages I'd suffered through mental anguish and emotional distress. I rolled the dice, and I just hoped the jury would infer that this arrest caused significant emotional distress. I could always, though, hope to rely on the punitive damages that the jury might award if they, first, decided that Jackson was responsible for my illegal arrest.

> **MR. MINOR:** It goes on to say that you cannot go about arbitrarily guessing. Well, he may have lost out on a trucking job, but you would be engaging in arbitrary guessing if you try to award him anything on that. You have no clue. He didn't testify about how much money he lost. You cannot award any money for this supposed loss. Now, this instruction is important. You can only award damages that Defendant James Jackson proximally caused the Plaintiff. Now, his mom paid to get Mr. Atwood out of jail. She paid for that. There's no evidence that he paid a nickel for that. His mom paid for it. You can only award him damages. Not his mom. Damages may not be awarded on speculation or guesswork, but instead must be established by the evidence. They haven't presented any evidence other than his mom's vague anecdotal testimony about losing a trucking job. You can't base damages off speculation or guesswork. You'll be doing that if you award him any damages for these supposed loses. This is the instruction on the emotional damages. He hasn't proved any emotional distress. He tried to establish that through his mom's testimony. She testified that she and the family were embarrassed because of the media coverage of the arrest. You can't compensate Mr. Atwood because his family was embarrassed. There's no evidence that he suffered mental distress. Maybe his mom did. But you can't compensate him for his mom's distress. And he didn't even take the stand to prove anything on how this affected him. He attempted in closing to make you sympathize with him about his grandfather. But he can't put on any evidence. The judge instructed you—closing argument is not evidence. No evidence was presented of emotional distress damages. The judge has also instructed you that anger, frustration, and hurt feelings are a part of life and is not the type of harm to establish mental anguish awards.

It was obvious from this part of the argument that Mr. Minor expected that Jackson would be held liable for my illegal arrest. I fully believe that. Jackson's conduct was inexcusable. The jurors' reactions to certain testimony and the way they interacted with me and responded to my words during my closing argument convinced everyone of that. But Mr. Minor had many important points in making the argument that he did.

I'd rolled the dice and decided not to testify, and he was making me pay dearly for that mistake. And knowing at that point that the jury was going to hold Jackson liable led Mr. Minor into making these specific damages arguments that he did. Whether from inexperience or deliberate strategy, I'd spent more time on proving Jackson liable for my false arrest than I did proving what damages I'd suffered. Mr. Minor was absolutely correct in going after my "proof" of damages arguments.

> **MR. MINOR:** This is what the Plaintiff established. On August 1st, 2011, he drove to Attala County and was booked into jail and remained there for about thirty minutes and then leaves. Then he has to go to a preliminary hearing before Judge Stewart, who found, after hearing testimony from my client and Sheriff Nail, and after my client was cross-examined by Mrs. Jordan, David Atwood's lawyer, probable cause for Mr. Atwood's case to be bound over to a grand jury. Ronnie Stewart found twice that there was probable cause. But Mr. Atwood wants you to believe that there wasn't. Finally, there's the instruction about nominal damages. According to the instruction, nominal damages are inconsequential. They are normally awarded to a plaintiff for technical violations of his constitutional rights or when a plaintiff has suffered no actual damages or loss. If you find that Mr. Jackson violated Mr. Atwood's constitutional rights by withholding relevant evidence from Judge Stewart, and is not entitled to qualified immunity, meaning no reasonable officer would have relied on Josh's third statement, you should award nominal damages. That is what you should do.
>
> **JUDGE AYCOCK:** Thank you Mr. Minor. Mr. Atwood, you may make a rebuttal argument.
>
> **ME:** Your Honor, I think that all that can be said has been said and I have no response.

The trial was now over except for the part where the jury goes to deliberate. I'd thought throughout Mr. Minor's closing argument that I might need to go to the podium once more and make an argument on why Mr. Minor's argument shouldn't be considered. But at that point in the trial there was nothing more that could be said that would have swayed the jury one way or another. So I sat quietly and trusted their good judgment to decide the case in my favor.

It had taken us four days to get to this point, but in a way, it was really an eight year journey from November 11, 2009. By the time Mr. Minor finished his closing argument it was nearly one o'clock. Everyone was hungry and worn out, but we were also excited about what we knew would be a big win. So as Mr. Minor finished his closing argument and sat back down, I leaned back in the chair and thought about all I had accomplished.

Even though we never really learned what caused the Atwood Lakehouse fire, we all were confident that it was not an arson except for the possibility that Emmett burned it himself so as to collect the insurance money. But not being able to prove the source did not take away from the fact that I'd been able to prove everything else that I'd believed and said all along. There did exist an Axis of Corruption and this trial had shed some light on it, and I was happy with that.

CHAPTER FORTY-SEVEN

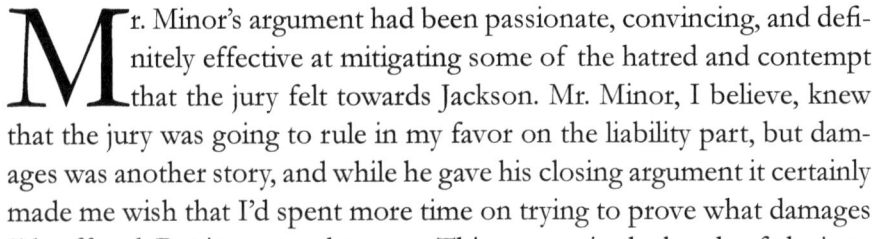

Mr. Minor's argument had been passionate, convincing, and definitely effective at mitigating some of the hatred and contempt that the jury felt towards Jackson. Mr. Minor, I believe, knew that the jury was going to rule in my favor on the liability part, but damages was another story, and while he gave his closing argument it certainly made me wish that I'd spent more time on trying to prove what damages I'd suffered. But it was too late now. Things were in the hands of the jury.

JUDGE AYCOCK: Ladies and gentlemen of the jury, I'm going to send you to the jury room with copies of the instructions and the exhibits. It will take a few minutes to gather up the exhibits and take them back there to you. I'm assuming that lunch will be back there waiting on you. Let me give you some further instructions. There are eight of you and all of you should deliberate. I've instructed that once you go back there you will find someone amongst yourselves that will be your foreperson. You may need to take a break. You may need to go to the restroom. But do not start your deliberations until all of you are together. If you find it necessary to take a break, stop your deliberations and wait until everyone is back at your table to continue deliberating. And you have been on my clock since Monday. We are now on your clock. There's no timeline. There's no time frame. There's no obligation on your side to hurry. What I will do is monitor you to say, "Are you still okay? Do you need to stop?

Do you need to come back in the morning?" I will monitor that, but it's strictly left up to you. Okay? So go to the jury room. We will deliver these things to you as soon as possible and you can start your deliberations.

At this point I could tell that the jurors were ready to get to the most important part of the case. As they got up to leave they began talking amongst themselves; some even had slight smiles on their faces. And let there be no doubt about this, all eyes were on the jury. Everyone in the courtroom wanted to know what their decision would be, although I am willing to bet, everyone also knew what that decision ultimately would be.

JUDGE AYCOCK: Okay. Mr. Atwood and Mr. Minor, we need your cell phone numbers. From time-to-time the jury has questions and we need a way to contact you to get you back to the courtroom. Come quickly if you're called. We will be in recess until we hear from the jury. Thank you.

I looked at my watch. It was fifteen minutes after one o'clock. Once Judge Aycock and her staff left the courtroom me, David, and Richard all immediately began discussing how long we expected the jury to deliberate. I guessed no more than two hours. David and Richard agreed.

The conduct of Jackson, Chaney, Emmett, and Sheriff Pace, proven through the testimony and circumstantial evidence, was some of the most despicable, deplorable, and illegal conduct that I'd ever heard of law enforcement officers in Mississippi committing as a collective unit. I felt almost certain that every juror would feel the same way. And even if I hadn't proved every penny and dollar that this false and illegal arrest cost me, I relied on the jury's emotions to make up for what I didn't exactly prove.

Any prosecutor worth his salt could easily bring obstruction of justice, conspiracy, RICO, perjury, and civil rights violation charges against the four members of the Axis of Corruption for their conduct and subsequent efforts to cover it up. At the head, of course, was Mike Chaney. And even without a law degree, I'd proven him the most culpable. If I had the power to convene grand juries, there'd be no doubt that I could secure indictments against them and, ultimately, convictions.

I hoped the jury would feel the same way and issue their own indictment of sorts—a verdict in my favor. Hopefully, they were as sickened by the Axis of Corruption as I was. There was an X-factor, however, in the equation. And that was Mr. Minor's excellent closing argument that he had made. It certainly mitigated some of the anger that I had for Jackson.

The real culprits behind the illegal arrest were Mike Chaney and Sheriff Pace, with some input from Emmett Atwood. Jackson was simply the pawn that had been used by them for an illegal purpose and, much like the game, was then sacrificed and thrown to the wolves (me) without their support when he'd gotten caught.

In a way, I kind of felt sorry for Jackson by the close of the trial. His conduct, under no extenuating circumstances, could be excused. Jackson knew what he was doing, he knew he was being used for an illegal purpose to retaliate against me for exercising my First Amendment rights, and even he knew that there was no excuse for his conduct. But Jackson was only a single link in a long chain of government-sanctioned corruption.

The idea of an Axis of Corruption, whose actions in isolation appear quite normal and legitimately related to a law enforcement purpose, but once set in motion forms a chain of evil that can best be described by using the example of Nazi guards in Jewish concentration camps.

This type of evil also refers to ordinary factors that together can add up to an illegal act. In the same tradition, an experiment conducted by Stanley Milgram showed that in "obedience to authority" ordinary people were willing to inflict apparent electric shocks on others to levels that would kill them.

Philip Zimbardo's Stanford Prison Experiment is also in this tradition. In that experiment, students were randomly assigned the roles of a guard or prisoner in a simulated prison, and those whom were "guards" quickly began acting cruel and inhumane to those whom were "prisoners."

Consider, for a moment, an example of the chain that led to millions of Jewish deaths during World War II:

> **PERSON #1:** I simply had the list of Jews in my municipality. I did not round up the Jews, but I did pass this list on when requested to do so.
>
> **PERSON #2:** I was told to go to these addresses, arrest these people, and take them to the train station. That's all I did.
>
> **PERSON #3:** My job was to open the doors of the train,

that's all.

> **PERSON #4:** My job was to direct the prisoners onto the train.
>
> **PERSON #5:** My job was to close the doors, not to ask where the train was going or why.
>
> **PERSON #6:** My job was simply to drive the train.

[Through all the other small links in the chain that could lead to . . .]

> **PERSON #7:** My job was simply to turn on the showers out of which the poison gas was emitted.

None of these individuals may have had overall responsibility for the deaths of so many millions, only part of it. But if one person—just one—had decided to contest their role in the evil that they were part of many souls may have survived the atrocity that was Nazi Germany.

In my specific case, anyone in the chain of the investigation, from Sheriff Nail down to Judge Stewart, could have at any point put the brakes on this sham investigation and illegal arrest. But courage is not common anymore in people in position of authority. And because everyone lacked the moral courage, the Axis of Corruption almost got away with framing an innocent person for a fire that was never proven to have been an arson.

Once Jackson finally gave up and quit trying to conceal the crimes that Chaney, Sheriff Pace, Emmett and he committed against me, it was fairly easy for him to disclose the truth. And Jackson's testimony couldn't have been clearer. He stated with utmost conviction that Chaney had ordered him to conduct this illegal arrest or face termination from his position as a deputy state fire marshal.

By every definition of the word, Mike Chaney committed the crime of extortion when he ordered Jackson to conduct an illegal, unlawful arrest or be fired from his job.

The federal and state courts have long held that extortion is the "act or practice of obtaining something or compelling some action by illegal means." By this definition, the Axis of Corruption, could be convicted and sent to prison for their illegal, felony conduct.

The unfortunate part of the situation was that Judge Aycock had dismissed Chaney from the lawsuit because there was not any direct evidence at the time of her order on summary judgment in July 2016 that Chaney was directly involved in my investigation or specifically ordered Jackson to make the arrest.

This changed once Jackson specifically testified that he had told Chaney that arresting me would be illegal and unlawful, but nevertheless had been ordered by Chaney to commit these felony crimes. This was direct proof that Chaney was responsible for my arrest.

If I had been representing James Jackson, such as Mr. Minor was, my foremost defense would be arguing to the jury that Jackson was only the sacrificial pawn in a horrible game of political chess that had gone terribly wrong. Chaney, however, was the big fish, the chess piece worth protecting the most. And sacrificing Jackson on the altar of judicial litigation was well worth the loss if Chaney was, at the end of the day, protected. But any jury verdict in my favor would still send a strong message to the Axis of Corruption—Mike Chaney the most—that never again would they be able to get away with committing crimes against me.

Once Judge Aycock had sent the jury to deliberate and dismissed us from the courtroom, David, Richard, and myself walked across the street to a Chinese restaurant. While we were eating lunch we saw on CNN a breaking news headlines that O.J. Simpson had been granted parole in Nevada and would soon be released from prison. I felt that was a good omen for my case, too.

Like most people, I originally thought Simpson was guilty of murder. Watching the 2016 FX television show about the Simpson murder trial changed my mind, and it reminded me a lot of what occurred in my case. Like his, my case involved corrupt law enforcement officers whom were motivated by an illegal purpose. In his, racism. In mine, retaliatory politics.

With the clearly racist investigators who hated blacks, none of the evidence in his murder trial could be trusted. His jury saw that, reached that conclusion, and set him free. Essentially, the corrupt cops framed a guilty man, and what the trial proved was that society (i.e., juries) would no longer tolerate such brazen, illegal, and corrupt behavior from law enforcement.

The Simpson jury sent a message that when corrupt cops are allowed to operate freely and without oversight from superiors, fabricate and destroy evidence, lie under oath, and let their personal biases infect their behavior in how they investigate and prosecute crime, those framed defendants would be set free and exonerated at trial.

Simpson was not set free because he was innocent of murder. He was set free because evil, corrupt, and malicious cops investigating his case allowed their racist hatred for a successful black man, who was married to an attractive white woman, overcome their sworn duty to uphold law and order through honest, legitimate means.

The analogy to my case is entirely appropriate, except, of course, I literally was innocent of starting the Atwood Lakehouse fire. By having, though, a group of corrupt law enforcement officers involved in investigating this case, it not only deprived me of my constitutional rights, but it also deprived Emmett and the rest of the family of the opportunity to know the true cause of the fire.

There is no doubt in my mind that had Jackson performed anything more than a cursory investigation, free from political pressure and motive, that today we'd know the true cause of the fire.

At the time of the 2017 trial, Emmett was ninety years old. Years after Emmett is dead and gone, other generations of the Atwood family will long remember the tragic fire on the night of November 10, 2009.

By their illegal actions, Chaney, Jackson, Sheriff Pace, and Emmett have denied future generations the truth about what really happened to that beloved lake house. And that is the true crime. The denial of knowledge they could have provided is the true travesty.

Of all the crimes that Chaney, Jackson, Sheriff Pace, and Emmett could be charged with, the biggest, in my mind, is the denial of our family's right to know what really happened to the lake house, because from now until eternity, rumors and innuendo will always swirl about its true cause.

I was glad that Simpson was getting out of prison. And I certainly interpreted it as a good omen of what was to come with my jury. I felt so good about a positive outcome that I rushed the others through their lunch so that we could make it back to the courtroom without risking being there late.

When we returned to the courtroom it was eerily silent. The only other people there were Mr. Minor and Jackson. One thing that I noticed after the first day of trial was that Jackson quit wearing suits. For the rest of the week he had worn slacks and a Polo-type shirt. If he was looking to make a good fashion statement with the jury, he'd certainly failed.

Once we passed the two-hour mark in the jury deliberations I began to get nervous. I firmly believed that I'd made such a good closing argument, not to mention I having undoubtedly proved my case, that the jury wouldn't need long to deliberate. But when the three-hour mark passed without any word I began to have my doubts. I'd totally believed that the case was open and shut.

Slowly, as time passed, more and more people began returning to the courtroom to await the ultimate verdict. At almost exactly the four-hour point since beginning their deliberations, the jury announced that they'd reached a verdict.

As Judge Aycock came into the courtroom and took her seat behind her bench, I quickly returned to my table with David behind me and Richard in the audience. Mr. Minor sat a little straighter in his chair and Jackson sat hunched back behind his table as though his vindication was imminent.

> **JUDGE AYCOCK:** You all may have a seat. I've been told the jury has reached a verdict. You may bring in the jury.

We all stood again as the deputy marshal brought the jury back into the courtroom. It was a few minutes after five o'clock and everyone was tense with anticipation.

> **JUDGE AYCOCK:** Ladies and gentlemen, I've been advised that you have a verdict. Can you pass it to me, please? [Judge Aycock takes a moment to look over the verdict form.] The verdict appears to be in proper form. At this time I am going to read the verdict.

I held my breath. I had a copy of the verdict form in my hand in front of me. I sat with rapt attention. Even though my life wasn't on the line, and even though if I lost I wouldn't really be losing anything of value, I knew that if the next few seconds didn't go my way that I would never be able to show my face in Vicksburg again.

If the jury verdict went against me it was game over, game over for everything I'd ever written about government corruption, game over for ever hoping to stop the Axis of Corruption, and game over in ever believing that I might be safe from government corruption again. I literally stopped breathing for the next few seconds.

> **JUDGE AYCOCK:** This jury has found the following: "*We the jury find that there was not probable cause to arrest the Plaintiff David Atwood; that Defendant James Jackson is not entitled to protection of the independent intermediary doctrine; that Defendant James Jackson is not entitled to qualified immunity. We the jury award the Plaintiff compensatory damages in the amount of five thousand dollars. We the jury award the Plaintiff emotional distress damages in the amount of zero dollars.*"

It was an immense relief. It was a win. And even though I didn't get more than $5,000.00, it was a huge win nevertheless. It had gone completely my way. Everything I'd ever said and written was finally vindicated. I'd proven the Axis of Corruption wrong and my jury had sent a message that their illegal behavior would not be tolerated. But I only had a few seconds of exhilaration before Judge Aycock continued with the trial.

> **JUDGE AYCOCK:** Ladies and gentlemen, we have one more issue to address. By virtue of you finding that the Plaintiff is entitled to compensatory damages, when he filed his lawsuit he also asked for punitive damages. The issue of punitive damages does not go to a jury until there is a determination of liability. So now that you have returned a verdict on liability, I need to go through with you the second phase of this trial. I will offer each of these parties an opportunity to call any additional witnesses they wish to call as part of their punitive damages phase of the trial. Mr. Atwood, Mr. Minor, do you have any additional witnesses?
>
> **ME:** No, Your Honor.
>
> **MR. MINOR:** No, Your Honor.
>
> **JUDGE AYCOCK:** There is a punitive damages instruction that I will now read. And I will do that now. I will read to you a punitive damages instruction that will give you some instructional law about how to award punitive damages. I am going to give both sides ten minutes to argue to you why it is that they believe they are entitled to or not entitled to punitive damages. At that point I will send you back to the jury room and you will make

a decision solely on the issues of punitive damages. So counselors, you have the jury instructions that were submitted earlier. If you've read it and are in agreement with it, or you want to have a conference about it outside the presence of the jury, I can send them out.

ME: Your Honor, I accept the jury instructions.

MR. MINOR: No objection, Your Honor.

JUDGE AYCOCK: Very well. Ladies and gentlemen of the jury, I will now read the instruction to you.

Since learning the procedure for which punitive damages are awarded, I've always thought that it was a little unfair to the jury. I fully believed that when the jury came back into court with their verdict they felt as though their duty was done and that it was time to go home. After all, it was well after five o'clock in the afternoon.

I think that the punitive damages instruction should have been given to the jury at the exact same time that the other instructions were read to them. That would have allowed them to deliberate whether it was appropriate or not to award punitive damages at the same time they deliberated the rest of the case.

Springing a last minute instruction on them at so late an hour no doubt caused some impatience in the jury to be done with the trial and go back to their normal lives. I'd depended a lot on hoping that the jury would award punitive damages since I'd not taken the witness stand myself and proved all of my compensatory damages. But I was determined to give it my best shot.

JUDGE AYCOCK: If you find that Defendant James Jackson is liable for Plaintiff David Atwood's injuries, you must award Plaintiff David Atwood the compensatory damages that he has proved. You may, in addition, award punitive damages if you find that Defendant James Jackson acted with malice or with reckless indifference to the rights of others. One acts with malice when one purposefully or knowingly violates another's rights or safety. One acts with reckless indifference to the rights of others when one's conduct, under the circumstances, manifests a complete lack of concern for the rights or safety of others. Plaintiff David Atwood has the burden of proving that punitive damages should be awarded proving by clear and convincing evidence that the Defendant James Jackson, against whom punitive damages are sought, acted with malice, gross negligence which evidences a willful, wanton or reckless disregard for the safety of others, or committed actual fraud. The purpose of punitive damages is to punish and deter, not to compensate. Punitive damages serve to punish a defendant for malicious or reckless conduct and, by doing so, to deter others from engaging in similar conduct in the future. You are not required to award punitive damages. If you do decide to award punitive damages, you must use sound reason in setting the amount. Your award of punitive damages must not reflect bias, prejudice, or sympathy toward any party. It should be presumed that Plaintiff David Atwood has been made whole by compensatory damages, so punitive damages should be awarded only if Defendant James Jackson's misconduct is so reprehensible as to warrant the imposition of further sanctions to achieve punishment or deterrence. If you decide to award punitive damages, the following factors should guide you in fixing the proper amounts. (1) The reprehensibility of Defendant James Jackson's conduct, including, but not limited to, whether there was deceit, cover-up, insult, intended or reckless injury, and whether Defendant James Jackson's conduct was motivated by a desire to augment profit; (2) The ratio between the punitive damages you are considering awarding and the amount of harm that was suffered by Plaintiff David Atwood or with which the Plaintiff David Atwood was threatened; and (3) You may consider the financial resources of Defendant James Jackson in fixing the amount of punitive damages.

This was the instruction, and I knew with all my heart that Jackson acted with malice and reckless disregard of my constitutional rights. He showed a complete lack of concern and he certainly put not only my life in danger, but that of the governor's son's too.

If there was any case which screamed out for a punishment to deter Chaney, Jackson, Sheriff Pace, and Emmett from committing any other serious felony crimes against a citizen whose political viewpoint they disagreed with, this was it. I needed punitive damages against them. What they did was not only reprehensible, it was patently illegal.

There was much more than just a simple jury verdict at stake in this trial. Every legal expert involved in this case or who knew its details had told me that it would be impossible for me to win a jury trial against a state law enforcement officer. My jury had proven them wrong. But what I wanted more than anything was a large monetary award in damages to send the clearest message of all that this type of illegal conduct by the Axis of Corruption would no longer be tolerated.

I needed a jury verdict so big that Sheriff Pace and every other corrupt cop would no doubt stop and consider what the potential consequences would be if they tried to frame me for a crime I didn't commit. I needed that punitive damages award.

Already, this trial had proven that I and my anti-corruption message was a force to be reckoned with and that the good citizens of Vicksburg and Warren County would no longer sit idly by while they were abused and victimized by people like Chaney, Jackson, and Sheriff Pace.

A few seconds after Judge Aycock had read my jury's verdict I turned and looked at Mr. Minor and Jackson. Both had gone white as a ghost and simply remained frozen in their chairs not sure if what they were hearing was the truth. But not only had Judge Aycock been clear, but Mr. Minor now knew that there was a serious possibility that this jury could award a very large amount of money in punitive damages if they were inclined to.

One must keep in mind that Jackson had admitted to committing multiple, serious felony crimes, he admitted to trying to conceal it, he admitted that he knew he was part of a crime, he admitted to being a dishonest, dirty cop who lied, schemed, and violated every constitutional right he could to achieve whatever personal goal he had in mind. However, it was also clear that Jackson was only the most expedient tool then available to be used by the Axis of Corruption and then discarded away when no longer needed.

If the jury was going to award punitive damages I needed them to understand that Jackson and Chaney were one in the same. If anyone needed punishment and deterrence from committing future felony crimes it was Mike Chaney, the Mississippi State Insurance Commissioner and State Fire Marshal. He was the real culprit, and although Jackson was the one facing the jury, I wanted my jury to face Chaney through Jackson.

Getting to this point in the trial, after a major win from the jury, was worth every struggle, every fight, every battle, and every ounce of energy I had in litigating this case. Seeing the abject look of horror on Jackson's face when the jury verdict was read was worth everything I'd been through. Jackson's fleeting look of disbelief at being proved wrong was worth more to me than the $5,000.00 written on the verdict form.

Against all odds, I'd overcome the Axis of Corruption. I'd done battle with one of the best assistant attorney generals that the Great State of Mississippi could throw at me. Without any legal training I'd overcome what should have been and open and shut case on day one with any judge not as fair and impartial as Judge Aycock and Magistrate Sanders. For the first time in my life I felt like I'd actually been treated fairly.

So as I patiently sat through the reading of the jury instruction on punitive damages I began formulating what I would say to the jury. After all, I'd not prepared a punitive damages argument to the jury. Whatever I was going to say in the next few minutes would all be ad-libbed. And as soon as Judge Aycock finished reading the punitive damages instruction to the jury I was asked to come to the podium once more and address the jury. The relay race was almost done.

CHAPTER FORTY-EIGHT

I detected a slight impatience with the jury. No doubt they wanted the day to end so that they could return to their normal daily lives. Unfortunately, I didn't expect them to award punitive damages because of their unwillingness to award anymore damages that they did for compensatory and emotional distress damages. I was going to give it my best shot, though.

>**ME:** May it please the Court?
>
>**JUDGE AYCOCK:** Yes, you may proceed.
>
>**ME:** I want to thank you first for finding in my favor. I told you that this case was not about winning. It was a case about what was right. It was a case about integrity and honesty. And I told you in my closing argument that this was like a relay race in many respects, and it has been. I thank you for participating and helping finish the race—almost. And Judge Aycock has just instructed you that you can give punitive damages against the defendant. And I want you to keep in mind a couple of things that the defendant testified to on Monday. That defendant [pointing to Jackson] sat right there in that chair and told you that what he was doing was wrong. He sat there and told you that he could have reported their illegal conduct to the FBI; he could have reported it to the Mississippi Attorney General's Office. But he didn't report it because it would have made life hard on him. Well, I want you to think how hard my life has been thanks to this

defendant. This defendant sat there and testified that he knew he didn't have any evidence of arson, but that he arrested me anyway and that he did it for an illegal purpose. And that illegal purpose was punishment for an outspoken stance that I took against certain members of law enforcement.

As I was ad-libbing this argument to the jury, the only thing that I kept thinking about was how this was such an easy, open and shut case. I didn't have to ask the jury to believe my side of the story because the single person with the most knowledge about this illegal conspiracy had sat on the witness stand on three different days and admitted to committing numerous state and felony crimes as part of that illegal conspiracy.

Jackson was the tool that the Axis of Corruption used to enforce their political retaliation, and because Jackson lacked any piece of internal integrity and honesty, he willingly allowed himself to be used by them for their illegal purposes. So, just as Chaney, Sheriff Pace, and Emmett were the organizers behind-the-scenes, Jackson was the strong-arm of the law that put their motives into practice.

I wanted and needed the jury to see that although Chaney was the power instigating this false arrest, Jackson should nonetheless be held accountable because he knew what he was doing was wrong, he knew what Chaney was doing was wrong, and he nevertheless willfully participated in helping them carry out their plans. So I kept pushing that argument.

ME: So, basically, he conducted this arrest in violation of my First Amendment rights. A person, no matter how unpopular his writings may be—a person has a right to publish what they feel and believe. And we went through a lot of that evidence with Sheriff Martin Pace. And Sheriff Pace did admit that there were quite a few things in that book about him, the Warren County Sheriff's Department, and others that were true and correct. And Emmett Ray Atwood sat there and eventually admitted that there were some things in that book that were true and correct. You saw the evidence of that. So there can be no room for doubt that the reason this defendant pursued this investigation and arrest was for an illegal purpose. And he didn't do it by mistake. He sat there and told you that what he was doing he knew to be a crime. He told you that he could have gone to the FBI, or the attorney general. That implies from the very beginning, before he obtained this arrest warrant, that he knew what he was doing was illegal. He knew it wasn't a mistake. He did not act in good faith. And you also know from the testimony that he didn't act alone. He acted in conjunction with his boss, Mike Chaney, an elected statewide official. That's reprehensible conduct.

So far I thought I had done a good job of bringing the separate pieces of this case together to form an argument as to why the jury should award punitive damages. One of the elements in the punitive damages instruction allows juries to award punitive damages to deter others from committing similar conduct.

As much as a win on liability and the award of $5,000.00 was, a large verdict in punitive damages would serve wonders to send a message and "deter" people like Sheriff Pace and the ilk that comprises most of his department from ever trying to frame me for a crime I didn't commit. I kept trying to bring the pieces together as best as my limited skills at ad-libbing closing arguments to a jury would allow.

ME: We should expect better from our elected leaders. We should expect better from our politicians. We should expect anyone in government service—we should expect better from them. But Mike Chaney and this defendant didn't expect you to rule in my favor. They didn't expect this false, illegal arrest lawsuit would come this far. I told you, it's a culture. It's a culture they're used to of people not questioning this type of reprehensible conduct. They've been doing it for a long time. And I believe it's safe to assume that if they did it to me, they've done it to others. Just imagine the number of innocent people that are in prison for decades right now because this defendant rushed to judgment and failed to conduct a competent, complete arson investigation. I shudder at the thought.

Awarding punitive damages in this case would send the ultimate message of all. It would set a high precedent that only corrupt cops like Chaney, Jackson, and Sheriff Pace would understand. Their culture of abusing the constitutional rights of unpopular defendants would never be immune to attack again. Their culture of using and selling drugs, committing rapes and murders, and framing innocent people for crimes they did not commit would never be committed again without the doubt in the back of their minds that they could be the next James O'Neal Jackson, forced to face a jury for their crimes.

> **ME:** So you have the power to send a message. And I told you in my closing argument that your verdict will send a message that this type of illegal, reprehensible conduct will not be tolerated. We expect better from our police. We expect better from our elected officials. And in this case we know this is the truth because that defendant sat there and told you that this is what occurred. I didn't tell you that what they did was illegal; the defendant told you that. So your verdict has power. It can send a message far beyond these walls. It can send a message to these other corrupt law enforcement officers that this type of reprehensible conduct will not be tolerated; that we will not put up with this kind of behavior in America. If we were in North Korea or Nazi Germany we could expect this. But we're not. We're in America. We should expect better from our law enforcement officers. We should expect better from our elected leaders. So you verdict has power. I don't have that power. The defendant and Mr. Minor don't have that power. They don't have the power to send this message. It's you and only you who have that power.

I reverted back to my line about asking the jury to empower themselves to send a message that these corrupt actions by this group of corrupt cops would not go unpunished. It was all I could think to say. I was still flushed with victory from the liability verdict twenty minutes before. I wished I had more time to prepare. But I was doing the best I could and I hoped that my best was good enough. There was just one thing left to do, and that was to ask the jury for money again—sort of.

> **ME:** So I'm not going to give you a number. I'm not going to ask for a million dollars. But I want you to consider, when you go back to the jury room, that this was not all just a bad mistake. This was a deliberate, calculated action by not only the defendant, but also Mike Chaney. It was a deliberate, calculated action to violate my constitutional rights. They knew what they

were doing from the very beginning. They knew because that defendant sat there and told you that he knew this was illegal. So I'm not going to ask for a specific sum. I'm not going to ask for that million dollars. But I ask you, that when you go back to that room, think, what is a number that will send a message to Mike Chaney—by the way, Mike Chaney isn't here, he hasn't been here the whole time, he didn't want to come—so think of a number that will send a message to Mike Chaney and other corrupt law enforcement officers—these alleged protectors of the law—that this type of illegal, reprehensible conduct will not be tolerated. I ask you, my family asks you, send this message that this will not be tolerated in Aberdeen, that it will not be tolerated at the state capitol in Jackson, that it won't be tolerated in Mississippi, and that it will not be tolerated in America. Thank you.

This was the best I could do at the spur of the moment. I hoped it was enough. I'd literally spent my entire focus and energy on the closing argument during the liability phase of the trial. But I'd had weeks to lay the groundwork for it, days to prepare, and plenty of time to practice it and fine tune it the night before.

Public speaking does not scare me. Whether it's eight unfamiliar people sitting in a jury box in a little small town in Mississippi, or a giant arena full of adoring, screaming fans, as long as I have time beforehand to practice and gather my thoughts about what I want to say, then I will have no problem. But I was utterly unprepared to give another rousing closing argument in furtherance of my request that the jury award punitive damages. But I tried with everything that I had. Now it was Mr. Minor's turn.

JUDGE AYCOCK: Thank you, Mr. Atwood. Mr. Minor.

MR. MINOR: This is not a case of intentional or malicious misconduct. My client legitimately believed that David Atwood set fire to that house. So did everyone else at the fire marshal's office. And they went out to find the evidence to support that finding. And they finally found Josh Chamblee and he told them what he knew. It wasn't obvious that what Josh Chamblee was saying was wrong. We still don't know that. My client, today, still maintains that Josh Chamblee wasn't lying. Obviously, y'all took a different view of the case. But my client didn't know he was doing anything wrong. He was trusting of his witness. He was not trying to harm Mr. Atwood. The plaintiff didn't write a book about James Jackson. He didn't write a book about Mike Chaney. He wrote the book about some people in Vicksburg. My client did not act with malice or reckless indifference to his rights. He acted according to the evidence he obtained to arrest this suspect. He didn't coerce Josh Chamblee. He just wanted to talk to him. Well, when he finally talked to him, Josh Chamblee told him what happened. If you do decide to award punitive damages, the judge directed that you may consider the financial resources of my client. You heard him testify, he's a retired state fire marshal. He does not have vast resources. So take that into account if you decide to award punitive damages. Thank you.

JUDGE AYCOCK: Thank you, Mr. Minor. So, ladies and gentlemen, I will send you back to the jury room and we will bring back this punitive damages instruction. Okay. [The jury is escorted from the courtroom and we are dismissed to await the verdict.]

Rather than leave the courtroom, I asked David and Richard to stay because I didn't believe the jury would have to deliberate long on whether to award punitive damages. It's not that I thought they wouldn't properly give consideration to my arguments, it's just that I detected a slight impatience with them to have this case finally done and over with. That's why I believed that giving a punitive damages instruction should have been given at the time that the jury first went to deliberate on liability and compensatory damages.

If Jackson and Mr. Minor had any specific feelings about what the jury would do on punitive damages I never found out. They remained at their respective counsel's table too. In fact, nearly everyone in the courtroom except Judge Aycock and her staff remained where they were. I even overheard some people talking about what the chances were of the jury awarding punitive damages. I was just as curious and, again, the time slowed to a crawl as we waited.

When Judge Aycock sent the jury to deliberate on the punitive damages request, I immediately grabbed my cell phone and began texting. Even though my first verdict had come about thirty minutes prior to the jury going to deliberate on punitive damages, it was only after they left the second time that I had time to text everyone and let them know about the big win. Everyone knew that I'd either vindicate myself or I would lose out on the longest and most hard-fought war I'd ever waged in my life. Truth be told, most everyone thought I'd lose.

In my haste to get the big win news out to as many people as possible, as quick as possible, I sent one short text to everyone in my contact's list. It consisted of two words and a bunch of exclamation points: "WE WON!!!!!!!!!!!."

Most people had been following the trial through either my Facebook Page, or through my short texts in between the testimony and evidence. Upon learning the news that I'd won, everyone began sending me congratulatory messages. With one exception, everyone's texts consisted of statements such as: "Wonderful," "I'm so proud of you," "Congratulations," "I knew you were going to win," "That's great," "I can't believe it," and "That's amazing."

The one exception was the text I received from my mother. Her first words were: "How much?" It was a hilarious encapsulation of the feeling that both she and I shared for the case. Only a large amount of money would send the message that the Axis of Corruption, and all the corrupt law enforcement officers and politicians like them, could no longer violate the constitutional rights of myself and others like me without fear of retributory justice.

Through texts, I had to quickly explain to everyone that the jury was again deliberating on a punitive damages request. But I did not leave anyone with false hope that a jury award of large amounts of money would be likely. I concentrated on the fact that I'd proven myself right and Mike Chaney, James Jackson, Sheriff Pace, and Emmett Atwood wrong. It was a repudiation of everything the Axis of Corruption had put me through. To those familiar with the case and my history, it was enough even without an award of punitive damages. The verdict I had was still good enough to prove that there was still justice, integrity, and honesty in our criminal justice system. I kept everyone informed, though, that we were still waiting on a second verdict.

As expected, our wait was short. About forty-five minutes after retiring to deliberate, the jury announced that they'd reached a decision on whether to award punitive damages. The bailiff quickly called the courtroom to order, we rose, and waited for Judge Aycock to take her seat behind her dais.

> **JUDGE AYCOCK:** Okay. You all may have a seat. I've been told the jury has reached a verdict. [Turning to the court bailiff.] You may bring in the jury.

I remained standing as the jury was led back into the courtroom for what would be the final time. They all walked with their heads level, gazing straight ahead. I could not detect any hint of what their verdict might be, but I knew I would shortly know.

> **JUDGE AYCOCK:** Let the record reflect that the jury has returned to the courtroom. Okay, ladies and gentlemen, do you have a verdict?
> **JURY FOREPERSON:** Yes, Your Honor.
> **JUDGE AYCOCK:** Okay. Please pass me the form. [Judge Aycock takes a moment to read over the verdict form.] Alright, the verdict form says, *We the jury, award punitive damages in the amount of zero dollars.*

I let out a big breath of air. As the air escaped my lungs I realized that my biggest hope for a resounding message to the Axis of Corruption had been lost. There would not be any additional money awarded to me for the damages, terror, complications, and distress that they had caused me and my family.

While I tried my best with the limited knowledge that I had, it was at this point that I realized that I would have to be satisfied with the victory I'd earned. A victory, after all, is still a victory. And I was still extremely proud of myself for proving that my beliefs about the illegal conspiracy committed by the Axis of Corruption was beyond a doubt true. But I wanted a million-dollar verdict more than I ever wanted something in my life. But I'd have to be happy with what I had.

> **JUDGE AYCOCK:** Okay. Thank you all. Ladies and gentlemen, I thank you so much for your jury service. You have been very attentive. I appreciate your service very much. I will ask you to go back to the jury room. I will follow you in there. I like to dismiss juries from in there. Okay. I'll be there shortly.

I remained standing as the deputy marshals led the jury from the courtroom. I knew that Judge Aycock was about to conclude the trial and dismiss us for the last and final time. I was actually still somewhat in shock and disappointed that the jury didn't award punitive damages. But the response that I'd received from everyone when I'd informed them that I'd won the $5,000.00 was enough to soothe my disappointment.

> **JUDGE AYCOCK:** Let the verdict form now be filed. Counselors, thank you. I've enjoyed trying the case with you. You've both done a very good job. Mr. Jackson, I've enjoyed having you in the courtroom. [I felt as though this was said tongue-in-cheek.] I'm going to retire to the jury room and talk to them. You are free to go. Thank you.
> **ME:** Thank you, Your Honor.
> **MR. MINOR:** Thank you, Your Honor.

I had never felt complimented more than I did when Judge Aycock told me that I'd done a very good job. I don't know what her personal feelings were, but I'd done my best not to antagonize her, argue with her, or show her the least disrespect. As a *pro se* litigant I wanted to be the antithesis of what most jailhouse lawyers are thought to be.

There had been several times when I'd crossed the line when I was interrogating Jackson, and Judge Aycock had shot me two or three disapproving looks while sustaining Mr. Minor's objections, but I felt that I'd done the best job that a prison-trained jailhouse lawyer could do. After all, I did win my case.

As Judge Aycock left the courtroom that late afternoon on July 20, 2017, I immediately walked over to Mr. Minor's table and offered my hand to him in gratitude of how he'd treated me during the litigation, the wonderful manner in which he interacted with me during trial, and the excellent job he had done under the circumstances.

There is no doubt in my mind that the only reason more money wasn't awarded was because of Mr. Minor's excellent closing arguments. Unfortunately, he was handicapped with a client that was almost impossible to defend. But as many criminal defense lawyers must do when representing guilty defendants, Mr. Minor had taken what good he could find from an overall bad situation and turned it into a viable and convincing defense of Jackson.

As I extended my hand to him, I saw a look of surprise come to his face. His facial surprise then turned into gratitude and recognition that my gesture was more than perfunctory; it was a genuine congratulations on how well he had done and an honest appreciation of how well he treated me throughout the proceedings.

Much as I tried, though, I could not force myself to turn and offer my hand to Jackson. In fact, I didn't even look at him. As far as I was concerned the jury had settled our score, the war was over, and he was now nothing but a distant memory, long laid to rest in a deeply buried judicial crypt. I will never forget, though, the utter look of shock on his face at the moment he realized that the jury had vindicated me and crucified him. It is a memory seared into my conscious forever, and it was worth every struggle, every fight, every battle, every ounce of energy I had in litigating this case to witness for that fleeting second that look of utter disbelief on Jackson's face.

Against all odds I'd overcome the Axis of Corruption that was Chaney, Jackson, Sheriff Pace, and Emmett Atwood. I'd done battle with one of the best assistant attorney generals that the Great State of Mississippi could throw at me.

Without any formal legal training, I'd overcome what should have been an open and shut case on day one. This victory was partially assured with competent, fair judges like Judge Aycock and Magistrate Sanders. For the first time in my life I felt that I'd actually gotten a fair hearing in a courtroom.

I was sure that Mr. Minor was disgusted that he'd lost. From day one he'd felt that the case should have gone his way. No doubt that every other case involving a *pro se* jailhouse lawyer had gone his way. I know that he has never been beat in court by someone without any legal training. So I perfectly understood the frustration and, one might say, slight embarrassment. But I made sure to express my sincere congratulations to him nevertheless on the excellent efforts that he expended during the proceedings.

What most impressed me with Mr. Minor was his willingness to treat me with respect and professionalism even though he doubted my ability to win. I admired that about Mr. Minor more than anything else, and I made sure to tell him that as he shook my hand.

I next turned to thanking Judge Aycock's staff and the courtroom deputy marshals. Judge Aycock's and Magistrate Sander's law clerks had made the entire complex and bewildering experience navigable for someone that didn't always know what to do or how to go about doing it. Without the assistance of Mr. Daniel McHugh, Mrs. Parker Kline, Mr. Rylee Zalanka, and Mrs. Melinda Tucker, it would have been much more difficult to litigate the case and prepare for trial. They deserve as much appreciation as Judge Aycock and Magistrate Sanders do.

One of the repeated refrains from myself and my family throughout the litigation was the apparent fairness exhibited by both Judge Aycock and Magistrate Sanders. I sincerely appreciated their effort to ensure justice, fairness, and honesty remained a constant part of the process.

There was no doubt about my pecking order in the courtroom, though. I was a convicted sex offender who'd been sent to prison numerous times by judges similar to Judge Aycock. But not once was I treated any different by her than she did Mr. Minor.

In hindsight, there was no doubt that some of my gay mannerisms tended to slip through the cracks of the tough persona that I tried to portray. I was playing a role, and the more ammunition Jackson provided me, the more I continued to shoot. I'm sure Judge Aycock found it amusing to hear me raise my voice, gesticulate wildly with my hands, and pace back and forth in front of the jury.

I had an idea of what an aggressive attorney would do when conducting a tough questioning of a hostile, dishonest witness, and I tried to mimic that, obviously with some success.

Once I'd made the rounds of the courtroom and thanked everyone for their assistance, David and Richard helped me pack all of my documents into my briefcase and we headed for the door. I walked out of the courthouse knowing that justice had been done and that I'd been vindicated.

David and I then loaded into our car, Richard into his, and we headed towards Vicksburg. That week in July 2017 had been one of the most rewarding experiences of my life and we were too excited to talk about anything other than the trial. We did get a good laugh at my mother's reaction to the news that I'd won.

There was no rule against contacting members of a jury after the trial was over, and I needed and wanted to know what went on behind-the-scenes. So one of the topics of conversation that we discussed was getting in touch with several of the jurors to see whether they'd talk to me. But winning a jury verdict and knowing what the jurors thought was only the first step.

I had the verdict in hand, but there was no guarantee that the $5,000.00 would be easily forthcoming. There would be time for that, though. At the moment, all anyone wanted to do was celebrate. I knew Mr. Minor would need a few days to think, but it wouldn't be long before we would have to talk again.

For the moment I was happy knowing that I'd won, and I'd won fair and square. The message was spreading, too. No doubt, Chaney, Sheriff Pace, Emmett, and the rest of the ilk of the Axis of Corruption were being made aware of my victory and their defeat. It was the message that I hoped most that they would get.

As I drove back to Vicksburg I knew that things would never be the same. The Axis of Corruption and their kind may have had thoughts of retaliating against me in the future, but after my victory there would always be doubt about whether or not they would be the next James O'Neal Jackson. And for that I was very thankful.

EPILOGUE

Several things occurred after the trial that are worth mentioning for one to fully understand the repercussions from the trial. One was what happened in the jury room. Before even trying to collect the money that the jury had awarded me, I needed to know why more money wasn't given.

I ended up contacting one of the jurors whom I thought had been most engaged with me in an overt and positive way throughout the trial. It was only then that I learned how close I'd actually come to winning the lottery.

This juror told me that during the deliberations four jurors had wanted to award $100,000.00 in emotional distress damages, two jurors wanted to award $25,000.00 in emotional distress damages, and the other two didn't want to award any damages at all except a nominal one. I was told these two jurors didn't necessarily see Jackson's conduct as excusable, they just didn't feel that I'd proved sufficient damages.

The entire four-hour jury deliberation had been spent trying to convince these two holdouts to award something. They all compromised at $5,000.00.

The juror that I spoke to also told me that all of the jurors would have been willing to award more compensatory damages had I been able to prove to them a more detailed monetary loss than what I did. There was no doubt that I'd proven a loss of $5,000.00 by having to pay to bond out of jail, but there wasn't much other evidence in the record to prove how much I lost by losing out on the employment opportunities that the arson arrest caused.

This was a gamble that I made because I didn't want to testify, and it was a gamble that I ultimately lost. However, I took consolation in the fact that the jury almost awarded me an extremely large amount of money and that they were going to do so because of the deplorable, dishonest, and despicable conduct of James Jackson.

There was no doubt in any of the jurors' minds that my entire arrest had been illegally motivated by retaliatory politics. The two holdouts just didn't seem to think that I suffered enough damages to want to award a substantial sum of money. They also surmised that any monetary award would come from the taxpayers of Mississippi rather than the pockets of Jackson's work jeans. I had to agree that this was correct.

I'd come so close, though. I'd come so close to obtaining an extremely large monetary award that would have been an earth shattering reckoning to the Axis of Corruption. And even though it wasn't what I wanted, I took comfort in the fact that I'd won nonetheless. I'd proven Chaney, Jackson, Sheriff Pace, and Emmett wrong. I just needed to actually to collect the money now.

About a week after the trial I gave Mr. Minor a call with the intention of inquiring about obtaining the money. He made it clear, though, that Jackson didn't have it, wouldn't be paying it, and that I'd probably never collect it from him. I disagreed, but my goal was to work out a settlement with Mr. Minor that would end the case once and for all.

For years I'd tried to get Mr. Minor to settle the case by having the $5,000.00 returned to me that I'd spent on bond. I was always told, however, that Chaney and Jackson would never settle. No one expected them to lose, though.

Once they lost, however, and once it became clear that Chaney was directly involved in an illegal conspiracy to violate my constitutional rights—not to mention ordering Jackson to commit numerous state and federal crimes—I had enough evidence to go back and have another trial with Mike Chaney as the defendant instead of Jackson. The prospect of having Chaney under my interrogation—much as I'd had Jackson and numerous psychotic ex-boyfriends that they were similar to—was something I relished, and Mr. Minor, no doubt, greatly feared. No one wanted another trial with Chaney sitting at the defendant's table—except me.

To this day I do not know what behind-the-scenes machinations went on between the Mississippi Attorney General's Office and the Office of the Mississippi Insurance Commissioner and State Fire Marshal, but I would assume that the Attorney General's Office recommended very strenuously that unless Mike Chaney wanted to be indicted by a federal grand jury for multiple felony crimes, it was probably best to go ahead and pay me my $5,000.00 and send me on my way. If I'd been Chaney's attorney, that would have been my best, most sincere advice. And with my recent victory at trial, my advice was worth a little weight.

There was another federal procedural rule to which I availed myself of in the hopes of forcing Chaney's and Jackson's hands to settle the case. I desperately wanted another trial. I craved as a dope-fiend would for another hit of heroin to have another trial with Chaney as the defendant and under my inquisition. I wanted him under my cross-examination more than I'd wanted anything in the world because I knew that I could destroy him like I did Jackson. And I also knew that there was a good chance that Chaney would end up in federal prison for decades if his crimes came out in another trial like Jackson's had. There was no doubt I would destroy him.

My other realistic consideration, however, was the fact that I needed to quit while I was ahead. There was no absolute guarantee that I could win another trial with Chaney as the defendant, and I didn't want to give the Axis of Corruption the ammunition that a loss on my part would give them. Trials are unpredictable—a sad fact that Mr. Minor learned the hard way—and I realized that. A loss with Chaney would only lessen the impact that my victory over Jackson had given me. But I needed to force their hand and make them consider the possibility.

As part of the settlement offer that I made to Mr. Minor, I offered to waive all claims that I had against Chaney for my false arrest and the crimes he committed in return for paying me the $5,000.00 immediately. If they would give me the money, I would give them a signed statement promising never to try and pursue any other legal claims against Chaney that arose out of my illegal arrest. It was a fair deal.

Because of the federal procedural rules I also had the opportunity to pursue a new trial against Jackson on damages only. A new trial on damages only essentially gave me a second chance to prove that I'd suffered more monetary damages than what the first jury had awarded.

If I was given a second trial on the question of damages only, there was a good chance that I could convince a jury to award more than the $5,000.00. It was a shot that I was going to take if I couldn't convince Mr. Minor to settle.

On August 2, 2017, I filed a motion for a new trial on damages only asking Judge Aycock to allow me to come back to Aberdeen and attempt to prove to a different jury that I'd suffered more monetary damages than what the first jury awarded.

Judge Aycock sat on the motion for a few days to give Mr. Minor, Chaney, and Jackson time to consider the potential loss that they might suffer if I was given a chance to address a jury again. I think that's when the ultimate decision was reached to immediately settle the case.

Twelve days after filing my motion for a new trial, Mr. Minor and I met on August 14, 2017, and came to an agreement where I would dismiss the recently filed motion and waive any legal claims that I had against Chaney. In return, they immediately paid me my $5,000.00. The case was almost finally over.

When I was handed my check, it was inside of an envelope with the return address of the Mississippi State Insurance Commissioner's Office. Mike Chaney had finally come to his senses, made his decision to avoid possibly going to prison, and sent me my check. There was no subliminal message in my check being given to me in an envelope from Chaney's office. It was his way of conceding defeat and accepting responsibility for his illegal actions.

For eight years Chaney had tried to fight me tooth-and-nail and deny me the ability to seek justice and compensation for the injuries that he caused. Yet, when I'd finally won, my check was given to me in an envelope with his name and address on it. I savored that envelope and I cherished that check. It was proof that justice could prevail over evil.

Upon signing and filing our settlement agreement, the lawsuit against the Axis of Corruption was over. Justice had been served, a wrong had been righted, and hopefully, a powerful message had been sent that corrupt and dishonest law enforcement officers were not above the law. There was one last battle, one last aftershock to deal with, though.

Emmett and Kade Atwood had failed to attend two different scheduled and duly subpoenaed depositions, and my motions to hold them in contempt of court had been pending for over a year. Their reckoning was to come on August 2, 2017, at 1:30 P.M. in Judge Aycock's courtroom in Aberdeen—the appropriate scene for another message of justice to be sent.

Richard attended their contempt hearing with me because he had actually served Kade with the two subpoenas that went to him. The process server that had served Emmett his subpoenas couldn't make it to court, but had, instead, provided affidavits under oath stating that the subpoenas were duly served on Emmett.

The contempt hearing began with me calling Emmett to the stand to testify. He and Kade were represented by Paul Kelly Loyacano—the attorney whom had made an absolute fool of himself in Judge Aycock's court back on the first day of the trial.

Much to his detriment, Emmett testified that he received both subpoenas but simply felt like he should not be obligated to have to attend any deposition that I had scheduled.

Even though Emmett was being as hostile as he had been at trial, I systematically established all of the elements that I needed to for him to be held in contempt of court for failing to follow the commandments of the subpoenas and Magistrate Sanders's direct orders to attend the depositions.

Apparently, it was clear, Emmett felt he was above the law and that he was accustomed to receiving preferential treatment by the corrupt courts in Vicksburg. He was sadly mistaken if he thought his money and political connections would protect him and Kade from justice in Aberdeen. Judge Aycock would make sure of that.

Kade's defense, when I called him to the stand, was that although he received the subpoenas, he was told by his Uncle Emmett that he didn't have to attend the depositions. Apparently, Kade felt that he, too, was beyond the power of the courts due to his familial relationship with Emmett. I felt that he was soon to realize otherwise.

After Emmett and Kade ruined themselves on the witness stand—just as Emmett had done at trial—I placed Richard on the stand to testify. He established that on both occasions when he served Kade the subpoenas he provided him with the court's order to appear and be deposed, or face contempt.

Richard only further solidified what Emmett and Kade had willingly admitted to. They received valid subpoenas and court orders, but utterly failed to abide by them because they felt they were above the law.

I placed myself on the stand last. I had to testify to precisely what expenses I'd suffered as a result of Emmett and Kade not attending the depositions—and they weren't insignificant.

I'd spent set-up and scheduling fees for the court reporter to appear and wait on Emmett and Kade to attend the depositions. I'd spent money having the subpoenas served. I'd spent money on filing the contempt motions, and both Richard and I also had significant traveling expenses for driving back and forth to Aberdeen to testify at the contempt hearing. We were, under federal law, entitled to be reimbursed for those reasonable expenses.

All in all, I had spent almost $2,000.00 behind the failed depositions. Split evenly between them, both owed around $900.00. When I testified, however, Loyacono spent the majority of his cross-examination asking me such irrelevant questions as to who my boyfriend was, how I paid for my vehicle, where I met my friend David, and several other questions that had absolutely nothing to do with why we were in court that day.

It was almost amusing. Loyacono was almost as interested in my gay lifestyle as I had apparently been during the trial about Emmett's past sexual trysts with women of all ethnic and racial nationalities—something amusing to me, but complexing as well, due to my intimate familiarity with Emmett's views on white supremacy.

Finally, Judge Aycock lost her temper at Loyacono after he continued to ask these irrelevant-type of questions despite him previously having been warned by her several times not to. Very pointedly, she asked Loyacono what these type of questions had to do with Emmett and Kade not showing up for their depositions. Loyacono couldn't answer.

Astonishingly, though, Loyacono continued until finally Judge Aycock slammed her hand down on her dais and told Loyacono that we were going to take a five minute break and that when we returned he better be ready to only ask questions directly related to why his two clients failed to appear for their depositions.

This had been the first time that I'd seen Judge Aycock truly upset. Jackson had strained her nerves at the first trial. But from three feet away, it looked as though Kelly Loyacono had made her furious. But he'd been warned. We weren't in a court in Vicksburg where the judges were scared of him and where they depended on Emmett's checkbook to get elected. We were in federal court in Aberdeen, and it was clear that Judge Aycock was not going to suffer Loyacono's dramatics.

When we reconvened after the five minute break, Loyacono stood up from behind his table, waved his arms in the air as one would when a gun is pointed at them, and announced that Emmett and Kade "surrenders" and that "the Court wins, we give up." It was a bizarre, disturbing display that made me question whether Kelly Loyacono retained all of his mental faculties. No doubt I wasn't the only one with doubts about his sanity after the fool he made of himself that day in court.

There was no doubt that Judge Aycock had not been impressed with Loyacono's performance and theatrics. If I'd done the same I'd been kicked out into the streets and my case dismissed.

We already knew that Emmett was a liar, that his testimony couldn't be trusted, and that he would lie about anything in order to advance his own version of events. The contempt hearing proved that Kade Atwood would do the same and that Loyacono was the absolute worst choice they could have picked to handle the case.

In rendering her decision, Judge Aycock was careful to lay out her rationale for why she was making the ruling that she was. Her opinion concluded that Emmett and Kade had twice been duly subpoenaed and ordered by the court to appear for two different depositions which they ultimately didn't attend.

Judge Aycock said that, "based on the testimony and evidence presented at the [contempt] hearing, Emmett Atwood and Kade Atwood never had any intention of appearing at the depositions" and that it is "clear that these witnesses have personal issues with the Plaintiff for a variety of reasons, some related to this case and some not, and that they willfully ignored the subpoenas."

When it came to how much money to award me for their failure to attend the depositions, Judge Aycock ordered that "splitting the costs of the hearing evenly between Emmett Atwood and Kade Atwood brings their respective totals to $885.42 for Emmett Atwood and $850.17 for Kade Atwood."

This was clearly another major victory for me. Not only had Jackson been sanctioned and fined nearly $2,000.00 in March 2017 for violating Judge Aycock's direct order not to mention anything about my criminal history, but I'd won at jury trial, and I'd also won a contempt hearing against Emmett and Kade.

Beating Emmett was almost as good as beating the Axis of Corruption. My entire life I'd always been told that Emmett and the Atwoods could never be beaten in court. Well, I'd proven that supposition wrong and I'd proven it big.

There was one last matter to handle before Judge Aycock dismissed us from the courtroom at the contempt hearing, though. Loyacono, the day before the contempt hearing, had filed a motion to hold me in contempt of court for "unduly burdening" Emmett and Kade by filing a "frivolous" (Loyacono's word) contempt motion against them. He even asked Judge Aycock to have me incarcerated. She dealt with their motion very quickly.

"Finally, the Court takes up Emmett Atwood and Kade Atwood's countermotion requesting sanctions against the Plaintiff. The countermotion was not timely filed, nor was leave of Court for a late filing requested. The countermotion also fails to comply with the federal rules. In addition, the countermotion fails to comply with the local federal rules. These procedural defects aside, the Court finds Emmett Atwood and Kade Atwood's request for sanctions against the Plaintiff to be wholly without merit, and it is denied." Slam dunk, in Loyacono's, Emmett's, and Kade's embarrassed faces.

Judge Aycock declared their motion against me to be completely frivolous. It was swatted away like one does a mosquito. And for good reason. It was laughable. Only an idiot like Loyacono—used to preferential treatment in the Vicksburg courts—could ever believe that there might even be a miniscule basis for filing such garbage.

Having won at jury trial, and now having won my request to have Emmett and Kade held in contempt of court, it was time for me to retire, so to speak. I'd made all the points that I needed to make.

Judge Aycock gave Emmett and Kade thirty days to pay the money, which, after seeing her erupt in court at them, I was, no doubt, sure they would. However, once thirty days had come and passed, no money had been sent to me.

On October 13, 2017, Judge Aycock entered her final order in the case. She ruled that if the contempt money was not provided to me by Emmett and Kade within ten days she would impose further harsh sanctions. There was no doubt in my mind that if they didn't pay the money she would have them incarcerated in jail until they did.

Exactly ten days later, a check was provided in the amount of $1,705.59. It was cherished as much as the check I'd received from Mike Chaney.

Both the Axis of Corruption and Emmett Atwood had been shown—probably for the first time in their lives—that they could not lie, manipulate, bully, and intimidate people. There were those who would fight back, and, no matter how small the chance of success, could win in a court of law and win big.

In the years since *Into Hell I Rode* had been published, and the legal saga began with the Axis of Corruption, I'd been extremely successful in using the federal courts to exact justice. Not only had I won against Chaney, Jackson, Sheriff Pace, and Emmett, but I'd also settled the lawsuits that I'd filed against Covington County and Rankin County for their false arrests of me. And most importantly to me, the City of Vicksburg and Warren County had conceded defeat, admitted my trespassing arrest at the Miss Mississippi Pageant in July 2011 had been illegal, dismissed the criminal charge, and paid me a substantial sum of money to settle the case.

With the exception of Chaney and Jackson, the other defendants in the other lawsuits recognized early on the inadvisability of proceeding to a full jury trial. To avoid an embarrassing result such as that handed to Chaney and Jackson, those other defendants decided to settle out-of-court with me rather than risk going to trial and losing.

If one were to judge the success in bringing justice to one whom had been victimized and abused by the corrupt cops by how much money one obtained in a legal proceeding, then I'd been very successful at distributing justice. Not once did I ever lose a legal battle with any of the corrupt cops I'd sued.

I will refuse, however, to become complacent in my search to bring to justice every corrupt law enforcement officer that I run across. I remain vigilant in this regard, not only for myself, but for others like me.

Throughout the litigation that bringing these types of anti-corruption lawsuits entails, I learned several very valuable lessons. There will always be those whom use and abuse the power given to them. This will never change. Police corruption and police abuse are tolerated to a certain extent because it is what the people in power ultimate want.

Corrupt law enforcement officers will only be disciplined when their behavior threatens the smooth operation of the institution that they are supposed to protect. We saw that with James Jackson.

Once it became obvious that Jackson had been caught, and would ultimately be held accountable for his illegal actions, he was abandoned by Chaney and his former superiors to fare as best as he could on his own. Jackson's screw-up—regardless if it was at the behest of Chaney—had begun to threaten the institution that he worked for and represented. If Jackson had to be sacrificed to protect his bosses, then he would be. And that is what occurred in Aberdeen in July 2017.

My trial proved that there has always been an uneasy truce between our law enforcement officers and our civilian heads of government. This also, certainly, includes the allegedly independent judicial system. Civilian oversight agencies and the courts have given law enforcement a certain amount of latitude and autonomy concerning police procedures, policies, and discipline when those officers commit crimes or violate the rules.

The only thing this does is provide the oversight agencies and courts a certain amount of plausible deniability when serious misconduct occurs. To have any kind of real control would mean implementing changes to our system of law enforcement that is so radical it would ultimately meet such resistance as to be impossible to enact.

But that doesn't change the fact that law enforcement's behavior and misconduct is reaching out-of-control proportions. Something will eventually have to be done to correct the slide into oblivion which Chaney, Jackson, Sheriff Pace, and the other corrupt law enforcement officers involved in my illegal arrests have taken us into.

Without change we will be a totalitarian police state worse than the regimes of the old Soviet Union and Nazi Germany. With advances in technology, which allows the police to monitor and control more and more aspects of our lives, immediate change must be implemented if we are to preserve our Constitution and the rights that our Founding Fathers insisted that we maintain to protect our life, liberty, and pursuit of happiness.

My biggest fear is that by the time we realize how far we've slid into the point of no-return, it'll be too late. It is the nature of those in power—such as law enforcement institutions—to preserve themselves. They will always actively oppose any person, organization, ideology, or opposing viewpoint that is counter to their perceived right to exist as a massive beast of constitutional destruction.

If history is any reminder of how these institutions preserve themselves, we can fairly predict that they will use propaganda, indoctrination, and other ideological means to accomplish their goals. And when that fails, the law enforcement institution as a whole will resort to more direct means like harassment, imprisonment, and violence. It is occurring today.

We are clearly past that point. My case is the beacon of light and the shining example to the world that the line of demarcation has been crossed. The police have resorted to violence, they have resorted to illegal arrests, and they have certainly resorted to harassment. But it's not too late.

We must immediately recognize that when the police intervene to suppress an organization, ideology, or countervailing viewpoint, it will always be a dissenting person or group that represents an idea or viewpoint opposite of those of the police. We saw this with the sniveling Vicksburg Police detective, Daniel Thomas, the Warren County Sheriff's Department, Mike Chaney, James Jackson, Judge Henry T. Wingate, and the other corrupt cops involved in suppressing my First Amendment rights.

Our only hope to survive as a nation of freedom, justice, fairness, and liberty for all lies in the hands of judges like Sharion Aycock and David Sanders. More than the victims of police abuse, these honest judges are literally on the front line of our war against evil totalitarianism. With them lies our only hope.

It can well be assumed that for every police abuse victim that files lawsuits against corrupt law enforcement officers there will be a hundred or more who simply sit idle and take no action to protect their rights. If every person—or at least half the number—whom is a victim of police corruption and abuse pursues legal litigation in the courts, then we may see positive changes. But even when victims pursue their rights, without honest, fair, and impartial judges justice will never be served. That's why Judge Aycock and Magistrate Sanders deserve so much praise for their handling of my case.

There is no doubt that these two judges faced latent pressure to grant Chaney's and Jackson's motions to dismiss my lawsuit. Judge Aycock's decision to hold them responsible for my illegal arrest is all the more surprising because Chaney is a popular, Republican statewide elected official who most people assume is an honest, law-abiding politician. We now know otherwise, though.

The fact that Judge Aycock could overlook political party affiliation—especially considering the fact that she was appointed by Republicans—and make a difficult choice in holding the defendants accountable for their illegal actions speaks volumes about her integrity. I will forever be indebted to her for that fairness and impartiality.

Pursuing litigation in the courts against corrupt law enforcement officers is only as effective as the judges who ultimate preside over the cases. With judges like Judge Aycock and Magistrate Sanders we can be assured that when deserving, justice will always prevail.

With judges like the deplorable idiot, Henry T. Wingate, who manage their role in legal cases more from a prosecutor's viewpoint than an impartial arbitrator, justice will never be served. Judges like Wingate pose more of a threat to our system of justice than the corrupt cops on the streets.

If our citizenry cannot count on our legal system and judges to preside over our disputes with fairness, honesty, integrity, and impartiality, then we will ultimately metamorphosis into a totalitarian police state.

Without effective citizen and judicial oversight of law enforcement's expansion beyond the limits of constitutionally-permissible activities we will no longer be the land of the free and the home of the brave. We will be at the mercy of a massive, unstoppable police machine that protects the powerful, protects themselves, and protects the ideology they wish for society to conform to.

Those who would oppose this police state through peaceful means can expect nothing but harassment, illegal incarceration, and unproportional violent responses from law enforcement. And as long as judges like Henry T. Wingate are allowed to remain in their positions, our defenders of freedom and liberty can offer little or no relief.

When we reach a point where our lives are directed by the police state, where our rights have been curtailed or eliminated, and no judicial court is willing to hold these destroyers of our Constitution accountable, no action other than revolution will preserve and restore our constitutional rights and freedoms. Our American society is at a crossroads of having to support and rely on our police to protect us from crime while also ensuring that the police maintain an acceptable level of conduct. Push too hard and we handcuff our police's ability to fight crime. Fail to hold them accountable for their illegal actions and their power and authority exceed acceptable limits. It's a very fine line.

Good cops exist, though. And the good cops exist farther in number than the bad. But where corruption is not checked it will spread. That is what has happened in Vicksburg. No one in authority has yet to stand up and challenge the corruption. I tried when I ran for constable in 2002 in my personal fight against law enforcement corruption. But everyone has their hands in the proverbial cookie jar.

To effect change in Vicksburg is not beyond the power of a strong leader to make. That leader does not consist of any law enforcement officer currently in existence there. At one time, though, our federal law enforcement agencies were not only the "creme de la creme" of law enforcement, but they could consistently be counted on and expected to seek out and prosecute government and police corruption. That's not so anymore.

Having hired Paul Leslie Amacker, Jr., who, in my opinion is a drug user, corrupt cop, sexual abuser, and is totally unsuited for the job, the FBI lost whatever respect they had from me, which was a considerable amount regardless of the fact that at one time they prosecuted me and sent me to prison.

Winning the false arrest trial against Jackson certainly sent a message to Chaney, Sheriff Pace, and their corrupt compatriots that I was a force to be reckoned with. But ultimately, an Axis of Corruption still exists. I simply replaced one dirty group of corrupts cops for another.

There is no doubt that my federal probation officer, Shameka Horton, has a personal, extremely biased attitude towards me. Upon my release from prison she did absolutely nothing to help me transition from prison to society and, in fact, took multiple steps to impede my positive progress and deny me needed medical care.

It was even clearer that Horton illegally and unethically used her position as a U.S. Probation officer to retaliate against me for filing the lawsuit against the probation officer in San Diego. This point cannot be stressed enough considering the fact that Horton filed a petition to revoke my probation the day after she learned that the lawsuit had been filed.

Shameka Horton's clear failure as a probation officer is only underscored by her failure at every employment opportunity given to her. Before, unexplainably, being hired as a probation officer, despite clearly not qualifying for the position, Horton had attempted to pass herself off as a therapist and counselor. But without ability and, most importantly, without patients, Horton failed, just as everyone knows she will fail as a probation officer. But she has plenty of judicial company.

Having continuously criticized Judge Wingate, both publicly and privately since my revocation hearing, I could expect no fair and impartial consideration from him at any future proceeding in his court.

Wingate had denied my 2255 petition that challenged my revocation violations even though both he and the prosecutor knew that I'd been prosecuted and sent to prison under a law that had been repealed by the legislature and was no longer in effect.

Shortly before U.S. Probation brought my new probation violations before Wingate for a hearing, a former employee of the U.S. Attorney's Office, Paulette Womack, who was the mother of Cody Womack, a guy I used to have a relationship with, posted on her personal Facebook account a message which said that she was friends was Judge Wingate, had spoken to him about my pending probation revocation violations, and that Wingate had assured her that he would send me back to prison.

Upon further investigation, we learned that Womack had also posted on her Facebook account a thread of conversation that she'd had with Wingate's adopted son, Antonio Bratton, wherein they discuss their actions in illegally influencing Wingate to revoke my probation.

Besides proving an extremely illegal conspiracy between a family member of my judge and a former employee—whom Judge Wingate admitted he was friends with—of the U.S. Attorney's Office that was prosecuting my case, their public Facebook comments, which were read by thousands of people, created a huge public appearance of bias and partiality on the part of Wingate.

Less than a week after Womack and Bratton illegally contacted Judge Wingate and asked him to violate my probation, Wingate signed a warrant for my arrest and had me locked in prison again. And despite filing multiple requests asking that he recuse himself and resign from my case, Wingate refused to do so and again found me guilty of ridiculous and false probation violations and sent me back to federal prison.

The false arrest trial in Aberdeen in July 2017 only proved beyond a doubt that an axis of law enforcement corruption exists and that they are very active in harassing, abusing, and violating the constitutional rights of anyone who would have the courage to stand against them.

Shameka Horton retaliating against me for exercising my right to avail myself of the courts only proves that the temporarily checked Axis of Corruption has migrated from the river bluffs of Vicksburg to the offices' of the federal law enforcement community in Jackson.

Unchecked, this Axis of Corruption will spread and infect the very veins that supply the life-blood of our Constitution. We must continue to fight and fight to the death if need be. Whether that fight is in the local, state, or federal courts, it must be waged. And if victims of police corruption—victims of the Axis of Corruption in Mississippi—cannot obtain justice in the courts from judges like Wingate, then revolution it will be, and a restoration of the United States Constitution of 1789 we must.

DAVID G. ATWOOD II

Be sure to check out David's other books:

She Walked Strong
And
Into Hell I Rode